Modern Financial Engineering

Counterparty, Credit, Portfolio and Systemic Risks

Topics in Systems Engineering

Print ISSN: 2810-9090
Online ISSN: 2810-9104

The Series aims to cover a wide spectrum of Engineering topics but with a strong characteristic of interdisciplinarity using less technical items. It could be a series including thinking aspects, history topics linked with engineering topics from civil engineering to industrial engineering and so on. The contributions will cover a wide series of engineering topics and could be useful both for educational purposes and for research information. The idea is to combine technology, science, arts and social science with some emerging subjects.

Published:

Vol. 2: *Modern Financial Engineering: Counterparty, Credit, Portfolio and Systemic Risks*
by Giuseppe Orlando, Michele Bufalo, Henry Penikas and Concetta Zurlo

Vol. 1: *Underwater Labriform-Swimming Robot*
by Farah Abbas Naser, Mofeed Turky Rashid and Luigi Fortuna

Topics in Systems Engineering — Volume 2

Modern Financial Engineering

Counterparty, Credit, Portfolio and Systemic Risks

Giuseppe Orlando
University of Bari, Italy

Michele Bufalo
University of Rome "La Sapienza", Italy

Henry Penikas
Bank of Russia, Russia

Concetta Zurlo
Accenture, Europe

World Scientific

NEW JERSEY • LONDON • SINGAPORE • BEIJING • SHANGHAI • HONG KONG • TAIPEI • CHENNAI • TOKYO

Published by

World Scientific Publishing Co. Pte. Ltd.
5 Toh Tuck Link, Singapore 596224
USA office: 27 Warren Street, Suite 401-402, Hackensack, NJ 07601
UK office: 57 Shelton Street, Covent Garden, London WC2H 9HE

Library of Congress Control Number: 2021056667

British Library Cataloguing-in-Publication Data
A catalogue record for this book is available from the British Library.

Topics in Systems Engineering — Vol. 2
MODERN FINANCIAL ENGINEERING
Counterparty, Credit, Portfolio and Systemic Risks

ISBN 978-981-125-235-8 (hardcover)
ISBN 978-981-125-236-5 (ebook for institutions)
ISBN 978-981-125-237-2 (ebook for individuals)

For any available supplementary material, please visit
https://www.worldscienti ic.com/worldscibooks/10.1142/12725#t=suppl

To Our Families

Foreword

Encountering Mathematical Finance during my studies was a game-changer for me. The realisation that one could apply advanced mathematical concepts and formulas in practice to the complex arcane of financial markets was mind-blowing. Moreover, I graduated when quants and financial engineers were the new fashionable tribes in demand at Wall Street and the City's finest institutions. I had started working towards the end of the nineties, full of the humble beginner's energy, for some of the most innovative financial institutions in the financial engineering and risk space. Having been on different sides of the financial services world (first working for banks and then for enterprise financial services firms) allowed me to gather different perspectives along the path and some certainties.

I witnessed the wonders of financial engineering in creating newly needed market instruments like credit default swaps or new innovative products in the Equity or Interest Rates derivatives (variance/volatility swaps, range accruals and many more exciting structures). However, I was also confronted with its ugly face when product engineering went rogue and out of control (Subprime CDOs and many other products that precipitated in the Global Financial Crisis to unfold, the absence of modelling standards at the most elementary level). The key lesson I learned back then was that expert risk management should adequately balance responsible financial engineering. The financial crisis of 2008 highlighted in no uncertain terms that all firms could suffer dramatic collapse. Therefore, an unprecedented level of measures was taken, following the 2008 GFC, focusing on risk management across all risk types (Market, Credit, Counterparty and Margin risk).

Financial companies and non-financial companies are all focused on their long-term success. Therefore, it is critical to embrace thorough credit risk management practices for their future survival. These firms face stricter regulations and higher constraints for sound risk management, governance and accountability. Since the financial crisis, credit risk has gone from the underdog in the risk taxonomy to a critical and strategic measure to assess firms' sustainability.

When looking at Credit risk and its relation to financial engineering in this post-GFC context, Giuseppe and his co-authors are some of the few people who have successfully bridged across both disciplines as a practitioner and a respected researcher. He is empowering new generations of "Risk Engineers", a terminology I took some freedom to coin to redefine the new mission-critical goal: using/creating mathematical techniques to solve current risk challenges. Instead of the old plan of harnessing those powerful tools at their disposal to develop new innovative financial products or weapons of mass destruction (depending on which extremes you are in the spectrum), one needs to use them to solve highly complex risk problems. The authors have been at the forefront of reconciling those two sides of the same coin to address credit risk-related issues. They have published extensively on the topic. The book you have in your hands is the result of many of his explorations, using the power of financial engineering foundational tools to turbocharge credit risk applications.

This book gives a detailed and compact description of the regulatory framework to set the scene and a comprehensive overview of the mathematical foundations necessary to model and assess credit risk in its various facets (Portfolio Risk, Counterparty Risk, and Systemic Risk). Giuseppe and his co-authors strike the right balance between exposing enough of the mathematical tools (foundations and modelling) to give the readers the necessary basis to lean on and deep-dive into the risk-specific concepts practically. The authors cover all the essential mathematical foundations with the rigour needed for a quantitative book of this format. I find his section on "Credit Risk Modelling Essentials" a must-read for any student, risk manager and practitioner in the credit risk field. In a clear, rigorous and comprehensive way, it explains all the building blocks in credit modelling: the probability of default, loss given default, and exposure at default.

The last section on systemic risk is a gem in itself as it gets rarely exposed in terms of credit risk. I particularly appreciated the thought process: starting from a case study on the Kingdom of Saudi Arabia, the authors use appropriate econometric methods (correlation, clustering, panel analysis) to work most recent and contemporary pandemic data to demonstrate how diversifying the economy would lead to substantial risk reduction for the country. From there, they extend their analysis to the western banking system and develop new and original implications to reflect systemic risk regulation.

I'm passionate about financial engineering and risk interactions, and credit risk is one risk type ripe for more evolution. Having entered the "risk engineering" era, new technologies used in credit risk will help solve complex challenges. To illustrate some of these new challenges, let us look at two specific examples.

The first example is the technological impact of the availability of big data in credit and the continuous improvements of Machine Learning/Artificial Intelligence techniques on screening methodologies for risky borrowing. One can then extend this to strengthen banking risk surveillance and enhance systemic risk appraisal.

The second example, closer to my heart, is climate risk. Credit risk will be one of the classical risk categories strongly impacted by climate transition and physical risk drivers. Indeed, it will probably lead to multiple impacts on borrowers' cash flows, capital and collateral leading to a change in their creditworthiness. Thanks to the worldwide mobilisation and coordinated efforts of various working and supervisory groups, several approaches to quantifying the impacts of climate-related risks on credit risk are under development. Due to the methodological challenges to quantifying climate-related risks and the variety of transition options, traditional credit risk models will need a dramatic upgrade to capture the causality between climate changes and macroeconomic and microeconomic variables.

This book might prove to be an essential foundation and a key reference to lean on to solve these new risk engineering challenges and many more to come in the credit risk space. I hope you will enjoy reading it as much as I did.

Rachid Lassoued
Global Head of Financial Engineering & Risk
Bloomberg L.P.

Preface

Nowadays we are living in an extraordinary and unprecedented situation. All world economies have experienced significant contractions because of lock-downs and COVID-19 pandemic of 2020-2021. However, we do not yet observe a spike in defaults as was during the financial crisis of 2007-2009. For instance, regarding the economy of the United States of America, defaults lag behind, see Figure 0.1. Thus, banks need to assure sustainability against a potential rise in credit risk that could have been temporarily mitigated by those policy measures aimed at supporting the economy.

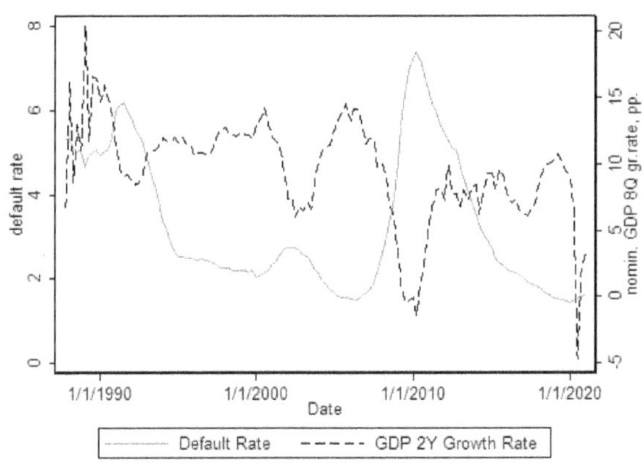

Fig. 0.1: USA economy drop in biannual nominal GDP growth rate in 2007-2009 and 2020-2021 versus charge-off and delinquency rates on loans and leases at commercial banks (default rates). Source: [FRB (2021)]

The purpose of this book is to illustrate the essential tools necessary for the estimation of the maximum loss attributable to the portfolio credit and counterparty risks. In recent years, financial institutions heavily invested human and technological resources in developing credit risk assessment, modeling, and management procedures. In particular, several models were developed to compute single asset credit risk, such as arising from a bond or derivative holding, or to a portfolio of such assets. We should also remember that credit risk may also arise from equity holdings, though it is less obvious. Among different models, we will focus on CreditRisk+. This is a model created by Credit Suisse Financial Products. Banks have widely adopted it for its simplicity and the small number of inputs required. We will quantify the portfolio loss using this model as an example. In this regard, we will choose as a risk measure, the Value-at-Risk (VaR). It is merely a loss distribution quantile. Therefore, having chosen this risk measure, the problem of estimating the potential portfolio loss boils down to the problem of deriving its loss distribution. CreditRisk+ helps us in obtaining the one. Furthermore, within this book, we will retrace the main components of the credit risk measurement, such as expected loss and unexpected loss, and the main credit risk factors, such as the Probability of Default, the Loss Given Default and the Exposure-At-Default. We present their respective estimation models as well as some implications in terms of systemic risk.

Structure of the Book

The book is structured in six parts and 21 chapters. In addition, the Appendices report the executable codes and data to replicate the applications discussed in the body of the book.

The first part is devoted to one of the pillars of the book i.e. the mathematical and statistical foundations. They include the discussion of the well-known analytical forms of univariate and multivariate distributions in Chapter 1. We specifically distinguish discrete and continuous univariate distributions. Then, in Chapter 2, we describe the Poisson process because of its centrality in credit and counterparty risk especially with regard to Credit Default Swap (CDS) modelling. Chapter 3 discusses approaches to data simulation including copulas as a tool to join marginal distributions. This background is essential for understanding the forthcoming material.

The second part concerns the finance background and regulation. Chapter 4 describes the types of risk as well as the main credit risk ratios. Chapter 5 guides the reader through the evolution of risk regulation in banks starting from the international banking regulation of credit risk in Basel I more than 30 years ago. Chapter 6 pays particular attention to how the financial crisis of 2007-2009 evolved. Chapter 7 discusses how the crisis impacted the regulatory approach to risk in general and credit in particular.

The third part revises the approaches to modeling the credit risk parameters, as well as obtaining the portfolio-level risk estimates. Chapter 8 discusses the approaches to modeling the most widely known credit risk parameter — Probability of Default (PD). Next Chapter 9 handles the second parameter by popularity, not maybe even the first one in impact on credit risk — Loss Given Default (LGD). Chapter 10 looks at the residual two credit risk parameters — Exposure-At-Default

(EAD) and Maturity (M). It also describes how all the parameters are linked together to obtain the values of the expected and unexpected losses, as well as the gross (total) risk. Chapter 11 deals with the most common approaches to model validation, as well as their shortcomings. We take the chance to offer useful solutions to outpace them.

The fourth part is devoted to a particular type of credit risk, i.e. to counterparty credit risk. Its specifics lie in the fact that it is somewhat similar to market risk as the EAD and it is largely driven by market factors such as interest rates, exchange rates, etc. That is why Chapter 12 focuses on its modeling. Chapter 13 includes materials that follow once the risk analyst has modeled EAD. Chapter 14 describes the cases where the independence assumption between risks is no longer valid and the risk manager has to account for the correlation.

The fifth part presents the applications of the counterparty and general credit risk modeling discussed in part three requiring the background of math from part one, of finance from part two, and of risk-modeling from part three. Chapter 15 discusses and remodels one of the most popular credit risk toolboxes, i.e. the Credit-Risk +. Chapter 16 provides an example of credit risk modeling across industries and sectors. Next, Chapter 17 focuses on the essential credit risk parameters — namely, PD and LGD — for the purpose of the non-performing loans forecasting. Chapter 18 extends the modeling approaches when there is a dependence between credit events, or there is non-zero default correlation. Chapter 19 focuses on the most common credit derivative that is credit default swap (CDS).

The sixth part encapsulates the preceding discussions. In Chapter 20 we consider both banking and insurance sectors and, for a specific example of an oil-dependent economy such as the Kingdom of Saudi Arabia (KSA), we show that the growing importance of insurance helped in diversifying the economy. This had positive consequences in terms of stability and resilience. Finally, in Chapter 21, we provide high-level implications for the entire financial system and its stability (which is what central banks target). We dare to suggest novel implications concerning the regulation of systemic risk. The last chapter concludes.

Appendices A and B list the code in R and Matlab, respectively, that can be run by the reader to perform simulations and model credit and counterparty risk at a portfolio level. Appendix C reports a dataset used for modeling non-performing loans (NPLs).

Giuseppe Orlando
University of Bari

Michele Bufalo
University of Rome "La Sapienza"

Henry Penikas
Bank of Russia

Concetta Zurlo
Accenture Italy

Acknowledgments

The authors wish to acknowledge Edward Bace (Middlesex University London), Nicola Basile (University of Bari), Fabrizio Durante (University of Lecce), Maximilian Härtel (MEAG Asset Management), Benjamin Jacot (La Française Group), Harvey Stein (Bloomberg) and Pascal Traccucci (La Française Group) for the valuable discussions concerning the book and credit risk-related issues. We also thank the editors of the series Luigi Fortuna (University of Catania) and Arturo Buscarino (University of Catania).

It was the untimely demise of Rosa Maria Mininni, with whom we spent a good deal of our academic research in finance in the last few years, that pushed us to write this book. That is why we dedicate this academic endeavour to her.

Contents

Useful Notations

$B(p)$	$:=$	Bernoulli distribution with success probability p;
$B(n,p)$	$:=$	Binomial distribution with parameters n and p;
$G(p)$	$:=$	Geometric distribution with parameters p;
$BN(n,p)$	$:=$	Negative Binomial distribution with parameters n and p;
$Pois(\lambda)$	$:=$	Poisson distribution with parameter λ;
$U(a,b)$	$:=$	Uniform distribution on $[a,b]$;
$N(\mu,\sigma^2)$	$:=$	Normal distribution with mean μ and variance σ^2;
$N(0,1)$	$:=$	Standard normal distribution;
$\chi^2(g)$	$:=$	Chi-squared distribution with g degrees of freedom;
$LN(\mu,\sigma^2)$	$:=$	Log-normal distribution with parameters μ and σ^2;
$Exp(\lambda)$	$:=$	Exponential distribution with parameter λ;
$Gamma(\alpha,\beta)$	$:=$	Gamma distribution with parameters α and β;
$Beta(\alpha,\beta)$	$:=$	Beta distribution with parameters α and β;
$\Gamma(\cdot)$	$:=$	Euler-Gamma function;
$\mathbb{E}[X]$	$:=$	Expected value of X;
$Var(X)$	$:=$	Variance of X;
G_X	$:=$	Probability generating function of X;
f_X	$:=$	Probability density function of X;
F_X	$:=$	Cumulative distribution function of X;
$\bar{X}$	$:=$	Sample mean of X;
S^2	$:=$	Sample variance of X;
$Cov(X,Y)$	$:=$	Covariance of X jointly with Y;
$Corr(X,Y)$	$:=$	Correlation between X and Y;
$=$	$:=$	Equation sign;
$:=$	$:=$	Definition sign;
$\lfloor\cdot\rfloor$	$:=$	Floor function;
bp	$:=$	Basis points (one hundredth of a percentage point, i.e. 0.0001);
Dates	$:=$	D - day; W - week; M - month; Q - quarter; Y - year;
Units order	$:=$	k - thousand; m - million; bn - billion; $trln$ - trillion.

PART 1
Mathematical and Statistical Foundations

Chapter 1

Distributions Commonly Used in Credit and Counterparty Risk Modeling

1.1 Common Distributions Families

Let $(\Omega, \mathcal{F}, \mathbb{P})$ be a probability space where Ω is the space of all elementary events, $\mathcal{F}$ is the set of measurable events and $\mathbb{P}$ is the probability measure in respect to $\mathcal{F}$. Let X be a random variable defined on such space. The probability distributions can be classified into

- Discrete distributions;
- Continuous distributions.

1.2 Discrete Distributions

Definition 1.1. A random variable X is said to be discrete if it can assume only a finite or countably infinite number of values $x_1, x_2, \ldots$. In this case, there exists a (discrete) probability mass function (PMF) $\mathbb{P}$ such that

- $0 \le \mathbb{P}(X = x_i) \le 1$ for any $i \ge 1$,
- $\sum_{i=1}^{+\infty} \mathbb{P}(X = x_i) = 1$.

The set of the values assumed by X is called support of X and it is generally denoted by *supp*(X).

Definition 1.2. Define the cumulative distribution function (CDF) of a given random variable X by $F_X : \mathbb{R} \to [0,1]$ such that

$$F_X(x) = \mathbb{P}(X \le x) \qquad (x \in \mathbb{R}).$$

Proposition 1.1. *The function F_X satisfies the following properties:*

i) F_X is not decreasing, i.e., $F_X(x_1) \le F_X(x_2)$ for any $x_1 < x_2$;
ii) F_X is bounded, i.e.,

$$\lim_{x \to -\infty} F_X(x) = 0, \qquad \lim_{x \to +\infty} F_X(x) = 1;$$

iii) F_X *is right continuous, i.e.,*

$$\lim_{h \to 0} F_X(x+h) = F_X(x).$$

Here, we list some discrete distributions, indicating the expected value and the variance for each of them.

1.2.1 *Bernoulli Distribution*

Definition 1.3. A random variable X is called a Bernoulli random variable with parameter $p \in [0, 1]$ if

$$\mathbb{P}(X = k) = \begin{cases} p & \text{if } k = 1 \\ 1 - p & \text{if } k = 0. \end{cases}$$

The events $\{X = 1\}$ and $\{X = 0\}$ denote the success and the failure of the experiment, respectively; in particular, the success has probability p. The expected value and the variance of X are given by

$$\begin{aligned} \mathbb{E}[X] &= p, \\ Var(X) &= p(1-p), \end{aligned} \tag{1.1}$$

respectively. The CDF of X is

$$F_X(x) = \begin{cases} 0 & \text{if } x < 0 \\ 1 - p & \text{if } 0 \leq x < 1 \\ 1 & \text{if } x \geq 1. \end{cases}$$

We will denote the Bernoulli distribution by $B(p)$ (see Figure 1.1).

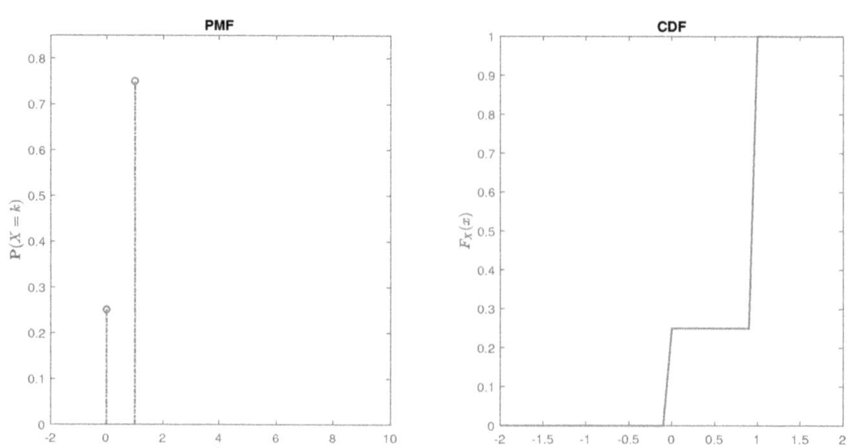

Fig. 1.1: PMF (left) and CDF (right) of a Bernoulli random variable X with $p = 0.75$.

1.2.2 *Binomial Distribution*

Definition 1.4. A random variable X follows a Binomial distribution with parameters $n \in \mathbb{N}$ and $p \in [0, 1]$ if

$$\mathbb{P}(X = k) = \binom{n}{k} p^k (1-p)^{n-k}, \quad k = 0, 1, 2...$$

where k denotes the number of successes in a sequence of n independent experiments and p is the probability of any success.

The expected value and the variance of X are

$$\mathbb{E}[X] = np,$$

$$Var(X) = np(1-p),$$

respectively. The CDF of X is

$$F_X(x) = \sum_{h=0}^{\lfloor x \rfloor} \binom{n}{h} p^h (1-p)^{n-h}.$$

We shall denote the Binomial distribution by $B(n, p)$ (see Figure 1.2).

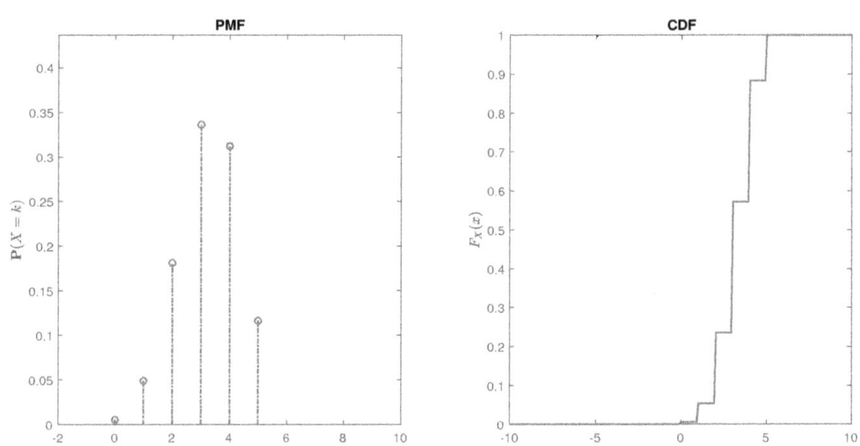

Fig. 1.2: PMF (left) and CDF (right) of a Binomial random variable X with $n = 5$ and $p = 0.65$.

Remark 1.1. The Bernoulli distribution is a special case of a Binomial distribution with just one experiment, i.e. $B(p) \equiv B(1, p)$.

1.2.2.1 *Correlated Bernoulli Distribution*

Let us consider a random variable $X = X_1+X_2+\cdots+X_n$ such that $Cor(X_i, X_j) = \rho$ for any two i and j ($i \neq j$); and each $X_i \sim B(p)$. The linearity of the expected value yields $\mathbb{E}[X] = np$, and, by setting $DR = X/n$, one has

$$Var(DR) = \frac{p(1-p)n}{n^2} + \frac{p(1-p)\rho\, n(n-1)}{n^2},$$

or, equivalently,

$$Var(DR) = \frac{\overline{DR}\,(1-\overline{DR})\big(1+\rho\,(n-1)\big)}{n}, \tag{1.2}$$

where $\overline{DR}$ indicates the mean value of DR (which is generally taken equal to p).

In a credit risk framework, DR and p shall denote the default rate and the default probability, respectively.

We can also make an inverse derivation of correlation ρ as follows (see [Merika *et al.* (2021)] for details)

$$\rho = \frac{n}{n-1}\frac{Var(DR)}{\overline{DR}\,(1-\overline{DR})} - \frac{1}{n-1}. \tag{1.3}$$

A granular portfolio is a type of portfolio that is well diversified and typically with a significant number of holdings. Formula (1.3) shows that the negative (default) correlation suits non-granular loan portfolios. In case $n \to +\infty$ we get a reduced form of Eq. (1.3) as follows

$$\rho = \frac{Var(DR)}{\overline{DR}\,(1-\overline{DR})}. \tag{1.4}$$

Remark 1.2. Formula (1.4) was made available to credit risk managers about 20 years ago by [Bluhm *et al.* (2003), p. 55] and it can easily be derived from the basics of probability theory. However, the version shown in Eq. (1.3) allows considering negative default correlations.

1.2.3 *Geometric Distribution*

If the number n of Bernoulli's trials goes to infinity, it is interesting to study the number of trials needed to get one success.

Definition 1.5. A random variable X has a Geometric distribution with parameters p if

$$\mathbb{P}(X = k) = (1-p)^{k-1}p, \quad k = 1, 2, \ldots \tag{1.5}$$

where $p \in [0, 1]$ is the probability of success.

The expected value and the variance of X are

$$\mathbb{E}[X] = \frac{1}{p},$$

$$Var(X) = \frac{1-p}{p^2},$$

respectively. The CDF of X is

$$F_X(x) = 1 - (1-p)^x.$$

We shall denote the Geometric distribution by $G(p)$ (see Figure 1.3). Notice that if $X \sim G(p)$ then X is a memoryless random variable, since

$$\mathbb{P}(X > k + a | X > k) = \frac{\mathbb{P}(X > k + a)}{\mathbb{P}(X > k + 1)} = \frac{(1-p)^{k+a-1}}{(1-p)^k} = (1-p)^{a-1} = \mathbb{P}(X > a).$$

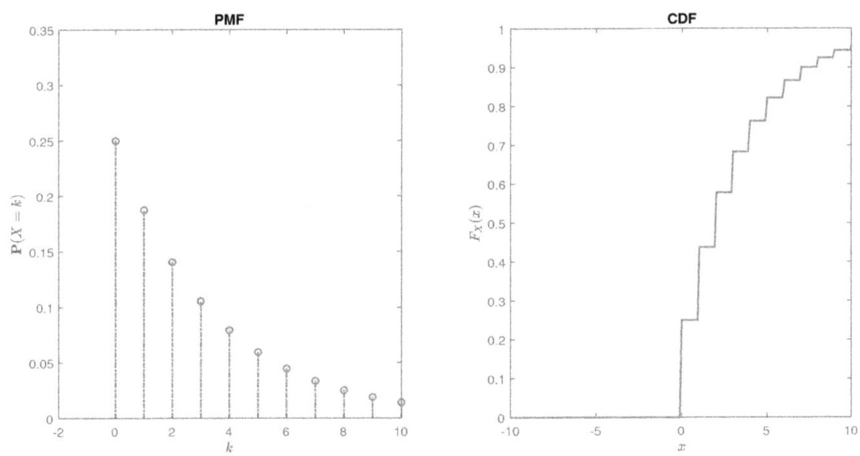

Fig. 1.3: PDF (left) and CDF (right) of a Geometric random variable X with $p = 0.25$.

Remark 1.3. A Geometric random variable can be defined in an alternative way through the number of failures before the first success. Hence, let $Y = X - 1$, where X is the number of Bernoulli's trials needed to get one success (distributed as in Definition 1.5). Then, Y is also a Geometric random variable, with

$$\mathbb{P}(Y = k) = (1-p)^k p, \quad k = 0, 1, \ldots$$

The expected value and the variance of Y are

$$\mathbb{E}[Y] = \frac{1-p}{p},$$

$$Var(Y) = \frac{1-p}{p^2},$$

respectively. The CDF of Y is

$$F_Y(y) = 1 - (1-p)^{k+1}.$$

1.2.4 *Negative Binomial Distribution*

The negative binomial distribution models the number of Bernoulli's trials needed to observe the n-th success.

Definition 1.6. Let $p \in [0,1]$ and $n \in \mathbb{N}$. A random variable X has a Negative Binomial distribution with parameters p and n if

$$\mathbb{P}(X = k) = \binom{k-1}{n-1} p^n (1-p)^{k-n}, \quad k = n, n+1, \ldots \tag{1.6}$$

where p is the probability of success and k is the number of independent experiments necessary to obtain n successes.

The expected value and the variance of a Negative Binomial random variable are

$$\mathbb{E}[X] = \frac{n}{p},$$

$$Var(X) = \frac{n(1-p)}{p^2},$$

respectively. The CDF of X has not a closed expression (it is related to the so-called regularized incomplete beta function) and can be numerically computed.
Denote by $BN(n,p)$ the Negative Binomial distribution (see Figure 1.4).

Remark 1.4. Analogously to the Geometric distribution, a Negative Binomial distribution can be defined in an alternative way as the number of failures before the n-th success. Hence, let $Y = X - n$, where X is the random variable defined in Definition 1.6. Then, Y is also a Geometric random variable with

$$\mathbb{P}(Y = r) = \binom{r+n-1}{r} p^n (1-p)^r, \quad r = 0, 1, \ldots$$

In this way, the support of Y does not depend on n. In particular, we have

$$\mathbb{E}[Y] = \frac{n(1-p)}{p},$$

$$Var(Y) = \frac{n(1-p)}{p^2}.$$

Moreover, the name Negative Binomial derives from the following identity

$$\binom{r+n-1}{r} = (-1)^r \binom{-n}{r}.$$

Finally, if $X \sim BN(n,p)$ then, by the memoryless property, can be proved that X is equal to the sum of n (independent) Geometric random variables with parameter p.

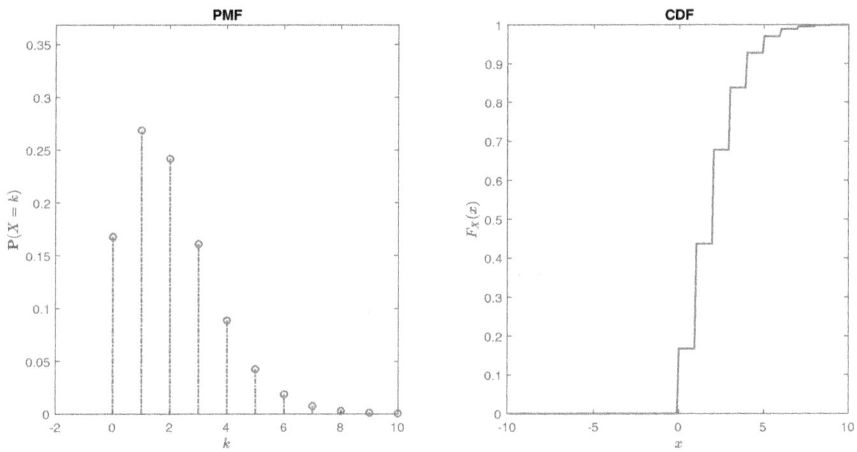

Fig. 1.4: PMF (left) and CDF (right) of a Negative Binomial random variable Y with $n = 8$ and $p = 0.8$.

1.2.5 *Poisson Distribution*

Differently from the previous cases, the Poisson distribution does not derive (directly) from a set of Bernoulli's trials. It regards the number of events occurring in a fixed interval of time and/or space when these events occur with a known constant mean rate and independently of the time since the last event.

Definition 1.7. Fixed $\lambda \in \mathbb{R}_+$, a random variable X follows a Poisson distribution with parameter λ if

$$\mathbb{P}(X = k) = \frac{e^{-\lambda}\lambda^k}{k!}, \qquad k = 0, 1, 2, ...$$

The expected value and the variance of X are

$$\mathbb{E}[X] = \lambda,$$

$$Var(X) = \lambda,$$

respectively. The CDF of X is

$$F_X(x) = e^{-\lambda} \sum_{i=0}^{\lfloor x \rfloor} \frac{\lambda^i}{i!}.$$

We will denote by $Pois(\lambda)$ the Poisson distribution (see Figure 1.5).

Poisson distribution is often used for operational risk to model the frequency of a negative event (see, e.g. Chapter 19).

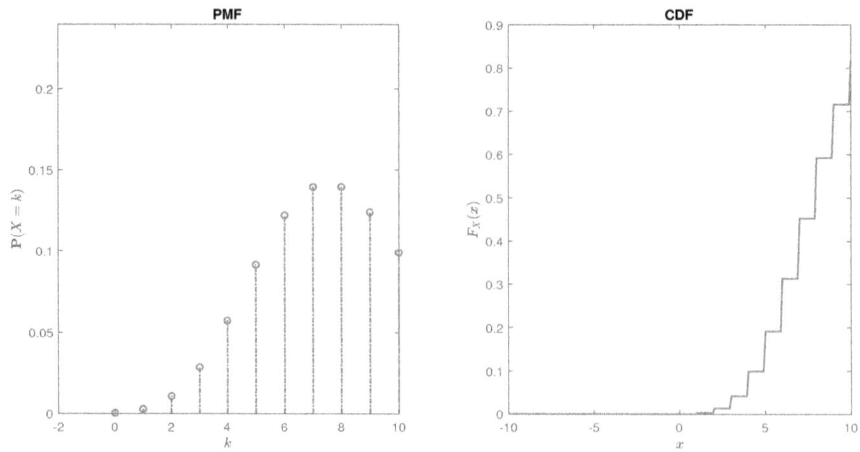

Fig. 1.5: PMF (left) and CDF (right) of a Poisson random variable X with $\lambda = 8$.

1.3 Continuous Distributions

Definition 1.8. A random variable X is said to be (absolutely) continuous if there exists a probability density function (PDF) $f_X : \mathbb{R} \to \mathbb{R}_+$, that is a non-negative Lebesgue-integrable function such that

- For any $I \in \mathcal{B}(\mathbb{R})$, where $\mathcal{B}(\mathbb{R})$ denotes the Borel σ-algebra on $\mathbb{R}$
$$\mathbb{P}(X \in I) = \int_I f_X(x)\,dx$$
- Its integral is
$$\int_{\mathbb{R}} f_X(x)\,dx = 1.$$

The support of a continuous random variable is an uncountable set, such as an interval of $\mathbb{R}$.

Recall an interesting property of the probability densities for continuous distributions.

Proposition 1.2. *If X is a continuous random variable with probability density f_X and CDF F_X, then*

$$\int_a^x f_X(t)\,dt = F_X(x) - F_X(a) \qquad (a \leq x). \tag{1.7}$$

This proposition is helpful if one wants to determine the PDF of a continuous random variable, knowing its CDF. Indeed, if a tends to $-\infty$ in Eq. (1.7), one has

$$\int_{-\infty}^x f_X(t)\,dt = F_X(x) \Rightarrow f_X(x) = \frac{d}{dx}F_X(x).$$

Below, we list some continuous distributions, indicating the expected value and the variance for each of them.

1.3.1 *Uniform Distribution*

Definition 1.9. The Uniform distribution on the (real) interval $[a, b]$ has the following density function

$$f_X(x) = \begin{cases} \frac{1}{b-a} & \text{if } x \in [a, b] \\ 0 & \text{otherwise.} \end{cases}$$

The expected value and the variance of a random variable X having Uniform distribution are

$$\mathbb{E}[X] = \frac{b+a}{2},$$

$$Var(X) = \frac{(b-a)^2}{12},$$

respectively. The CDF of X is

$$F_X(x) = \begin{cases} 0 & \text{if } x < a \\ \frac{x-a}{b-a} & \text{if } a \le x \le b \\ 1 & \text{if } x > b. \end{cases}$$

We denote the Uniform distribution on the interval $[a, b]$ by $U(a, b)$ (see Figure 1.6).

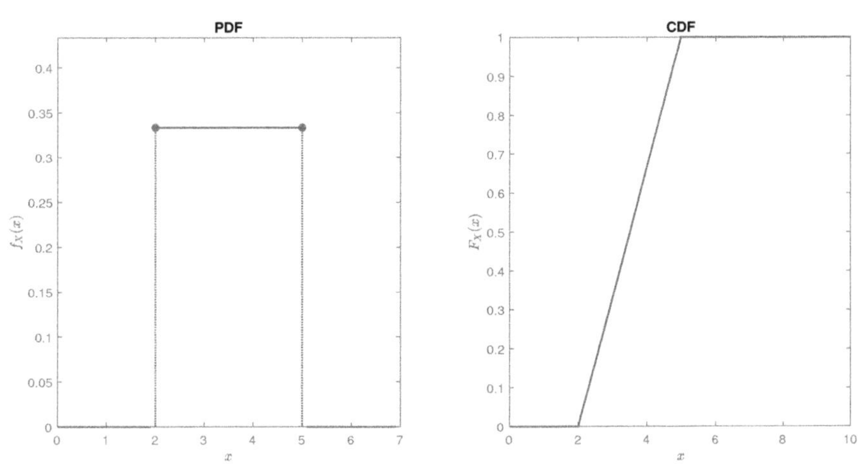

Fig. 1.6: PDF (left) and CDF (right) of a Uniform random variable X with $a = 2$ and $b = 5$.

Remark 1.5. Usually, one gets $[a, b] = [0, 1]$. This is because, if $Y \sim U(a, b)$, it can be rewritten as

$$Y = a + (b - a)X,$$

with $X \sim U(0, 1)$. In this case the density function is $f_X(x) = 1$ for any $x \in [0, 1]$. X is called a Uniform standard random variable if $X \sim U(0, 1)$.

1.3.2 *Normal Distribution*

The Normal (or Gaussian) distribution is a continuous probability distribution for a real-valued random variable, that is parametrized by its mean and variance, denoted by μ and σ^2, respectively, where $\mu \in \mathbb{R}$ and $\sigma^2 \in \mathbb{R}_+$.

Definition 1.10. The normal density function with parameters μ, σ^2 is defined as

$$f_X(x) = \frac{1}{\sigma\sqrt{2\pi}} e^{-\frac{1}{2}\left(\frac{x-\mu}{\sigma}\right)^2} \qquad (x \in \mathbb{R}). \tag{1.8}$$

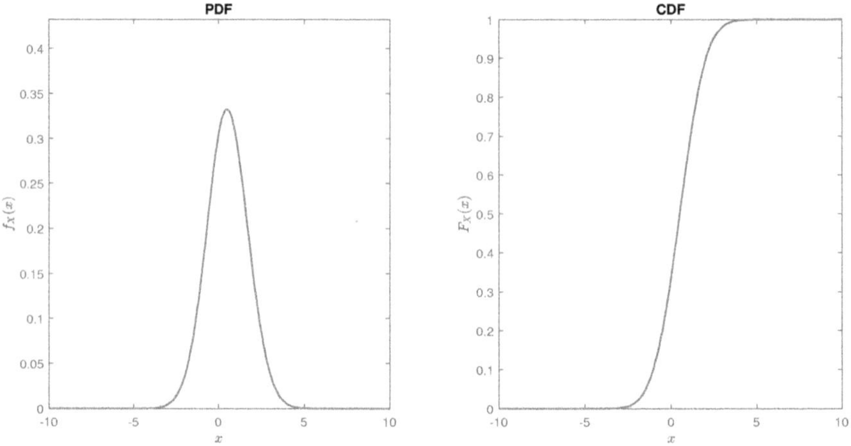

Fig. 1.7: PDF (left) and CDF (right) of a Normal random variable X with $\mu = 0.5$ and $\sigma = 1.2$.

The CDF of X is not available in closed form but can be easily computed numerically. A popular expression of this function is given by

$$F_X(x) = \frac{1}{2}\left(1 + erf\left(\frac{x - \mu}{\sigma\sqrt{2}}\right)\right),$$

where

$$erf(u) := \frac{2}{\sqrt{\pi}} \int_0^u e^{-t^2}\, dt \qquad (u \in \mathbb{R})$$

indicates the Gaussian error function. The above CDF is commonly denoted by Φ (see Figure 1.7).

We will indicate the Normal distribution with $N(\mu, \sigma^2)$.

Remark 1.6. If $X \sim N(\mu, \sigma^2)$, then the variable $Z = \frac{X-\mu}{\sigma}$ is normally distributed with $\mu = 0$ and $\sigma^2 = 1$, i.e. $Z \sim N(0,1)$. Z is known as standard Normal random variable.

Recall some helpful properties.

Proposition 1.3. *If $X \sim N(\mu, \sigma^2)$, then the following properties hold true.*

i) The density f_X defined in Eq. (1.8) is an even function with respect to the variable $x - \mu$, i.e. $f_X(x-\mu) = f_X(\mu - x)$;
ii) Given $a, b \in \mathbb{R}$ and $X \sim (\mu, \sigma^2)$, then $Y = aX + b \sim N(a\mu + b, a^2\sigma^2)$.

1.3.3 *Log-Normal Distribution*

The Log-normal distribution is often used when one wants to maintain the tractability of the Normal distribution, but for modeling phenomena that assume positive values. For a better understanding, we recall the following result.

Theorem 1.1. *Let X be a continuous random variable with density function f_X. Let $g : \mathbb{R} \to \mathbb{R}$ be a strictly monotone function over the support of X. Then $Y = g(X)$ is a continuous random variable with density*

$$f_Y(y) = f_X(g^{-1}(y)) \left| \frac{d}{dy} g^{-1}(y) \right| \qquad (y \in supp(g(X))),$$

where g^{-1} denotes the inverse function of g.

Definition 1.11. A Log-normal random variable X is defined as $X = e^Y$, where $Y \sim N(\mu, \sigma^2)$. Hence, by virtue of Theorem 1.1 it is easy to see that

$$f_X(x) = \frac{1}{\sigma x \sqrt{2\pi}} e^{-\frac{1}{2}\left(\frac{\ln x - \mu}{\sigma}\right)^2} \qquad (x > 0).$$

The expected value and the variance of X are given by

$$\mathbb{E}[X] = e^{\mu + \frac{\sigma^2}{2}},$$

$$Var(X) = (e^{\sigma^2} - 1)e^{2\mu + \sigma^2},$$

respectively. The CDF of X is

$$F_X(x) = \frac{1}{2}\left(1 + erf\left(\frac{\ln x - \mu}{\sigma\sqrt{2}}\right)\right).$$

We will indicate the Log-normal distribution with $LN(\mu, \sigma^2)$ (see Figure 1.8).

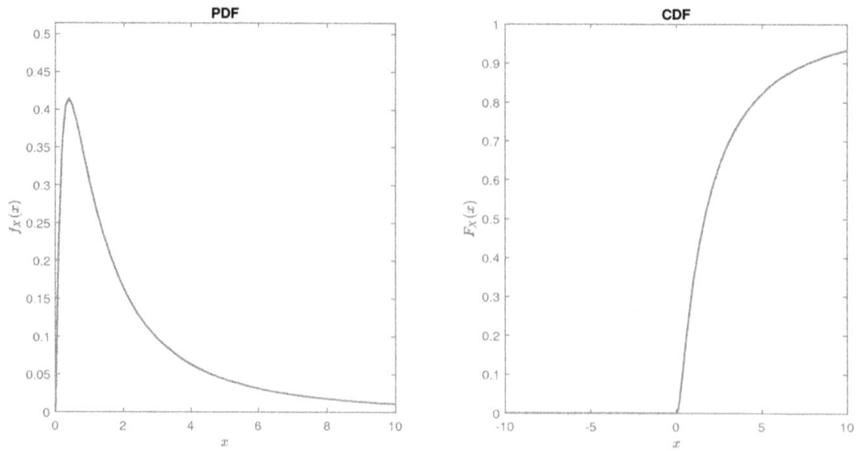

Fig. 1.8: PDF (left) and CDF (right) of a Log-normal random variable X with $\mu = 0.5$ and $\sigma = 1.2$.

1.3.4 *Exponential Distribution*

The exponential random variable generally describes phenomena whose (time) duration might be of some interest.

Definition 1.12. The Exponential density function with rate parameter $\lambda > 0$ is given by

$$f_X(x) = \lambda e^{-\lambda x} \qquad (x \geq 0).$$

The expected value and the variance of a random variable X having Exponential distribution are

$$\mathbb{E}[X] = \frac{1}{\lambda},$$

$$Var(X) = \frac{1}{\lambda^2},$$

respectively. The CDF of X is

$$F_X(x) = 1 - e^{-\lambda x}.$$

We denote the Exponential distribution by $Exp(\lambda)$ (see Figure 1.9).

Proposition 1.4. *The following properties hold true.*

i) If $X \sim Exp(\lambda)$, then it is a memoryless variable, i.e.

$$\mathbb{P}(X > s + t | X > t) = \mathbb{P}(X > s) \qquad (s, t \in \mathbb{R}_+);$$

ii) If $X_1, X_2, ..., X_n$ are n independent random variables with $X_i \sim Exp(\lambda_i)$, then

$$Y = \min\{X_i | 1 \leq i \leq n\} \sim Exp\left(\sum_{i=1}^{n} \lambda_i\right).$$

Moreover,

$$\mathbb{P}(X_j = Y) = \frac{\lambda_j}{\sum_{i=1}^{n} \lambda_i} \qquad (1 \leq j \leq n).$$

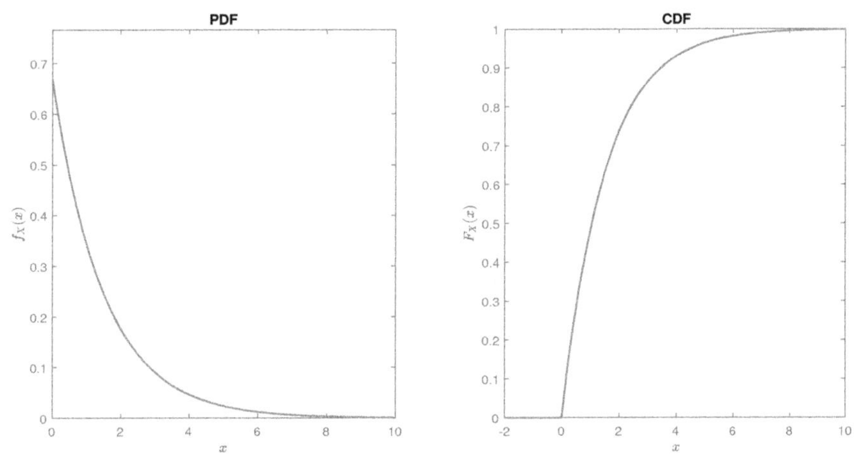

Fig. 1.9: PDF (left) and CDF (right) of an Exponential random variable X with $\lambda = 1.5$.

1.3.5 *Gamma Distribution*

The Gamma family of distributions is made up of some continuous distributions having $\mathbb{R}_+$ as support, which can be parameterized in terms of a shape parameter $\alpha > 0$ and a rate parameter $\beta > 0$.

Definition 1.13. The Gamma density function is given by

$$f_X(x) = \frac{e^{-\frac{x}{\beta}} x^{\alpha-1}}{\beta^\alpha \Gamma(\alpha)} \qquad (x > 0),$$

where $\Gamma(\alpha)$ is the Euler-Gamma function, defined as

$$\Gamma(\alpha) := \int_0^{+\infty} t^{\alpha-1} e^{-t}\, dt. \tag{1.9}$$

The expected value and the variance of a Gamma random variable X are

$$\mathbb{E}[X] = \alpha\beta,$$

$$Var(X) = \alpha\beta^2,$$

respectively. It is not possible to make explicit the CDF of X since it depends on the so-called incomplete Gamma function; but, if $\alpha \in \mathbb{N}$, one has

$$F_X(x) = 1 - \sum_{i=0}^{\alpha-1} \frac{x^i}{\beta^i i!} e^{-\frac{x}{\beta}}.$$

Denote the Gamma distribution with $Gamma(\alpha, \beta)$ (see Figure 1.10).

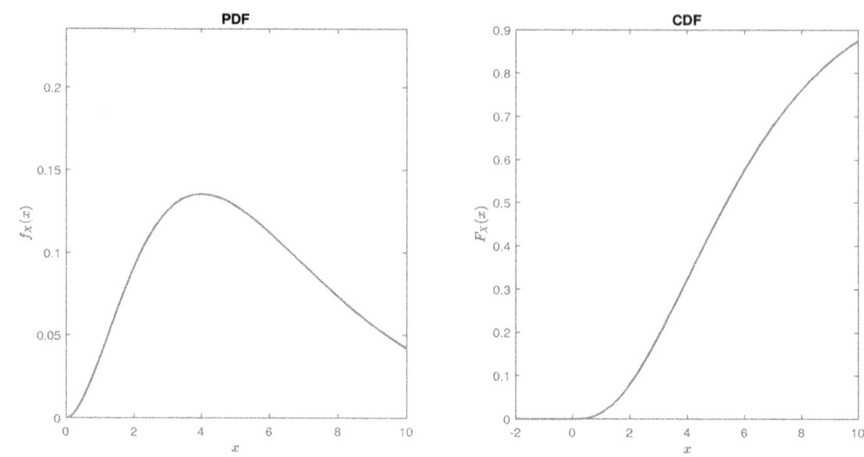

Fig. 1.10: PDF (left) and CDF (right) of a Gamma random variable X with $\alpha = 3$ and $\beta = 0.5$.

Proposition 1.5. *The following properties hold true.*

i) Let $X_1, X_2, ...X_n$ be n independent random variables with $X_i \sim Gamma(\alpha_i, \beta)$. Then

$$X = \sum_{i=1}^{n} X_i \sim Gamma\left(\sum_{i=1}^{n} \alpha_i, \beta\right);$$

ii) Given $\lambda > 0$, the distribution $Gamma(1, \frac{1}{\lambda})$ coincides with the exponential distribution $Exp(\lambda)$;

iii) Let $X_1, X_2, ...X_n$ be n independent random variables with $X_i \sim Exp(\lambda)$, $\lambda > 0$. Then

$$X = \sum_{i=1}^{n} X_i \sim Gamma(n, \lambda).$$

1.3.6 *Beta Distribution*

Beta distribution generalizes various situations ranging from unimodal to bimodal distributions (see Figure 1.11).

Definition 1.14. The Beta density function is given by

$$f(x) = \frac{\Gamma(\alpha+\beta)}{\Gamma(\alpha)\Gamma(\beta)} x^{\alpha-1}(1-x)^{\beta-1} \qquad (0 \leq x \leq 1),$$

where $\Gamma(\cdot)$ is the Euler-Gamma function (see Eq. (1.9)) and α, β are the (positive) shape parameters.

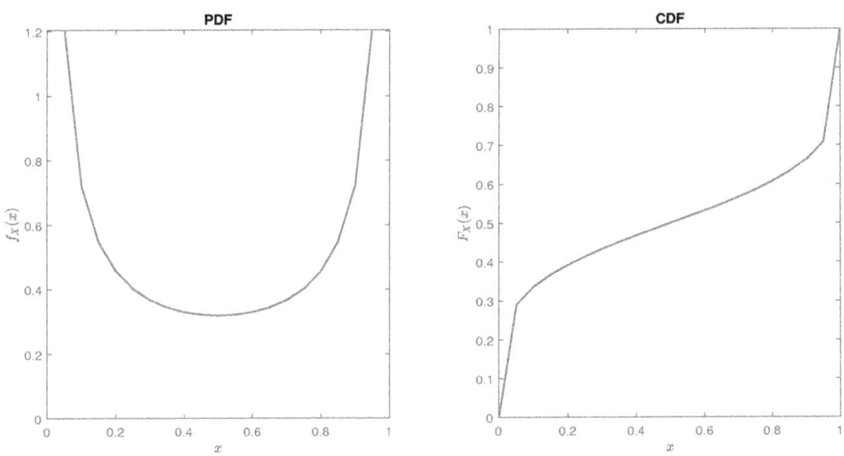

Fig. 1.11: PDF (left) and CDF (right) of a Beta random variable X with $\alpha = 0.2$ and $\beta = 0.2$.

Beta distribution with parameters below unity is often used for the loss given default (LGD) modeling.

1.4 Indicator Function

Definition 1.15. Let $(\Omega, \mathcal{F}, \mathbb{P})$ be a probability space. The indicator random variable of an event A is a measurable function $\mathbb{1}_A : \Omega \to \{0,1\}$ defined as

$$\mathbb{1}_A(\omega) := \begin{cases} 1 & \omega \in A, \\ 0 & \omega \notin A. \end{cases}$$

Proposition 1.6. *The mean and the variance of* $\mathbb{1}_A$ *are*

$$\mathbb{E}[\mathbb{1}_A(\omega)] = \mathbb{P}(A)$$

and

$$Var(\mathbb{1}_A(\omega)) = \mathbb{P}(A)(1 - \mathbb{P}(A)),$$

respectively.

Proof. Let $A \in \mathcal{F}$. We have

$$\mathbb{E}[\mathbb{1}_A] = \int_\Omega \mathbb{1}_A(\omega) d\mathbb{P} = \int_A d\mathbb{P} = \mathbb{P}(A)$$

$$Var(\mathbb{1}_A) = \mathbb{E}[(\mathbb{1}_A)^2] - \mathbb{E}\left[\mathbb{1}_A\right]^2 = \mathbb{P}(A) - \mathbb{P}(A)^2 = \mathbb{P}(A)\left(1 - \mathbb{P}(A)\right),$$

where we used the variance definition and the fact that the n-th power of $\mathbb{1}_A$ is equal to 1 if $\omega \in A$, and 0 otherwise. ■

Proposition 1.7. *Let* $(\Omega, \mathcal{F}, \mathbb{P})$ *be a probability space. If* $A, B \in \mathcal{F}$, *then*

i) $\mathbb{1}_{A \cap B} = \mathbb{1}_A \mathbb{1}_B$.
ii) $\mathbb{1}_{A \cup B} = \mathbb{1}_A + \mathbb{1}_B - \mathbb{1}_A \mathbb{1}_B$.

Proof. i) It easily comes from

$$\omega \in A \cap B \Longleftrightarrow \{\omega \in A \wedge \omega \in B\} \Longleftrightarrow \{\mathbb{1}_A(\omega) = 1 \wedge \mathbb{1}_B(\omega) = 1\} \Longleftrightarrow \mathbb{1}_A(\omega)\mathbb{1}_B(\omega).$$

ii) It holds

$$\omega \in A \cup B \Longleftrightarrow \{\omega \in A \vee \omega \in B\} \Longleftrightarrow \{\mathbb{1}_A(\omega) = 1 \vee \mathbb{1}_B(\omega) = 1\} = \mathbb{1}_A(\omega) + \mathbb{1}_B(\omega) - \mathbb{1}_A \mathbb{1}_B.$$

■

1.5 Multivariate Distributions

In this section, we introduce the main definitions and propositions about the multivariate distributions, which generalize the concepts of previous sections. The discrete and the continuous cases are treated simultaneously, for the sake of the synopsis.

Definition 1.16. Let $\boldsymbol{X} = (X_1, ..., X_m)$ be a random vector on $\mathbb{R}^m$.

- If the components X_i are discrete random variables, then $\boldsymbol{X}$ is said to be a discrete random vector with probability mass function $\mathbb{P} : \mathbb{R}^m \to [0, 1]$. The above distribution is called joint probability mass function and verifies

$$\sum_{x_1=0}^{+\infty} \cdots \sum_{x_m=0}^{+\infty} \mathbb{P}(X_1 = x_1, ..., X_m = x_m) = 1.$$

- If the components X_i are continuous random variables, then $\boldsymbol{X}$ is said to be a (absolutely) continuous random vector with joint probability density function $f_{\boldsymbol{X}} : \mathbb{R}^m \to \mathbb{R}_+$, that is a non-negative and Lebesgue-integrable function such that

$$\mathbb{P}(\boldsymbol{X} \in I) = \int_I f_{\boldsymbol{X}}(\boldsymbol{x})\, d\boldsymbol{x} \qquad (I \in \mathcal{B}(\mathbb{R}^m))$$

and

$$\int_{\mathbb{R}^m} f_{\boldsymbol{X}}(\boldsymbol{x})\, d\boldsymbol{x} = 1,$$

where the above integrals denote a m-manifold integral. If $I = I_1 \times ... \times I_m$ and $\boldsymbol{x} = (x_1, ..., x_m)$, with $I_i \subseteq \mathbb{R}$, shall denote

$$\int_I f_{\boldsymbol{X}}(\boldsymbol{x})\, d\boldsymbol{x} = \int_{x_1 \in I_1} ... \int_{x_m \in I_m} f_{\boldsymbol{X}}(x_1, ..., x_m)\, dx_1 ... dx_m.$$

Definition 1.17. Define the CDF of a random vector $\boldsymbol{X}$ by the function $F_{\boldsymbol{X}} : \mathbb{R}^m \to [0,1]$ such that

$$F_{\boldsymbol{X}}(\boldsymbol{x}) = \mathbb{P}(X_1 \leq x_1, ..., X_m \leq x_m) \qquad (\boldsymbol{x} = (x_1, ..., x_m) \in \mathbb{R}^m).$$

Proposition 1.8. *A continuous function $F_{\boldsymbol{X}} : \mathbb{R}^m \to [0,1]$ is a CDF if and only if*

i) $\lim\limits_{x_i \to -\infty} F_{\boldsymbol{X}}(x_1, ..., x_m) = 0 \qquad (i = 1, ..., m)$;

ii) $\lim\limits_{\boldsymbol{x} \to +\infty} F_{\boldsymbol{X}}(\boldsymbol{x}) = 1$;

iii) For all $\boldsymbol{a} = (a_1, ..., a_m)$, $\boldsymbol{b} = (b_1, ..., b_m)$, with $a_i < b_i$ for any $i = 1, ..., m$, it holds

$$\sum_{i_1=1}^{2} \cdots \sum_{i_m=1}^{2} (-1)^{i_1+...+i_m} F_{\boldsymbol{X}}(x_{1,i_1}, ..., x_{m,i_m}) \geq 0, \qquad (1.10)$$

where $x_{i,1} = a_i$, $x_{i,2} = b_i$, for any $i = 1, ..., m$.

In particular,

- *If $F_{\boldsymbol{X}}$ has m-th order derivatives, then condition iii) is equivalent to $\frac{\partial^m F_{\boldsymbol{X}}}{\partial x_1 ... \partial x_m} \geq 0$;*
- *If $a_2, ..., a_m \to -\infty$ in Eq. (1.10), then*

$$F_{\boldsymbol{X}}(b_1, b_2, ..., b_m) - F_{\boldsymbol{X}}(a_1, b_2, ..., b_m) \geq 0,$$

and $F_{\boldsymbol{X}}$ is increasing in the first variable. Analogously, for symmetry, $F_{\boldsymbol{X}}$ is increasing in the remaining variables.

Definition 1.18. Let $\boldsymbol{X} = (X_1, ..., X_m)$ be a random vector on $\mathbb{R}^m$.

- If $\boldsymbol{X}$ is discrete, with joint PMF $\mathbb{P}$, define the marginal distribution of X_i $(1 \leq i \leq m)$ by

$$\mathbb{P}(X_i = x_i) = \sum_{x_1=0}^{+\infty} \cdots \sum_{x_{i-1}=0}^{+\infty} \sum_{x_{i+1}=0}^{+\infty} \cdots \sum_{x_m=0}^{+\infty} \mathbb{P}(x_1, ..., x_m).$$

- If $\boldsymbol{X}$ is continuous, with joint PDF $f_{\boldsymbol{X}}(\boldsymbol{x})$, define the marginal distribution of X_i $(1 < i < m)$ by

$$f_{X_i}(x_i) = \underbrace{\int_{\mathbb{R}} \dots \int_{\mathbb{R}}}_{m-1} f_{\boldsymbol{X}}(x_1, \dots, x_m)\, dx_1 \dots dx_{i-1}\, dx_{i+1} \dots dx_m.$$

By virtue of the previous Definitions we introduce the notion of independence between random variables.

Definition 1.19. Two random variables X_1, X_2 with CDF's F_1 and F_2, respectively, are said to be independent (stochastically independent), and it is denoted by $X_1 \perp\!\!\!\perp X_2$, if and only if

$$F_{(X_1,X_2)}(x_1, x_2) = F_1(x_1)F_2(x_2),$$

for any $(x_1, x_2) \in \mathbb{R}^2$.
Equivalently, if f_1, f_2 are the marginal distributions of X_1, X_2, respectively, and $f_{(X_1,X_2)}$ is the joint PDF, then $X_1 \perp\!\!\!\perp X_2$ if and only if

$$f_{(X_1,X_2)}(x_1, x_2) = f_1(x_1)f_2(x_2).$$

In particular, if $f_{X_1|X_2}(x_1|X_2 = x_2)$ denotes the conditioning PDF of X_1 with respect to X_2, i.e.

$$f_{X_1|X_2}(x_1|x_2) = \frac{f_{(X_1,X_2)}(x_1, x_2)}{f_2(x_2)},$$

then $X_1 \perp\!\!\!\perp X_2$ if and only if

$$f_{X_1|X_2}(x_1|x_2) = f_1(x_1).$$

Finally, observe that Theorem 1.1 may be generalized in $\mathbb{R}^m$. This will be helpful in order to study the distributions of functions of some random variables.

Theorem 1.2. *Let $\boldsymbol{X}$ be a continuous random vector on $\mathbb{R}^m$ with PDF $f_{\boldsymbol{X}}$. If $g : \mathbb{R}^m \to \mathbb{R}^m$ is a continuous, differentiable and invertible function on supp($\boldsymbol{X}$), then the random vector $\boldsymbol{Y} = g(\boldsymbol{X})$ is a continuous random vector with PDF*

$$f_{\boldsymbol{Y}}(\boldsymbol{y}) = f_{\boldsymbol{X}}(g^{-1}(\boldsymbol{y}))\left|det(J_{x,y})\right|\mathbb{1}_{g(S)}(y) \qquad (y \in g(supp(\boldsymbol{X}))),$$

where

$$J_{\boldsymbol{x},\boldsymbol{y}} = \begin{pmatrix} \frac{\partial x_1}{\partial y_1} & \dots & \frac{\partial x_1}{\partial y_m} \\ \vdots & & \vdots \\ \frac{\partial x_m}{\partial y_1} & \dots & \frac{\partial x_m}{\partial y_m} \end{pmatrix}$$

denotes the Jacobian matrix, being $\boldsymbol{x} = g^{-1}(\boldsymbol{y})$.

Example 1.1. Let X_1, X_2 be two i.i.d. standard Normal random variables. Consider the transformation $g : \mathbb{R}^2 \to \mathbb{R}^2$ mapping (X_1, X_2) into its polar coordinates, i.e.

$$g(X_1, X_2) = (R, \theta),$$

with

$$\begin{cases} X_1 = R\, cos\theta \\ X_2 = R\, sin\theta \\ R = \sqrt{X_1^2 + X_2^2}. \end{cases}$$

The Jacobian matrix is

$$J_{(x_1,x_2),\,(R,\theta)} = \begin{pmatrix} cos\theta & -R\, sin\theta \\ sin\theta & R\, cos\theta \end{pmatrix}$$

whose determinant is R. Hence, from Theorem 1.2, one has

$$f_{(R,\theta)}(R, \theta) = \frac{R}{2\pi} e^{-\frac{1}{2}R^2}.$$

In particular, one can deduce that

- $R \perp\!\!\!\perp \theta$,
- $\theta \sim U(0, 2\pi)$,
- $f_R(R) = R\, e^{-\frac{R^2}{2}}$ (which is known in physics as the Rayleigh distribution).

Remark 1.7. An alternative way to express the joint PDF coming from a transformation of m independent random variables regards the case of the sum. More specifically, given $X_1, ..., X_m$ are independent random variables having PDF equal to f_{X_i}, respectively, then the joint PDF of the variable $Z = X_1 + ... + X_m$ has the following form

$$f_Z(z) = \int_{\mathbb{R}^{m-1}} f_{X_1}(x_1)...f_{X_{m-1}}(x_{m-1}) f_{X_m}(z - x_1 - ... - x_m)\, dx_1...dx_{m-1}. \quad (1.11)$$

The above expression is known as the convolution formula.

1.5.1 *Multivariate Gaussian Distribution*

The Gaussian (or Normal) distribution can be generalized in $\mathbb{R}^m$, as follows.

Definition 1.20. Let $\boldsymbol{X} = (X_1, ..., X_m)$ be a random vector. $\boldsymbol{X}$ follows a *multivariate Gaussian distribution* on $\mathbb{R}^m$ if there exist $\boldsymbol{\mu} \in \mathbb{R}^m$ and $\Sigma \in \mathbb{R}^{m\times m}$ such that

$$Y = \boldsymbol{a}^T \boldsymbol{X} \sim N(\boldsymbol{a}^T \boldsymbol{\mu}, \boldsymbol{a}^T \Sigma \boldsymbol{a}) \qquad (\boldsymbol{a} \in \mathbb{R}^m),$$

where $\boldsymbol{a}^T$ is the transpose of $\boldsymbol{a}$.

The above definition implies that any linear combination of X_i, i.e.

$$Y = a_1 X_1 + \cdots + a_m X_m,$$

is a (univariate) Normal random variable. We write $\boldsymbol{X} \sim N(\boldsymbol{\mu}, \Sigma)$ to say that X follows a multivariate normal distribution with mean $\boldsymbol{\mu}$ and covariance matrix Σ. We say X follows a multivariate standard Normal distribution if $\boldsymbol{\mu}$ is null and Σ is the identity matrix.

Remark 1.8. The above definition is valid if $\boldsymbol{a}^T \Sigma \boldsymbol{a} \geq 0$, i.e. if the covariance matrix Σ is positive semidefinite.

The density function of a multivariate Normal random variable $\boldsymbol{X} \in \mathbb{R}^m$ is given by

$$f_{\boldsymbol{X}}(\boldsymbol{x}) = \frac{1}{\sqrt{(2\pi)^k \, det(\Sigma)}} \exp\left(-\frac{1}{2}(\boldsymbol{x} - \boldsymbol{\mu})^T \Sigma^{-1} (\boldsymbol{x} - \boldsymbol{\mu}) \right) \qquad (\boldsymbol{x} \in \mathbb{R}^m). \quad (1.12)$$

Definition 1.21. By virtue of Definition 1.17 and Eq. (1.12), define the cumulative distribution function of a multivariate Normal random variable $\boldsymbol{X} \in \mathbb{R}^m$ as

$$F_{\boldsymbol{X}}(\boldsymbol{x}) = \int_{-\infty}^{x_1} \cdots \int_{-\infty}^{x_m} f_m(t_1, ..., t_m) \, dt_1 \cdots dt_m$$

for any $\boldsymbol{x} = (x_1, ..., x_m) \in \mathbb{R}^m$.

In the case of a m-dimensional standard Gaussian density, we denote the CDF with Φ_m (see Figure 1.12).

The Gaussian distribution density from the above is often referred to as the bell-shaped curve distribution and it also resembles the sandhill in the sand watch.

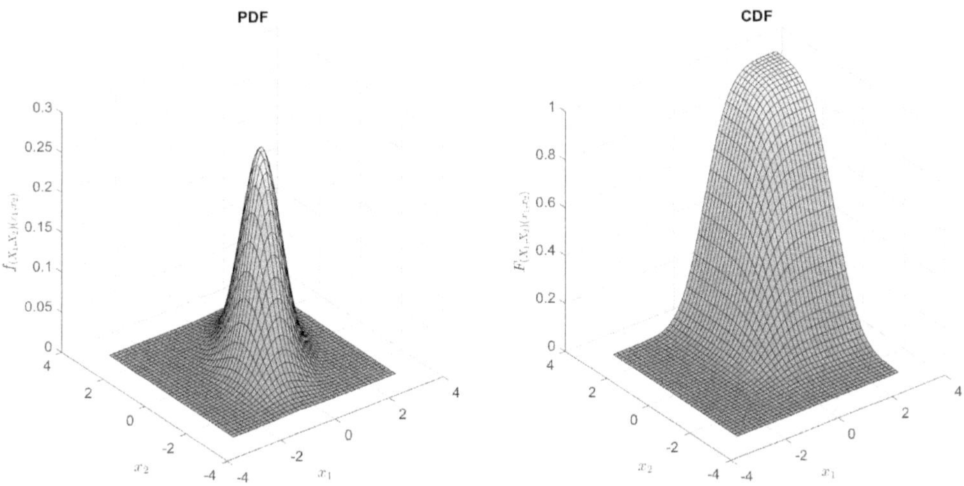

Fig. 1.12: PDF (left) and CDF (right) of a bivariate Gaussian random vector $\boldsymbol{X} = (X_1, X_2)$ with $\boldsymbol{\mu} = (0.4, 0.1)$ and $\Sigma = \begin{pmatrix} 0.5 & 0.3 \\ 0.3 & 0.9 \end{pmatrix}$.

Chapter 2

Poisson Processes

In this chapter, we provide some useful notions about Poisson processes which will be later used in Chapter 19 to explain how defaults are modeled by the first jump of a Poisson process. A detailed analysis of the Poisson process can be found in [Ross (2014)].

2.1 Homogeneous Poisson Process

A Poisson process is a stochastic process (defined on a suitable probability space $(\Omega, \mathcal{F}, \mathbb{P})$ reflecting the *probabilistic environment* related to the phenomenon under observation) whose events occur continuously in time and independently of one another. Mathematically, the Poisson process is described by the so-called counting process $(N_t)_{t\geq 0}$, where N_t counts the number of arrivals of the event that have occurred in the interval $(0, t]$ (in our case N_t is the number of defaults of a counterparty in a period of length t). The variable $t > 0$ denotes the time, whereby $t = 0$ stands for the observation time, i.e. today. For mathematical reasons, it is important to include the endpoints. The Poisson process must be right-continuous. So, we take $(a, b] := \{t \geq 0 \mid a < t \leq b\}$.

Definition 2.1. A counting process $N_t = (N(t))_{t\geq 0}$ is said to be a *time homogeneous Poisson process* with intensity λ if it satisfies the following properties:

i) $N(0) = 0$;
ii) $(N(t))_{t\geq 0}$ has independent increments;
iii) Number of events in any time interval of length t is Poisson distributed with mean λt, i.e. for any $t > 0$

$$\mathbb{P}(N(t) = n) = e^{-\lambda t} \frac{(\lambda t)^n}{n!}, \quad n \in \mathbb{N}. \tag{2.1}$$

By definition N_0 is 0 with a probability of 1, which means that we are considering only defaults at strictly positive times. This makes sense because we know whether a counterparty has defaulted at the time of observation or not. If we want to know the number of defaults between the times a and b, we have to calculate the *increment* $N_b - N_a$.

Based upon the above definition, we can deduce the following properties:

- $(N(t))_{t\geq 0}$ has stationary increments;
- $(N(t))_{t\geq 0}$ has mean equal to λt. In fact, for $t \geq 0$:

$$\begin{aligned}\mathbb{E}[N(t)] &= \sum_{k=1}^{+\infty} k\mathbb{P}(N(t) = k)\\ &= \sum_{k=1}^{+\infty} ke^{-\lambda t}\frac{(\lambda t)^k}{k!}\\ &= \sum_{k=1}^{+\infty} e^{-\lambda t}(\lambda t)\frac{(\lambda t)^{k-1}}{(k-1)!}\\ &= (\lambda t)e^{-\lambda t}\sum_{j=0}^{+\infty}\frac{(\lambda t)^j}{j!}\\ &= \lambda t.\end{aligned} \tag{2.2}$$

  Hence, $\lambda = \frac{\mathbb{E}[N(t)]}{t}$ can be seen as the average arrival rate per unit of time.
- The probability of having no jumps up to a certain time t is a (negative) exponential function of such time, i.e.

$$\mathbb{P}(N(t) = 0) = e^{-\lambda t}.$$

  It can be easily proved by replacing $n = 0$ in (2.1) and by using i) of Definition 2.1.

Now, we give an equivalent definition of the Poisson process.

Definition 2.2. A counting process $(N(t))_{t\geq 0}$ is said to be a *time homogeneous Poisson process* with intensity λ if the following conditions hold true:

i) $N(0) = 0$;
ii) $(N(t))_{t\geq 0}$ has independent and stationary increments;
iii) $\mathbb{P}(N(h) = 1) = \lambda h + o(h)$;
iv) $\mathbb{P}(N(h) \geq 2) = o(h)$.

Based on this definition, we deduce that:

- (Time-rescaled) probability of having one jump in an arbitrarily small time is exactly the intensity of the process, i.e.

$$\lim_{h\to 0}\frac{\mathbb{P}(N(h) = 1)}{h} = \lambda;$$

- Probability of having more than one jump in an arbitrarily small time goes to zero faster than such time, i.e.

$$\lim_{h\to 0} \frac{\mathbb{P}(N(h) \geq 2)}{h} = 0.$$

Theorem 2.1. *Definitions 2.1 and 2.2 are equivalent.*

Proof. First, we show that Definition 2.2 implies Definition 2.1. The first two conditions are the same, so they do not need to be proved. On the contrary, the third condition of Definition 2.1 cannot be easily deduced from Definition 2.2. Put $P_n(t) = \mathbb{P}(N(t) = n)$. For $n = 0$, by independence, we get

$$\begin{aligned} P_0(t+h) &= \mathbb{P}(N(t+h) = 0) = \mathbb{P}(N(t) = 0, N(t+h) - N(t) = 0) \\ &= \mathbb{P}(N(t) = 0)\mathbb{P}(N(t+h) - N(t) = 0). \end{aligned} \tag{2.3}$$

Observe that

$$\begin{aligned} \mathbb{P}(N(t+h) - N(t) = 0) &= \mathbb{P}(N(h) = 0) = 1 - \mathbb{P}(N(h) > 0) \\ &= 1 - \mathbb{P}(N(h) = 1) - \mathbb{P}(N(h) \geq 2) \\ &= 1 - \lambda h + o(h), \end{aligned} \tag{2.4}$$

where, in the last equality, we have used the assumptions *iii)* and *iv)* of Definition 2.2. Thus, we obtain

$$P_0(t+h) = \mathbb{P}(N(t) = 0)(1 - \lambda h + o(h)).$$

Rearranging and dividing by h, we have

$$\frac{P_0(t+h) - P_0(t)}{h} = -\lambda P_0(t) + \frac{o(h)}{h},$$

and consequently,

$$P_0'(t) = -\lambda P_0(t)$$

if $h \to 0$. By integrating this differential equation, we obtain

$$\ln(P_0(t)) = -\lambda t + c \qquad (c \in \mathbb{R}),$$

that is

$$P_0(t) = e^{-\lambda t + c} = K e^{-\lambda t} \qquad (K \in \mathbb{R}).$$

We can determine the value of the constant K since $P_0(0) = \mathbb{P}(N(0) = 0) = 1$.

This yields

$$P_0(t) = e^{-\lambda t}.$$

In a similar way, for any $n > 0$,

$$\begin{aligned}P_n(t+h) &= \mathbb{P}(N(t+h)=n)\\ &= \mathbb{P}(N(t)=n, N(t+h)-N(t)=0) + \mathbb{P}(N(t)=n-1, N(t+h)-N(t)=1)\\ &\quad - \sum_{k=2}^{n} \mathbb{P}(N(t)=n-k, N(t+h)-N(t)=k)\\ &= \mathbb{P}(N(t)=n)\mathbb{P}(N(t+h)-N(t)=0) + \mathbb{P}(N(t)=n-1)\mathbb{P}(N(t+h)-N(t)=1)\\ &\quad - \sum_{k=2}^{n} \mathbb{P}(N(t)=n-k)\mathbb{P}(N(t+h)-N(t)=k),\end{aligned} \tag{2.5}$$

by independence of the increments. Moreover, by assumption *iv*)-Definition 2.2, the last term of the above equality is $o(h)$ since

$$\begin{aligned}0 \leq &\sum_{k=2}^{n} \mathbb{P}(N(t)=n-k)\mathbb{P}(N(t+h)-N(t)=k) = \sum_{k=2}^{n} \mathbb{P}[(N(t)=n-k)o(h)\\ &\leq o(h)\sum_{k=0}^{n} \mathbb{P}(N(t)=n-k) = o(h)\mathbb{P}(N(t)\leq n) \leq o(h).\end{aligned} \tag{2.6}$$

Hence, by assumptions *i*) and *ii*) of Definition 2.2 we deduce that

$$\begin{aligned}P_n(t+h) &= P_n(t)P_0(t) + P_{n-1}(t)P_1(t) = P_n(t)(1-\lambda h + o(h)) + P_{n-1}(t)(\lambda h + o(h)) + o(h)\\ &= (1-\lambda h)P_n(t) + \lambda h P_{n-1}(t) + o(h).\end{aligned}$$

Rearranging and dividing by h, we get

$$\frac{P_n(t+h)-P_n(t)}{h} = -\lambda P_n(t) + \lambda P_{n-1}(t) + \frac{o(h)}{h}.$$

If $h \to 0$, then

$$P_n'(t) = -\lambda P_n(t) + \lambda P_{n-1}(t)$$

and, by rearranging and multiplying both elements by $e^{\lambda t}$,

$$e^{\lambda t}(P_n'(t) + \lambda P_n(t)) = e^{\lambda t}\lambda P_{n-1}(t),$$

or equivalently

$$\frac{d}{dt}(e^{\lambda t}P_n(t)) = \lambda e^{\lambda t}P_{n-1}(t).$$

But $P_0(t) = e^{-\lambda t}$; so that

$$\frac{d}{dt}(e^{\lambda t}P_1(t)) = \lambda e^{\lambda}e^{-\lambda} = \lambda.$$

Integrating this differential equation, we have

$$e^{\lambda t}P_1(t) = \lambda t + c \implies P_1(t) = (\lambda t + c)e^{-\lambda t}.$$

Since $P_1(0) = 0$, we may conclude that

$$P_1(t) = \lambda t e^{-\lambda t}.$$

Now proceed by induction on n. Assume that $P_{n-1}(t) = e^{-\lambda t}\frac{(\lambda t)^{n-1}}{(n-1)!}$, then

$$\frac{d}{dt}(e^{\lambda t}P_n(t)) = \lambda e^{\lambda t}P_{n-1}(t) = \lambda e^{\lambda t}e^{-\lambda t}\frac{(\lambda t)^{n-1}}{(n-1)!} = \lambda^n\frac{t^{n-1}}{(n-1)!}.$$

By integration, we get

$$e^{\lambda t}P_n(t) = \frac{\lambda^n t^n}{n!} + c, \quad c \in \mathbb{R} \implies P_n(t) = \left(\frac{\lambda^n t^n}{n!} + c\right)e^{-\lambda t}.$$

Since $P_n(0) = 0$, we can compute the value of the constant $c \in \mathbb{R}$, that is equal to 1. Hence, we can conclude that

$$P_n(t) = e^{-\lambda t}\frac{(\lambda t)^n}{n!},$$

as claimed. Conversely, we show that Definition 2.1 implies Definition 2.2. Again, the assumptions $i)$ and $ii)$ are the same. By assumption iii)-Definition 2.1 we deduce that a Poisson process has stationary increments, that means

$$\mathbb{P}(N(t+s) - N(s) = n) = e^{-\lambda t}\frac{(\lambda t)^n}{n!} \qquad (n \in \mathbb{N}^*).$$

Due to the stationarity of the process, if $n = 0$, we have

$$\mathbb{P}(N(t+h,t) = 0) = \mathbb{P}(N(t+h) - N(t) = 0) = e^{-\lambda h} = 1 - \lambda h + o(h),$$

where we used the first order Taylor expansion at $h = 0$.
For $n = 1$, it holds

$$\begin{aligned}\mathbb{P}(N(t+h,t) = 1) &= \mathbb{P}(N(t+h) - N(t) = 1) \\ &= e^{-\lambda h}\lambda h \\ &= (1 - \lambda h + o(h))\lambda h \\ &= \lambda h + o(h).\end{aligned} \tag{2.7}$$

Finally, for $n \geq 2$, we get

$$\begin{aligned}\mathbb{P}(N(t+h,t) > 1) &= 1 - \mathbb{P}(N(t+h,t) = 1) - \mathbb{P}(N(t+h,t) = 0) \\ &= 1 - \lambda h + o(h) - 1 + \lambda h + o(h) \\ &= o(h),\end{aligned} \tag{2.8}$$

which concludes the proof. ■

Given a time homogeneous Poisson process $(N(t))_{t\geq 0}$, let $\tau^1, \tau^2, ...,$ be its first, second jump, etc. For these processes, there exists a positive constant λ such that

$$\mathbb{P}(N(t) = 0) = \mathbb{P}(\tau^1 > t) = e^{-\lambda t}.$$

Define the default time τ as the *first jump* of the Poisson process.

Corollary 2.1. *Let τ be the default time. Then, $\mathbb{P}(\tau > t) = e^{-\lambda t}$.*

Proof. The proof comes immediately from the equivalence that $\mathbb{P}(\tau > t) = \mathbb{P}(N(t) = 0)$ and from Definition 2.1. ■

Generally, the equivalence

$$\{\tau^n > t\} \iff \{N_t \leq n-1\},$$

for all $n \geq 1$ holds true. This allows to compute the distribution of the random jump τ^n by the Gamma distribution with integer parameter $n > 1$.

Proposition 2.1. *For $n \geq 1$, τ^n is distributed as a Gamma, i.e. for all $t > 0$,*

$$\mathbb{P}(\tau^n \geq t) = \lambda^n \int_t^{+\infty} e^{-\lambda u} \frac{u^{n-1}}{(n-1)!} du.$$

Proof. If $n = 1$, Corollary 2.1 yields

$$\mathbb{P}(\tau^1 > t) = \mathbb{P}(N_t = 0) = e^{-\lambda t} \qquad (t > 0).$$

By induction on n, if

$$\mathbb{P}(\tau^{n-1} > t) = \lambda \int_t^{+\infty} e^{-\lambda u} \frac{(\lambda u)^{n-2}}{(n-2)!} du,$$

then,

$$\begin{aligned} \mathbb{P}(\tau^n > t) &= \mathbb{P}(\tau^n > t \geq \tau^{n-1}) + \mathbb{P}(\tau^{n-1} > t) \\ &= \mathbb{P}(N_t = n-1) + \lambda \int_t^{+\infty} e^{-\lambda u} \frac{(\lambda u)^{n-2}}{(n-2)!} du \\ &= e^{-\lambda t} \frac{(\lambda t)^{n-1}}{(n-1)!} + \lambda \int_t^{+\infty} e^{-\lambda u} \frac{(\lambda u)^{n-2}}{(n-2)!} du \\ &= \lambda \int_t^{+\infty} e^{-\lambda u} \frac{(\lambda u)^{n-1}}{(n-1)!} du, \end{aligned} \tag{2.9}$$

for any $n \geq 2$. ■

Hence, for any $n \in \mathbb{N}$ and $t > 0$, we can write

$$\mathbb{P}(N_t = n) = p_n(t) = e^{-\lambda t} \frac{(\lambda t)^n}{n!},$$

where p_{n-1}, $n \geq 1$, is the probability density function of the random jumps time τ^n.

Proposition 2.2. *The random times $\tau^{k+1} - \tau^k$ $(k \in \mathbb{N})$, with $\tau^0 = 0$, form a sequence of i.i.d. random variables having exponential distribution with parameter $\lambda > 0$, i.e.*

$$\mathbb{P}(\tau^1 > t_0, ..., \tau^n - \tau^{n-1} > t) = e^{-(t_0 + t_1 + ... t_n)\lambda} \qquad (t_0, t_1, ..., t_n) \in \mathbb{R}^n.$$

As a consequence, we can deduce that

$$\mathbb{E}[\tau^k - \tau^{k-1}] = \lambda \int_0^{+\infty} x e^{-\lambda x} dx = \frac{1}{\lambda} \qquad (k \in \mathbb{N}).$$

Moreover, the n-th jump τ^n has the mean equal to

$$\mathbb{E}[\tau^n] = \frac{n}{\lambda}.$$

2.2 Time-Varying Intensity Model

Now, consider an intensity model with a deterministic time-varying intensity $\lambda(t)$.

Proposition 2.3. *The function*

$$\lambda(t) = \frac{\mathbb{P}(\tau \leq t + dt | \tau > t)}{dt}$$

satisfies the following condition

$$\mathbb{P}(\tau > t) = exp\Big(- \int_0^t \lambda(u) du \Big) \qquad (t > 0). \tag{2.10}$$

Proof. Firstly, observe that

$$\begin{aligned}
\lambda(t) &= \frac{\mathbb{P}(\tau \leq t + dt | \tau > t)}{dt} \\
&= \frac{1}{\mathbb{P}(\tau > t)} \frac{\mathbb{P}(t < \tau \leq t + dt)}{dt} \\
&= \frac{1}{\mathbb{P}(\tau > t)} \frac{\mathbb{P}(\{\tau \leq t + dt\} \cap \{\tau > t\})}{dt} \\
&= \frac{1}{\mathbb{P}(\tau > t)} \frac{\mathbb{P}(\{\tau > t\} \backslash \{\tau > t + dt\})}{dt} \\
&= \frac{1}{\mathbb{P}(\tau > t)} \frac{\mathbb{P}(\tau > t) - \mathbb{P}(\tau > t + dt)}{dt} \\
&= -\frac{1}{\mathbb{P}(\tau > t)} \frac{\mathbb{P}(\tau > t + dt) - \mathbb{P}(\tau > t)}{dt} \\
&= -\frac{1}{\mathbb{P}(\tau > t)} \frac{d}{dt} \mathbb{P}(\tau > t).
\end{aligned} \tag{2.11}$$

So, we have to solve the following first order differential equation

$$\frac{d}{dt} \mathbb{P}(\tau > t) = -\lambda(t) \mathbb{P}(\tau > t).$$

By integration, we obtain

$$\mathbb{P}(\tau > t) = K \exp\Big(\int_0^t \lambda(u)\, du \Big).$$

The value of the constant K comes from the initial condition $\mathbb{P}(\tau > 0) = 1$, i.e.

$$1 = \mathbb{P}(\tau > 0) = K.$$

Thus, we can conclude that

$$\mathbb{P}(\tau > t) = \exp\Big(- \int_0^t \lambda(u)\, du \Big) \qquad (t > 0),$$

as claimed. ■

The integral in Eq. (2.10) is known as the *cumulative intensity, or cumulative hazard rate, or Hazard function* and is denoted by

$$\Gamma(t) = \int_0^t \lambda(u)\, du \qquad (t > 0).$$

2.3 Inhomogeneous Poisson Process

Definition 2.3. Let $(N(t))_{t \geq 0}$ be a time homogeneous Poisson process with intensity 1. A *time inhomogeneous Poisson process* $(M(t))_{t\geq 0}$ with intensity λ is defined as

$$M(t) = N(\Gamma(t)) \quad (t > 0).$$

By construction, we have that $(M(t))_{t\geq 0}$ jumps the first time at τ if and only if $(N(t))_{t\geq 0}$ jumps the first time at $\Gamma(\tau)$. Moreover, since $(N(t))_{t\geq 0}$ is a Poisson process with intensity 1, the first jump time is an exponential random variable, i.e.

$$\Gamma(\tau) = \xi \sim Exp(1).$$

So, if we transform the first jump time of a Poisson process according to its cumulative intensity, we obtain a standard exponential random variable. It is easy to see that

$$\tau = \Gamma^{-1}(\xi).$$

and

$$\mathbb{P}(\tau > t) = \mathbb{P}(\Gamma(\tau) > \Gamma(t)) = \mathbb{P}(\xi > \Gamma(t)) = 1 - \mathbb{P}(\xi \leq \Gamma(t)) = e^{-\Gamma(t)} = e^{-\int_0^t \lambda(u) du}.$$

The next proposition summarizes the above results.

Proposition 2.4. *Given $t > 0$, if $NDP(t)$ is the survival probability at time t, then*

- $NDP(t) = \mathbb{P}(\tau > t) = e^{-\lambda t}$, *if λ is constant in the time;*
- $NDP(t) = \mathbb{P}(\tau > t) = e^{-\int_0^t \lambda(u) du}$, *if λ is time-varying.*

Moreover, the conditional probability of no defaults at time s is given by

$$NDP(t,s) = \mathbb{P}(\tau > s | \tau > t) = \frac{\mathbb{P}(\tau > s \cap \tau > t)}{\mathbb{P}(\tau > t)} = \frac{\mathbb{P}(\tau > s)}{\mathbb{P}(\tau > t)}. \qquad (2.12)$$

More specifically, the expression (2.12) is equivalent to say that

- $NDP(t,s) = e^{-\lambda(s-t)}$, if λ is constant;

- $NDP(t,s) = e^{-(\Gamma(s)-\Gamma(t))} = e^{-\int_t^s \lambda(u)du}$, if λ is time-varying.

Moreover, the properties below hold true:

- *Superposition of independent Poisson processes:* if $N_{1,t}$ and $N_{2,t}$ are independent Poisson processes with rates λ_1 and λ_2, their combination into a single process by taking the union of both sets of events (or equivalently $N_t = N_{1,t} + N_{2,t}$) is a Poisson process with rate $\lambda_1 + \lambda_2$.
- *Approximation of the Binomial distribution:* when n is large and p is small, the Poisson distribution is an accurate approximation to the binomial distribution.
- *Likelihood equivalence:* the Poisson model is a likelihood equivalent to a model in which defaults are modeled by independent exponential, see [Caffo (2007)]. If $X \sim Pois(t\lambda)$, then the likelihood for λ is

$$\mathcal{L} = \frac{(\lambda t)^x e^{-\lambda t}}{x!} \quad \propto \quad \lambda^x e^{-\lambda t}.$$

Chapter 3

Estimation Techniques

3.1 Estimator Finite Sample Properties

Let X be a random variable whose distribution depends upon a parameter $\theta \in \Theta \subset \mathbb{R}^n$, $n \geq 1$. Under the unrealistic hypothesis that θ is known, we can compute the probability of all the events concerning X. Herein, there is a problem to estimate θ, or, more generally, a function of θ, e.g. $g(\theta) = (g_1(\theta), ..., g_k(\theta))$ $(k \leq n)$, where g is a real evaluated function. Assume $k = 1$, i.e. $g(\theta) \in \mathbb{R}$, for convenience. We start by introducing the notions of parameter estimator and estimate. Let $(X_1, ..., X_n)$ be an n-dimensional random sample generated by the random variable X, where $X_1, ..., X_n$ are independent and identically distributed (i.i.d.).

Definition 3.1. Any statistic $U = U(X_1, ..., X_n)$ used to estimate the unknown quantity $g(\theta)$ is called estimator of $g(\theta)$. The value of U for given realizations (observations) of X, i.e. $U(x_1, ..., x_n)$, is called estimate of $g(\theta)$.

3.1.1 *Estimator Selection Criteria*

In this subsection, we recall some helpful criteria about the estimators' selection. To choose the estimator of $g(\theta)$, we have to look among all the estimators satisfying some optimal properties.

Definition 3.2. Let g be a real evaluated function. The estimator $U = U(X_1, ..., X_n)$ of $g(\theta)$ is called *unbiased* if

$$\mathbb{E}_\theta[U(X_1, ..., X_n)] = g(\theta),$$

for any $\theta \in \Theta$ (where the notation $\mathbb{E}_\theta$ denotes the dependency on θ).

Equivalently, we say that the estimator U is unbiased if $B_\theta(U) = 0$, where

$$B_\theta(U) := \mathbb{E}_\theta[U] - g(\theta)$$

is the bias.

Hence, we restrict our search to the class of unbiased estimators. Let us provide an example for the Normal distribution.

Proposition 3.1. *Consider $X \sim N(\mu, \sigma^2)$ and let $(X_1, ..., X_n)$ be a random sample generated by X. Assume that X_i's are i.i.d. with $X_i \sim N(\mu, \sigma^2)$, for any i. The following properties hold true.*

i) An unbiased mean-estimator is given by

$$\bar{X} := \frac{1}{n}\sum_{i=1}^{n} X_i. \tag{3.1}$$

The estimator $\bar{X}$ is called sample mean.

ii) If the mean μ is unknown, an unbiased variance-estimator is

$$S^2 := \frac{1}{n-1}\sum_{i=1}^{n}(X_i - \bar{X})^2. \tag{3.2}$$

The estimator S^2 is named sample variance.

Proof. i) Due to the independence of X_i's and by the linearity of the expected value, we have

$$\mathbb{E}_\theta[\bar{X}] = \frac{1}{n}\sum_{i=1}^{n}\mathbb{E}_\theta[X_i] = \frac{1}{n}n\mu = \mu.$$

ii) We can write

$$\begin{aligned} S^2 &= \frac{1}{n-1}\sum_{i=1}^{n}\left((X_i-\mu)+(\mu-\bar{X})\right)^2 \\ &= \frac{1}{n-1}\sum_{i=1}^{n}\left((X_i-\mu)^2 + 2(X_i-\mu)(\mu-\bar{X}) + (\mu-\bar{X})^2\right) \\ &= \frac{1}{n-1}\left(\sum_{i=1}^{n}(X_i-\mu)^2 - 2n(\mu-\bar{X})^2 + n(\mu-\bar{X})^2\right) \\ &= \frac{1}{n-1}\left(\sum_{i=1}^{n}(X_i-\mu)^2 - n(\mu-\bar{X})^2\right). \end{aligned} \tag{3.3}$$

The expected value of S^2 is given by

$$\begin{aligned} \mathbb{E}_\theta[S^2] &= \frac{1}{n-1}\sum_{i=1}^{n}\mathbb{E}_\theta[X_i-\mu]^2 - \frac{n}{n-1}\mathbb{E}_\theta[\mu-\bar{X}]^2 \\ &= \frac{n}{n-1}\sigma^2 - \frac{n}{n-1}Var(\bar{X}), \end{aligned} \tag{3.4}$$

where

$$Var(\bar{X}) = \frac{1}{n^2}\sum_{i=1}^{n} Var(X_i) = \frac{1}{n^2}n\sigma^2 = \frac{1}{n}\sigma^2;$$

hence, we soon obtain

$$\mathbb{E}_\theta[S^2] = \frac{n}{n-1}\sigma^2 - \frac{1}{n-1}\sigma^2 = \sigma^2.$$

■

Since the class of the unbiased estimators is very large, we have to consider a further criterion that, jointly with the unbiasedness, may help us in selecting the best estimator. The criterion presented in the next definition, suggests choosing the estimator with the smallest variance among the other unbiased estimators. This is because the variance measures the closeness between the realizations of a random variable and its mean.

Definition 3.3. The unbiased estimator U of $g(\theta)$ is called *minimum-variance unbiased estimator* (MVUE) or *uniformly minimum-variance unbiased estimator* (UMVUE) if it has lower variance than any other unbiased estimator for all possible values of the parameter. In other words, given any other unbiased estimator $U^\star$ of $g(\theta)$, the following inequalities hold true

- $\frac{Var(U)}{Var(U^\star)} \leq 1$ for any $\theta \in \Theta$,
- There exists $\theta \in \Theta$ such that $\frac{Var(U)}{Var(U^\star)} < 1$.

Observe that the quantity $\frac{Var(U)}{Var(U^\star)}$ can be used to test the efficiency of $U^\star$. An MVUE estimator U of $g(\theta)$ is also named *efficient* estimator of $g(\theta)$.

Definition 3.4. An unbiased and MVUE estimator U of $g(\theta)$ is said to be *optimal* estimator of $g(\theta)$.

3.1.2 *Cramer-Rao Inequality*

Unfortunately, the optimal estimator is not always available. In this case, we have to use alternative methods. One of these, known as the Cramer-Rao inequality, suggests choosing the estimator with the variance as close as possible to the lower bound on the unbiased estimator variance. The next theorem explains how to determinate such a bound.

Theorem 3.1 (Cramer-Rao inequality). *Let X be a random variable with density function $f(x,\theta)$, $\theta \in \Theta \subset \mathbb{R}$, and let $(X_1, ..., X_n)$ be a random sample generated by X. Assume that*

- *$f(x;\theta)$ is positive over a set S which is independent of $\theta \in \Theta$;*
- *Θ is an open interval of $\mathbb{R}$;*

- *For any* $\theta \in \Theta$ *and* $x \in S$, *there exists* $\frac{\partial}{\partial \theta} f(x;\theta)$ *a.s. except subsets* $N \subset S$ *such that* $\mathbb{P}_\theta(X \in N) = 0$ *for any* $\theta \in \Theta$.;
- $\frac{\partial}{\partial \theta} \int_S \cdots \int_S f(x_1; \ldots, x_n, \theta)\, dx_1 .. dx_n = \int_S \cdots \int_S \frac{\partial}{\partial \theta} f(x_1; \ldots, x_n \theta)\, dx_1 .. dx_n$, *i.e.* $f(x;\theta)$ *is differentiable under the integral sign;*
- *The quantity* $I(\theta) := \mathbb{E}_\theta \left[\frac{\partial}{\partial \theta} \log f(X;\theta)\right]^2 < \infty$ *for any* $\theta \in \Theta$;
- *If* $W = W(X_1, .., X_n)$ *is an estimator of* $g(\theta)$ *such that* $\mathbb{E}_\theta[W] < \infty$ *one has*

$$\frac{\partial}{\partial \theta} \mathbb{E}_\theta[W] = \int_S \cdots \int_S W \frac{\partial}{\partial \theta} f(x_1, .., x_n; \theta)\, dx_1 .. dx_n.$$

Then, for every unbiased estimator $U = U(X_1, \ldots, X_n)$ *of* $g(\theta)$, *we have*

$$Var(U) \geq \frac{(g'(\theta))^2}{nI(\theta)} \qquad (\theta \in \Theta).$$

The right-side quantity is known as Cramer-Rao bound (CRB), while $I(\theta)$ *is said to be the Fisher information.*

Remark 3.1. If an unbiased estimator U of $g(\theta)$ has variance equal to the Cramer-Rao bound, then it is an optimal estimator of $g(\theta)$. Otherwise, we can use the following quantity as a measure of efficiency for U

$$e(U) = \frac{B_n(\theta)}{Var(U)},$$

where $B_n(\theta) = \frac{1}{nI(\theta)}$.

Definition 3.5. An unbiased estimator $U = U(X_1, \ldots, X_n)$ of $g(\theta)$ is said to be efficient if its variance coincides with the Cramer-Rao bound, i.e. $e(U) = 1$ for any θ.

Remark 3.2. Define the mean square error (MSE) of an estimator U of $g(\theta)$ by the following

$$MSE(U) := \mathbb{E}_\theta[U - g(\theta)]^2.$$

If U is an unbiased estimator of $g(\theta)$, then the MSE coincides with its variance, and the efficiency reduces to the MVUE property.

3.2 Probability Generating Functions (PGF)

Let X be a discrete random variable on $(\Omega, \mathcal{F}, \mathbb{P})$.

Definition 3.6. The probability generating function (PGF) of X, $G_X : \mathbb{R} \to \mathbb{R}$, is given by

$$G_X(z) = \mathbb{E}\left[z^X\right] = \sum_{k=0}^{+\infty} \mathbb{P}(X = k) z^k. \qquad (3.5)$$

$G_X(z)$ represents a power series in z, which converges if there exists a real number $r \in (0, +\infty)$ such that $|z| \leq r$. The quantity r is known as the radius of convergence.

Example 3.1. Consider $X \sim B(p)$. The PGF of X is

$$G_X(z) = \sum_{k=0}^{+\infty} \mathbb{P}(X = k)z^k = \sum_{k=0}^{+\infty} p^k(1-p)^{1-k}z^k = (1-p) + pz, \tag{3.6}$$

where the last equality comes from the binomial theorem.

Example 3.2. Consider $X \sim Pois(\lambda)$. The PGF of X is

$$\begin{aligned} G_X(z) &= \sum_{k=0}^{+\infty} \mathbb{P}(X = k)z^k = \sum_{k=0}^{+\infty} \frac{\lambda^k e^{-\lambda}}{k!} z^k = e^{-\lambda} \sum_{k=0}^{+\infty} \frac{(\lambda z)^k}{k!} \\ &= e^{-\lambda} e^{\lambda z} = e^{-\lambda(1-z)}, \end{aligned}$$

where we have used the Taylor series expansion of the exponential function.

Example 3.3. Consider $X \sim BN(n, p)$. The PGF of X is

$$\begin{aligned} G_X(z) &= \sum_{k=0}^{+\infty} \mathbb{P}(X = k)z^k = \sum_{k=n}^{+\infty} \binom{k-1}{n-1} p^n (1-p)^{k-n} z^k \\ &= \left(\frac{p}{1-p}\right)^n \sum_{k=n}^{+\infty} \binom{k-1}{n-1} (1-p)^k z^k \\ &= \left(\frac{pz}{1-z(1-p)}\right)^n. \end{aligned}$$

3.2.1 *PGF Properties*

The next theorem summarizes some properties concerning the probability generating functions.

Theorem 3.2. *Let X, Y be two discrete random variables, with PGF G_X and G_Y, respectively. Then, following properties hold true.*

i) If $Y = a + bX$, with $a, b \in \mathbb{R}$, then $G_Y(z) = z^a G_X(z^b)$;
ii) If X and Y are independent, then $G_{X+Y}(z) = G_X(z)G_Y(z)$;
iii) $\mathbb{P}(X = n) = \frac{1}{n!}G^{(n)}(0)$, for any $n \in \mathbb{N}$, where $G^{(n)}(z) := \frac{d^n}{dz^n}G(z)$.

Proof. i) For fixed $a, b \in \mathbb{R}$, we have

$$G_Y(z) = \mathbb{E}[z^{a+bX}] = z^a \mathbb{E}\big[(z^b)^X\big] = z^a G_X(z^b).$$

ii) Due to the independence between X and Y, we can write

$$G_{X+Y}(z) = \mathbb{E}\big[z^{(X+Y)}\big] = \mathbb{E}\big[z^X z^Y\big] = \mathbb{E}\big[z^X\big]\mathbb{E}\big[z^Y\big] = G_X(z)G_Y(z).$$

iii) Let p_k be the probability $\mathbb{P}(X = k)$, so that

$$G_X(z) = \sum_{k=0}^{+\infty} p_k z^k.$$

It is easy to see that

$$\begin{aligned} G_X^{(n)}(z) &= \sum_{k=n}^{+\infty} k(k-1)\cdots(k-n+1)p_k z^{k-n} \\ &= n!\, p_n + \sum_{k=n+1}^{+\infty} k(k-1)\cdots(k-n+1)p_k z^{k-n}, \end{aligned} \tag{3.7}$$

which soon implies $G_X^{(n)}(0) = n! p_n$.

■

Observe that the property *iii*)-Theorem 3.2 allows us to compute the PMF of a random variable X by the knowledge of its PGF. For this reason, the PGFs will be widely used in Chapter 15 and 16.

The property *ii*)-Theorem 3.2 can be generalized as follows.

Theorem 3.3 (Convolution theorem). *Let $X_1, ..., X_n$ be independent discrete random variables with PGF $G_{X_1}(z), ..., G_{X_n}(z)$, respectively. Then*

$$G_{X_1+\cdots+X_n}(z) = \prod_{i=1}^{n} G_{X_i}(z). \tag{3.8}$$

Theorem 3.4. *Let X, Y be two random variables. Then X and Y have the same probability distribution if and only if $G_X = G_Y$.*

This result implies that the probability generating function of a random variable X uniquely determines its probability distribution, and vice versa.

3.3 Monte Carlo Methods

The so-called Monte Carlo method (MC) is a non-parametric statistical tool used to evaluate mathematical formulas, such as definite integrals from partial or stochastic differential equations, which are generally difficult to solve explicitly. The basic idea is to use randomness to describe the observations of a random variable. We owe Stanislav Ulam for the Monte Carlo method development (see [Metropolis, N. and Ulam, S. (1949)]). The name of the method comes from the city in the south of France, famous for its casinos. This is because the idea of the method came when Stanislav Ulam was thinking over the chances to win in the solitaire card game (see [Los Alamos Science (1987)]). The MC methods belong to a broad class of computational algorithms relying on repeated random sampling. The approach is the same also for problems arising from different fields. The basic assumption in the

MC methods is the possibility to generate sample paths of a given random variable. Below, we show the most common application of the MC method, i.e. the integral evaluation.

3.3.1 *Integral Evaluation*

We want to solve the following integral

$$\theta = \int_{\mathcal{S}} f(x)\, dx,$$

for some domain $\mathcal{S}$. From a probabilistic point of view, this problem is equivalent to computing the expected value of a certain random variable. Indeed, let X be a random variable with $supp(X) = \mathcal{S}$ and density function f_X. Given a real function g, the new random variable $g(X)$ has expected value

$$\mathbb{E}[g(X)] = \int_{\mathcal{S}} g(x) f_X(x)\, dx = \int_{\mathcal{S}} f(x)\, dx = \theta, \tag{3.9}$$

being $f = g \circ f_X$.

Example 3.4. Consider $\mathcal{S} = [a, b]$, $X \sim U(a, b)$ and $g = f$, the relationship (3.9) becomes:

$$\mathbb{E}[f(X)] = \int_{\mathcal{S}} f(x) \cdot f_X(x)\, dx = \int_a^b \frac{f(x)}{b-a}\, dx = \frac{1}{b-a}\theta, \tag{3.10}$$

that is

$$\theta = (b-a)\mathbb{E}[f(X)]. \tag{3.11}$$

Then, in order to evaluate θ, it will be sufficient to take an unbiased estimator of $\mathbb{E}[f(X)]$, i.e. the sample mean (see Eq. (3.1)),

$$\widehat{\mathbb{E}}[f(X)] = \frac{1}{n} \sum_{i=1}^{n} f(X_i), \tag{3.12}$$

where $(X_1, ..., X_n)$ is a random sample generated by X. Hence, the estimator of θ is

$$\hat{\theta} = \frac{(b-a)}{n} \sum_{i=1}^{n} f(x_i), \tag{3.13}$$

where $(x_1, ..., x_n)$ is a set of realizations $(X_1, ..., X_n)$.
Moreover, the above estimator $U = (b-a)\widehat{\mathbb{E}}[f(X)]$ is an unbiased estimator of θ. In fact,

$$\mathbb{E}[U] = (b-a)\widehat{\mathbb{E}}[f(X)] = (b-a)\mathbb{E}[f(X)] = \theta. \tag{3.14}$$

3.3.2 *Estimator Variance*

We want to compute the variance of the unbiased estimator U of θ,

$$\begin{aligned} Var(U) &= \frac{(b-a)^2}{n^2}\sum_{i=1}^{n} Var(f(X_i)) = \frac{(b-a)^2}{n} Var(f(X)) \\ &= \frac{(b-a)^2}{n}\int_a^b \left(f(x) - \int_a^b f(t)\,dt\right)^2 dx. \end{aligned} \tag{3.15}$$

Look for an estimator of the unknown $Var(f(X))$. Observe that $f(X_i)$'s ($i = 1, ..., n$), are independent random variables (like the X_i's are too), then, by Eq. (3.2), the unbiased estimator of the variance is given by the sample variance, i.e.

$$Var(U) = \frac{(b-a)^2}{n}\frac{\sum_{i=1}^{n}(f(X_i) - \widehat{\mathbb{E}}[f(X)]^2)}{n-1}. \tag{3.16}$$

Note that Eq. (3.16) is valid if the X_i's are independent; otherwise, the variance of the sum is different from the sum of the variances.

3.4 Variance Reduction

One of the main sampling goals is the reduction of the estimators' variance without affecting their properties, such as unbiasedness. A possible way to do this is provided by the antithetic variates.

3.4.1 *Antithetic Variates*

Consider the integral evaluating problem described in Example 3.4,

$$\theta = \int_a^b f(x)\,dx.$$

From the MC method we find the following unbiased estimator of θ

$$U = (b-a)\widehat{\mathbb{E}}[f(X)],$$

whose variance is given by Eq. (3.15). Our goal is the variance reduction of U. Set X_i equal to

$$\tilde{X}_i = a + (b - X_i) \qquad (i = 1, ..., n), \tag{3.17}$$

with n an even integer. $\tilde{X}_i$ is called *antithetic variate*. If $X_i \sim U(a, b)$, then $\tilde{X}_i \sim U(a, b)$ with the same expected value and variance of X_i, since

$$\mathbb{E}[\tilde{X}_i] = a + b - \mathbb{E}[X_i] = a + b - \frac{a+b}{2} = \frac{a+b}{2} = \mathbb{E}[X_i],$$

$$Var(\tilde{X}_i) = Var(X_i).$$

By using the antithetic variates we built a new unbiased estimator of θ, given by

$$\bar{\theta} = \frac{b-a}{n}\sum_{i=1}^{\frac{n}{2}}(f(X_i) + f(\tilde{X}_i)). \tag{3.18}$$

Indeed,

$$\mathbb{E}[\bar{\theta}] = \frac{b-a}{n} n\mathbb{E}[f(X)] = (b-a)\mathbb{E}[f(X)] = \theta.$$

Moreover,

$$\begin{aligned} Var(\bar{\theta}) &= \frac{(b-a)^2}{n^2}\sum_{i=1}^{\frac{n}{2}}(Var(f(X_i)) + Var(f(\tilde{X}_i)) + 2Cov(f(X_i), f(\tilde{X}_i))) \\ &= \frac{(b-a)^2}{n}(Var(f(X)) + Cov(f(X), f(\tilde{X}))) \\ &= \frac{(b-a)^2}{n}(Var(f(X)) + Var(f(X))Corr(f(X), f(\tilde{X}))) \\ &= \frac{(b-a)^2}{n}Var(f(X))(1 + Corr(f(X), f(\tilde{X}))), \end{aligned} \tag{3.19}$$

If we set $\sigma^2_{f(X)} = Var(f(X))$ and $\rho = Corr(f(X), f(\tilde{X}))$, relation (3.19) may be rewritten as

$$Var(\bar{\theta}) = \frac{(b-a)^2}{n}\sigma^2_{f(X)}(1+\rho). \tag{3.20}$$

By comparing Eqs. (3.15) and (3.20), we conclude that

$$Var(\bar{\theta}) = Var(U)(1+\rho). \tag{3.21}$$

Finally, $Var(\bar{\theta}) < Var(U)$ if ρ is negative, since

$$Var(\bar{\theta}) < Var(U) \iff (1+\rho) < 1 \iff \rho < 0,$$

as desired. The next result provides a necessary condition for a negative correlation.

Proposition 3.2. *Consider $Y = f(X_1, .., X_n)$ with X_i i.i.d. random variables, $X_i \sim U(a,b)$, and set $\tilde{Y} = f(\tilde{X}_1, ..., \tilde{X}_n)$, where $\tilde{X}_i$ are given in Eq. (3.17). If $a = 0$, $b = 1$ and f is monotone (in each variable), then $Corr(Y.\tilde{Y}) < 0$.*

3.5 Copulas

3.5.1 *Definitions*

Definition 3.7. Let X_1, X_2 be two random variables defined on the probability space $(\Omega, \mathcal{F}, \mathbb{P})$. We say X_1 and X_2 are of the same type if there exist $a > 0$ and $b \in \mathbb{R}$ such that

$$X_2 = aX_1 + b.$$

3.5.1.1 *Generalized Inverse Function*

Let T be a real-evaluated and increasing function (i.e. $T(x) \leq T(y)$ if $x \leq y$). The next lemma cares about some properties of increasing functions of random variables.

Lemma 3.1.

i) Let X be a random variable and T an increasing function, then, for $x \in \mathbb{R}$, one has

$$\{X \leq x\} \subset \{T(X) \leq T(x)\}$$

and

$$\mathbb{P}(T(X) \leq T(x)) = \mathbb{P}(X \leq x) + \mathbb{P}(T(X) \leq T(x), X > x).$$

ii) If F_X is the CDF of X, then

$$\mathbb{P}(F_X(X) \leq F_X(x)) = \mathbb{P}(X \leq x).$$

Definition 3.8. Let T be an increasing and real-evaluated function. We define the generalized inverse function of T as

$$T^{(-1)}(y) = inf\{x \in \mathbb{R} | T(x) \geq y\} \qquad (y \in \mathbb{R}). \tag{3.22}$$

Below, we give some properties of $T^{(-1)}$.

Proposition 3.3. *Let T be an increasing and real-valued function. Then*

i) $T^{(-1)}$ is increasing;
ii) T is continuous $\Longleftrightarrow$ $T^{(-1)}$ is strictly increasing;
iii) T is strictly increasing $\Longleftrightarrow$ $T^{(-1)}$ is continuous;
iv) $(T^{(-1)} \circ T)(x) \leq x$;
v) $(T \circ T^{(-1)})(y) \geq y$;
vi) T is strictly increasing $\Longleftrightarrow$ $(T^{(-1)} \circ T)(x) = x$;
vii) If T is continuous, then $(T \circ T^{(-1)})(y) = y$.

Now, let us apply the generalized inverse function to the probability distributions.

Definition 3.9. Let F_X be the CDF of a random variable X, then the generalized inverse of F_X is called the *quantile function* of F_X, i.e.

$$F_X^{(-1)}(q) = \inf\{x \in \mathbb{R} | F_X(x) \geq q\}, \tag{3.23}$$

for any $q \in [0, 1]$.

Remark 3.3. Since the CDF is an increasing function, Proposition 3.3 implies that $(F_X^{(-1)} \circ F_X)(x) \leq x$.
However the event $\{(F_X^{(-1)} \circ F_X)(x) \neq x\}$ has null probability, and so the next proposition holds on.

Proposition 3.4. *If X is a random variable with CDF F_X, then*

$$\mathbb{P}\big((F_X^{(-1)} \circ F_X)(X) = X\big) = 1.$$

Proposition 3.5. *Let F_X be the CDF of a random variable X.*

i) If $U \sim U(0,1)$, then $\mathbb{P}(F_X^{(-1)}(U) \leq x) = F_X(x)$, i.e. the random variable $F_X^{(-1)}(U)$ has CDF equal to F_X, or equivalently, $X = F_X^{(-1)}(U)$.
ii) If F_X is continuous, then $F_X(X) \sim U(0,1)$.

Proof. i) If $x \in \mathbb{R}$ and $u \in [0,1]$, by virtue of *i*)-Proposition 3.3 and Proposition 3.4, we have

$$F_X(x) \geq u \iff F_X^{(-1)}(u) \leq x.$$

Therefore,

$$\mathbb{P}(F_X^{(-1)}(U) \leq x) = \mathbb{P}(U \leq F_X(x)) = F_X(x).$$

ii) Observe that

$$\begin{aligned}\mathbb{P}(F_X(X) \leq u) &= \mathbb{P}\big((F_X^{(-1)} \circ F_X)(X) \leq F_X^{(-1)}(u)\big)\\ &= \mathbb{P}(X \leq F_X^{(-1)}(u))\\ &= F_X(F_X^{(-1)}(u))\\ &= u,\end{aligned}$$

where the first equality comes from *ii*)-Proposition 3.3, the second one from Proposition 3.4 and the last one from *vii*)-Proposition 3.3.

■

A formal definition of a copula is given below.

Definition 3.10. An m-dimensional copula is a cumulative distribution function $C : [0,1]^m \to [0,1]$ having uniform marginals.

Any copula C is such that

i) $C(u_1, ..., u_m)$ is increasing with respect to each component u_i, for any $(u_1, ..., u_m) \in [0,1]^m$;
ii) $C(1, ..., 1, u_i, 1, ..., 1) = u_i$, for any $u_i \in [0,1]$, $i \in \{1, ..., m\}$.

The first property comes from the definition of multivariate CDF, while the second holds true since the marginal distributions are (standard) uniformly distributed. Copulas can be used to establish the relationship between marginal distributions and their joint cumulative distribution. Given the marginal cumulative distributions $F_1(\cdot), ..., F_m(\cdot)$, the function

$$F(x_1, ..., x_m) := C(F_1(x_1), ..., F_m(x_m)), \quad (x_1, ..., x_m) \in \mathbb{R}^m,$$

defined by the copula C, represents the multivariate CDF having marginal distributions $F_1, ..., F_m$. Indeed, if $(u_1, ..., u_m) = (F_1(x_1), ..., F_m(x_m)) \in [0,1]^m$, from *ii*)-Proposition 3.5 and since $U_i \sim U(0,1)$, we have

$$\begin{aligned} C(u_1, ..., u_m) &= \mathbb{P}(U_1 \le F_1(x_1), ..., U_m \le F_m(x_m)) \\ &= \mathbb{P}(F_1^{(-1)}(U_1) \le x_1, ..., F_m^{(-1)}(U_m) \le x_m) \\ &= \mathbb{P}(X_1 \le x_1, ..., X_m \le x_m) \\ &= F(x_1, ..., x_m), \end{aligned}$$

for any $(x_1, ..., x_m) \in \mathbb{R}^m$, where $X_i = F_i^{(-1)}$.

3.5.2 *Sklar Theorem*

In probability theory and statistics, copulas are usually used to describe the dependence between random variables. A copula is a multivariate CDF such that the marginal probability distribution of each variable is uniform on the interval $[0,1]$.

The importance of copulas is due to the following Sklar theorem which states that copulas can be used to link the marginal cumulative distributions with their joint cumulative distribution.

Theorem 3.5 (Sklar theorem). *Let F be a multivariate m-dimensional distribution function with marginal distributions $F_1, ..., F_m$. Then there exists an m-copula C such that, for every $(x_1, \ldots, x_m) \in \mathbb{R}^m$, we have*

$$F(x_1, \ldots, x_m) = C(F_1(x_1), \ldots, F_m(x_m)). \tag{3.24}$$

Moreover, if the marginal distributions are continuous, then C is unique. Conversely, if C is a m-copula and $F_1, \ldots, F_m$ are distribution functions, then the function F defined by Eq. (3.24) *is an m-dimensional distribution function with marginals $F_1, \ldots, F_m$.*

To show the corollary to the Sklar theorem, we first need to define the quantile function F^{-1} that is the generalized inverse function of a univariate cumulative distribution function F.
For every $q \in [0,1]$: $F^{-1}(q) = inf\{x \in \mathbb{R} \mid F(x) \ge q\}$.

Corollary 3.1. *Let F be a multivariate m-dimensional distribution function with continuous marginal distributions $F_1, ..., F_m$ and C is an m-copula. Then, for every $(u_1, \ldots, u_m) \in [0,1]^m$, we have*

$$C(u_1, \ldots, u_m) = F(F_1^{(-1)}(u_1), \ldots, F_m^{(-1)}(u_m)),$$

where $F_1^{(-1)}, \ldots, F_m^{(-1)}$ are quantile functions of $F_1, ..., F_m$, respectively.

Through this result, a joint cumulative distribution with continuous marginals is linked to its copula if and only if its arguments are the quantile functions of the marginals.

To prove Sklar's theorem we consider a distributional transform defined as follows.

Let Y be a random variable with distribution function F and let V be a random variable independent of Y, such that V is uniformly distributed on $(0, 1)$. The modified distribution function $F(x, \lambda)$, for $\lambda \in \mathbb{R}$, is defined by

$$F(x, \lambda) = \mathbb{P}(X < x) + \lambda \mathbb{P}(Y = x).$$

Then, we call

$$U = F(Y, V) \tag{3.25}$$

the generalized distributional transform of Y.
If F is continuous, $F(x, \lambda) = F(x)$ for all $\lambda \in \mathbb{R}$.
So we have the following result.

Proposition 3.6. *(Distributional transform) Let $U = F(Y, V)$ be the generalized distributional transform of Y as defined in Eq. (3.25). Then U is uniformly distributed on $(0, 1)$ and $Y = F^{-1}(U)$ almost surely.*

Now we use the generalized distributional transform to provide the proof of Sklar's theorem in the general case.

Proof. (**Proof of Sklar's theorem**) If $F_1, ..., F_m$ are continuous, then $F_i(X_i) \sim U(0, 1)$ for $i = 1, \ldots, m$ and so, for every $(u_1, \ldots, u_m) \in [0, 1]^m$:

$$\begin{aligned} C(u_1, \ldots, u_m) &= \mathbb{P}(F_1(X_1) \leq u_1, \ldots, F_m(X_m) \leq u_m) \\ &= \mathbb{P}(X_1 \leq F_1^{-1}(u_1), \ldots, X_m \leq F_m^{-1}(u_m)) \\ &= F(F_1^{-1}(u_1), \ldots, F_m^{-1}(u_m)). \end{aligned}$$

Let $(x_1, \ldots, x_m) \in \mathbb{R}^m$, because C is a copula

$$\begin{aligned} F(x_1, \ldots, x_m) &= \mathbb{P}(X_1 \leq x_1, \ldots, X_m \leq x_m) \\ &= \mathbb{P}(F_1(X_1) \leq F_1(x_1), \ldots, F_m(X_m) \leq F_m(x_m)) \\ &= C(F_1(X_1), \ldots, F_m(X_m)). \end{aligned}$$

In the case the marginal is not continuous, let V be a random variable independent of $X = (X_1, \ldots, X_m)$ and uniformly distributed on $(0, 1)$. Considering the distributional transforms $U_i = F_i(X_i, V)$ for $i = 1, \ldots, m$, the previous theorem yields U_i are uniformly distributed on $(0, 1)$ and $X_i = F_i^{-1}(U_i)$ almost surely. Thus, let $(x_1, \ldots, x_m) \in \mathbb{R}^m$ and defining C to be the distribution function of $U_1, \ldots, U_m$, we have

$$\begin{aligned} F(x_1, \ldots, x_m) &= \mathbb{P}(X_1 \le x_1, \ldots, X_m \le x_m) \\ &= \mathbb{P}(F_1^{-1}(U_1) \le x_1, \ldots, F_m^{-1}(U_m) \le x_m) \\ &= \mathbb{P}(U_1 \le F_1(x_1), \ldots, U_m \le F_m(x_m)) \\ &= C(F_1(X_1), \ldots, F_m(X_m)), \end{aligned}$$

i.e. C is a copula.

■

The property *ii*) of Definition 3.10, implies that the marginal distribution of X_i is

$$\begin{aligned} C(F_1(+\infty), .., F_i(x_i), .., F_m(+\infty)) &= C(1, ..., F_i(x_i), ..., 1) \\ &= \mathbb{P}(X_i \le x_i) \\ &= F_i(x_i), \end{aligned}$$

for any $x_i \in \mathbb{R}$.
The vice versa is still valid, as shown by the Sklar theorem.

3.5.3 *Properties*

3.5.3.1 *Invariance*

A useful property of the copula is the invariance to strictly increasing transformations of the marginal distributions.

Theorem 3.6 (Invariance). *Let $\boldsymbol{X} = (X_1, ..., X_m)$ be a random vector having continuous marginal CDF $F_1, ..., F_m$ and copula C. Consider $T_1, ..., T_m$ a strictly increasing function. Then, also $(T_1(X_1), ..., T_m(X_m))$ has copula equal to C.*

Proof. First of all, let us show that the CDF of $T_i(X_i)$'s are $\tilde{F}_i(y) = \left(F_i \circ T_i^{(-1)}\right)(y)$, for any $i = 1, ..., m$. Indeed,

$$\begin{aligned} \tilde{F}_i(y) &= \mathbb{P}(T_i(X_i) \le y) = \mathbb{P}\big((T_i^{(-1)} \circ T_i)(X_i) \le T_i^{(-1)}(y)\big) \\ &= \mathbb{P}(X_i \le T_i^{(-1)}(y)) \qquad (y \in \mathbb{R}), \end{aligned}$$

where we have used *vi*)-Proposition 3.3. Since F_i and $T_i^{(-1)}$ are continuous, by *iii*)-Proposition 3.3, then also $\tilde{F}_i$ is continuous, for any i. Consequently, $T_i(X_i)$'s have continuous CDF. Because $T_i^{(-1)}$ is increasing, from *i*)-Lemma 3.1 we have

$$\tilde{F}_i(y) = \mathbb{P}(T_i(X_i) \le y) + \mathbb{P}(X_i \le T_i^{(-1)}(y), T_i(X_i) > y),$$

where the second probability is null due to the continuity of F_i, for any i, and so

$$\tilde{F}_i(y) = \mathbb{P}(T_i(X_i) \leq y). \tag{3.26}$$

It remains to prove that C is the copula of $(T_1(X_1), ..., T_m(X_m))$. From the relationship (3.26), we may write

$$\begin{aligned} C(u_1, ..., u_m) &= \mathbb{P}(F_1(X_1) \leq u_1, ..., F_m(X_m) \leq u_m) \\ &= \mathbb{P}(\tilde{F}_1(T_1(X_1)) \leq u_1, ..., \tilde{F}_m(T_m(X_m)) \leq u_m). \end{aligned}$$

Moreover, due to vi)-Proposition 3.3,

$$(\tilde{F}_i \circ T_i)(x) = (F_i \circ T_i^{(-1)} \circ T_i)(x) = x \qquad (x \in \mathbb{R}),$$

and this concludes the proof. ■

3.5.3.2 *Fréchet-Hoeffding Copula Boundaries*

Another important result for the copulas, which ensures the existence of its upper and lower boundaries, is given below.

Theorem 3.7. *Consider a copula C. For any $\boldsymbol{u} = (u_1, ..., u_m) \in [0,1]^m$ one has*

$$\max\left\{\sum_{i=1}^{m} u_i + 1 - m, 0\right\} \leq C(\boldsymbol{u}) \leq \min\{u_1, ..., u_m\}. \tag{3.27}$$

Proof. To prove the first (left) inequality, observe that

$$\begin{aligned} C(\boldsymbol{u}) = \mathbb{P}\left(\bigcap_{1\leq i\leq m} \{U_i \leq u_i\}\right) &= 1 - \mathbb{P}\left(\bigcup_{1\leq i\leq m} \{U_i > u_i\}\right) \\ &\geq 1 - \sum_{i=1}^{m} \mathbb{P}(U_i > u_i) = 1 - m + \sum_{i=1}^{m} u_i \end{aligned}$$

The second (right) inequality follows from the inclusion

$$\bigcap_{1\leq j\leq m} \{U_j \leq u_j\} \subset \{U_i \leq u_i\}$$

which holds true if $U_j \sim U(0,1)$ $(j = 1, ..., m)$, for any $i = 1, ..., m$. ■

We denote the lower and upper Fréchet-Hoeffding boundaries by $W(\boldsymbol{u})$ and $M(\boldsymbol{u})$, respectively.
Note that $M(\boldsymbol{u})$ is a copula for any m, while $W(\boldsymbol{u})$ is never a copula for $m > 2$. Anyway, $W(\boldsymbol{u})$ represents the best possible lower boundary; i.e. given $\boldsymbol{u} \in [0,1]^m$ and $m \geq 3$, there exists a copula C such that $C(\boldsymbol{u}) = \max\{\sum_{i=1}^{m} u_i - m + 1, 0\}$. W and M are both copulas only when $m = 2$.

Remark 3.4. The previous result can be extended also to the CDF. In fact, for a multivariate distribution F with marginal distributions $F_1, ..., F_m$, we have

$$\max\left\{\sum_{i=1}^{m} F_i(x_i) + 1 - m, 0\right\} \leq F(\boldsymbol{x}) \leq \min\{F(x_1), ..., F(x_m)\}, \tag{3.28}$$

for any $\boldsymbol{x} = (x_1, .., x_m) \in \mathbb{R}^m$.

3.5.4 *Popular Families*

3.5.4.1 *Independence Copula*

The notion of independence between random variables can be explained by the copulas.

In Chapter 1 we introduced the definition of stochastic independence (see Definition 1.19), where events are independent if the probability of the joint event occurrence is equal to the product of the single event occurrence probabilities. Now, we express independence through copulas.

Theorem 3.8. *Let $\boldsymbol{X} = (X_1, ..., X_m)$ be a continuous random vector with joint cumulative distribution and marginal distributions $F_{\boldsymbol{X}}$ and $F_1, ..., F_m$, respectively. Then $X_1, ..., X_m$ are independent if and only if*

$$C_{\boldsymbol{X}}(\boldsymbol{u}) = \prod_{i=1}^{m} u_i,$$

for any $\boldsymbol{u} = (u_1, ..., u_m) \in \mathbb{R}^m$.

Proof. By virtue of Theorem 3.6 and from the independence of X_i's, the copula of $\boldsymbol{X}$ is

$$\begin{aligned} C_{\boldsymbol{X}}(\boldsymbol{u}) &= F_{\boldsymbol{X}}(F_1^{(-1)}(u_1), ..., F_m^{(-1)}(u_m)) = F_{\boldsymbol{X}}(x_1, ..., x_m) \\ &= \prod_{i=1}^{m} F_i(x_i) = \prod_{i=1}^{m} F_i(F_i^{(-1)}(u_i)) = \prod_{i=1}^{m} u_i. \end{aligned}$$

■

Based on the above result, we give the following definition.

Definition 3.11. Let $\boldsymbol{X} = (X_1, ..., X_m)$ be a vector of independent random variables. Then we define the *independence copula* by

$$\Pi_{\boldsymbol{X}}(\boldsymbol{u}) = \prod_{i=1}^{m} u_i, \tag{3.29}$$

with $\boldsymbol{u} = (u_1, ..., u_m) \in \mathbb{R}^m$.

3.5.4.2 Comonotonic Copula

Definition 3.12. Let $\boldsymbol{X} = (X_1, ..., X_m)$ be a random vector. The X_i's are *comonotonic* if their copulas admit the upper Fréchet-Hoeffding boundary, i.e.

$$M(\boldsymbol{u}) = \min\{u_1, ..., u_m\}, \tag{3.30}$$

with $\boldsymbol{u} = (u_1, ..., u_m) \in \mathbb{R}^m$. M defined in Eq. (3.30) is called *comonotonic copula.*

Note that the comonotonic copula represents the joint distribution of the random vector $(U_1, ..., U_m)$, where $U_i \sim U(0,1)$ for any i. Indeed, let $X_1, ..., X_m$ be m (continuous) random variables, such that $X_i = T_i(X_1)$, where T_i's are real-evaluated and strictly increasing functions; by virtue of Theorem 3.6 we know that each CDF F_i of X_i is given by $F_i = F_1 \circ T_i^{(-1)}$. Then, the copula of $\boldsymbol{X} = (X_1, ..., X_m)$ is equal to the CDF of

$$\left(F_1(X_1), (F_1 \circ T_2^{(-1)} \circ T_2)(X_1), ..., (F_1 \circ T_m^{(-1)} \circ T_m)(X_1)\right). \tag{3.31}$$

Setting $U_i = F_i(X_i)$, from vi)-Proposition 3.3, we have that Eq. (3.31) is the distribution of $(U_1, ..., U_m)$, coincident with Eq. (3.30). Therefore, the comonotonic copula highlights the perfect dependence between the random variables X_i.
The next proposition gives a characterization of the comonotonic copula.

Proposition 3.7. *Consider a random variable Z and m increasing functions $v_1, ..., v_m$. Then $X_1, ..., X_m$ are comonotonic random variables if and only if*

$$(X_1, ..., X_m) = (v_1(Z), ..., v_m(Z)).$$

Proof. Let $\boldsymbol{X} = (X_1, ..., X_m)$ be a random vector with joint cumulative distributions and marginal distributions given by $F_{\boldsymbol{X}}$ and $F_1, ..., F_m$, respectively. Assume that X_i are comonotonic for any i. Let U be a uniform random variable. By virtue of Eq. (3.30), we have

$$\begin{aligned} F_{\boldsymbol{X}}(x_1, ..., x_m) &= \min\{F_1(x_1), ..., F_m(x_m)\} \\ &= \mathbb{P}(U \le \min\{F_1(x_1), ..., F_m(x_m)\}) \\ &= \mathbb{P}(U \le F_1(x_1), ..., U \le F_m(x_m)) \\ &= \mathbb{P}(F_1^{(-1)}(U) \le x_1, ..., F_m^{(-1)}(U) \le x_m). \end{aligned}$$

This means that

$$(X_1, ..., X_m) = (F_1^{(-1)}(U), ..., F_m^{(-1)}(U)).$$

Vice versa,

$$\begin{aligned} F_{\boldsymbol{X}}(x_1, ..., x_m) &= \mathbb{P}(X_1 \le x_1, ..., X_m \le x_m) \\ &= \mathbb{P}(v_1(Z) \le x_1, ..., v_m(Z) \le x_m) \\ &= \mathbb{P}(Z \in A_1, ..., Z \in A_m) \\ &= \mathbb{P}(Z \in \cap_{i=1}^m A_i) \end{aligned}$$

where each $A_i := v_i^{-1}(-\infty, x_i]$ represents an interval of type $(-\infty, k_i)$ o $(-\infty, k_i]$. Therefore,

$$\begin{aligned} F_{\mathbf{X}}(x_1, ..., x_m) &= \min \{\mathbb{P}(Z \in A_1), ..., \mathbb{P}(Z \in A_m)\} \\ &= \min \{F_1(x_1), ..., F_m(x_m)\}; \end{aligned}$$

and the proof is complete. ■

In the case of continuous marginal distributions, the next result holds true.

Corollary 3.2. *Let $X_1, ..., X_m$ be random variables with continuous marginal distributions $F_1, ..., F_m$. Then $X_1, ..., X_m$ are comonotonic if and only if, for any pair (i, j), there exists an increasing function T_{ji} such that $X_j = T_{ji}(X_i)$.*

Proof. The proof comes from Proposition 3.7, since there exists i such that $U = F_i(X_i)$. Without loss of generality, we can choose $m = 2$ and $i = 1$. Then, $U = F_1(X_1)$ and

$$(X_1, X_2) = ((F_1^{(-1)} \circ F_1)(X_1), (F_2^{(-1)} \circ F_1)(X_1)) = (X_1, (F_2^{(-1)} \circ F_1)(X_1)).$$

■

Analogously, define countermonotonicity.

3.5.4.3 *Countermonotonic Copula*

Definition 3.13. Two random variables X_1, X_2 are said to be *countermonotonic* if they admit the lower Frèchet-Hoeffding boundary

$$W(u_1, u_2) = \max \{u_1 + u_2 - 1, 0\}. \tag{3.32}$$

The term W in Eq. (3.32) is called a *countermonotonic copula.*

This copula represents the joint cumulative distribution of the random vector $(U, 1 - U)$, with $U \sim U(0, 1)$.

If X_1, X_2 are two continuous and negative-dependent, i.e. X_2 is a strictly decreasing function of X_1, random variables, then their copula is given by Eq. (3.32).

Proposition 3.8. *Consider a random variable Z, an increasing function v_1 and a decreasing function v_2. Then, X_1 and X_2 are counteromonotonic variables if and only if*

$$(X_1, X_2) = (v_1(Z), v_2(Z)).$$

Proof. If $U \sim U(0, 1)$, we get

$$\begin{aligned} (X_1, X_2) &= (F_1^{(-1)}(U), F_2^{(-1)}(1 - U)) \\ &= (F_1^{(-1)}(U), (F_2^{(-1)} \circ g)(U)), \end{aligned}$$

where $g(x) = 1 - x$. Therefore, $v_1 = F_1^{(-1)}$ and $v_2 = F_2^{(-1)} \circ g$ are increasing and decreasing functions, respectively. Vice versa, assume that

$$(X_1, X_2) = (v_1(Z), v_2(Z)),$$

with v_1 and v_2 being increasing and decreasing functions, respectively. We have

$$\begin{aligned} F(x_1, x_2) &= \mathbb{P}(v_1(Z) \leq x_1, v_2(Z) \leq x_2) \\ &= \mathbb{P}(A_1 \cap A_2), \end{aligned}$$

with $A_1 := \{Z \in v_1^{-1}((-\infty, x_1])\}$, $A_2 := \{Z \in v_2^{-1}((-\infty, x_2])\}$. As first step, assume $A_1 \cap A_2 \neq \emptyset$. Due to the monotonicity of v_1, v_2, we can write

$$\mathbb{P}(A_1 \cap A_2) = \mathbb{P}(A_1) + \mathbb{P}(A_2) - 1.$$

Hence,

$$\mathbb{P}(A_1 \cap A_2) = \mathbb{P}(v_1(Z) \leq x_1, v_2(Z) \leq x_2) = F_1(x_1) + F_2(x_2) - 1.$$

Secondly, assume $A_1 \cap A_2 = \emptyset$. Then, $F_1(x_1) + F_2(x_2) - 1 \leq 0$. In both cases, we may conclude that

$$\mathbb{P}(v_1(Z) \leq x_1, v_2(Z) \leq x_2) = \max\{F_1(x_1) + F_2(x_2) - 1, 0\}.$$

■

The independence, comonotonic and countermonotonic copulas are called *fundamental copulas.*

3.5.4.4 *Gaussian Copula*

If $\boldsymbol{X} = (X_1, ..., X_m)$ is a Gaussian random vector, its copula is named *Gaussian copula.* If $\boldsymbol{Y}$ denotes the standardized vector of $\boldsymbol{X}$, then, $\boldsymbol{Y} \sim N(\mathbf{0}, \mathcal{S})$, where $\mathcal{S} = \rho(\Sigma)$ is the correlation matrix of $\boldsymbol{X}$. It is easy to see that $\boldsymbol{X}$ and $\boldsymbol{Y}$ have the same following copula

$$\begin{aligned} C_m(\boldsymbol{u}) &= \mathbb{P}(\Phi(X_1) \leq u_1, ..., \Phi(X_m) \leq u_m) \\ &= \Phi_m(\Phi^{-1}(u_1), ..., \Phi^{-1}(u_m)) \qquad \boldsymbol{u} \in \mathbb{R}^m, \end{aligned}$$

where Φ, Φ_m represent the CDF of the (univariate) standard normal density and the joint cumulative distribution of Y, respectively. The Gaussian copula cannot be defined in a closed form but can be expressed as a manifold integral with respect to the density of $\boldsymbol{Y}$. In two dimensions, if $|\rho| < 1$, one has

$$C(u_1, u_2) = \int_{-\infty}^{\Phi^{-1}(u_1)} \int_{-\infty}^{\Phi^{-1}(u_2)} \frac{1}{2\pi(1-\rho^2)^{\frac{1}{2}}} \exp\left(-\frac{s_1^2 - 2\rho s_1 s_2 + s_2^2}{2(1-\rho^2)}\right) ds_1\, ds_2. \tag{3.33}$$

Observe that the independence and comonotonic copulas, defined by Eqs. (3.29) and (3.30), respectively, are particular cases of Gaussian copulas. In fact, the independence copula reduces to a Gaussian copula if $\mathcal{S}$ is the diagonal matrix (with zeros everywhere except the principal diagonal); similarly holds true for the comonotonic copula if $\mathcal{S}$ is the identity matrix, when m tends to infinity.

The popularity of the Gaussian copula is due in some way to the publication of [Li (2000)]. This is because, in that paper, an example of pricing collateralized debt obligations (CDO) was presented.

3.5.5 *Examples*

Let us introduce three additional families that one may often meet in modeling dependence. Those are Cauchy, Clayton and Gumbel copulas. The first one belongs to the family of symmetric copulas. It is similar to the Gaussian in that it replicates the Student-t multivariate distribution with one degree of freedom $df = 1$. That is why it is often called an extreme copula. The latter two copulas belong to the Archimedean type.

Clayton copula from Eq. (3.34) enables us to model the distributions when joint downside events tend to occur more often than upsides. This is typical for stocks as they tend to fall at the same time, but they do not rise in tandem (see [Longin and Solnik (2014)]). This was confirmed by [Penikas (2014)] when fitting hierarchical copulas to joint distributions of international stock returns. Gumbel copula from Eq. (3.35), on the opposite, allows capturing simultaneous upside movements, rather than the downside ones. Moreover, [Penikas and Simakova (2014)] have found that such copula best fits the joint distribution of the interest rates before the introduction of the inflation targeting. These dependencies at the extremes, or the tails, of the joint distribution, are known as tail dependence. We would look at it closer in Subsection 3.6.3.

$$C = \left(\left(\sum_{i=1}^{d} u_i^{-\theta}\right) + 1 - d\right)^{-1/\theta} \qquad (\theta > 0), \tag{3.34}$$

$$C = exp\left(-\left(\sum_{i=1}^{d}(-log(u_i))^{\theta}\right)^{1/\theta}\right) \qquad (\theta \geq 1), \tag{3.35}$$

where u_i is the cumulative distribution function of the i-th marginal distribution; d is the number of dimensions in the joint distribution (for instance, the number of industry sectors like in Chapter 16).

In Figures 3.1-3.4 we demonstrate a bivariate case where each dimension might be regarded as a separate country or industry. As in Section 16.1, we use Gamma distribution to model marginal distributions. *Gross risk* is the sum of X_1 and X_2 realisations. Importantly, in all four cases, the correlation equals 70%. We make 10k simulations for $X_1 \sim Gamma(2.4; 4.0)$ and $X_2 \sim Gamma(4.4; 2.5)$. These parameters correspond to mean values of 10 and 11 and the variances of 6.2 and 5.2, respectively.

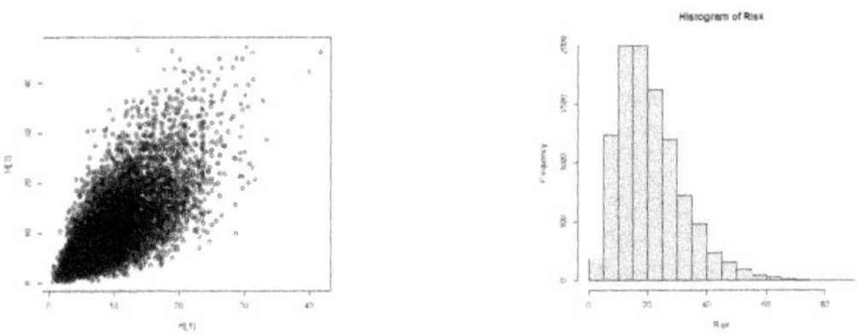

Fig. 3.1: Bivariate plot (left) and gross risk PDF (right) for a *Normal* copula.

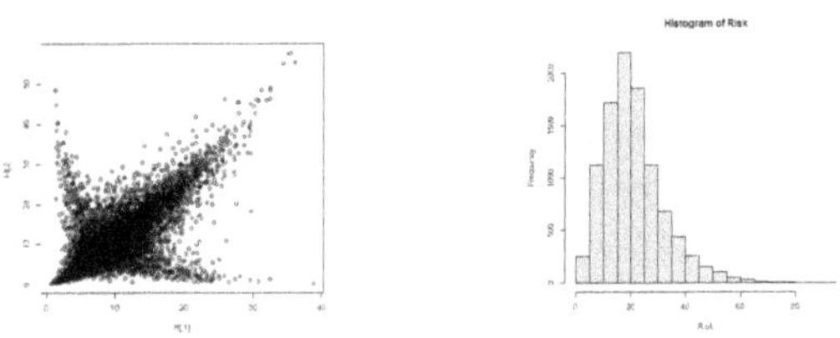

Fig. 3.2: Bivariate plot (left) and gross risk PDF (right) for a *Cauchy* copula.

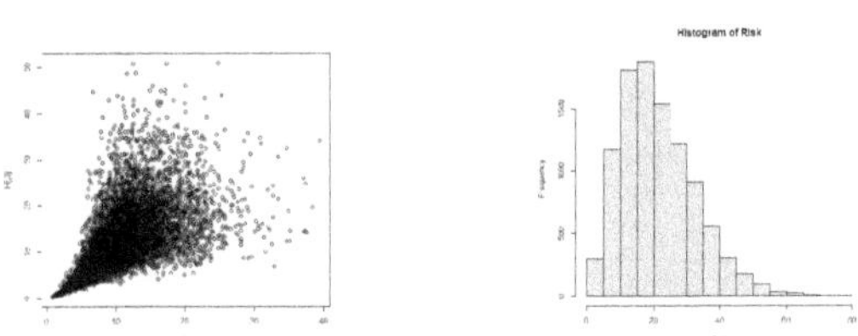

Fig. 3.3: Bivariate plot (left) and gross risk PDF (right) for a *Clayton* copula.

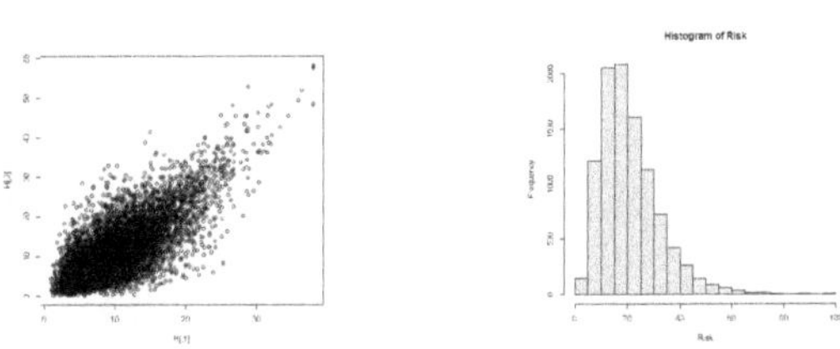

Fig. 3.4: Bivariate plot (left) and gross risk PDF (right) for a *Gumbel* copula.

We are interested in the quantiles of the gross risk distributions depending on the copulas. We consider five most popular confidence levels in Table 3.1. The *95.0%* is the most widespread confidence level in statistics. *97.5%* was introduced as a part of the fundamental review of the market risk for the new risk measure called expected shortfall (see Definition 10.1), see [BCBS (2016a), p. 56, par. 181(b)]. *99.0%* was a Basel II confidence level for the market risk since [BCBS (1996)]. *99.5%* was a temporarily proposed confidence level for the credit risk Internal Ratings-Based (IRB) approach, see [BCBS (2001a), p. 36, par. 172]. *99.9%* is the ultimate level for the credit risk IRB approach since Basel II. It was also the level for the operational risk Advanced Measurement Approach (AMA) in Basel II, but it was abandoned in Basel III.

If X_1 and X_2 are default rates or losses from two country exposures or two industry ones, then the larger the gross risk is, the higher are the total losses. As expected, the downside dependency in Clayton copula results in systematically lower quantile estimates for a chosen level of α. Upside dependency in the Gumbel copula yields higher risk estimates mostly for any confidence level, except the highest one of 99.9% where the extreme Cauchy copula delivers the largest gross risk estimate. As expected, the downside dependency in Clayton copula results in systematically lower quantile estimates for a chosen level of α. Upside dependency in the Gumbel copula yields higher risk estimates mostly for any confidence level, except the highest one of 99.9% where the extreme Cauchy copula delivers the largest gross risk estimate.

Table 3.1: Gross risk quantiles by copulas.

	Copula			
1-α	Normal	Cauchy	Clayton	Gumbel
95.0%	41.28	41.96	41.52	42.69
97.5%	47.41	48.51	46.91	48.34
99.0%	54.35	55.59	52.30	57.50
99.5%	59.73	61.74	56.09	64.02
99.9%	69.44	76.59	64.09	75.90

When discussing copulas, the reader may come across the notation of *rotation*. It is a characteristic of how we treat the inputs to copula function. The direct inputs are the values of the cumulative distribution functions (CDFs). This is the case of zero rotation. Should we look at the inverse to any of the inputs — i.e. $1 - CDF$ — in a bivariate setup, we obtain 90 or 270 degrees rotation. In case when we take the inverse for each of the inputs, we have 180 degrees rotation. It is also called a survival copula.

For illustration we present in Figures 3.5 and 3.8 the rotation for a bivariate Clayton copula with gamma marginals. We use 10k simulated observations and fit the copula parameter in order to have close to +70% correlation when there is zero rotation. Next, we compare the quantiles of the gross risk distribution in Table 3.2 assuming that it is a portfolio of two equally weighted assets.

The reader may think that a survival Clayton copula should be an exact replica of the Gumbel one as after 180 degree rotation the Clayton copula also gets upper

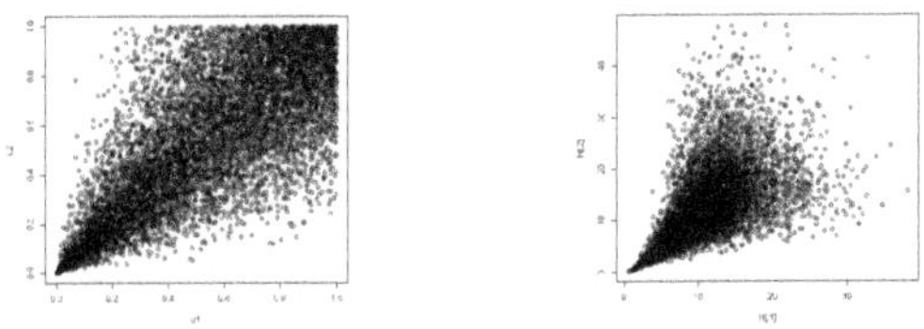

Fig. 3.5: Bivariate plots: in probabilities (left) and in levels (right) for a *0 degree rotation* of Clayton copula.

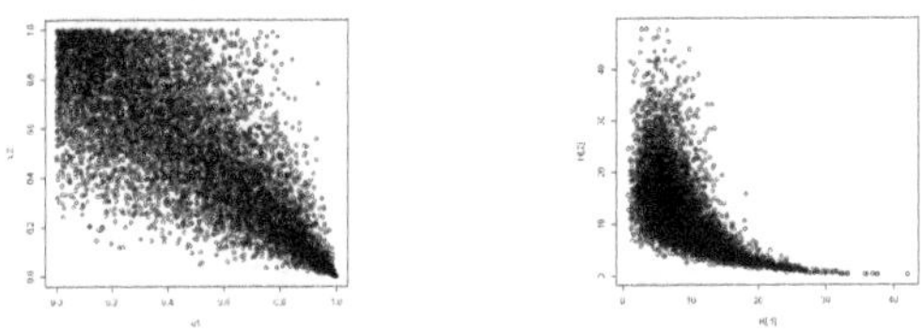

Fig. 3.6: Bivariate plots: in probabilities (left) and in levels (right) for a *90 degree rotation* of Clayton copula.

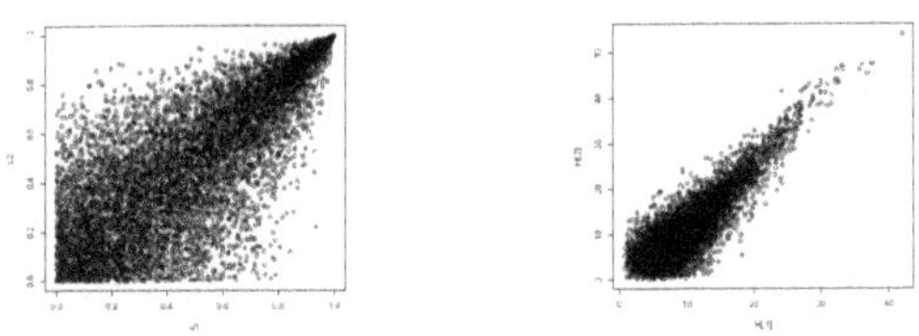

Fig. 3.7: Bivariate plots: in probabilities (left) and in levels (right) for a *180 degree rotation* of Clayton copula.

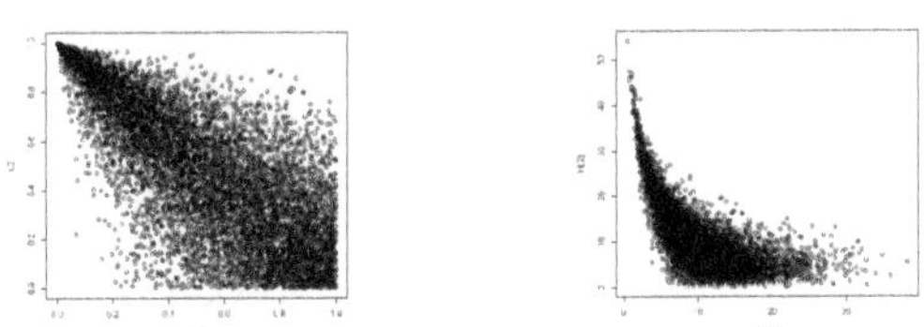

Fig. 3.8: Bivariate plots: in probabilities (left) and in levels (right) for a *270 degree rotation* of Clayton copula.

tail dependence like the Gumbel one. As we may see from the pairwise comparison of Figure 3.7 to 3.9 and Figure 3.5 to 3.10, it does not hold true. The Clayton copula has more concentration of the observations than the Gumbel one. As a result, the extreme quantiles for the survival Clayton copula tend to be larger than those for the Gumbel one. This comes from the different functional forms of two copulas. An

Table 3.2: Gross risk quantiles by rotated copulas.

Copula	Clayton				Gumbel	
Parameter	3.2				1.93	
Rotation, degrees	0	90	180	270	0	180
Correlation, %	+65.29	-68.00	+87.28	-69.89	73.01	59.45
95.0%	42.05	31.24	44.23	30.44	41.64	40.20
97.5%	46.48	34.90	51.23	33.81	48.52	44.68
99.0%	51.59	39.96	59.79	38.08	57.17	50.83
99.5%	55.80	44.23	65.96	41.32	61.76	54.36
99.9%	62.81	51.22	78.08	48.56	71.47	62.82

important implication comes from this observation. The rotation parameter offers a risk manager a much richer variety of joint distributions that can be modeled.

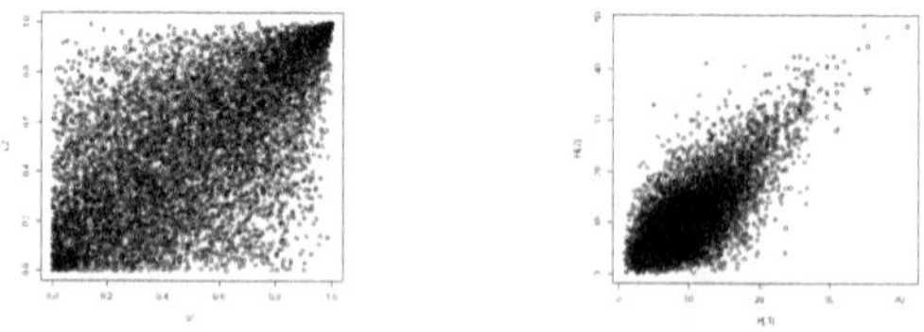

Fig. 3.9: Bivariate plots: in probabilities (left) and in levels (right) for a *0 degree rotation* of Gumbel copula.

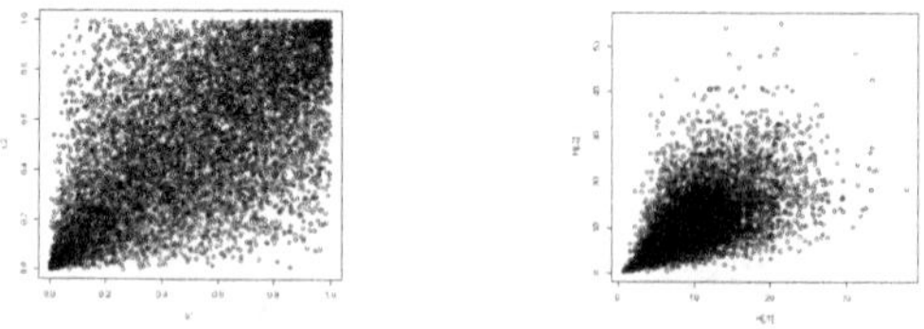

Fig. 3.10: Bivariate plots: in probabilities (left) and in levels (right) for a *180 degree rotation* of Gumbel copula.

We wished to demonstrate examples of different copulas so that the reader can see different parametric estimations of portfolio credit risk. That is why it is particularly important to fit accurately the copula. Otherwise, modelers and not copulas should be blamed, opposite to what [Salmon (2009)] and [MacKenzie and Spears (2012)] did. For more discussion of the latter issue, please, refer to Section 6.

For additional discussion of copulas we may recommend referring to [Joe (1997)], [Cherubini *et al.* (2004)], [Nelsen (2006)], [Shemyakin and Kniazev (2017)].

3.6 Dependence Measures

Among the most common dependence measures we list the following:

- (Linear) Pearson correlation;
- Kendall and the Spearman rank correlation;
- Tail dependence.

Definition 3.14. Given two random variables X_1, X_2, define the Pearson correlation as the ratio of the covariance between X_1 and X_2 to the product of their standard deviations, i.e.

$$\rho(X_1, X_2) = \frac{Cov(X_1, X_2)}{\sigma(X_1)\sigma(X_2)}.$$

The above definition is well posed if $\sigma(X_i) \neq 0$, $i = 1, 2$. The Pearson correlation is a measure of the linear dependence between two random variables. It satisfies the following properties.

Proposition 3.9. *Consider two random variables X_1, X_2. Then*

i) $\rho(X_1, X_2) \in [-1, 1]$;

ii) If X_1, X_2 are independent, then $\rho(X_1, X_2) = 0$;

iii) If $|\rho(X_1, X_2)| = 1$, then there is a perfect (linear) dependence between X_1 and X_2, i.e.

$$\mathbb{P}(X_1 = \alpha + \beta X_2) = 1, \quad \alpha, \beta \in \mathbb{R}.$$

In particular, if $\beta > 0$, X and Y are said to be positively correlated; while if $\beta < 0$ they are negatively correlated;

iv) $\rho(X_1, X_2)$ is invariant with respect to positive linear transformations, i.e.

$$\rho(\alpha_1 + \beta_1 X_1, \alpha_2 + \beta_2 X_2) = \rho(X_1, X_2),$$

where $\alpha_1, \beta_1, \alpha_2, \beta_2 \in \mathbb{R}$;

v) $\rho(X_1, X_2)$ is not invariant with respect to strictly increasing transformations, i.e. $\rho(T(X_1), T(X_2)) \neq \rho(X_1, X_2)$ for a given strictly increasing transformation $T : \mathbb{R} \to \mathbb{R}$.

Remark 3.5. The state $\rho(X_1, X_2) = 0$ does not imply the independence between X_1 and X_2. Such implication holds if and only if X_1 and X_2 are jointly normal random variables.

Lemma 3.2. *Consider a random vector $\boldsymbol{X} = (X_1, X_2)$ with the continuous joint cumulative distribution and marginal distributions $F_{\boldsymbol{X}}$ and F_1, F_2, respectively. Then, if the covariance between X_1 and X_2 is finite, it is defined by*

$$Cov(X_1, X_2) = \int_{\mathbb{R}} \int_{\mathbb{R}} \left(F_{\boldsymbol{X}}(x_1, x_2) - F_1(x_1)F_2(x_2)\right) dx_1\, dx_2 \qquad ((x_1, x_2) \in \mathbb{R}^2). \tag{3.36}$$

Proof. Consider a random vector $(\tilde{X}_1, \tilde{X}_2)$ which is independent of (X_1, X_2). Then,

$$2\,Cov(X_1, X_2) = \mathbb{E}[(X_1 - \tilde{X}_1)(X_2 - \tilde{X}_2)].$$

Indeed,

$$\begin{aligned}\mathbb{E}[(X_1 - \tilde{X}_1)(X_2 - \tilde{X}_2)] &= \mathbb{E}[X_1X_2] - \mathbb{E}[X_1\tilde{X}_2] - \mathbb{E}[\tilde{X}_1X_2] + \mathbb{E}[\tilde{X}_1\tilde{X}_2] \\ &= \mathbb{E}[X_1X_2] - 2\mathbb{E}[X_1]\mathbb{E}[X_2] + \mathbb{E}[X_1X_2] \\ &= 2(\mathbb{E}[X_1X_2] - \mathbb{E}[X_1]\mathbb{E}[X_2]) \\ &= 2\,Cov(X_1, X_2),\end{aligned}$$

Now, by applying the relationship

$$a - b = \int_{\mathbb{R}} (\mathbb{1}_{\{b\le x\}} - \mathbb{1}_{\{a\le x\}})dx \qquad (a, b \in \mathbb{R}), \tag{3.37}$$

to the variables $X_1 - \tilde{X}_1$ and $X_2 - \tilde{X}_2$, we obtain

$$\begin{aligned}2\,Cov(X_1, X_2) &= \mathbb{E}\left[\int_{\mathbb{R}}\int_{\mathbb{R}} (\mathbb{1}_{\{\tilde{X}_1\le x_1\}} - \mathbb{1}_{\{X_1\le x_1\}})(\mathbb{1}_{\{\tilde{X}_2\le x_2\}} - \mathbb{1}_{\{X_2\le x_2\}})\,dx_1\,dx_2\right] \\ &= 2\int_{\mathbb{R}}\int_{\mathbb{R}} \Big(\mathbb{P}(X_1 \le x_1, X_2 \le x_2) - \mathbb{P}(X_1 \le x_1)\mathbb{P}(X_2 \le x_2)\Big)\,dx_1\,dx_2 \\ &= 2\int_{\mathbb{R}}\int_{\mathbb{R}} (F_{\boldsymbol{X}}(x_1, x_2) - F_1(x_1)F_2(x_2))\,dx_1\,dx_2.\end{aligned}$$

■

Theorem 3.9. *Consider a random vector $\boldsymbol{X} = (X_1, X_2)$ having finite variance, marginal cumulative distributions F_1, F_2 and unknown joint cumulative distribution. Assume that $Var(X_1) > 0$ and $Var(X_2) > 0$. Then*

i) The minimum correlation $\rho = \rho_{min}$ is reached if and only if X_1, X_2 are countermonotonic. The maximum correlation $\rho = \rho_{max}$ is reached if and only if X_1, X_2 are comonotonic;
ii) $\rho \in [\rho_{min}, \rho_{max}]$, with $\rho_{min} < 0 < \rho_{max}$;
iii) $\rho_{min} = -1$ if and only if the variables $X_1, -X_2$ are of the same type. $\rho_{max} = 1$ if and only if the variables X_1, X_2 are of the same type.

Proof. i) By virtue of Theorem 3.7, the CDF $F_{\boldsymbol{X}}$ of $\boldsymbol{X}$ satisfies

$$\max\{F_1(x_1) + F_2(x_2) - 1, 0\} \le F_{\boldsymbol{X}}(x_1, x_2) \le \min\{F_1(x_1), F_2(x_2)\}. \tag{3.38}$$

Due to Eq. (3.38), we obtain that the integrand function in Eq. (3.36) is controlled by

$$\int_{\mathbb{R}}\int_{\mathbb{R}} (\max\{F_1(x_1) + F_2(x_2) - 1, 0\} - F_1(x_1)F_2(x_2))\,dx_1\,dx_2$$

$$\leq \int_{\mathbb{R}} \int_{\mathbb{R}} \left(F_{\boldsymbol{X}}(x_1, x_2) - F_1(x_1)F_2(x_2) \right) dx_1\, dx_2$$

$$\leq \int_{\mathbb{R}} \int_{\mathbb{R}} \left(\min\left\{ F_1(x_1), F_2(x_2) \right\} - F_1(x_1)F_2(x_2) \right) dx_1\, dx_2.$$

Therefore, the correlation is maximum when X_1, X_2 are comonotonic, i.e. when their copula is $M(F_1, F_2)$. Analogously, the correlation is minimum when X_1, X_2 are countermonotonic, i.e. when their copula is given by $W(F_1, F_2)$.

ii) Observe that $\rho_{max} > 0$. In fact, if $\rho_{max} = 0$, then

$$\min\left\{ F_1(x_1), F_2(x_2) \right\} = F_1(x_1)F_2(x_2),$$

and so F_1, or F_2 should be a degenerate distribution, i.e. a probability distribution whose support is only a single point. In this case the variance will be null, which contradicts the initial assumptions. Analogously, we may prove that $\rho_{min} < 0$.

Moreover, the linear combination

$$\lambda W(F_1, F_2) + (1 - \lambda) M(F_1, F_2), \quad 0 \leq \lambda \leq 1,$$

has correlation equal to

$$\lambda \rho_{min} + (1 - \lambda) \rho_{max}.$$

Hence, for any $\rho \in [\rho_{min}, \rho_{max}]$, we can set $\lambda = \frac{(\rho_{max} - \rho)}{(\rho_{max} - \rho_{min})}$ so that the joint distribution admits ρ as correlation index.

iii) Note that saying $\rho_{min} = -1$, or $\rho_{max} = 1$, it is equivalent to say X_1, X_2 are perfectly dependent, i.e. the variables X_1, X_2 are of the same type. ■

Show an application of the above theorem.

Example 3.5. Consider a random vector $\boldsymbol{X} = (X_1, X_2)$ with $\ln X_1 \sim N(0, 1)$ and $\ln X_2 \sim N(0, \sigma^2)$. If $\sigma \neq 1$, the variables are not of the same type. Neither are $X_1, -X_2$. This implies that $-1 < \rho_{min} < \rho_{max} < 1$.

In order to compute the bounds of the interval $[\rho_{min}, \rho_{max}]$, note that if X_1, X_2 are comonotonic, then $(X_1, X_2) = (e^Z, e^{\sigma Z})$, with $Z \sim N(0, 1)$. Therefore, $\rho_{max} = \rho(e^Z, e^{\sigma Z})$ and $\rho_{min} = \rho(e^Z, e^{-\sigma Z})$. Finally, it is easy to verify that

$$\rho_{min} = \frac{e^{-\sigma} - 1}{\sqrt{(e - 1)(e^{\sigma^2} - 1)}}, \quad \rho_{max} = \frac{e^{\sigma} - 1}{\sqrt{(e - 1)(e^{\sigma^2} - 1)}}.$$

3.6.1 *Rank Correlation*

In order to compare different copulas, we need a correlation measure that is independent of the marginal cumulative distributions. Since the Pearson correlation depends on the marginal cumulative distributions (see Section 3.6), we are looking for different measures, such as the Kendall and Spearman rank correlations.

3.6.1.1 *Kendall Rank Correlation*

First of all, introduce the concordance definition.

Definition 3.15. Consider two observations (x_1, x_2), $(\tilde{x}_1, \tilde{x}_2) \in \mathbb{R}^2$ of the random vector (X_1, X_2). The variables X_1, X_2 are said to be concordant if $(x_1 - \tilde{x}_1)(x_2 - \tilde{x}_2) > 0$, while they are discordant if $(x_1 - \tilde{x}_1)(x_2 - \tilde{x}_2) < 0$.

Now we can define the Kendall rank correlation originally proposed in [Kendall (1948)].

Definition 3.16. Let $(X_1, X_2), (\tilde{X}_1, \tilde{X}_2)$ be two i.i.d. random vectors with joint cumulative distribution F. Then the *Kendall rank correlation* is defined as the difference between the concordance and the discordance probability, i.e.

$$\rho_\tau(X_1, X_2) = \mathbb{P}((X_1 - \tilde{X}_1)(X_2 - \tilde{X}_2) > 0) - \mathbb{P}((X_1 - \tilde{X}_1)(X_2 - \tilde{X}_2) < 0). \quad (3.39)$$

Remark 3.6. The relation (3.39) may be rewritten as

$$\rho_\tau(X_1, X_2) = \mathbb{E}\big[sgn\big((X_1 - \tilde{X}_1)(X_2 - \tilde{X}_2)\big)\big]. \quad (3.40)$$

Indeed,

$$sgn\big((X_1 - \tilde{X}_1)(X_2 - \tilde{X}_2)\big) = \mathbb{P}\big((X_1 - \tilde{X}_1)(X_2 - \tilde{X}_2) > 0\big) - \mathbb{P}\big((X_1 - \tilde{X}_1)(X_2 - \tilde{X}_2) < 0\big);$$

hence, by taking the expectation one soon obtains Eq. (3.39).

In order to understand the copulas role in the concordance, we shall define the *concordance function* Q by the difference between the concordance and the discordance probability of two random vectors $(X_1, X_2), (\tilde{X}_1, \tilde{X}_2)$ with joint cumulative distributions and marginal distributions given by $F, \tilde{F}$ and F_1, F_2, respectively; i.e.

$$Q = \mathbb{P}\big((X_1 - \tilde{X}_1)(X_2 - \tilde{X}_2) > 0\big) - \mathbb{P}\big((X_1 - \tilde{X}_1)(X_2 - \tilde{X}_2) < 0\big). \quad (3.41)$$

Q depends on the distributions of (X_1, X_2) and $(\tilde{X}_1, \tilde{X}_2)$ through their copulas.

Theorem 3.10. *Consider two independent random vectors $(X_1, X_2), (\tilde{X}_1, \tilde{X}_2)$ with joint cumulative distributions and marginal distributions given by $F, \tilde{F}$ and F_1, F_2, respectively. Let C_1, C_2 be their copulas, respectively, so that $F(x_1, x_2) = C_1(F_1(x_1), F_2(x_2))$ and $\tilde{F}(x_1, x_2) = C_2(F_1(x_1), F_2(x_2))$. If Q is the concordance function, defined in Eq. (3.41), then*

$$Q(C_1, C_2) = 4 \int_0^1 \int_0^1 C_2(u_1, u_2)\, dC_1(u_1, u_2) - 1. \quad (3.42)$$

Proof. Since our random variables are continuous, it holds

$$\mathbb{P}\big((X_1 - \tilde{X}_1)(X_2 - \tilde{X}_2) < 0\big) = 1 - \mathbb{P}\big((X_1 - \tilde{X}_1)(X_2 - \tilde{X}_2) > 0\big),$$

and so

$$Q(C_1, C_2) = 2\mathbb{P}\big((X_1 - \tilde{X}_1)(X_2 - \tilde{X}_2) > 0\big) - 1.$$

However,

$$\mathbb{P}\big((X_1 - \tilde{X}_1)(X_2 - \tilde{X}_2) > 0\big) = \mathbb{P}\big(X_1 > \tilde{X}_1, X_2 > \tilde{X}_2\big) + \mathbb{P}\big(X_1 < \tilde{X}_1, X_2 < \tilde{X}_2\big),$$

where the above probabilities can be computed by using the distributions of the random vector (X_1, X_2) or $(\tilde{X}_1, \tilde{X}_2)$. Choose (X_1, X_2) for convenience. We have

$$\begin{aligned}\mathbb{P}\big(X_1 > \tilde{X}_1, X_2 > \tilde{X}_2\big) &= \mathbb{P}\big(\tilde{X}_1 < X_1, \tilde{X}_2 < X_2\big)\\ &= \int_{\mathbb{R}}\int_{\mathbb{R}} \mathbb{P}\big(\tilde{X}_1 \le x_1, \tilde{X}_2 \le x_2\big)\, dC_1(F_1(x_1), F_2(x_2))\\ &= \int_{\mathbb{R}}\int_{\mathbb{R}} C_2(F_1(x_1), F_2(x_2))\, dC_1(F_1(x_1), F_2(x_2))\\ &= \int_0^1\int_0^1 C_2(u_1, u_2)\, dC_1(u_1, u_2).\end{aligned}$$

Similarly,

$$\mathbb{P}\big(X_1 < \tilde{X}_1, X_2 < \tilde{X}_2\big) = \int_{\mathbb{R}}\int_{\mathbb{R}} \mathbb{P}\big(\tilde{X}_1 > x_1, \tilde{X}_2 > x_2\big)\, dC_1(F_1(x_1), F_2(x_2))$$

$$= \int_{\mathbb{R}}\int_{\mathbb{R}} (1 - F_1(x_1) - F_2(x_2) + C_2(F_1(x_1), F_2(x_2))\, dC_1(F_1(x_1), F_2(x_2))$$

$$= \int_0^1\int_0^1 (1 - u_1 - u_2 + C_2(u_1, u_2))\, dC_1(u_1, u_2).$$

Since C_1 is the joint distribution of the pair (U_1, U_2), with $U_i \sim U(0,1)$, $i = 1, 2$, then $\mathbb{E}[U_1] = \mathbb{E}[U_2] = \frac{1}{2}$, and so

$$\begin{aligned}\mathbb{P}\big(X_1 < \tilde{X}_1, X_2 < \tilde{X}_2\big) &= 1 - \frac{1}{2} - \frac{1}{2} + \int_0^1\int_0^1 C_2(u_1, u_2)\, dC_1(u_1, u_2)\\ &= \int_0^1\int_0^1 C_2(u_1, u_2)\, dC_1(u_1, u_2)\end{aligned}$$

Consequently, we have

$$\mathbb{P}\big((X_1 - \tilde{X}_1)(X_2 - \tilde{X}_2) > 0\big) = 2\int_0^1\int_0^1 C_2(u_1, u_2)\, dC_1(u_1, u_2).$$

Replacing the above relation in Q, soon obtain

$$Q(C_1, C_2) = 4\int_0^1\int_0^1 C_2(u_1, u_2)\, dC_1(u_1, u_2) - 1.$$

■

Due to the previous theorem, we may express the Kendall rank correlation in terms of copula as follows.

Definition 3.17. Consider two random variables X_1, X_2 both with copula C. Then the Kendall rank correlation of X_1 and X_2 is given by

$$\rho_\tau(X_1, X_2) = Q(C, C) = 4\int_0^1\int_0^1 C(u_1, u_2)\, dC(u_1, u_2) - 1. \tag{3.43}$$

Proof. The proof comes soon from Theorem 3.10, taking $F = \tilde{F}$. ■

Remark 3.7. Note that the integral in Eq. (3.43) can be seen as the expected value of $C(U_1, U_2)$, where U_1, U_2 are uniform random variables on $[0, 1]$ with joint cumulative distribution C, i.e.

$$\rho_\tau = 4\,\mathbb{E}[C(U_1, U_2)] - 1. \tag{3.44}$$

3.6.1.2 *Spearman Rank Correlation*

Definition 3.18. Consider (X_1, X_2), $(\tilde{X}_1, \tilde{X}_2)$ and $(\bar{X}_1, \bar{X}_2)$ three independent random vectors with the same joint cumulative distribution F and copula C. In particular, $(\tilde{X}_1, \tilde{X}_2), (\bar{X}_1, \bar{X}_2)$ have marginal distributions F_1 and F_2, respectively. The *Spearman rank correlation*, ρ_s, is a quantity which is proportional to the difference between the concordance and the discordance probability of $(X_1, X_2), (\tilde{X}_1, \bar{X}_2)$, i.e.

$$\rho_S(X_1, X_2) = 3\left(\mathbb{P}((X_1 - \tilde{X}_1)(X_2 - \bar{X}_2) > 0) - \mathbb{P}((X_1 - \tilde{X}_1)(X_2 - \bar{X}_2) < 0)\right). \tag{3.45}$$

Remark 3.8. Due to the independence between $\tilde{X}_1$ and $\bar{X}_2$, the joint cumulative distribution of (X_1, X_2) is $F(x_1, x_2)$, and the joint cumulative distribution of $(\tilde{X}_1, \bar{X}_2)$ is $F_1(x_1)F_2(x_2)$. Therefore, the copula of $\tilde{X}_1$ and $\bar{X}_2$ is the independence copula Π, defined in Eq. (3.29).

Theorem 3.11. *Let X_1 and X_2 be two continuous random variables with copula C. Then the Spearman rank correlation of X_1 and X_2 is given by*

$$\rho_s(X_1, X_2) = 12 \int_0^1 \int_0^1 C(u_1, u_2)\, du_1\, du_2 - 3. \tag{3.46}$$

Proof. The proof comes directly from Theorem 3.10, being

$$\rho_s(X_1, X_2) = 3\,Q(C, \Pi) = 12 \int_0^1 \int_0^1 u_1 u_2\, dC(u_1, u_2) - 3.$$

So, it remains to prove that

$$\int_0^1 \int_0^1 u_1 u_2\, dC(u_1, u_2) = \int_0^1 \int_0^1 C(u_1, u_2)\, du_1\, du_2.$$

We get

$$\int_0^1 \int_0^1 u_1 u_2\, dC(u_1, u_2) = \int_0^1 \int_0^1 u_1 u_2 \frac{\partial^2}{\partial u_1 \partial u_2} C(u_1, u_2) du_1\, du_2$$

$$= \int_0^1 u_2 \left(\int_0^1 u_1 \frac{\partial^2}{\partial u_1 \partial u_2} C(u_1, u_2)\, du_1 \right) du_2.$$

The above nested integral is equal to

$$\int_0^1 u_1 \frac{\partial^2}{\partial u_1 \partial u_2} C(u_1, u_2)\, du_1 = u_1 \frac{\partial}{\partial u_2} C(u_1, u_2)\Big|_{u_1=0}^1 - \int_0^1 \frac{\partial}{\partial u_2} C(u_1, u_2)\, du_1$$

$$= 1 - \int_0^1 \frac{\partial}{\partial u_2} C(u_1, u_2)\, du_1,$$

where we use the integration by parts in the first equality, and the last equality comes from the fact that $C(1, u_2) = u_2$.
Summing up,

$$\int_0^1 \int_0^1 u_1 u_2\, dC(u_1, u_2) = \int_0^1 \int_0^1 u_1 u_2 \frac{\partial^2}{\partial u_1 \partial u_2} C(u_1, u_2) du_1\, du_2$$

$$= \int_0^1 u_2 \left(1 - \int_0^1 \frac{\partial}{\partial u_2} C(u_1, u_2)\, du_1\right) du_2 = \int_0^1 u_2\, du_2 - \int_0^1 \int_0^1 u_2 \frac{\partial}{\partial u_2} C(u_1, u_2)\, du_1 du_2$$

$$= \frac{1}{2} - \int_0^1 \left(\int_0^1 u_2 \frac{\partial}{\partial u_2} C(u_1, u_2)\, du_2\right) du_1 = \frac{1}{2} - \int_0^1 \left(u_1 - \int_0^1 C(u_1, u_2)\, du_2\right) du_1$$

$$= \frac{1}{2} - \int_0^1 u_1\, du_1 + \int_0^1 \int_0^1 C(u_1, u_2)\, du_2 du_1 = \int_0^1 \int_0^1 C(u_1, u_2)\, du_1 du_2,$$

which concludes the proof. ■

This theorem interprets the Spearman rank correlation in the following way. Consider two random variables X_1, X_2 with same joint cumulative distribution F, same copula C and with marginal distributions F_1 and F_2, respectively. Given $U_1 = F(X_1)$, $U_2 = F(X_2)$, with $U_i \sim U(0, 1)$ $(i = 1, 2)$, then the Spearman rank correlation of X_1 and X_2 is equal to

$$\begin{aligned} \rho_S(X_1, X_2) &= 12 \int_0^1 \int_0^1 C(u_1, u_2) du_1 du_2 - 3 \\ &= 12\, \mathbb{E}[U_1 U_2] - 3 \\ &= \frac{\mathbb{E}[U_1 U_2] - \frac{1}{4}}{\frac{1}{12}} \\ &= \frac{Cov(U_1, U_2)}{\sqrt{Var(U_1) Var(U_2)}} \\ &= \rho(U_1, U_2) \\ &= \rho(F_1(X_1), F_2(X_2)), \end{aligned}$$

where ρ denotes the Pearson correlation coefficient. Therefore, the Spearman rank correlation of X_1, X_2 coincides with the Pearson correlation of $F_1(X_1), F_2(X_2)$.

Theorem 3.12. *The Spearman rank correlation, ρ_S, satisfies the following properties*

- ρ_S *is symmetric, i.e.* $\rho_S(X_1, X_2) = \rho_S(X_2, X_1)$*;*
- ρ_S *is bounded, i.e.* $-1 \leq \rho_S(X_1, X_2) \leq 1$*;*

- *$\rho_S(X_1, X_2) = 1 \iff X_1$ and X_2 are comonotonic;*
- *$\rho_S(X_1, X_2) = -1 \iff X_1$ and X_2 are counteromonotonic;*
- *If h is a strictly monotone function, then*

$$\rho_S\big(h(X_1), h(X_2)\big) = \begin{cases} \rho_S(X_1, X_2), & \text{if } h \text{ is increasing} \\ -\rho_S(X_1, X_2), & \text{otherwise.} \end{cases}$$

Analogous results hold true for the Kendall rank correlation ρ_τ.

3.6.2 *Dependence Measurement with Copulas*

To compare the different copulas we need a correlation measure that is independent of the marginal cumulative distributions. The Pearson's correlation is unstable, depends on both the distributions (joint cumulative and marginal), and requires the mean-squared linear dependence of random vectors. For these reasons, it is excluded and we consider the rank correlations of Kendall and Spearman.

Let $(X_1, Y_1), (X_2, Y_2)$ be independent and identically distributed random vectors, with joint distribution function F. We say that $(X_1, Y_1), (X_2, Y_2)$ are concordant (comonotone) if $(X_1 - X_2)(Y_1 - Y_2) > 0$ and discordant (countermonotone) if $(X_1 - X_2)(Y_1 - Y_2) < 0$. Then, Kendall's rank correlation is defined as the probability of concordance minus the probability of discordance

$$\rho_\tau(X, Y) = \mathbb{P}((X_1 - X_2)(Y_1 - Y_2) > 0) - \mathbb{P}((X_1 - X_2)(Y_1 - Y_2) < 0).$$

In terms of the copula C, this is given by

$$\rho_\tau(X, Y) = 4 \int_0^1 \int_0^1 C(u, v) dC(u, v) - 1.$$

Spearman's rank correlation is also based on concordance and discordance definitions.

Let $(X_1, Y_1), (X_2, Y_2), (X_3, Y_3)$ be independent random vectors with a common joint distribution function F (with marginals F_1 and F_2) and copula C. Spearman's rank correlation is defined to be proportional to the probability of concordance minus the probability of discordance for the two vectors (X_1, Y_1) and (X_2, Y_3) (that is a pair of vectors with the same marginals, but one vector has distribution function F and the other has independent components; the pair (X_3, Y_2) could be used equally as well)

$$\begin{aligned} \rho_S(X, Y) &= 3(\mathbb{P}((X_1 - X_2)(Y_1 - Y_3) > 0) - \mathbb{P}((X_1 - X_2)(Y_1 - Y_3) < 0)) \\ &= 12 \int_0^1 \int_0^1 uv\, dC(u, v) - 3 = 12 \int_0^1 \int_0^1 C(u, v)\, du\, dv - 3. \end{aligned}$$

Note that while the joint distribution function of (X_1, Y_1) is $F(x, y)$, the joint distribution function of (X_2, Y_3) is $F_1(x)F_2(y)$ because X_2 and Y_3 are independent and so their copula is Π (analogously, if we consider the pair (X_3, Y_2)).

The rank correlation τ for Clayton and Gumbel copulas introduced in Eq. (3.34) and (3.35) equals to $\tau = \theta/(\theta+2)$ and $\tau = (\theta-1)/\theta$, respectively.

3.6.3 *Tail Dependence*

Differently from the Kendall and Spearman rank correlation, which may be called a global dependence measure, the tail correlation coefficient, between the random variables X_1, X_2, is a local dependence measure. Indeed, it quantifies the dependence level between two extreme values, that is the tail value of $F_1(X_1), F_2(X_2)$.

Definition 3.19. Suppose X_1, X_2 are two random variables with CDF F_1, F_2, respectively. We define the *upper tail dependence* as

$$\lambda_U(X_1, X_2) = \lim_{q\to 1^-} \mathbb{P}\big(X_2 > F_2^{(-1)}(q) | X_1 > F_1^{(-1)}(q)\big). \tag{3.47}$$

If $\lambda_U \in (0,1]$, then X_1, X_2 are said to be upper tail-asymptotically dependent; while if $\lambda_U = 0$, they are upper tail-asymptotically independent.
Similarly define the *lower tail dependence* by

$$\lambda_L(X_1, X_2) = \lim_{q\to 0^+} \mathbb{P}\big(X_2 \le F_2^{(-1)}(q) | X_1 \le F_1^{(-1)}(q)\big). \tag{3.48}$$

If $\lambda_L \in (0,1]$, then X_1, X_2 are said to be lower tail-asymptotically dependent; while if $\lambda_L = 0$, they are lower tail-asymptotically independent.

Like the Kendall and Spearman correlations, the coefficients λ_U, λ_L may be expressed in terms of a copula. In fact, Eqs. (3.47) and (3.48) give

$$\lambda_L = \lim_{q\to 0^+} \frac{\mathbb{P}\big(X_2 \le F_2^{(-1)}(q), X_1 \le F_1^{(-1)}(q)\big)}{\mathbb{P}\big(X_1 \le F_1^{(-1)}(q)\big)} = \lim_{q\to 0^+} \frac{C(q,q)}{q}$$

and

$$\lambda_U = \lim_{q\to 1^-} \frac{\mathbb{P}\big(X_2 > F_2^{(-1)}(q), X_1 > F_1^{(-1)}(q)\big)}{\mathbb{P}\big(X_1 > F_1^{(-1)}(q)\big)} = \lim_{q\to 1^{-1}} \frac{1 + C(q,q) - 2q}{1-q},$$

if the above limits exist. Observe that the probability

$$\mathbb{P}\big(X_2 > F_2^{(-1)}(q) | X_1 > F_1^{(-1)}(q)\big)$$

can be written as

$$\frac{1 - \mathbb{P}\big(X_2 \le F_2^{(-1)}(q)\big) - \mathbb{P}\big(X_1 \le F_1^{(-1)}(q)\big) + \mathbb{P}\big(X_2 \le F_2^{(-1)}(q), X_1 \le F_1^{(-1)}(q)\big)}{1 - \mathbb{P}\big(X_1 \le F_1^{(-1)}(q)\big)},$$

which is equal to

$$\frac{1 - 2q + C(q,q)}{1-q}.$$

Clayton copula in Eq. (3.34) has the lower tail dependence of $2^{-1/\theta}$, while the Gumbel one in Eq. (3.35) — the upper tail one of $2 - 2^{1/\theta}$, where θ is the copula dependence parameter (it is not equal to correlation for Archimedean copulas).

For an illustrative comparison of correlation and copula as measures of dependence let us look at the following chart. The higher the correlation is, the closer observations from our two-dimensional case lie to the trend, while the higher the copula dependence is the more observations are located to the extremes of the trend line (see Figure 3.11).

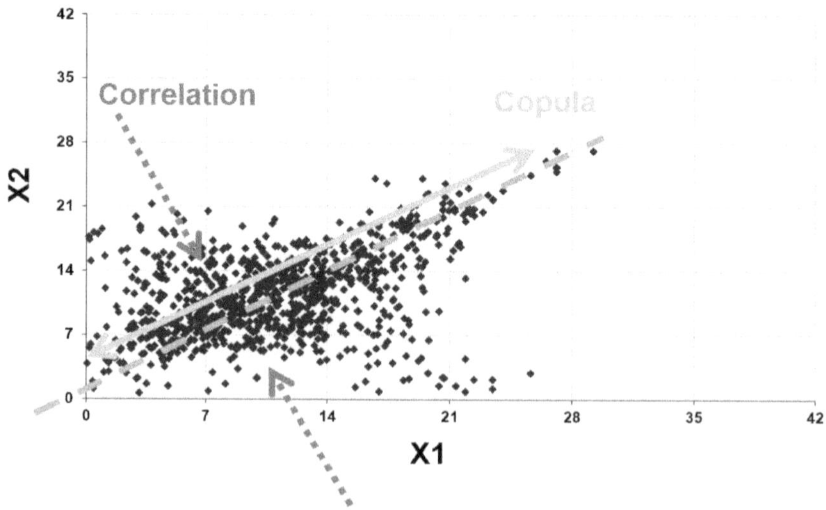

Fig. 3.11: Higher correlation implies observation concentration around the trend, while higher copula dependence implies more concentration around the extreme values of the trend line.

PART 2
Finance Background and Regulatory Framework

Chapter 4

Basic Definitions

4.1 Risk Types

In the contemporary economy, the identification and management of risk are now the pillars on which the healthy and prudent management of banking activities is concerned. Analysis and operational experience led to the identification of four major classes of risk:

- *Market risk*, which includes the risks of losses following unfavorable movements in market prices, including interest rates, exchange rates, and share prices;
- *Operational risk*, which includes the risks of losses due to human errors, fraud (internal and external), business interruptions, fraud-driven defaults, IT system failures, natural disasters, vandalism and terrorist acts;
- *Credit risk*, the most traditional of the banking business risks linked to the possibility of *insolvency* of the counterparty entrusted. One of its sub-types worth covering is a *counterparty credit risk*. The latter one is the result not only of the deterioration in borrower creditworthiness but also because of the change in market prices that lead to the existence of a non-nil exposure. Take a derivative transaction as an example. Initially, the profit and loss (P&L) is the initially transferred margin (collateral requirement). If market prices do not change, the fair value of a derivative depends only upon the counterparty's stability. In case the latter neither changes, the fair value for the residual cash-flows is nil. However, when the market prices change, though the counterparty creditworthiness is unchanged, the exposure is not nil anymore.
- *Liquidity risk*, associated with banking panics and bank runs. Deposit insurance systems are established to calm people's intents to withdraw money from turbulent times. However, the fundamental cause for the liquidity risk existence is the *fractional reserve* nature of the modern banking systems. If banking deposit was not legitimized in addition to debt (rent) and storage

contracts, no liquidity risk would ever be, unless those driven by the credit one. For more discussions, please, refer to [Huerta de Soto (2006)].

The former three risks may be called capital-demanding ones as the existing banking regulation requires holding capital against those, while it is not necessarily for the latter one. The credit risk is the most important in the modern financial systems, see Table 4.1.

Table 4.1: Total risk decomposition by risk types.

Country	Source	Proportion of total risk*		
		Credit	Market	Operational
China	[BCBS (2013b), pp. 8, 66]	91.30	0.80	7.90
The European Union	[BCBS (2014c), p. 62]	81.96	6.09	9.88
Japan	[BCBS (2012a), p. 31]	91.30	2.90	5.80
The USA	[BCBS (2014d), p. 73]	65.76	10.03	19.90
Average by countries		84.07	4.82	10.25

Note: * Percent of the total risk-weighted assets (RWA).

The *credit risk* constitutes a fundamental component of any transition of a financial nature, in consideration of the fact that the contractual performance of one of the two parties is opposed by a performance of the other deferred over time or not contextually in the settlement. The party who first fulfils its contractual obligations is therefore exposed to the risk that the counterparty does not fulfill its obligations, due to insolvency or default. Consider, for example, the case of a bank that grants financing to an enterprise. In this case, the creditor is exposed to the risk that the debtor will fail in the periodic payment of interest and the repayment of the principal at maturity. Similar is the case of an investor who, by investing in bonds, takes on the credit risk towards the issuer.

The assets producing credit risk are generally grouped into the banking book, while the remaining ones generating market risk belong to the trading book.

4.2 Credit Risk Ratios

Based on financial reports, the following ratios may help in assessing the exposure to credit risk of a bank.

4.2.1 *Loan Loss Provision (LLP)*

Loan Loss Provision (LLP) is defined in Eq. (4.1). In general, the lower LLP rate is, the better. We may say that LLP rate presents the bank's opinion about the loan book, i.e. it is a more subjective indicator, than NPL ratio that follows. However, in front of investors, the bank might wish to look better than it actually is. That is why it may be prone to underprovision. Such behaviour is called "window-dressing". That is why financial analysts look at the so-called balanced scorecard or at the dashboard consisting of several indicators like the ones that follow below.

$$LLP = \frac{Total\ Allowance}{Total\ Loans} \tag{4.1}$$

4.2.2 *Coverage Ratio (CovR)*

Coverage Ratio (CovR) is presented in Eq. (4.2). This indicator helps detect the extent of the adequateness in a bank's credit risk assessment. The lower it is, the more drastic changes might occur to the financial statements if the taken credit risks materialize. However, making full allowance against the amount of NPLs would materially reduce bank earnings. In case the credit risk does not take place to a full extent then the bank would need to restore allowances. From one side, this is going to be good news as profits would appear in the income statement or P&L. On another side, this is a negative signal to investors as it adds to the performance indicators' volatility. This means that the financial and risk management in a bank is somewhat chaotic. That is why Chief Financial Officer (CFO) and Chief Risk Officer (CRO) should search for an optimal balance. As a somewhat result, we observe that in 2019 the coverage ratio for the Eurozone banks was around 45%, according to [EBA (2019a), p. 9].

$$CovR = \frac{Total\ Allowance}{Total\ NPLs} \tag{4.2}$$

4.2.3 *Cost of Risk (CoR)*

Cost of Risk (CoR) is from Eq. (4.3). Any business requires its owner to bear the corresponding costs. Offering money for temporary use requires costs when making a deal or in the time of the loan that stays on the book. The former case reflects the general tendencies (for instance, the central tendency for the default probability PD that we will cover in more detail in Chapter 8 and onwards in Chapter 9). The latter case is relevant in the event of a change in the economic environment. In general, the lower the CoR, the more attractive the loan portfolio. However, extremely low values can signal hidden problems or concerns. For instance, zero CoR may reflect the situation that the bank stopped lending. This may require deeper inspection into the origins of the situation for the interested stakeholders. To feel the figures, the CoR for the Italian banks rose from around 0.8-1.0% right after the crisis in 2010 to 1.2-1.6% in 2013. This happened to a large extent due to the pressure by the prudential authorities, according to [Avantage Reply Observatory on Banking System Solidity (2013), p. 19].

$$CoR = \frac{Change\ in\ Allowances}{Total\ Loans} \tag{4.3}$$

4.2.4 *Non-Performing Loans (NPL)*

Non-Performing Loans (NPL) ratio is available in Eq. (4.4). If a bank experiences problems from the borrower's side in servicing the loan, the loan is said to be non-performing. The degree of severity of problems is defined by the bank in consideration of the regulatory requirements and financial reporting standards (we will discuss those more in Section 8.1 devoted to default definition). Opposite to LLP rate, NPL is a more objective indicator. It reflects not the bank's perspective on the loan, but the naturally occurred situation. This does not mean that this is an ideal indicator. The bank may deliberately manipulate this indicator by not recognising problems in servicing debt (for instance, by readjusting the payment schedule) or this may have a hazardous nature when the schedule was wrongly inputted from the start. Disregarding whether the adjustment is of fraud nature like in the first case or a human or operational mistake, it is already an operational risk event, and not a credit one. That is why, all else being equal, the NPL ratio may be called the most informative credit risk indicator. The lower it is, the better. We will discuss the empirical data on NPLs further in Chapter 17. To get a sense of the figures, the NPL ratio for the Eurozone is reduced from around 6% in 2016 to 3% in 2019, according to [EBA (2019a), p. 8].

$$NPL\ Ratio = \frac{Total\ NPLs}{Total\ Loans} \tag{4.4}$$

As the reader might have noticed, the above credit risk ratios are interlinked in the following manner, see Eq. (4.5). This means that knowing NPL and coverage ratio for the Eurozone from the above, we may deduct the LLP for the banks in the region. It equals to $45\% * 3\% = 0.135\%$.

$$LLP = NPL * CovR = \frac{Total\ NPLs}{Total\ Loans} * \frac{Total\ Allowance}{Total\ NPLs} = \frac{Total\ Allowance}{Total\ Loans} \tag{4.5}$$

To illustrate those let us introduce an illustrative set of three loans in Table 4.2. For simplicity let us assume there is no interest on these loans. The first loan out of three is a good loan with no impairment. The second one has some impairment. That is why a non-zero allowance is created against it. The third one is a bad loan as the prospects of its repayment are non-realistic. That is why full allowance is made against it. To sum up, the total loan amount is €(100) and the total allowance equals to €(20). The loan book is the amount of total loans net of allowances. It is the loan book that in the end contributes to the bank's total assets. In our example, the loan book is €80. In case a loan has an impairment, it is called a non-performing loan (NPL). Here the amount of performing loans is €60 and that of non-performing — disregarding the amount of allowance — is €40. As the reader may see, for simplicity we distinguished between three loan categories: no impairment; partial and full impairment. To compute the credit risk ratios, it does

Table 4.2: An input set of loans.

#	Principal, €	Allowance, €	Impairment	Type
1	60	0	No	Good
2	25	5	Partial	NPL
3	15	15	Full	NPL
Total	100	20		

Table 4.3: Comparing the credit risk ratios in pp. for the two banks.

#	Indicator	Bank A	Bank B
1	LLP	20.0	5.9
2	NPL	40.0	29.4
3	CovR	50.0	20.0

not matter how many loans are in each category. What matters is the amount in the currency units. That is why it is sufficient to look at three broads, but distinctly different loan categories.

4.3 Write-Offs

Now let us compute the bank-wide credit risk indicators using this data about the loan portfolio. They are summed up in Table 4.3 in the column under the header *Bank A*. For comparison we added a column with indicators of *Bank B*. Bank B has all indicators lower than for Bank A. A natural question comes — if you were a bank supervisor, which bank would you most likely inspect first: Bank A or B?

As the reader can remember, the lower the LLP and NPL ratios are, the better. From this perspective, Bank B seems to have taken less credit risks. The only concern or a hint comes from the coverage ratio (CovR) which is also lower. From the most independent perspective, one may try to acquit the situation supposing that the CRO and CFO of Bank B believe in this lower optimal value of the coverage ratio. However, expect that your perception may drastically change when you know that actually, Bank B is a Bank A with the written-off loan No. 3, i.e. the one with a full impairment. Such write-off results in the decrease of both total loans volume from € 100 to € 85 and that of NPLs from € 40 to € 25. If the reasonable time for loan recovery has passed away — as we will consider in Chapter 17 — then writing the loan off is a justified strategy. However, keeping the loan on the book for a very long time might be as suspicious, as writing it off too soon. The latter case might be a form of fraudulent charity, while the former one might help in creative accounting as it reduces the volatility of the credit risk ratios. If we get back to the initial question, we may recommend inspecting first bank B who had written off the loan earlier all else being equal.

Our general finding from this is to accompany the credit risk analysis via the above credit risk ratios with the credit risk indicators like expected and unexpected losses, probability of default, loss given default, exposure at default that we are going to discuss in greater detail now.

4.4 Prepayment Risk

There is a risk worth mentioning when undertaking credit risk management for fixed income securities and debt-like products. It is called the *prepayment risk*. It is a probable loss of a creditor because the debtor may pay back earlier than anticipated. This risk has two interesting features related to the credit risk being the core topic of this book. First, similar to the counterparty credit risk, the prepayment risk often may be triggered by the change in the market prices or because of a change in expectations with respect to these prices. Suppose there is a foreign currency denominated debt or a floating-rate instrument. If the exchange rate of local currency is appreciated or an interest rate is expected to fall, the debtor — subject to availability of free funds with him — may decide to pay back earlier, so that he may borrow soon after the expectation comes true at more lucrative terms.

Second, in some sort, the prepayment risk is equivalent to the survival probability of the credit risk. The credit risk demonstrates losses from the counterparty being unable to pay. The prepayment risk is actually the wished outcome from the credit risk perspective as the counterparty pays. Though the prepayment is then a sort of anti-credit risk it does not produce the diversification benefit and does not reduce the credit risk amount. To demonstrate it let us look at the following case.

Consider the following simplified example to get better the interrelationship of the credit and prepayment risks. There is a €1000 credit for a year. Suppose, that you know that on average, one in ten borrowers does not pay back. Same time you noticed that every one borrower in twenty can pay off within half a year. Looking separately at each of these risks you would most likely obtain the following estimates. The credit risk is one tenth of the loan amount for a full year, i.e. €100. Disregarding the time value of money, the minimum interest rate on the loan should be 10% per annum to earn the expected loss of €100 for a €1000 loan. The prepayment risk tells us that we may expect to receive only half of the interest income from one twentieth of borrowers on average as they redeem the loan within six months. Then given the interest rate is set at 10%, the prepayment risk is $€1000 \cdot 5\% \cdot 6M/12M = 25$. This means that if the interest rate was 10%, the creditor would receive only $€100 - €25 = €75$. This amount is insufficient to cover the credit loss of €100. That is why the baseline breakeven interest rate seems to be no less than 12.5%.

However, we need to recall our observation that the prepayment risk is by nature a sort of survival case for the credit events. This means that those borrowers that tend to redeem earlier are the least likely to default and vice versa. That is why we should reasonably disentangle the probability space into three distinct groups of non-intersecting events.

The first group consists of the expected defaults. Those form a 10% portion in our example. It is the default probability PD. They cannot prepay, otherwise they would fall outside of the defaulted cohort. This means that we should consider the prepayment risk for only those borrowers that are unlikely to default. We assumed that the prepayment risk is attributable to only each in twenty borrowers. Those are 5% of the pool in headcount. This means that the prepayment probability PP is not 5%, but $5\%/(1-10\%) = 5.5\%$. The residual 85% of the total borrowers are those who are expected to neither default nor prepay.

Now we should also consider the feedback loop. In the baseline computation above we evaluated the prepayment risk departing from the credit loss amount. However, we noticed that the prone-to-prepay and the prone-to-default populations do not intersect. This means that our calculation of the 10% rate may be inadequate. Let us write down the complete set of cash flow scenarios and solve the equation with respect to the interest rate r that yields us with the breakeven P&L. There are three scenarios corresponding to the above three cohorts. The defaulted cohort yields the creditor zero return at the end of the year. The second prone-to-prepay cohort yields the creditor the relative yield of $1+(m/M*r)$, where m is the number of months within which there is a prepayment (for simplicity we took six months); M is the loan maturity (also for simplicity it equals to twelve months, i.e. one year); r — is the loan interest rate (we assumed zero time value of money for ease of illustration). The third cohort yields to the creditor the full interest income and the repayment of principal for one year of $1+r$. Now, we need to weigh these three scenarios according to their relative probabilities and equate the weighted sum to the initial funds of the creditor as in Eq. (4.6).

$$PD \cdot 0 + (1-PD) \cdot PP \cdot \Big(1 + (\frac{m}{M} \cdot r)\Big) + (1-PD) \cdot (1-PP) \cdot (1+r) = 1. \quad (4.6)$$

After simple arithmetic, we obtain in Eq. (4.7) the breakeven interest rate that considers both the credit and prepayment risks.

$$r = \frac{PD}{1 - PD \cdot \Big(1 + PP \cdot (\frac{m}{M} - 1)\Big)}. \quad (4.7)$$

When we input the parameters from our illustrative case ($PD = 10\%, PP = 5.5\%, m = 6, M = 12$), we may derive the sufficient breakeven interest rate. It is not 12.5% as came from the rough straight-forward computation above, but $r = 11.1\%$. Thus, the credit risk component is 10%, while the prepayment risk is the residual 1.1% for the situation when every borrower in twenty tends to early redeem the loan.

Chapter 5

Banking Regulation Before the Crisis

5.1 Basel Committee and Basel I

Inadequate management and assessment of the credit risk has been and still is one of the main causes of bank problems and bankruptcies. The first attempts to manage credit risk date back to individual practices of local Central Banks of the XX-th century. [Goodhart (2011)] refers to Belgium, Germany, Japan, Luxembourg, the Netherlands, Sweden, Switzerland, the UK and the USA. In fact, following banking crises such as that of 1974, the need arose among central banks to improve international collaboration in order to avoid accidents similar to those that occurred in the past and strengthen the banks' capacity to absorb shocks coming from economic and financial tensions. In 1974, the G10 countries deemed it appropriate to form a committee, under the auspices of the Bank for International Settlements, located in Basel, the *Basel Committee on Banking Supervision (BCBS)* (hereafter — BCBS or the Basel Committee), whose mandate was to strengthen regulation, supervision and banking practices worldwide to increase financial stability. The *Basel Committee on Banking Supervision (BCBS)* is still the main body for defining international standards for the prudential regulation of the banking sector and is made up of high representatives of central banks and bodies directly responsible for banking regulation and supervision.

The Basel Committee is made up of senior representatives of central banks and supervisory authorities of Argentina, Australia, Belgium, Brazil, Canada, China, Korea, France, Germany, Japan, Hong Kong SAR, India, Indonesia, Italy, Luxembourg, Mexico, Netherlands, United Kingdom, Russia, Saudi Arabia, Singapore, Spain, South Africa, Sweden, Switzerland, United States, Turkey. The Committee usually meets at the Bank for International Settlements (BIS) in Basel, Switzerland, where its Permanent Secretariat is located. The Group of Governors and Heads of Supervision (GHOS) is the governing body of the Basel Committee and is made up of central bank Governors and supervisors.

In 1988, the Basel Committee introduced the first regulation on the capital adequacy of banks with the *Capital Agreement*, known as *Basel I*. Basel I required banks to hold assets of at least 8% of the total risk-weighted assets (RWA), a condition of bank solvency. This rule got the name of the capital ratio, capital adequacy ratio, or CAR. In its simplest form, it equals the following

$$\text{CAR} = \frac{\text{Capital}}{\text{RWA}_{CR}}, \tag{5.1}$$

where Capital is the amount of own funds deducted by the amount of expected losses EL ($EL = \sum_{i=1}^{n}(EL_i)$). The definition of EL_i depends upon the jurisdiction. However, most often it is the amount of provisions per i-th exposure. As the reader may imagine, the difference between the risk estimate of EL and the prudential requirements towards provisions may give rise to inconsistencies in prudential requirements. To partially account for those, the Pillar I minimal requirements got amended by the add-ons within the Basel II Pillar II, or economic capital, or internal capital adequacy assessment process (ICAAP).

RWA_{CR} is the amount of total credit risks only. The total risks, or the risk-weighted assets, are defined as follows

$$\text{RWA}_{CR} = \sum_{i=1}^{n}\Big(RW_i\,(A_i - EL_i)\Big), \tag{5.2}$$

where the risk-weight RW_i per exposure depends on the type of the debtor as follows:

- 0% for loans to central governments, central banks and the European Union;
- 20% for loans to public bodies, banks and investment firms;
- 50% for mortgage loans and leasing transactions on properties;
- 100% for loans to the private sector;
- 200% for investments in non-financial companies with financial statement results.

There was an important step in bank regulation. That was the Amendment to incorporate market risks (see [BCBS (1996)]). That was the first intent to allow banks to use their own statistics and own (internal) models to evaluate risks and use the output for the prudential capital ratios. Thus the latter became as follows

$$\text{CAR} = \frac{\text{Capital}}{\text{RWA}_{CR} + \text{RWA}_{MR}}, \tag{5.3}$$

where RWA_{MR} is the total risk-weighted assets against the market risk.

5.2 Basel II

With time, the limits inherent in this agreement became increasingly evident, such as: the mere consideration of credit risk in the calculation of the regulatory capital to be set aside; poor differentiation of credit risk measures (there were only five of them). Therefore in 2004 *Basel II* was issued. With *Basel II*, the minimum capital requirements of banks were revised, making them more sensitive to the risk of individual loans. Such sensitivity came from linking the risk-weights RW_i to the external ratings provided by the External Credit Assessment Institutions (ECAIs), like Fitch, Moody's, Standard&Poor's. This was called a Standardized Approach (ST). New risk measurement systems for bank investments were offered. Banks continued to have an obligation to set aside a regulatory capital of at least 8% of their risk-weighted assets. In addition, the risk of bank lending was divided into credit risk, market risk and operational risk. Thus, the capital ratio took the following form

$$\text{CAR} = \frac{\text{Capital}}{\text{RWA}_{CR} + \text{RWA}_{MR} + \text{RWA}_{OR}}, \tag{5.4}$$

where RWA_{OR} is the total risk-weighted assets against the operational risk. We should mention that Basel II immediately allowed for the use of internal models for this risk type also. It was called Advanced Measurement Approach (AMA). However, later after the financial crisis of 2007-2009 the Basel III significantly limited such model use for the operational risk, though the Basel Committee preserved recommendations to continue collecting operational loss data.

The real novelty of the Agreement was the introduction of a new credit risk assessment methodology. It was called the Internal Ratings-Based (IRB) approach. It allowed banks to determine the risk-weights for individual assets themselves. *Basel II*, in fact, allowed to abandon the fixed credit risk-weights according to the type of debtor (0, 20%, 50%, 100%, and 200%), and to use more appropriate own models to rate each debtor (governments, banks, individuals, independently). Therefore, debtors of the same type (for example, private companies) could have different risk-weights. This means that the capital ratio was once again adjusted to the following

$$\text{CAR} = \frac{\text{Capital}}{\text{RWA}_{CR,ST} + \text{RWA}_{CR,IRB} + \text{RWA}_{MR} + \text{RWA}_{OR}}, \tag{5.5}$$

where $\text{RWA}_{CR,ST}$ stands for the credit risk attributable to that share of assets that are still subject to the application of the fixed risk-weights; $\text{RWA}_{CR,IRB}$ denotes the amount of assets subject to new treatment within the Internal Ratings-Based (IRB) approach. For details on its computation, please, refer to Eq. (5.6).

However, such opportunity is offered subject to having successfully passed the prudential validation by the local regulator. Conceptually, the regulator wishes a bank to minimize assets subject to fixed risk-weights, i.e. being under the standardized approach (ST), after the transition period of three to five years. To remember, upon the application for IRB approval a bank should cover above 50% of its exposures by the novel approach. However, it might be inefficient to develop models for the entire book of assets. It may be costly for a bank to develop those and also costly for a regulator to validate those. That is why the regulator accepts that the IRB asset coverage may not converge to 100% of the exposures. There are no formal criteria, though an implicit threshold of 85% is expected.

Transition to IRB approach might occur in two different modes. The most typical is the one exercised by the European Union. It has been voluntary since 2004. By 2021 there were more than 160 banks that adopted IRB in the EU. The second format is a mandatory one. It was accepted by the Unites States, though ten years later after the financial crisis of 2007-2009, i.e. in 2014. At that time, fifteen of the largest American banks adopted internal models for all risk types (credit, market, operational). Same time the transition to the internal models (including IRB for the credit risk) was forbidden for the other banks. Moreover, [Penikas *et al.* (2021)] find that such a monopoly over the internal models in the US might have been more positively perceived by investors, than the voluntary transition format in the EU. The preference towards the American format might be additionally fueled by the larger share of market-risk-exposed assets in the US banks (recall Table 4.1) and the necessity to apply advanced approaches to each risk type internal modeling in the US, while in the EU some banks might have stayed with the foundation only.

5.2.1 *Standardized Approach (ST)*

Under the standardized approach, banks rely on external institutions to assess counterparty risk. In detail, they turn to the external rating agencies, known as ECAIs ("External Credit Assessment Institution") to obtain assessments on the creditworthiness of customers. The estimates of the remaining risk-weights are predetermined directly by the Supervisory Authority in relation to the economic legal category of the individual counterparties. Therefore, banks have the task of identifying the different types of counterparties and of associating each of them with a specific risk-weight. There are four exposure classes, each of which must be weighted for credit risk net of provisions. These exposure classes are: sovereign entities, banks and financial institutions, corporate companies, and retail portfolios.

5.2.2 *Internal Ratings-Based (IRB) Approach*

In the IRB approach, credit risk assessments are carried out through an internal rating system of the banks. Banks are required to spread banking book loans into broad asset classes with different risk characteristics. These classes are represented by the following exposures:

- Corporate exposures;
- Sovereign exposures (governments, central banks, etc.);
- Banks;
- Retail;
- Equity items.

Definition 5.1. A corporate exposure is defined as a debt obligation of a public company, partnership or individual business. There is a subsegment of small and medium enterprises (SME) here. SMEs are the corporate borrowers with annual sales between €1m and €50m. Loans to smaller entities are treated as retail exposures.

Within this class, there are five sub-classes of specialized lending (SL) represented by the financing of projects (project finance, tangible assets for specific purposes (lease, or object finance), goods (commodity finance), investment properties (income producing real estate (IPRE)) and highly volatile commercial real estate (HVCRE). The credits present in these sub-classes have the following characteristics:

- Exposure to an entity (usually SPVs) created ad hoc to finance and/or administer tangible assets;
- Debtors with few tangible assets, and therefore unable to repay the debt independently, apart from the income received from the financed assets;
- Terms of the debt (which give the creditor a substantial degree of control over the assets and income they produce);
- Primary source of debt repayment (i.e. income generated by assets, rather than autonomous entrepreneurial capacity).

Definition 5.2. An exposure to governments includes exposures to sovereign entities. They include governments, multilateral development banks that meet the criteria for 0% risk-weight in the standardized approach.

Definition 5.3. By exposure to banks, we mean more in general exposures to financial companies such as banks, real estate brokerage companies and multilateral development banks that do not have a 0% risk-weight in the standardized approach.

Definition 5.4. A retail exposure means an exposure that meets the following criteria:

- Category of debtors
  - Exposures to individuals — loans, personal loans and leasing with a limited duration (loans for the purchase or leasing of motor vehicles, student loans) — regardless of their amount;
  - Mortgage loans on residential properties, regardless of their amount, provided that the credit is granted to the owner or tenant of the property; loans guaranteed by a single housing unit or by a small number of housing units in a single building or complex of buildings.
  - Loans to SMEs provided that the banking group's total exposure to the company is less than €1m;
- High number of exposures. The exposure must be part of a large pool of assets managed by the bank. Supervisors may decide to set a minimum

number of exposures within the pool for them to be admitted to be treated as retail ones.

Within this class, banks must identify three sub-classes: exposures secured by residential real estate, qualifying revolving retail exposures (QRRE) and other retail exposures.

Definition 5.5. Equity exposure means exposure satisfying the following criteria:

- It is irredeemable, i.e. the return on the invested funds can only be obtained with the sale of the investment or in the event of liquidation of the issuer;
- Does not include any obligation on the part of the issuer;
- Confers a portion of the residual credit on the issuer's assets or income.

In addition, the following instruments are considered equity exposures:

- Instruments with the same structure as those making up Tier 1;
- Instruments that include bonds issued by the issuer provided they satisfy certain conditions;
- Instruments that transfer the economic content of the shareholder;
- Liabilities whose return is linked to that of the shares.

For each asset class, three fundamental elements must be considered:

- The components of risk, such as:
  - Probability of default (PD);
  - Loss on insolvency (LGD);
  - Exposure in the event of insolvency (EAD);
  - Maturity (M);
- The risk-weighting functions, that is the procedure by which the components of the risk are transformed into risk weighted assets, and therefore into capital requirements;
- The minimum requirements, or minimum standards that banks must meet in order to apply the IRB approach to an asset class.

In this regard, the IRB approach is divided into foundation IRB (F-IRB) and advanced IRB (A-IRB). With the basic model, banks are allowed to determine: the customer's rating grade through appropriate calculation systems and PD estimates. The remaining elements are determined by the Supervisory Authority in relation to the customer they have before them. By combining the inputs provided by the banks and the inputs provided by the local regulator, it is possible to calculate the bank's capital ratios. With the advanced IRB method, banks enjoy full autonomy as the customer's risk assessment is carried out entirely by the bank itself; therefore, the banks not only determine the customer's merit class, but also the entire set of components. However, in order to carry out these activities, banks must adopt methods that have been validated by the supervisory authority of the home country and that are based on historical data series deriving from the bank's past experience for all risk components listed above.

5.2.2.1 *Minimum Requirements for the IRB Approach*

For a bank to adopt the IRB approach, it must comply with minimum requirements, such as:

- Conception of the rating system;
- Functioning of the rating system;
- Corporate governance and supervision;
- Use of internal ratings;
- Quantification of risk;
- Validation of internal estimates;
- Regulatory estimates of LGD and EAD for F-IRB;
- Calculation of capital ratios for equity exposures;
- Disclosure requirements.

We will examine only a few of the aforementioned requirements, such as: the design of the rating system, the functioning of the rating system and the quantification of risk. For more information on the remaining requirements see [BCBS (2006)].

5.2.2.2 *IRB Risk-Weighted Assets (RWA)*

The determination of the *Risk Weighted Assets (RWA)*, with reference to a given asset class, depends on the estimates of PD, LGD, EAD and, in some cases, of M. In this section, PD and LGD are expressed as a decimal number, while EAD is measured in terms of currency (for example, euro). The formula for calculating RWA is as follows

$$\text{RWA}_{CR,IRB} = 12.5 \cdot K \cdot EAD, \tag{5.6}$$

where K is the capital requirement from Eq. (5.7). The product of the capital requirement, K, by the factor 12.5 $\left(\frac{1}{12.5} = 0.08\right)$ guarantees that the capital is not less than 8% of the RWA.

The capital requirement K is defined as a function of PD, an asset correlation factor R (defined through Eq. (5.11)) and LGD

$$K = LGD \cdot \left(N\left(N^{-1}(PD) \cdot \sqrt{\frac{1}{1-R}} + N^{-1} \cdot (0.999)\sqrt{\frac{1}{1-R}}\right) - PD \right), \tag{5.7}$$

where N denotes the cumulative distribution function of a standard normal random variable and N^{-1} denotes its inverse. The used confidence level of 99.9% relates to the realization of a single systemic risk factor. That is why the model is also referred to as an asymptotic single risk factor (ASRF).

Remark 5.1. Asymptotic Single Risk Factor (ASRF) Model
The name of the model comes from its following set-up. It assumes that an obligor is a publicly listed company. Then there exists a company asset value A_i. Same time there is the amount of debt D_i. There are two widespread interpretations. First, we may think of the entire company value and the total debt amount. If a company ends its activity, it sells all of its assets. If the market value is insufficient to pay off the raised debt, the obligor is deemed insolvent. Second, one may think of debt servicing. For instance, A_i might be the total asset return, i.e. the sum of dividends from the owned assets and change in its market value. Then the obligor is solvent until the total asset proceeds (or asset returns) exceed the debt-servicing payments, i.e. the interest rate on the borrowed funds. That is why A_i may be called asset value or asset return. Fundamentally, the two approaches to interpretation make no difference, as ultimately all the inputs are assumed standard normally distributed. The inquisitive reader should readily notice several fundamental flaws in the model assumptions when applying them to the real-life risk management and banking regulation:

- There are many borrowers — particularly, the retail loans — that are not publicly listed. This means that there is no actual market data to model the asset value or the asset returns;
- Any sort of mass liquidation of assets on the market does not come without its cost. This phenomenon is known as fire sales. When trades of unprecedented size are traded on an exchange, this causes other market participants to sell and drain the liquidity of the market as well. Both effects cause market prices to drop much more than initially expected. This means that in the ideal model set-up, the marked-to-market assets might exceed the debt amount. However, when physically settled the assets might yield the cash pool inferior to that of the debt one. Thus, a theoretically solvent company by the model logic is prone to be insolvent, though the model does not capture this.

Disregarding the important shortcomings from the above, the ASRF is used in practice with the additional assumptions imposed in [Vasicek (1987)] and [Vasicek (2002)] works. The value A_i is a result of the two risk factors contribution as in Eq. (5.8): the single common factor Z and the idiosyncratic one ϵ_i. The acronym ASRF comes from having a single common risk factor. Possible extensions to multi-factor model are discussed in [Pykhtin (2004)].

$$A_i = Z \cdot \rho_i + \epsilon_i \cdot \sqrt{1 - R_i}, \tag{5.8}$$

where $R_i = \rho_i^2$.

For the purpose of ASRF, it is assumed that $Z \sim N(0,1)$ and $\epsilon_i \sim N(0,1)$. Hence, $A_i \sim N(0,1)$. We then take a hypothetical threshold D and introduce an indicator $I_i = \mathbf{1}(A_i \leq D|Z)$. Then we are interested in the distribution of the sum of such indicators — $\sum_i I_i$ — given a realisation of a systemic risk factor Z (supposedly, an adverse one). This is actually the distribution of defaults for our hypothetical loan portfolio in the event of a crisis (e.g. see Figure 5.1).

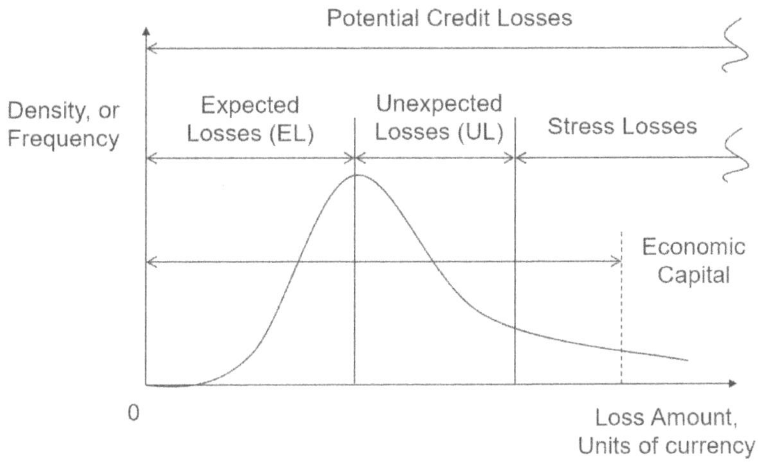

Fig. 5.1: The ASRF model defines capital requirement as the credit value at risk (VaR) in excess of the expected loss (EL). (Concept borrowed from [BCBS (2005a)]) *EL is the normal cost of doing business covered by provisioning and pricing policies; UL is the potential unexpected loss for which capital should be held; Stressed Losses are the potential unexpected losses against which it is judged to be too expensive to hold capital against. Unexpected losses of this extent lead to insolvency.*

Hence ASRF is based on a widely criticized assumption of perfect granularity. The loan portfolio is assumed to consist of an infinite number of infinitely small homogeneous loans. The interesting feature of this configuration is that the impact of idiosyncratic factors is completely compensated and the distribution of default depends exclusively on the correlation with the systemic factor and on the unconditional probability of default PD for each single loan. It also allows the contributions of individual loans to be added to the total value of portfolio defaults. This means that the credit risk capital is the amount of unexpected losses as shown in Figure 5.1:

$$Capital = (VaR - PD) \cdot LGD \cdot EAD\,, \tag{5.9}$$

and the VaR at the confidence level α is

$$VaR(\alpha) = N\left(N^{-1}(PD) \cdot \sqrt{\frac{1}{1-R}} + N^{-1}(\alpha) \cdot \sqrt{\frac{R}{1-R}}\right). \tag{5.10}$$

This set of assumptions brings us to another set of fundamental flaws of the ASRF model underlying the adopted IRB approach:

- Although the properties of the model are convenient thanks to the assumptions introduced, they are not realistic. Hence, it is a challenge to rely on such a model in real life. A sort of remedy is to adjust the model parameters by introducing a conservative margin. However, this may not be sufficient due to the presence of model risk.
- The systemic factor is not observed. There are many proxy options but the choice requires consistency in terms of model and correlation of assets R.
- The ASRF baseline model from Eq. (5.10) takes PD as an input to compute conditional probability of default, or VaR, at some α level of the systemic risk factor realisation. It is an industry standard to measure PD using the observed default data via probit, logit models etc. (we will discuss the PD modeling approaches in more detail in Chapter 8). However, the observed defaults are already driven by the realisation of the systemic factor. This means that we do a sort of double-counting when using the PD from the observed defaults.

In this remark we wanted to shed light on the popular single risk factor asymptotic model. The reader may now be able to appreciate the beauty of the model's approach, as well as the challenges and distortions that this ideal could entail if implemented in banks in the manner prescribed by the IRB approach. For further discussion of the ASRF model we can recommend [Tarashev and Zhu (2007); Lütkebohmert (2009); Radkov and Minkova (2011)].

Asset Correlation (R)

The correlation factor (R) is determined on the basis of the portfolio under examination. For example, for exposures to companies, governments and banks, the asset correlation factor R is given by

$$R = 0.12 \cdot \left(\frac{1 - \exp^{-50 \cdot PD}}{1 - \exp^{-50}} \right) + 0.24 \cdot \left(1 - \frac{1 - \exp^{-50 \cdot PD}}{1 - \exp^{-50}} \right). \tag{5.11}$$

[Repullo (2013)], from the Centro de Estudios Monetarios y FInancieros (CEMFI) founded by the Bank of Spain, suggested a more elegant way to model the same dependence of asset correlation R factor and the probability of default PD as follows

$$R = 0.12 \cdot (1 + \exp^{-50 \cdot PD}). \tag{5.12}$$

The IRB approach provides an adjustment to the asset correlation formula for the SME loans in the following form:

$$R = 0.12\left(\frac{1-\exp^{-50PD}}{1-\exp^{-50}}\right) + 0.24\left(1-\frac{1-\exp^{-50PD}}{1-\exp^{-50}}\right) - 0.04\left(1-\frac{S-5}{45}\right), \tag{5.13}$$

where S indicates the size of the firm, or more precisely its annual sales expressed in € m subject to the SME definition of S being below € 50 m.

Since LGD and EAD determine RWA, it is important to have models that allow you to get as accurate estimates of LGD and EAD as possible. For more information on the evolution of the IRB parameters, see [Penikas (2020a)].

Pillar II Requirements (ICAAP)

Both the standardized approach and the IRB one form part of the so-called Pillar I regulation of Basel II. This means the approach to risk measurement under certain minimum requirements. However, "one size fits all" may not work well for quite different banks by size and by business model. That is why the Basel Committee suggested having a tailored approach to risk management. Due to existing differences between banks, one cannot list minimum requirements to capture all the forms. The only solution is to recommend pathways on how to account for them. To do this, the Basel Committee added Pillar II requirements to the Basel II. It may also be called economic capital or Internal Capital Adequacy Assessment Process (ICAAP). An illustrative economic capital decomposition for one of the world's largest banks is available in Figure 5.2.

Overall risk position as measured by economic capital usage by risk type

in € m. (unless stated otherwise)	Jun 30, 2015	Dec 31, 2014
Credit risk	12,510	12,885
Market risk	18,062	14,852
Trading market risk	5,360	4,955
Nontrading market risk	12,701	9,898
Operational risk	9,006	7,598
Business risk	2,480	3,084
Diversification benefit[1]	(7,249)	(6,554)
Total economic capital usage	**34,808**	31,866

1 Diversification benefit across credit, market, operational and strategic risk (largest part of business risk)

Fig. 5.2: Deutsche Bank economic capital decomposition.
Source: [Deutsche Bank (2015)].

Bank of England specified two Pillar II (ICAAP) subformats:

- Pillar IIA. Here auxiliary risks are considered within the denominator of the capital ratio. Among the most typical ones is the credit concentration risk. It may also capture extra risks revealed during the stress-test;
- Pillar IIB. Here the bank may change the approach to risk measurement. For instance, a bank has PD, LGD, EAD models, but it did not apply for an IRB approval for these parameters' use to compute prudential capital ratios. Thus, a bank cannot use IRB for Pillar I, but a bank may use IRB models for the economic capital derivation, i.e. for Pillar IIB.

Figure 5.2 demonstrates a Deutsche Bank economic capital decomposition (its total RWAs) within the Pillar II approach. For instance, business risk is an additional risk considered as part of Pillar IIA. Diversification benefit may be deemed a part of Pillar IIB as it recomputes the aggregate (gross) risk of a bank.

In addition to Pillar I and Pillar II, the Basel II accord has the third component, Pillar III. It describes the recommendations for more granular and more uniform information disclosure on the risks taken.

Chapter 6

The Financial Crisis of the XXI-st Century

6.1 Stock Market Turmoil

On September 15, 2008, the Wall Street Journal published:
"Crisis on Wall Street as Lehman Totters, Merrill is Sold, AIG Seeks to Raise Cash", manifest of the outbreak of the financial crisis.
The origins of this crisis are far more remote. After the terrorist attack on the Twin Towers on September 11, 2001, the main US stock markets, such as the *New York Stock Exchange (NYSE)*, the *National Association of Securities Dealers Automated Quotation (Nasdaq)* and *Wall Street*, anticipating market chaos, panic sales and disastrous losses, remained closed until September 17, 2001. Upon reopening, the NYSE suffered a 7.1% decline, the NASDAQ 6.8% and Wall Street 4.9% which declined to -11% on September 21 [Mollenkamp, Carrick and Craig, Susanne and Ng, Serena and Lucchetti, Aaron (2001)]. The share prices of the main American airlines, such as *American Airlines* (NYSE: AMR) and *United Airlines* (NYSE: UAL), fell sharply: the first recorded a loss of 39% and the second of 42% (see Figure 6.1). Strong declines also occurred in the financial sector (Merrill Lynch suffered a loss of 11.5% and Morgan Stanley fell by 13%), as well as in the tourism and hotel sector.

In response to what happened, on September 17 of the same year, the *Federal Reserve (FED)*, the American central bank, deemed it necessary to act by promoting an expansive monetary policy, based on the fall in interest rates, which historically reached record low (see Figure 6.2).

6.2 Fuel for the Crisis

Given the very low interest rates, starting from 2003, there was a dizzying growth in the demand for mortgage loans by households for the purchase of properties (see Figure 6.3), which led to a rise in the relative housing prices (see Figure 6.4) and therefore to the generation of a housing bubble. Lending institutions, provided there was a continuous rise in prices, granted low rate mortgages to applicants, even to those with a high risk of default (*subprime mortgages*).

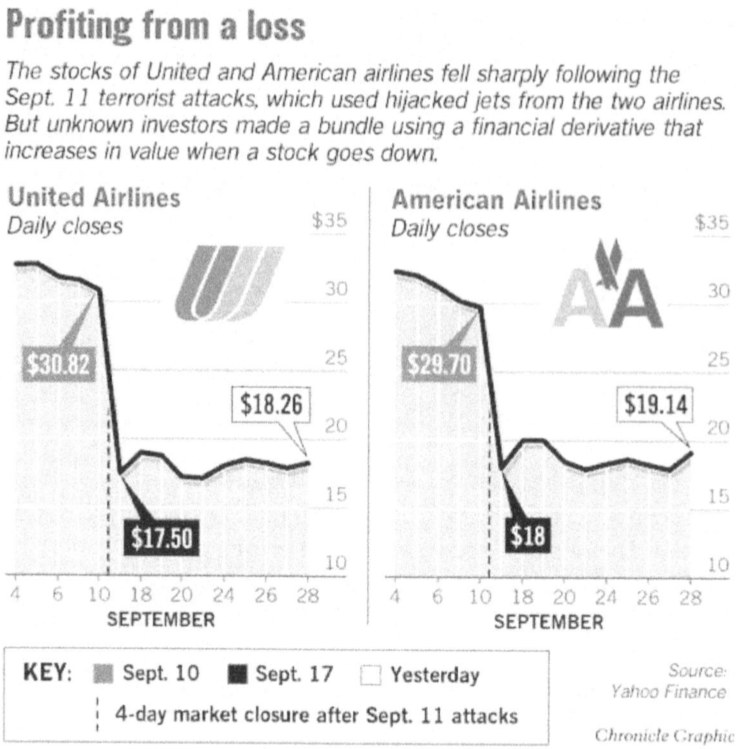

Fig. 6.1: Collapse of the shares of the two airlines.
The graph shows the collapse of the share prices of United Airlines and American Airlines immediately after the attack on the Twin Towers. It can be observed that the market value of the former share went from \$ 30.82 to \$ 17.50, while the market value of the latter one plummeted from \$ 29.70 to \$ 19.14.

The huge concession of mortgages and subprime mortgages (see Figure 6.5) was stimulated by securitisation transactions and high financial leverage, also prompted by a real estate bubble. In fact, securitisation of credits such as mortgages, is a financial transaction consisting in the sale of a portfolio of credits or other non-negotiable financial assets, which can also be identified in bulk, capable of generating cash flows.

Receivables are assigned by one or more companies (Originator) to a special purpose vehicle (SPV) which, in exchange for the assets sold, issues negotiable securities to be placed on the markets. The transferring company does not provide guarantees to the special purpose vehicle in the event of non-payment by the debtors. A special purpose vehicle or SPV is a legal entity created to fulfil a specific task. Typically, SPVs are subsidiaries of another (parent) company (called originator or sponsor) that are distinct from this one. Their structure is aimed at isolating it from the credit risk of the originator. SPVs are usually used as financing vehicles to

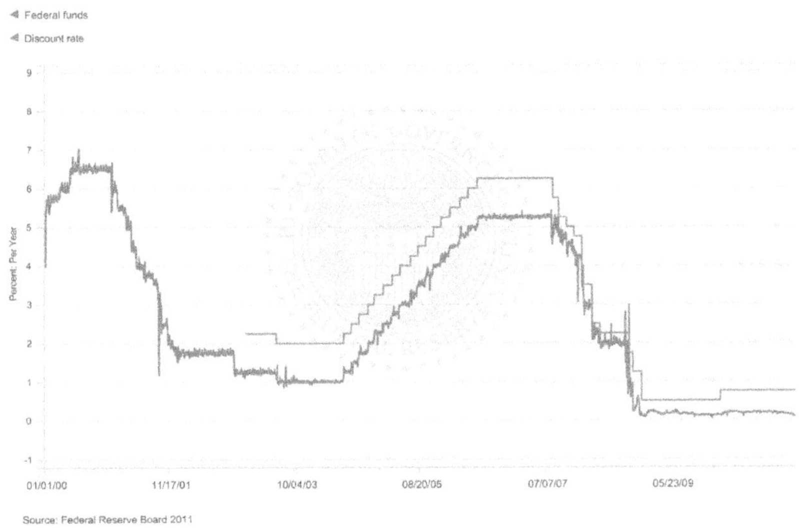

Fig. 6.2: Fed funds rates.

The graph shows the trend of rates on FED Funds. Following the attack on the Twin Towers, interest rates dropped from 6% to 3% on 17 September 2001. Then, in October 2001, they dropped again to 2.5% and in December of the same year to 1.75%. The FED in June 2003 further reduced its rates up to 1%. Following the recovery of the economy, the FED in 2004 began to raise rates, which peaked in 2006. In that year, the rates reached around 5.5%, and then declined drastically in 2009, the year in which rates touched zero.

which exposures are sold in exchange for money or other financed activities. Another task of the SPV is the management of a single activity characterized by complex financial transactions and which requires numerous permits for its operation, such as a factory or a power plant. With the use of securitisation processes, the company can make movable those capital otherwise tied up in the form of financing to third parties, obtaining in exchange for liquidity. Lending institutions had the possibility of reselling mortgages to third parties, called vehicle companies, transferring the risk of insolvency to them and immediately recovering a large part of the credit, which they would have collected only at the end of the mortgages themselves, for example to finance other mortgages.

With high financial leverage (see Figure 6.6), lenders had the opportunity to increase their credit offerings and at the same time to increase their available means, using borrowed money.

In 2004, when the US economy showed signs of recovery, interest rates rose following a FED decision, which made mortgages more expensive for families. Despite the rise in mortgages, the demand for real estate as well as the demand for mortgages did not decline, on the contrary, it grew more and more fueling prices, which reached their peak in 2006. The high prices and high rates reached in 2006 accentu-

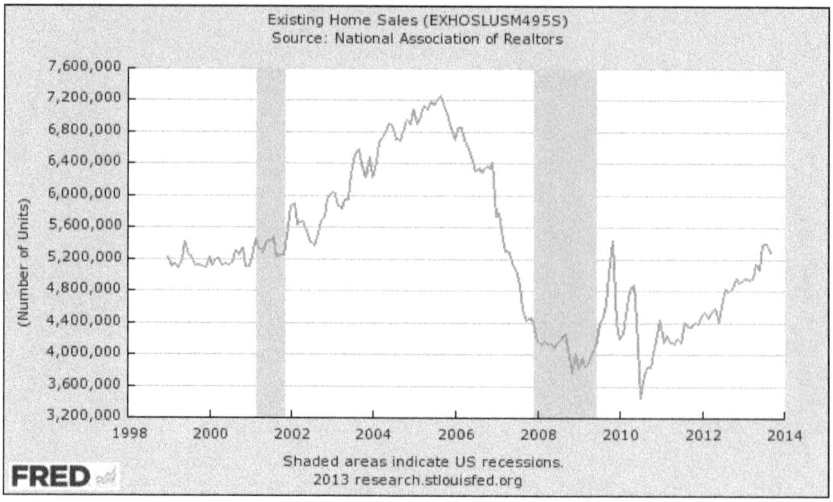

Fig. 6.3: Sales performance in the real estate market.
The graph shows the changes that the real estate market has undergone from 2001 to 2013. We are witnessing its growth from 2003 to 2006, and then its decline from 2006 to 2009.

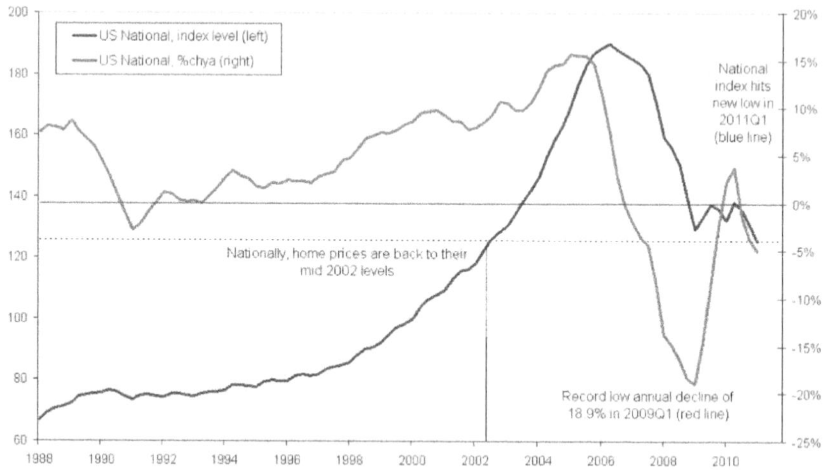

Fig. 6.4: Case-Shiller Home Price Index.
Source: Standard&Poor's (S&P). The graph shows the trend of property price indices in the time interval 1988-2010. A significant rise in prices of more than 10% can be observed, from 2003 to 2006, when they reach their maximum peak, to then decrease by more than 15% starting from 2007. Source: [S&P Dow Jones Indices (2012); FRED (2012)]

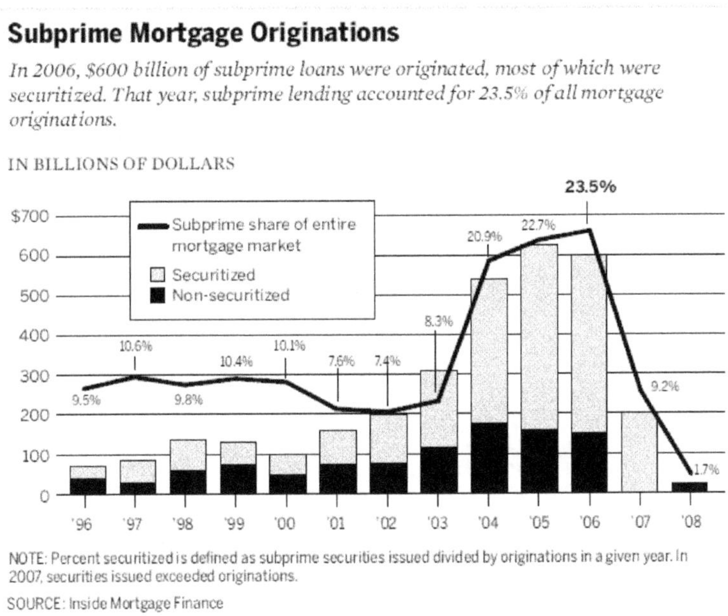

Fig. 6.5: Subprime mortgage payments.
The graph shows that 600 billion subprime mortgages were disbursed in 2006, most of which were securitised. In that year, subprime mortgages made up 23.5% of all mortgages.

ated the cases of insolvency of borrowers already occurred in the past and led to a contraction in demand for mortgages and real estate. The situation was exacerbated by the extensive use of floating-rate mortgages instead of fixed-rate ones. The decline in the real estate market negatively affected property prices, which drastically dropped; then the real estate bubble burst. This event had serious repercussions on credit institutions which recorded significant losses due to both: the devaluation of mortgages following the downfall of property prices (especially those with a high leverage ratio) and the increase in insolvencies.

6.3 Complexity Tree of Securitizations

Furthermore, the various downgrades of the creditworthiness of the SPVs resulted in a devaluation of the securitized securities, which became illiquid. The situation got worse due to the "complexity tree" effect coined by [Haldane (2009)]. The former Chief Economist of the Bank of England, Andrew Haldane, claimed that investors were unable to understand the underlying risks. He brings an example of a special form of a derivative known as the collateralized debt obligation, or more precisely a CDO-squared. On average, one CDO-squared comports 125 CDOs on asset backed securities (ABS). Each simple CDO consists of 150 residential mortgage

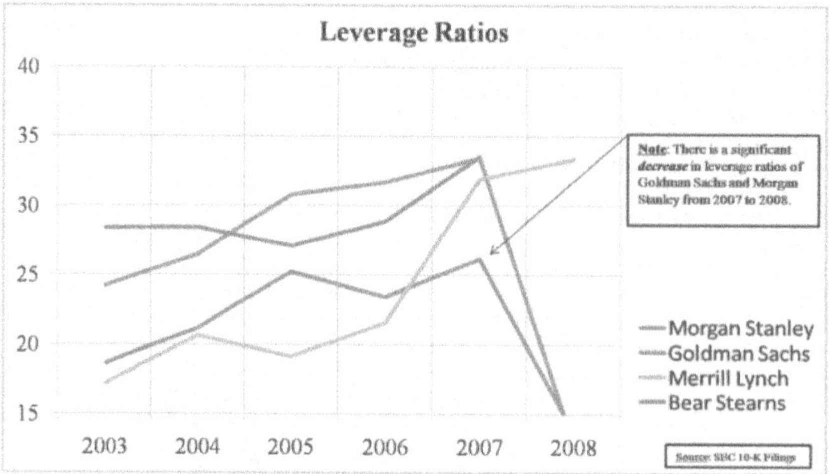

Fig. 6.6: Leverage ratios.

The graph shows the leverage ratios of the four major US banks from 2003 to 2008. Of the four lenders, only two survived during the financial crisis: Goldman Sachs and Morgan Stanley, who since 2007 have significantly reduced the use of leverage, about 15%.

backed securities. Each security comprises of five thousand mortgage loans. Thus, a typical CDO-squared includes 90 mln of mortgage loans. Each mentioned stage of securitisation (RMBS, ABS etc.) is accompanied by a thick book of documentation, or information memorandum (infomemo). Then one CDO-squared has a description on around 1.1 bn pages per one investor in CDO-squared. Such volume is generally unfeasible to absorb, not to say within the shortest terms of the CDO-squared underwritting process. Not surprisingly that even with the presence of the warning marks within such infomemos, probably none of the investors even noticed as they did not open it. That is why Andrew Haldane names the complexity of the credit derivatives as the cause of the financial crisis 2007-2009.

To combat the risks and crisis there came a parallel rise in the complexity of the banking regulation established by the Basel Committee. For instance, [Penikas (2015)] and the current Chairman of the Basel Committee [Hernández de Cos (2019)] proxied such complexity by thirty thousand pages of regulatory documents published by the Basel Committee since its establishment (see Figure 6.7). On one side, a rise in banking regulation is just a particular realisation of the global trend to strengthen regulation. [Shleifer (2012)] argues that this tendency arose to balance the inefficiencies of the court litigation. At least, it takes too much time. That is why there is an implicit consensus to invest in regulation in order to prevent going to litigation. From another side, there is a direct benefit from regulation. The primary beneficiaries are the regulated entities. Their return on investment becomes more guaranteed. The reason is simple. The more complicated the regulation is, the fewer new entrants may distort the envisaged yields. This idea was coined mostly a decade before the establishment of the Basel Committee by [Demsetz (1968)] with reference to utilities regulation in the United States.

However, such a rise in banking regulation complexity did not pay off. That is why Andrew Haldane was the only Central Bank official to promote banking regulation simplification (see [Zhong (2013)]).

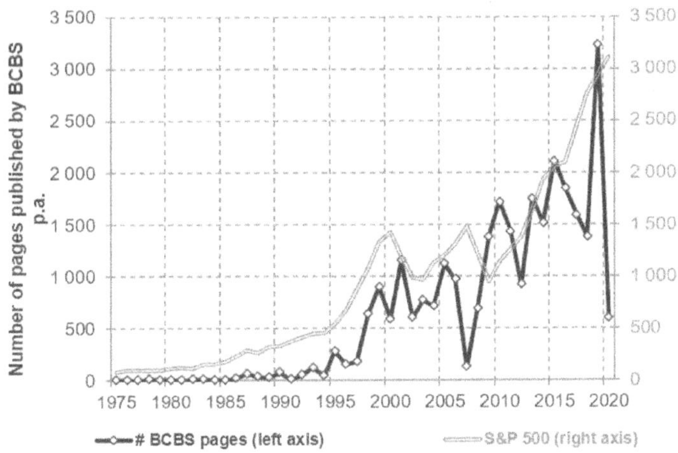

Fig. 6.7: The increasing complexity of banking regulation.
Methodology Source: [Penikas (2015)] %

The "Complexity tree" effect was not the only one to blame for the 2007-2009 crisis. Another culprit was copula. As it often happens, the more just the arguments are, the less popular and less promoted they are. This was the case with the "complexity tree" of Andrew Haldane. However, criticism of copulas was to the same extent wrong, to what it was loudly announced. Take, for instance, [Salmon (2009)] or [MacKenzie and Spears (2012)]. They argued that those were copulas who killed the Wall Street in 2007-2009. The roots of the copulas criticism lie with the already mentioned article by [Li (2000)]. We would like to recall that David Li merely showed that a Gaussian copula may be used for modeling default correlation within the CDO. David neither promoted the use of Gaussian copula nor did select the best copula to fit the default data. All he did was demonstrate a particular mathematical tool application. What risk managers and underwriters should have done was to validate whether Gaussian copula indeed fits the data well. But they did not. They only relied on [Li (2000)], though he demonstrated one of possible and not necessarily the optimal copula family. To recall, the Basel Committee listed copulas as one of the preferred tools to aggregate risks (see [BCBS (2010c), p. 25]). However, it did not claim that the banks are limited to a Gaussian copula only.

6.4 Lehman Brothers Collapse and the Change in Deposit Insurance

This is a typical situation when the theoretical paper is used for empirical use either without proper understanding of the underlying message or by referring to it in the case when the actual implementation falls far from the modeled one. For instance, we observe a similar situation with the deposit insurance systems. The paper by [Diamond and Dybvig (1983)] is known as the first solid justification for the positive effects of the state deposit insurance systems. However, the original paper suggested a simple and quite logical approach. The idea was to impose fines on the depositors who withdrew their funds early from a bank thus provoking a bank run and causing bankruptcy. The total amount of fines was suggested to be equal to the volume of deposits lost subject to bank bankruptcy. Thus, the proposed *ex post* deposit insurance was super-optimal and implied no bank runs. However, the implementation was at least twice different. First, the fines of deposit insurance fees are collected *ex ante*, i.e. before any bank bankruptcy. Second, all the depositors are subject to indirectly paying these fees, and not only those who withdrew early. As a result, there is nothing novel in the discovery by the former Chairman of the Basel Committee [Ingves (2017)] that the state deposit insurance systems have systematic budget deficits worldwide. Though the negative result is spoken about, the paper by [Diamond and Dybvig (1983)] is brought back to justify the need for state deposit insurance or the need to increase its limits. For instance, the latter step was one of the measures to combat the infamous consequences of the Lehman Brothers collapse. Thus, FED increased the state deposit insurance limit in September 2008 from USD 100k to USD 250k. Otherwise, people could have withdrawn all the deposits from a system within a couple of days.

The vehicle companies, therefore, were forced to ask for funds from the banks that had issued them and that had guaranteed liquidity lines to pay the interest to the savers who had purchased the securities they issued. Some banks, however, were unable to find the necessary liquidity, as no financial institution was willing to lend them credit. In such a context, the interbank market experienced a sharp rise in interest rates and a significant contraction in banks' willingness to grant credit to other financial institutions. Thus a *liquidity crisis* developed. In response to this crisis, central banks acted by buying government bonds, reducing interest rates to encourage consumption and investments, but their interventions were insufficient.

In fact, the situation continued to worsen and reached its culmination on September 15, 2008, when the Treasury and the monetary authorities of the United States allowed the large investment bank *Lehman Brothers* to go bankrupt, without intervening, as they had done in other cases. These circumstances led some of the major US lenders to bankruptcy (see Figure 6.8), including Lehman Brothers who filed for bankruptcy on September 15, 2008. The bankruptcy of this lender shook shareholder confidence in the market and banks, and fuelled concerns about the effects of all other market participants on exposure to these institutions. The increase in counterparty risk caused a further reduction in liquidity on the interbank deposit market. The crisis became real and in a short time extended its roots even overseas. Its consequences were evident. The fastest-to-react was the stock market.

Non-US lenders recorded high losses by investing in derivative securities linked to subprime mortgages or to the shares of the US banks that had gone bankrupt or gone into crisis. Only the banks that were able to absorb these losses with their own capital remained solvent, the others became insolvent and went bankrupt.

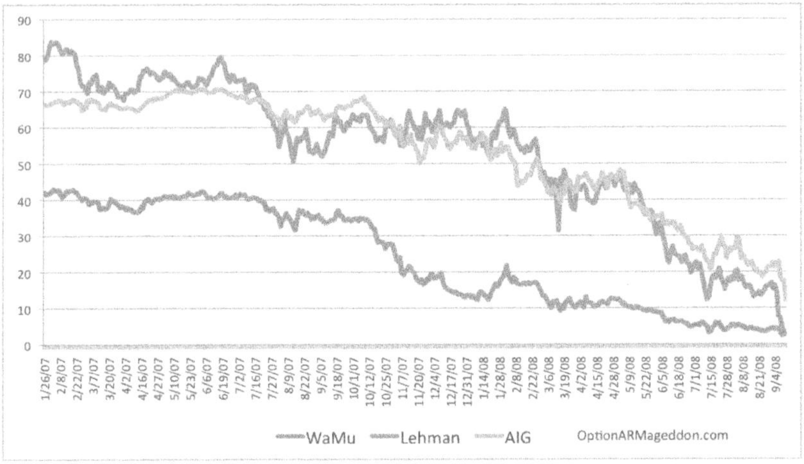

Fig. 6.8: The stock market crash 2007 to 2008.

6.5 Wider Macroeconomic Implications of the Great Recession

However, that was not only the stock market to react. The real economy was also materially hurt.

Investments and consumption fell due to the crisis of confidence in the international financial system, with a consequent propensity to save (see Figure 6.9).

The prices of goods and services rose dramatically. Suffice it to say that oil prices reached record levels on the eve of the crisis in 2007, reaching $ 145 per barrel (Brent quality), up 470% compared to the beginning of 2000; metal prices measured on the London Metal Exchange index, which includes aluminium, nickel, lead, copper, tin and zinc, showed increases of 200%. Food prices measured on the Spot Index of Foodstuffs also increased by 150%. According to the Food and Agriculture Organisation of the United Nations (FAO), many factors had determined the rise in food prices, such as: unfavourable weather conditions; devaluation of the US dollar; long-term economic growth in several developing countries which had put upward pressure on oil and fertilizer prices and led to increased demand for meat; the increase in production and transport costs as a result of rising oil and fertilizer prices; increased demand on commodity futures markets as a result

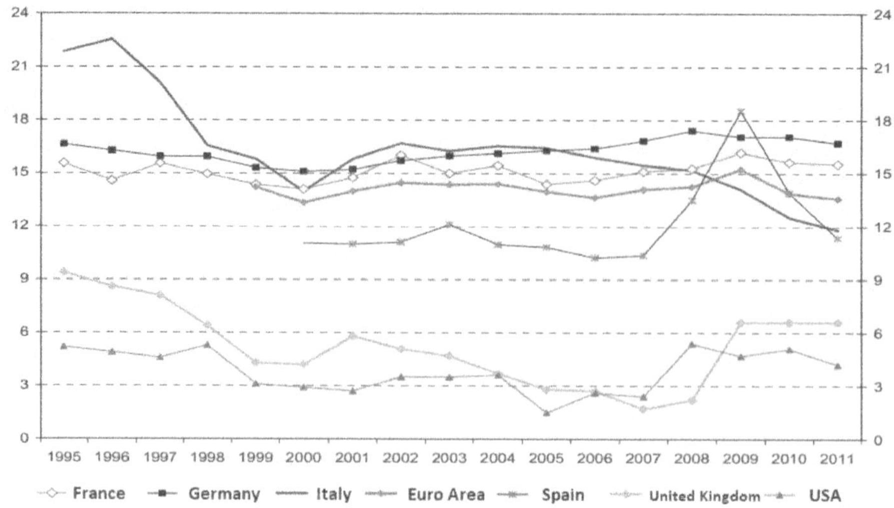

Fig. 6.9: Propensity to save.
Source: Eurostat, for euro area countries; ONS for the United Kingdom; BEA for the United States. It is an international comparison on the propensity to save by families during the financial crisis. It shows that from 2007 to 2009 there has been a growth in the propensity to save.

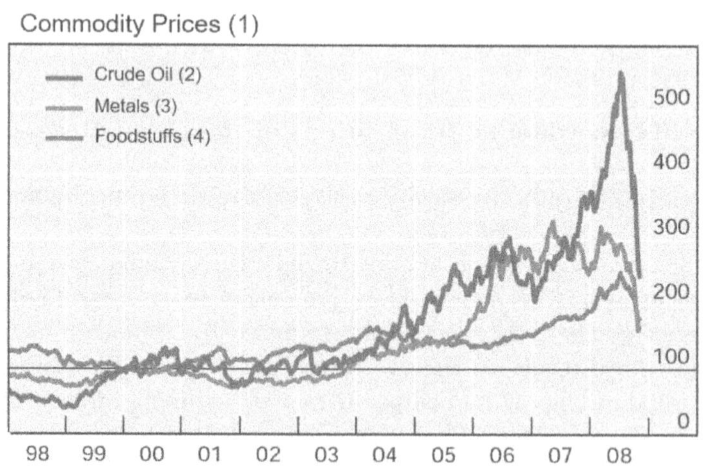

Fig. 6.10: Commodity prices.
Sources: IMF; OECD; CEIC; Datastream; national statistics; BRI processing. (1) Early 2000 = 100. (2) Brent quality. (3) London Metal Exchange Index including aluminium, nickel, lead, copper, tin and zinc. (4) Spot Index Foodstuffs of the Commodity Research Bureau.

of portfolio speculation and diversification; low stock levels [FAO (2011)]. But in mid-2008, with the outbreak of the crisis, the price of goods declined drastically to very low values (see Figure 6.10).

As for food prices, they also rose significantly; one of the causes is found in the increase in food consumption induced by higher per capita incomes in emerging economies, which occurred in conjunction with temporary supply interruptions.

The rise in food and energy prices pushed world inflation upwards. In mature economies, inflation doubled, from around 2% some years before the crisis to 4% in mid-2008, while in emerging economies it increased from around 4% to 8%. The relatively more significant increase in the latter group of economies was at least partly attributable to the greater weight attributed to food within the consumption basket in the countries with the lowest per capita income. In the sample of countries analyzed, the weighting of food in the consumer price index (CPI) of the emerging economies was equal to about 30%, or more than double the 13% found on average in mature ones. This was one of the reasons why in mid-2008 food price increases made a contribution of almost 4 percentage points to the growth of overall inflation in emerging economies, compared to just about one percentage point in mature economies (see Figure 6.11).

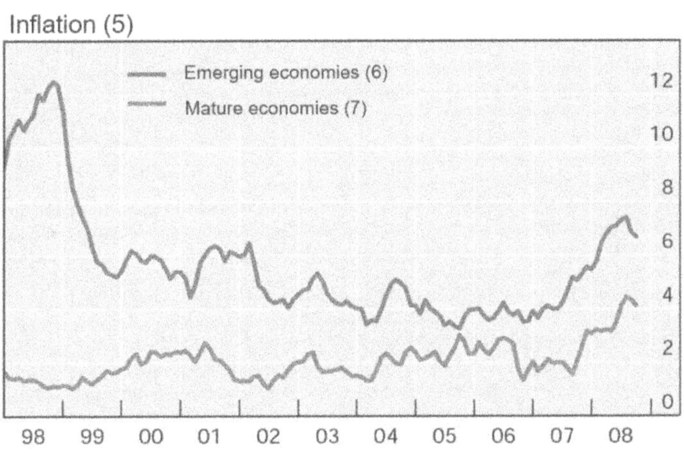

Fig. 6.11: Inflation.
Sources: IMF; OECD; CEIC; Datastream; national statistics; BIS calculations. Twelve-month percentage changes in consumer prices. Weighted average based on 2005 GDP and PPP exchange rates. (6) Brazil, China, Korea, Philippines, Hong Kong SAR, India, Indonesia, Malaysia, Mexico, Poland, Czech Republic, Singapore, Slovakia, South Africa, Chinese Taipei, Thailand, Turkey and Hungary. (7) Euro area, Canada, Denmark, Japan, Norway, United Kingdom, United States, Sweden and Switzerland.

In addition, consumer price inflation tended to be higher in emerging economies than in mature ones over the same period. By contrast, the weight of energy within the consumption basket in the two groups of economies was more similar and therefore did not have a significant influence, disregarding the increase in inflation in various parts of the world.

Chapter 7

Credit Risk Regulation After the Crisis

7.1 From Basel II to Basel III

Basel II had become the point of reference for many banks and it was a huge step forward in the direction of credit risk management with the construction of models and rating systems for estimating risk components. However, it was not enough to safeguard the financial system from further crises, and the recent financial crisis has been a confirmation. The aforementioned crisis of 2007-2009 highlighted the various gaps inherent in the regulatory framework of *Basel II*, such as excessive leverage, inadequate and low-quality capital, insufficient liquidity reserves, procyclical deleveraging process and interconnections between systemically important financial institutions (SIFIs). To address these shortcomings, in response to the financial crisis and the problems related to Basel II, the Basel Committee on Banking Supervision and its governing body, the Group of Governors and Heads of Supervision (GHOS) of the member countries, developed a program of reforms aimed at strengthening the financial system in terms of assets and liquidity, known as *Basel III*.

In July 2009, the Committee issued a further package of documents in order to strengthen the Basel II capital framework, in particular with regards to complex securitisations, off-balance-sheet vehicles and exposures of the trading book. These improvements have been part of a wider effort to strengthen the regulation and supervision of internationally active banks, in light of the shortcomings revealed by the financial market crisis. In September 2010, the GHOS announced the rise in the minimum global capital standards for commercial banks. This followed an agreement reached in July regarding the overall design of the capital and liquidity reform package, now called "Basel III". In November 2010, the new capital and liquidity standards were approved by the leaders of the G20 summit in Seoul and subsequently agreed at the Basel Committee meeting in December 2010.

Basel III, which entered into force on January 1, 2013, is an articulated set of reform measures, prepared by the Basel Committee. These reforms aim to improve the banking sector's ability to absorb shocks resulting from economic and financial tensions, risk management, governance and strengthen the transparency and reporting of banks. Broadly speaking, one may classify them into two kinds: *microprudential* (i.e. concerning regulation at the level of individual banks) and *macroprudential* (i.e. concerning system-wide risks that can accumulate in the banking sector).

The main innovations introduced with Basel III are:

- Improvement of the quality, consistency and transparency of regulatory capital;
- Strengthening of risk coverage;
- Introduction of a new coefficient called leverage ratio;
- Reduction of procyclicality and promotion of a countercyclical buffer;
- Introduction of liquidity requirements;
- Remuneration regulation.

7.1.1 *Basel III Credit Risk Amendments*

With regards to the credit risk and RWA assessment, Basel III reconfirmed the methods introduced by Basel II. Thus, banks can choose to adopt one of the following approaches:

- *Standardized approach (ST)*;
- *Internal Ratings-Based (IRB)*; approach divided into *Foundation IRB* and *Advanced IRB*.

There were some principal changes to the credit risk evaluation in Basel III both in ST and IRB approaches. The major change in the standardized approach is that it became more flexible. For instance, for retail borrowers loan-to-value (LTV) became another differentiating criteria.

There were two major changes within IRB regulation. First, the Lehman Brothers demonstrated that banks are not equally destructive to the banking system when the financial crisis strikes. Particularly, there are systemically important financial institutions like Lehman that are more interconnected with other market participants. Therefore, a SIFI collapse is much more detrimental to the stability than that of an ordinary bank. That is why the Basel Committee suggested recognizing higher credit risks related to exposures against SIFIs. To do this, the asset correlation R_{SIFI} was a quarter enhanced compared to the general asset correlation R from Eq. (5.11) (see Eqs. (7.1) and (7.2)),

$$R_{SIFI} = 1.25 \cdot R, \tag{7.1}$$

or,

$$R_{SIFI} = 0.15 \cdot \left(\frac{1 - e^{-50 \cdot PD}}{1 - e^{-50}}\right) + 0.30 \cdot \left(1 - \frac{1 - e^{-50 \cdot PD}}{1 - e^{-50}}\right). \tag{7.2}$$

Second, the applicability of the Advanced IRB was limited. Specifically, concerning the so-called Low Default Portfolios (LDP). Those are typically observed either in innovative retail products that have not yet accumulated default statistics or in mature portfolios where the defaults are rare. The LDP-alike asset classes are large corporates with annual sales exceeding €500m, banks and other financial institutions (see [BCBS (2017)]). However, F-IRB is still applicable for the mentioned asset classes. This means that there still exist opportunities for regulatory arbitrage due to distortions in PD prediction for the segment with no observation for one of the two classes.

Consider a simple example of LDP-driven regulatory arbitrage in Table 7.1. Suppose we have a portfolio of $N = 1000$ borrowers, of which there are $D = 100$ defaults. We compare two cases: either we break down the sample into either part with similar default rates (i.e. $DR = 10\%$ of borrowers per each group), or we differentiate those by making a more risky segment and a lower one. In both cases, we start with the capital before the expected loss EL deduction of $K_0 = 210$ units of currency. Thus, using the very same dataset we can reduce the total credit risk estimate from 199.5 to 184.0 (see rows 3, 6 in column 8 above). As a result, the capital ratio CAR rises from 8.5 to 9.5% (see column 11). To do so, one merely has to segment LDP with a significantly lower default rate (see rows 4 and 6 in column 5).

Table 7.1: Illustrative case when there appears internal regulatory arbitrage from LDP.

CAR when there is no LDP										
No.	Portfolio	N	D	DR	EL	UL	VaR	EL, % of VaR	K_0	CAR
1	Segment 1	500	50	10%	22.5	77.2	99.7	22.6%		
2	Segment 2	500	50	10%	22.5	77.2	99.7	22.6%		
3	Total	1000	100	10%	45.0	154.5	199.5	22.6%	210.0	8.5%
CAR in the presence of the LDP segmentation										
No.	Portfolio	N	D	DR	EL	UL	VaR	EL, % of VaR	K_0	CAR
4	LDP	500	10	2%	4.5	45.9	50.4	8.9%		
5	Other	500	90	18%	40.5	93.1	133.6	30.3%		
6	Total	1000	100	10%	45.0	139.0	184.0	24.5%	210.0	9.5%

To bring the problem of PD prediction for an LDP portfolio think of the following example. Assume that a portfolio consists of perfectly correlated exposures where each borrower has the same individual default probability (PD). This means that the default correlation is equal to 100%. Then the default rate (DR) distribution is as follows. It implies that there are only two possible DR realisations: 0% and 100%. The nice property of the correlated Bernoulli distribution is that its mean equals the individual success (default) probability. Then the mean DR equals the individual PD, while the density of $DR = 0\%$ equals $1 - PD$ (see Figure 7.1). This is a pure LDP portfolio. There are no defaults observed. However, in a crisis, there might occur another extreme. The default rate may trigger to 100%. This is the very unpleasant cliff-effect for risk-managers. It is much easier to model, optimize and hedge risk distributions that are continuous and do not demonstrate such rapid jumps from 0% to 100%. That is why from the financial stability perspective it would be much more beneficial to prohibit any IRB approach for an LDP portfolio like it was entirely forbidden for the credit risk in equity holdings exposures.

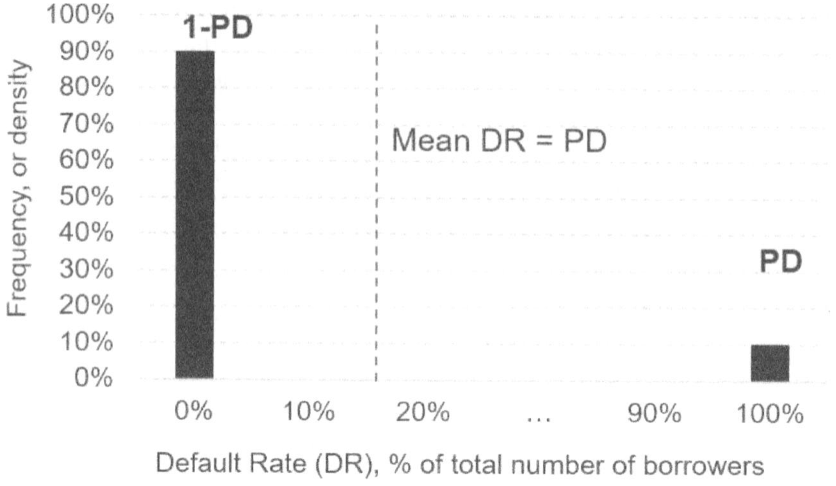

Fig. 7.1: Default Rate (DR) distribution under perfect default correlation.

7.2 Basel III Liquidity Ratios

One of the probable rationales for the introduction of two minimum liquidity ratios was the following. Before the financial crisis, markets were characterized by the availability of low-cost financing. The rapid change in market conditions had highlighted both the speed with which liquidity could evaporate and how illiquid situations could last for a long time. All this led to serious tensions within the banking system, which required the intervention of central banks to support both the functioning of the money markets and, in some cases, of individual institutions. Many of the difficulties encountered by some banks were due to the failure to comply with the basic principles of liquidity risk management. In this regard, in 2008 the Basel Committee published the document [BCBS (2008)], which provided guidelines for the management and control of liquidity funding risk (funding risk) and intend to contribute to promoting better risk management in this important area. The Basel Committee wished to have more rigorous coordination of supervisors as a follow-up to the document. Therefore, it wanted to ensure banks were complying with the fundamental principles. Furthermore, the Basel Committee developed two minimum quantitative requirements for liquidity risk:

- *Liquidity Coverage Ratio* (LCR);

- *Net Stable Funding Ratio* (NSFR).

7.2.1 *Liquidity Coverage Ratio (LCR)*

The Liquidity Coverage Ratio measures the bank's probable reaction to a liquidity crisis lasting 30 days, ensuring that it has sufficient high-quality liquid assets to deal with the crisis. The scenario must simulate significant stress. It may assume a downgrade of the bank's rating, withdrawal of a portion of deposits, a reduction in unsecured wholesale funding, an increase in both: margin requirements and haircuts applied in guaranteed financing operations. A haircut is the discount to the value of an asset real or financial, given as a guarantee, requested by the creditor to protect against the risk of a loss of the asset itself.

The coefficient requires that

$$\text{LCR} = \frac{HQLA}{\text{Net outflows}} \geq 100\%, \tag{7.3}$$

where HQLA stands for the amount of the high-quality liquid assets. Those are assets that can be converted immediately into cash and with negligible losses. *Net outflows* are the gross outflows net of expected inflows in the thirty days following the stress event.

7.2.2 *Net Stable Funding Ratio (NSFR)*

The Net Stable Funding Ratio requires banks to maintain a minimum amount of stable sources of funding depending on the degree of liquidity of on-balance sheet assets and off-balance sheet commitments and exposures. The scenario must simulate the stress conditions that a bank can face over a year and assumes:

- A significant reduction in profitability or solvency following an increase in risk exposures;
- A rating downgrade;
- An event that can negatively affect the bank's reputation.

The NSFR requires that

$$NSFR = \frac{\text{Amount of stable funding available}}{\text{Amount of mandatory stable funding}} \geq 100\% \tag{7.4}$$

The amount of the available stable funding (ASF) is measured based on the general characteristics of the relative stability of an institution's sources of funding, including maturity of its liabilities and the different propensity of the various lenders to withdraw the loans disbursed. When determining the maturity of an equity instrument or liability, investors are expected to redeem any call options on the earliest possible date. For sources of funding with options exercisable at the bank's discretion, banks will have to assume that they will exercise the options at the earliest possible date unless they can demonstrate — to the satisfaction of the competent supervisory authority — that under no circumstances they would exercise the option. For long-term liabilities, only the portion of cash flows due at or after the six-month and one-year maturities should be considered as having an effective residual maturity equal to or greater than six months and one year, respectively. It is calculated first by classifying the carrying amount of equity and liabilities of an institution in one of the five categories presented below. The carrying amount represents the amount at which the liability or equity instrument is recorded gross of the application of any deductions, filters, or other regulatory adjustments. The amount attributed to each category is subsequently multiplied by an ASF factor; the total available stable funding corresponds to the sum of the weighted amounts. The table presents the specific types of activities to be attributed to each category and the associated ASF factor.

ASF factor	Components of ASF category
100%	• Total regulatory capital • Other capital instruments and liabilities with effective residual maturity of one year or more
95%	• Stable non-maturity (demand) deposits and term deposits with residual maturity of less than one year provided by retail and SME customers
90%	• Less stable non-maturity deposits and term deposits with residual maturity of less than one year provided by retail and SME customers
50%	• Funding with residual maturity of less than one year provided by non-financial corporate customers • Operational deposits • Funding with residual maturity of less than one year from sovereigns, public sector entities (PSEs), and multilateral and national development banks • Other funding with residual maturity of not less than six months and less than one year not included in the above categories, including funding provided by central banks and financial institutions
0%	• All other liabilities and equity not included in above categories, including liabilities without a stated maturity • Derivatives payable net of derivatives receivable if payables are greater than receivables

Fig. 7.2: Summary of the categories of liabilities and the ASF factors associated with them.

Instead, the required stable funding is measured against the general characteristics of an institution's asset liquidity risk profile and potential liquidity exposures. It is calculated first by classifying the book value of an institution's assets into one of the categories listed below. The amount attributed to each category is subsequently multiplied by the corresponding required stable funding factor (RSF); the total of the mandatory stable funding will correspond to the sum of the weighted amounts and the amount of the potential liquidity exposure transactions multiplied by the associated RSF factor. The table presents the specific types of assets to be attributed to each category and the associated RSF factor. For more details see [BCBS (2014b)].

RSF factor	Components of RSF category
0%	• Coins and banknotes • All central bank reserves • Unencumbered loans to banks subject to prudential supervision with residual maturities of less than six months
5%	• Unencumbered Level 1 assets, excluding coins, banknotes and central bank reserves
15%	• Unencumbered Level 2A assets
50%	• Unencumbered Level 2B assets • HQLA encumbered for a period of six months or more and less than one year • Loans to banks subject to prudential supervision with residual maturities six months or more and less than one year • Deposits held at other financial institutions for operational purposes • All other assets not included in the above categories with residual maturity of less than one year, including loans to non-bank financial institutions, loans to non-financial corporate clients, loans to retail and small business customers, and loans to sovereigns, central banks and PSEs
65%	• Unencumbered residential mortgages with a residual maturity of one year or more and with a risk weight of less than or equal to 35% • Other unencumbered loans not included in the above categories, excluding loans to financial institutions, with a residual maturity of one year or more and with a risk weight of less than or equal to 35% under the Standardised Approach

Fig. 7.3: Summary of liability categories and associated RSF factors.

This new scheme for liquidity risk is complemented by a set of monitoring tools aimed at improving the consistency of supervisory activity at the international level. They are:

- Misalignment of contractual deadlines;
- Concentration of deposits;
- Unencumbered assets available;
- LCR for significant currency;
- Monitoring tools through the market.

LCR and NSFR are widely known as Basel III novelties. However, the liquidity risk regulation is not that novel for the Basel Committee, at least when considering its inner work. For instance, [Goodhart (2011)] claims that such regulation was on the committee agenda since its inaction in the 1970s. Unfortunately, four decades were needed to get to a compromise. It was quickly reached when the Lehman Brothers defaulted.

Although LCR and NSFR assume stress modeling, they are still of the nature of the minimum requirements. This means that, like the Basel II first pillar requirements for credit risk, they cannot capture the wide variety of risk combinations of a given bank. Likewise, LCR and HSFR cannot do this due to liquidity risk. That is why the regulator has developed the second pillar for liquidity risk management. Similarly to the ICAAP, it was called Internal Liquidity Adequacy Assessment (ILAA). To improve them, the Basel Committee has published some guidelines on intraday liquidity management in [BCBS (2012c)] although they have not obtained any final regulatory status.

7.3 Basel III Capital Definition

The Basel Committee has redefined the regulatory capital, capital held by banks, as follows:

- Basic capital (Tier 1 Capital), in turn made up of
  - Primary quality assets, Common Equity Tier 1 (CET1) capital;
  - Additional Tier 1;
- Additional capital (Tier 2).

Tier 1 capital is understood to be the primary component of regulatory capital intended to absorb losses in conditions of business continuity. It is made up of share capital and balance sheet reserves from retained earnings after tax. The share capital is made up of issued and fully paid-up ordinary shares and non-cumulative perpetual preferred stock. The former are shares with no maturity that are not necessarily entitled to dividends, the latter are preference shares with no maturity that are entitled to dividends at a fixed rate. Unpaid dividends do not accumulate, i.e. dividends that have not been paid in a certain year are not carried over to the next year.

To increase the banks' capacity to absorb losses and therefore increase the latter's resilience to stressful situations, the Basel Committee deemed it appropriate to improve the quality of the equity by increasing primary quality financial instruments, such as ordinary shares and retained earnings reserves, and eliminate the hybrid capital from Tier 1. The latter consisted of innovative hybrid capital instruments whose amount should not exceed 15% of the Tier 1 capital. With Basel III, therefore, the Tier 1 capital is redefined as follows: Common Equity Tier 1 and additional Tier 1. The first consists of ordinary shares and undistributed earnings reserves, the amount of which must be at most 85% of Tier 1, the second is composed of financial instruments subordinated to deposits, unsecured credits, with no expiry date, incentives for early redemption and clauses that allow the temporal deferral of coupons. For more details see the additional Tier 1 compatibility criteria.

7.3.1 *Additional Capital Instruments*

Supplementary capital means the secondary component of the regulatory capital intended to absorb losses in the event of a liquidity crisis. It is made up of revaluation reserves, hybrid capital instruments, innovative and non-innovative capital instruments not included in Tier 1 capital, subordinated bonds, implicit net capital gains on equity investments and other instruments satisfying Tier 2 compatibility criteria (see [BCBS (2009)]).

Tier 2 can be broken down into two levels: *upper* and *lower*. The *lower Tier 2* is characterized by subordinated bank securities that are less risky in terms of repayment of the payments envisaged by the bond. They are subordinated only to non-subordinated bonds and for them, a duration of 10 years is envisaged. The option of early repayment of the nominal value (starting from the fifth year) can only take place if requested by the issuer. However, such an option is subject to authorization by the supervisory body. Finally, there are no clauses that allow a time deferral of coupons, or the possibility of paying interest in a period after that established by the loan.

The *upper Tier 2* is characterized by non-subordinated bonds only with respect to those of Tier 1. These instruments provide for the *loss absorption* mechanism, i.e. in the event of significant losses that reduce the share capital and the reserve below the regulatory limits, the issuer can use principal and interest to smooth out such negative results, reducing the nominal value of the loan or converting it to equity. Basel III aims to harmonize the instruments computed in Tier 2 and to eliminate those present in Tier 3. Tier 3 is the third-level capital used by banks to provision against market risks. It includes a large amount of short-term (up to 3 years) debt including subordinated bonds, hidden reserves and general loss of reserves. For it to be classified as Tier 3, assets must be limited to 250% of a bank's Tier 1 and must be unsecured, subordinated and have a minimum maturity of two years. Basel II introduced Tier 3 capital, but with Basel III it was excluded from the regulatory capital.

In addition to increasing the quality of capital, Basel III aims to increase the amount of capital of banks by raising the minimum capital requirements established in Basel II. In detail:

- Tier 1 capital must be at least equal to 6% of the assets weighted for their risk instead of 4%;
- The Common equity Tier 1 must be at least equal to 4.5% of the assets weighted for their risk instead of 2%.

As regards the regulatory capital, it is required that it must be at least equal to 8% of the assets weighted for their risk, as was required in Basel II.

To improve risk coverage of the balance sheet, the Committee has elaborated a series of reforms aimed at raising capital requirements both concerning exposures linked to the trading portfolio or securitisations, and exposures to counterparty credit risk deriving from bank transactions in derivative instruments. With reference to the former, it introduced a capital requirement based on the value at risk in conditions of acute stress (stressed value), calculated assuming an uninterrupted period of 12 months of significant financial stress and more stringent capital requirements for re-securitisations. With regard to the latter, the measures envisage an increase in capital resources to face exposures and a strengthening of counterparty risk management. In this regard, the Committee has established that each bank determines the capital requirement in the face of stress conditions and is subject to a capital requirement to deal with any losses it may incur due to a change in market prices. It also strengthened the requirements in terms of collateral management, supported by the initiatives of the Committee on Payment and Settlement Systems (CSPR) and the International Organization of Securities Commissions (IOSCO) on systemic risk and assessed a series of measures aimed to reduce the use of external ratings under the Basel II framework. These measures include the obligation for banks to internally assess exposures to securitisations with external ratings.

Procyclicality is the tendency of the financial system to amplify the oscillations of the economic cycle. History has shown that the economy has a cyclical trend, characterized by the alternation of recessive phases with expansion phases. While in times of economic recession banks tend to contract their supply of credit, in times of expansion they tend to increase their supply. In fact, if in periods of recession, banks increase the cost of money or require greater guarantees or more collateral in the granting of credit following the deterioration of the creditworthiness of debtors or capital shortages, causing a contraction in supply, in periods of expansion there happens exactly the opposite. One of the first discussions on procyclicality can be found in [Gordy and Howells (2006)].

This is counterproductive for the economic system as a credit crunch by credit institutions accentuates the recession, and therefore procyclicality. The interested reader may refer to the first discussions on the topic. The Basel Committee has therefore introduced a series of measures to limit procyclicality. These measures concern the promotion of countercyclical provisions, capital conservation and credit growth.

Provisions, or allowances, are budgetary allocations for the establishment of funds to cover certain or probable future expenses. This category includes costs, charges or losses that contribute to the determination of operating income whose existence, amount or date of occurrence is probable. This category includes costs, charges, or losses concurrent to the determination of operating income, the existence, amount or date of occurrence of which is probable. On this front, the Committee has introduced more robust estimation methodologies, based on *expected losses* (EL) and no longer on incurred losses (*incurred loss*), and has evaluated an incentive system that promotes higher provisions in the context of capital adequacy.

This coincides with IFRS 9 standard and it, also, requires life-time credit risk assessment for assets with significant deterioration in credit risk. The other two objectives, capital preservation and credit growth are achieved through a capital buffer and a countercyclical buffer, which we will now describe.

Let us remind the difference between the mentioned provisions and reserves that look like synonyms in English. Provisions are "above the line" charges to profit made mostly by the bank itself, whereas reserves stand for the "below the line" non-distributable appropriations of profit required by a supervisor in addition to provisions (see [BCBS (2019)]).

The introduction of an additional emergency capital *buffer* is meant to absorb any losses that banks may incur and can be achieved by setting aside capital without the minimum capital requirements being violated. The course of events has shown that the alternation of recessive and expansionary phases has led to huge losses that destabilized the banking system, in some cases triggering a contraction of the economy. Therefore, it becomes necessary for the banks to equip themselves with capital reserves to face periods of recession. Once the available reserves have been used, banks must immediately replenish them, for example by reducing the distribution of profits.

However, there are cases when banks, despite having exhausted their buffers, have continued to distribute capital. This behaviour is not tolerable both because the interests of shareholders are privileged over those of depositors, and because it could lead to bankruptcy in other banks. Nevertheless, this is a dilemma known from the establishment of the Basel Committee and the introduction of the capital ratio. We may call it a "taxi phenomenon". [Goodhart (2011)] reminds us that one of the most famous Chairman of the Basel Committee was Peter Cooke from the Bank of England. When designing the capital ratio, he always challenged his colleagues at the committee whether the ratio should be targeted and not be subject to the famous minimum of 8% of the RWA. He presented a taxi case. Suppose there is a rule that at the taxi parking lot there should always be at least a taxi. Let there be a car at such a lot. When a potential passenger approaches it, the taxi refuses to give him a ride. The reason is simple. The taxi cannot leave the taxi parking lot according to the established rule as there should always be a single car. The situation is ridiculous. However, the rule is a rule. Somewhat two decades have passed to think over this "taxi phenomenon". It is only after the financial crisis of 2007-2009 that the Basel Committee made a step towards targeting instead of strict minimum imposition. Capital buffers — that we discuss below — could be dispersed in crisis meaning that the minimum became adjustable. However, there are two specifics, not truly abolishing the "taxi phenomenon". First, the capital buffers were introduced above the existing minimum, and not within the current minimum levels. Second, the minimum — even with all the buffers dispersed — is still there.

From historical retrospect, it seems that Peter Cook and Andrew Haldane both were misunderstood by their employer the Bank of England. Though Peter Cook is known for having introduced the international standard on the capital ratio measurement in Basel I, he had to spend several years working mostly independently of his parent institution, i.e. without any support from the Bank of England on the eve of accepting Basel I in 1988 according to [Goodhart (2011)]. Moreover, in parallel to their representative's work, the Bank of England started parallel discussions with Americans and other regulators on the capital ratio design without informing Peter Cooke. The stories of Peter Cooke and Andrew Haldane with their ideas on the "taxi phenomenon" and "simplicity" in banking regulation show that correct ideas when being unpopular may cost a career to their promoters.

The new prudential framework aims to prevent banks that have already used buffers from further reducing them through the distribution of profits and to encourage capital conservation. There are two types of buffers:

- *Capital conservation buffer*;
- *Countercyclical buffer*;
- *Systemically Important Financial Institutions (SIFI) buffer.*

7.3.2 *Capital Conservation Buffer*

The capital conservation buffer is equal to 2.5% of the risk-weighted assets (RWA) and consists of the Common Equity Tier 1, in addition to the minimum capital adequacy requirements. Before contributing to the buffer, the Common Equity Tier 1 capital must be used to meet minimum capital requirements. If the assets fall below this limit, constraints will be imposed on the distribution of the capital. The elements considered as distributions include dividends, repurchases of own shares, payments on other instruments of the basic capital. These constraints only affect the distribution of profits and not the operations of the institutions and increase as the capital of the banks approaches the minimum requirements. Profits are defined as the distributable profits calculated before their eventual distribution. Table 7.2 illustrates the minimum capital conservation ratios that a bank must comply with at different levels of The Common Equity Tier 1 coefficient that includes the amounts used to meet the minimum CET1 requirement of 4.5%, but not the Common Equity Tier 1 used to meet the other minimum capital requirements (6% of the core capital or 8% of the regulatory capital). Therefore, if a bank has a CET1 of 8%, then it meets all the minimum capital requirements, but has a buffer of 0 and therefore is subject to a 100% constraint on the distribution of profits.

Table 7.2: Individual bank minimum capital conservation standards.

CET1 Ratio	Minimum Capital Conservation Ratios (expressed as a percentage of earnings)
(4.500% - 5.125%]	100%
(5.125% - 5.750%]	80%
(5.750% - 6.375%]	60%
(6.375% - 7.000%]	40%
above 7.000%	0%

Note: round brackets "(" indicate open interval, i.e. not including, whereas rectangular bracket "]" stands for closed interval, i.e. including.

Source: [BCBS (2010a), p. 56].

For example, a bank with a CET1 coefficient between 5.75% and 6.37% must set aside 60% of its profits in the financial year.

7.3.3 *Countercyclical Buffer*

The countercyclical buffer was designed to strengthen the relationship between the capital requirements of the banking sector and the macro-financial context in which banks operate. It is activated by national authorities to ensure that the banking system has a capital reserve that protects it from possible future losses. In general, each bank is subject to a countercyclical buffer of between 0 and 2.5% of risk-weighted assets. The buffer applied to each bank reflects the geographical composition of the credit exposure portfolio. Banks must meet the requirement for this buffer with Common Equity Tier 1 and other capital tiers. Otherwise, they will be subject to profit distribution constraints. The levels and constraints on the distribution of profits are identical to those seen for the capital conservation buffer. In particular, for banks operating internationally, the countercyclical buffer is obtained as a weighted average of the buffers applied in the various jurisdictions to which they are exposed.

Table 7.3 illustrates the minimum capital conservation ratios that a bank must comply with at different levels of the Common Equity Tier 1 ratio.

Table 7.3: Individual bank minimum capital conservation standards.

CET1 Ratio (including other fully loss absorbing capital)	Minimum Capital Conservation Ratios (expressed as a percentage of earnings)
Within *first* quartile of buffer	100%
Within *second* quartile of buffer	80%
Within *third* quartile of buffer	60%
Within *fourth* quartile of buffer	40%
Above top of buffer	0%

Source: [BCBS (2010a), p. 60].

7.3.4 *Systemically Important Financial Institutions (SIFI) Buffer*

We already stated that the financial crisis of 2007-2009 has revealed the non-proportionate risks related to the largest or, more precisely, to the more systemically important financial institutions. Before Lehman Brothers collapse in 2008, those were deemed "too big to fail" (TBTF) ones. As the crisis revealed that there are no TBTF banks, the Basel Committee decided to capture the associated credit risks. That is why the asset correlation was raised against SIFI exposures within the IRB approach (see Eq. (7.1)). However, not all banks run IRB. As we remember from [Penikas *et al.* (2021)], in the USA banks other than the 15 largest ones are prohibited from using IRB for prudential purposes. That is why the Basel Committee decided to require SIFIs to be more resilient. This implies that they have to assure higher capital ratio levels.

There are two principal SIFI qualifications to define the applicable SIFI capital buffer. The first and the largest buffer is associated with the Globally Systemically Important Banks (G-SIBs). The G-SIB capital buffer ranges from 1% of RWA to 3.5%. Till 2019 including, there was always a bank assigned 2.5% G-SIB add-on. In 2019 it was J.P. Morgan Chase. Citigroup and HSBC got 2% (see [FSB (2019)]). However, in 2020 all three mentioned banks got assigned with 2% add-on, having left a 2.5% bucket empty first in history (see [FSB (2020)]). Nordea and Royal Bank of Scotland have left the G-SIB list since 2019. The full 2020 bank allocation by G-SIB buffer applicable for 2021 is available in Table 7.4.

Table 7.4: 2021 G-SIB capital buffers.

CET1 Ratio Bucket	Banks in the Bucket
2.0%	Citigroup, HSBC, J.P. Morgan Chase
1.5%	Bank of America, Bank of China, Barclays, BNP Paribas, China Construction Bank (CCB), Deutsche Bank, Industrial and Commercial Bank of China (ICBC), Mitsubishi UFJ FG
1.0%	Agricultural Bank of China, Bank of New York Mellon, Credit Suisse, Goldman Sachs, Groupe Banco Populaire CdE (BPCE), Groupe Credit Agricole, ING Bank, Mizuho FG, Morgan Stanley, Royal Bank of Canada, Santander, Societe Generale, Standard Chartered, State Street, Sumitomo Mitsui FG, Toronto Dominion, UBS, UniCredit, Wells Fargo

Source: [FSB (2020)].

The second buffer is attributable to Domestic Systemically Important Banks (G-SIBs). In the European Union such institutions are called other systemically important institutions (OSII) to distinguish them from G-SIBs. Their respective D-SIB capital buffer reaches 1% of the RWA.

As one can see, for the IRB banks here comes a double-treatment when lending to SIFIs. From one side, the IRB-lender is limited because of the higher asset correlation requirement. On another side, SIFI-borrower is also constrained by the need to keep a higher capital ratio. This means that given the higher capital requirement for SIFIs, asset correlation against SIFI exposure within IRB should not be raised.

7.3.5 *Minimum Capital Ratio Level*

Figure 7.4 shows the consecutive increases in the minimum threshold for the capital ratio. The Basel Committee argues that CET1 level was around 2% of RWA in Basel II times according to [Caruana (2010)]. This implied low bank solvency on

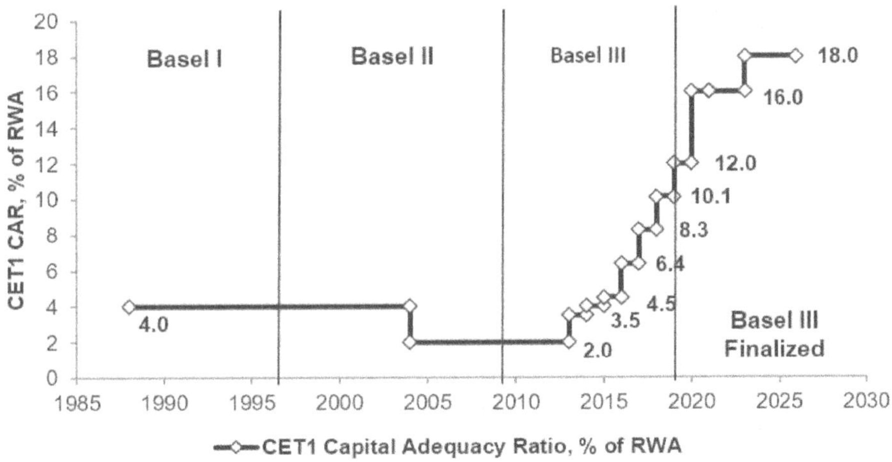

Fig. 7.4: The time evolution of the minimum requirement for the capital ratio.
Source: For references on the thresholds, refer to [Penikas (2021a), p. 6].

the eve of the 2007-2009 financial crisis. As a sequence of capital buffer applications, the minimum is forecasted to rise to 18% of RWA by 2027. The hike in the last fast years is driven by the new capital measures. It is the Total Loss Absorbing Capacity (TLAC) for international application (see [BCBS (2016b)]) and the Minimum Requirements for own funds and Eligible Liabilities (MREL) (see [SRB (2021)]) in the European Union.

Though capital is considered a safety cushion for a bank, it cannot be used for loss absorption at no cost. Such immediate absorption at a crisis — targeted by the regulators via increasing the minimum thresholds — results in higher risk-taking by banks in the forthcoming medium- and long-run. This implies an increase in systemic risks and deterioration of financial stability. Though such logic is apparent to any practitioner, it took regulators mostly a couple of decades to recognize this. Therefore, only in the mid-2021, they acknowledged that raising the minimum capital adequacy threshold does not improve banks' stability [Goel and Agarwal (2021)]. That is why we may expect that so long argued position of Andrew Haldane to simplify regulation may in the end realize.

It is important to recognize that the rise in the CET1 capital ratio minimum requirements should imply that it is sufficient for a bank to substitute the entire numerator of the capital ratio with the highest quality capital instruments. However, this will be called still the minimum requirements for CET1 ratio. The Basel Committee gives an explicit illustration in [BCBS (2010a), p. 56, par. 131] that the requirement applies buffers to all tiers of capital if a bank wishes to distribute profits. For instance, the application of the 2.5% capital conservation buffer implies that the CET1 capital ratio should rise from 4.5% of RWA to 7.0%, as well as the total capital ratio — from 8.0% to 10.5%.

7.3.6 *Capital Ratio for Islamic Banks*

The period after the financial crisis of 2007-2009 was remarked by an important novelty in terms of the credit risk regulation. It relates to the practices within the Islamic banks. Islamic banking has many differences compared to traditional banking. Interested readers may refer to [Kahf (2005)], [Abedifar *et al.* (2015)]. However, we would like to focus on the restricted agency investment accounts (RPSIA) of the Islamic Banks, as opposed to unrestricted accounts (UPSIA). The former (RPSIA) is equivalent to the assets under management. Assets under management are off-balance sheet exposures for a traditional bank. Any profits attributable to such investments are only those of an investee, i.e. the bank client, and not the bank. It is also the bank client solely to bear the associated risks and losses. Thus, the assets or funds at RPSIA fully belong to the bank client. It is the bank client who decides where to invest those funds, though such a decision may be, of course, driven by a recommendation from the bank client-relationship manager, or from the assigned private banker.

However, Islamic banking principles allow sharing profits and risks arising from unrestricted accounts (UPSIA). This means that a bank may be allocated with an entire amount of the associated risks or only with its portion. Those risks form a special type of credit risk i.e. the so-called credit risk in equity holdings. The Basel Committee had issued relevant guidance for such risks in traditional banks in [BCBS (2006), par. 344, 345] and [BCBS (2013a)].

To capture those special credit risks, the Islamic Financial Services Board (IFSB) — not to be mistaken with the International Financial Standards Board (IFSB) that introduced IFRS 9 standard on expected losses — modified the capital ratio when applied to Islamic banks according to [IFSB (2013), p. 67] and [CBB (2015), par. CA-1.1.17]

$$\text{CAR} = \frac{\text{Capital}}{RWA_{SF} + \alpha\Big(RWA_{UPSIA} - PER\&IRR_{UPSIA}\Big)}, \tag{7.5}$$

where $\text{RWA}_{SF} = \text{RWA}_{CR,ST} + \text{RWA}_{CR,IRB} + \text{RWA}_{MR} + \text{RWA}_{OR}$ is the amount of investments self-funded by an Islamic bank; RWA_{UPSIA} are the credit and market risk-weighted assets related to the unrestricted investment accounts and $PER\&IRR_{UPSIA}$ is the amount of reserves created by the Islamic bank against UPSIA assets; α is the regulatory parameter which is set locally (its values for the selected countries are available in Table 7.5; we should note that the Kingdom of the Saudi Arabia decided not to implement specific regulation of this type for the Islamic banks operating in its jurisdiction). The latter component in brackets $(RWA_{UPSIA} - PER\&IRR_{UPSIA})$ is equivalent to the deduction of the expected loss amount as discussed above with reference to Eq. (5.2).

Table 7.5: Alpha parameter for the capital regulation of the Islamic banks in selected countries.

Country	α, %
Bahrain	30
Jordan	30
Kuwait	50
Oman	30
Qatar	100
Sudan	50

Source: [IMF (2020), p. 215].

7.4 Basel III Leverage Ratio

Basel III has introduced the so-called *leverage ratio*. This is because the excessive leverage, both on and off-balance sheet, was one of the causes that fueled the financial crisis. Indeed, in times of crisis, the banking sector was forced to reduce its leverage, thus amplifying the downward pressure on the prices of its assets. All this has accentuated the losses, the erosion of capital of the banks and the contraction of the availability of credit. Given what happened, the Basel Committee, therefore, considered it appropriate to introduce a financial leverage ratio in order to:

- Limit the degree of leverage in the banking sector;
- Strengthen capital requirements by introducing an alternative and more reliable non-risk-based measure;
- Limit the effects of model errors resulting from the calculation of risk-weighted assets (RWA).

This index is defined as the ratio of capital and the measure of exposure. It is expressed in percentage terms as

$$\text{Leverage ratio} = \frac{\text{Capital measure}}{\text{Exposure measure}}, \tag{7.6}$$

where the measure of capital corresponds to CET1 capital, while the exposure measure corresponds to the sum of the bank's total assets not weighted for risk plus off-balance sheet exposures. For more details, see [BCBS (2014a)]. A minimum leverage ratio of 3% is being tested until January 1, 2017. There were discussions to raise it to 6% for the systemically important financial institutions.

Actually, it is more correct to say that Basel III reinvented the leverage ratio, and not introduced brand-new metrics. Historically before the approval of the risk-weighted capital ratio in Basel I, the United Kingdom and the United States regulated local banks used risk-unweighted capital ratio, i.e. what we now call a leverage ratio, according to [Goodhart (2011)].

7.5 Remuneration Regulation

The financial crisis of 2007-2009 is notoriously known for revealing deficient banking practices. One of them relates to remuneration. As [Penikas (2020b)] describes, the Royal Bank of Scotland (RBS) had a loss of around GBP 55bn. It got rescue funds from Bank of England for approximately GBP 20bn. However, upon receipt of the funds RBS transfered GBP 1bn as a bonus payment to its top management on the basis that they promised to pay such an amount disregarding the unprecedented crisis and bank individual loss. This is the most vivid case of suboptimality of the existing remuneration schemes. Their principal drawback was the lack of an adequate link to the risks taken.

To address the drawback in remuneration practices, the Basel Committee suggested how it should be designed in [BCBS (2011b)]. All the staff was divided into risk-takers (sales persons and underwriters) and risk-controllers (risk-managers, internal auditors and internal controllers). The remuneration earned was decomposed into variable and fixed parts. Risk-takers should mostly have variable remuneration, whereas the risk-managers predominantly the fixed one. Going even further, the remuneration of the risk-takers should be at material part deferred up for at least three years to be able to offset part of losses, like in RBS case. Figure 7.5 illustrates the newly introduced rules regulating the remuneration payments to bank employees.

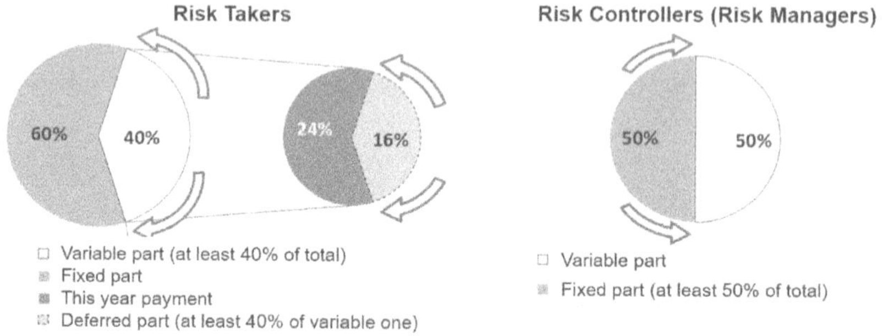

Fig. 7.5: Remuneration decomposition into fixed/variable and actual/deferred parts for risk-takers and risk-controllers.

The European regulator offered clarification on who's remuneration to regulate in the above-described fashion. If a person meets one of the below criteria, his or her remuneration should be regulated as follows:

- The banker is responsible for managing a unit, book or segment that gets an allocation of at least 2% of the economic capital;
- The banker has the right to approve a deal with the notion in excess of 0.5% of the CET1 capital or in excess of €5m;

- The banker may decide (accept or veto) deals in excess of 5% of the trading book Value-at-Risk evaluated at 99% confidence level;
- The person falls into top -0.3% of the total headcount when sorting in descending order by the amount of remuneration paid out in the last year.

Though the above remuneration regulation guidelines demonstrate a clear link with the risks taken by a person and by the institution, there resides a controversy. Modern lending processes — particularly, that for the retail loans — are quite automated. This means that the loan approval and granting depend upon the developed prescriptive models. In such a situation there is almost no place for a salesperson or a risk-taker, while the most risks taken depend upon the models and, more precisely, upon the modelers. In case the modelers are risk managers, there comes a contradiction. Due to the lending process automation, their remuneration should be mostly completely dependent upon the risks taken and risks realised. It should be totally variable, while by the above rules it should be mostly fixed. Today, each financial institution decides on its own how to handle the described case. A lot also depends on the position of the local regulator.

The remuneration issues were, are and definitely will be one of the most sensitive topics when managed and regulated. That is why they constantly provoke discussions. Leaving aside the fact that ten years have passed since the Basel Committee proposals in [BCBS (2011b)], the topic is still hot. For instance, the interested reader may refer to the recent consultation on the identification of the material risk-takers launched by [Bank of England (2021)].

PART 3
Credit Risk Modeling Essentials

Chapter 8

Probability of Default (PD)

8.1 Default Definition

A *default* is deemed[1] to have occurred in relation to a particular obligee if at least one of the following events occurs, see [EBA (2017)]:

- The creditor considers it unlikely that the obligor will fulfil his credit obligations in full, i.e. it is unlikely to pay (UTP);
- The obligor is in default for a period of time set by the creditor on a credit obligation relevant to the latter. In particular, for banks, the obligee is considered in default if he has exceeded the 90 days past due. Overdrafts are considered in default from the moment in which the obligor has exceeded the limit granted or received notification of a limit lower than the current balance.

Among the elements to be considered as indicative of the improbable fulfilment we find the following circumstances:

- The creditor assigns the credit undergoing a significant economic loss following the deterioration of the credit quality;
- The creditor has filed for bankruptcy in relation to the debtor's credit obligation;
- The debtor has declared bankruptcy or has been placed in bankruptcy or similar situations that prevent and delay the payment of the credit obligation;
- The creditor makes a write-down considering that a significant deterioration in the credit quality has occurred after taking the exposure on the book.

[1] Part of this chapter has been published in [Orlando and Härtel (2014)] and [Orlando and Pelosi (2020)].

8.2 Rating System

After the banks have outlined the criteria that characterize a specific rating grade, the assignment of the rating to each entity to which they are exposed and the periodic review of the ratings must take place through third parties who do not benefit from the granting of credit. Following the assignment of ratings, banks are required to update their ratings at least once a year, except in the cases below:

- Presence of debtors with a high risk of default. In this case, it is advisable for the bank to carry out more checks in order not to incur unexpected losses;
- Presence of new relevant information on the debtor. In this case, banks are required to recalculate the rating on the basis of this information.

Finally, banks must have effective procedures in place in order to acquire and update information on the borrower's financial situation, as well as to reconsider the borrower's rating based on the new information.

When designing a rating system, a risk-manager should decide upon its two fundamental aspects: the rating philosophy and the rating type. The rating philosophy tells us whether the rating grades will change during a crisis or not, according to [Ozdemir and Miu (2009)].

For instance, look at Figure 8.1. Suppose, we are in point C at good times. When the crisis comes, most probably either the default probability PD or the default rate is going to rise. However, there are two paths on how to reflect such a rise in PD. We can move to either point F or D. Point D belongs to the very same rating curve $A-A$. This means that the rise in PD implies a deterioration in rating grade. However, a rating is a relative category. It helps in ranking bank borrowers. Then a borrower C may not change its relative creditworthiness compared to other borrowers. Therefore, we can preserve its credit rating grade by moving to another rating curve $B-B$ at point F.

The second cross-road for a risk manager is the approach to rating estimate. Generally, there are two extremes. The least volatile estimate is called Through-the-Cycle (TTC). Ideally, it coincides with the PD central tendency. The more volatile alternative is a Point-in-Time (PIT) estimate. [Ozdemir and Miu (2009)] say that the external credit rating agencies tend to provide more TTC ratings, whereas IRB estimates are more PIT ones. However, one should think about how a TTC estimate can be obtained. The industry practice is to assess the PD central tendency and its PIT values. As [Penikas (2020d)] shows, that is the only solution if one wishes to fit the central tendency as close as possible. It is to take the weight for the PIT estimate equal to zero. Developing a PD model is in vain then. This is an important example to demonstrate that targeting CT has no mathematical solution. Then any non-zero weight is just an expert judgment. Such judgments should be rejected during prudential IRB validation.

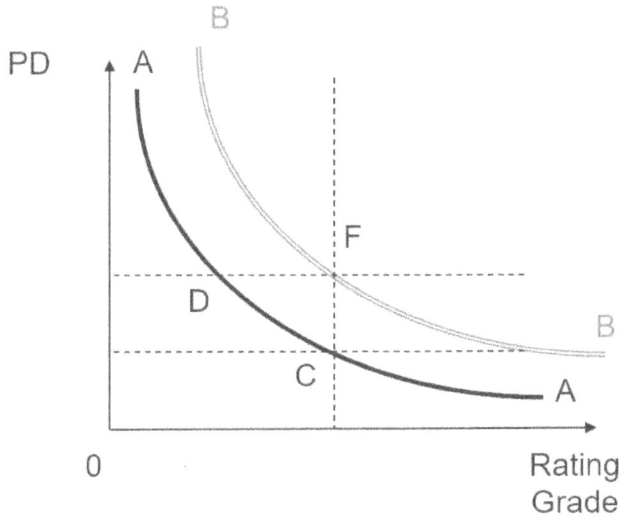

Fig. 8.1: Rating philosophy.

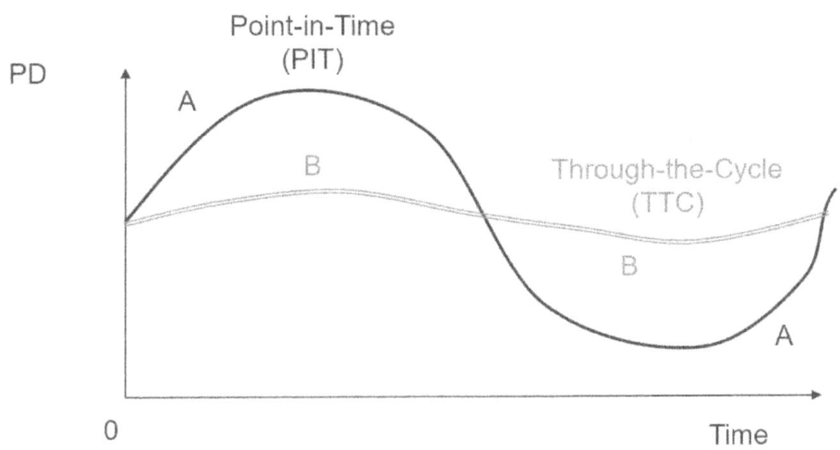

Fig. 8.2: Rating types.

8.2.1 *Rating System Concept*

By a rating system we mean a set of data, models, methods and IT systems used for the assessment of credit risk, for the attribution of internal credit rating grade and for the quantitative estimate of defaults and losses. In order for a rating system to be considered qualified, it must have two distinct dimensions: the risk of default by the debtor (the solvency of the debtor) and the specific characteristics of the transaction (guarantees, the degree of pre-emption, the type of product, etc.).

Having defined the *"rating grade"* as the assessment of the debtor's counterparty credit risk carried out according to predetermined criteria, the bank must show an adequate distribution of exposures among the various rating grades. In this regard, the bank must provide at least seven rating grades for non-defaulting debtors and one for defaulting debtors. This is also referred to as a Rating Master Scale. Each rating grade must outline both a certain risk profile of default of the debtors assigned to the same rating grade and the criteria with which they have outlined this risk profile. This description must be somewhat detailed in such a way as to allow those assigned to the same rating to be debtors who present the same credit risk. Before assigning a rating grade to any debtor, banks must take into account all the information available and relevant at the time, and in the event that there are updates or new information, they are required to reassess the debtor's rating grade. Furthermore, if banks do not have sufficient information to assess the creditworthiness of the debtor, then they will have to be much more careful and prudent in assigning the rating grade. On the basis of the above, it is clear that if a bank was to present a large number of credit portfolios in the same range of default risk, then it would have to increase the number of credit ratings in order to obtain an appropriate distribution of exposures. The procedures and criteria by which banks assign rating grades to each exposure must be intuitive and plausible, detailed and clear in such a way as to be easily legible and understandable to third parties.

During the rating assignment processes, banks could apply statistical models to obtain more precise estimates and assessments. Also in this case, banks are required to:

- Provide very detailed documentation of the theory, the assumptions and the mathematical basis used for the estimates of the rating grade;
- Establish a rigorous statistical procedure for the validation of the model;
- Indicate any circumstances in which the model is ineffective.

8.2.2 *Rating Grades*

In order to quantify the credit risk associated with each class of assets to which they are exposed, banks are required to estimate the PD, the LGD, the EAD and the M. As noted above, banks adopting the IRB approach must estimate a PD for each rating grade. PD estimates must be based on the long-term averages of the effective default rates of debtors with the same credit rating, i.e. on the central tendency. Banks adopting the advanced IRB approach must also provide a long-term average LGD and an average EAD weighted based on observed defaults for each exposure. These estimates can be made using available data, information and methods. However, such data must not be chosen at random, but with criterion: the banks must prove that the economic and market conditions on which the data are based are consistent with the current macroeconomic situation and with the bank credit policy. Furthermore, for the estimates to be accurate, banks should

Table 8.1: Rating grades.

Moody's	S&P's	Risk	Description
Aaa	AAA	Minimum	Good asset quality - Wide diversification and consolidated size - Excellent market positioning - Distinctive managerial skills - Very high debt coverage capacity
Aa1 Aa2 Aa3	AA+ AA AA-	Modest	Good asset quality - Good market integration and diversification of outlets - Good quality of management - Strong debt coverage capability.
A1 A2 A3	A+ A A-	Medium low	Satisfactory asset quality and liquidity - Market entry and management quality average - Normal credit standards - Average credit coverage capacity.
Baa1 Baa2 Baa3	BBB+ BBB BBB-	Acceptable	Acceptable quality and liquidity, albeit with significant risk - Normal credit standards, with slight surpluses liquidity and weaker debt coverage capacity.
Ba1 Ba2 Ba3	BB+ BB BB-	Acceptable carefully	Acceptable quality and liquidity, albeit with a significant degree of risk - Poor diversification of assets - Low liquidity and limited debt coverage margins.
B1 B2 B3	B+ B B-	Monitor continuously	Credit under observation - Asset quality acceptable, albeit with temporary liquidity difficulties - High financial leverage - Some managerial, positioning and market entry weaknesses.
Caa1 Caa2 Caa3 Ca C	CCC+ CCC CCC- CC C	Close observation / doubtful outcome	As above, but with evident difficulties and sometimes tense and labored debt management - Uncertainties on the possibility of paying interest and even the capital

have sufficient data. It follows that the estimates obtained are based on past and empirical experience, and not only on subjective evaluations. Since the estimates involve errors, to avoid over-optimistic estimates, banks must incorporate a caution factor (conservative margin) in their measurements commensurate with the presumed margin of error.

8.3 PD Estimation Methods

There are three possible methods of estimating the PD and they are:

- Qualitative-quantitative models, based on the internal experience of default;
- Mapping to external data;
- Statistical models (see [Siarka (2011)]).

Banks are free to choose which of the methods to adopt and use to obtain more accurate estimates with less margin for error. They are required to justify their choice to the prudential authority. Here, by *prudential* we mean regulatory (coming from the objective to ensure prudent behavior of economic agents and banks), and not *Prudential* as the name of the American insurance company. The term *prudent* was first coined right after the adoption of Basel I by [Polizatto (1989)] and was later populated by [Dewatripont and Tirole (1994)] and [Dewatripont *et al.* (2010)]. By adopting the first method, banks use data on defaults from past experience (historical series of at least 5 years). In this case, they must prove that the estimates are in perfect agreement with the credit rating criteria and with the ratings. By adopting the second method, banks classify their exposures both according to the rating master scale adopted by external agencies and according to their own internal rating scale. By adopting the third method, banks can average the estimates of the PD for individual borrowers assigned to a certain credit rating grade, assuming that these estimates were obtained through the use of statistical methods of default forecasting. Regardless of the method used, the time horizon used to estimate the PD is one year. In the following section, we will present some methods that allow you to obtain an estimate of the probability of default of a loan portfolio. The characteristics of the individual debtors play a key role in these methods.

The methods we are about to present can be used to estimate the probability of default of both a single obligor and a class of obligors. In this subsection, the probability of default is a function of the characteristics of the obligors. In particular, the probability that the i-th debtor becomes insolvent PD is modeled as

$$PD_i = F(\boldsymbol{x}_i),$$

where PD_i denotes the probability of default of the i-th debtor and $F(\boldsymbol{x}_i)$ is a function of the vector $\boldsymbol{x}_i$ (characteristics of the debtor). One of the simplest approaches for estimating PD is the linear model

$$PD_i = F(\boldsymbol{x}_i^T \boldsymbol{\beta}_i) = \boldsymbol{x}_i^T \boldsymbol{\beta}_i,$$

where $\boldsymbol{\beta}_i$ is the parameter vector (the parameter set can differ from borrower to borrower in this setup). Since the PD takes values in the $[0, 1]$ range, the following condition must be met:

$$0 \leq \boldsymbol{x}_i^T \boldsymbol{\beta}_i \leq 1.$$

But since very often the linear regression function assumes values that are not in the allowed range, we can overcome this problem by redefining the model as follows

$$PD_i = \begin{cases} 0 & \boldsymbol{x}_i^T \boldsymbol{\beta}_i \leq 0 \\ \boldsymbol{x}_i^T \boldsymbol{\beta}_i & 0 \leq \boldsymbol{x}_i^T \boldsymbol{\beta}_i \leq 1 \\ 1 & \boldsymbol{x}_i^T \boldsymbol{\beta}_i \geq 1. \end{cases}$$

8.3.1 *Probit and Logit Models*

One way to break free from this assumption is to resort to the *probit model* Eq. (8.1), specification of the linear model in which the dependent variable is a binary variable that takes the value 0 if the debtor is solvent or 1 if the debtor is insolvent. This method allows arriving at an estimate of the probability of default or default probability — PD — through the use of the cumulative distribution function of a normal random variable. It was originally coined by [Bliss (1934)]. In this model, the probability of default relating to the i-th debtor is given by

$$PD_i = F(\boldsymbol{x}_i^T \boldsymbol{\beta}_i) = \int_{-\infty}^{\boldsymbol{x}_i^T \boldsymbol{\beta}_i} \frac{1}{\sqrt{2\pi}} e^{-\frac{t^2}{2}}\, dt. \tag{8.1}$$

Another widely used binomial model is the *logit* model Eq. (8.2). Logit analysis or logistic regression is in many ways the natural complement of ordinary linear regression whenever the regressand is not a continuous variable but a state, which may or may not hold, or a category in a given classification. Historically it was first introduced in [Berskon (1944)]. The recent discussions are available in [Cramer (2003)]. According to this model, the F function is the logistic cumulative distribution function defined as follows

$$PD_i = F(\boldsymbol{x}_i^T \boldsymbol{\beta}_i) = \frac{1}{1 + e^{-\boldsymbol{x}_i^T \boldsymbol{\beta}_i}} = \frac{e^{\boldsymbol{x}_i^T \boldsymbol{\beta}_i}}{e^{\boldsymbol{x}_i^T \boldsymbol{\beta}_i} + 1}. \tag{8.2}$$

The logistic regression model then takes the form

$$logit(PD_i) = \boldsymbol{x}_i^T \boldsymbol{\beta}_i = F_i^{-1}(PD_i) = \ln\left(\frac{PD_i}{1 - PD_i}\right),$$

which is a linear function of the parameters.

The mean of the Bernoulli distribution is equal to the probability of success and the variance depends on the mean. In this case, the natural approach is to make the probability of $Y = 1$, not the value of Y itself, a suitable function of the regressors X_i $i = 1, 2, \cdots k$. This leads to a probability model, which specifies the probability of the outcome as a function of the stimulus, see [Cramer (2003)]. Within probability models, a linear one does not fit very well to the data:

$$P(Y) = \alpha + \beta X + U, \quad E(U) = 0 \Rightarrow E(Y|X) = P(Y = 1|X) = \alpha + \beta X$$

- The Y has Bernoulli distribution and is not normal;
- The homoskedasticity hypothesis is not verified; and
- The estimated value of $E(Y|X)$ does not necessarily fall into $(0, 1)$.

For these reasons, it is necessary to transform the outcome into a variable consistent with the linear relationship which can take any value between $-\infty$ and $+\infty$. The so-called "logit transformation" consists of considering the natural logarithm of the odd ratio (called Logit) as the new dependent variable in a linear relationship with its covariates — where the odd ratio is the probability of the occurring event divided by its complementary probability. The new model implies a non-linear relationship between probability and explanatory variable(s):

$$P(X) = P(Y = 1|X) = \exp(\alpha + \beta X)/[1 + \exp(\alpha + \beta X)];$$
$$Q(X) = 1 - P(X) = P(Y = 0|X) = 1/(1 + \exp(\alpha + \beta X)]. \tag{8.3}$$

so that the logit is:

$$L = \ln \text{odds}[P(X)] = \ln(P(X))/[1 - P(X)]) = \ln[\exp(\alpha + \beta X)] = \alpha + \beta X.$$

The probability $P(X)$ is the inverse of the logistic function ($Q(X)$): an S-shaped curve that flattens at both ends, so it must remain in the limited range from 0 to 1.

Applications of the logit model in the field of risk assessment have been numerous and still are, due to its simplicity as well as its effectiveness. However, over the years, although rather slowly compared to the evolution of corresponding literature [Jones and Hensher (2004)], there has been the development of innovative techniques regarding this approach, which have made it increasingly performing. [Tsai (2013)] overcame the usual failed–non-failed dichotomy to also consider companies that are not bankrupt but that face slight financial distress events. He adopted the multinomial logit model in which the dependent variable assumes three different values, depending on whether the company is "not distressed", "slightly distressed" or "in reorganization or bankruptcy". For this purpose, within the covariates are included corporate governance factors (insiders' ownership ratio, pledge of ownership ratio of the insiders, deviation ratio between voting and cash flow rights—where insiders include directors, supervisors, managers and large shareholders), in addition to the financial ratios (current assets to current liabilities, total liabilities to total assets, working capital to total assets, retained earnings to total assets, sales to total assets and net income to total assets) and market variables (market equity to total liabilities, abnormal returns, the logarithm of the firm's relative size, the idiosyncratic standard deviation of each firm's stock returns and the logarithm of age). The idea stems from the assumption that many companies facing financial difficulties mask the accounting results to prevent their financial statements from showing losses recorded at the end of the year. This phenomemon is sometimes called "window-dressing". The use of only financial ratios and market variables, in fact, would generate estimates polluted by such a lack of transparency of financial statements.

The investigation aims to evaluate whether the corporate governance (CG) variables are useful in order to reveal further information regarding the occurrence of slight distress events and, in general, whether the use of a model that includes these variables (CG model) better predicts PD compared to what a model based only on financial ratios and market variables (non-CG model) does [Tsai (2013)]. Comparing the average of each covariate calculated for each group of companies, the results of the previous study are confirmed: in all financial ratios, the group of "not distressed" ranks first, with the best means; the "slightly distressed firms rank second and the "reorganized or bankrupt" ones are third. Unlike that study, however, in this case, all the financial variables are significant for the model, certainly due to the greater representativeness of the sample. Once the coefficients of the CG model have been estimated, it results that, compared to the corporate governance variables, financial ratios are less relevant to the occurrence of slight distress events. This shows and confirms what was assumed at the beginning: managers of companies subject to slight financial difficulties tend to manipulate financial results. Conversely, financial ratios are more closely related to reorganization and bankruptcy events than corporate governance variables are. Although the CG model estimates show that market variables are significantly related to the occurrence of financial distress, it appears that they are more connected to reorganization and bankruptcy events than to slight distress ones; this is because reorganized and bankrupt firms show greater candor in divulging operational difficulties in their financial statements and investors can react in a timely fashion to their devaluation. Moreover, once the estimates of both models have been made and the respective probabilities that a company is in a group of three have been obtained, the accuracy tests show that, in general, the CG model outperforms the non-CG model.

According to Jones and Hensher (2004): "considering the case of firm failures, the main improvement is that mixed logit models include a number of additional parameters that capture observed and unobserved heterogeneity both within and between firms" that is the heterogeneity characterizing the behavior of subjects, i.e. the individual changes in tastes and preferences. In fact, while in the case of the traditional logit model the influences deriving from behavioral heterogeneity flow incorrectly into the error term and the functional form of utility that each company q associates with each outcome i is given by

$$U_{iq} = \beta_q X_{iq} + e_{iq}$$

where X_{iq} is the vector of observed characteristics of companies, β_q is the parameter vector, $e_i q$ is the term of residuals, containing the effects not observed and it is assumed that the unobserved influences are distributed identically and independently among the alternative outcomes (therefore, it is possible to remove the subscript i from the term e), mixed logit model maximizes the use of behavioral information incorporated in the analyzed dataset through the partition of stochastic component e into two uncorrelated parts:

$$U_{iq} = \beta_q^{'} X_{iq} + (\eta_{iq} + \epsilon_{iq})$$

where η_{iq} is the random term correlated with each alternative outcome, heteroscedastic and with generic density function $f(\eta_{iq}|\Omega)$ (Ω the fixed parameters of the distribution) and ϵ_{iq} is the part i.i.d. over alternative outcomes and firms. For a given value of η_{iq}, the conditional probability of each outcome i is the logit

$$L_i(\eta) = \frac{\exp(\beta' X_{iq} + \eta_{iq})}{\sum_j \exp(\beta' X_{jq} + \eta_{jq})}.$$

Since η is not given, the outcome probability is this logit formula integrated overall value of η weighted by the density of η:

$$P_i = \int L_i(\eta) f(\eta|\Omega) d\eta.$$

hence the name "mixed", indicating that the probability of an outcome i occurring is given by the mix of logits and f. Comparing the results of the analysis on financial distress events conducted by researchers, first with a standard logit model and then with the mixed logit model, the second is far better than the first.

Here, too, the dataset is made up of companies divided into three groups: non-failed firms, insolvent firms and firms which filed for bankruptcy. The independent variables are financial ratios (total debt to gross operating cash flow, working capital to total assets, net operating cash flow to total assets, total debt to total equity, cash flow cover and sales revenue to total assets). Both measures of goodness-of-fit and statistical tests provide indications of the best performance of the mixed logit model. Results of the latter indicate that some variables have only one fixed parameter while others have up to three parameters, indicating the influence of behavioral heterogeneity not considered by other models. The multinomial logit model is rather poor in classifying financial distress firms: in its best performance, it predicts corporate default in 29% of cases. Conversely, mixed logit works very well in both cases of financial distress, even when one moves away from the reporting period: the accuracy rate in the five years following data collection drops to a minimum of 98.73% [Jones and Hensher (2004)].

Regarding the regressors, we aligned our analysis to the methodology available in the literature. For example, on **debt to equity**, [Achleitner *et al.* (2011)], when evaluating value creation and pricing in buyouts, brought empirical evidence confirming that it is the "better proxy to account for the influence of leverage on equity returns". On the same line, [Penman *et al.* (2007)] stated "net debt divided by the market value of equity is the generally accepted measure of leverage that captures financing risk" and [Phongmekin and Jarumaneeroj (2018)] affirmed that "according to the regression coefficients, a stock with a higher value of third year's net debt to equity ratio also has a high tendency for positive return". The reason for that is quite straightforward as "the net debt would account for the available cushion and represent a more accurate measure of financial risk emanating from capital structure". "An increasing net debt would put constraints on raising incremental capital and firms with high leverage would find it difficult and costly to access funds as compared to firms with less leverage" [Nawazish *et al.* (2013)]. More in general, on the use of **financial ratios**, [Tian and Yu (2017)] found them useful as predictors in forecasting corporate default and [Phongmekin and Jarumaneeroj (2018)] found them useful to develop a predictive model about companies listed on the Stock Exchange of Thailand (SET).

A different approach to modeling the PD is the use of a *logarithmic linear model*, in which the F function is defined as follows:

$$PD_i = F(\boldsymbol{x}_i^T \boldsymbol{\beta}) = \exp(\boldsymbol{x}_i^T \boldsymbol{\beta}). \tag{8.4}$$

Like the linear model, here too the same problem could arise, namely that the function assumes values greater than 1. In order to prevent it, we can impose the following condition $\boldsymbol{x}_i^T \boldsymbol{\beta} < 0$.

For the completeness of coverage, one would also mention the Copula Discriminant Analysis (CODA) as an alternative to *PD* modeling. The conventional discriminant analysis relies upon the assumption of joint normality of default factors' distribution within both classes of defaulted and non-defaulted borrowers. The difference between Linear (LDA) and Quadratic DA (QDA) is the assumption of covariance matrix equality in the former LDA case and its inequality in the latter QDA case. CODA allows moving away from the joint normality distribution of default factors within each of the classes. For more discussion about CODA, we recommend referring to [Penikas (2020d)].

8.3.2 *Calibration*

The default probability *calibration* is a process that assigns a probability of default to each possible rating. Analytically, calibration can be seen as an application

$$Rating \rightarrow \; PD$$

The probability of default of a portfolio of debtors can be seen as a vector $\boldsymbol{p}$ which has the probability of default for the different rating classes as elements. Assuming that the internal rating system consists of R rating grades, the vector $\boldsymbol{p}$ looks like this: $\boldsymbol{p} = (p_1, ..., p_R)$, where each p_i, denotes the probability of default relative to the i-th rating grade. The quality of the calibration depends on how close the *PD* estimated through the rating models are to the actual default rates. The data used for calibration are:

- Estimated *PD* on a rating class and the loan portfolio for a given observation period;
- Number of obligors assigned to each rating class;
- State of default of the debtors at the end of the observation period.

Finally, to show how good the estimates of the *PD* obtained from the model are, once two confidence levels have been set, 95% and 99.9%, we calculate the confidence intervals. According to the Basel Committee for exposures to companies and banks, the *PD* is the maximum between 0.03% and the annual *PD* corresponding to the internal rating grade of the borrower to whom the exposure in question is assigned. For exposures to governments, the *PD* is equal to the annual *PD* relating to the internal rating grade to which the exposure in question is assigned. For exposures classified in the "default" category, the *PD* is equal to 100%.

8.3.3 *Bernoulli Distribution and Binomial Process*

The Bernoulli distribution is the probability distribution of a random variable L which takes the value 1 with success (default) probability of p and the value 0 with the probability of $1-p$ (see Subsection 1.2.1). We can define a vector of random losses $\boldsymbol{L} = (L_1, ..., L_n)$, where L_i denotes the loss variable associated to counterparty i, as a Bernoulli vector where all marginal distributions of $\boldsymbol{L}$ are Bernoulli, that is

$$L_i \sim B(p_i) \quad \text{where} \quad L_i = \begin{cases} 1 \text{ with probability } p_i, \\ 0 \text{ with probability } 1 - p_i. \end{cases}$$

Assuming no dependence among counterparties and a uniform default probability $p_i = p$, for all $i = 1, ..., n$, which means $L_i \sim B(p)$ and $L_1, ..., L_n$ are independent. Then the portfolio loss L defined as $L = \sum_{i=1}^{n} L_i$ is a *Binomial* distributed random variable with parameters n and p, i.e. $L \sim B(n, p)$. When independent counterparties have different default probabilities, i.e. $L_i \sim B(p_i)$ and $L_1, ..., L_n$ independent, then the probability distribution of L is still a convolution of the single Bernoulli ones with mean and variance given by

$$\mathbb{E}[L] = \sum_{i=1}^{n} p_i, \qquad Var(L) = \sum_{i=1}^{n} p_i(1 - p_i).$$

As mentioned above, we assume that defaults of a counterparty are modeled as events of a Poisson counting process whose important properties are presented in Subsection 19.3.1.

8.4 Time Scaled Default Probabilities

In our context, we denote the intensity of the Poisson process modeling the number of defaults of a R-rated counterparty, by $\lambda(\bar{t}, R)$, since it will depend on the valuation horizon $\bar{t}$, assumed to be the unit of time, and the rating R associated to a specified counterparty. To compute $\lambda(\bar{t}, R)$ we refer to Moody's and display the historic default probabilities for companies admitting different ratings in Table 8.2. For the default rates of different time horizons, the values of Exhibit 36 of [Ou (2011)] are used. The time horizons are from one year to nine years. According to this matrix, we have nine different intensities for every rating. For our purposes, we need to compute the default probabilities in a time horizon of one week. To be conservative, the yearly intensity is taken as a basis and then it is scaled to one week.

A reader familiar with the risk management basics may challenge the approach and suggest using alternative forms of interpolation. For instance, we may use the compound interest rule and put the return in the power of 1/52. The comparison of the two approaches yields us an immaterial difference. For instance, the linear interpolation to a week from a 10% annual yield is 0.18%, while the power approach gives 0.19%. More formally, we recommend running a back-test to validate which of

Table 8.2: Probability of default matrix.

Rating\Year	1	2	3	4	5	6	7	8	9
Aaa	0%	0.016%	0.016%	0.048%	0.086%	0.132%	0.182%	0.186%	0.186%
Aa1	0%	0%	0%	0.094%	0.141%	0.158%	0.158%	0.158%	0.158%
Aa2	0%	0.014%	0.088%	0.192%	0.334%	0.431%	0.495%	0.561%	0.635%
Aa3	0.048%	0.127%	0.182%	0.254%	0.327%	0.380%	0.415%	0.435%	0.444%
A1	0.061%	0.217%	0.461%	0.672%	0.855%	0.992%	1.089%	1.180%	1.297%
A2	0.065%	0.174%	0.351%	0.578%	0.788%	1.073%	1.463%	1.918%	2.324%
A3	0.058%	0.214%	0.439%	0.627%	0.923%	1.235%	1.550%	1.907%	2.255%
Baa1	0.146%	0.380%	0.643%	0.897%	1.204%	1.501%	1.801%	2.016%	2.207%
Baa2	0.176%	0.486%	0.897%	1.519%	2.078%	2.686%	3.226%	3.723%	4.337%
Baa3	0.302%	0.876%	1.558%	2.219%	3.099%	3.993%	4.840%	5.847%	6.790%
Ba1	0.709%	1.986%	3.721%	5.546%	7.226%	9.012%	10.455%	11.506%	12.537%
Ba2	0.800%	2.286%	4.198%	6.249%	8.077%	9.538%	10.953%	12.522%	13.97%
Ba3	1.826%	5.291%	9.371%	13.66%	17.163%	20.379%	23.342%	26.385%	29.384%
B1	2.512%	6.969%	11.678%	15.866%	20.159%	24.509%	29.191%	33.167%	36.694%
B2	3.986%	9.863%	15.713%	21.076%	25.701%	29.903%	33.774%	37.281%	40.724%
B3	7.584%	16.097%	24.299%	31.262%	37.199%	42.764%	47.117%	51.039%	53.727%
Caa1	9.940%	21.715%	32.211%	40.782%	48.782%	54.343%	57.144%	60.441%	65.864%
Caa2	19.045%	30.446%	39.104%	46.371%	51.475%	55.336%	58.498%	61.973%	65.153%
Caa3	29.542%	45.41%	54.642%	61.612%	67.565%	69.136%	71.854%	75.593%	80.516%
Ca	38.739%	50.58%	59.678%	66.353%	71.652%	73.385%	75.92%	78.884%	78.884%
C	38.739%	50.58%	59.678%	66.353%	71.652%	73.385%	75.92%	78.884%	78.884%

the two approaches is more relevant for the specific data the reader has at disposal. As for our purpose of the approach illustration — given the negligible difference between the two — we proceed with the linear interpolation.

After that, we can compute the probability of default for a time horizon of one week.

For further calculations, we need a day count convention. The day-count convention is computed for the residual time from a time $t \geq 0$ up to a fixed date T, namely $T - t$, as follows

$$\frac{T-t}{365}, \tag{8.5}$$

where we assume 1-year $=$ 365 days. For two different times $0 \leq s < t$ the difference $t - s$ is measured in years, cf. [Miron and Swannel (1991)] for a complete discussion of day-count conventions. The default probability p of a counterparty with rating R in a time interval of length $\bar{t}$ is given by

$$\begin{aligned} p &= \mathbb{P}(N_{\bar{t}} > 0) = \mathbb{P}(N_{\bar{t}} \geq 1) = 1 - \mathbb{P}(N_{\bar{t}} = 0) \\ &= 1 - \frac{(\lambda(\bar{t}, R)\,\bar{t})^0}{0!} e^{-\lambda(\bar{t},R)\,\bar{t}} = 1 - e^{-\lambda(\bar{t},R)\,\bar{t}}, \end{aligned}$$

which yields the intensity of the Poisson process with respect to the time horizon $\bar{t}$

$$\lambda(\bar{t}, R) = -\frac{1}{\bar{t}} \ln(1-p) \ . \tag{8.6}$$

Let us take an example. We want to calculate the probability of default for a B1-rated company in a time horizon of one week. From Table 8.2, the corresponding row of the default probability matrix is as follows in Table 8.3.

Table 8.3: Probability of default matrix for B1 rated borrower.

Rating\Year	1	2	3	4	5	6	7	8	9
B1	2.512%	6.969%	11.678%	15.866%	20.159%	24.509%	29.191%	33.167%	36.694%

Thus, from Eq. (8.6) the 1-year intensity (i.e. $\bar{t} = \frac{365}{365} = 1$) of the Poisson process by considering the default probability of a B1-rated company in a 1-year time horizon (i.e. $p = 0.02512$) is given by

$$\lambda(1 \text{ year}, B1) = -\frac{1}{1} \log(1 - 0.02512) = 0.0254409. \tag{8.7}$$

We are now able to evaluate the default probability of a B1-rated company in a week horizon by using the day-count convention (8.5) (i.e. $\frac{T-t}{365} = \frac{7}{365}$)

$$p_{B1} := \mathbb{P}\left(N_{\frac{7}{365}} > 0\right) = 1 - e^{-\lambda(1 \text{ year}, B1)\frac{7}{365}} = 1 - e^{-0.0254409 \cdot \frac{7}{365}} = 0.04878\%. \tag{8.8}$$

The whole calculation shown for a B1-rated company can be done for all other ratings resulting in the following

- $\lambda(1 \text{ year}, Aaa) = 0.0$, $p_{Aaa} = 0.0\%$.
- $\lambda(1 \text{ year}, Aa1) = 0.0$, $p_{Aa1} = 0.0\%$.
- $\lambda(1 \text{ year}, Aa2) = 0.0$, $p_{Aa2} = 0.0\%$.
- $\lambda(1 \text{ year}, Aa3) = 0.0004801$, $p_{Aa3} = 0.00092\%$.
- $\lambda(1 \text{ year}, A1) = 0.0006102$, $p_{A1} = 0.00117\%$.
- $\lambda(1 \text{ year}, A2) = 0.0006502$, $p_{A2} = 0.00125\%$.
- $\lambda(1 \text{ year}, A3) = 0.0005802$, $p_{A3} = 0.00111\%$.
- $\lambda(1 \text{ year}, Baa1) = 0.0014611$, $p_{Baa1} = 0.00280\%$.
- $\lambda(1 \text{ year}, Baa2) = 0.0017615$, $p_{Baa2} = 0.00338\%$.
- $\lambda(1 \text{ year}, Baa3) = 0.0030246$, $p_{Baa3} = 0.00580\%$.
- $\lambda(1 \text{ year}, Ba1) = 0.0071152$, $p_{Ba1} = 0.01364\%$.
- $\lambda(1 \text{ year}, Ba2) = 0.0080322$, $p_{Ba2} = 0.01540\%$.
- $\lambda(1 \text{ year}, Ba3) = 0.0184288$, $p_{Ba3} = 0.03534\%$.
- $\lambda(1 \text{ year}, B1) = 0.0254409$, $p_{B1} = 0.04878\%$.
- $\lambda(1 \text{ year}, B2) = 0.0406762$, $p_{B2} = 0.07798\%$.
- $\lambda(1 \text{ year}, B3) = 0.0788701$, $p_{B3} = 0.15114\%$.
- $\lambda(1 \text{ year}, Caa1) = 0.1046941$, $p_{Caa1} = 0.20058\%$.

- $\lambda(1 \text{ year}, Caa2) = 0.2112767$, $p_{Caa2} = 0.40437\%$.
- $\lambda(1 \text{ year}, Caa3) = 0.3501534$, $p_{Caa3} = 0.66928\%$.
- $\lambda(1 \text{ year}, Ca) = 0.4900268$, $p_{Ca} = 0.93537\%$.
- $\lambda(1 \text{ year}, C) = 0.4900268$, $p_C = 0.93537\%$.

Note that the above default probabilities have been computed without considering the evolution in time of rating quality for a counterparty. Then to calculate the final probability of default of a counterparty with actual rating R by considering possible jumps to other rating classes over the observed time horizon, we need to know the rating transition probabilities as explained in the next chapter.

8.5 Time Scaled Rating Transitions

Transition matrices are widely used as a model to explain the dynamics of changes in rating quality for a counterparty over a given time horizon.

Table 8.4 lists the yearly probabilities of transition from one rating class to another one averaged over a period from 1975 to 2010. The last column in the matrix refers to the category Not Rated when no rating is available at all. The original document does not have the row for the transition from the non-rated (NR) borrowers to other rating categories. However, for the matrix to be complete, we add the last row in Table 8.4 taking the rather strong assumption that every unrated borrower remains unrated.

Table 8.4: 1Y Rating transition matrix (cf. [Saldanha and Beers (2011), Table 1]).

	Aaa	Aa	A	Baa	Ba	B	Caa -C	NR
Aaa	94.2%	3.6%	0.0%	0.0%	0.0%	0.0%	0.0%	2.2%
Aa	1.7%	93.3%	2.1%	0.0%	0.0%	0.0%	0.0%	2.9%
A	0.0%	3.0%	91.7%	1.4%	0.0%	0.0%	0.0%	4.0%
Baa	0.0%	0.0%	3.8%	86.4%	3.2%	0.0%	0.0%	6.6%
Ba	0.0%	0.0%	0.0%	2.3%	88.9%	1.1%	1.5%	6.1%
B	0.0%	0.0%	0.0%	0.0%	12.8%	75.4%	3.8%	8.1%
Caa -C	0.0%	0.0%	0.0%	0.0%	0.0%	32.4%	62.1%	5.4%
NR	0.0%	0.0%	0.0%	0.0%	0.0%	0.0%	0.0%	100.0%

Let $T_{i,j}$ denote the i,j-th entry of the rating transition matrix, e.g. for $i,j = Aaa$, from Table 8.4 we get

$$T_{Aaa,Aaa} = 94.2\%.$$

Therefore, $T_{i,j}$ is the probability of a counterparty being in class j at time $t+1$ (e.g. at the end of a year) given that they were in class i at time t (e.g. at the beginning of a year).

Here our goal is to calculate the total probability of default for a rated counterparty in a one week time horizon by taking into account also possible changes in asset quality rating. To do that, we consider a Poisson process to describe the evolution of an asset credit quality. With similar arguments as in Subsection 8.4, let us compute the transition matrix as in Table 8.4 but in a time horizon of one week. Indeed, using the yearly rating transition matrix given in Table 8.4, we first compute by Eq. (8.7) the yearly intensity of the Poisson process counting the number of transitions of a counterparty from one rating to another, and then we use Eq. (8.8), suitably normalized, to compute the weekly transition probabilities. For example, for a counterparty whose rating downgraded in one year from *Aaa* to *Aa*, Eq. (8.7) yields

$$\lambda(1\,year, Aa) = -\ln(1 - T_{Aaa,Aa}) = -\ln(1 - 0,036) = 0.037.$$

Thus the 1-week corresponding unadjusted transition probability is computed as in Eq. (8.8), i.e.

$$T^{Unadj}_{Aaa,Aa} = 1 - e^{-0.037\cdot\frac{7}{365}} = 0.0703\%. \tag{8.9}$$

Table 8.5 lists the weekly unadjusted rating transition probabilities for all rating classes in Table 8.4.

Table 8.5: 1W unadjusted rating transition matrix.

	Aaa	Aa	A	Baa	Ba	B	Caa -C	NR
Aaa	5.3142%	0.0703%	0.0%	0.0%	0.0%	0.0%	0.0%	0.0427%
Aa	0.0329%	5.0519%	0.0407%	0.0%	0.0%	0.0%	0.0%	0.0564%
A	0.0%	0.0584%	4.6611%	0.0270%	0.0%	0.0%	0.0%	0.0783%
Baa	0.0%	0.0%	0.0743%	3.7539%	0.0624%	0.0%	0.0%	0.1309%
Ba	0.0%	0.0%	0.0%	0.0446%	4.1281%	0.0212%	0.0290%	0.1206%
B	0.0%	0.0%	0.0%	0.0%	0.2623%	2.6537%	0.0743%	0.1619%
Caa -C	0.0%	0.0%	0.0%	0.0%	0.0%	0.7481%	1.8435%	0.1064%

Observe that the sum of elements in each row of the above matrix is less than 1. To get the sum equal to 1, each element of a row is divided by a normalization factor given by the sum of all unadjusted probabilities in that row. For example, Eq. (8.9) normalized by the sum of all unadjusted probabilities in the first row of the matrix in Table 8.5, becomes

$$T_{Aaa,Aa} = \frac{T^{Unadj}_{Aaa,Aa}}{\sum_j T^{Unadj}_{Aaa,j}} = \frac{0.000703}{0.05427} = 1.29\%.$$

Table 8.6 lists the weekly rating transition matrix corresponding to Table 8.5.

An inquisitive reader may again recall the compound interest for the Markov chains and challenge the used approach of normalisation. This means that the

1Y-transition matrix is a 52-times product of 1W matrix, i.e.

$$(M_{1W})^{52} = M_{1Y}, \tag{8.10}$$

where M is a 8x8 transition matrix like in Table 8.6. However, the compound interest would yield us a less realistic 1W transition matrix of the type in Table 8.7, where mostly each rating preserves it with a probability around 99%. Once again, we would recommend properly back-testing the particular probability transformation for a given dataset at the reader's disposal. For our future needs, we proceed with the transition matrix from Table 8.6 since a near-diagonal matrix from Table 8.7 does not allow us to demonstrate all the richness of the modeling tools.

Table 8.6: 1W adjusted rating transition matrix.

	Aaa	Aa	A	Baa	Ba	B	Caa -C	NR
Aaa	97.92%	1.29%	0.0%	0.0%	0.0%	0.0%	0.0%	0.79%
Aa	0.63%	97.49%	0.78%	0.0%	0.0%	0.0%	0.0%	1.09%
A	0.0%	1.21%	96.61%	0.56%	0.0%	0.0%	0.0%	1.62%
Baa	0.0%	0.0%	1.85%	93.35%	1.55%	0.0%	0.0%	3.25%
Ba	0.0%	0.0%	0.0%	1.03%	95.04%	0.49%	0.67%	2.78%
B	0.0%	0.0%	0.0%	0.0%	8.32%	84.19%	2.36%	5.13%
Caa -C	0.0%	0.0%	0.0%	0.0%	0.0%	27.73%	68.33%	3.94%

Table 8.7: 1W rating transition matrix from the Markov Chain Product.

	Aaa	Aa	A	Baa	Ba	B	Caa -C	NR
Aaa	99.982%	0.011%	0.0%	0.0%	0.0%	0.0%	0.0%	0.007%
Aa	0.005%	99.979%	0.007%	0.0%	0.0%	0.0%	0.0%	0.009%
A	0.0%	0.010%	99.974%	0.005%	0.0%	0.0%	0.0%	0.012%
Baa	0.0%	0.0%	0.013%	99.956%	0.011%	0.0%	0.0%	0.020%
Ba	0.0%	0.0%	0.0%	0.008%	99.965%	0.003%	0.006%	0.019%
B	0.0%	0.0%	0.0%	0.0%	0.045%	99.913%	0.016%	0.026%
Caa -C	0.0%	0.0%	0.0%	0.0%	0.0%	0.140%	99.855%	0.014%
NR	0.0%	0.0%	0.0%	0.0%	0.0%	0.0%	0.0%	100.0%

Now we want to calculate the 1-week probability of default for a counterparty knowing its rating class among those considered in Table 8.2 at the beginning of the week, and assuming possible credit quality changes during the week. We still have to solve the problem that the rating transition probabilities are not on a very granular level. Indeed, from Table 8.6 it is only known that the probability of moving from rating Aaa to Aa is about 1.5%, but the probability to move from Aaa to Aa2 is not known. Without any loss of generality, we may assume that lower credit rating classes than those in Table 8.6 show the same rating transition matrix. Thus, for example, for a company with an initial rating B1 the 1-week probability of default D_{B1} is given by

$$\mathbb{P}(D_{B1}) = p_{B1} + p_{Aaa}T_{B,Aaa} + \cdots + p_B T_{B,B} + \cdots + p_C T_{B,C}\,, \tag{8.11}$$

where, by using the weekly probabilities of default computed in Subsection 8.4 we get

- $p_{Aaa} = 0.0\%$.
- $p_{Aa} = \frac{1}{3}\left(p_{Aa1} + p_{Aa2} + p_{Aa3}\right) = 0.0003\%$.
- $p_A = \frac{1}{3}\left(p_{A1} + p_{A2} + p_{A3}\right) = 0.0012\%$.
- $p_{Baa} = \frac{1}{3}\left(p_{Baa1} + p_{Baa2} + p_{Baa3}\right) = 0.0040\%$.
- $p_{Ba} = \frac{1}{3}\left(p_{Ba1} + p_{Ba2} + p_{Ba3}\right) = 0.0215\%$.
- $p_B = \frac{1}{3}\left(p_{B1} + p_{B2} + p_{B3}\right) = 0.0926\%$.
- $p_{Caa} = \frac{1}{3}\left(p_{Caa1} + p_{Caa2} + p_{Caa3}\right) = 0.4247\%$.
- $p_{Ca} = p_C = 0.9354\%$.

With these figures we can now calculate the final weekly probabilities of default according to Eq. (8.11)

- $\mathbb{P}(D_{Aaa}) = 0.00000\%$, $\mathbb{P}(D_{Aa1}) = 0.00001\%$, $\mathbb{P}(D_{Aa2}) = 0.00001\%$, $\mathbb{P}(D_{Aa3}) = 0.00091\%$.
- $\mathbb{P}(D_{A1}) = 0.00116\%$, $\mathbb{P}(D_{A2}) = 0.00123\%$, $\mathbb{P}(D_{A3}) = 0.00110\%$. One could argue that $\mathbb{P}(D_{A3})$ should be higher than $\mathbb{P}(D_{A2})$. This counterintuitive case is due to empirical data. Exhibit 36 of [Ou (2011)] is taken as basis and the empirical data yielded a lower $p(D_{A3})$ than $p(D_{A2})$.
- $\mathbb{P}(D_{Baa1}) = 0.00311\%$, $\mathbb{P}(D_{Baa2}) = 0.00368\%$, $\mathbb{P}(D_{Baa3}) = 0.00606\%$.
- $\mathbb{P}(D_{Ba1}) = 0.02884\%$, $\mathbb{P}(D_{Ba2}) = 0.03051\%$, $\mathbb{P}(D_{Ba3}) = 0.04946\%$.
- $\mathbb{P}(D_{B1}) = 0.09703\%$, $\mathbb{P}(D_{B2}) = 0.12161\%$, $\mathbb{P}(D_{B3}) = 0.18321\%$.
- $\mathbb{P}(D_{Caa1}) = 1.44103\%$, $\mathbb{P}(D_{Caa2}) = 1.58028\%$, $\mathbb{P}(D_{Caa3}) = 1.76129\%$.
- $\mathbb{P}(D_{Ca}) = \mathbb{P}(D_C) = 1.59420\%$.

If a company is not rated, we assume its rating is Baa2. For OTC counterparty risk reporting, the values of derivatives are not affected by a change in the rating class.

For the discussion purpose, we mention here an alternative formula to Eq. (8.11) which corresponds to the formula of total probability when a finite number of mutually exclusive events are available (in our case different rating classes)

$$\mathbb{P}(D_{B1}) = \frac{p_{B_1}}{p_{B_1} + p_{B_2} + p_{B_3}} \left(p_{Aaa}T_{B,Aaa} + \cdots + \mathbf{p}_B T_{B,B} + \cdots + p_C T_{B,C} \right). \tag{8.12}$$

In this formula, it is not necessary to calculate p_B, but one can use p_{B1}, which is known. The same argument is valid for all rating classes in Table 8.2.

8.6 Modeling Tails

According to [Koyluoglu and Hickman (1998)] and [Crouhy *et al.* (2000)] the models are quite similar across a broad range of parameters provided that the parameters are the same across the models (cf. Table 8.8). However, as the parameters vary by estimation technique, this may lead to estimates which are inconsistent with the reported results.

By defining the tail as the area more than twice the standard deviation above the mean, i.e. $z = \bar{p} + 2\sigma$, results in Table 8.8 demonstrate "the similarity of the models holds for a reasonably wide range of parameters. The models begin to diverge at a very high ratio of default rate volatility to default probability, particularly for very low or very high default probabilities (upper right and lower right regions of the table). In the case of very low default probabilities (upper right), the conditional default rate functions of the Merton-based and econometric models become much more concave than that of the actuarial model. In the case of very high default probabilities (lower right), the gamma distribution's lack of upper bound begins to have a significant effect. Accordingly, in very high quality (AA or better) or very low quality (B or worse) portfolios, model selection can make a difference, though there is scant data on which to base such selection. In a portfolio where very high or very low quality sub-portfolios have only moderate weight, these differences should not be significant in aggregation" [Koyluoglu and Hickman (1998), p. 15]. We will explain what Merton model is later in Subsection 13.3. For now we would like to briefly mention that it forms the basis for the PortfolioManager credit risk model that we cover in more detail in Chapter 15.

We describe here how to link a rating transition to price variation. The price change is discussed in [Benzschawel *et al.* (2011)]. To calculate this, we take the market-implied rating (MIR) because it reflects more promptly the variation of the expected loss according to the markets than the stationary ratings.

8.7 Additional Thoughts on PD

In this subsection, we show how to calculate the probability of default of counterparties admitting different ratings.

Mathematically, the default event is usually associated with a Bernoulli random variable, which takes the value zero (no default) or one (default) with a fixed probability. In the literature, the most used stochastic processes for modeling a portfolio of losses are the Binomial and the Poisson processes. In the following sections we will briefly illustrate their probabilistic properties while, here, we explain why we prefer the Poisson process. Apart from some modeling benefit that follows from (very strong) assumptions (e.g. if counterparties are unrealistically assumed to be independent, then the sum of the corresponding Poisson losses is still a Poisson random variable), the main reason to prefer the Poisson model to the Bernoulli one is that in reality, a counterparty may default multiple times. A famous case of

Table 8.8: Tail agreement statistics from [Koyluoglu and Hickman (1998)].

$\bar{\rho}$	$\sigma/\bar{\rho}$ = 0.5	1.00	2.00	3.00	
0.05%	98.10%	95.94%	91.16%	89.12%	Ξ (Merton vs. Econometric)
	93.53%	88.50%	81.17%	78.99%	Ξ (Merton vs. Actuarial)
	91.71%	84.70%	73.13%	69.04%	Ξ (Econometric vs. Actuarial)
0.10%	97.92%	95.57%	91.15%	88.40%	
	93.75%	88.94%	82.16%	80.40%	
	91.73%	84.78%	73.95%	69.73%	
0.25%	97.61%	94.93%	90.35%	87.86%	
	94.11%	89.73%	83.87%	82.92%	
	91.79%	84.97%	74.83%	71.60%	
0.50%	97.33%	94.41%	89.91%	88.09%	
	94.42%	90.56%	85.71%	85.61%	
	91.88%	85.30%	76.15%	74.28%	
1.00%	97.06%	93.97%	89.89%	88.97%	
	94.93%	91.69%	88.29%	89.38%	
	92.04%	85.93%	78.57%	78.72%	
2.50%	96.62%	93.62%	90.77%	91.33%	
	95.82%	93.94%	93.65%	94.68%	
	92.62%	87.79%	84.77%	87.53%	
5.00%	96.33%	93.85%	92.79%	94.59%	
	97.02%	96.70%	95.24%	81.79%	
	93.55%	90.87%	91.38%	79.96%	
10.00%	96.21%	94.92%	95.79%		
	98.55%	95.57%	72.95%	N/A*	
	95.45%	95.22%	72.41%		

*Not a reasonable combination of parameters – model results become unstable.

multiple defaults is former President of the United States Donald Trump. He went bankrupt six times: in 1991, 1992 for three times, 2004 and 2009 [Newman (2015)].

As an example, in Table 8.9 we show the probabilities of multiple defaults (in a one-year time horizon) referred to counterparties with three different S&P ratings (see [McNeil *et al.* (2005)]). For each rating, the estimated Poisson intensity λ is given by the sample mean of the number of observed defaults over a group of assets admitting a particular credit rating.

Table 8.9: Probability of multiple events for a Poisson random variable with various intensity parameters.

	BBB	B	CCC
Intensity λ	0.00230	0.05296	0.26231
Zero events	99.770%	94.970%	79.220%
One event	0.230%	4.901%	18.454%
Two events	0.000%	0.126%	2.149%

Chapter 9

Loss Given Default (LGD)

9.1 Basic Definition

By *Loss Given Default* or rate of loss in the event of insolvency we mean the loss that a bank, or more generally a credit institution, suffers on a certain credit exposure when the counterparty becomes insolvent[1]. Defining the recovery rate as the percentage that the creditor recovers, compared to the outstanding exposure for the credit, when the issuing counterparty defaults, the LGD is equal to the difference between one and the recovery rate RR, or

$$LGD = 1 - RR, \tag{9.1}$$

where it is expected that

$$0 \leq LGD \leq 1.$$

However, real-world data provides evidence that both boundaries might be breached. For instance, the LGD extremes on the left may be negative which means banks earn more upon the default than the principal and the interest income with applicable time discounting. That might happen after getting full ownership over the collateral that has significantly risen in price during the boom after the turbulent times that forced a borrower to go bust and to leave the collateral to the creditor. As for the extremes on the right, [Yao *et al.* (2014), p. 2] demonstrate value up to 1.7 and [Frontczak *et al.* (2017), p. 658] — up to 1.5. This implies that court fees and accompanying expenses incurred may not be offset during the debt recovery process.

Alternatively, following [Ye and Bellotti (2019)], LGD may be calculated as the proportion of money financial institutions successfully collected minus the administration fees during the collection period, given the borrower has already defaulted:

$$LGD = 1 - RR = 1 - (VR - AC)/EAD \tag{9.2}$$

[1]Part of this chapter has been published in [Orlando and Härtel (2014)]

where EAD is the exposure at default of each loan (including the related interest), AC stands for the administration costs incurred, discounted at the time of default, and VR is the present value of the recovered amount. We would discuss the empirical LGD determinants such as the collateral availability and the recovery timing in Section 17.3.2.

9.2 Recovery Rating Scale

Here we list the recovery ratings from [Fitch Ratings (2016)]. The scale "is based upon the expected relative recovery characteristics of an obligation upon the curing of a default, emergence from insolvency or following the liquidation or termination of the obligor or its associated collateral". It must be noted that the factors affecting the recovery rates are seniority, collaterals, the expected value of the company or underlying collateral in distress, etc.

Table 9.1: The Recovery Rating (RR) Scale, percent of current principal and related interest.

RR No.	Category Name (prospects given default)	recovered amount
1	outstanding	91 - 100
2	superior	71 - 90
3	good	51 - 70
4	average	31 - 50
5	below average	11 - 30
6	poor	0 - 10

9.3 LGD Modeling Approaches

In general, the LGD is never known at the time of granting a loan and in the event of default in primary market activity. However, if the exposure is traded on a secondary market, it is possible to estimate this variable based on the market price after insolvency. By secondary market, we mean the market in which securities already outstanding are traded and remain there until their possible maturity. Several factors influence this variable and these can be grouped into four main categories. For further information see "Risk management and shareholders' value in banking: from risk measurement models to capital allocation policies" by [Sironi and Resti (2007)]. They are:

- Technical characteristics of the loan, such as collateral, personal guarantees;
- Characteristics of the financed entity. Among these, we find the production sector to which it belongs, which affects the degree of liquidity of the company's activities and the country or geographic region in which the debtor

is located;

- Specific characteristics of the individual bank, such as the internal policy relating to credit recovery processes;
- External factors, such as the state of the business cycle and the level of interest rates.

An ordered logit model can be well suited to the case of estimating LGD, considering that we usually would observe three ordered categories of values, including '0' (in case of total recovery), '1' (in case of total loss) and 'in-betweens', as a dependent variable.[2] In ordered response models, it is assumed that the observed variable Y_i is the result of a single continuous latent variable Y_i^*, which depends linearly on a set of individual characteristics:

$$Y_i^* = (\beta^*)'X_i + e_i^*$$

where X_i is the vector of independent variables, (β^*) is the parameter vector and e_i^* is the error term. Considering three alternatives, as in our case, the observed variable Y_i assumes the following values:

$$\begin{cases} Y_i = 0 & \text{if } Y_i^* = 0 \\ Y_i = 1 & \text{if } 0 < Y_i^* 0 < \alpha_c^* \\ Y_i = 2 & \text{if } Y_i^* = \alpha_c^* \end{cases} \tag{9.3}$$

where α^* represents the so-called thresholds or cut-off points between categories; in general, there are as many thresholds as categories of the ordinal variable minus one. The probability distribution of the observable variable Y_i is given by:

$$\begin{aligned} P(Y_i = 0|X_i) &= P(e_i^* \leq (\beta^*)'X_i) = F(-(\beta^*)'X_i) \\ P(Y_i = 1|X_i) &= P(-(\beta^*)'X_i \leq e_i^* \leq \alpha_c^* - (\beta^*)'X_i) = F(\alpha_c^* - (\beta^*)'X_i) - F(-(\beta^*)'X_i) \\ P(Y_i = 2|X_i) &= P(e_i^* > \alpha_c^* - (\beta^*)'X_i) = 1 - F(\alpha_c^* - (\beta^*)'X_i) \end{aligned} \tag{9.4}$$

Using the logistic cumulative distribution function, we obtain the ordered logistic regression model:

$$\begin{aligned} P(Y_i = 0|X_i) &= P(Y_i \leq 0|X_i) = \exp(\alpha_c - \beta'X_i)/[1 + \exp(\alpha_c - \beta'X_i)] \\ P(Y_i = 1|X_i) &= P(Y_i \leq 1|X_i) - P(Y_i \leq 0|X_i) \\ P(Y_i = 2|X_i) &= 1 - P(Y_i \leq 1|X_i) \end{aligned} \tag{9.5}$$

The cumulative probabilities are related to a linear predictor $\beta'X_i = \beta_0 + \beta_1 X_1 + \beta_2 X_2 + \cdots$ through the logit function:

$$\text{logit}[P(Y_i)] = \ln(P(Y_i)/[1 - P(Y_i)]) = \alpha_c - \beta'X_i$$

[2]This material has been partly published as [Orlando and Pelosi (2020)].

The parameters β and the thresholds α_c are estimated using the Maximum Likelihood method. Regressors for the LGD might be industry classification, size of the loan, collateral, seniority of debts, product type, firm size, creditworthiness, firm age, macroeconomic condition, etc. "However, different studies suggest different factors and there is no consensus on these factors except collateral" [Han and Jang (2013)]. This is in line with our findings as the only two relevant variables are collateral and recovery time.

9.4 LGD Proxy Indicators

Based on the above given LGD definitions, we deduce that the problem of estimating the LGD can be traced back to the problem of estimating the recovery rate. There are several methods for calculating the recovery rate (see Committee of European Banking Supervision, Guidelines on the implementation, validation and assessment of Advanced Measurement (AMA) and Internal Ratings Based (IRB) Approaches):

- Market LGD (see [Altman (2006)]);
- Implied Market LGD (see [Seidler and Jakubik (2009)]);
- Implied Historical LGD (see [Porto (2011)]);
- Workout LGD (see [Sironi and Resti (2007)]).

The *Market LGD* allows you to obtain an estimate of the LGD by analyzing the market prices of the defaulted exposures. In other words, the prices of the defaulted exposures are used as an estimate of the recovery rate, so that an estimate of the LGD is obtained by subtracting the estimate of the recovery rate from 1. The LGD obtained is called the Market LGD. For example, if a bond issued by an insolvent company is traded at 30 cents for each Euro of nominal capital, the recovery rate estimated by the market will be about 30%, so the estimated LGD will be about 70%.

A limitation of this approach is that it can only be applied to secondary market exposures and it is at large extent driven by the current market liquidity conditions. To overcome this problem, two variants of the model have been created:

- *Implied Market LGD*, which allows an estimate of the LGD of the bonds traded on the market not yet in default. It is often based on a structural model of the Merton-Vasicek type. Thus, it assumes Brownian motion in the dynamics of the stock returns, lognormal distribution of the firm value. The actually observed quotes are treated then as a combination of PD and LGD. Wherever PD comes from the structural model, the residual variation is attributed to LGD. However, the theoretical setting has limitations. Then the implied market LGD estimates may not be reliable. As a counter-evidence, they are not accepted by the supervisors when a bank applies for IRB approach.

- *Implied Historical LGD* which allows you to obtain a long-term LGD estimate based solely on the past loss experiences and PD estimates at the portfolio level rather than at the individual exposure level. This approach is more trustworthy, than the implied market ones. However, they also have a limitation. The portfolio level estimate considers yet non-defaulted exposures weighted by the PD estimates. As the reader may expect, an error in PD results in inverse deviation for the LGD estimates. Such errors might be netted to an extent due to a portfolio-wide view. However, when the loan offering and loan collection processes are managed by separate divisions driven mostly by PD and LGD, respectively, such error redistribution may produce incorrect signals. Such LGD estimates are neither accepted within an IRB application.

Above we touched the three out of four proxy LGD indicators. Each of them has some attractive features — be it ease and speed of computation or a linkage to a theoretical model — none of them is accepted by a regulator for the IRB approach. The only one out of the four indicators left is exactly the one that is accepted for IRB. It is workout LGD. That is why we are going to focus more on it below.

Workout LGD

Market data certainly provide objective estimates of LGD (subject to controlling for the securities liquidity). However, they are only available for bonds. Most bank loans are not negotiated, and therefore their market prices cannot be observed. In such circumstances, one must then find a different method, alternative to the previous one, which is based on the recoveries experienced by the banks in the months or years after insolvency has occurred. This method is the *Workout LGD*. For definition clarity, the term *workout* is more often used when applied to corporate exposures, whereas it is the term *collection* with respect to retail claims. It is based on discounting the positive and negative cash flows associated with the recovery of defaulted positions. Such recovery cash flows may come from the collateral sell-off, though not necessarily. Here is a dilemma for a credit risk manager as to whether the collateral signals lower or higher credit risk. On the one hand, all things being equal, the presence of collateral is definitely welcome. Therefore, the collateral should signal lower credit risk. However, on the other hand, collateral is often required of riskier borrowers. This means that when the credit risk is high — or more precisely, when the PD is high — the collateral is most often required. Thus, the credit risk of a deal with collateral may be the same as the one without it. This may be due to the re-balancing between PD and LGD. In case of no collateral PD may be low, but LGD is high. When the guarantee is present, it is often due to the low LGD rather than a high PD. We will additionally discuss the interrelationship of PD and LGD in Section 10.3 devoted to expected and unexpected losses.

These are the cash flows discounted at the recovery rate and the costs discounted at the recovery rate of the recovery process. IFRS 5 standard requires estimating the recovered amount subject to collateral sale within one year past default.

The ratio between the net present value of these flows at the date of default and the exposure amount at the time of default (EAD) constitutes the recovery rate of the defaulted asset, the completion of which to the unit provides the measure of the Workout LGD. Although the calculation of Workout LGD is more complex than Market LGD, the advantage of this method is that it is applicable to all types of exposures and the results it produces are more accurate.

To arrive at an estimate of the LGD, we need to calculate the observed Workout LGD. In detail, let S be a set of credits and $i \in S$ a single credit. The i-th credit Workout LGD is expressed as follows

$$\mathrm{LGD}_i = 1 - \frac{RCF_i(r) - C_i(r)}{EAD_i}, \tag{9.6}$$

where

- EAD_i is the Exposure at Default of credit i;
- RCF_i is the sum of the discounted cash flows at rate r during the credit recovery process i;
- C_i is the sum of direct and indirect costs discounted at the same rate during the i-th credit recovery process.

We observe that if the sum of the discounted cash flows equals the EAD plus the costs of the recovery process, then the $LGD = 0$. If the exposure fully defaults, the LGD can be greater than 1 as there are additional costs that arise during the recovery process.

Remark 9.1. To calculate the LGD, it is important to distinguish the defaulted credits in *Recoveries* and *Write-off*.

- *Recoveries* are the credits recovered. For example, a debtor has paid the backlog or a new payment plan has been set up (we may say it was restructured). In this case, the credit is managed as a normal credit not in default. However, we would preserve this event as default for the purpose of PD modeling;
- *Write-offs* are the cancelled credits. If the possibility of recovering money from the debtor is minimal, the credit will be written off from the balance sheet assets.

Based on this distinction, the equation is correct for write-offs, but not for Recoveries as the exposure at the time of recovery ($EARC$) is the amount that has been recovered, must be considered. Since the $EARC$ reduces the economic loss resulting from insolvency but is not included in the cash flows, it must be added to the discounted cash flows:

$$\text{LGD}_{\ i} = 1 - \frac{RCF_i(r) - C_i(r) + EARC_i}{EAD_i},$$

where $EARC_i$ is the exposure at the time of credit recovery i.

Although the calculation of the Workout LGD for each i credit is not complicated, the choice of an appropriate data set, which serves as the basis for the estimates of the *LGD*, is difficult. First, it should be noted that banks are primarily interested in the total *LGD* to apply to an asset class. Therefore, the input data chosen by the banks, in general, are historical defaulted positions with complete recovery processes. For each of them, all information relating to the amounts recovered and the recovery procedures adopted must be recorded. After which these data are segmented according to the type of exposure, debtor, recovery process adopted, to obtain a finite number of clusters, each of which consists of similar elements and therefore similar *LGD*. Finally, these clusters are used to estimate the expected *LGD* for future defaults, by calculating the weighted average for each cluster.

In the F-IRB approach, a value of *LGD* of 45% is assigned for unsecured loans to sovereigns, companies and banks, while 75% for subordinated loans to the same exposures. In case the collateral is available, LGD in F-IRB can go down to 35%. In the A-IRB approach, *LGD* is measured as a percentage of the exposure at the time of default, most preferably in the form of the workout *LGD* described above, and not that of market *LGD*. One of the immediate implications of the financial crisis of 2007-2009 was a request by the Basel Committee to limit the value of the model *LGD* estimate to 10% of the *EAD* from below.

9.5 Additional Thoughts on LGD

In an ideal world sufficient data would be available with the required data quality.

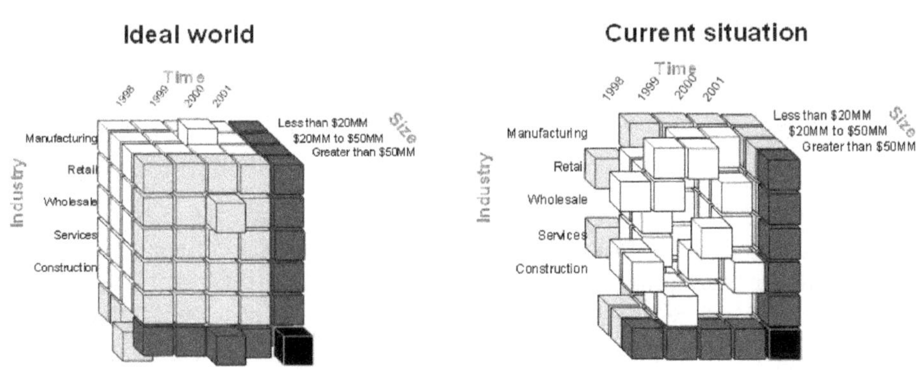

Fig. 9.1: Comparison of the ideal and the real world concerning data (figure taken from [Kofman (2011)]).

From the statistical point of view, a low number of defaults is not significant and cannot be used for validation. It is common to require at least 100 defaults. Otherwise, portfolios are called low default portfolios (LDP). When LDPs are present as a particular IRB segment, this may give rise to regulatory arbitrage opportunities. This means that the capital ratio may be artificially improved by mere data perturbation, i.e. by segmenting the pooled dataset into several segments with high and low default rates, respectively. Such segmentation might even seem natural when it is done according to a size or indebtedness criteria. For instance, the largest or the least indebted borrowers form one segment and the others fall into the second segment. For more discussion of LDP we recommend referring to Subsection 7.1.1 or to [Penikas (2020c)].

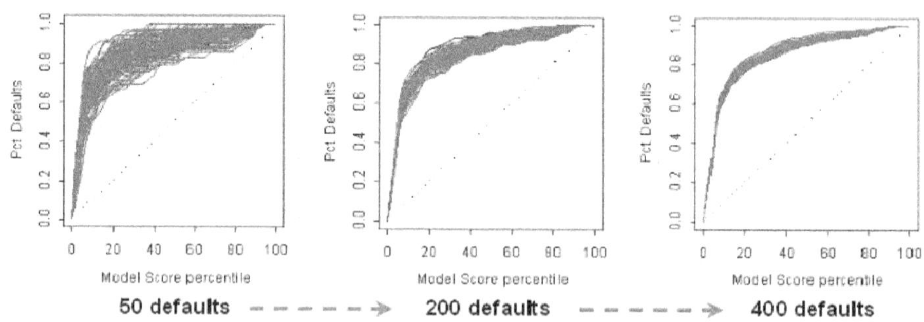

Fig. 9.2: Comparison of the number of defaults and the variability of PD modeling in case of LDP (figure of [Kofman (2011)]).

The most common remedies in the presence of data limitations can be:

- Data pooling or use of external datasets;
- Addition of "quasi-defaults" near to default issuers, see relevant methodology when applied to shipping companies' PD model in [Lozinskaia *et al.* (2017)];
- Economic losses determined at obligor or family level;
- Estimation at LGD "segment level" (e.g. secured vs. unsecured) and applied to the defaulted instrument in a segment.

There can be several key factors for being able to service the debt, e.g. region, industry sector, seniority, state of the economy, assets of the obligor. The segmentation imposes further splits of already scarce data. In addition, the need to isolate data from economic down-turn conditions to calculate a downturn LGD compliant with §468 of the Basel II framework (cf. [BCBS (2004)]) aggravates the problem even further.

A pragmatic approach that we are considering is to add an LGD score similarly to the one proposed in [Glößner *et al.* (2006)]. In this approach, instead of segmenting the observed loss data, an LGD score (based on a combination of expert judgment analysis and statistical analysis) can be added with the aim to reflect the relative order of the expected loss rate. In a second step, the score is calibrated to the internal loss history and it should provide a robust approximation of data.

Chapter 10

Other Credit Risk Components and Portfolio Risk

10.1 Exposure at Default (EAD)

By *exposure to risk* we mean a transaction resulting from an agreement between the bank,[1] or more generally a creditor, and the customer who benefits from the credit made available to him. Let us distinguish two types of exposures:

- Exposure to a certain amount;
- Exposure to uncertain amount.

The former are exposures for which the bank has not made any commitment to provide credit to the customer in the future and the book value gives the exposure value. For example, the granting of a mortgage loan without the option of early repayment represents an exposure with a certain value since there is a coincidence between the amount disbursed and that agreed upon at the time of signing the contract. For these exposures, the EAD is set equal to the nominal value of the exposure itself

$$EAD = \text{Part of credit used.}$$

The latter are exposures for which the amount cannot be quantified immediately, but only upon the occurrence of insolvency. An example of exposure to an uncertain value is represented by the opening of a current account credit as the value of the risk exposure will be known only at the end of the risk time horizon. Not knowing *a priori* the value of the exposure, it becomes necessary to determine its estimate with reference to the moment in which it is assumed that the default may occur. To determine the exposure at risk, it is important to estimate only the part of the credit to be used by the counterparty in the event, should it go into insolvency as only this can be subject to losses since the remainder is retained by the financial institution. In this regard, we divide the maximum disbursement commitment (or credit limit), called *commitment*, made available by the creditor to the debtor into two components: risky and non-risky.

[1]Part of this chapter has been published in [Orlando and Härtel (2014)].

The risky component is equal to

$$Risky\ Component = OS + \alpha \cdot COM$$

while the non-risky component is equal to

$$Non\ Risky\ Component = (1 - \alpha) \cdot COM,$$

where

- α is the *Credit Conversion Factor (CCF)*, that is the percentage that has been estimated to be used by the customer at the time of insolvency;
- OS is the *outstanding* amount, that is the part of the amount already used by the debtor;
- COM is the *undrawn commitment*, which is part of the amount not used by the customer.

The risky component is the EAD for exposure to uncertain value. As we can see, it depends on the amount currently used and on the estimate of future uses of the credit line not yet used. Potential future uses are expressed as a percentage of the unused amount. Since the total financed amount and the one currently used are known, the problem of estimating the EAD goes back to the problem of estimating the credit conversion factor. For credit institutions that adopt the IRB method, the calculation of the EAD depends upon the approach chosen:

- Foundation approach (F-IRB);
- Advanced approach (A-IRB).

With the first approach, the EAD associated with a credit line, for off-balance sheet transactions, is calculated as just said, where the CCF is provided by the local regulator. In particular, a CCF of 75% is applied to credit line, to the Note Issuance Facilities (NIF) and Revolving Underwriting Facilities (RUF), regardless of the duration of the underlying credit. On the other hand, credit lines with no firm commitment, revocable at any time and without prior notice or with an automatic revocation clause (for example, following a deterioration of creditworthiness), a CCF of 0% is applied. A CCF of 20% applies to self-liquidating letters of credit for merchant transactions (for example, documentary credits in which the shipment of the merchandise serves as a guarantee). A CCF of 20% and 50% respectively applies to credit openings with an original maturity of no more than one year and those with a maturity of more than one year. A CCF of 100% applies to securities lending (financing) or security collateral transactions. With the second approach, banks are allowed to use their own proxies, and they have the flexibility in choosing templates. In this case, the CCF is not provided by the regulator and must therefore be calculated.

In the next subsection, we will see how it is possible to arrive at estimates of CCF by providing some methods.

10.1.1 *Modeling the CCF*

The definition of the CCF requires credit institutions to estimate how much of the amount not yet used by the debtor will be used at the time of insolvency. To obtain estimates of CCF, credit institutions use all observations of defaulted receivables before insolvency as input data. Most of the models adopted by credit institutions are based on the calculation of certain statistics, and one of these is the CCF *achieved.* Let us consider a credit in default, g, with time-varying exposure, $E(t)$, and with a credit limit, $L(t)$. If the credit defaults at time t_d, considered t_r as reference time, with $t_r < t_d$, the pair $i = \{g, t_r\}$ is called *observation index.* If EAD_i denotes the observed exposure at the time of default, $E(t_d)$, it can be expressed in terms of the observed exposure and credit limit at time t_r as follows

$$EAD_i = E(t_r) + CCF_i(L(t_r) - E(t_r)),$$

where

$$CCF_i = \frac{E(t_d) - E(t_r)}{L(t_r) - E(t_r)},$$

or also

$$CCF_i = \frac{\frac{E(t_d)}{L(t_r)} - \frac{E(t_r)}{L(t_r)}}{1 - \frac{E(t_r)}{L(t_r)}}.$$

Therefore, given the observation O_i, with $i = \{g, t_r\}$, $L(t_r) \neq E(t_r)$, the first formula can be used to calculate the associated CCF for a realized observation O_i. However, this formula has some limitations:

- It is not defined when $L(t_r) = E(t_r)$. This implies that it is not possible to estimate the EAD if you use the statistic;
- It is not stable when $L(t_r) \approx E(t_r)$.

For these reasons, lenders sometimes prefer to use other statistics to estimate the EAD. One of these statistics is defined as follows

$$CCF_i = \frac{L(t_r)}{EAD_i(t_r)}.$$

Despite being little used, it has two advantages:

- It is well defined when $L(t_r) = E(t_r)$;
- It is stable when $L(t_r) \approx E(t_r)$.

10.1.2 *CCF Estimation Models*

Given a set of credits in default, there are several methods of obtaining the conversion factors through which it is possible to arrive at estimates of the EAD of the credits, not in default. These methods are *Fixed Time Horizon, Cohort Approach* or *Variable Time Horizon.* They use observations of loans in default dating back to times prior to the moment of insolvency and are based on the identification of two time points, the reference date and the date of default, which define the observation period.

We will provide a brief description of each method, highlighting its disadvantages or advantages.

10.1.2.1 *Cohort Approach*

In this method, the observation period is divided into time intervals of equal length, called *cohorts* (e.g. one-year intervals). After that, the credits are grouped into the cohorts based on the range that includes their default date. In order to calculate the CCF factor for each credit, the first extreme of the interval containing its default date is used as the reference date, $\{t_1, t_2, ..., t_n\}$,

$$CCF(t_i) = \frac{E(t_d) - E(t_i)}{L(t_i) - E(t_i)}.$$

The disadvantages are:

- The lengths of the cohorts are conventional;
- The reference dates are conventional;
- Does not use all available information because for each g credit in default during the observation period only the observation $\{g, t_i\}$ is used.

10.1.2.2 *Fixed Time Horizon*

In this method, a T time horizon is set, which is usually one year. After that, for each credit in default, the CCF factor is calculated using $t_d - T$ as the reference date

$$CCF(t_d - T) = \frac{E(t_d) - E(t_d - T)}{L(t_d - T) - E(t_d - T)}.$$

The disadvantages of this method are:

- Fixed time horizon T is conventional;
- It does not consider all relevant information because for each g credit in default during the observation period, only the observation $\{g, t_d - T\}$ is used;
- It does not consider the possibility that the current exposure may default at any time during the following year. Estimates based on this approach assume that the default dates for any credit that will default during the next 12 months will be at the end of this period.

10.1.2.3 *Variable Time Horizon*

In this method, a range of horizon values, in correspondence with which we are going to calculate the CCF_i factors, is fixed. For each credit in default, the CCF_i

factors associated with a set of reference dates are calculated (for example, for 1 month, 2 months, .. before the default)

$$CCF(t_d - j) = \frac{E(t_d) - E(t_d - j)}{L(t_d - j) - E(t_d - j)} \qquad (j = 1, ..., 12 \text{ months}). \tag{10.1}$$

In principle, twelve CCF factors could be associated with each credit in default. However, these $CCFs$ are non-homogeneous in the sense that some of these values are calculated using observations very close to the default date and others are based on observations from one year before the default. The advantages of this method are that, unlike the previous methods, it has a greater number of observations. In addition, the estimation procedures based on these data should produce more stable (because it uses more observations) and accurate (because it uses more information) estimates.

10.2 Maturity (M)

The *maturity* denotes the repayment or maturity date of a loan or other financial instrument. Defined the *effective maturity* of the underlying as the maximum remaining (not contractual or original) period before the counterparty is called to fulfil its obligations, M is the maximum between 1 year and the remaining effective maturity expressed in years. The latter is 2.5 years except for transactions of the repurchase agreement type, which is 6 months if the foundation IRB approach is used, while it must be calculated for each transaction if the advanced IRB approach is used. In all cases, M will not be greater than 5 years. In detail, for financial instruments that have a predetermined cash flow profile, M is calculated as follows, see [BCBS (2006), p. 75, par. 320]:

$$M = \frac{\sum_t t \cdot CF_t}{\sum_t CF_t}$$

where CF_t denotes the cash flows owed by the debtor in terms of principal, interest and commissions at time t. If the bank is unable to calculate the actual *duration* of the contractual payments, it can use a more conservative measure of M, such as the maximum time the debtor has to pay off his obligations. For short-term exposures, less than three months, the duration should be calculated as the greater value between one day and the actual duration. For exposures to smaller companies, an average duration of 2.5 years is assumed. The Basel Committee requires no maturity adjustment for the retail exposures.

IRB risk-weighting Eq. (5.7) considers the maturity adjustment — where applicable to non-retail exposures — in the form of the following multiplier $\tilde{\mathrm{M}}$

$$K = LGD \cdot \left(\phi\left(\sqrt{\frac{1}{1-R}} \cdot \phi^{-1}(PD) + \sqrt{\frac{1}{1-R}} \cdot \phi^{-1}(0.999) \right) - PD \right) \cdot M. \tag{10.2}$$

The Basel Committee revised the maturity adjustment M three times. Table 10.1 presents its evolution. We consider two representative PD values. The value of 1% is typical for the corporate exposures in stable times and the developed economies, while the value of 30% gives maximum to the unexpected loss component in K. The 2004 version was preserved later on in [BCBS (2005b)], [BCBS (2006)] and Basel III. Minimum M_{min} and maximum M_{max} maturity values are expressed in years. As we may see from Figure 10.1, the major changes relate to low PD values, while for the larger ones the maturity is comparable and negligible.

Table 10.1: Maturity adjustment M evolution.

Type	Source	M_{min}	M_{max}	M	b
$Mult\_01$	[BCBS (2001b)]	1	7	$1 + b \times (M - 3)$	$\frac{0.0235 \times (1-PD)}{(PD^{0.44} + 0.0470 \times (1-PD))}$
$Mult\_03$	[BCBS (2003)]	1	5	$\frac{(1+(M-2.5)\times b)}{(1-1.5\times b)}$	$(0.08451 - 0.05898 \times \log(PD))^2$
$Mult\_04$	[BCBS (2004)]	1	5	$\frac{(1+(M-2.5)\times b)}{(1-1.5\times b)}$	$(0.11852 - 0.05478 \times \log(PD))^2$

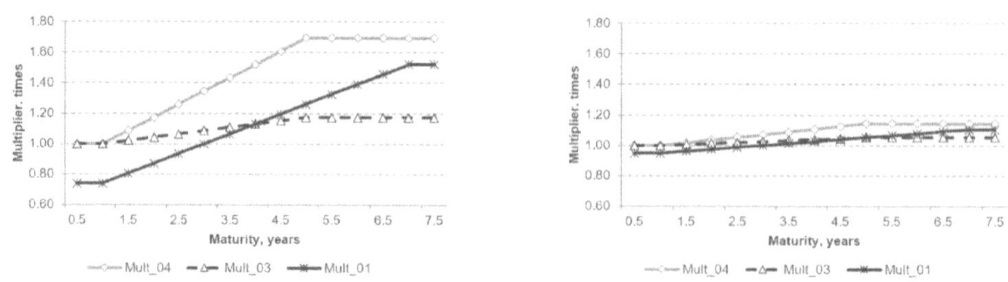

Fig. 10.1: Maturity adjustment M for $PD = 1\%$ (left) and $PD = 30\%$ (right).
For $Mult\_$ definitions, please, refer to Table 10.1, source: [Penikas (2020a)]

However, the IRB maturity adjustment has its peculiarities. [Osadchiy (2021)] draws attention to the case of low default portfolios (LDP), when $0 < PD < 2.927 \times 10^{-6}$. In such a case, the capital requirements might become negative for the maturity over one year, see Figure 10.2. This represents the logic of [Merton (1974)] when he argued that in the long run, the borrower has more opportunities to find sources to redeem its debt, rather than in the shorter run.

10.3 Expected and Unexpected Losses

The gross credit risk measurement components are: *expected loss* and *unexpected loss*. Schematically we may present it in Figure 10.3.

Let us examine each of the two components of the gross credit risk in detail.

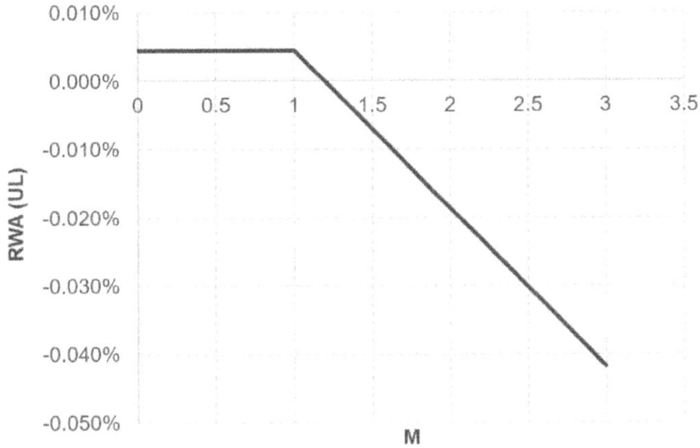

Fig. 10.2: Negative capital requirements arise for small PD in excess of one year.

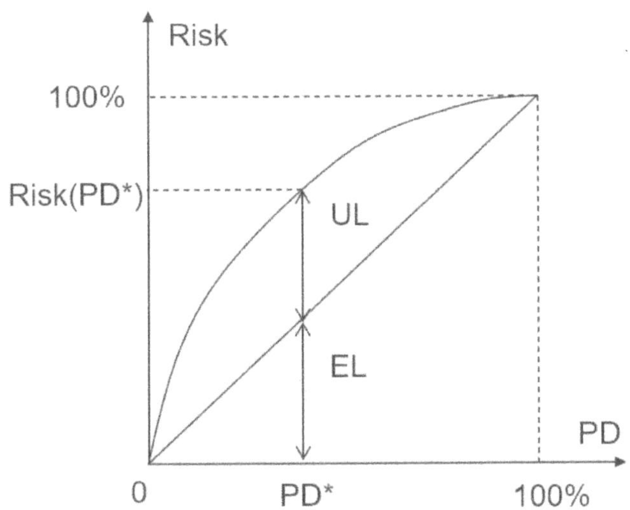

Fig. 10.3: Gross risk decomposition into EL and UL.

Expected Loss

According to what has been said, it is natural to think that the creditor has an interest in observing the economic and financial situation of the counterparty in order to be able to estimate any losses he may incur, and therefore estimate the expected losses. *Expected loss* means the loss that a bank, or more generally a creditor, expects to suffer from a credit exposure. It is expressed as a function of the three elements:

- Probability of Default (PD);
- Loss rate in case of insolvency — Loss Given Default (LGD);
- Expected exposure in the event of insolvency — Exposure at Default (EAD);

and, by the very definition, it is the expected value of the *loss variable.*

Denoted by D the event that the counterparty is insolvent, with $PD = \mathbb{P}(D)$ the probability of default, the loss variable is defined for each open position as

$$\tilde{L} = EAD \cdot LGD \cdot L,$$

where

$$L := \begin{cases} 1 & \text{with probability } PD \\ 0 & \text{with probability } 1 - PD, \end{cases}$$

can be modeled as a Bernoulli variable.

Assuming that EAD and LGD are constant, we have

$$\mathbb{E}[\tilde{L}] = EAD \cdot LGD \cdot PD, \tag{10.3}$$

since the expected value of a Bernoulli variable equals the probability of a single event (success, default) occurrence. So, if for example the $PD = 2\%$, the $LGD = 40\%$ and the $EAD =$ EUR 10k, then the expected loss will be equal to Euro 80.

Remark 10.1. In the representation given for the expected loss, we have assumed that EAD and LGD are constants. These are quite strong assumptions, but they are not always realistic: there are several situations in which EAD and LGD are described by random variables. In fact, the exposure value and the loss rate generally depend on various random circumstances, such as the technical form of the loan, debt seniority, any guarantees and other factors that may affect the timing and methods of quantifying losses and credit shares that can be recovered. If the EAD is described by a random variable, the expected loss is always given by the previous relationship, provided that the default D is assumed to be an event independent of the other variables of the model and that the EAD and the LGD are expected values. The hypothesis of PD-LGD-EAD independence is also quite arbitrary.

Equation (10.3) is the model that describes the expected loss in the simplest possible way. One moves away from it as soon as the assumptions are removed. Furthermore, from Eq. (10.3) we deduce that the expected loss of a single credit is a function of the probability of default of the counterparty and the expected recovery rate. Denoting by EL the expected loss variable, from now on, we will assume that the default exposure (EAD) is a deterministic quantity and that the default loss rate (LGD) is the expected value of a random variable, independent of the variable L.

Unexpected loss

After defining the expected loss of an open position, it is also necessary to define the unexpected loss. *Unexpected loss* means a loss on a financial instrument that was not foreseen by the creditor. To prevent such losses, the creditor must set aside some capital in addition to the intended losses to cover the unexpected losses. Let us denote the loss severity as SEV. Assuming that $\mathbb{E}[SEV] = LGD$, we can define the unexpected loss as the standard deviation of the loss variable $\tilde{L}$, or

$$UL = \sqrt{Var(\tilde{L})} = \sqrt{Var(EAD \cdot SEV \cdot L)}. \tag{10.4}$$

Under appropriate hypotheses, the following result exists.

Proposition 10.1. *If the severity and the default event are uncorrelated, then the unexpected loss variable is given by:*

$$UL = EAD \cdot \sqrt{Var(SEV) \cdot DP + (DP \cdot (1 - DP) \cdot LGD)^2}.$$

Proof. Recalling that the variance of a random variable X is $Var(X) = \mathbb{E}[X^2] - (\mathbb{E}[X])^2$, we explicitly calculate the variance of the variable $\tilde{L}$.

$$\begin{aligned}
Var(\tilde{L}) &= Var(EAD \cdot SEV \cdot L) = EAD^2 \cdot Var(SEV \cdot L) \\
&= EAD^2 \cdot (\mathbb{E}[SEV]^2 \cdot Var(L) + \mathbb{E}[L]^2 \cdot Var(SEV) \\
&\quad + Var(SEV) \cdot Var(L)) \\
&= EAD^2 \cdot (LGD^2 \cdot DP \cdot (1 - DP) + DP^2 \cdot Var(SEV) \\
&\quad + Var(SEV) \cdot DP \cdot (1 - DP)) \\
&= EAD^2 \cdot Var(SEV) \cdot (DP^2 + DP \cdot (1 - DP)) \\
&\quad + EAD^2 \cdot LGD^2 \cdot DP \cdot (1 - DP) \\
&= EAD^2 \cdot (Var(SEV) \cdot DP + LGD^2 \cdot DP \cdot (1 - DP)),
\end{aligned}$$

where we used the following results in the order:

- $Var(aX) = a^2 Var(X) \qquad (a \in \mathbb{R})$;
- $Var(L) = DP(1 - DP)$;
- If X and Y are independent random variables then

$$\begin{aligned}
Var(XY) = \mathbb{E}[X]^2 \cdot Var(Y) + \mathbb{E}[Y]^2 \cdot Var(X) \\
+ Var(X) \cdot Var(Y).
\end{aligned}$$

By extracting the root, the assertion is obtained. ■

We observe that the hypothesis of the proposition is almost always unrealistic. In fact, it is not unlikely that on average the recovery rate will decrease as economic conditions worsen.

So far we have defined the expected and unexpected losses related to a single open position. Now, let us move on to define the expected and unexpected loss variables of a loan portfolio.

10.4 Portfolio Loss

Let us consider a portfolio of m credits. Define the variable of loss on the single open position as

$$\tilde{L}_i = EAD_i \cdot SEV_i \cdot L_i,$$

with $L_i = 1$ and $P(D_i) = DP_i$, we define the *portfolio loss variable* as follows

$$\tilde{L}_{PF} = \sum_{i=1}^{m} L_i = \sum_{i=1}^{m} (EAD_i \cdot SEV \cdot L_i).$$

Also for the loss portfolio, we can define the expected loss and the unexpected loss. The variable is called an *expected loss of a portfolio*

$$EL_{PF} = \mathbb{E}[\tilde{L}_{PF}] = \sum_{i=1}^{m} \mathbb{E}[\tilde{L}_i] = \sum_{i=1}^{m} (EAD_i \cdot LGD_i \cdot DP_i),$$

where we exploited the linearity of the expected value. While the *unexpected loss of a portfolio* is

$$UL_{PF} = \sqrt{Var(\tilde{L}_{PF})}$$

$$= \sqrt{\sum_{i=1}^{m}\sum_{j=1}^{m} EAD_i \cdot EAD_j \cdot Cov(SEV_i \cdot L_i, SEV_j \cdot L_j)}.$$

Also in this case there is a result similar to that seen previously.

Proposition 10.2. *For a portfolio with constant severities, we have*

$$UL_{PF}^2 = \sum_{i,j=1}^{m} EAD_i \cdot EAD_j \cdot LGD_i \cdot LGD_j \cdot \sqrt{DP_i \cdot (1 - DP_i) \cdot DP_j \cdot (1 - DP_j)} \cdot \rho_{ij},$$

where $\rho_{ij} = Corr(L_i, L_j) = Corr(1_{D_i}, 1_{D_j})$ *is the default correlation between counterparties* i *and* j.

Proof. We actually just have to prove that

$$Cov(SEV_i \cdot L_i, SEV_j \cdot L_j) = LGD_i \cdot LGD_j \cdot \sqrt{DP_i \cdot (1 - DP_i) \cdot DP_j \cdot (1 - DP_j)} \cdot \rho_{ij}.$$

For simplicity of notation, let us set

$$\sigma_{ij} = Cov(SEV_i \cdot L_i, SEV_j \cdot L_j).$$

Recalling that the covariance of two random variables X, Y is by definition

$$Cov(X, Y) = \mathbb{E}\left[(X - \mathbb{E}[X])(Y - \mathbb{E}[Y])\right]$$

and remember that the correlation coefficient is

$$\rho = \frac{Cov(X, Y)}{\sqrt{Var(X) \cdot Var(Y)}},$$

we have

$$\begin{aligned}
\sigma_{ij} &= \mathbb{E}\left[(SEV_i \cdot L_i - \mathbb{E}[SEV_i \cdot L_i])(SEV_j \cdot L_j - \mathbb{E}[SEV_j \cdot L_j])\right] \\
&= \mathbb{E}\left[(SEV_i \cdot L_i - SEV_i \cdot \mathbb{E}[L_i])(SEV_j \cdot L_j - SEV_j \cdot \mathbb{E}[L_j])\right] \\
&= \mathbb{E}\left[(SEV_i(L_i - \mathbb{E}[L_i])(SEV_j(L_j - \mathbb{E}[L_j])\right] \\
&= SEV_i \cdot SEV_j \cdot Cov(L_i, L_j) \\
&= SEV_i \cdot SEV_j \cdot \sqrt{Var(L_i) \cdot Var(L_j)} \cdot \frac{Cov(L_i, L_j)}{\sqrt{Var(L_i) \cdot Var(L_j)}} \\
&= LGD_i \cdot LGD_j \cdot \rho_{ij},
\end{aligned}$$

where we used the fact that $SEV_i = \mathbb{E}[SEV_i] = LGD_i$.

■

Let us interpret this result. For simplicity, we assume that our portfolio consists of only two credits with $LGD = 100\%$ and $EAD = 1$. Denoting by $p_i = DP_i$, based on the previous proposition, we know that

$$UL_{PF}^2 = p_1(1-p_1) + p_2(1-p_2) + 2\rho\sqrt{(p_1(1-p_1)}\sqrt{p_2(1-p_2)}.$$

Let us examine the three possible cases:

i) $\rho = 0$. In this case the previous relation becomes

$$UL_{PF}^2 = p_1(1-p_1) + p_2(1-p_2).$$

ii) $\rho > 0$. In this case, the two counterparties are positively correlated, which is why if one counterparty defaults, the other also has a high probability of default. To justify what has been said, we calculate the probability that the second counterparty goes into default conditional on the event that the first counterparty goes into default. We have

$$\mathbb{P}(L_2 = 1 | L_1 = 1) = \frac{\mathbb{P}(L_2 = 1, L_1 = 1)}{\mathbb{P}(L_1 = 1)}$$

$$= \frac{\mathbb{E}[L_1 L_2]}{\rho_1} = \mathbb{E}[L_1]\mathbb{E}[L_2] + \frac{Cov(L_1, L_2)}{p_1} = p_1 p_2 + \frac{Cov(L_1, L_2)}{p_1}$$

$$= p_2 + \frac{Cov(L_1, L_2)}{p_1} > p_2,$$

where $Cov(L_1, L_2) > 0$. So if $\rho > 0$, the two counterparties follow the same direction. The extreme case is $\rho = 1$; in this case, the riskiness of the portfolio is maximum.
Another interesting case is $p_1 = p_2 = p$. We have

$$UL = 2\sqrt{p(1-p)},$$

that is, the riskiness of the portfolio is exactly twice the riskiness of a single counterparty.

iii) $\rho < 0$. In this case, the two counterparties are negatively correlated, which means that they follow opposite directions. To realize this, we calculate conditional probability. We have

$$\mathbb{P}(L_2 = 1|L_1 = 1) = \frac{\mathbb{P}(L_2 = 1, L_1 = 1)}{\mathbb{P}(L_1 = 1)} = \frac{\mathbb{E}[L_1 L_2]}{p_1}$$

$$= \mathbb{E}[L_1]\mathbb{E}[L_2] + \frac{Cov(L_1, L_2)}{\rho_1} = p_1 p_2 + \frac{Cov(L_1, L_2)}{p_1}$$

$$= p_2 + \frac{Cov(L_1, L_2)}{p_1} < p_2,$$

being the $Cov(L_1, L_2) < 0$. [Preisser and Qaqish (2014)] present the limit to the lower default correlation value as follows, supposing there exists a single value for any pair of borrowers

$$\rho \geq -\frac{1}{n-1},$$

where n is the number of borrowers in the loan portfolio in our case. Extreme case is $\rho = -1$. This is the case with *perfect coverage.*
We remind the reader that hedging means an operation that eliminates or reduces the portfolio risk. This is the case with *perfect diversification.* Recall that diversifying a portfolio means reducing the risk by investing in those assets that have independent or negatively correlated returns.

10.5 Economic Capital

Risk capital refers to the risk that an investor will lose all or a part of the invested capital. One of the most common ways of quantifying venture capital is *economic capital.* It is precisely a measure of the amount of capital necessary to face the losses resulting from a given risk portfolio and can be defined as follows

$$EC_\alpha = q_\alpha - EL_{PF},$$

where q_α denotes the α quantile and α is a predefined confidence level of $\tilde{L}_{PF}$, i.e.

$$q_\alpha = \inf\{q > 0|\mathbb{P}(\tilde{L}_{PF} \leq q) \geq \alpha\}.$$

From the given definition, we deduce that the economic capital depends on the quantile and the expected loss of the portfolio (recall Figure 5.1). This is a possible definition of economic capital; in fact, there is another which is based on the *Expected Shortfall.* But before defining the Expected Shortfall, it is worth remembering the definition of *Value-at-Risk (VaR).*

Definition 10.1. Given a probability measure $\mathbb{P}$ and a confidence level α, *Value-at-Risk (VaR)* is defined as the order quantile α of the loss variable X, i.e.

$$VaR_\alpha(X) = inf\{x \geq 0 \mid \mathbb{P}(X \leq x) \geq \alpha\}. \tag{10.5}$$

VaR is a risk measure defined on L^∞ invariant for translation, positively homogeneous, monotonous, but not sub-additive; therefore, it is a non-coherent risk measure. [Artzner *et al.* (1999)] introduced the requirements for a risk measure to be *coherent*. Through the VaR, we are now able to define the Expected Shortfall.

Definition 10.2. The *Expected Shortfall (ES)*, or *Tail Conditional Expectation (TCE)*, or Tail VaR (TVaR), with confidence level α is a measure of risk that describes the magnitude of the potential losses of a portfolio if they exceed the VaR and is defined as follows

$$TCE_\alpha(X) = \mathbb{E}[X \mid X \geq VaR_\alpha(X)]. \tag{10.6}$$

Indicated with $c = VaR_\alpha(X)$ the critical loss threshold, the economic capital (EC), based on the Expected Shortfall, can be defined as follows

$$EC_{TCE}(c) = \mathbb{E}[X \mid X \geq c] - \mathbb{E}[X].$$

The use of expected EL and unexpected UL loss concepts for the economic capital purpose may produce regulatory arbitrage opportunities of two types. First, the increase of the expected loss proportion may improve the capital ratio if the amount of capital before EL is above the gross risk amount, see Figure 10.4. Otherwise, a rise in EL implies a deterioration in the capital ratio. Second, the use of unlikely to pay UTP criteria enable to earlier recognize defaults. All else being equal, this also improves the capital ratio for a bank running A-IRB. However, the same UTP use yields more conservative credit risk estimates for an F-IRB bank, see Figures 10.5 and 10.6.

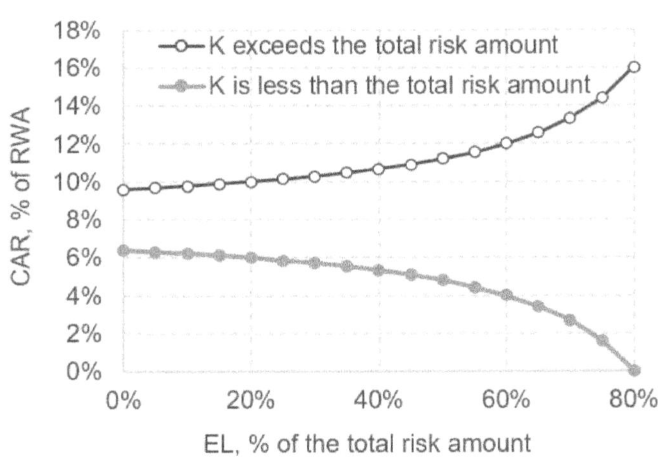

Fig. 10.4: Regulatory Arbitrage from EL portion of gross risk manipulation. *Source: [Penikas (2020a)].*

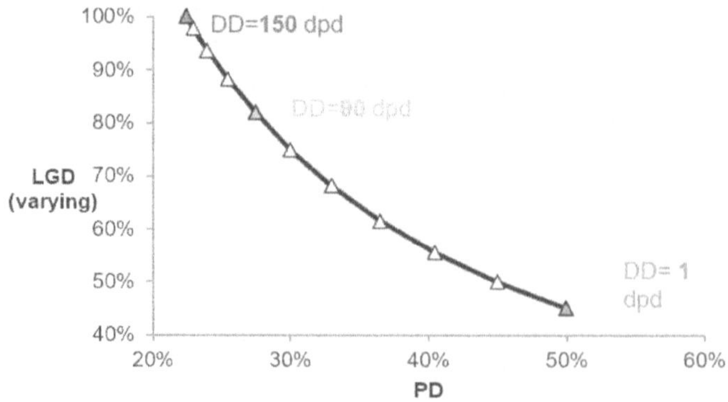

Fig. 10.5: *PD-LGD* dependence for different default definitions subject to *UTP*.
Source: [Penikas (2020a)]

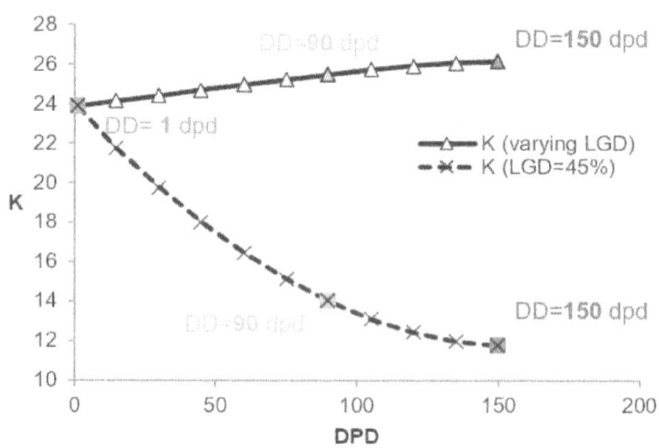

Fig. 10.6: Regulatory Arbitrage from different default definitions because of *UTP*.
Source: [Penikas (2020a)]

Chapter 11

Model Validation and Audit

The Basel Committee has released recommendations on how to validate the IRB models right after Basel II adoption (see [BCBS (2005c)]). These recommendations cover PD, LGD, EAD properties validation. They involve the description of the applicable statistical procedures. However, there are no thresholds to decide whether a risk model is compliant or not. Another shortcoming is the absence of guidance regarding the validation of the predicted total (gross) risk. Below we present the most important findings to overcome the shortcomings of the published regulatory guidelines.

11.1 Validating Credit Risk Parameters

[BCBS (2005c)] suggests validating separate properties of the credit risk parameters (i.e. the PD, LGD and EAD) and they are:

- Discriminatory power;
- Accuracy or calibration;
- Stability.

For the different parameters, sometimes there are separate tests for the same property. First, we describe the basic tests and then discuss more evolved ones where applicable.

11.1.1 *Discriminatory Power*

11.1.1.1 *PD*

Discriminatory power shows how a model (a credit risk parameter) can distinguish opposite cases. For instance, a model on the *PD* performs well when separates, most of the time, good (reliable, creditworthy) borrowers from the bad ones. Therefore, each risk parameter can be validated for the presence of this feature.

The most common tool to validate a discriminatory power of a *PD* model is the Receiver Operating Curve (ROC) and the area underneath (AUROC). Its widespread alternative is a Gini coefficient or a Cumulative Accuracy Profile (CAP).

We focus on the ROC because of its popularity. The ROC is built in the dimensions of the Hit Rate (HR) and false alarm rate (FR) defined as follows

$$HR = \frac{H(C)}{N_D}, \quad FR = \frac{F(C)}{N_{ND}}, \tag{11.1}$$

where $H(C)$ is the number of correctly predicted defaults subject to a cut-off C; $F(C)$ is the number of incorrectly predicted defaults given the same cut-off; N is the total number of defaults D and non-defaults ND.

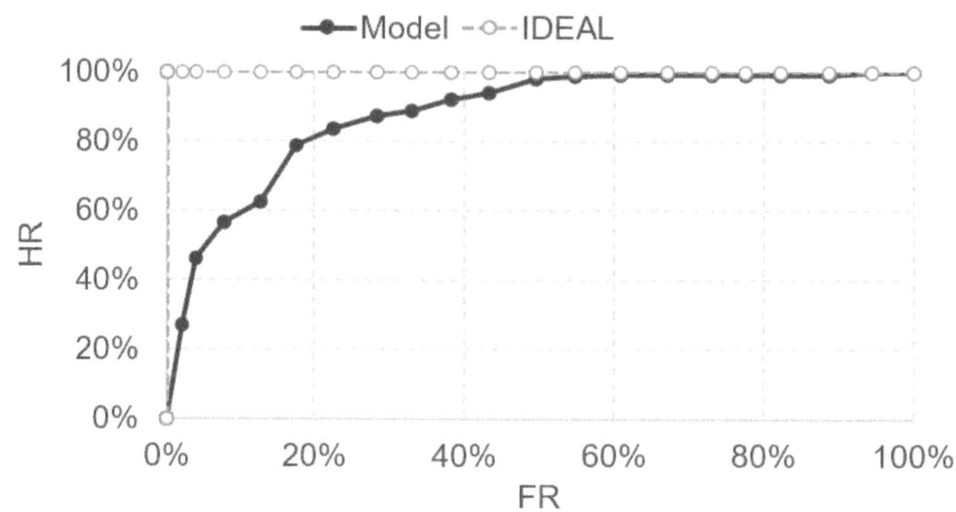

Fig. 11.1: Receiver Operating Curve (ROC).
$AUROC = 90\%$, equivalent to 75% correlation of actual and predicted PD.

Thus, simplistically, to build a ROC curve we run the cut-off values from $PD = 0\%$ to $PD = 100\%$. The surface under the curve reflects the discriminatory power of a parameter of interest. The larger it is, the higher the discriminatory power is, the better a parameter (a model) differentiates observations from good to bad. However, for validation purposes, the Accuracy Ratio, *AR*, is more often used instead of the area under the curve (AUROC), though they have the following linear relationship

$$AR = (2 \cdot AUROC) - 1. \tag{11.2}$$

The following thresholds may be recommended to assess whether the PD model well discriminates the borrowers. Here the retail models are broken down into two classes by the history of the relationship with a given client. A PD model is called *applicative* when it assesses the credit risk when the client just started operating with the bank. Conventionally, such models are used for the first *three months* after granting the first loan. In case the operational history with a client is not that scarce, then a *behavioral* model is used. When the bank has lots of data, a validator expects the model to better discriminate compared to an applicative PD model. That is why the acceptance criteria for a *behavioral* model are higher than for a *applicative* one.

Table 11.1: PD discriminatory power validation thresholds for AR, in %.

	Corporates	Retail - Behavioral	Retail - Applicative
Development Stage			
Good	60 - 100	70 - 100	60 - 100
Satisfactory	40 - 60	50 - 70	40 - 60
Bad	0 - 40	0 - 50	0 - 40
Validation Stage			
Good	50 - 100	60 - 100	50 - 100
Satisfactory	40 - 50	40 - 60	35 - 50
Bad	0 - 40	0 - 40	0 - 35

Source: [Bank of Russia (2012)]

However, thresholds from Table 11.1 should be taken with caution. The AR is by itself a random variable. That is why there exists a confidence interval for each point estimate. If a mean point estimate falls into some category from the table, it may not be necessary that the entire confidence range belongs to the same category. For instance, [Engelmann *et al.* (2003)] uses the German data of 325k borrowers with 3k defaults. The default rate is around 1%. We may call it a low default portfolio (LDP). The nice thing is that the absolute number of defaults is large. The point estimate of the area under the ROC curve for the entire sample with the logit score equals 0.84. Its point estimate for a subsample with only 10 defaults is 0.855. That is well comparable and yields the AR of around 70%. Such a model seems to be *good*. However, the 95% confidence interval for the entire sample is [0.8278, 0.8526], whereas it is much wider for the subsample and equals to [0.7317, 0.9777]. The lower boundary for a subsample of 0.7317 corresponds to the AR of around 45%. Such a model has a better *satisfactory* discriminatory power. At worst, if it was a retail behavioral model, it would fail at the development stage.

There is an alternative procedure to the PD discriminative power validation. It is known as the *Weight of Evidence (WoE)*. The concept is to decompose all the data into several m buckets by values of the indicator which discriminatory power is going to be validated. For instance, that might be PD buckets or the ones for particular default driver X. For each bucket j is calculated by the number of defaults n_j^D and non-defaults n_j^{ND}, where the total numbers of defaults and non-defaults equal N^D and N^{ND}, respectively. Then the weight-of-evidence for a given bucket j is as follows

$$WoE_j = ln\left(\frac{n_j^{ND}}{N^{ND}} \cdot \frac{n_j^D}{N^D}\right). \tag{11.3}$$

Then, the *Information Value (IV)* is obtained as an alternative benchmark for the PD discriminatory power as follows

$$IV = \sum_{j=1}^{m}\left(WoE_j \cdot \left(\frac{n_j^{ND}}{N^{ND}} - \frac{n_j^D}{N^D}\right)\right). \tag{11.4}$$

The following thresholds may be applicable to validate the PD discriminatory power using the WoE and IV.

Table 11.2: PD Discriminatory power validation thresholds for IV, in %.

	IV
Suspiciously Good	50 - 100
Good	30 - 50
Satisfactory	10 - 30
Bad	2 - 10
Useless	0 - 2

Source: [Upadhyay (2014)]

When validating the discriminatory power of a PD model, one should consider the recent trend of developing a non-discriminative (fair, ethical) PD model. The origins date back to cases when people of a certain race either did not get loans or were offered exorbitantly high ones. Then there came a movement for the models to be fair. This means that the models should not yield any preferences when accepting loan applications. The natural solution is not to feed a model with data on discriminatory features (e.g. race, age). This is an *unawareness* requirement. However, it turns out that often the key default determinants like income are highly correlated to race, age, etc. as [Fuster *et al.* (2018)] shows. That is why merely excluding the discriminating data is not a solution.

[Szepannek and Luebke (2021)] offer an alternative. First, they explain that a PD (scoring) model is fair if it does not change the PD prediction subject to changing the discriminatory indicator value, i.e.

$$PD(X, P = 0) = PD(X, P = 1) \tag{11.5}$$

should hold, where P is the indicator that may cause discrimination and X are all the other non-discriminatory variables. Then, [Szepannek and Luebke (2021)] suggests building a model in two steps. First, derive the L^* as the residual from the regression of L on the discriminatory factors P, where L is the default indicator.

Thus, we obtain the values uncorrelated to the discriminatory factors P. Second, develop a PD model with the dependent variable L^*, and not L. Then the resultant PD model may be considered fair and satisfying Eq. (11.5).

11.1.1.2 *LGD*

When validating the discriminatory power of an LGD model, there is an equivalent procedure to the AR for PD models. It is called *Cumulative LGD Accuracy Ratio* (CLAR). Its idea is to compare the prediction accuracy by LGD buckets. The number of such buckets is chosen heuristically. This resembles the approach of *WoE*. For instance, we use 20 in Figure 11.2. As one can see, the $CLAR$ curve is de facto a Lorenz curve used for income inequality measurement.

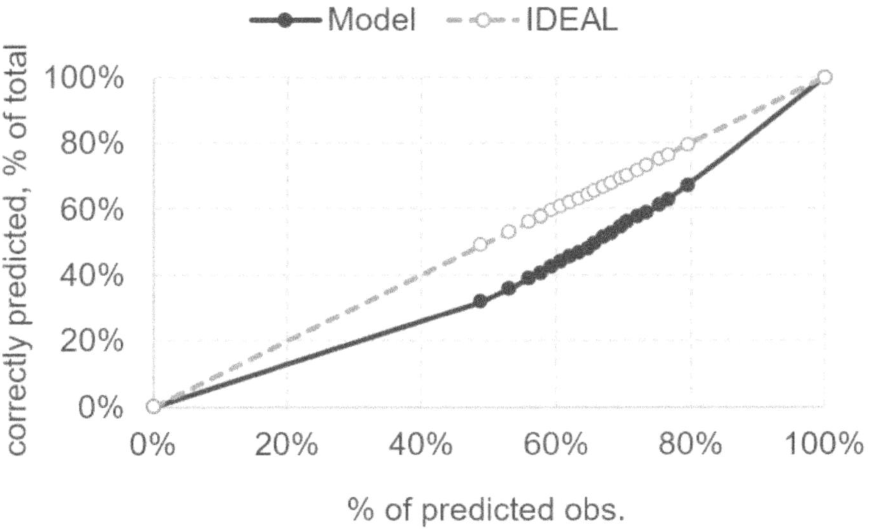

Fig. 11.2: CLAR curve.
CLAR = 75%, equivalent to 50% correlation of actual and predicted LGD.

We agree with the following $CLAR$ thresholds from [Maarse (2012)] when validating the LGD discriminatory power, see Table 11.3.

Table 11.3: LGD discriminatory power validation thresholds for $CLAR$, in %.

	CLAR
Good	75 - 100
Satisfactory	60 - 75
Bad	50 - 60

Source: [Maarse (2012), pp. 53, 76-77]

11.1.2 *Accuracy (Calibration)*

11.1.2.1 *General: Anchor Point (AP) Test*

Calibration means that the model should yield credit risk parameter prediction comparable to the historical values, or the central tendency (CT). One may notice that there might be two approaches to CT computation: the mean of all fractions in CT_1 or the fraction of two sums in CT_2,

$$CT_1 = \frac{1}{T}\sum_{t=1}^{T}\left(\frac{n_t^D}{N_{t-1}}\right) \tag{11.6}$$

$$CT_2 = \frac{\sum_{t=1}^{T}(n_t^D)}{\sum_{t=1}^{T}(N_{t-1})} \tag{11.7}$$

Consider the following Table 11.4 to illustrate the differences in two approaches to CT calculation, where $DR = \frac{n_t^D}{N_{t-1}}$. We have the data on defaults for actually two time slots: for $t = 2$ and $t = 3$. There are two trends in this portfolio. First, there is a rise in default rate DR. Second, the entire lending expands and the number of borrowers N_t grows. In such a case, mean of $DR_2 = 15\%$ and $DR_3 = 20\%$ yields a $CT_1 = 16\%$ in accordance to Eq. (11.6). However, the alternative approach yields a more conservative estimate of $CT_2 = 18\%$ according to Eq. (11.7). From the conservative perspective, a validator is advised to look at the default rate trends and choose which central tendency definition is to be applied to aim at obtaining a more conservative estimate.

Table 11.4: Comparing approaches to central tendency calculation.

t	N_t	N_{t-1}	n_t^D	DR
1	100			10%
2	200	100	15	15%
3	400	200	40	20%
sum		300	55	

When a validator has a CT estimate, it is possible to run a general heuristic calibration test for any parameter. It is called an *anchor point (AP)* test. It compares the portfolio-level credit risk parameter prediction to the central tendency. The model may be evaluated according to the thresholds from Table 11.5.

11.1.2.2 *PD*

There are several procedures suggested to validate the PD model calibration. They can be grouped into two classes:

Table 11.5: *LGD* discriminatory power validation thresholds for *CLAR*, in %.

	AP, % of CT
Good	80 - 120
Satisfactory	70 - 80 & 120 - 130
Bad	below 70 & above 130

- Procedures in the *absence* of default correlation;
- Procedures in the *presence* of default correlation.

When there is no default correlation, we would consider the *Hosmer–Lemeshow test* and the *binomial test*, or normal approximation, out of the many procedures described by the Basel Committee original validation guidelines in [BCBS (2005c)].

The Hosmer–Lemeshow test in essence is similar to the Weight-of-Evidence (WoE) concept discussed above. It also needs data decomposition by groups, for instance, by rating grades g ranging from 1 to G. It is more appealing than WoE as it has an asymptotic chi-squared distribution with G degrees of freedom. This means that the critical values for the test are statistically grounded and not subjectively chosen. However, those thresholds are applicable only when the assumptions of the test hold true. Primarily, it is the absence of the default correlation that is unlikely to be absent in real life. However, the formal formula for the test is the following:

$$\chi^2_{HL} = \sum_{g=1}^{G} N_g \cdot \frac{(y_g - PD_g)^2}{PD_g \cdot (1 - PD_g)} \sim \chi^2(g), \tag{11.8}$$

where y_g is the actual proportion of defaults in grade g and PD_g is the predicted proportion; N_g is the total number of borrowers in grade g.

The Hosmer–Lemeshow test validates the null hypothesis that the actual proportion of defaults is equal to the predicted one grade-wise against the alternative hypothesis that there is at least a grade where the actual and forecasted proportions are statistically significantly unequal.

The binomial test relies on the following formula:

$$DR_0 - N^{-1}_{1-\alpha/2} \cdot Var_{DR} \leq \widetilde{DR} \leq DR_0 + N^{-1}_{1-\alpha/2} \cdot Var_{DR}, \tag{11.9}$$

where the Var_{DR} is the default rate variance for the independent Bernoulli trials and equals to

$$Var_{DR} = \frac{DR_0 \cdot (1 - DR_0)}{n}, \tag{11.10}$$

n is the number of borrowers in the portfolio; N^{-1}_u is the u-quantile of the standard Normal distribution.

The test idea is quite natural. If there is a series of independent Bernoulli trials (defaults), the default rate distribution takes the Gaussian bell-shaped form. Then the precise $\widetilde{DR}$ is the one that falls into the α confidence interval of the Normal distribution around the value of the central tendency DR_0.

However, the general normal approximation has deficiencies described by [Brown *et al.* (2001)] in detail. That is why [EBA (2019b)] suggests using a Jeffreys interval of the form:

$$Beta(a,b)_{\alpha/2} \leq \widetilde{DR} \leq Beta(a,b)_{1-\alpha/2}, \tag{11.11}$$

where $a = n \cdot DR + 1/2$ and $b = n - n \cdot DR + 1/2$.

Disregarding the fact that Jeffreys' confidence interval is more accurate, it is limited to the case of independent defaults. When defaults are correlated, the Basel Committee recommends adjusting the *binomial test* for correlation. Two options naturally come to mind. The first option is to substitute variance Var_{DR} for independent defaults in Eq. (11.10) with the variance for the correlated defaults from Eq. (1.2). Naturally, a higher default correlation implies a rise in default rate variance. Hence, one may expect the expansion (widening) of the confidence intervals for the PD model calibration validation. The second option is conceptually similar. It derives the quantile from the Vasicek-based IRB model, see [Blochwitz *et al.* (2006), p. 295]. It yields the same in essence output, i.e. the widening confidence interval when the default correlation rises. However, this is a wrong way of thinking.

Let us recall the default rate DR dynamics in the United States in the last 40 years from Figure 0.1. The corresponding DR distribution is given in Figure 11.3. We vividly see that a DR rate distribution is bimodal. Bimodal distributions were already discussed in the literature, see, for instance, [Witt (2014)]. However, only in [Borzykh and Penikas (2021)] its implications were examined for the PD calibration validation.

When a distribution is bimodal, the probability mass concentrates around the modes, and not the mean. Then the optimal confidence interval is not the widest, but the one consisting of two parts. [Borzykh and Penikas (2021)] call it "*twin confidence intervals*". For illustration consider Table 11.6.

Notice that ρ is the default correlation; *Jeffreys* is the interval taken from [Brown *et al.* (2001)]; $BTWC$ stands for the binomial test with correlation from [Blochwitz *et al.* (2006)]; *Twin CIs* is the approach from [Borzykh and Penikas (2021)]; *left* and *right* and are the respective boundaries of the confidence interval.

11.1.3 *Stability*

11.1.3.1 *General*

The idea behind validating the credit risk parameter stability is that the distribution of parameters should not change much when time goes by. However, we one has to admit that such a requirement might hold true if the macroeconomic environment is

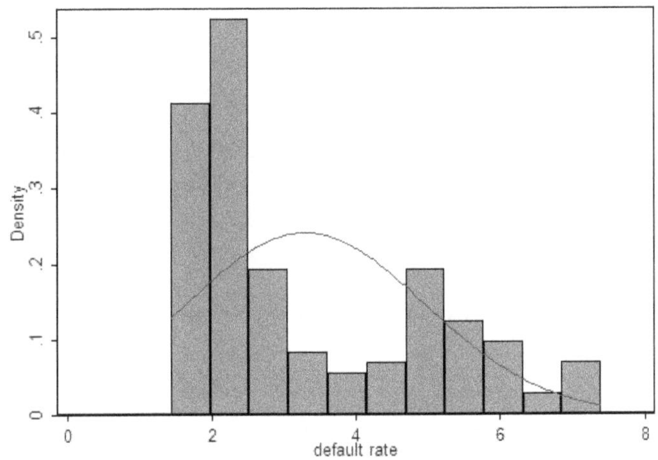

Fig. 11.3: The DR distribution for the American data of all loans for 1985-2021. *Source:* `https://www.federalreserve.gov/releases/chargeoff/delallsa.htm`

Table 11.6: Confidence Intervals (CIs) comparison for PD calibration validation for $PD = 20\%$ and $\alpha = 5\%$.

Approach	ρ	Coverage	CI length	left 1	right 1	left 2	right 2
Jeffreys	0%	92.3%	27.9%	8.8%	36.7%		
BTWC	80%	84.2%	88.7%	0.0%	88.7%		
BTWC	30%	81.1%	32.8%	6.7%	39.5%		
BTWC	0%	15.8%	0.0%	20.0%	20.0%		
BTWC	-3%	28.0%	3.3%	18.4%	21.7%		
Twin CIs	80%	95.8%	20.0%	0.0%	10.0%	90.0%	100.0%
Twin CIs	30%	95.9%	40.0%	4.0%	24.0%	40.0%	60.0%
Twin CIs	0%	97.2%	33.0%	7.0%	40.0%		
Twin CIs	-3%	97.2%	24.0%	10.0%	34.0%		

stable (e.g. we are not in pandemics of 2020-2021) and neither the bank strategy nor its credit policy changes with time. Nevertheless, the Basel Committee in [BCBS (2005c)] recommends validating stability. The general approach, in this case, is to use the weight of evidence and information value criteria already described in Eqs. (11.3) and (11.4) with two changes. First, we build buckets not over the X parameter values, but over time t. This yields us a slightly modified formula in Eq. (11.12).

$$IV = \sum_{t=1}^{T} \left(WoE_t \times \left(\frac{n_t^{ND}}{N^{ND}} - \frac{n_t^{D}}{N^{D}} \right) \right), \tag{11.12}$$

where WOE_t is defined in (11.3) by substituting j with t.

Second, we treat the threshold values from Table 11.2 in the opposite way. What was good before, i.e. was well discriminating, becomes bad because it is different, i.e. not stable when applied to the time dimension. Thus, we propose the following values.

Table 11.7: Stability validation thresholds for IV, in %.

	IV
Useless	50 - 100
Bad	30 - 50
Satisfactory	10 - 30
Good	2 - 10
Suspiciously Good	0 - 2

Source: [Upadhyay (2014)], authors' interpretation

11.1.3.2 *Rating Grade Concentration*

Concerning the developed master scale, there might be another view on stability. The idea is that the borrowers should be more or less equally distributed along with the rating classes. As the reader may recall from the discussion on rating philosophy in Section 8.2, given the same credit policy, the ranking of borrowers may not change with time because the ranking is a relative category of comparison. That is why the Basel Committee requires a bank to have a dispersed distribution of borrowers by rating grades or equally avoid their grade concentration. The most widespread measure of concentration is the Herfindahl-Hirshman Index (HHI) from Eq. (11.13).

$$HHI = \left(\sum_{i=1}^{I} \left(\frac{N_i}{\sum_{i=1}^{I} N_i} \right)^2 \right) \cdot 100\%, \tag{11.13}$$

where N_i is the number of borrowers in rating grade i. When validating an IRB rating system, the following thresholds with respect to HHI are conventionally applied as in Table 11.8.

However, the presented HHI thresholds might be easily manipulated. If a bank extends the number of grades, the grade concentration declines, see Figure 11.4. [Penikas (2020d)] discusses the probable origins of 20% and 30% limit values. The major corollary from this observation is that the HHI thresholds should be dynamic

Table 11.8: Grade concentration validation thresholds for HHI.

	HHI, %
Good	below 20
Satisfactory	20 - 30
Bad	above 30

and be linked to the number of grades. For instance, if there are 25 grades, the *good* category requires at most $HHI \leq 10\%$ (look at the TTC curve plus a 5% mark-up), and not $HHI \leq 20\%$.

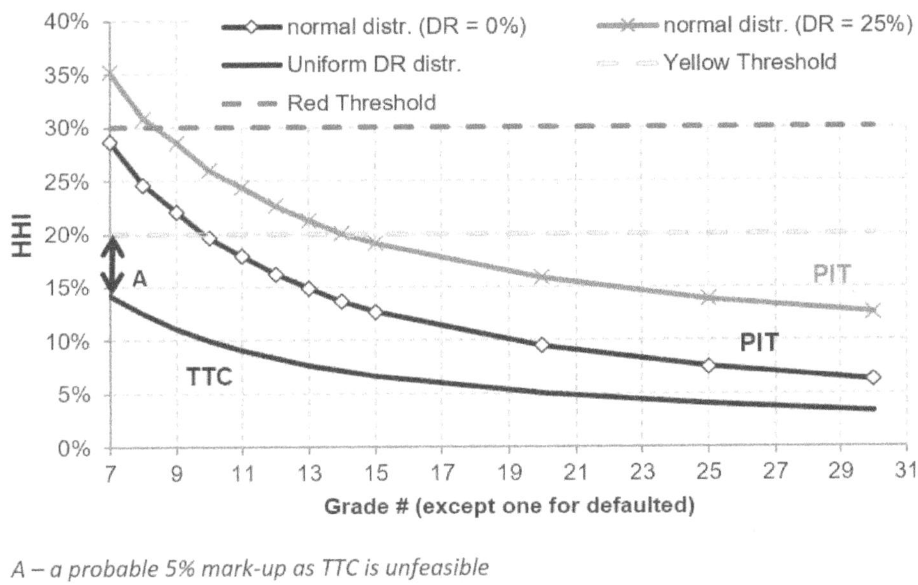

Fig. 11.4: Grade concentration thresholds by HHI.
Source: [Penikas (2020d)]

11.2 Back-Testing Gross Risk

A validator might have well verified separate credit risk model parameters using the approach described above. However, this may occur to be insufficient for the stability of a bank. In the end, the bank is interested in obtaining correct loss prediction which is not limited to the correct prediction of PD, LGD and EAD taken separately. The conventional way to assure the risk is correctly predicted is to run back-testing. However, here comes a challenge. In the above, we discussed the concepts of the expected and unexpected losses. In reality, we are not aware which type of loss had occurred: was it an expected, or an unexpected one. Sometimes, a bank provisions for both types. The expected loss is directly deducted from the capital numerator in the capital ratio and the unexpected ones are considered in its denominator. Thus, a natural approach to back-testing gross (total) risk is to compare the total actual losses to the sum of the predicted expected and unexpected ones.

Even when the validator has assured himself that not only credit risk parameters and the total risk are of adequate (*good*) quality in terms of discriminatory power, calibration and stability, there is still a potential hurdle to the bank's stability. We may call it a model risk. These problems are particularly important for a bank running IRB approach. When the PD models are not perfectly discriminating (what is always the case in real life), there are the envisaged defaults or borrowers mostly prone to it and actual (unforeseen) defaults. Ideally, we might have wished to offset actual losses by capital provisioned for the predicted defaults. But this is impossible. By trusting the developed models, the capital is locked with the model predictions. Actual defaults bring *extra* losses. That is the source of earlier unforeseen model risk in credit risk management. Table 11.9 provides a validator with the proxy. It has model risk add-ons to total risk depending on the discriminatory power in PD and LGD models as well as the list of probable calibration indicators. Its positive values of $+5$ stand for the more conservative models, whereas the negative ones of -5 are for more optimistic ones. These values are differences in percentage points to the central tendencies in PD (in rows) and LGD (in columns). Calibration indicators are brought here to show that even conservative models underestimate total risk when the discriminatory power is good, but not perfect. For instance, take a PD model with $AUROC = 75\%$ and LGD with $CLAR = 75\%$. Let both models have a conservative margin (calibration) of $+5$ pp. Still, the actual risk underestimation is 11.3% of the total predicted risks (see value in bold in Table 11.9). We may even see that conservative margin in PD increases distortions in risk assessment (compare the rows with PD calibration +5% pp. against 0% or -5%).

Table 11.9: Model risk add-ons in percentage points of the IRB gross risk for PLC = 50%.

PD \LGD	CLAR, pp.	99			91			81			**75**			71		
AUROC, pp.	Calibration, pp.	+5	0	-5	+5	0	-5	+5	0	-5	**+5**	0	-5	+5	0	-5
100	+5	0.0	0.2	1.3	0.0	1.9	3.3	5.1	8.8	5.5	15.1	14.9	15.3	10.7	18.4	21.8
	0	0.0	0.1	1.1	0.1	3.2	2.8	7.6	9.0	8.8	12.3	18.1	21.7	14.3	13.8	25.1
	-5	0.0	0.1	1.1	0.0	2.2	1.8	7.4	7.4	9.5	15.6	9.2	11.9	13.5	18.4	18.1
88	+5	0.0	0.7	2.0	0.7	1.5	2.4	7.7	13.7	12.8	12.6	13.6	17.4	15.1	18.0	16.2
	0	0.0	0.8	2.2	1.2	2.3	3.7	6.6	9.0	11.7	13.7	11.3	13.5	17.9	16.3	22.1
	-5	0.0	0.8	2.2	0.0	4.1	4.2	5.3	11.5	10.8	12.2	14.7	11.3	16.7	12.1	15.5
75	**+5**	1.1	2.6	3.1	1.7	4.8	4.9	8.6	14.0	5.5	**11.3**	18.0	16.5	16.2	12.9	19.6
	0	1.5	2.7	3.5	2.0	4.2	5.9	8.0	10.8	13.2	12.4	12.8	12.1	18.7	16.3	17.1
	-5	0.6	2.6	2.9	3.6	3.0	6.6	8.4	10.1	13.4	18.8	21.3	15.7	20.7	15.6	20.0
64	+5	3.5	5.2	7.1	4.4	6.9	8.1	11.3	14.0	9.9	16.4	14.4	17.2	16.0	24.4	18.5
	0	2.3	4.2	5.3	2.4	3.6	4.8	13.8	12.1	13.9	15.4	14.5	16.3	12.2	18.1	31.1
	-5	2.6	3.8	5.1	5.7	4.1	7.5	10.8	9.1	13.7	16.5	22.1	16.0	18.6	16.0	22.3
50	+5	3.8	8.4	7.1	7.2	9.8	11.4	12.0	13.4	12.1	14.5	17.4	18.9	17.1	18.3	20.8
	0	5.6	7.0	8.4	4.4	8.3	10.5	18.3	13.3	11.0	18.1	18.8	17.1	21.6	14.1	16.5
	-5	6.8	7.0	8.5	7.6	7.9	10.1	9.3	12.1	16.9	14.5	19.5	18.6	20.6	23.9	23.4

11.3 Correlation

Practitioners can find here some useful suggestions relating to a key factor in developing accurate estimates of the expected losses. Correlations must be carefully handled because of lack of historical data, data quality, interpretation and instability.

To measure the risk associated with a portfolio of exposures, it is necessary to determine the associated correlation structure. For this purpose, we need to identify the joint cumulative distribution function of the default events, given the marginals.

In this fashion, a statistical tool important in credit risk modeling is the copula. An m-dimensional copula, or m-copula, is a multivariate distribution whose marginal distributions are standard uniform and m denotes obligors, assets or latent variables. For more details we invite the reader to refer to Section 3.5.

11.4 Lack of Data

Regarding the lack of data, a fairly simple approach would be recurring to the bootstrapping in combination with a GARCH(1,1) to preserve the volatility structure. A simple description can be found in [Deblauwe and Ha Le (1997)]. For example, in case we want to estimate the returns, the method consists in deriving the standardised residuals z_t, first, and scrambling them. Given the estimates for the parameters of the GARCH model, it is possible to recompute the returns while preserving the main volatility structure. After acquiring the returns, the correlations, as well as other statistics such as volatilities, kurtosis, etc., can be computed over different holding periods. Every series of log returns y_t can be modeled as

$$y_t := m + e_t$$

with m being the unconditional average and e_t is the residual at time t defined as

$$e_t := \sqrt{h_t} z_t \,,$$

where h_t follows a GARCH(1,1) process. From this, we may derive a formula for the standardised residuals.

11.5 Data Quality

The first two issues are connected and our suggestion is to adopt the following unified approach for computing the between- and within-netting group correlation coefficients while adjusting for the effect of an error factor Z. A suitable model for our purpose is the following multilevel regression model with random-effects (see [Ferrari (2005)]),

$$Y_{ij} := \alpha_j + \beta_{Wj}\left(X_{ij} - \bar{X}_j\right) + \beta_B \bar{X}_j + \gamma_W\left(Z_{ij} - \bar{Z}_j\right) + \gamma_B \bar{Z}_j + \epsilon_{ij}$$

with

$$\alpha_j := \alpha + u_{0j}\,, \text{ and } \beta_{Wj} = \beta_W + u_{1j}\,.$$

The index $j = 1, \ldots, J$ denotes a group variable, respectively, and $i = 1, \ldots, n_j$ are the individual measurements within group j. The variables $\bar{X}_j$, $\bar{Z}_j$ are the respective group means. Further, the term β_B reflects the between-group component of the association between Y and X, and the within-group component is denoted by β_{Wj}. It is decomposed in a random part u_{1j} and a fixed one β_W. Then, the variable α_j captures the individual group effects and can also be split into a random and fixed part, denoted by u_{0j} and α, respectively. Similar to β_B and β_W, γ_B and γ_W model the between- and the within-group effects for the individual and aggregate level of the confounding variables, $Z_{ij} - Z_j$ and Z_j. The variable ϵ_{ij} is an error term that is normally distributed with a standard deviation of σ_ϵ

$$\epsilon_{ij} \sim N(0, \sigma_\epsilon^2) \ .$$

The random effects u_{0j} and u_{1j} are also jointly normally distributed, i.e.

$$\begin{pmatrix} u_{0j} \\ u_{1j} \end{pmatrix} \sim N\left(\begin{pmatrix} 0 \\ 0 \end{pmatrix}, \begin{pmatrix} \sigma_B^2 & \sigma_{B,\beta_W} \\ \sigma_{B,\beta_W} & \sigma_{\beta_W}^2 \end{pmatrix}\right) ,$$

where σ_B^2 denotes the variance between groups, $\sigma_{\beta_W}^2$ reflects the variability across groups, and the corresponding covariance is σ_{B,β_W}.

11.6 Data Interpretation

Regarding data interpretation, as we deal with time series, it could be useful to warn the reader about Simpson's paradox in which a trend that appears in different groups of data disappears when these groups are combined, and the reverse trend appears for the aggregate data. The interested reader may also look for a reversal paradox and amalgamation paradox or the Yule–Simpson effect in [Wagner (1982)].

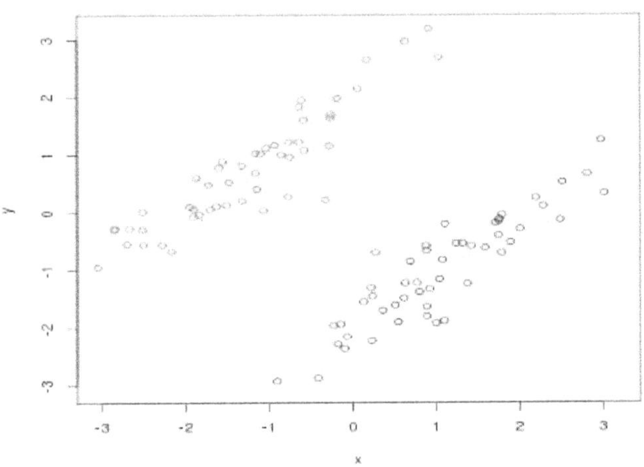

Fig. 11.5: Illustration of Simpson's paradox.
The correlation coefficient between x and y within each cluster is 0.9, but the overall correlation coefficient is zero. Source: [Marzban (2013)]

The reversal effect can arise when the common variable between data is time. For instance, in [Berman (2012)], a dataset is shown from which it seems that the demand is positively correlated with price (that is, higher prices induce more demand). From the analysis, it can be seen that time is the confounding variable. In fact, plotting both price and demand against time reveals the expected negative correlation over various periods, which then reverses to become positive if the influence of time is ignored by simply plotting demand against price.

11.7 Heteroskedasticity

It is well known that correlation coefficients are distorted due to the *heteroskedasticity* in the data. The two more widely used tests are the Breusch and Pagan and the White test, but they require a large data sample. For a small set of data, the Goldfeld-Quandt test can be used (cf. [Breusch and Pagan (1979)] and [White (1980)]).

A simple way to correct for heteroskedasticity is to apply the Weighted Least Squares (WLS) which produces unbiased and efficient estimates but it depends on knowing the variance structure (which must be known in advance or requires making some assumptions).

The alternative strategy can be used even when the form of the heteroskedasticity is unknown. It consists in retaining the ordinary least squares (OLS) (which is still unbiased, though not efficient) and the use of a Heteroskedasticity Consistent Covariance Matrix (HCCM) to estimate the standard errors of the estimates (which are robust standard errors) as below

$$\mathrm{HC}_1 = \frac{n-p}{n}\left(X^\top X\right)^{-1} X^\top \operatorname{diag}(e_i^2)\, X \left(X^\top X\right)^{-1}.$$

11.8 Tails

Because of long-tailed distributions of credit risk models, "the range of required capital corresponding to the choice of a target loss quantile within the 99.0 – 99.8 interval can be wider than the range corresponding to the 95.0 – 99.0 interval used in market risk models" (see [BCBS (1999)]). In terms of model validation, this implies that:

- The estimation error may be big;
- The shape of the distribution matters even more;
- Plausible, but alternative assumptions may lead to very different results.

PART 4
Counterparty Risk Modeling

Chapter 12

EAD Modeling

12.1 Counterparty Credit Risk for OTC Instruments

In [1] the course of the financial crisis starting in 2008, counterparty risk has become very important for participants on the global financial markets and in particular over-the-counter (OTC) derivatives have become instruments of interest since risks cannot be controlled by an exchange. Especially given the huge amount traded in the OTC derivatives market — there were notional amounts of \$ 633 trillion and gross market values of \$ 24.7 trln outstanding at the end of 2012 (cf. [BIS (2013)]). For comparison, the world nominal GDP in 2012 equaled to \$ 75 trln. Figure 12.1 presents the evolution of the total notional of all registered derivative contracts to the world GDP.

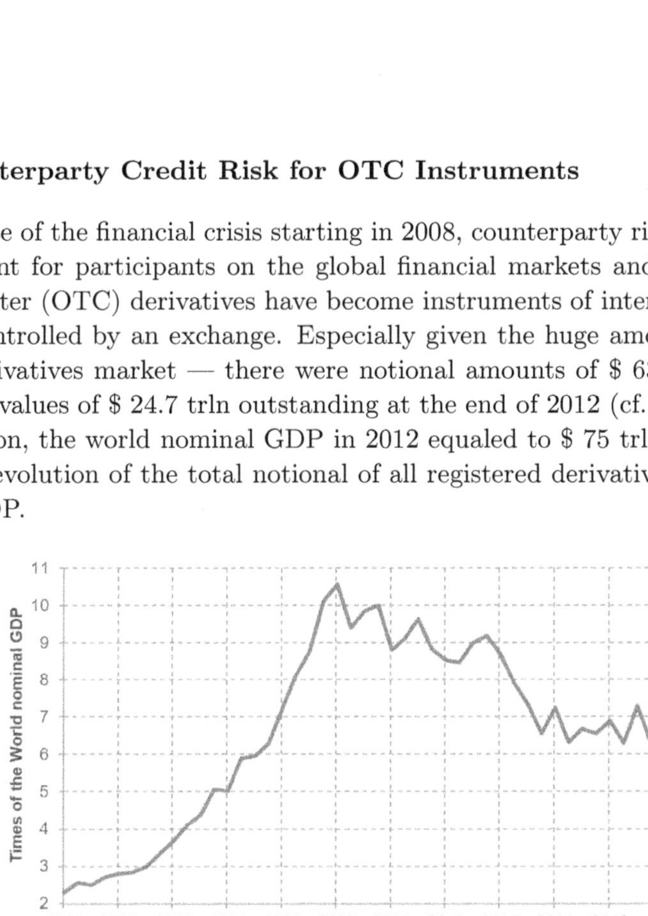

Fig. 12.1: On the eve of the 2007-2009 financial crisis the total notional amount of all registered derivative contracts exceeded the world nominal GDP ten times. Due to regulators' efforts it recently fell to around seven times.
Sources: [BIS (2020)].

[1]Part of this chapter has been published in [Orlando and Härtel (2014)].

Governments were driven to higher regulation of these financial instruments. Apart from the size, regulators' concerns are fueled by the systemic risk perspective. Counterparty risk was quite concentrated and post-Lehman data from the Office of the Comptroller of the Currency (OCC) highlighted that five U.S. banks (J.P. Morgan, Citi, Bank of America, Goldman Sachs and Morgan Stanley) were the major players in the derivatives market (cf. [Singh and Aitken (2009)]). Some of these initiatives for better regulation and monitoring are described in [BIS (2009)], but the most important regulatory requirement is that all OTC derivative contracts have to be reported to trade repositories (cf. [G20 State Leaders (2009)]). Besides regulatory changes, there has been a heavy impetus to trade all OTC derivatives with the help of collateralisation, higher margins, and central counterparties (CCP) as stated in [Singh (1999)].

This book describes a pragmatic approach to credit and counterparty risk where the first is defined by the Credit Valuation Adjustment (CVA) risk and the second is defined as the risk to each party of a contract that the counterparty will not fulfil its contractual obligations (cf. [Pykhtin and Zhu (2007)]). Only contracts which were privately negotiated between counterparties are subject to counterparty credit risk, hence OTC derivatives constitute the main focus describing counterparty risk. Of course, cash accounts, bonds or other instruments that were privately arranged also bear the risk of default by a counterparty, but for all other instruments, we can apply the upcoming formulas in a simplified way. Therefore, we look only at OTC derivatives throughout this book except for paragraphs where it is necessary to elaborate on the specific instruments, for instance, in the investigation of the recovery rate.

Non-fulfillment can be regarded as default or late delivery, or otherwise, failure to complete/settle a transaction as previously agreed upon. In fact, as mentioned by the Basel Committee, "during the financial crisis, however, roughly two-thirds of losses attributed to counterparty credit risk were due to CVA losses and only about one-third were due to actual defaults" (cf. [BCBS (2011a)]). For this reason, the Basel Committee has determined that "Banks will be subject to a capital charge for potential mark-to-market losses (i.e. credit valuation adjustment – CVA – risk) associated with a deterioration in the creditworthiness of a counterparty" (cf. [BCBS (2010b)]) that was not covered by the Basel II standard.

As mentioned by [Segoviano and Singh (2008)], with regards to OTC derivatives, notional amounts i.e. the gross notional values "provide a measure of the size of the market, but do not provide a measure of risk. Risk in derivatives stems from various other variables including price changes, volatility, leverage and hedge ratios, duration, liquidity, and counterparty risk".

In this book we will show a pragmatic approach to address most of the factors mentioned above by explaining in detail how to deal with data and risk mitigations as netting, collateral, diversification (through correlation) and CCPs. Starting with data, the availability of it determines the granularity of the calculated risk. In our framework, a position is specified by: counterparty, fund, netting group and instrument. This is because some mitigations as netting apply only within the same netting group at fund level as regulated by the netting agreement such as ISDA (or by cross-margining agreement). In addition, the risk is further reduced by collateral.

The risk is defined for the current exposure as well as for the Potential Future Exposure (PFE) and depends on the probability of default for the counterparty as derived from the company's implied rating (which, in turn, is a measure of counterparty creditworthiness). It is important to note that "strong capital requirements are a necessary condition", "but by themselves are not sufficient" (cf. [BCBS (2010b)]), hence potential collateral requirement is introduced to take into account liquidity risk.[2]

What does a negative or a positive net exposure of a contract mean from a risk perspective for the investor? As described by [Segoviano and Singh (2008)], there is an asymmetry of in-the-money contracts in favor of the defaulting counterparty because clients terminate contracts in their favor, but not those where the counterparty is in favor. As mentioned by [Segoviano and Singh (2008)] "Lehman's bankruptcy illustrates the asymmetry between the treatment of derivatives payables and derivatives receivables. Moody's (2008) mentions that when Lehman's default was being considered at the year-end session (September 13-14) at NY Fed, only a limited amount of outstanding derivatives payable trades were re-priced as participants expected significant price changes and operational difficulty in replacing a sizeable volume of trades." In addition, it must be noted that the replacement cost for the residual derivatives payable obligations (i.e. the unsecured receivables for those who have lost their counterparty) can be very high (cf. Figure 12.2).

To understand the exposure at risk, it is required to measure first the net current exposure with each counterparty. Netting is not only between trades but is also between collaterals. In this respect, good data is crucial as some credit support annex (CSA) claim collateral on a fund level, whilst others on a position level. CSA is a legal document that regulates the mitigation of credit risk for transactions of derivatives. It is explained in detail in [Brigo *et al.* (2013), Chapter III, Section 5.1]. In addition to the above, net potential future exposure is calculated in an adverse market scenario. The credit loss is calculated for both current exposure as well as for the potential future exposure (PFE) and we introduce the concept of unexpected loss, i.e. the deviation of the actual loss as well as we show the influence of CCPs on mitigating counterparty risk.

[2]During the early "liquidity phase" of the financial crisis, many banks — despite adequate capital levels — still experienced difficulties because they did not prudently manage their liquidity. The crisis again drove home the importance of liquidity to the proper functioning of financial markets and the banking sector. Before the crisis, asset markets were buoyant and funding was readily available at low cost. The rapid reversal in market conditions illustrated how quickly liquidity can evaporate and that illiquidity can last for an extended time. The banking system came under severe stress, which necessitated central bank action to support both the functioning of money markets and, in some cases, individual institutions (cf. [BCBS (2010b)]).

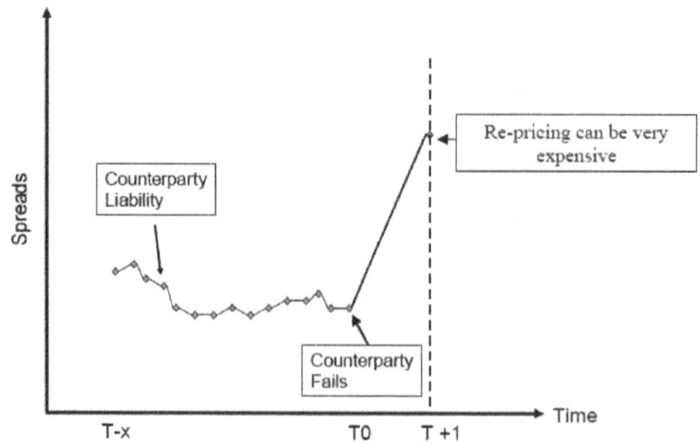

Fig. 12.2: Spread-time combination (Figure 1 of [Singh and Aitken (2009)]).

To measure the risk for an investor, and to avoid a cumbersome computation, a hybrid between Value-at-Risk (VaR), explained in the textbooks [McNeil *et al.* (2005)] and [Jorion (2007)], and the add-on is introduced to get both the potential future exposure and its corresponding credit loss. This hybrid VaR is calculated for every position and depends on the risk of a specific asset type (e.g. futures/forwards on equity, options on equity, futures/ forwards on commodities, swaptions, etc.) and it is used for determining the potential future exposure. As netting can only be done within the same netting group, we need to distinguish assets by netting groups.

In Table 12.1 we summarize asset types and netting groups:

The netting groups are CERT, GMRA, ISDA, TBA, OTHER, and WARRANT. Where CERT stands for "certificates", GMRA for "Global Master Repurchase Agreement", ISDA for "International Swaps and Derivatives Association", WARRANT for "warrants" and OTHER for investments that cannot be allocated to the netting group, TBA for "to be announced". The netting group TBA contains forwards on mortgage pools. The composition of these pools is not known when the contract is issued as this is announced later.

For other instruments that bear counterparty risk besides OTC derivatives, netting also has to be considered, but unless there are other different agreements, instruments of the same type can be netted against each other, e.g. a bond with any other bond.

12.2 Current Exposure Method (CEM)

The current exposure is defined as the amount at risk should the counterparty default know. It is normally assumed to be the market value, or the mark-to-market (MtM) value (cf. [le Roux (2008)]). Due to the changes of the contract values over time as the market moves, the current exposure independent from its observation level is the only exposure known with certainty at the observation date,

Table 12.1: Instrument types and corresponding netting groups.

Instrument Type	Netting Group
CDS	ISDA
Certificate	CERT
Forward/Future on loans, equity, commodity, swaptions	ISDA
Inflation linked forward/future	ISDA
Foreign exchange forward/future	ISDA
Forward/Future on bonds	GMRA
Forward/Future on mortgage	TBA
Swap	ISDA
Bond swap	ISDA
Not specified option	OTHER
Option on future	TBA
All other options	ISDA
Repurchase agreement	GMRA
Warrant	WARRANT

whereas all future exposures are uncertain. To measure the current exposure, the granularity of data is crucial. First, we define current exposure at the contract level. Then we derive the exposure at the counterparty level without and with netting arrangements and lastly we show the impact of collateral as a tool for reducing the current exposure. In general, the current exposure is defined as the Net Aggregate Value (NAV) of all contract positions minus collateral, where collateral can be posted on contract or netting group or fund level for the respective counterparty depending on CSA. The value of a position is its price used for calculating the NAV of the account (mandate/ mutual fund/ etc.) to which the position belongs. In the whole methodology, the term "value" is used for describing this value of a position.

If a counterparty defaults, we are interested in the Net Replacement Value (NRV) that the affected investor has to deposit. In our setting the NRV of a counterparty k is the current exposure of the investor with counterparty k, denoted by NRV_k. For calculating the NRV of a specific counterparty, we use the following notations. All notations are for the current date $t = 0$.

K := number of counterparties;

$\text{NRV}_{i,g,f,k}$:= net replacement value of position i in netting group g, fund f and with counterparty k;

$\text{NRV}_{i,f,k}$:= net replacement value of position i in fund f and with counterparty k (no consideration of netting groups);

NRV_k := aggregated net replacement value of counterparty k;

F_k := number of funds with positions with counterparty k;

$G_{f,k}$	:=	number of netting groups in fund f and with counterparty k;
$N_{g,f,k}$	:=	number of positions in netting group g, fund f and with counterparty k;
$N_{f,k}$	:=	number of positions in fund f and with counterparty k (no consideration of netting groups);
$\text{Col}_{i,g,f,k}$	:=	collateral or margin amount of position i in netting group g, fund f and with counterparty k. Collateral net of haircuts in case of OTC derivatives or margin amount in case of exchange traded and trades processed through central clearing;
$\text{Col}_{g,f,k}$	:=	collateral or margin amount of counterparty k for fund f and netting group g;
$\text{Col}_{i,f,k}$	:=	Collateral or margin of position i in fund f and with counterparty k (no consideration of netting groups);
$V_{i,f,k}$	:=	value of position i in fund f and with counterparty k (no consideration of netting groups);
$V_{i,g,f,k}$	:=	value of position i in netting group g, fund f and with counterparty k.

As we have to specify every single position by counterparty, fund, netting group and instrument type, we need four indices. Therefore $V_{i,g,f,k}$ is the most granular description of the derivative position's value and $\text{NRV}_{i,g,f,k}$ is the corresponding NRV if all information is available. If netting is not allowed or should not be considered, the respective notations are $V_{i,f,k}$ and $\text{NRV}_{i,f,k}$, whereas $\text{Col}_{i,f,k}$ denotes the collateral in this case. Depending on the CSA, collateral can be available on contract or netting group level for the counterparty, hence these amounts are denoted by $\text{Col}_{i,g,f,k}$ and $\text{Col}_{g,f,k}$ respectively. As described in [Brigo *et al.* (2013), Chapter II, Section 5] the bilateral collateral account has to be adjusted mark-to-market: if the mark-to-market NRV of the collateralised position is positive the investor receives collateral payments and if it is negative the investor has to post collateral onto the account. The collateral amount can also be positive or negative in the case of collateral only on a netting group level, depending on the fact if the client collateral exceeds the broker collateral in the respective netting group or the other way round. In this chapter, we will mainly consider broker collateral, i.e. collateral the investor receives, which is positive. In the chapter on potential collateral requirements (Section 13.10), we consider, also, the client collateral to be posted by the investor (which is negative).

12.3 Exposure at Contract Level

The value of contract i with a counterparty k is known only for the current date ($t = 0$). For any future date t, this value $V_{i,g,f,k}(t)$ is uncertain. Regarding the current date we write $V_{i,g,f,k}(0) := V_{i,g,f,k}$. If the counterparty defaults at a time before the contract maturity, maximum economic loss equals the replacement cost of the contract:

- If the contract value is positive, the investor does not receive anything from the defaulted counterparty, but has to pay this amount to another counterparty to replace the contract;
- If the contract value is negative, the investor receives this amount from another counterparty, but has to forward it to the defaulted counterparty.

Thus the $\mathrm{NRV}_{i,g,f,k}$ on contract-level at time t is

$$\mathrm{NRV}_{i,g,f,k}(t) = \max(V_{i,g,f,k}(t)\,, 0)\ .$$

Hence, today the $\mathrm{NRV}_{i,g,f,k}$ on contract-level is

$$\mathrm{NRV}_{i,g,f,k} := \mathrm{NRV}_{i,g,f,k}(0) = \max(V_{i,g,f,k}, 0)\ . \tag{12.1}$$

12.4 Exposure at Counterparty Level

The NRV_k on counterparty-level at future time t can be defined as the loss if the counterparty k defaults at time t under assumption of no recovery. If counterparty risk is not mitigated in any way, i.e. there are no netting and collateral agreements, the counterparty-level NRV at time t equals the sum of contract-level exposures

$$\mathrm{NRV}_k(t) = \sum_{f=1}^{F_k}\sum_{i=1}^{N_{f,k}} \mathrm{NRV}_{i,f,k}(t) = \sum_{f=1}^{F_k}\sum_{i=1}^{N_{f,k}} \max(V_{i,f,k}(t)\,, 0)\ . \tag{12.2}$$

Let us look at the current date $t = 0$, then (12.2) becomes

$$\mathrm{NRV}_k = \sum_{f=1}^{F_k}\sum_{i=1}^{N_{f,k}} \mathrm{NRV}_{i,f,k} = \sum_{f=1}^{F_k}\sum_{i=1}^{N_{f,k}} \max(V_{i,f,k}, 0)\,. \tag{12.3}$$

If netting agreements exist between the considered counterparties $N_{g,f,k}$ and do not exist for other $G_{f,k}$, then the exposure at time t is given by the following net positive value

$$\mathrm{NRV}_k(t) = \sum_{f=1}^{F_k}\sum_{g=1}^{G_{f,k}} \max\left(\sum_{i=1}^{N_{g,f,k}} V_{i,g,f,k}(t)\,, 0\right)\,, \tag{12.4}$$

that for the current date becomes

$$\mathrm{NRV}_k = \sum_{f=1}^{F_k}\sum_{g=1}^{G_{f,k}} \max\left(\sum_{i=1}^{N_{g,f,k}} V_{i,g,f,k}, 0\right)\,. \tag{12.5}$$

In case of several specific netting agreements with one counterparty, where not all trades have to be covered by netting agreements, we denote by NA_m the m-th netting agreement. Then the counterparty NRV with and without netting agreements at time t, is given by (cf. [Pykhtin and Zhu (2007), Eq. (4)])

$$\mathrm{NRV}_k(t) = \sum_{f=1}^{F_k} \left[\sum_{m=1}^{G_{f,k}} \max\left(\sum_{i\in \mathrm{NA}_m} V_{i,m,f,k}(t), 0 \right) + \sum_{i\notin\{\mathrm{NA}\}} \max\left(V_{i,f,k}(t), 0\right) \right], \quad (12.6)$$

where $\{\mathrm{NA}\}$ denotes the set of all netting agreements and $V_{i,m,f,k}$ is the value of position i in the netting group m of fund f with counterparty k. When $t = 0$, Eq. (12.6) becomes

$$\mathrm{NRV}_k = \sum_{f=1}^{F_k} \left[\sum_{m=1}^{G_{f,k}} \max\left(\sum_{i\in \mathrm{NA}_m} V_{i,m,f,k}, 0 \right) + \sum_{i\notin\{\mathrm{NA}\}} \max\left(V_{i,f,k}, 0\right) \right]. \quad (12.7)$$

12.5 Exposure with Collateral Payments

Now, we want to measure the current exposure including collateral payments. Without any loss of generality, in this section, we will always consider $t = 0$. Suppose the counterparty posts collateral for every specific position and each position is encompassed by a netting agreement. Then the NRV of counterparty k is given by

$$\mathrm{NRV}_k = \sum_{f=1}^{F_k} \sum_{g=1}^{G_{f,k}} \max\left(\sum_{i=1}^{N_{g,f,k}} V_{i,g,f,k} - \mathrm{Col}_{i,g,f,k}, 0 \right). \quad (12.8)$$

In case when not every position is covered by a netting agreement, the following formula for the NRV of counterparty k holds

$$\mathrm{NRV}_k = \sum_{f=1}^{F_k} \left[\sum_{m=1}^{G_{f,k}} \max\left(\sum_{i\in \mathrm{NA}_m} V_{i,m,f,k} - \mathrm{Col}_{i,m,f,k}, 0 \right) + \sum_{i\notin\{\mathrm{NA}\}} \max\left(V_{i,f,k} - \mathrm{Col}_{i,f,k}, 0\right) \right], \quad (12.9)$$

where $\mathrm{Col}_{i,m,f,k}$ is the collateral amount corresponding to the contract of position i of netting agreement m in fund f with counterparty k.

Now assume that collateral is posted on a netting group level. Hence the NRV of counterparty k is given by

$$\mathrm{NRV}_k = \sum_{f=1}^{F_k} \max\left\{ \sum_{g=1}^{G_{f,k}} \left[\max\left(\sum_{i=1}^{N_{g,f,k}} V_{i,g,f,k}, 0 \right) - \mathrm{Col}_{g,f,k} \right], 0 \right\}. \quad (12.10)$$

First, we add all the positions which belong to the same netting group, that are contained in the same fund, and that belong to the same counterparty. If this sum is positive we continue with summing over all netting groups of the same fund belonging to the same counterparty and subtracting the respective collateral. If the figure, after subtraction, is still positive, this value represents the exposure of the fund with counterparty k. The sum over all funds is the NRV of counterparty k.

Further, if not every position is covered by a netting agreement and the collateral is posted on a netting group level, the NRV of a counterparty k is given by

$$\mathrm{NRV}_k = \sum_{f=1}^{F_k} \max\left\{ \sum_{m=1}^{G_{f,k}} \left[\max\left(\sum_{i \in \mathrm{NA}_m} V_{i,m,f,k}, 0 \right) - \mathrm{Col}_{m,f,k} \right] + \sum_{i \notin \{\mathrm{NA}\}} \max\left(V_{i,f,k}, 0\right), 0 \right\}, \tag{12.11}$$

where $\mathrm{Col}_{m,f,k}$ denotes the collateral amount of the netting agreement m.

In the presence of netting agreements and collateral payments, from Eq. (12.10) the current exposure is defined as the NRV over all counterparties k

$$\mathrm{NRV} = \sum_{k=1}^{K} \mathrm{NRV}_k .$$

It is worth pointing out that whenever collateral amounts are considered throughout the book, a collateral amount is meant after applying a corresponding haircut. This haircut is regulated by the respective CSA and depends on the instrument type, the instrument issuer and the maturity of the collateral.

12.6 Potential Future Exposure (PFE)

The calculation of potential future exposure is much more complex compared to the current exposure. The following two methods are the most widely used for the quantification of potential future exposure:

- Regulatory Current Exposure Method (CEM)/Standardised Method (SM);
- Full revaluation/Monte Carlo simulation.

The choice between these two methodologies is driven by the trade-off among accuracy, time, budget and level of computational complexity. Therefore, we will explain in detail a third approach that is, in our opinion, an efficient trade-off. Figure 12.3 illustrates the idea of the potential future exposure described in the subsequent sections. The shaded area indicates that only positive outcomes of position values (MtM positive values) are counted to the relevant exposure.

12.7 Regulatory Methodology

The regulatory Current Exposure Method (CEM) was proposed by the Basel Committee in 1988 (cf. [BCBS (1988)]) and amended in 1996 (cf. [BCBS (1996)]). This

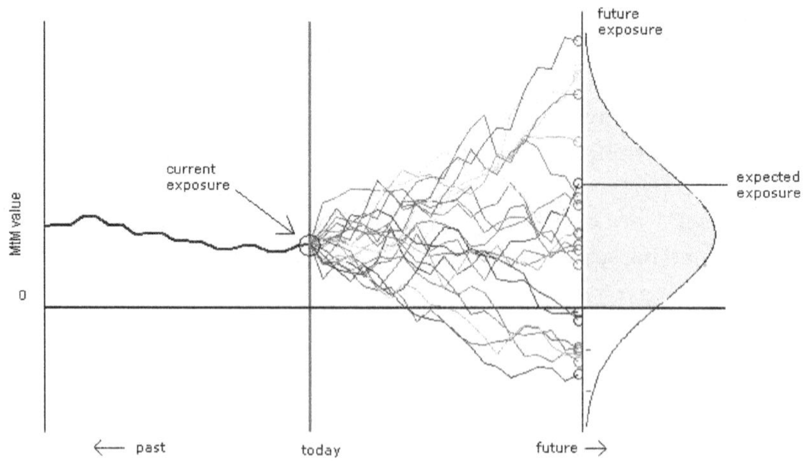

Fig. 12.3: Simulated paths.

amendment was updated in 2005 to assess the volatility of future exposure changes. That was a big step forward with respect to the exposure measurement based on a percentage of notional depending on the residual time to maturity. Moreover, it has been considered as a straightforward method to assess the potential future exposure in a meaningful way. The Basel Committee stated that "under the Current Exposure Method, banks must calculate the current replacement cost by marking contracts to market, thus capturing the current exposure without any need for estimation, and then adding a factor (the "add-on") to reflect the potential future exposure over the remaining life of the contract". Hence "in order to calculate the credit equivalent amount of these instruments under this current exposure method, a bank would sum the replacement cost" ([BCBS (2006), p. 274]), i.e. the MtM of all its contracts with a positive value, plus an add-on amount.

The table below shows the percentage, i.e. the Credit Conversion Factor (CCF), to be multiplied by the notional of a contract in order to estimate the potential future exposure as suggested by the BCBS (cf. [BCBS (2006)]).

Table 12.2: Add-on matrix ([BCBS (2006), p. 274]).

CCF/Add-on Matrix					
Residual Maturity	Interest Rate	Exchange Rate and Gold	Equity	Precious Metals (Except Gold)	Other Commoditites
<1Y	0.0%	1.0%	6.0%	7.0%	10.0%
1-5Y	0.5%	5.0%	8.0%	7.0%	12.0%
>5Y	1.5%	7.5%	10.0%	8.0%	15.0%

The add-on amount, which is supposed to capture the potential future exposure, is defined as

$$\text{Add-onAmount} = \text{CCF} \cdot \text{Notional}\,.$$

Then the Exposure-At-Default (EAD) is given by

$$\text{EAD} = \text{RC} \cdot \text{Add-onAmount} - \text{C}_{adj},$$

where

RC	=	replacement cost, i.e. MtM or variation margin to be paid by the Clearing Member in case of CCPs/Exchange derivatives;
C_{adj}	=	collateral net of haircut adjusted to its volatility.

In the case of netting the regulator allows for a discount (cf. [BCBS (2004), p. 275]) on the add-on amount as follows: the add-on for netted transactions (Add-on_{net}) will equal the weighted average of the gross add-on (Add-on_{gr}) and the gross add-on adjusted by the Net-to-Gross-Ratio (NGR), that is

$$\text{Add-on}_{net} = 0.4 \cdot \text{Add-on}_{gr} + 0.6 \cdot \text{NGR} \cdot \text{Add-on}_{gr},$$

with

Add-on_{gr}	=	sum of individual add-on amounts (calculated by multiplying the notional principal amount by the appropriate add-on factors) of all transactions subject to legally enforceable netting agreements with one counterparty;
NGR	=	level of net replacement cost/level of gross replacement cost for transactions subject to legally enforceable netting agreements.

12.8 From the Add-on Factors to the Parametric Approach

The CEM approach has been widely criticised as (cf. [BCBS (2012b)]):

- It does not differentiate between margined and unmargined transactions;
- It does not sufficiently capture the level of volatilities as observed over the recent stress periods;
- The recognition of hedging and netting benefits through the NGR is too simplistic and does not reflect economically meaningful relationships among the derivative positions.

As a criticism follow-up, the CEM approach is under review by the regulator and a Non-Internal Model Method (NIMM) has been recently proposed in June 2013.

Our methodology, instead, is to interpret the add-on amount as the maximum credit exposure, i.e. the VaR corresponding to a prescribed level of statistical confidence α (we set α=99.5%). For this purpose, we assume arbitrary annual volatility (abbreviated as Vol_a in Table 12.3) and weekly Delta values for the different underlyings as listed in Table 12.3. The values are based on historical data. Assumptions on volatility, correlations and other parameters can be set by the user who has to define a customized (potential stress) scenario.

For interest rate/fixed income derivatives the VaR factor increases with maturity. The Basel Committee proposes to distinguish among the following maturity buckets: up to 1 year, 1 to 5 years and more than 5 years (cf. [BCBS (2006), p. 272]). Table 12.4 states some assumptions for the level of increase. Under the assumption of normally distributed collateralised positions, we calculate the yearly VaR as follows

$$\text{VaR}_{yearly} = z_\alpha \cdot \frac{\text{Vol}_a}{\sqrt{52}} \cdot \text{Delta} \cdot T,$$

where z_α is the α-quantile of the standard normal distribution ($z_\alpha = 2.3263$ if $\alpha = 99.5\%$) and T denotes the Time Factor proportionate to annual frequency. For the sake of simplicity, we assume that the probability distribution is normal (a more refined approach, e.g. the Cornish–Fisher expansion, can be used in case the skewness and kurtosis are calculated). The reporting frequency in many companies involved at capital markets is yearly as they would like to understand the potential future exposure in one year i.e. the time required for liquidating the positions. For uncollateralised positions the time required for liquidating a position is two years.

Table 12.3: Arbitrary volatility and delta values.

Assumptions for the extended VaR Matrix										
	Equity		Commodity		FI / IR		Credit		FX	
	Futures or Forwards	Options	Futures or Forwards	Options	Futures or Forwards or Swaps	Options or Swap-tions	Futures or Forwards or Swaps	Options or Swap-tions	Futures or Forwards	Options
Vol_a	30%	30%	30%	30%	5%	5%	40%	40%	10%	10%
Delta	1.00	0.50	1.00	0.50	1.00	0.50	1.00	0.50	1.00	0.50

Table 12.4: Time factor for interest rate and fixed income derivatives.

Assumptions for the extended VaR Matrix			
Time to Maturity	below 1 year	1 - 5 years	above 5 years
Time Factor	1	3.5	10

For uncollateralised positions we calculate the fortnightly (2-week) VaR, since we assume that it will take one year longer to liquidate the position compared to a collateralised position

$$\text{VaR}_{fortnightly} = z_\alpha \cdot \frac{\text{Vol}_a}{\sqrt{26}} \cdot \text{Delta} \cdot T \ .$$

For example, the VaR factor for an uncollateralised interest rate swap (IRS) with time to maturity in 4 years is equal to 8%, since

$$\text{VaR}_{fortnightly} = 2.3263 \cdot \frac{0.05}{\sqrt{26}} \cdot 1.00 \cdot 3.5 = 0.08 \ .$$

Tables 12.5 and 12.6 list the yearly and fortnightly VaR (computed for all different instrument types, underlying and time to maturities) depending on whether the positions are collateralised or uncollateralised. Of course, these figures depend on the figures from the add-on matrix.

Table 12.5: Weekly VaR factors.

VaR Factors - Weekly						
Instrument Type	Instrument Subtype	Underlying	Netting Group	below 1Y	1Y - 5Y	above 5Y
Certificate		CTY	CERT	13.7%	13.7%	13.7%
Certificate		EQ	CERT	13.7%	13.7%	13.7%
Certificate		IR	CERT	2.3%	8.0%	22.8%
Fwd/Future		CR	ISDA	2.3%	8.0%	22.8%
Fwd/Future		CTY	ISDA	13.7%	13.7%	13.7%
Fwd/Future		EQ	ISDA	13.7%	13.7%	13.7%
Fwd/Future		FX	ISDA	4.6%	4.6%	4.6%
Fwd/Future	Bond Fwd	IR	GMRA	2.3%	8.0%	22.8%
Fwd/Future	TBA	IR	TBA	2.3%	8.0%	22.8%
Fwd/Future		IR	ISDA	2.3%	8.0%	22.8%
Fwd/Repo		IR	GMRA	2.3%	8.0%	22.8%
Option	Option	CR	ISDA	8.0%	28.2%	80.5%
Option	Warrant	CTY	WARRANT	13.7%	13.7%	13.7%
Option	Option	EQ	ISDA	6.8%	6.8%	6.8%
Option	Option	EQ	OTHER	6.8%	6.8%	6.8%
Option	Warrant	EQ	WARRANT	6.8%	6.8%	6.8%
Option	Option	FX	ISDA	2.3%	2.3%	2.3%
Option	Warrant	FX	WARRANT	2.3%	2.3%	2.3%
Option	Option	IR	ISDA	2.3%	8.0%	22.8%
Option	TBA	IR	TBA	2.3%	8.0%	22.8%
Option	Warrant	IR	WARRANT	2.3%	8.0%	22.8%
Option/Swap	Swaption	CR	ISDA	8.0%	28.2%	80.5%
Option/Swap	Swaption	IR	ISDA	2.3%	8.0%	22.8%
Swap		EQ	ISDA	13.7%	13.7%	13.7%

Swap		FX	ISDA	4.6%	4.6%	4.6%
Swap		IR	ISDA	2.3%	**8.0%**	22.8%
Swap/CDS		CR	ISDA	2.3%	8.0%	22.8%

Table 12.6: Fortnightly VaR factors.

VaR Factors - Fortnightly						
Instrument Type	Instrument Subtype	Underlying	Netting Group	below 1Y	1Y - 5Y	above 5Y
Certificate		CTY	CERT	9.7%	9.7%	9.7%
Certificate		EQ	CERT	9.7%	9.7%	9.7%
Certificate		IR	CERT	1.6%	5.6%	16.1%
Fwd/Future		CR	ISDA	1.6%	5.6%	16.1%
Fwd/Future		CTY	ISDA	9.7%	9.7%	9.7%
Fwd/Future		EQ	ISDA	9.7%	9.7%	9.7%
Fwd/Future		FX	ISDA	3.2%	3.2%	3.2%
Fwd/Future	Bond Fwd	IR	GMRA	1.6%	5.6%	16.1%
Fwd/Future	TBA	IR	TBA	1.6%	5.6%	16.1%
Fwd/Future		IR	ISDA	1.6%	5.6%	16.1%
Fwd/Repo		IR	GMRA	1.6%	5.6%	16.1%
Option	Option	CR	ISDA	8.0%	22.6%	64.5%
Option	Warrant	CTY	WARRANT	13.7%	13.7%	13.7%
Option	Option	EQ	ISDA	4.8%	4.8%	4.8%
Option	Option	EQ	OTHER	4.8%	4.8%	4.8%
Option	Warrant	EQ	WARRANT	4.8%	4.8%	4.8%
Option	Option	FX	ISDA	1.6%	1.6%	1.6%
Option	Warrant	FX	WARRANT	1.6%	1.6%	1.6%
Option	Option	IR	ISDA	1.6%	5.6%	16.1%
Option	TBA	IR	TBA	1.6%	5.6%	16.1%
Option	Warrant	IR	WARRANT	1.6%	5.6%	16.1%
Option/Swap	Swaption	CR	ISDA	8.0%	22.6%	64.5%
Option/Swap	Swaption	IR	ISDA	1.6%	5.6%	16.1%
Swap		EQ	ISDA	9.7%	9.7%	9.7%
Swap		FX	ISDA	3.2%	3.2%	3.2%
Swap		IR	ISDA	1.6%	5.6%	16.1%
Swap/CDS		CR	ISDA	1.6%	5.6%	16.1%

Let us take an example for calculating the yearly VaR factor for an uncollateralised interest rate swap with notional of €100 million and a residual maturity of 4 years. For the corresponding VaR factor, please, consult the row before the last and the column before in Table 12.5. It is in bold font and yields 8.0%. The add-on amount is then

$$\text{VaR} = €\,100{,}000{,}000 \cdot 0.08 = €\,8{,}000{,}000\,.$$

Thus, for this interest rate swap we have to add €8,000,000.

12.9 Parametric Potential Future Exposure

The potential NRV of a counterparty k is the future exposure of the investor with counterparty k, denoted by NRV-VaR$_k$ where VaR stands for the add-on amount. For calculating the potential future NRV of a specific counterparty, we use the notations stated at the beginning of Section 12.2. Furthermore, if we take into account the VaR (i.e. the so-called add-on factor) of all positions, the following additional notations are required

$\text{VaRFactor}_{i,g}$	:=	VaR factor of position i in netting group g;
$\text{VaR}_{i,g,f,k}$	:=	VaR of position i in netting group g, fund f and with counterparty k;
$\text{Not}_{i,g,f,k}$	:=	notional of position i in netting group g, fund f and with counterparty k;
NRV-VaR_k	:=	aggregated net replacement value including add-on of counterparty k.

Each add-on factor refers to a specific instrument in each netting group. This factor is independent of the fund and counterparty. As the add-on amount is calculated on the position level, four indices to the VaR and notional terms are needed. The following formula is used to calculate the add-on amount

$$\text{VaR}_{i,g,f,k} = \text{Not}_{i,g,f,k} \cdot \text{VaRFactor}_{i,g}\ , \tag{12.12}$$

where the VaR factor depends on the investment type. As mentioned in Section 12.7, the Basel Committee suggested fixed add-on amounts for the different types of investments, depending on the tenor and type of investment (cf. [BCBS (2006)]). As we want to distinguish the add-on factor by derivative type and underlying, more information is required.

The add-on amount computed in Eq. (12.12) is used for computing the potential NRV of a counterparty k as follows

$$\text{NRV-VaR}_k = \sum_{f=1}^{F_k} \max\left\{ \sum_{g=1}^{G_{f,k}} \left[\max\left(\sum_{i=1}^{N_{g,f,k}} V_{i,g,f,k} + \text{VaR}_{i,g,f,k}, 0 \right) - \text{Col}_{g,f,k} \right], 0 \right\}. \tag{12.13}$$

The following two figures show the NRV-VaR for the three types of derivatives: the NRV-VaR is positive for the green and red derivative types when collateral payments are not considered (Figure 12.4), whereas the NRV-VaR remains positive only for the green derivative type when collaterals payments are considered (Figures 12.5).

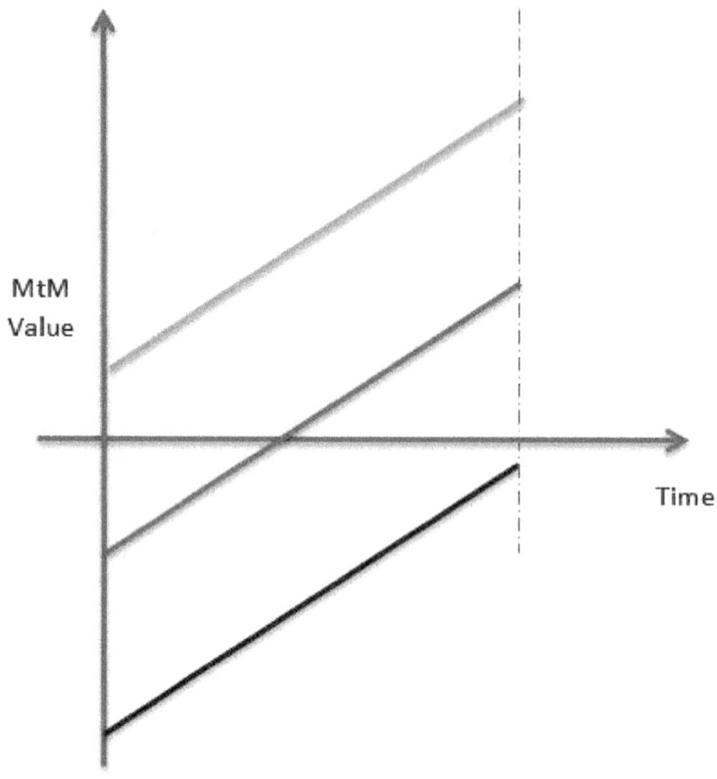

Fig. 12.4: NRV-VaR without collateral.

It is worth noting that the NRV-VaR is not the classic linear VaR mentioned in the literature since formula (12.13) sums up the VaR of each position and takes the maximum of this sum (after having subtracted the collateral) and 0. The method iterates this procedure through netting groups and funds introducing a non-linear effect which is what needs to be captured. As a consequence of the non-linearity introduced by the max term, i.e. considering the positive values that the investor could lose in case of default, this method yields a better view on the investor's risk towards its counterparties than the linear VaR (or the regulatory CEM approach).

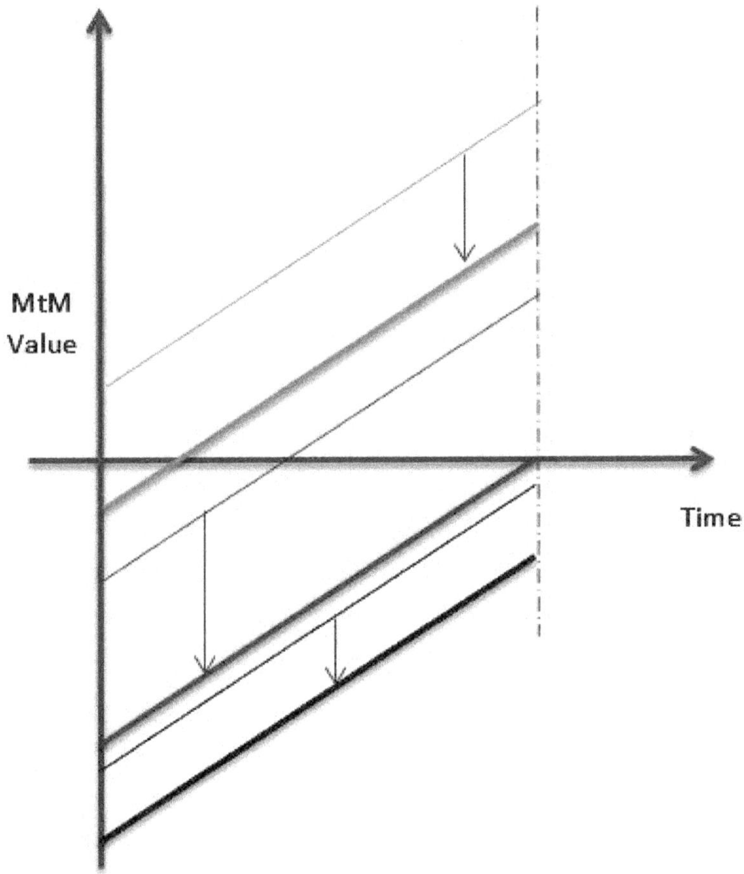

Fig. 12.5: NRV-VaR with collateral payments.

Chapter 13

EAD-Related Issues

13.1 Credit Loss

The [1] credit loss (CL) is defined as the difference between the asset's current value and its future value at the end of some time horizon (cf. [BCBS (1999)]). There are two widely conceptual approaches for defining the CL: the default-mode (DM) and the mark-to-market (MtM) paradigm. In the first case, only defaults (within the so-called planning horizon) are considered while in the second creditworthiness deterioration due to, for example, short to default events is also considered. DM models derive the first two moments of the portfolio's credit losses whilst MtM models employ either a discounted contractual cash flow (DCCF) or a risk-neutral valuation (RNV) approach for deriving current and future MtM values of credit instruments.

13.2 Discounted Contractual Cash Flow (DCCF)

The DCCF approach is well known because of J.P. Morgan's *CreditMetrics*^{TM}. Within this methodology, the current value of an asset is determined as the discounted value of its future contractual cash flows where the discount factors (credit spreads) are those corresponding to the asset's rating. The problem with this approach is the asset value does not depend on the expected LGD. In other terms "senior and subordinated loans to a single firm would have the same future discount price, regardless of differences in expected recovery in the event of future default" [BCBS (1999)]. Furthermore "loans to two identically rated firms receive the same discount rates, even if the two firms are not equally sensitive to the business cycle or to other systematic factors" [BCBS (1999)] (which is against the principle that correlation of returns affects asset's value). As this method is non-parametric, it does not require many modeling assumptions but performs poorly where data are scant or noisy.

[1]Part of this chapter has been published in [Orlando and Härtel (2014)].

Change in Value

Let us assume that the value of a security is derived from the zero-curve corresponding to the rating of the obligor as listed in Table 13.1.

Table 13.1: One-year forward zero-curves for each credit rating (%).

	Year			
Category	1	2	3	4
Aaa	3.6	4.17	4.73	5.12
Aa	3.65	4.22	4.78	5.17
A	3.72	4.32	4.93	5.32
Baa	4.1	4.67	5.25	5.63
Ba	5.55	6.02	6.78	7.27
B	6.05	7.02	8.03	8.52
Caa-C	15.05	15.02	14.03	13.52

Source: CreditMetrics, JP Morgan.

Therefore the 1-year forward price of a bond rated B, paying a coupon of 2.5 annually, is

$$2.5 + \frac{2.5}{1.0605^1} + + \frac{2.5}{1.07.02^2} + \frac{2.5}{1.0803^3} + \frac{2.5}{1.0852^4} = 82.9299. \tag{13.1}$$

By discounting each bond according to its rating spread, it is possible to determine the value of all of them. The last column of Table 13.2 shows the price's change when a bond rated B is upgraded or downgraded following a credit event.

Table 13.2: 1-year forward prices of bonds discounted according to their spread.

Rating	Value	Transition Prob.	Δ Value
Aaa	93.33592743	0.0000%	10.41
Aa	93.16992079	0.0000%	10.24
A	92.67828857	0.0000%	9.75
Baa	91.66082576	0.0000%	8.73
Ba	86.55851943	8.3221%	3.63
B	82.92994258	84.1868%	0.00
Caa-C	69.96996378	2.3561%	-12.96
Default	39.10936559	5.1350%	-43.82

In case of default the recovery rate is 50%.

13.3 Risk-Neutral Valuation (RNV)

According to the RNV approach by [Merton (1973)] commonly adopted for pricing derivatives, as well as by Moody's KMV's *PortfolioManager*^{TM}, a firm goes into default when the value of its underlying assets falls beneath the required level to support its debt. This approach is also called structural and the default process is endogenous. "Instead of discounting contractual payments, the RNV method discounts contingent payments: if payment is contractually due at date t, the payment received by the lender will be the contractual amount only if the firm has not defaulted by date t; the lender receives a portion of the loan's face value equal to $1 - LGD$ if the borrower defaults at date t, and the lender receives nothing at date t if the borrower has defaulted before date t. A loan can thus be viewed as a set of derivative contracts on the underlying value of the borrower's assets" [BCBS (1999)]. Therefore a loan is the sum of present values of contingent payments (risk-neutral valued) provided that the company has not defaulted (where the discount rate is risk-free). Because the risk-neutral evaluation assets' values reflect both: correlation with the market and seniority. This method prices each asset in a single unified framework and it is calibrated by using the market risk premium (credit spreads). Given the large use of modeling assumptions data is used efficiently but results can be hampered by the model's misspecification.

First, the credit migration approach, as proposed by J.P. Morgan with CreditMetrics, is based on the probability of moving from one credit quality to another, including default, within a given time horizon. Second, the option pricing, or structural approach, as initiated by KMV and which is based on the asset value model originally proposed by [Merton (1974)]. In this Merton model, the default process is endogenous and relates to the capital structure of the firm. Default occurs when the value of the firms' assets falls below some critical level. Third, the actuarial approach is as proposed by Credit Suisse Financial Products (CSFP) with CreditRisk+ and which only focuses on default. The default for individual bonds or loans is assumed to follow an exogenous Poisson process. Finally, McKinsey proposes CreditPortfolioView which is a discrete-time multi-period model where default probabilities are conditional on the macro-variables like unemployment, the level of interest rates, the growth rate in the economy,

13.4 Parametric Approach

For calculating the so-called credit loss within our framework [Orlando and Härtel (2014)], we need to know the probability of default of the respective counterparty with its rating. This is computed by using the calculations shown in Subsection 8.7.

After evaluating the default probability, the loss given default (LGD)[2] is needed for the credit loss calculation. Observe that the recovery rate depends on the priority of the claim. With the help of [Emery and Ou (2009)] we distinguish between the following priorities of investments.[3]

Table 13.3: Recovery rates for different instrument types.

Instrument Type	**RR**
Cash	0.4
Covered Bonds	0.95
Covered Loans	0.95
Government Guaranteed Bonds	0.6
Loans	0.6
Senior Secured Bonds	0.6
Senior Unsecured Bonds	0.3
Subordinated Bonds (Senior & Junior)	0.2
Derivatives	0.2

The LGD is dependent on the specific instrument. For instance, if instrument i is a derivative, we get

$$\mathrm{LGD}_i = 1 - \mathrm{RR}_i = 1 - 0.2 = 0.8 \; .$$

Therefore, the LGD corresponding to the instrument types listed in Table 13.3 are 0.6, 0.05, 0.4, 0.7 or 0.8, respectively.

The credit loss is calculated for the current exposure (CL^{curr}) as well as for the future exposure in a worst case scenario (CL^{future}). Thus by using the notations introduced at the beginning of Section 12.2 and in Section 12.9, the credit loss of a position i in a netting group g and in a fund f with counterparty k is given by

$$\mathrm{CL}^{curr}_{i,g,f,k} = V_{i,g,f,k} \cdot \mathrm{LGD}_i \cdot p_k \tag{13.2}$$

$$\mathrm{CL}^{future}_{i,g,f,k} = (V_{i,g,f,k} + \mathrm{VaR}_{i,g,f,k}) \cdot \mathrm{LGD}_i \cdot p_k, \tag{13.3}$$

where p_k denotes the probability of default for a counterparty k with its specific rating, i.e. if a counterparty k has market implied rating Aa1 thus $p_k = \mathbb{P}_{Aa1}$

[2]As the recovery rate (RR) is usually modeled as a random variable, the LGD, which is defined as LGD = 1 - RR, is also a random variable. To compute the expected loss, the expected value of the LGD is needed. That is a number between 0 and 1, not a random variable anymore, often called loss on default (LD). Thus we take the LGD as a deterministic quantity equal to its expected value.

[3]The recovery rate figures are average numbers derived from Exhibits 25 and 26 of [Emery and Ou (2009)].

($\mathbb{P}_{Aa1}$ has been computed in Subsection 8.7). The add-on amount is calculated as described in Section 12.9, that is

$$\mathrm{VaR}_{i,g,f,k} = \mathrm{Not}_{i,g,f,k} \cdot \mathrm{VaRFactor}_{i,g} .$$

As shown in Eqs. (13.2) and (13.3), the credit loss is firstly calculated for every investment regardless of netting class, fund or counterparty. Then it is aggregated by netting class and fund resulting in the following formulas for a counterparty k based on the current exposure

$$\mathrm{CL}_k^{curr} = \sum_{f=1}^{F_k} \max\left[\sum_{g=1}^{G_{f,k}} \max\left(\sum_{i=1}^{N_{g,f,k}} \mathrm{CL}_{i,g,f,k}^{curr}, 0\right) - \mathrm{Col}_{g,f,k}, 0\right],$$

and the future exposure

$$\mathrm{CL}_k^{future} = \sum_{f=1}^{F_k} \max\left[\sum_{g=1}^{G_{f,k}} \max\left(\sum_{i=1}^{N_{g,f,k}} \mathrm{CL}_{i,g,f,k}^{future}, 0\right) - \mathrm{Col}_{g,f,k}, 0\right] . \tag{13.4}$$

Logically these formulas are similar to Eqs. (12.10) and (12.13), respectively. Finally, the credit loss is aggregated by counterparty resulting in the total credit loss for an investor in OTC derivatives based on the current exposure

$$\mathrm{CL}^{curr} = \sum_{k=1}^{K} \mathrm{CL}_k^{curr} , \tag{13.5}$$

as well as on the potential future exposure in a worst case scenario

$$\mathrm{CL}^{future} = \sum_{k=1}^{K} \mathrm{CL}_k^{future} , \tag{13.6}$$

where, as mentioned before, K is the number of different counterparties.

13.5 Unexpected Loss

Besides the credit loss, we are interested in the unexpected loss (UL) that indicates the potential deviation from the expected loss, i.e. the credit loss that the investor can expect to incur (recall Figure 5.1). The idea of modeling the first two moments of the portfolio's credit losses is, also, defined as the "unexpected losses approach".

In [Ong (1999), Chapter V] and [Schroeck (2002), Chapter V] a detailed analysis of the unexpected loss is given. In this section, we describe briefly the concept of the unexpected loss and its application to counterparty risk measurement.

First, we define the actual loss of a position i, denoted by $\mathrm{L}_{i,g,f,k}$, as a random variable (on a suitable probability space $(\Omega, \mathcal{F}, \mathbb{P})$ of type

$$\mathrm{L}_{i,g,f,k} = V_{i,g,f,k} \cdot \mathrm{LGD}_i \cdot \mathbb{1}_{\{X_k=1\}}, \tag{13.7}$$

where $X_k(\bar{t})$, $\bar{t} \geq 0$, denotes the default random variable for the counterparty k in a time horizon of length t (defined on the same probability space $(\Omega, \mathcal{F}, \mathbb{P})$). For our purposes we consider a time horizon of one year. Thus $X_k := X_k(1)$ and the event $\{X_k = 1\} = \{\omega \in \Omega : X_k(\omega) = 1\}$ denotes all default states with probability $p_k = \mathbb{P}(X_k = 1)$, whereas $\{X_k = 0\} = \{\omega \in \Omega : X_k(\omega) = 0\}$ is the set of all non-default states, with probability $1 - p_k$. Further, $1_{\{X_k=1\}}$ is a random variable assuming only two values: 1 if the event $\{X_k = 1\}$ is realized with probability p_k, and 0 if the event $\{X_k = 0\}$ is realized with probability $1 - p_k$. As observed in Section 13.1, p_k is the probability of default for a counterparty k admitting a specific rating and is evaluated by using the same arguments as in Subsection 8.7. Since at time $t = 0$ we know which state $\omega \in \Omega$ is realised, then the actual loss of a position i is either 0 with probability $1 - p_k$ or $V_{i,g,f,k} \cdot \mathrm{LGD}_i$ with probability p_k.

It is worth noting that the credit loss for the current exposure defined in (13.2) is the expected value of the actual loss $\mathrm{L}_{i,g,f,k}$ given in (13.7) (the expectation of $\mathbb{1}_{\{X_k=1\}}$ is $\mathbb{E}\left[\mathbb{1}_{\{X_k=1\}}\right] = p_k$). Thus, as a natural choice, the unexpected loss can be defined as the standard deviation of $\mathrm{L}_{i,g,f,k}$, i.e. the square root of $Var(\mathrm{L}_{i,g,f,k})$, the variance of $\mathrm{L}_{i,g,f,k}$.

Observe that

$$\begin{aligned} Var(\mathrm{L}_{i,g,f,k}) &= \mathbb{E}\left[\mathrm{L}^2_{i,g,f,k}\right] - \mathbb{E}[\mathrm{L}_{i,g,f,k}]^2 = \mathbb{E}\left[\mathrm{L}^2_{i,g,f,k}\right] - \left(\mathrm{CL}^{curr}_{i,g,f,k}\right)^2 \\ &\overset{(13.7)}{=} V^2_{i,g,f,k} \cdot \mathrm{LGD}^2_i \cdot \mathbb{E}\left[\mathbb{1}^2_{\{X_k=1\}}\right] - V^2_{i,g,f,k} \cdot \mathrm{LGD}^2_i \cdot p^2_k \\ &= V^2_{i,g,f,k} \cdot \mathrm{LGD}^2_i \cdot p_k \cdot (1 - p_k), \end{aligned} \tag{13.8}$$

with $\mathbb{E}\left(\mathbb{1}^2_{\{X_k=1\}}\right) = p_k$.

As in the case of credit loss, the unexpected loss is calculated for the current exposure (UL^{curr}) as well as for the future exposure in a worst case scenario (UL^{future}). Then by using the notations introduced at the beginning of Section 12.2 and in Section 12.9, from Eq. (13.8) the unexpected loss for the current exposure of a position i in a netting group g and in a fund f with counterparty k, is defined as

$$\mathrm{UL}^{curr}_{i,g,f,k} := \sqrt{Var(\mathrm{L}_{i,g,f,k})} = \sqrt{V^2_{i,g,f,k} \cdot \mathrm{LGD}^2_i \cdot p_k \cdot (1 - p_k)}\ . \tag{13.9}$$

According to computations given in Section 12.9, we calculate an add-on amount which is added to the current value of position i

$$\mathrm{VaR}_{i,g,f,k} = \mathrm{Not}_{i,g,f,k} \cdot \mathrm{VaRFactor}_{i,g}\ .$$

Thus the unexpected loss of the future exposure is given by

$$\mathrm{UL}^{future}_{i,g,f,k} = \sqrt{(V_{i,g,f,k} + \mathrm{VaR}_{i,g,f,k})^2 \cdot \mathrm{LGD}^2_i \cdot p_k \cdot (1 - p_k)}\ . \tag{13.10}$$

The credit loss is firstly calculated for every investment regardless of netting class, fund or counterparty. Then it is aggregated by netting class and fund resulting in the following formulas for a counterparty k based on the current exposure. Finally, the credit loss is aggregated by counterparty resulting in the total credit loss for an investor in OTC derivatives based on the current exposure

$$\mathrm{CL}^{curr} = \sum_{k=1}^{K} \mathrm{CL}_k^{curr} , \tag{13.11}$$

as well as on the potential future exposure in a worst case scenario.

First, the unexpected loss is calculated using Eqs. (13.9) and (13.10) for every investment regardless of netting class, fund or counterparty. Second, it is aggregated by netting class, fund and counterparty level, resulting in the following formulas for a counterparty k based on the current exposure

$$\mathrm{UL}_k^{curr} = \sum_{f=1}^{F_k} \max\left[\sum_{g=1}^{G_{f,k}} \max\left(\sum_{i=1}^{N_{g,f,k}} \mathrm{UL}_{i,g,f,k}^{curr}, 0\right) - \mathrm{Col}_{g,f,k}, 0\right] ,$$

and the future exposure

$$\mathrm{UL}_k^{future} = \sum_{f=1}^{F_k} \max\left[\sum_{g=1}^{G_{f,k}} \max\left(\sum_{i=1}^{N_{g,f,k}} \mathrm{UL}_{i,g,f,k}^{future}, 0\right) - \mathrm{Col}_{g,f,k}, 0\right] .$$

Afterwards, it is aggregated for the respective counterparties. Finally, the unexpected loss for an investor in OTC derivatives based on the current exposure

$$\mathrm{UL}^{curr} = \sum_{k=1}^{K} \mathrm{UL}_k^{curr} , \tag{13.12}$$

as well as on the potential future exposure, in a worst case scenario,

$$\mathrm{UL}^{future} = \sum_{k=1}^{K} \mathrm{UL}_k^{future} , \tag{13.13}$$

are given with respect to the total number K of different counterparties.

13.6 Economic Capital

In line of this work and according to current regulation and market practices, we set the level of capital in a way that it equals the amount the company needs for absorbing unexpected losses over a certain time horizon at a given confidence level (cf. [Kuritzkes and Schuermann (2007)]). We follow the standard convention and measure the economic capital as the difference between the unexpected and expected losses (a detailed discussion of economic capital can be found in [Schroeck (2002), Chapter V]). Therefore a current and a future economic capital can be distinguished as we distinguish current and future credit loss, current and future unexpected loss. Hence the following formula for the economic capital (which is denoted by EC) is as below

$$\mathrm{EC}_{i,g,f,k}^{curr} = \mathrm{UL}_{i,g,f,k}^{curr} - \mathrm{CL}_{i,g,f,k}^{curr} , \tag{13.14}$$

$$\mathrm{EC}_{i,g,f,k}^{future} = \mathrm{UL}_{i,g,f,k}^{future} - \mathrm{CL}_{i,g,f,k}^{future} . \tag{13.15}$$

The calculations for the economic capital are similar to the calculations for the credit loss in Sections 13.1 and 13.5. The economic capital for each counterparty k based on Eqs. (13.14) and (13.15) are

$$\mathrm{EC}_k^{curr} = \sum_{f=1}^{F_k} \max\left[\sum_{g=1}^{G_{f,k}} \max\left(\sum_{i=1}^{N_{g,f,k}} \mathrm{EC}_{i,g,f,k}^{curr}, 0\right) - \mathrm{Col}_{g,f,k}, 0\right] ,$$

$$\mathrm{EC}_k^{future} = \sum_{f=1}^{F_k} \max\left[\sum_{g=1}^{G_{f,k}} \max\left(\sum_{i=1}^{N_{g,f,k}} \mathrm{EC}_{i,g,f,k}^{future}, 0\right) - \mathrm{Col}_{g,f,k}, 0\right] .$$

Then we calculate the economic capital based on the current exposure as well as the economic capital for a future worst case based on the potential future exposure

$$\mathrm{EC}^{curr} = \sum_{k=1}^{K} \mathrm{EC}_k^{curr} , \tag{13.16}$$

$$\mathrm{EC}^{future} = \sum_{k=1}^{K} \mathrm{EC}_k^{future} . \tag{13.17}$$

Note that it is important to calculate first the economic capital for every investment i, then for each counterparty k. Finally, the sum of the values for each counterparty gives us the economic capital for the investor. In fact, if we had used Eqs. (13.2) and (13.9) to calculate Eq. (13.16) (respectively, Eqs. (13.3) and (13.10) to calculate Eq. (13.16)), we would have subtracted the collateral twice.

13.7 Central Counterparty (CCP)

"Central Counterparties (CCPs) are designed to mitigate counterparty risk through multi-lateral netting, high levels of collateralisation as well as loss mutualisation" ([Arnsdorf (2011), p. 1]). Due to the financial crisis of 2008 there has been a concerted regulatory drive to substantially increase the proportion of derivatives that are centrally cleared. The primary motivation is to reduce bilateral counterparty risk, increase transparency and avoid contagion in the case of the default of a large financial institution. For derivatives cleared through a CCP, we use the LGD shown in Table 13.4 (cf. [Arnsdorf (2011), p. 15]) that is dependent upon the underlying. There is no figure for the LGD of derivatives with underlying commodity stated in [Arnsdorf (2011)], so we take the same as for equity underlying, because of similarities in the volatility levels for these underlyings.

Note that the used probability of default for a CCP-cleared position depends on the assumed rating of the CCP.

Table 13.4: LGD of CCP-cleared derivatives according to their respective underlying.

	Equity	Commodity	Fixed Income / IR	Foreign Exchange	Credit
LGD	10.3%	10.3%	11.5%	17.4%	6.9%

13.8 Cox Process

In reality, events often exhibit dependencies that cannot be captured by the Poisson process because of the assumption that the number of events that occur in two non-overlapping time intervals must be independent. One way to capture such dependencies is to consider Cox processes, which are Poisson processes with a random mean measure. In particular, consider mean measures that takes the form of latent Markov processes. In queuing theory, this kind of model is referred to as a Markov-Modulated Poisson Process, see [Ryden (1996)], and it has been used as a model for packets in networks, see [Fischer and Meier-Hellstern (1993)].

13.9 Business Cycles

Depending on the state of the economy creditworthiness may change dramatically. UL, *CreditMetrics*^{TM} and *CreditRisk*$^{+TM}$ models incorporate some counterparty facility-specific information, but they fall in the category of the so-called *unconditional models.* McKinsey's *CreditPortfolio View*^{TM}, instead, captures some macroeconomic information such as employment, inflation, interest rates, etc. Therefore it is called a *conditional model* as transition matrices evolve according to the state of the economy. A different approach is adopted by KMV's *PortfolioManager*^{TM} in which the "estimates of asset values, rates of return and volatility are based, in part, on current equity prices, which are inherently forward-looking" [BCBS (1999)].

13.10 Potential Collateral Requirements

In this paragraph, we develop the concept of how collateral requirements might have an impact on a fund's/account's liquidity and risk. When the value of a position decreases, it does not only have an impact on the NAV, but also on the collateral. Three cases might happen:

- The position changes from positive to negative, i.e. the fund has to give back the collateral received and to post additional collateral;
- The position remains positive, i.e. the fund has to give back part of the collateral received;
- The position remains negative, i.e. the fund has to post additional collateral.

The above shows that a market/credit event might put stress on the liquidity of the fund which, if not carefully managed, could, in turn, lead to a sale of assets at unfavorable conditions.

In the following, we present the formula which describes the potential collateral requirements (PCR) of counterparty k, that has to be compared with the fund's liquidity, potential borrowing needs and eligible assets for collateral by using the known notations of Sections 12.2 to 14

$$\mathrm{PCR}_k = \sum_{f=1}^{F_k} \max\left[-\sum_{g=1}^{G_{f,k}} \min(V_{g,f,k} + \mathrm{VaR}_{g,f,k} - \mathrm{Col}_{g,f,k}, 0), 0\right], \qquad (13.18)$$

where the sum of the NRVs of all positions of a netting group g in a fund f with counterparty k is denoted by

$$V_{g,f,k} := \sum_{i=1}^{N_{g,f,k}} V_{i,g,f,k}\,.$$

The difference between available assets (i.e. liquidity, borrowing and eligible assets for collateral) and PCRs can be used for managing liquidity risk as a shortfall measure.

Note that in Eq. (13.18) the collateral amount of a certain netting group $\mathrm{Col}_{g,f,k}$ can be positive or negative, i.e. broker and client collateral respectively have to be taken into consideration. As far as collateral received is booked off balance, a reduction of this collateral does not affect the assets of the fund. Since often there is not sufficient information, it is difficult to gauge, whether collateral received is on- or off-balance. For this reason, the PCR is reported as a value independent from the way broker collateral is booked. In such an instance, the PCR will overstate the real requirements, that have to be covered by the fund's assets, by the amount of broker collateral booked off-balance. To correct that, to evaluate whether the eligible assets of a fund are sufficient to cover potential collateral requirements, the PCR has to be reduced by the amount of the off-balance broker collateral before comparing it to the amount of assets available. Further, $\mathrm{VaR}_{g,f,k}$ denotes the diversified add-on amount, described in Chapter 14.

In the book, we have shown a pragmatic solution to the problem of measuring credit and counterparty risk and dealing with liquidity risk via collateral requirements. It is worth mentioning that the figures shown in the tables should be estimated/calibrated to obtain a number of exceptions in the back-testing consistent with the confidence level set for the VaR (e.g. if the VaR is set at 99.5%, the figures in the table should lead to a maximum number of exceptions of 5 over 1,000 runs).

Estimation and calibration can be carried out through Monte Carlo simulation (which presents some issues in terms of modeling the nonlinearities) or by historical simulation which accurately reflects the historical multivariate probability distribution but requires some corrections to incorporate volatility updating (cf. [Hull and White (1998)]). A possible extension could be to illustrate how to address the matter pragmatically. Finally, it goes without saying that, in the context of this work, VaR is the Shortfall/CVaR for a lower confidence level.

Chapter 14

Correlation-Driven Issues

This chapter[1] describes a method to include the correlation between different positions within a netting group at the first stage and between netting groups at a second stage. A change in the value of a derivative might impact the value of other derivatives with this counterparty. This effect can be properly captured on a netting group level, as we cannot net positions from different netting groups. Therefore, the next sections explain how to include the correlation into the future net replacement value and the credit loss.

A credit event that may cause a loss on a portfolio can be either a significant change in:

- Probability of Default (PD);
- Loss Given Default (LGD);
- Applicable Credit Spread (CS) to discount the cash-flows;
- Exposure-At-Default (EAD).

14.1 Correlation in the Future Exposure

First, we need a correlation matrix with the dependencies between the different positions of a netting group g. Let us denote this matrix by $\Sigma_{g,f,k}$. If the specific netting group consists of n positions, then it is a $n \times n$-matrix as below

$$\Sigma_{g,f,k} := \begin{pmatrix} c_{11} & c_{12} & \cdots & c_{1n} \\ c_{21} & c_{22} & \cdots & c_{2n} \\ \vdots & \vdots & \ddots & \vdots \\ c_{n1} & c_{n2} & \cdots & c_{nn} \end{pmatrix},$$

where c_{kl} denotes the correlation between position k and position l of a netting group g. Next, a factor measuring the risk of a position in a netting group is needed for each position of the respective netting group. For this purpose, we take the respective VaR factor which can be found in the Tables 12.5 and 12.6 in Section

[1] Part of this chapter has been published in [Orlando and Härtel (2014)].

12.8. For the n positions of the netting group, we get a n-variate vector as VaR factor vector of this netting group g which we denote by $\beta_{g,f,k}$

$$\beta_{g,f,k} := (\text{VaRFactor}_{1,g,f,k}, \cdots, \text{VaRFactor}_{n,g,f,k})^\top .$$

Then, we need a weight for each position within the netting group as a derivative with a very large notional having apparently a more significant effect on the future exposure than a derivative with a small notional. Therefore, the notional of all positions of the netting group is as follows

$$\text{Not}_{g,f,k} := \sum_{i=1}^{N_{g,f,k}} \text{Not}_{i,g,f,k} .$$

The weight of a position i in the netting group is then

$$w_{i,g,f,k} := \frac{\text{Not}_{i,g,f,k}}{\text{Not}_{g,f,k}} .$$

Hence, the weighting vector of the netting group is

$$w_{g,f,k} := (w_{1,g,f,k}, \cdots, w_{n,g,f,k})^\top .$$

Then, we define the vector $v_{g,f,k}$ as $w_{g,f,k}^\top \cdot \beta_{g,f,k}$. We obtain the VaR factor for the netting group g as

$$\text{VaRFactor}_{g,f,k} := \sqrt{v_{g,f,k}\, \Sigma_{g,f,k}\, v_{g,f,k}},$$

and hence the amount that has to be added to the values of the positions of the netting group g for calculating the future exposure is

$$\text{VaR}_{g,f,k} := \text{Not}_{g,f,k} \cdot \text{VaRFactor}_{g,f,k} .$$

In the end, the future exposure of a counterparty k, i.e. the aggregated net replacement value including add-on for the counterparty k with the incorporation of correlation, equals to the following

$$\text{NRV-VaR}_k = \sum_{f=1}^{F_k} \max\left[\sum_{g=1}^{G_{f,k}} \max\left(\sum_{i=1}^{N_{g,f,k}} V_{i,g,f,k}, 0\right) + \text{VaR}_{g,f,k} - \text{Col}_{g,f,k}, 0\right] . \tag{14.1}$$

14.2 Correlation in Credit Loss and Unexpected Loss

This section describes how to include the correlation within a netting group into the credit loss and unexpected loss. The current credit loss of a counterparty k remains unchanged as well as the unexpected loss

$$\mathrm{CL}_k^{curr} = \sum_{f=1}^{F_k} \max\left[\sum_{g=1}^{G_{f,k}} \max\left(\sum_{i=1}^{N_{g,f,k}} \mathrm{CL}_{i,g,f,k}^{curr}, 0\right) - \mathrm{Col}_{g,f,k}, 0\right],$$

with

$$\mathrm{CL}_{i,g,f,k}^{curr} = V_{i,g,f,k} \cdot \mathrm{LGD}_i \cdot p_k$$

and

$$\mathrm{UL}_k^{curr} = \sum_{f=1}^{F_k} \max\left[\sum_{g=1}^{G_{f,k}} \max\left(\sum_{i=1}^{N_{g,f,k}} \mathrm{UL}_{i,g,f,k}^{curr}, 0\right) - \mathrm{Col}_{g,f,k}, 0\right],$$

with

$$\mathrm{UL}_{i,g,f,k}^{curr} = \sqrt{V_{i,g,f,k}^2 \cdot \mathrm{LGD}_i^2 \cdot p_k \cdot (1 - p_k)}\ .$$

To calculate the credit loss and unexpected loss for the future exposure, we have to integrate the severity of position i of netting group g to the respective weight, i.e.

$$w_{i,g,f,k}^{\mathrm{CL}} := w_{i,g,f,k} \cdot \mathrm{LGD}_i,$$

or respectively

$$w_{i,g,f,k}^{\mathrm{UL}} := w_{i,g,f,k} \cdot \mathrm{LGD}_i\ .$$

We again define an auxiliary variable

$$v_{i,g,f,k}^{\mathrm{CL}} := (w_{g,f,k}^{\mathrm{CL}})^\top \cdot \beta_{g,f,k},$$

or respectively

$$v_{i,g,f,k}^{\mathrm{UL}} := (w_{g,f,k}^{\mathrm{UL}})^\top \cdot \beta_{g,f,k}\ .$$

Then, the VaR factor of the netting group is

$$\mathrm{VaRFactor}_{g,f,k}^{\mathrm{CL}} := \sqrt{v_{i,g,f,k}^{\mathrm{CL}}\ \Sigma_{g,f,k}\ v_{i,g,f,k}^{\mathrm{CL}}},$$

or respectively

$$\mathrm{VaRFactor}_{g,f,k}^{\mathrm{UL}} := \sqrt{v_{g,f,k}^{\mathrm{UL}}\ \Sigma_{g,f,k}\ v_{g,f,k}^{\mathrm{UL}}}\ .$$

Hence the amount that has to be added is

$$\mathrm{VaR}^{\mathrm{CL}}_{g,f,k} := \mathrm{Not}_{g,f,k} \cdot \mathrm{VaRFactor}^{\mathrm{CL}}_{g,f,k},$$

or respectively

$$\mathrm{VaR}^{\mathrm{UL}}_{g,f,k} := \mathrm{Not}_{g,f,k} \cdot \mathrm{VaRFactor}^{\mathrm{UL}}_{g,f,k} \ .$$

Next, we can calculate the future credit loss for the netting group g as

$$\mathrm{CL}^{future}_{g,f,k} := \mathrm{CL}^{curr}_{g,f,k} + \mathrm{VaR}^{\mathrm{CL}}_{g,f,k} \cdot p_k - \mathrm{Col}_{g,f,k},$$

where

$$\mathrm{CL}^{curr}_{g,f,k} := \max\left(\sum_{i=1}^{N_{g,f,k}} \mathrm{CL}^{curr}_{i,g,f,k}, 0\right).$$

Then, the calculation of the future unexpected loss regarding netting group g is

$$\mathrm{UL}^{future}_{g,f,k} := \mathrm{UL}^{curr}_{g,f,k} + \mathrm{VaR}^{\mathrm{UL}}_{g,f,k} \cdot p_k - \mathrm{Col}_{g,f,k} \ ,$$

where

$$\mathrm{UL}^{curr}_{g,f,k} := \max\left(\sum_{i=1}^{N_{g,f,k}} \mathrm{UL}^{curr}_{i,g,f,k}, 0\right).$$

In the end, the future credit loss of a counterparty k with correlation is

$$\mathrm{CL}^{future}_{k} = \sum_{f=1}^{F_k} \sum_{g=1}^{G_{f,k}} \max\left(\mathrm{CL}^{future}_{g,f,k}, 0\right) \ , \tag{14.2}$$

and the future expected loss of a counterparty k with correlation can be calculated in the following way

$$\mathrm{UL}^{future}_{k} = \sum_{f=1}^{F_k} \sum_{g=1}^{G_{f,k}} \max\left(\mathrm{UL}^{future}_{g,f,k}, 0\right) \ . \tag{14.3}$$

Using Eqs. (14.2) and (14.3) the credit loss as well as the unexpected loss based on the potential future exposure with the correlation between different positions within a netting group is as follows (where K denotes the number of different counterparties)

$$\mathrm{CL}^{future} = \sum_{k=1}^{K} \mathrm{CL}^{future}_{k} \ ,$$

$$\mathrm{UL}^{future} = \sum_{k=1}^{K} \mathrm{UL}^{future}_{k} \ .$$

14.3 Correlation between Netting Groups

In addition to the correlation of positions inherent into a specific netting group, there is also a correlation between the different netting groups. Therefore, a correlation matrix is needed displaying the dependences of the netting groups of a fund f and is denoted by $\Sigma_{f,k}$. If the specific fund consists of n positions, then it is a $n \times n$-matrix as below

$$\Sigma_{f,k} := \begin{pmatrix} k_{11} & k_{12} & \cdots & k_{1n} \\ k_{21} & k_{22} & \cdots & k_{2n} \\ \vdots & \vdots & \ddots & \vdots \\ k_{n1} & k_{n2} & \cdots & k_{nn} \end{pmatrix}$$

with k_{lm} denoting the correlation between netting groups l and m of fund f. Then, the correlation of the netting groups is incorporated in the calculations as described for positions in a netting group in the previous section, whereas the weight of each netting group in the fund f is calculated via the sum of all notionals of all positions of the specific netting group.

14.4 Cross-Correlations between Different Types of Credit Events

The discussions above assumed independence of various credit events related to PD, LGD, EAD. However, in real life, this assumption might be often violated. For instance, [Altman (2006)] used the United States data for 30 years from 1982 to 2009, see Figure 14.1. We may see significant dependence of PD and LGD. This effect is also known as the *PD-LGD Correlation (PLC)*. [Ermolova and Penikas (2017)] find similar, but less significant dependence for the Russia data for 1999-2015 for the largest corporate borrowers with publicly listed bonds, see Figure 14.2.

[Ozdemir and Miu (2009)] discuss the possible modification of [Vasicek (1987)] and IRB approaches for the presence of *PD-EAD* correlation. The key implication for it, as well as for the PLC, is that the credit risk is underestimated when the parameter independence is mistakenly assumed. However, PLC to be properly estimated requires reliable data on recoveries. Particularly, when a bank prefers an *F-IRB*, then such data is not available to it. That is why regulators suggest using a more conservative LGD value to offset credit risk underestimation due to PLC. It is called a *downturn LGDDownturn LGD*. However, as we have shown in Section 11.2, the use of conservative values might not be sufficient to completely estimate the portfolio credit risk. [Osadchiy and Sidorov (2020)] discuss an additional shortcoming of a model with independent PD and LGD. They show that due to correct accounting of the parameter dependence, the loss distribution takes a unique springboard form. No conservative margin can compensate for risks in such a case.

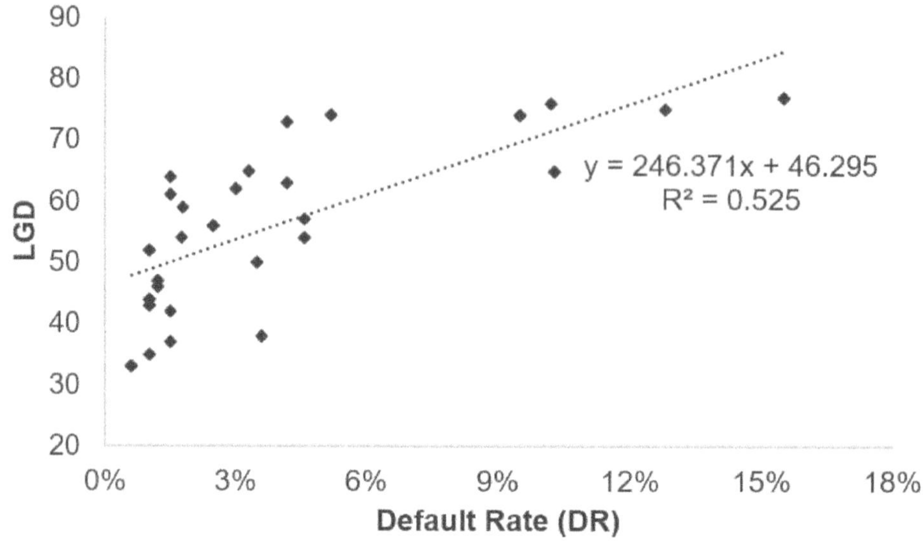

Fig. 14.1: PD-LGD correlation in the United States Data for 1982-2009.
Adapted by authors from [Altman (2006)]

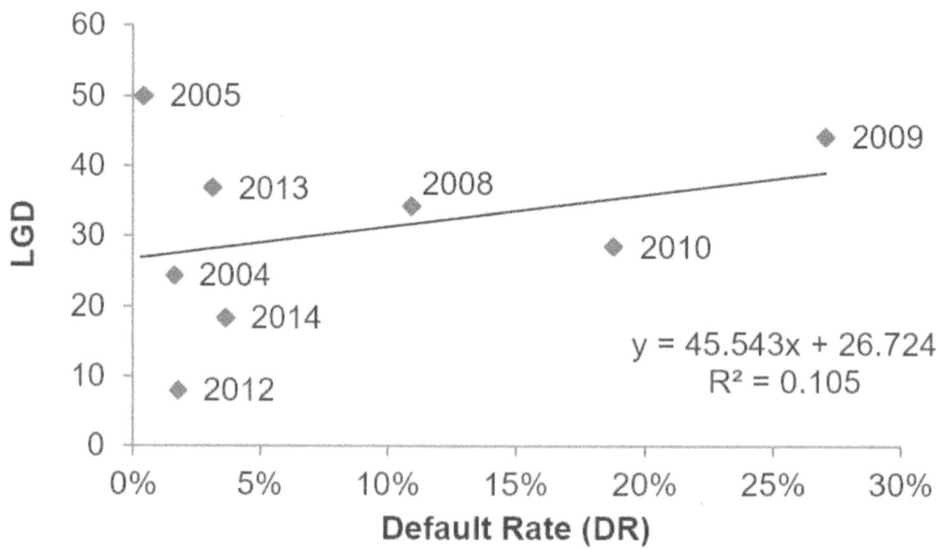

Fig. 14.2: PD-LGD correlation in the Russian Data for 2003-2015.
Source: [Ermolova and Penikas (2017)]

PART 5

Portfolio Credit Risk Management Applications

Chapter 15

Credit Risk Models

In Section 10.3 we defined the loss variables as indicators of default events. A very common approach in actuarial mathematics is modeling the defaults by Bernoulli or Poisson random variables. This approach is preferred by the following credit risk models:

- *CreditMetrics*^{TM}, an original model proposed by the US bank J.P. Morgan, under which the default probabilities of debtors belong to different rating classes;
- *CreditPortfolioView*^{TM}, a model developed by McKinsey, based on an econometric analysis of the relationships between default probabilities or default migrations and the state of the macroeconomic cycle;
- *CreditRisk*+, a model proposed by Credit Suisse Financial Products, based on some actuarial mathematical models;
- *PortfolioManager*^{TM}, a model developed by Moody's KMV, based on the default probability estimation methods through the Merton model. The original name of the company is an acronym for its founders' family names: Stephen Kealhofer, John McQuown, and Oldrich Vasicek (see [Vasicek (2012), p. 1]). It is sometimes mistakenly called Kealhofer-Merton-Vasicek (see [Tetereva (2012), p. 1]) most probably because the [Vasicek (1987)] paper is an extension of the [Merton (1974)] one.

In Section 15.2 we analyze the *CreditRisk* +, which describes the probability distribution of the amount of defaults over a fixed time horizon through the Poisson distribution. For more discussion of the models, we recommend referring to [Gordy (2000)].

Here we start by describing the well-known Poisson model; all the random variables that will be considered are assumed to be defined on a probability space $(\Omega, \mathcal{F}, \mathbb{P})$.

15.1 Poisson Model

Assume the portfolio consists of n counterparties $L_1, ..., L_n$, with $L_i \sim Pois(\lambda_i)$, for any $i = 1, ..., n$, i.e.

$$\mathbb{P}(L_i = l_i) = \frac{e^{-\lambda_i}\lambda_i^{l_i}}{l_i!} \qquad (l_i \in \mathbb{N}).$$

Each L_i stands for the number of defaults of the i-th counterparty during the fixed time horizon, e.g. one year. Denoted by $p_i = \mathbb{P}(L_i \geq 1)$ the probability that the default event occurs at least once, the probability that the i-th counterparty default occurs more than once is given by

$$\mathbb{P}(L_i \geq 2) = 1 - e^{-\lambda_i}(1 + \lambda_i).$$

Indeed,

$$\begin{aligned}\mathbb{P}(L_i \geq 2) &= 1 - \mathbb{P}(L_i < 2) = 1 - (\mathbb{P}(L_i = 0) + \mathbb{P}(L_i = 1)) \\ &= 1 - (e^{-\lambda_i} + e^{-\lambda_i}\lambda_i) = 1 - e^{-\lambda_i}(1 + \lambda_i).\end{aligned}$$

Generally, this probability is very small. For example, if $\lambda = 0.02$, then $\mathbb{P}(L_i \geq 2)$ $= 0.0002$. One of the possible ways to calibrate the parameter λ_i is to choose $\lambda_i \geq 0$ so that $p_i = 1 - e^{-\lambda_i}$. In fact, suppose that λ_i takes on sufficiently small values and consider the MacLauren series development up to the first order of the function $e^{-\lambda_i}$. We have

$$e^{-\lambda_i} = 1 - \lambda_i + o(\lambda_i^2). \tag{15.1}$$

Neglecting the terms with order higher than one, from Eq. (15.1) we soon obtain

$$p_i = \mathbb{P}(L_i \geq 1) = 1 - e^{-\lambda_i} \approx \lambda_i.$$

Set $L = \sum_{i=1}^{n} L_i$ be the random variable describing the number of defaults in the book. Let us model the distribution of L. If L_i are two by two independent, it is clear that $L \sim Pois(\lambda)$, where $\lambda = \sum_{i=1}^{n} \lambda_i$. If all L_i are not independent, there is no guarantee that L follows a Poisson distribution. In this case, it is necessary to take into account the correlations existing between the variables L_i. This correlation will be introduced in the mixed Poisson model, described in the following subsection.

15.1.1 *Mixed Poisson Model*

Let $\boldsymbol{L} = (L_1, ..., L_n)$ be a vector of Poisson random variables, $L_i \sim Pois(\Lambda_i)$, where $\boldsymbol{\Lambda} = (\Lambda_1, ..., \Lambda_n)$ is a random vector with continuous distribution function $F_{\boldsymbol{\Lambda}}$ having support $[0, +\infty)^n$.

Definition 15.1. $\boldsymbol{L} = (L_1, ..., L_n)$ is said to follow a mixed Poisson model with parameter $\boldsymbol{\Lambda} = (\Lambda_1, ..., \Lambda_n)$ if there exists a vector $\boldsymbol{\lambda} = (\lambda_1, ..., \lambda_n)$, which is a realisation of $\boldsymbol{\Lambda}$, such that $(L_i|\Lambda_i = \lambda_i) \sim Pois(\lambda_i)$ and the conditioned random variables $(L_i|\boldsymbol{\Lambda} = \boldsymbol{\lambda})$ are independent, for any i.

Observe that the default probability of the i-th debtor is given by

$$\mathbb{P}(L_i = l_i|\Lambda_i = \lambda_i) = \frac{e^{-\lambda_i}\lambda_i^{l_i}}{l_i!}. \tag{15.2}$$

Furthermore, the conditional probability of $\boldsymbol{L}$ is given by

$$\begin{aligned}
&\mathbb{P}(\boldsymbol{L}|\boldsymbol{\Lambda} = \boldsymbol{\lambda}) \\
&\qquad = \mathbb{E}[\mathbb{1}_{\{L_1=l_1,...,L_n=l_n\}}|\Lambda_1 = \lambda_1, ..., \Lambda_n = \lambda_n] \\
&\qquad = \prod_{i=1}^{n} \mathbb{P}(L_i = l_i|\Lambda_i = \lambda_i) \\
&\qquad = \prod_{i=1}^{n} \frac{e^{-\lambda_i}\lambda_i^{l_i}}{l_i!},
\end{aligned} \tag{15.3}$$

where we have used Eq. (15.2). Consequently, the unconditional joint distribution of $\boldsymbol{L}$ is obtained by integrating Eq. (15.3) as follows

$$\mathbb{E}\Big[\mathbb{P}(\boldsymbol{L}|\boldsymbol{\Lambda} = \boldsymbol{\lambda})\Big] = \int_{[0,+\infty)^n} \prod_{i=1}^{n} \frac{\lambda_i^{l_i}}{l_i!} e^{-(\lambda_1+...+\lambda_n)}\, dF_{\boldsymbol{\Lambda}}(\boldsymbol{\lambda}).$$

Recalling that $L = \sum_{i=1}^{n} L_i$, the expected value and variance of L can be deduced from the properties of the parameter. We start by calculating the first moment and variance of L_i:

i) $\mathbb{E}[L_i] = \mathbb{E}[\mathbb{E}[L_i|\Lambda_i]] = \mathbb{E}[\Lambda_i]$;
ii) $Var(L_i) = \mathbb{E}[Var(L_i|\Lambda_i)] + Var(\mathbb{E}[L_i|\Lambda_i]) = \mathbb{E}[\Lambda_i] + Var(\Lambda_i)$.

From the relations *i)*, *ii)* and from the properties of the expected value and variance, we deduce that

$$\mathbb{E}[L] = \sum_{i=1}^{n} \mathbb{E}[L_i] = \sum_{i=1}^{n} \mathbb{E}[\Lambda_i], \tag{15.4}$$

$$\begin{aligned}
Var(L) &= \sum_{i=1}^{n} Var(L_i) + \sum_{\substack{i,j=1,\\ i\neq j}}^{n} Cov(L_i, L_j) \\
&= \sum_{i=1}^{n} \mathbb{E}[\Lambda_i] + \sum_{i=1}^{n} Var(\Lambda_i) + \sum_{\substack{i,j=1,\\ i\neq j}}^{n} Cov(L_i, L_j).
\end{aligned} \tag{15.5}$$

Observe that, if $i \neq j$,

$$\begin{aligned} Cov(L_i, L_j) &= \mathbb{E}[L_i L_j] - \mathbb{E}[L_i]\mathbb{E}[L_j] \\ &= \mathbb{E}[\Lambda_i \Lambda_j] - \mathbb{E}[\Lambda_i]\mathbb{E}[\Lambda_j] \\ &= Cov(\Lambda_i, \Lambda_j), \end{aligned} \tag{15.6}$$

where we have used the independence of the variables, i.e.

$$\mathbb{E}[L_i L_j] = \mathbb{E}[\mathbb{E}[L_i L_j | \Lambda_i, \Lambda_j]] = \mathbb{E}[\mathbb{E}[L_i | \Lambda_i]\mathbb{E}[L_j | \Lambda_j]] = \mathbb{E}[\Lambda_i \Lambda_j].$$

Therefore, Eq. (15.5) can be rewritten as

$$Var(L) = \sum_{i=1}^{n} \mathbb{E}[\Lambda_i] + \sum_{i=1}^{n} Var(\Lambda_i) + \sum_{\substack{i,j=1, \\ i \neq j}}^{n} Cov(\Lambda_i, \Lambda_j). \tag{15.7}$$

The correlation between the L_i's (the default correlation) can also be deduced from the properties of Λ_i's. Indeed,

$$\begin{aligned} Corr(L_i, L_j) &= \frac{Cov(L_i, L_j)}{\sqrt{Var(L_i) Var(L_j)}} \\ &= \frac{Cov(\Lambda_i, \Lambda_j)}{\sqrt{\Big(Var(\Lambda_i) + \mathbb{E}[\Lambda_i]\Big)\Big(Var(\Lambda_j) + \mathbb{E}[\Lambda_j]\Big)}}, \end{aligned}$$

where we used relation *ii*) and Eq. (15.6).

15.1.2 *Homogeneous Portfolio*

In the case of a homogeneous portfolio, we assume that each Λ_i is equal to a certain $\Lambda \sim F_\Lambda$, for any $i = 1, ..., n$, where F_Λ is a continuous distribution function with support $[0, +\infty)$. In this case, the unconditional joint distribution of L_i is given by

$$\mathbb{P}(L_1 = l_1, ..., L_n = l_n) = \int_0^{+\infty} \frac{e^{-n\lambda} \lambda^{(l_1 + ... + l_n)}}{l_1! \cdots l_n!} \, dF_\Lambda(\lambda).$$

Since L_i are equally distributed and conditionally independent, it follows that the conditional distribution of $L = \sum_{i=1}^{n} L_i$ still follows a Poisson distribution with parameter $n\lambda$, i.e. $(L_{|\Lambda = n\lambda}) \sim Pois(n\lambda)$. Hence, the probability that k defaults occur is

$$\begin{aligned} \mathbb{P}(L = k) &= \int_0^{+\infty} \mathbb{P}(L = k | \Lambda = n\lambda) \, dF_\Lambda(\lambda) \\ &= \int_0^{+\infty} \frac{e^{-n\lambda} n^k \lambda^k}{k!} \, dF_\Lambda(\lambda). \end{aligned}$$

In this particular case, we have:

i') $\mathbb{E}[L_i] = \mathbb{E}[\mathbb{E}[L_i|\Lambda]] = \mathbb{E}[\Lambda]$;
ii') $Var(L_i) = \mathbb{E}[Var(L_i|\Lambda)] + Var(\mathbb{E}[L_i|\Lambda]) = \mathbb{E}[\Lambda] + Var(\Lambda)$;

while the expected value and variance of L become

$$\mathbb{E}[L] = \sum_{i=1}^{n} \mathbb{E}[L_i] = \sum_{i=1}^{n} \mathbb{E}[\Lambda] = n\mathbb{E}[\Lambda], \tag{15.8}$$

$$\begin{aligned} Var(L) &= \sum_{i=1}^{n} Var(L_i) + \sum_{\substack{i,j=1,\\ i\neq j}}^{n} Cov(L_i, L_j) \\ &= \sum_{i=1}^{n} \mathbb{E}[\Lambda] + \sum_{i=1}^{n} Var(\Lambda) + \sum_{\substack{i,j=1,\\ i\neq j}}^{n} Cov(L_i, L_j) \\ &= n\big(\mathbb{E}[\Lambda] + Var(\Lambda)\big), \end{aligned} \tag{15.9}$$

where we have used the following relationship

$$Cov(L_i, L_j) = \mathbb{E}[L_iL_j] - \mathbb{E}[L_i]\mathbb{E}[L_j] = Cov(\Lambda_i, \Lambda_j) = Var(\Lambda).$$

The correlation between the variable L_i's is

$$\begin{aligned} Corr(L_i, L_j) &= \frac{Cov(\Lambda_i, \Lambda_j)}{\sqrt{\Big(Var(\Lambda_i) + \mathbb{E}[\Lambda_i]\Big)\Big(Var(\Lambda_j) + \mathbb{E}[\Lambda_j]\Big)}} \\ &= \frac{Var(\Lambda)}{Var(\Lambda) + \mathbb{E}[\Lambda]}. \end{aligned} \tag{15.10}$$

Based on these results, we are ready to analyze the *CreditRisk +* model.

15.2 CreditRisk +

In October 1997, Credit Suisse Financial Products (CSFP) published its portfolio model, i.e. the *CreditRisk +*. The model, created by Tom Wilde, is still the only one of the various existing portfolio models to involve actuarial mathematics in calculating the expected loss distribution of a portfolio. One of the main reasons for the success of this model is that it is the only credit risk model that focuses its analysis on the event of default. Furthermore, it can be easily applied to various financial instruments, such as derivatives and bonds. This model is based on some fundamental ideas, which can be summarized as follows:

- Default of an obligor is described like a purely random event, characterized by its default probability PD;
- Default probability of a debtor is not considered constant, but as a random quantity whose variability depends on the presence of one or more risk factors;
- Portfolio losses are represented by integer multiples of a unit exposure;
- Loss distribution is derived from the PGF of the individual losses;
- In order to obtain the distribution of the portfolio defaults, we may use an approximation of the default probability generating function, like the Poisson distribution.

Based on these assumptions, the *CreditRisk +* provides the portfolio loss distribution obtained by the sum of independent negative binomial variables.

Let us consider a credit portfolio made up of n distinct counterparties and let L_i be the Bernoulli variable describing the default number of the i-th debtor, for $i = 1, ..., n$. Therefore,

$$L_i = \begin{cases} 1 & \text{if the } i\text{-th debtor defaults,} \\ 0 & \text{otherwise.} \end{cases}$$

We assume L_i are two by two independent variables and we denote $p_i = \mathbb{P}(L_i = 1)$ as the default probability of the i-th debtor. The first step to derive the probability distribution of the portfolio loss is the computation of the probability distribution of the portfolio defaults' number L. In this regard, we distinguish the following two cases:

- Probability of default (PD) is constant;
- Probability of default (PD) is a random variable.

In the first case, L follows a Poisson distribution, while in the second one L follows a Negative Binomial distribution (see Chapter 16).

15.2.1 *Distribution of Defaults with Constant PD*

Let L be the total number of defaults of the considered portfolio. We obtain it by summing up the defaults of each counterparty within a portfolio, i.e. $L = \sum_{i=1}^{n} L_i$. Our aim is to determine the probability distribution of L. Since L is the sum of independent and discrete random variables, we can reach this probability distribution by its PGF. Let

$$G_L(z) = \sum_{k=0}^{+\infty} \mathbb{P}(L = k) z^k,$$

be the PGF of L (see Eq. (3.5)). By the convolution theorem (see Theorem 3.3), G_L can be obtained as the product of the PGF G_{L_i} of L_i, i.e.

$$G_L(z) = \prod_{i=1}^{n} G_{L_i}(z).$$

Since L_i's follow a Bernoulli distribution with parameter p_i, their PGFs are given by $G_{L_i}(z) = (1 - p_i) + p_i z$, (see Example 3.1) which can be rewritten as

$$G_{L_i}(z) = \exp\left(\ln\left(1 + p_i(z - 1)\right)\right). \tag{15.11}$$

If p_i is sufficiently small, the same holds true for $p_i(z-1)$, if $|z| \leq 1$. Now, set $w = p_i(z-1)$, and apply the Taylor's series expansion, at $w = 0$, to $\ln(1 + w)$,

$$\ln(1 + w) = w - \frac{w^2}{2} + \frac{w^3}{3} \cdots$$

Neglecting the terms of order higher than one, we get

$$\ln(1 + p_i(z - 1)) \approx p_i(z - 1).$$

Substituting this approximation into Eq. (15.11), we have

$$G_{L_i}(z) \approx \exp\left(p_i(z - 1)\right).$$

Therefore, the PGF of L can be approximated by

$$\begin{aligned} G_L(z) &= \prod_{i=1}^{n} G_{L_i}(z) \approx \prod_{i=1}^{n} \exp\left(p_i(z - 1)\right) \\ &= \exp\left(\sum_{i=1}^{n} p_i(z - 1)\right) = \exp\left(\lambda(z - 1)\right) \\ &= \exp(-\lambda)\exp(\lambda z), \end{aligned}$$

where we have set $\lambda = \sum_{i=1}^{n} p_i$. Using again the Taylor's series expansion, for $z = 0$, to $\exp(\lambda z))$, we get

$$G_L(z) \approx \exp\left(-\lambda(1 - z)\right) = e^{-\lambda} \sum_{k=0}^{+\infty} \frac{(\lambda z)^k}{k!},$$

which is the PGF of the Poisson distribution of parameter λ (see Example 3.2). It follows that, for small values of p_i, the probability that k defaults occur in one year is approximately equal to

$$\mathbb{P}(L = k) = \frac{e^{-\lambda}\lambda^k}{k!}. \tag{15.12}$$

Remark 15.1. From Eq. (15.12) we deduce that the probability distribution of the number of defaults is approximately a Poisson, which

- Depends on a single parameter, λ, representing the expected number of defaults in the fixed time horizon. In particular, such distribution does not depend on the number of exposures in the portfolio, or on the individual PD (assuming that these are sufficiently small);

- Does not require that the exposures have the same PD. Indeed, it can be calculated for each exposure, if there is sufficient information. Recall that our goal is to model the distribution of losses rather than the number of defaults.

  Figure 15.1 shows the PD distribution of a portfolio consisting of 25 counterparties. We deduce that the probability of 0 defaults, $\mathbb{P}(L = 0)$, is less than 5%, while the probability that there are more than 10 defaults, $\mathbb{P}(L > 10)$, is almost null. Furthermore, the graph shows that the probability of 3 defaults, $\mathbb{P}(L = 3)$, is approximately 22%. To see the code related to this graph, refer to Appendix B.2.1.

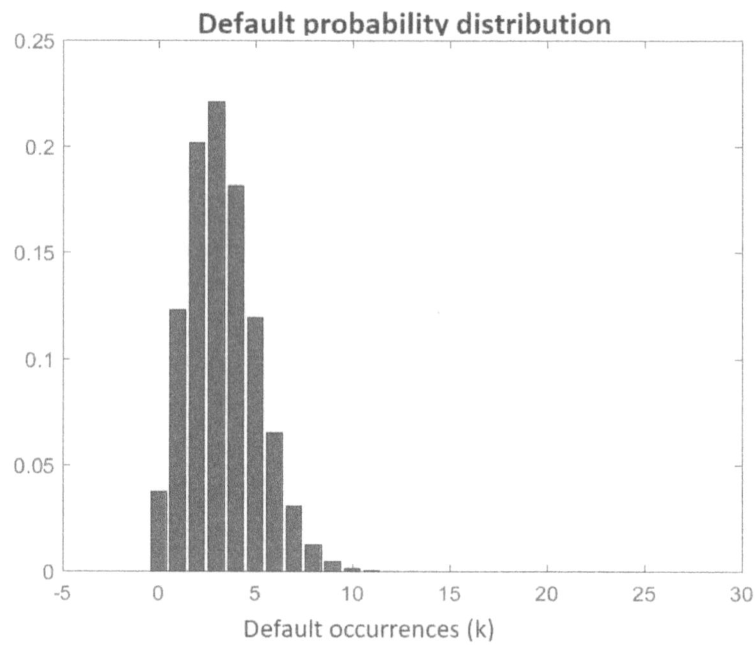

Fig. 15.1: PD for a portfolio consisting of 25 counterparties.

15.2.1.1 *Exposure Bands*

After deriving the probability distribution of L, we group the exposures into some bands. The main purpose of the division of debtors into these bands is to reduce the computational cost. In this regard, we set a unit exposure, E, and for each counterparty i we denote by EL_i, EAD_i and LGD_i the expected loss, the default exposure and the loss given default, respectively.

We denote the risk exposure of the i-th debtor by E_i, defined as

$$E_i = EAD_i \cdot LGD_i,$$

It represents the loss that a credit institution suffers on a certain credit exposure when an obligor defaults. For each debtor i, we define the quantities

$$E_i = \nu_i E, \qquad EL_i = \varepsilon_i E, \tag{15.13}$$

which are the exposure and expected loss of an obligor, respectively, expressed as multiples of the unit exposure E.

From now on, the *CreditRisk +* replaces any exact exposure E_i by the nearest integer multiple of the unit exposure E.

Therefore, an appropriate choice of E is essential in order to obtain a fine approximation of the distribution of the original portfolio exposure. In particular, this approximation has to partition the portfolio into m exposure bands, with m significantly less than the real number of debtors.

We denote by $[j]$ and $L_{[j]}$, for $j \in \{1,..,m\}$, the j-th exposure band and the total number of defaults in the band $[j]$, respectively . We write $i \in [j]$ to indicate that the debtor i is in the band $[j]$. Thus, $L_{[j]}$ and L can be expressed in terms of L_i as follows

$$L_{[j]} = \sum_{i\in[j]} L_i \qquad \text{and} \qquad L = \sum_{j=1}^{m} L_{[j]} = \sum_{j=1}^{m}\sum_{i\in[j]} L_i.$$

After partitioning of the portfolio into these bands, the debtors belonging to the same band have an exposure equal to $\nu_{[j]}E$, where $\nu_{[j]} \in \mathbb{N}_0$ such that

$$\min_{n\in\mathbb{N}_0}\{|\nu_i - n|\} = |\nu_i - \nu_{[j]}|,$$

with $i = 1, ..., n$, $i \in [j]$, $j = 1, ..., m$.

Consider, for example, a portfolio consisting of $n = 5$ counterparties, each with its own exposure. Let us assume that E = \$ 1,000,000. Table 15.1 shows the exposures and their respective exposure bands.

The next step is to compute the expected default amount for any exposure band. We observe that $L_{[j]}$ follows a Poisson distribution because it is obtained as sum of Bernoulli variables. Recalling that the expectation of a Poisson variable coincides with its parameter and that the expectation is a linear operator, it follows that the expected default amount in the exposure band $[j]$ is given by the sum of the defaults of the counterparties in the band $[j]$, i.e.

$$\lambda_{[j]} = \mathbb{E}[L_{[j]}] = \sum_{i\in[j]} \mathbb{E}[L_i] = \sum_{i\in[j]} p_i,$$

Table 15.1: Example of division into bands.

Debtor	Exposure	Net exposure $\nu_i = \text{Ei}/\text{E}$	Approximate exposure $\nu_{[j]}$	Band $[j]$
1	358,475	0,3585	1	1
2	1,089,819	1,0898	2	2
3	1,799,710	1,7997	2	2
4	1,933,116	1,9331	2	2
5	2,317,327	2,3173	3	3

with $p_i = \frac{\varepsilon_i}{\nu_i}$. Indeed, based on (15.13), the expected value of L_i can be also obtained as ratio of EL_i to E_i, that is equal to the ratio of ε_i to ν_i.

Hence, the expected loss in the band $[j]$, denoted by $\varepsilon_{[j]}$, is obtained by multiplying the expected default amount $\lambda_{[j]}$ by the band exposure $\nu_{[j]}$, i.e.

$$\varepsilon_{[j]} = \lambda_{[j]}\nu_{[j]}. \tag{15.14}$$

Since we have approximated $\nu_{[j]}$ with an integer, the expected loss $\varepsilon_{[j]}$ will be rounded unless this is offset.

If the default number of each exposure band is known, we can determine the expected default amount in the portfolio, which we indicate with λ_{PF}. From Eq. (15.14), λ_{PF} is equal to the sum of the expected defaults of each exposure band,

$$\lambda_{PF} = \mathbb{E}[L] = \sum_{j=1}^{m} \mathbb{E}[L_{[j]}] = \sum_{j=1}^{m} \lambda_{[j]} = \sum_{j=1}^{m} \frac{\varepsilon_{[j]}}{\nu_{[j]}}. \tag{15.15}$$

Thus, $L_{[j]}$ and L follow a Poisson distribution with parameters $\lambda_{[j]}$ and λ_{PF}, respectively, i.e.

$$L_{[j]} = \sum_{i\in[j]} L_i \sim Pois(\lambda_{[j]}) \tag{15.16}$$

where $\lambda_{[j]} = \sum_{i\in[j]} p_i$, and

$$L = \sum_{j=1}^{m} L_{[j]} \sim Pois\left(\sum_{j=1}^{m} \lambda_{[j]}\right) = Pois(\lambda_{PF}). \tag{15.17}$$

15.2.2 *Portfolio Loss Distribution with Constant PD*

From the above results, we want to derive the loss distribution of the portfolio. For each risk exposure $E_i = EAD_i \cdot LGD_i$, we determine the loss variable (see Subsection 10.3)

$$\tilde{L}_i = E_i \cdot L_i, \qquad i = 1, ..., n.$$

In the aftermath of the division of the n counterparties into bands, the variable loss relating to the j-th band, $\tilde{L}_{[j]}$, is obtained from the product of the exposure $\nu_{[j]}$ by

$L_{[j]}$, i.e. $\tilde{L}_{[j]} = \nu_{[j]} L_{[j]}$. Consequently, the expected losses in each band and in the portfolio are given respectively by

$$\mathbb{E}[\tilde{L}_{[j]}] = \nu_{[j]}\lambda_{[j]} \quad \text{and} \quad \mathbb{E}[\tilde{L}] = \sum_{j=1}^{m} \nu_{[j]}\lambda_{[j]}, \tag{15.18}$$

where $\tilde{L}$ denotes the portfolio loss variable. Wanting to determine the probability distribution of the portfolio loss variable, we first derive its probability generating function, which we denote by $G_{\tilde{L}}$,

$$\begin{aligned}
G_{\tilde{L}}(z) &= \prod_{j=1}^{m} G_{\tilde{L}_{[j]}}(z) = \prod_{j=1}^{m}\sum_{k=0}^{+\infty} \mathbb{P}(\tilde{L}_{[j]} = \nu_{[j]}k) z^{\nu_{[j]}k} \\
&= \prod_{j=1}^{m}\sum_{k=0}^{+\infty} \mathbb{P}\left(\frac{\tilde{L}_{[j]}}{\nu_{[j]}} = k\right) z^{\nu_{[j]}k} \\
&= \prod_{j=1}^{m}\sum_{k=0}^{+\infty} \mathbb{P}(L_{[j]} = k) z^{\nu_{[j]}k} \\
&= \prod_{j=1}^{m}\sum_{k=0}^{+\infty} \frac{e^{-\lambda_{[j]}}\lambda_{[j]}^{k}}{k!} z^{\nu_{[j]}k} \\
&= \prod_{j=1}^{m} e^{-\lambda_{[j]}} e^{\lambda_{[j]} z^{\nu_{[j]}}} \\
&= \exp\left(\sum_{j=1}^{m} \lambda_{[j]}(z^{\nu_{[j]}} - 1)\right),
\end{aligned} \tag{15.19}$$

where we used the independence of L_i's and Eqs. (15.16), (15.18).
If we define the polynomial

$$p(z) = \frac{\sum_{j=1}^{m} \frac{\varepsilon_{[j]}}{\nu_{[j]}} z^{\nu_{[j]}}}{\sum_{j=1}^{m} \frac{\varepsilon_{[j]}}{\nu_{[j]}}} = \frac{\sum_{j=1}^{m} \lambda_{[j]} z^{\nu_{[j]}}}{\lambda_{PF}}, \tag{15.20}$$

then we may define the PGF of $\tilde{L}$ in terms of p as follows

$$G_{\tilde{L}}(z) = \exp\left(\lambda_{PF}(p(z) - 1)\right) = G_L(p(z)). \tag{15.21}$$

Observe that $G_{\tilde{L}}(z)$ depends on $\nu_{[j]}$ and $\varepsilon_{[j]}$. Therefore, to obtain the loss distribution of a loan portfolio, it is necessary to know the different portfolio exposures and the respective expected losses.

Given the PGF of $\tilde{L}$, we are able to determine its probability distribution. By virtue of Theorem 3.2, we know that

$$\mathbb{P}(\tilde{L} = \nu_{[j]}k) = \frac{1}{k!}\frac{d^k G_{\tilde{L}}(z)}{dz^k}\bigg|_{z=0} := A_k.$$

Compute A_k using the Leibniz's rule. From Eq. (15.19), we have

$$\begin{aligned}\frac{1}{k!}\frac{d^k G_{\tilde{L}}(z)}{dz^k}\bigg|_{z=0} &= \frac{1}{k!}\frac{d^{k-1}}{dz^{k-1}}\left(G_{\tilde{L}}(z)\frac{d}{dz}\sum_{j=1}^{m}\lambda_{[j]}z^{\nu_{[j]}}\bigg|_{z=0}\right)\\ &= \frac{1}{k!}\sum_{l=0}^{k-1}\binom{k-1}{l}\frac{d^{k-l-1}}{dz^{k-l-1}}G_{\tilde{L}}(z)\frac{d^{l+1}}{dz^{l+1}}\left(\sum_{j=1}^{m}\lambda_{[j]}z^{\nu_{[j]}}\right)\bigg|_{z=0}.\end{aligned} \tag{15.22}$$

Observe that

$$\frac{d^{l+1}}{dz^{l+1}}\left(\sum_{j=1}^{m}\lambda_{[j]}z^{\nu_{[j]}}\right)\bigg|_{z=0} = \begin{cases}\lambda_{[j]}(l+1)! & \text{if } l = \nu_{[j]}-1 \text{ for some } j\\ 0 & \text{otherwise,}\end{cases} \tag{15.23}$$

and

$$\frac{d^{k-l-1}}{dz^{k-l-1}}G_{\tilde{L}}(z)\bigg|_{z=0} = (k-l-1)!A_{k-l-1}. \tag{15.24}$$

Substituting Eqs. (15.23) and (15.24) into Eq. (15.22), we obtain

$$A_k = \frac{1}{k!}\sum_{\nu_{[j]}=1}^{k}\binom{k-1}{\nu_{[j]}-1}(k-\nu_{[j]})!(\nu_{[j]})!\lambda_{[j]}A_{k-\nu_{[j]}}, \tag{15.25}$$

where

$$\begin{aligned}\frac{1}{k!}\binom{k-1}{\nu_{[j]}-1}(k-\nu_{[j]})!\nu_{[j]}! &= \frac{1}{k!}\frac{(k-1)!}{(\nu_{[j]}-1)!(k-\nu_{[j]})!}(k-\nu_{[j]})!\nu_{[j]}!\\ &= \frac{1}{k(k-1)!}\frac{(k-1)!}{(\nu_{[j]}-1)!}\nu_{[j]}l!\\ &= \frac{\nu_{[j]}}{k}.\end{aligned}$$

and so,

$$A_k = \sum_{\nu_{[j]}=1}^{k}\frac{\nu_{[j]}}{k}\lambda_{[j]}A_{k-\nu_{[j]}} \tag{15.26}$$

Being $\varepsilon_{[j]} = \nu_{[j]}\lambda_{[j]}$, Eq. (15.26) can be rewritten as

$$A_k = \sum_{\nu_{[j]}=1}^{k}\frac{\varepsilon_{[j]}}{k}A_{k-\nu_{[j]}} \tag{15.27}$$

The above relationship allows us to determine the probability distribution of the portfolio loss. In particular, the probability that there are no losses is given by A_0, where

$$A_0 = G_{\tilde{L}}(0) = G_L(p(0)) = e^{-\lambda_{PF}} = \exp\left(- \sum_{j=1}^{m} \frac{\varepsilon_{[j]}}{\nu_{[j]}} \right).$$

Figure 15.2 shows the probability distribution of loss for a portfolio consisting of $n = 25$ counterparties. We deduce that the probability that there are no losses is greater than 3.5%, the probability that there is a loss of \$ 25,000,000 is slightly less than 2%.
To see the code that generates this graph, refer to Appendix B.2.2.

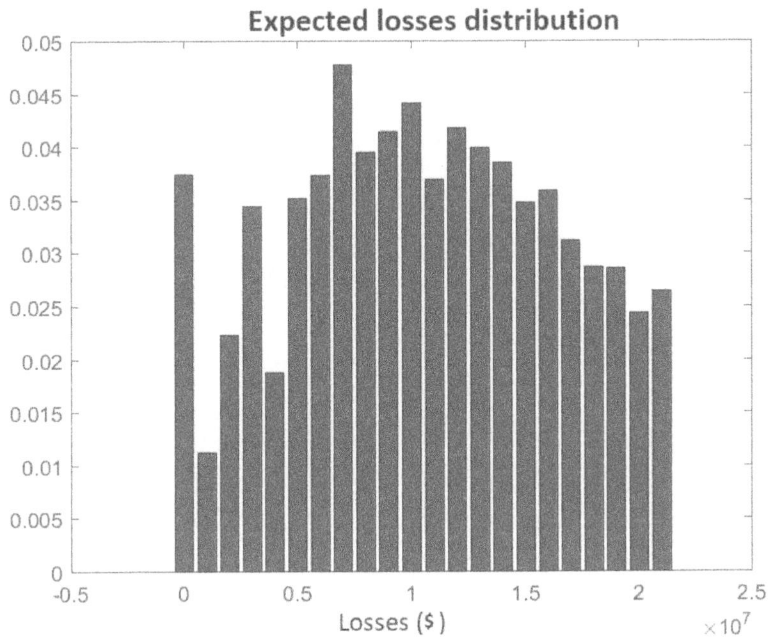

Fig. 15.2: Portfolio loss probability distribution for a portfolio consisting of 25 counterparties.

Chapter 16

Sector Analysis

Generally, the *CreditRisk +* assumes that the default probability (PD) of each debtor is random and its variability depends on some factors, present in the portfolio, named *risk factors*. The debtors may be divided into *sectors*, i.e. sets of debtors that are affected by the influence of a particular (systemic) risk factor. Any factor influences the sector through the total PD, which is modeled as a random variable $\Lambda_{[s]}$, with mean $\lambda_{[s]}$ and standard deviation $\sigma_{[s]}$. If we have k sectors, the *CreditRisk +* assumes that $\Lambda_{[s]} \sim Gamma(\alpha_s, \beta_s)$, so that the default number in each sector s follows a Gamma-Poisson distribution with parameter $\Lambda_{[s]}$. Furthermore, it assumes that the variables $\Lambda_{[1]}, ..., \Lambda_{[k]}$ are two by two independent. Analogously to the procedure adopted in Chapter 15, first, we compute the PGF of the default amount in the sector s. Second, we derive the probability distribution of the default events in s. Third, we obtain the PGF for the portfolio loss.

16.1 Distribution of Defaults with Random PD

Let $L_{[s]}$ be a Poisson distributed variable describing the number of defaults in the sector s with stochastic parameter $\Lambda_{[s]}$, for $s = 1, ..., k$. We denote by $\lambda_{[s]}$ and $\sigma_{[s]}$, respectively, the mean and the standard deviation of $\Lambda_{[s]}$. Let L be the total number of portfolio defaults obtained as the sum of the defaults of each sector

$$L = \sum_{s=1}^{k} L_{[s]}.$$

To derive the probability distribution of L, we start by computing its PGF, G_L. If the sectors are independent, by the convolution theorem (see Theorem 3.3), the PGF of L is expressed as the product of the generating functions of $L_{[s]}$, that is

$$G_L(z) = \prod_{s=1}^{k} G_{L_{[s]}}(z), \tag{16.1}$$

where $G_{L_{[s]}}$ denotes the probability generating function of $L_{[s]}$. If $f_s(\cdot)$ denotes the probability density function of $\Lambda_{[s]}$, then the PGF of the default events in the sector s is equal to

$$G_{L_{[s]}}(z) = \mathbb{E}\left[z^{L_{[s]}}\right] = \mathbb{E}_{\Lambda_{[s]}}\left[\mathbb{E}\left[z^{L_{[s]}}|\Lambda_{[s]} = x_s\right]\right] = \mathbb{E}_{\Lambda_{[s]}}\left[G_{L_{[s]}}(z)|\Lambda_{[s]} = x_s\right]$$
$$= \int_0^{+\infty} (G_{L_{[s]}}(z)|\Lambda_{[s]} = x_s) f_s(x_s)\, dx_s = \int_0^{+\infty} e^{x_s(z-1)} f_s(x)\, dx_s,$$

where we have used the fact that $(L_{[s]}|\Lambda_{[s]} = x_s) \sim Pois(x_s)$, i.e.

$$(G_{L_{[s]}}(z)|\Lambda_{[s]} = x_s) = e^{x_s(z-1)}.$$

In order to obtain an explicit representation for the PGF $G_{L_{[s]}}$, we must choose an appropriate distribution for $\Lambda_{[s]}$. Assume $\Lambda_{[s]}$ follows a Gamma distribution (see Subsection 1.3.5) with parameters α_s and β_s,

$$\Lambda_{[s]} \sim Gamma(\alpha_s, \beta_s),$$

where

$$\alpha_s = \frac{\lambda_{[s]}^2}{\sigma_{[s]}^2} \quad \text{and} \quad \beta_s = \frac{\sigma_{[s]}^2}{\lambda_{[s]}}. \tag{16.2}$$

In this way, we require that the default number in each sector s follows a Poisson-Gamma distribution.

Remark 16.1. Now, the (unconditional) PGF of $L_{[s]}$ is completely known. In fact, if the rate parameter $\Lambda_{[s]}$ follows a Gamma distribution, then the random variable $L_{[s]}$ follows a Negative Binomial distribution. Recalling that the dispersion of a random variable X is defined as the ratio of the variance to the expected value, i.e.

$$D_X = \frac{Var(X)}{\mathbb{E}[X]},$$

then $D_X = 1$ if $X \sim Pois(\lambda)$. Therefore, in a mixed Poisson model, D_X is always greater than one, meaning there is a persistent over-dispersion. In fact, using the relations $i)$ and $ii)$ of Subsection 15.1.1, we obtain

$$D_X = \frac{Var(X)}{\mathbb{E}[X]} = \frac{\mathbb{E}[\Lambda] + Var(\Lambda)}{\mathbb{E}[\Lambda]} = 1 + D_\Lambda > 1,$$

where Λ denotes the Poisson parameter. When Λ follows a Gamma distribution, the above inequality is always true because in a Negative Binomial distribution the variance is greater than the expected value.

With the sectoral analysis, there are cases in which several counterparties in the same sector have different ratings, (and different risks), or cases in which a counterparty admits several ratings. While the Poisson distribution models the cases where the risks are homogeneous, the Poisson distribution with random rate parameter allows to capture heterogeneous risks. In particular, if the rate parameter follows a Gamma distribution, we obtain a Poisson mixture distribution which is very suitable for modeling non-homogeneous and clustered risks.

With the choice of the Gamma distribution, the PGF of $L_{[s]}$ can be evaluated directly,

$$G_{L_{[s]}}(z) = \int_0^{+\infty} e^{x_s(z-1)} \frac{e^{-\frac{x_s}{\beta_s}} x_s^{\alpha_s - 1}}{\beta_s^{\alpha_s}\Gamma(\alpha_s)}\, dx_s = \frac{1}{\beta_s^{\alpha_s}\Gamma(\alpha_s)} \int_0^{+\infty} e^{-x_s(1+\beta_s^{-1}-z)} x^{\alpha_s - 1}\, dx_s. \tag{16.3}$$

Through the variable change $y_s = x_s(1 + \beta_s^{-1} - z)$, $dx_s = \frac{dy_s}{(1+\beta_s^{-1}-z)}$, obtain

$$\begin{aligned} G_{L_{[s]}}(z) &= \frac{1}{\beta_s^{\alpha_s}\Gamma(\alpha_s)} \int_0^{+\infty} \left(\frac{y_s}{1+\beta_s^{-1}-z}\right)^{\alpha_s - 1} e^{-y_s} \frac{dy_s}{1+\beta_s^{-1}-z} \\ &= \frac{\Gamma(\alpha_s)}{\beta_s^{\alpha_s}\Gamma(\alpha_s)(1+\beta_s^{-1}-z)^{\alpha_s}} = \frac{1}{\beta_s^{\alpha_s}(1+\beta_s^{-1}-z)^{\alpha_s}}. \end{aligned} \tag{16.4}$$

If we set $p_s = \frac{\beta_s}{1+\beta_s}$, Eq. (16.4) can be written in a more compact form

$$G_{L_{[s]}}(z) = \left(\frac{1-p_s}{1-p_s z}\right)^{\alpha_s}. \tag{16.5}$$

This is PGF of $L_{[s]}$ in the sector s. By applying the binomial expansion with negative exponent

$$\begin{aligned} (1-p_s z)^{-\alpha_s} =& 1 + (-\alpha_s)(-p_s z) + \frac{(-\alpha_s)(-\alpha_s - 1)}{2!}(-p_s z)^2 \\ &+ \frac{(-\alpha_s)(-\alpha_s - 1)(\alpha_s - 2)}{3!}(-p_s z)^3 + \cdots \\ &= \sum_{k=0}^{+\infty} \binom{-\alpha_s}{k} (-p_s z)^k \\ &= \sum_{k=0}^{+\infty} \binom{k+\alpha_s - 1}{k} p_s^k z^k \end{aligned}$$

to Eq. (16.5), we get

$$G_{L_{[s]}}(z) = (1-p_s)^{\alpha_s} \sum_{k=0}^{+\infty} \binom{k+\alpha_s - 1}{k} p_s^k z^k,$$

Hence, the probability that k defaults occur in the sector s is equal to

$$\mathbb{P}(L_{[s]} = k) = \binom{k+\alpha_s - 1}{k} p_s^k (1-p_s)^{\alpha_s}, \quad k = 0, 1, \ldots \tag{16.6}$$

Equation (16.6) yields $L_{[s]} \sim BN(\alpha_s, 1-p_s)$. The expected value and the variance of $L_{[s]}$ are given by

$$\mathbb{E}[L_{[s]}] = \frac{\alpha_s p_s}{1-p_s} = \frac{\alpha_s \frac{\beta_s}{1+\beta_s}}{1 - \frac{\beta_s}{1+\beta_s}} = \alpha_s \beta_s = \mathbb{E}[\Lambda_{[s]}], \tag{16.7}$$

and

$$Var(L_{[s]}) = \alpha_s \frac{p_s}{(1-p_s)^2} = \alpha_s \beta_s (1+\beta_s) = \mathbb{E}[\Lambda_{[s]}] + Var(\Lambda_{[s]}), \tag{16.8}$$

which soon imply the over-dispersion condition.

Observe that α_s is generally not an integer. Substituting Eq. (16.5) into (16.1), we obtain

$$G_L(z) = \prod_{s=1}^{k} G_{L_{[s]}}(z) = \prod_{s=1}^{k} \left(\frac{1-p_s}{1-p_s z} \right)^{\alpha_s}, \tag{16.9}$$

that represents the PGF of the total number of defaults L.

16.2 Portfolio Loss Distribution with Random PD

Given the PGF of the default number $L_{[s]}$ in the sector s, we compute the loss distribution of the portfolio. Assume that the portfolio is divided into m exposure bands as well as k sectors. Thus, each sector can be considered as the set of bands that are affected by the same risk factor. We denote by $\nu_{[j]}^{(s)}$ and $\varepsilon_{[j]}^{(s)}$, respectively, the exposure and expected loss of the j-th band in sector s, that are computed in the same way as described in Subsection 15.2.1. Since $L_{[s]}$ is the variable that counts the number of defaults in sector s, it can be obtained by summing up the defaults of each band in s, i.e.

$$L_{[s]} = \sum_{j=1}^{m(s)} L_{[j]}^{(s)},$$

where $L_{[j]}^{(s)}$ denotes the exposure band $[j]$ in the sector s. Hence, the expected defaults amount in the sector s is given by

$$\lambda_{[s]} = \mathbb{E}[\Lambda_{[s]}] = \mathbb{E}[L_{[s]}] = \sum_{j=1}^{m(s)} \frac{\varepsilon_{[j]}^{(s)}}{\nu_{[j]}^{(s)}}, \tag{16.10}$$

where we used Eq. (16.7) and the linearity of expected value.

We define the loss variable relating to the s-th sector $\tilde{L}_{[s]}$ as the sum of loss variables of each exposure band in sector s, i.e.

$$\tilde{L}_{[s]} = \sum_{j=1}^{m(s)} \nu_{[j]}^{(s)} \tilde{L}_{[j]}^{(s)}.$$

Thus, the portfolio loss variable $\tilde{L}$ is given by the sum of the losses of sectors, i.e.

$$\tilde{L} = \sum_{s=1}^{k} \tilde{L}_{[s]}.$$

In order to get the probability distribution of $\tilde{L}$ we derive its PGF, denoted by $G_{\tilde{L}}$. Since the sectors are independent, by virtue of Theorem 3.3, the loss generating function of the portfolio is obtained as the product of the loss probability generating functions of each sector, namely

$$G_{\tilde{L}}(z) = \prod_{s=1}^{k} G_{\tilde{L}_{[s]}}(z).$$

In this regard, we introduce for all sectors $s = 1, ..., k$ the following polynomials

$$p_{[s]}(z) = \frac{\sum_{j=1}^{m(s)} \frac{\varepsilon_{[j]}^{(s)}}{\nu_{[j]}^{(s)}} z^{\nu_{[j]}^{(s)}}}{\sum_{j=1}^{m(s)} \frac{\varepsilon_{[j]}^{(s)}}{\nu_{[j]}^{(s)}}} = \frac{1}{\lambda_{[s]}} \sum_{j=1}^{m(s)} \frac{\varepsilon_{[j]}^{(s)}}{\nu_{[j]}^{(s)}} z^{\nu_{[j]}^{(s)}}, \tag{16.11}$$

where we used the relation (16.10). Since $\left(L_{[s]} | \Lambda_{[s]} = x_s\right) \sim Pois(x_s)$, by (15.21) the probability generating function of $\tilde{L}_{[s]}$ conditional on $\Lambda_{[s]} = x_s$ is given by

$$(G_{\tilde{L}_{[s]}}(z) | \Lambda_{[s]} = x_s) = (G_{L_{[s]}}(p_{[s]}(z)) | \Lambda_{[s]} = x_s) = \exp(x_s(p_{[s]}(z) - 1)).$$

Hence, the unconditional probability generating function of $\tilde{L}_{[s]}$ is obtained by integrating over the space of possible values of $\Lambda_{[s]}$, i.e.

$$G_{\tilde{L}_{[s]}}(z) = \int_0^{+\infty} \exp(x_s(p_{[s]}(z) - 1)) f_s(x_s) dx_s = \left(\frac{1 - p_s}{1 - p_s p_{[s]}(z)}\right)^{\alpha_s},$$

where we used the relation (16.5). Thus, the PGF of $\tilde{L}$ is equal to

$$G_{\tilde{L}}(z) = \prod_{s=1}^{k} G_{\tilde{L}_{[s]}}(z) = \prod_{s=1}^{k} \left(\frac{1 - p_s}{1 - p_s p_{[s]}(z)}\right)^{\alpha_s} = \prod_{s=1}^{k} \left(\frac{1 - p_s}{1 - \frac{p_s}{\lambda_{[s]}} \sum_{j=1}^{m(s)} \frac{\varepsilon_{[j]}^{(s)}}{\nu_{[j]}^{(s)}} z^{\nu_{[j]}^{(s)}}}\right)^{\alpha_s}.$$

Given the loss probability generating function, we are now able to derive the loss probability distribution of the portfolio through the next arguments.

General Recursive Relation

Let X be a random variable. Consider the PGF $G_X(z) = \sum_{k=0}^{+\infty} A_k z^k$, with $A_k = \mathbb{P}(X = k)$ and assume that it satisfies the following differential equation

$$\frac{d}{dz} \log G(z) = \frac{1}{G(z)} \frac{dG(z)}{dz} = \frac{A(z)}{B(z)}, \tag{16.12}$$

where

$$A(z) = \sum_{i=0}^{r} a_i z^i \quad \text{and} \quad B(z) = \sum_{j=0}^{s} b_j z^j. \tag{16.13}$$

To calculate the terms A_k, start by noting that Eq. (16.12) can be rewritten as

$$B(z)\frac{dG}{dz} = A(z)G(z), \tag{16.14}$$

or, equivalently,

$$\left(\sum_{j=0}^{s} b_j z^j\right)\left(\sum_{k=0}^{+\infty}(k+1)A_{k+1}z^k\right) = \left(\sum_{i=0}^{r} a_i z^i\right)\left(\sum_{k=0}^{+\infty} A_k z^k\right). \tag{16.15}$$

For any $n \geq 0$, the coefficients of z^n in Eq. (16.15) are given, respectively, by

$$\sum_{j=0}^{\min(s,k)} b_j(k+1-j)A_{k+1-j} \quad \text{and} \quad \sum_{i=0}^{\min(r,k)} a_i A_{k-i}.$$

Therefore, it holds

$$\sum_{j=0}^{\min(s,k)} b_j(k+1-j)A_{k+1-j} = \sum_{i=0}^{\min(r,k)} a_i A_{k-i},$$

that is

$$\begin{aligned} b_0(k+1)A_{k+1} &= \sum_{i=0}^{\min(r,k)} a_i A_{k-i} - \sum_{j=1}^{\min(s,k)} b_j(k+1-j)A_{k+1-j} \\ &= \sum_{i=0}^{\min(r,k)} a_i A_{k-i} - \sum_{j=0}^{\min(s-1,k-1)} b_{j+1}(k-j)A_{k-j}. \end{aligned}$$

From the above relation, deduce that the coefficients A_{k+1} satisfy the following recurrence

$$A_{k+1} = \frac{1}{b_0(k+1)}\left(\sum_{i=0}^{\min(r,k)} a_i A_{k-i} - \sum_{j=0}^{\min(s-1,k-1)} b_{j+1}(k-j)A_{k-j}\right). \tag{16.16}$$

Now, we are ready to compute the loss probability distribution of the portfolio. We proved that the PGF of $\tilde{L}$ is given by

$$G_{\tilde{L}}(z) = \prod_{s=1}^{k} \left(\frac{1 - p_s}{1 - \frac{p_s}{\lambda_{[s]}} \sum_{j=1}^{m(s)} \frac{\varepsilon_{[j]}^{(s)}}{\nu_{[j]}^{(s)}} z^{\nu_{[j]}^{(s)}}} \right)^{\alpha_s}.$$

By calculating the derivative of log $G_{\tilde{L}}$, with respect to z, we get

$$\frac{d}{dz} \log G_{\tilde{L}}(z) = \frac{d}{dz} \left(\sum_{s=1}^{k} \log G_{\tilde{L}_{[s]}}(z) \right) = \sum_{s=1}^{k} \left(\frac{G'_{\tilde{L}_{[s]}}(z)}{G_{\tilde{L}_{[s]}}(z)} \right)$$
$$= \sum_{s=1}^{k} \left(\frac{\frac{p_s \alpha_s}{\lambda_{[s]}} \sum_{j=1}^{m(s)} \varepsilon_{[j]}^{(s)} z^{\nu_{[j]}^{(s)} - 1}}{1 - \frac{p_s}{\lambda_{[s]}} \sum_{j=1}^{m(s)} \frac{\varepsilon_{[j]}^{(s)}}{\nu_{[j]}^{(s)}} z^{\nu_{[j]}^{(s)}}} \right).$$

Hence, we can express the derivative of log $G_{\tilde{L}}$ by the ratio of two polynomials A and B of type (16.13). By the polynomial identity, we can compute the coefficients of A and B through Eq. (16.16). Given the terms A_k, we know the loss probability distribution of the portfolio.

Figure 16.1 shows the loss probability distribution of a portfolio consisting of 25 counterparties, each of them is fully concentrated in one of the two considered sectors. Deduce that the probability that there are no losses is just over 3.5%, the probability that there is a loss greater than \$ 35,000,000 is about 0.5%.
To see the related code, refer to Appendix B.3.1.

Remark 16.2. Up till now, we have assumed the default probabilities are random. However, there are some circumstances in which they may be considered constant, for example, when the standard deviation of $\Lambda_{[s]}$ is close to 0. In this case, the portfolio loss probability function converges to the portfolio loss function with constant PD (see Subsection 15.2.2). Indeed, we know that

$$G_{\tilde{L}}(z) = \prod_{s=1}^{k} \left(\frac{1 - p_s}{1 - \frac{p_s}{\lambda_{[s]}} \sum_{j=1}^{m(s)} \frac{\varepsilon_{[j]}^{(s)}}{\nu_{[j]}^{(s)}} z^{\nu_{[j]}^{(s)}}} \right)^{\alpha_s},$$

where

$$\alpha_s = \frac{\lambda_{[s]}^2}{\sigma_{[s]}^2}, \quad \beta_s = \frac{\sigma_{[s]}^2}{\lambda_{[s]}}, \quad p_s = \frac{\beta_s}{1 + \beta_s} \quad \text{and} \quad \lambda_{[s]} = \sum_{j=1}^{m(s)} \frac{\varepsilon_{[j]}^{(s)}}{\nu_{[j]}^{(s)}}.$$

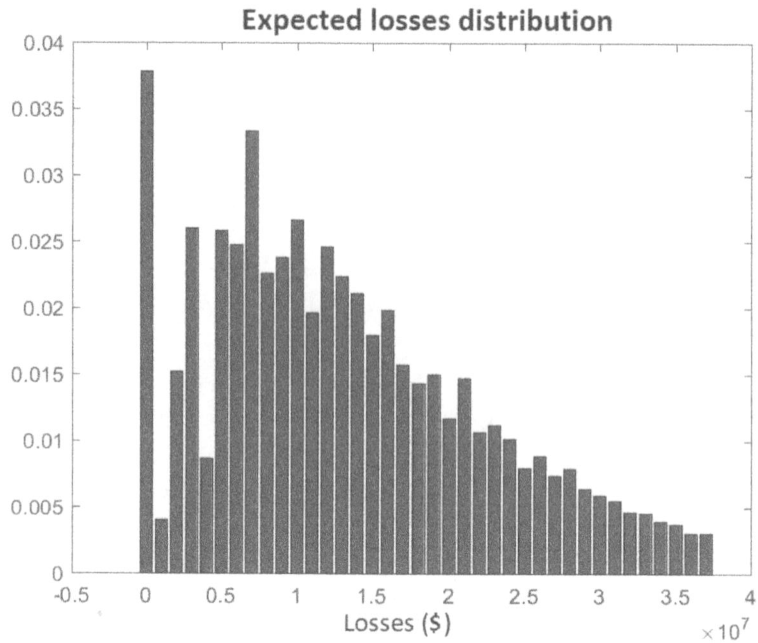

Fig. 16.1: Probability distribution of portfolio loss — Sectoral analysis.

If $\sigma_{[s]} \to 0$, then $\beta_s \to 0$ and $p_s \to 0$ with the same order, so that $\alpha_s = \frac{\lambda_{[s]}}{\beta_s} \approx \frac{\lambda_{[s]}}{p_s}$. and, consequently,

$$\prod_{s=1}^{k} \left(\frac{1-p_s}{1-\frac{p_s}{\lambda_{[s]}} \sum_{j=1}^{m(s)} \frac{\varepsilon_{[j]}^{(s)}}{\nu_{[j]}^{(s)}} z^{\nu_{[j]}^{(s)}}} \right)^{\alpha_s} \approx \prod_{s=1}^{k} \left(\frac{1-p_s}{1-\frac{p_s}{\lambda_{[s]}} \sum_{j=1}^{m(s)} \frac{\varepsilon_{[j]}^{(s)}}{\nu_{[j]}^{(s)}} z^{\nu_{[j]}^{(s)}}} \right)^{\frac{\lambda_{[s]}}{p_s}}.$$

Recalling that

$$\lim_{x \to \pm\infty} \left(1 + \frac{1}{x}\right)^x = e,$$

we get

$$G_{\tilde{L}}(z) \to \prod_{s=1}^{k} \exp\left(-\lambda_{[s]} + \sum_{j=1}^{m(s)} \frac{\varepsilon_{[j]}^{(s)}}{\nu_{[j]}^{(s)}} z^{\nu_{[j]}^{(s)}} \right). \tag{16.17}$$

as $p_s \to 0$. Indeed, note that the factor in Eq. (16.17) can be rewritten as

$$\left(\frac{1-p_s}{1-p_s p_{[s]}(z)} \right)^{\frac{\lambda_{[s]}}{p_s}} = (1-p_s)^{\frac{\lambda_{[s]}}{p_s}} \left(1 - p_s p_{[s]}(z)\right)^{-\frac{\lambda_{[s]}}{p_s}},$$

due to Eq. (16.11). Through the variable changes $y_s = -\frac{1}{p_s}$ and $t_s = \frac{y_s}{p_{[s]}(z)}$, obtain

$$\lim_{p_s \to 0} (1-p_s)^{\frac{\lambda_{[s]}}{p_s}} = \lim_{y_s \to -\infty} \left[\left(1+\frac{1}{y_s}\right)^{y_s} \right]^{-\lambda_{[s]}} = e^{-\lambda_{[s]}} \tag{16.18}$$

and

$$\begin{aligned}\lim_{p_s \to 0} \left(1-p_s p_{[s]}(z)\right)^{-\frac{\lambda_{[s]}}{p_s}} &= \lim_{y_s \to -\infty} \left[\left(1+\frac{1}{y_s} p_{[s]}(z)\right)^{y_s} \right]^{\lambda_{[s]}} \\ &= \lim_{t_s \to -\infty} \left[\left(1+\frac{1}{t_s}\right)^{t_s} \right]^{\lambda_{[s]} p_{[s]}(z)} \\ &= e^{\lambda_{[s]} p_{[s]}(z)}. \end{aligned} \tag{16.19}$$

By virtue of Eqs. (16.18) and (16.19), we have

$$\lim_{p_s \to 0} \left(\frac{1-p_s}{1-p_s p_{[s]}(z)} \right)^{\frac{\lambda_{[s]}}{p_s}} = e^{-\lambda[s]} e^{\lambda_{[s]} p_{[s]}(z)} = \exp\left(-\lambda_{[s]} + \sum_{j=1}^{m(s)} \frac{\varepsilon_{[j]}^{(s)}}{\nu_{[j]}^{(s)}} z^{\nu_{[j]}^{(s)}} \right).$$

As the exponent of Eq. (16.17) is equal to

$$\begin{aligned}\prod_{s=1}^{k} \exp\left(-\lambda_{[s]} + \sum_{j=1}^{m(s)} \frac{\varepsilon_{[j]}^{(s)}}{\nu_{[j]}^{(s)}} z^{\nu_{[j]}^{(s)}} \right) &= \exp\left[-\sum_{s=1}^{k} \left(\lambda_{[s]} - \sum_{j=1}^{m(s)} \frac{\varepsilon_{[j]}^{(s)}}{\nu_{[j]}^{(s)}} z^{\nu_{[j]}^{(s)}} \right) \right] \\ &= \exp\left[-\sum_{s=1}^{k} \left(\sum_{j=1}^{m(s)} \frac{\varepsilon_{[j]}^{(s)}}{\nu_{[j]}^{(s)}} - \sum_{j=1}^{m(s)} \frac{\varepsilon_{[j]}^{(s)}}{\nu_{[j]}^{(s)}} z^{\nu_{[j]}^{(s)}} \right) \right] \\ &= \exp\left[\sum_{s=1}^{k} \sum_{j=1}^{m(s)} \frac{\varepsilon_{[j]}^{(s)}}{\nu_{[j]}^{(s)}} \left(z^{\nu_{[j]}^{(s)}} - 1 \right) \right] \\ &= \exp\left[\sum_{j=1}^{m} \lambda_{[j]} (z^{\nu_{[j]}} - 1) \right], \end{aligned}$$

then $G_{\tilde{L}}$ converges to the loss PGF with constant PD when $\sigma_{[s]} \to 0$.

16.3 Multifactor Analysis over Several Sectors

In the previous Section 16.2 we derived the loss portfolio distribution through a partition into independent sectors. Furthermore, we assumed that each debtor was affected by a single systemic risk factor. Obviously, these hypotheses may not be valid. In fact, most of the time it happens that one or more counterparties depend on several factors; in this case we are talking about multisectoral analysis. To understand how to generalize the sectoral analysis previously presented, we compute again the PGF of the portfolio loss. Assuming that the sectors are independent, the PGF loss is obtained by the product of the PGF of $\tilde{L}_{[s]}$, i.e.

$$G_{\tilde{L}}(z) = \prod_{s=1}^{k} G_{\tilde{L}_{[s]}}(z) = \prod_{s=1}^{k} \int_0^{+\infty} e^{x_s(p_{[s]}(z)-1)} f_s(x_s)\, dx_s, \tag{16.20}$$

which can be rewritten as the following manifold

$$G_{\tilde{L}}(z) = \int_0^{+\infty} \cdots \int_0^{+\infty} \exp\left(\sum_{s=1}^{k} x_s(p_{[s]}(z)-1)\right) \prod_{s=1}^{k} f_s(x_s)\, dx_s. \tag{16.21}$$

The exponent in the above integral can be rewritten as

$$\begin{aligned}\sum_{s=1}^{k} x_s(p_{[s]}(z)-1) &= \sum_{s=1}^{k}\sum_{i\in[s]} \frac{x_s}{\lambda_{[s]}}\frac{\varepsilon_i}{\nu_i}(z^{\nu_i}-1)\\ &= \sum_{s=1}^{k}\sum_{i\in[s]} \frac{x_s}{\lambda_{[s]}} p_i(z^{\nu_i}-1)\\ &= \sum_{s=1}^{k}\sum_{i=1}^{n} \delta_s(i)\frac{x_s}{\lambda_{[s]}} p_i(z^{\nu_i}-1),\end{aligned} \tag{16.22}$$

where we used the following relationship

$$p_{[s]}(z) = \frac{1}{\lambda_{[s]}}\sum_{i\in[s]}\frac{\varepsilon_i}{\nu_i} z^{\nu_i} = \frac{1}{\lambda_{[s]}}\sum_{i\in[s]} p_i z^{\nu_i}, \tag{16.23}$$

and the delta function defined as follows

$$\delta_s(i) = \begin{cases} 1 & \text{if the obligor } i \text{ belongs to sector } s,\\ 0 & \text{otherwise.}\end{cases}$$

This representation is valid if the default probability of each obligor is influenced by one risk factor, otherwise the *CrediRisk+* model assumes that the default probability p_i is a linear function of $(\Lambda_{[1]}, ..., \Lambda_{[k]})$, i.e.

$$p_i(\Lambda_{[1]}, ..., \Lambda_{[k]}) = p_i \sum_{s=1}^{k} \omega_{s,i}\Lambda_{[s]}, \quad i = 1, ..., n, \tag{16.24}$$

where

$$0 \le \omega_{s,i} \le 1 \quad \text{and} \quad \sum_{s=1}^{k} \omega_{s,i} = 1, \quad i = 1, ..., n.$$

The numbers introduced above are called *weights* and measure the sensitivity of the obligor i with respect to the risk factor $\Lambda_{[s]}$. Moreover, by (16.24), p_i is the average default probability of the obligor i. If we replace the delta function by $\omega_{s,i}$ in (16.22), we have

$$\sum_{s=1}^{k} x_s(p_{[s]}(z)-1)=\sum_{s=1}^{k}\sum_{i=1}^{n}\omega_{s,i}\frac{x_s}{\lambda_{[s]}}p_i(z^{\nu_i}-1).$$

with $p_{[s]}(z)$ equal to

$$p_{[s]}(z)=\frac{1}{\lambda_{[s]}}\sum_{i=1}^{n}\omega_{s,i}p_i z^{\nu_i}.$$

Therefore, the portfolio loss PGF is given by

$$G_{\tilde{L}}(z)=\prod_{s=1}^{k}\left(\frac{1-p_s}{1-\frac{p_s}{\lambda_{[s]}}\sum_{i=1}^{n}\omega_{s,i}p_i z^{\nu_i}}\right)^{\alpha_s}. \tag{16.25}$$

Figure 16.2 shows the probability distribution of loss of a portfolio consisting of two counterparties, each of them is classified on its rating and country. In this example, we are considering the *AAA* and *BBB* rating classes, the *USA* and *Europe* countries. The two counterparties are fully concentrated in *AAA-USA* and *AAA-Europe*, respectively. Consequently, the probability of zero losses is just over 75%, the probability that there is a loss equal to the overall exposure is less than 10%. To see the code that generated this graph, refer to Appendix B.3.2.

16.4 Advantages and Limitations of CreditRisk +

The *CreditRisk +* has two important advantages:

- Small number of inputs required. In fact, the data required are just the probabilities of default and the exposures of each debtor;
- Possibility of deriving the probability distribution of the portfolio loss analytically, i.e. without the usual Monte Carlo simulations, with a considerable computational advantage.

However, the *CreditRisk +* has the following limitations:

- It considers default risks, but not the migration risks from a rating class to another one. This is an important limit for those exposures that do not expire within one year. Indeed, we consider a long-term exposure incurring a rating downgrade. This suggests that the possible losses in the next years will be greater than those initially estimated;

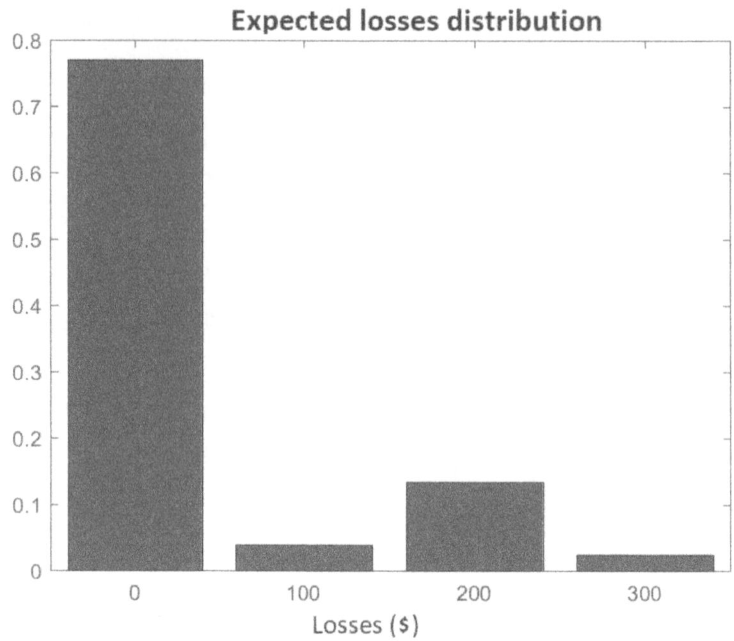

Fig. 16.2: Portfolio loss probability distribution — multisector analysis.

- The recovery risks are neglected (the model assumes that expected recovery rates are estimated without error) and risk exposures are assumed to be known with certainty.

Chapter 17

Estimating PD and LGD for Modeling Non-Performing Loans: The Case of Italy

17.1 Introduction

The purpose of this chapter[1] is to show how to fit a logit model to estimate PD and LGD for modeling Non-Performing Loans (NPLs). The 1997 research by the Italian Central Financial Statements Database (CFSD) of [Laviola and Trapanese (1997)] as mentioned in [BCBS (2000), p. 110] motivated us to undertake this endeavor. They applied the linear discriminant analysis (LDA) to distinguish 1920 sound Italian firms from 1885 unsound ones.

In recent years, there has been an impressive development of loans characterized by a difficult or uncertain degree of recoverability, defined as non-performing loans. Several factors have contributed to the growth of these "problematic" credits in the balance sheets of European creditors, mainly related to the recession triggered out by the collapse of so-called subprime mortgages, American real estate financing and the subsequent international crisis of structured finance products (recall our discussion of the crisis in Section 6). This recession has had heavy consequences even for the European economic system, and in countries such as Italy, where the business funding is mainly supplied by credit institutions, the economic difficulties of underlying borrowers could not fail to influence banking activity, leading to a significant increase in credit risk. The recent economic and financial crisis in Europe has led to progressive deterioration in credit quality and to the consequent immobilization of financial resources, which could, conversely, be used in granting new loans for economic development. To manage this problem and restore the sound and prudent management of credit institutions, it is necessary to speed up the enactment process of regulatory measures. Regulation of the European banking system is still facing a harmonization process that will promote comparability between the Member States on this matter, as well as increasing financial stability.

[1]Part of this chapter has been partly published as [Orlando and Pelosi (2020)].

17.2 Materials and Methods

17.2.1 *Non-Performing Exposure and Regulation*

The centrepiece of technical regulations and harmonized definitions of non-performing exposures is the European Banking Authority (EBA) final draft of Implementing Technical Standards (ITS) on Supervisory reporting on forbearance and non-performing exposures, enacted in July 2014 and lately amended in 2017. Remember the default definition from Section 8.1

The ITS provides guidance for three classes of NPEs (Non-Performing Exposures):

(a) Overdrawn and/or past-due exposures (aside from those classified among bad loans and unlikely-to-pay exposures) are those that are overdrawn and/or past-due by more than 90 days and for above a predefined amount.
(b) Unlikely-to-pay exposures (aside from those included among bad loans) are those in respect of which banks believe debtors are unlikely to meet in full their contractual obligations unless taking actions such as the enforcement of guarantees. However, this category of exposures can be still carried out. According to this definition, banks' evaluation is autonomous and regardless of the presence of any past due or unpaid amounts.
(c) Bad loans are exposures to debtors that are insolvent or in substantially similar circumstances. Debtor's insolvency is not necessarily declared procedurally but can be presumed by the debtor's behavior. Bad loans classification does not refer to the individual risk items of the debtor but to his overall exposure.

17.2.2 *Asymptotic Methods and Data Separation*

In Section 17.3, we apply the methodology from Sections 8.3 and 9.3 to the dataset reported in Appendix C. As our database is limited, one may argue that the Maximum Likelihood (ML) requires a larger dataset as it only performs well *asymptotically*. In fact, standard testing methods that rely on the asymptotic behavior of the estimators do not preserve the Type I error rate. That has the effect to distort the quantile-quantile plot and the testing p-values [Wang (2014)]. In the literature, there are available penalized likelihood based methods such as the Firth logistic regression [Firth (1993)] which provides a solution. The Firth logistic regression adds, to the score function, a penalization that counteracts the first-order term from the asymptotic expansion of the bias of the maximum likelihood estimation. The aforesaid penalization goes to zero as the sample size increases [Firth (1993); Heinze and Schemper (2002)].

An additional problem is related to the so-called *data separation*, i.e. when the outcome variable separates a predictor variable which typically happens when there are subgroups where the same event occurs. For the logistic regression, the ML assumes that data are free from separation, but that may not be the case. Then, mathematically, the ML estimate for the predictor does not converge (i.e. it becomes infinite) [Gim and Ko (2017)]. The said issue of separation "primarily occurs in small samples with several unbalanced and highly predictive risk factors" [Heinze and Schemper (2002)] and it has been shown that the Firth regression (originally developed to reduce the bias of maximum likelihood estimates) provides an ideal solution to the said problem. Penalized likelihood ratio tests and profile penalized likelihood confidence intervals are often preferable to corresponding Wald tests and confidence intervals. Moreover, Firth logistic regression, compared to alternative approaches such as permutation or bootstrapping, has the advantage that is easier to implement and less computationally intensive [Wang (2014)].

In our case, we are dealing with corporate default forecasting. Moscatelli *et al.* (2020), when trying to estimate corporate default forecasting with machine learning, found that "tree-based models outperform statistical models over the entire period, with an average increase in discriminatory power over the Logistic (LOG) model of about 2.6 percent. Linear Discriminant Analysis (LDA) and Penalized Logistic Regression (PLR) display results very close to the LOG model, probably due to similarities in their functional forms". We perform a Firth logistic regression, comparing the results with the ML estimations and we reach similar conclusions (i.e. LOG and PLR display close results). Evidently, data separation, as well as ML distortion, is not a matter of concern in our specific example.

17.3 Experimental Results on a Portfolio of Italian Companies

The sample taken into consideration consists of 51 companies — listed on the Italian Stock Exchange, for simplicity of data retrieval — randomly chosen from sectors in consumer and services goods (see Table C.1). Data collected for the analysis refer to the year 2018. The analysis has been carried out with SPSS and R.

17.3.1 *Results for the PD*

Based on the value of Net-Debt-to-Equity ratio (ND/E), a measure of company's financial leverage calculated by dividing its net liabilities by stockholders' equity, the dependent variable follows this rule:

$$Y = \begin{cases} 1 & \text{if ND/E } \geq 1 \\ 0 & \text{if ND/E } < 1 \end{cases} \tag{17.1}$$

In fact, according to analysts, to be a "healthy" company, this ratio should be at most equal to 1; conversely, a ratio equal to or greater than 1 would mean the company is "risky" and that in the next year it could become insolvent. According to this rule, in the sample, there are 37 healthy companies (72.5%) and 14 risky ones (27.5%) (see Appendix C for the complete dataset). In our case, following (Tsai, 2013), the explanatory variables are six financial ratios (they well correspond to the 1997 study by the Italian CFSD where 10 balance sheet ratios were considered according to [BCBS (2000), p. 110] with more details in [Laviola and Trapanese (1997), p. 16]. Note that one may often come across them as covenants in loan agreements):

- **Current ratio** (current assets to current liabilities) measures the ability of an entity to pay its near-term obligations. "Current" usually is defined as within one year. In business practice, it is believed that this ratio must be equal to 2 to have an optimal liquidity situation, or between 1.5 and 1.7 to have a satisfactory liquidity situation. A current ratio lower than 1.5 is symptomatic of a liquidity situation to be kept under control, and, if it is lower than unity, then this would mean facing a liquidity crisis. It should, however, be specified that an excess of liquidity that generates a ratio higher than 2 means that the company has money in cash or safe investments that could be put to better use in the business.
- **Debt ratio** (total liabilities to total assets) is a leverage ratio. Recall that we already introduced the leverage ratio for banks in Eq. (7.6) where it measures capital over assets, i.e. it is opposite in interpretation compared to industrial companies. That is why using the term "leverage ratio" requires always clarifications whether banks or enterprises are considered. As for the debt ratio, it shows the degree to which a company has used debt to finance its assets. The higher is the ratio, the higher is the degree of leverage and, consequently, the higher is the risk of investing in that company. A debt ratio equal to or lower than 0.4 means that a company's assets are financed by creditors; if it is equal to or greater than 0.6, the assets are financed by owners' (shareholders') equity.
- **Working Capital (WC) to total assets** ratio is a solvency ratio; it measures a firm's short-term solvency. Working capital is the difference between current assets and current liabilities. A ratio greater than 0.15 represents a satisfactory solvency situation; a ratio lower than 0 means that the company's working capital is negative, and its solvency is critical.
- **ROE** (Earnings Before Interests and Taxes (EBIT) to total assets) is an indicator that expresses the company's ability to produce income from only the core business for all its lenders (investors and external creditors). In fact, both financial and tax activity are excluded from EBIT.
- **Asset turnover** (sales to total assets) is a key efficiency metric for any business as it measures how efficiently a business is using its assets to produce revenue.
- **ROI** (net income to cost of investment): a profitability ratio that provides how much profit a company is able to generate from its investments. The higher the number, the more efficient the company is at managing its invested capital to generate profits.

Before proceeding with the evaluation of the model results, the statistical analysis involves a detailed exploration of the characteristics of the data. Table 17.1 shows frequencies of healthy and risky companies within the sample, means, medians and standard deviations of the Net-Debt-to-Equity ratio for each of the two groups:

Table 17.1: Descriptive statistics for Net-Debt-to-Equity ratio.

	Frequency	**Mean**	**Median**	**Std. Dev.**
Healthy	37	0.328	0.240	0.249
Risky	14	1.656	1.302	0.749
Total	51	0.692	0.434	0.741

It is easy to notice that both the mean and median of the healthy group are much lower than 1 while those of the risky group are much greater than 1. The average of total observations is lower than 1, and this is evident because healthy firms make up almost three quarters of the sample. Standard deviations of the two groups also diverge by 0.5 points. This is because among risky companies there is a greater dispersion from the average of observed ratios. Looking at each explanatory variable (Table 17.2), data show that the current ratio average for the healthy group is equal to 1.6, meaning a good liquidity situation, while the same average for the risky one is equal to 1.1, signs of a liquidity situation to be kept under control. The mean of ROI is clearly different between the two groups: for the healthy one, it is 15.41%, and, for the risky one, it is equal to 0.1%. The working capital to assets ratio is negative for the risky companies, showing a critical solvency situation, where current liabilities, on average, are greater than current assets; conversely, the healthy companies' working capital to assets is greater than 0.15, meaning a satisfactory solvency situation. As expected, the debt ratio is higher for the risky group, while asset turnover and ROA are higher for healthy companies. It should be emphasized that the latter is on the average negative for the risky ones, resulting from a negative net income (from incurred losses).

The first estimated model includes all the six independent variables introduced above, under the assumption of the absence of multicollinearity. However, looking at the parameter estimates (Table 17.3), it is clear that for the discussed sample only two of these six regressors are significant for the PD model at 5% significance level (ROI and WC to assets).

Proceeding to the sequential elimination of covariates through the Wald test, the variables discarded in increasing order of significance are: ROA (p-value = 0.360), asset turnover (0.207), current ratio (0.242) and debt ratio (0.091). The only two remaining significant variables are ROI and Working-capital-to-Asset ratio. The second estimated model contains precisely these two variables for both ML estimation (Table 17.4) and Firth penalized logistic regression (Table 17.5).

Table 17.2: Descriptive statistics for covariates.

		Current Ratio	ROI	WC to Asset	Debt Ratio	Asset Turnover	ROA
Healthy	Mean	1.558	0.154	0.272	1.301	1.991	0.046
	Median	1.454	0.137	0.292	1.052	1.952	0.092
	S.D	0.611	0.094	0.450	1.177	0.960	0.308
Risky	Mean	1.101	0.001	−0.137	1.554	1.850	−0.059
	Median	0.827	0.030	−0.159	1.370	1.578	0.012
	S.D	0.795	0.124	0.308	0.622	1.205	0.167
Total	Mean	1.432	0.112	0.160	1.370	1.952	0.017
	Median	1.244	0.105	0.215	1.107	1.827	0.058
	S.D	0.689	0.123	0.452	1.054	1.022	0.279

Table 17.3: Model 1 parameter estimates.

	Coef.	S.E.	Wald	df	p-Value
Current Ratio	1.424	1.217	1.371	1	0.242
ROI	−4.454	13.297	6.713	1	0.010
WC to Asset	−8.3344	3.661	5.183	1	0.023
Debt Ratio	−1.423	0.842	2.855	1	0.091
Asset Turnover	0.779	0.616	1.596	1	0.207
ROA	2.387	2.608	0.838	1	0.360
Constant	1.056	2.026	0.272	1	0.002

Table 17.4: Model 2 parameter estimates.

	Coef.	S.E.	Wald	df	p-Value
ROI	−26.642	9.88	7.271	1	0.007
WC to Asset	−2.782	1.203	5.348	1	0.021
Constant	1.453	0.891	2.663	1	0.003

Table 17.5: Model 2 parameter estimates with Firth PLR.

	Coef.	S.E.	Lower 0.95	Upper 0.95	Chi-Sq.	p-Value
ROI	−22.31	8.413	−44.009	−8.290	15.509	8.21×10^{-5}
WC to Asset	−2.372	1.0806	−4.767	−0.463	5.773	0.016
Constant	1.155	0.798	−0.280	3.047	2.367	0.124

As expected, both coefficients are negative: this means that both variables have a positive effect on company health. The log-likelihood ratio test provides a chi-square with six degrees of freedom equal to 26.974, whose p-value is 0.000. Therefore, the null hypothesis that at least one of the parameters of the model is equal to zero is rejected. The measures of goodness-of-fit are also acceptable either with the classical ML estimation (Table 17.6) or with the Firth penalized logistic regression (Table 17.7). Likelihood ratio represents the dependent variable that is not explained after considering covariates: the bigger it is, the worse it is. Cox–Snell R-Squared provides how much the independent variables explain the outcome; it is between 0 and 1, where the bigger, the better. The Nagelkerke R-Squared is similar to the previous one, but reaches 1.

Table 17.6: Goodness of fit for the logistic regression (ML estimates).

−2 Log-Likelihood	**Cox–Snell R-Squared**	**Nagelkerke R-Squared**
32.971	0.411	0.594

Table 17.7: Goodness of fit for the logistic regression (Firth PLR estimates).

−2 Log-Likelihood	**p-Value**	**Wald Test**	**p-Value**
23.378	8.39×10^{-6}	7.889	0.019

A pseudo R-squared equals to 40% is good if it is considered that PD is certainly not determined exclusively by these two variables. The Hosmer–Lemeshow test from Eq. (11.8) provides a high enough p-value to accept the hypothesis that the model is correctly specified (0.914). The contingency table for the test is available in Table 17.8.

Observations are divided into deciles based on observed frequencies. The table shows that expected frequencies are very close to the observed ones for each decile except for the ninth, where the deviation of the two values is more marked. The percentage correctly predicted is equal to 82.4%: 42 are the cases rightly estimated; of the nine classified incorrectly, six (42.9%) are among the risky companies and three (8.1%) are among the healthy ones (Table 17.9).

The model ranks health companies better, but this is mainly because the majority of the sample is made up of Type 0 ("healthy") companies. The effects of the individual regressors are graphically described in Figures 17.1 and 17.2. Both coefficients are negative showing that PD decreases with increasing covariates. As the Return on!Investment (ROI) increases, the riskiness of the company decreases (Figure 17.1); as the Working Capital to Asset ratio increases (and, therefore, as the difference between current assets and current liabilities increases), the company becomes safer (Figure 17.2).

Table 17.8: Contingency table for Hosmer–Lemeshow test.

	Healthy		Risky		
	Observed	**Expected**	**Observed**	**Expected**	**Total**
1	5	4.999	0	0.001	5
2	5	4.980	0	0.020	5
3	5	4.923	0	0.077	5
4	5	4.743	0	0.257	5
5	4	4.438	1	0.562	5
6	3	3.981	2	1.019	5
7	4	3.678	1	1.322	5
8	3	2.842	2	2.158	5
9	3	2.015	2	2.985	5
10	0	0.401	6	5.599	6

Table 17.9: Percentage correctly predicted by Model 2.

		Predicted		
		Healthy	**Risky**	**Correct Percentage**
Observed	Healthy	34	3	91.9
	Risky	6	8	57.1
	Overall Percentage			82.4

The points of the P(Y) constitute an inverse sigmoid: as the ROI increases, P(Y) decreases. They are concentrated mainly in the lower part of the graph, where P(Y) is less than 0.4. This is because in the sample there are more Type 0 ("healthy") firms than Type 1 ("risky") ones. A probability function of this type is better suited to the observations, remaining within the constraints of 0 and 1.

This second inverse sigmoid has the same trend as the previous one. However, it is truncated, as no observation of the sample presents a probability as a function of the WC to asset ratio lower than 0.3.

17.3.2 *Results for the LGD*

Our dataset contains 55 defaulted loans, of which are known historical accounting movements, year of default, EAD, recovery time and presence of collateral (see Tables C.2 and C.2). LGD is calculated according to Definition 9.2.

Recovery time is standardized through the equation $1 - e^{-rt}$. The discount rate used is 10%. All data are shown in Appendix C. As in [Jones and Hensher (2004); Tsai (2013); Hartmann-Wendels *et al.* (2014)], and to avoid data separation that

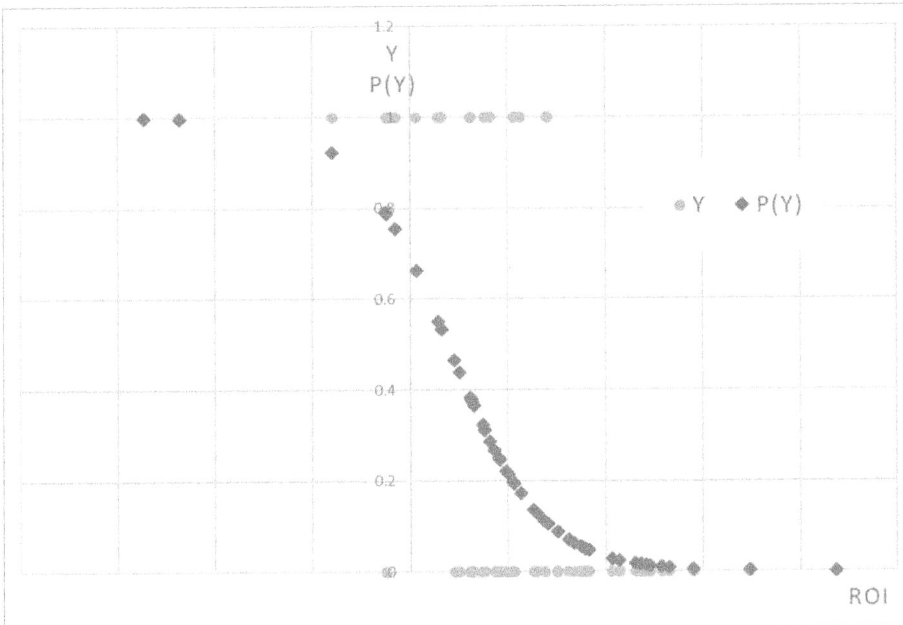

Fig. 17.1: PD as the ROI changes.

could be introduced by a finer partition of the dataset, we split the sample into three buckets so that the "$LGD*$" column is categorized as (0, 1, 2) of each loan in relation to the LGD level. Therefore, the following rule applies:

$$\begin{cases} Y_i = 0 & \text{if } LGD \leq 30\% \\ Y_i = 1 & \text{if } 30\% < LGD \leq 70\% \\ Y_i = 2 & \text{if } LGD > 70\%. \end{cases} \tag{17.2}$$

In the "COLLATERAL*" column, the presence or absence of collateral is, respectively, indicated by 1 and 0.

At this point, the goal is to demonstrate in this sample how the presence of collateral and the length of the recovery time affects LGD. Loans with the lowest loss level form 15% of the sample; Category 1, where the loss was between 30% and 70% of exposure, constitute 49% of the total; loans with LGD greater than 0.7 form the residual 36%. It is easy to understand that the average and the median of latent LGD are lower than 0.1 for the first category of loans, close to 0.5 — and to the total average of the sample — for the second category, and almost 1 for the third. Moreover, only 17 credits of 55 were guaranteed by collateral (31%), 7 out of 8 in the first category, 6 out of 27 in the second one and 4 out of 20 in the third groups. Both mean and median of the latent response variable are higher for loans without collateral than for the ones with collateral, confirming that collateral has a positive effect on credit recovery. Both mean and median of recovery time grow

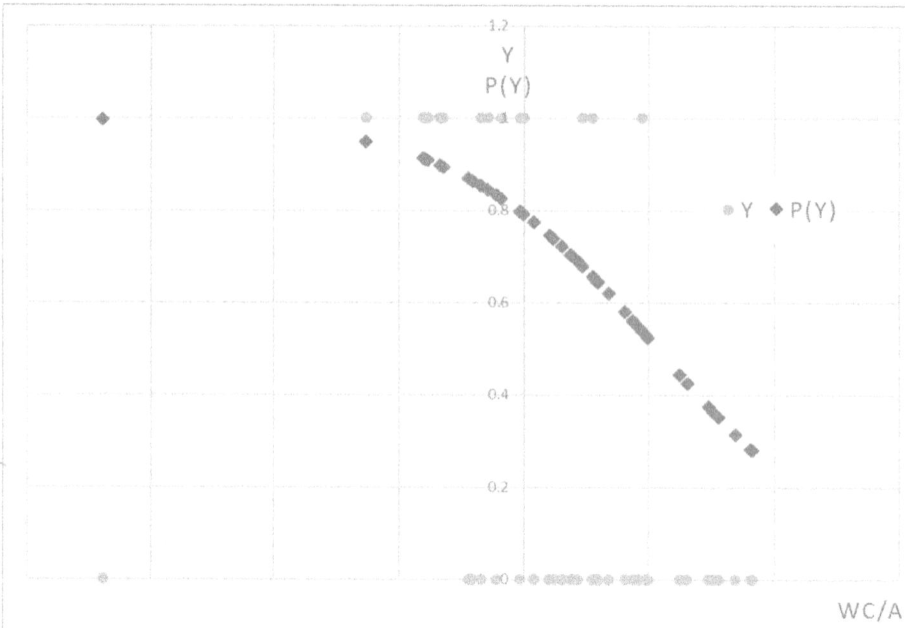

Fig. 17.2: PD as the WC/A changes.

as the *LGD* increases: as more time passes, it becomes more difficult to recover a loan. The first model shows the relationship between *LGD* trend and the presence of collateral. Estimating the model, it can be immediately noticed that this model does not fit very well to the data: Pearson's chi-square corresponds to a small *p*-value that does not allow us to reject the null hypothesis according to which the model is good. Pseudo R-squared is also very low and therefore unconvincing. The results are shown below (Tables 17.10 and 17.11).

Table 17.10: Model 1 goodness of fit.

	Chi-Squared	**df**	***p*-Value**
Pearson	5.111	1	0.024
Deviance	5.343	1	0.021

Table 17.11: Model 1 pseudo R-squared.

Cox–Snell	**Nagelkerke**	**McFadden**
0.136	0.157	0.073

Certainly, a large part of this low fit score is attributable to the sample size, which is extremely small. However, the estimates of the model parameters are shown below (Table 17.12), which are still significant.

Table 17.12: Model 1 parameter estimates.

		Estimate	**S.E.**	**Wald**	**df**	***p*-Value**
Threshold	[LGD=0]	−0.720	0.488	2.177	1	0.140
	[LGD=1]	1.941	0.583	11.079	1	0.001
Location	[COLL=0]	1.748	0.628	7.742	1	0.005
	[COLL=1]	0 *	.	.	0	.

* The parameter is set to zero because it is redundant.

The second estimated model is the one that includes recovery time as regressor. Estimating the model, data fit measures are obtained first. The "Final" model has a better fit than the first one (Table 17.13).

Table 17.13: Model 2 measures of fit.

Model	**−2 Log-Likelihood**	**Chi-Squared**	**df**	***p*-Value**
Intercept Only	61.495			
Final	44.729	16.775	1	0.000

LR Chi-Squared test allows verifying if the predictor's regression coefficient is not equal to zero. The test statistic is obtained from the difference between LR of Model 0 and LR of the final model. p-value (equal to 0.000 — it represents the probability of obtaining this chi-square statistic (31.56) if in reality there is no effect of the predictive variables) compared with a specified alpha level — i.e. our willingness to accept a Type I error, which is generally set equal to 0.05 — leads us to conclude that the regression coefficient of the model is not equal to zero. Pearson's chi-square statistics and deviance-based chi-squared statistics give us information on how suitable the model is for empirical observations. The null hypothesis is that the model is good; therefore, if p-value is large, then the null hypothesis is accepted, and the model is considered good. In this case, it is possible to say that the model is acceptable, as its results are satisfactory: it has a Pearson's chi-squared equal to 22.0, df = 19, p-value = 0.283; Deviance's chi-squared is equal to 23.5, df = 19, p-value = 0.218; the pseudo R-squared measurements are also acceptable (Table 17.14), considering that the *LGD* is determined by many factors and recovery time is not the only feature.

In Table 17.15, it is possible to notice that recovery time is significant as well as directly proportional to *LGD*: the positive coefficient tells us that, as recovery

Table 17.14: Pseudo R-square of Model 2.

Cox–Snell	Nagelkerke	McFadden
0.263	0.304	0.153

time increases, LGD also increases, as expected. In fact, it is known that the best way to manage a bad credit is to act promptly and that, over time, the chances to recover a loan worsen.

Table 17.15: Model 2 parameter estimates.

		Estimate	S.E.	Wald	df	p-Value
Threshold	[LGD=0]	0.463	0.674	0.472	1	0.492
	[LGD=1]	3.412	0.847	16.237	1	0.000
Location	RECOV. TIME	6.624	1.785	13.768	1	0.000

The "threshold" section contains estimates, in terms of logit, of cut-off points between categories of the response variable. The value for $[LGD = 0]$ is the estimate of cut-off between the first and second classes of LGD; the value corresponding to $[LGD = 1]$ is the estimate of cut-off between the second and the third LGD classes. Basically, they represent points, in terms of logit, from which loans should be predicted in the upper class of LGD. For the purposes of this analysis, their interpretation is not particularly significant, nor is it useful to interpret these values individually. The only estimate of logit ordered regression coefficient that appears in the parameter estimates table is the one relating to the regressor. Conceptually, interpretation of this value is that when the explanatory variable increases by one unit the level of the response variable is expected to change, according to its ordered log-odd regression coefficient. In our case, a unit time increment generates a variation of the ordered log-odd of being in a higher LGD category of 6.624. A corresponding p-value (0.000) that remains below the acceptance threshold of the null hypothesis ensures the significance of recovery time determining LGD. Figure 17.3 shows the probability curves of occurrence of each category related to recovery time.

Circles belong to a probability curve that Y is equal to 0 — the category with the lowest loss rate. Over time, this probability decreases until it is almost zero for loans, among the observed, with the longest recovery times. Diamonds, instead, define the curve of probability that Y is equal to 2: here, loans have very high expected LGD, almost equal to one. This probability increases considerably over time. Finally, triangles outline the probability curve that Y is equal to 1, the class in which the expected LGD is between 0.30 and 0.70. It is increasing in the first part; starting from the moment in which the probabilities of the other two classes

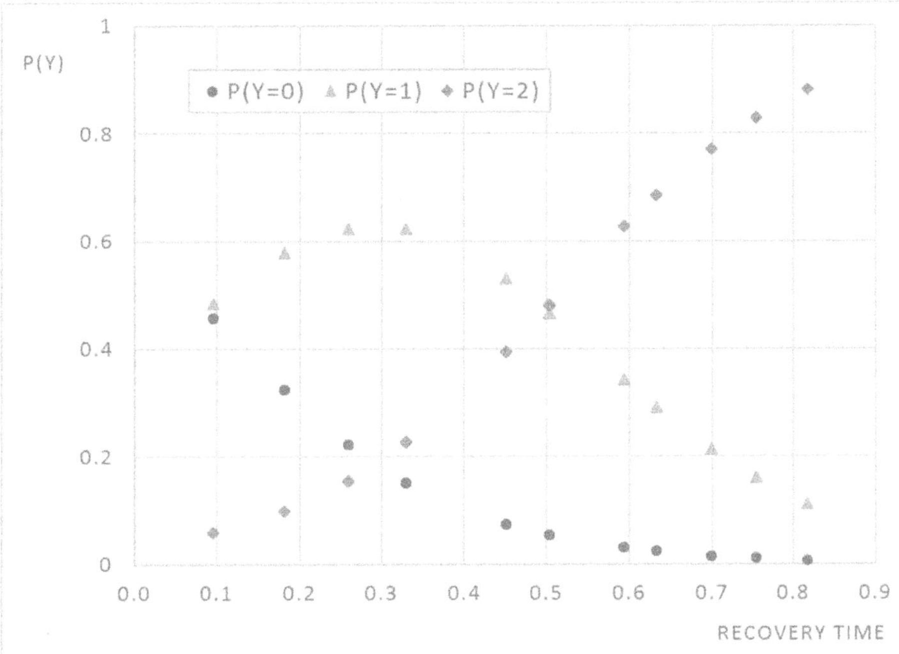

Fig. 17.3: Probability of occurrence of each category for recovery time.

are equal and the respective curves intersecting starts to decrease till the end of the time axis.

17.3.2.1 *Poisson Estimation and Suitability Analysis*

We divide the dataset into three groups as in [Jones and Hensher (2004)], [Tsai (2013)], [Hartmann-Wendels *et al.* (2014)]. We found the ranges in Equation (17.2) to suit well our analysis but, in other contexts, it could be that these ranges are different. The logistic regression answers the question of how many cases belong to a certain category. To assess the suitability of the classification, we ran a generalized linear model (GLM) Poisson regression. Tables 17.16 and 17.17 provide the estimates for the models with (Model 1) or without the intercept (Model 2), respectively. The dispersion of the results is shown in Table 17.18. As illustrated, Model 2 (i.e. the model without intercept) performs better than Model 1 with little loss in terms of dispersion of residuals. Moreover, this analysis confirms that the most important factor is time.

17.4 Discussion

On the classification model, a study made on a similar dataset in [Phongmekin and Jarumaneeroj (2018)] has shown that classification techniques such as logistic

Table 17.16: GLM Poisson Model 1 parameter estimates.

	Coef.	**Std. Error**	**z Value**	**p-Value**
Time	1.5352	0.6650	2.309	0.0210
Collateral	−0.5255	0.3005	−1.749	0.0804
Constant	−0.3327	0.3337	−0.997	0.3187

Table 17.17: GLM Poisson Model 2 parameter estimates.

	Coef.	**Std. Error**	**z Value**	**p-Value**
Time	0.922	0.276	3.339	0.001
Collateral	−0.581	0.294	−1.978	0.048

Table 17.18: GLM Poisson estimate: dispersion analysis.

	Deviance of the Residuals				
	Min	**1Q**	**Median**	**3Q**	**Max**
Pois. mod. 1	−1.452	−0.286	−0.066	0.343	1.370
Pois. mod. 2	−1.478	−0.383	−0.172	0.312	1.249

regression (LR), decision tree (DT), linear discriminant analysis (LDA) and K-nearest neighbor (KNN), are comparatively good. In addition, they found that LR and LDA are "the most useful classifiers for risk averse investors — as both are not subject to uncertainty due to true positive counting bias".

On the PD, we showed that the ROI and the WC to Asset are the most relevant variables. To check the quality of our results, we complemented the analysis by running the Firth's penalized likelihood. The latter is a method of addressing issues of separability, small sample sizes and bias of the parameter estimates. Then, we demonstrated that the outcomes are similar.

On the LGD, several studies have certainly led to the assertion that there are no universally valid models for any type of loans' technical form [Yashkir and Yashkir (2013)]. If a single solution has not yet been found on the issue of LGD modeling, it is because the loss rate depends on both external macroeconomic factors and the individual characteristics of each credit institution. However, those who have tried to incorporate the effects of the economy by adding some macroeconomic variables to the model (see, for example, [Bruche and González-Aguado (2010)], [Bellotti and Crook (2012)], [Leow *et al.* (2014)]) did not report any significant improvement. For this reason, we share the opinion that LGD estimates should reflect the practice of each individual institution [Dahlin and Storkitt (2014)]. Furthermore, the analysis carried out in this specific case shows how recovery time assumes great importance in determining the degree of loss, more than the presence of collateral to guarantee the credit. To maximize the recovery of a non-performing credit, the time taken to recover the credit should therefore be minimized.

Chapter 18

Default Correlations

In Chapter 15 we have analyzed the *CreditRisk+*, i.e. a credit risk model able to derive the loss probability distribution, the default probabilities and all the counterparty weights in a given portfolio, once the exposures are known (see also Chapter 16). More generally, this model splits the counterparties into independent sectors (i.e. independent groups of counterparties each of them being influenced by the same systemic risk factor).

However, this assumption is not realistic, and we need to understand what happens if this hypothesis is abandoned. In this case, the dependence between the sectors must be measured through some standard measure, such as the linear correlation, the rank correlation, or the tail dependence. Among them, the linear correlation is the least efficient because it requires the knowledge of both the joint distribution and the marginal distributions.

To introduce a correlation structure, we have to compute the joint cumulative distribution of the default events, given their marginal distributions. This problem does not admit a unique solution. Generally, we may obtain the marginal distributions and the correlation structure from the joint cumulative distribution, but the converse is not easy to do. In statistics, copulas are the simplest instruments able to solve this issue. A *copula* is a statistical instrument that connects the joint distribution to the marginal distributions. It is specially used to compute the joint cumulative distribution from a mixture of the marginal distributions, and vice versa. This is a very important result guaranteed by the Sklar theorem. For more details on copulas see Section 3.5.

18.1 Correlated Bernoulli Baseline Model

We have already shown the formula for the default correlation supposing the sequence of default events is a correlated Bernoulli process by Eqs. (1.3) and (1.4). Then we can apply to real-world data. For instance, the American data on total loans allows us to capture the following dependency. The worse the crisis is, the larger the drop in the GDP growth rate is, the higher the default correlation is.

This reconfirms the findings of [Longin and Solnik (2014)]. They observed during the Asian financial crisis of 1997 that the asset correlation rose. A similar effect was observed 20 years later during the pandemics of 2020 by [Aramonte and Avalos (2020)]. They found that the default correlation between CDS quotes unprecedentedly rose above the levels observed even during the financial crisis of 2007-2009.

[Merika *et al.* (2021)] provide an empirical verification of the finding that the default correlation rises in crisis. They look at the shipping companies as borrowers and notice that indeed those are both *PD* and *default correlation* that rise in crisis. Specifically, one of the stress scenarios they consider is a world GDP decline of -5%, as was expected by the World Bank for the 2020 pandemics. They argue that such stress scenario is characterized by an increase in *PD* from 1.1% of the total number of borrowers to 2.8%, while the default correlation also rises from 0.7% to 2.4%. The IRB formula would have yielded a credit risk of 21.9% of the total exposure (EAD), while it is actually around 32%, i.e. the credit risk underevaluation is mostly half as much as the IRB estimate.

18.2 Computation of Correlation Matrix through the Copula

Here we apply the results presented in Subsection 3.6.2 to determine the correlation matrix and the related risk for a given exposures portfolio. The software used in the next two examples are *Matlab* and *R*, respectively.

Consider a portfolio consisting of $m = 8$ counterparties with the default probabilities matrix from Table 18.1 where they belong to two distinct sectors (industries) S_1 and S_2.

Table 18.1: Default probabilities matrix.

S_1	S_2
0.1	0.2
0.3	0.5
0.6	0.8
0.7	0.9

S_1 and S_2 represent two co-dependent sectors of the economy. Each cell contains the default probability per particular borrower.

Table 18.2: Estimated gamma parameters.

	i=1	i=2
α_i	2.2548	3.5607
β_i	0.1885	0.1685

Assume that the columns of this matrix, named S_1, S_2, follow a Gamma distribution with parameters $(\alpha_1, \beta_1), (\alpha_2, \beta_2)$, respectively. In order to estimate the Gamma parameters in Table 18.2, we use the Matlab function *gamfit*.

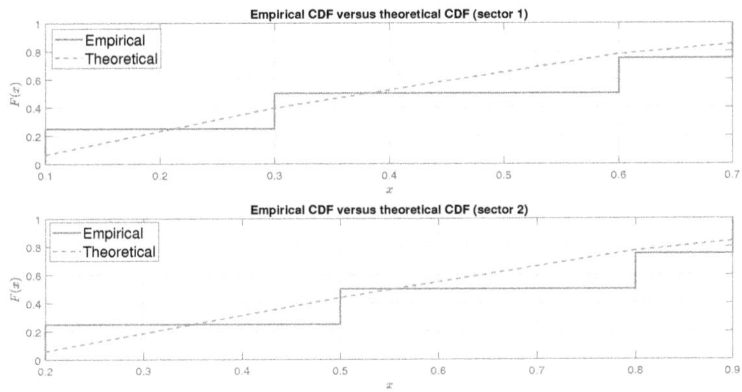

Fig. 18.1: Theoretical CDF versus empirical CDF.
Observe that the theoretical CDF's do not intercept the middle points of the empirical CDF's. Hence, there is no compensation between upward and downward errors.

Now, to compute the CDF of S_1 and S_2 (see Figure 18.1), we generate $n = 1,000$ random numbers from the Gamma distribution with parameters (α_1, β_1) and (α_2, β_2), representing the default rates (to recall its properties, please, refer to Section 1.3.5). As the reader may recall from Table 18.1 and see the horizontal axis at Figure 18.1, the default rate ranges from 10% of the total borrowers to 70% for the first sector S_1 and from 20% to 90% for the second one S_2.

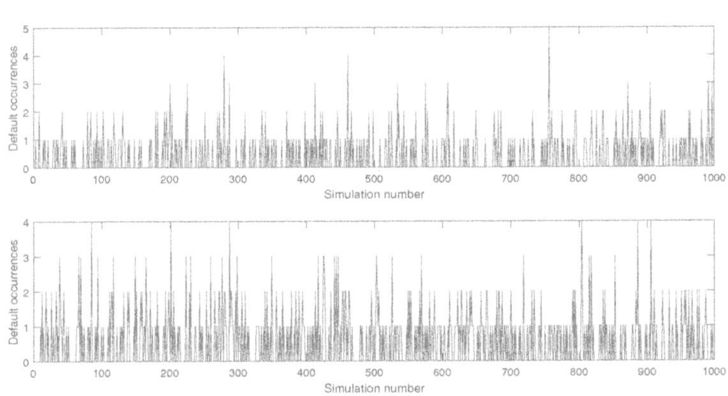

Fig. 18.2: Default occurrences by sectors (S_1 above and S_2 below).

Then, we generate two n-dimensional samples distributed like a Poisson, by using the Matlab function *poissrnd*, see Figure 18.2 (as a reminder, please, consult a corresponding Section 1.2.5). We switch to Poisson from Gamma as we wish to transit from default rates to the discrete number of defaults. As the reader may see from the vertical axis in Figure 18.2, the number of defaults ranges from zero to four-five by sectors.

Since the two marginals are Poisson distributed and assuming a Gaussian copula to join them (to refresh the key relevant concepts, please, check Section 3.5.4.4), we will test the dependence between these samples. The Matlab function *copulafit* gives us the correlation matrix between the Gamma parameters. Finally, by computing the Kendall rank correlation matrix using Eq. (3.43) in Table 18.3, we obtain Figure 18.3.

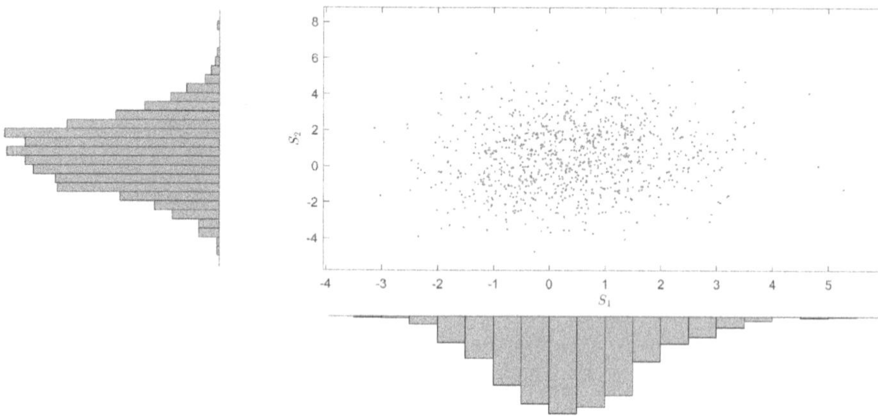

Fig. 18.3: Scatterplot between S_1 and S_2.
The plot suggests there is no correlation between variables.

Table 18.3: Kendall correlation matrix.

1	0.0045
0.0045	1

By looking at the scatter plot in Figure 18.3 and the correlation matrix in Table 18.3, we conclude that there is no dependence between the variables of interest. For more details about the coding, see Appendix B.4. This is an expected outcome as we did not set up the non-zero co-dependence when generating a set of eight borrowers. When a credit risk manager deals with the real loan portfolio data, he starts with the joint distribution and evaluates co-dependence between marginals as done in Table 18.3. Below we look at the case when such dependence is far from a zero-correlation case.

18.3 Portfolio Risk Evaluation

18.3.1 *Description of the Input Bond Return Data*

In this section, we show how to compute the risk by factoring in the credit migration of a fixed income portfolio containing two secured bonds with a recovery rate equal to 60% (see Table 18.4). We set equal weights for these bonds and an $EAD = \$100$ to each of them. The code for the computations here displayed is reported in Appendix A.2.

Table 18.4: Fixed income portfolio.

Bond	Issue	Price	Coupon	Maturity	Moody's Rating
1	Bond A	95.22	0.5%	5	Aaa
2	Bond B	99.61	1.3%	2	Aa

Table 18.5 shows the log return statistics for the two bonds. Figure 18.4 displays the histogram of log returns for Bond A and Bond B.

Table 18.5: Log return statistics for Bond A and Bond B.

Bond A		Bond B	
Min.	-0.1377	Min.	-0.1595
1st Qu.	-0.0065	1st Qu.	-0.0055
Median	0.0011	Median	0.0011
Mean	0.0014	Mean	0.0013
Std. Dev.	0.0191	Std. Dev.	0.0172
3rd Qu.	0.0103	3rd	0.0097
Max.	0.1132	Max.	0.1329
Skewness	-0.3403	Skewness	-0.3481
Kurtosis	-0.3403	Kurtosis	-0.3481

Our goal is to compute the correlation matrix through the copulas. To do this, we first start from the raw data of bond returns, see Figure 18.5. We see that the returns are quite codependent. They demonstrate joint extreme realisations both in the positive and negative domains. This points to the best fit of a symmetric copula with upper and lower tail dependences.

Then, recall the default transition probabilities matrix in Table 18.6.

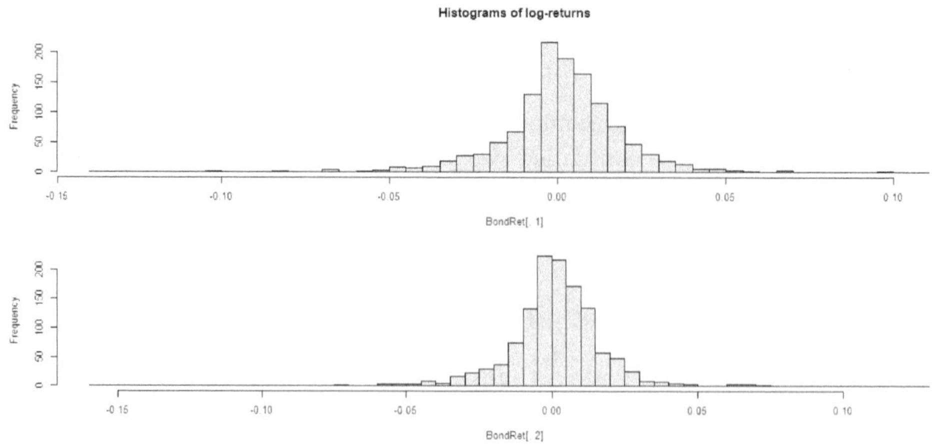

Fig. 18.4: Histogram of log returns of Bond A (above) and Bond B (below).

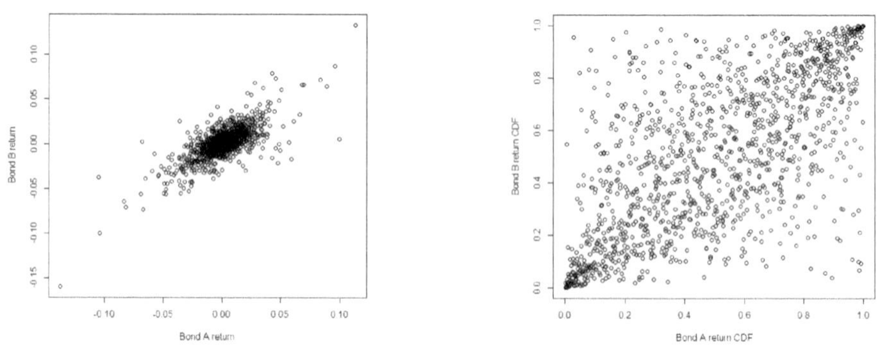

Fig. 18.5: The bond returns are codependent with joint fat upper and lower tails in our illustrative example (left part — data in levels, the right one — in probability).

Table 18.6: 1Y Rating transition matrix (cf. [Saldanha and Beers (2011), Table 1]).

	Aaa	Aa	A	Baa	Ba	B	Caa - C	NR
Aaa	94.2%	3.6%	0.0%	0.0%	0.0%	0.0%	0.0%	2.2%
Aa	1.7%	93.3%	2.1%	0.0%	0.0%	0.0%	0.0%	2.9%
A	0.0%	3.0%	91.7%	1.4%	0.0%	0.0%	0.0%	4.0%
Baa	0.0%	0.0%	3.8%	86.4%	3.2%	0.0%	0.0%	6.6%
Ba	0.0%	0.0%	0.0%	2.3%	88.9%	1.1%	1.5%	6.1%
B	0.0%	0.0%	0.0%	0.0%	12.8%	75.4%	3.8%	8.1%
Caa -C	0.0%	0.0%	0.0%	0.0%	0.0%	32.4%	62.1%	5.4%

18.3.2 *Risk Evaluation of Credit Migration*

We use the *R* package *mlCopulaSelection* and can fit the best copula and estimate the marginal probabilities. Then, we compute the correlation matrix through the Spearman rank correlation.

We use the function *mlcbbsel* of package *mlCopulaselection.* It provides the parameter estimates for a copula through the Maximum Likelihood (ML) method. Based on the data, the best copula is BB9 with zero rotation (to recall what the copula *rotation* parameter is, please, refer to Subsection 3.5.5 and its illustration in Figures 3.5–3.10). The functional form for the BB9 copula CDF C_{BB9} is given in Eq. (18.1) (see [Joe (1997), p. 154, formula (5.13)]). The parameters of the best fitted BB9 copula are $\theta = 3.16$ and $\delta = 0.45$, and

$$C_{BB9}(u, v; \theta, \delta) = \exp\{-[(\delta - \log(u))^{\theta} + (\delta - \log(v))^{\theta} - \delta^{\theta}]^{1/\theta} + \delta\}, \tag{18.1}$$

where u, v are the corresponding CDFs of the marginal distributions from the right part of Figure 18.5.

From this output, it is possible to obtain the copula density with the corresponding function *dcbb9*. Given the copula generated by the above model, we are able to compute the Spearman correlation by using the representation from Eq. (3.46). In this way, we obtain the correlation for our two bonds. It equals to +69%, while the direct Spearman rank correlation when applied to bond returns yields only +65%.

Once the correlation is known, we may evaluate the portfolio risk by the *R* package *CreditMetrics*. Therefore, we conclude that the 99% VaR is equal to \$ 38.08. This means that the maximum expected portfolio loss will be less than \$ 38.08, with a probability of 99.9%. Moreover, given the confidence level $\alpha = 95\%$, we have that the 95% VaR is \$ 0.43, i.e. the maximum expected portfolio loss will be less than \$ 0.43, with a probability of 95%. We remember that these figures should be pronounced with the following additions: for the time horizon of interest (for instance, during ten days holding period for which we obtained the returns) and given no changes in the market liquidity.

We should note that in the extreme case — when the transition matrix is degenerated to a diagonal one, i.e. there is no ratings' migration — the *CreditMetrics* package yields a zero level of the conditional credit risk arising from the ratings' transition.

18.3.3 *Portfolio Risk Evaluation: Selecting the Copulas*

In this section, we show an example on how to select the correct copula for measuring the risk. The code for the computations here displayed is reported in Appendix A.2 and has been inspired by [Bolancé Losilla *et al.* (2015)].

Table 18.7 shows the tail dependence (to recall the definition and properties the reader may consult Section 3.6.3). Notice that both Gaussian and Frank copulas have zero dependence while t-Student have symmetric tail dependence. Finally, Gumbel and Clayton have asymmetric positive and negative tail dependence, respectively.

Table 18.7: Tail dependence for Bond A and Bond B.

	Tail dependence	
Copula	Lower	Upper
Normal	0	0
t-Student	0.459	0.459
Gumbel	0	0.558
Clayton	0.693	0
Frank	0	0

Fitting is obtained by running the MLE (maximum likelihood estimation) over the data. According to both Bayesian information criterion (BIC) and Akaike information criterion (AIC), Table 18.8 shows that the best fit is given by the t-Student copula. It demonstrates the lowest values for AIC and BIC criteria.

Table 18.8: AIC and BIC for Bond A and Bond B.

Copula	AIC	BIC
Normal	-788.238	-783.101
t-Student	-933.741	-923.468
Gumbel	-788.002	-782.865
Clayton	-784.834	-779.698
Frank	-717.563	-712.426

Tables 18.9 and 18.10 show, respectively, the VaR from Eq. (10.5) and the Tail VaR (TVaR) from Eq. (10.6) of a portfolio composed of Bond A and Bond B. As the reader may see, the most conservative measures are with t-Student copula and t-Student marginals and with Clayton copula and t-Student marginals. We derive this conclusion by observing the largest values in the last column of both tables, i.e. 0.7218 and 0.5509 in Table 18.9 and 1.2176 and 1.1541 in Table 18.10 (recall that the worst values for us are the positive ones as they are equivalent to the default rates).

Table 18.9: VaR of a portfolio composed by Bond A and Bond B.

		VaR		
Copula	Marginal	99%	99.50%	99.90%
Gaussian	Normal	0.0815	0.0894	0.1059
	t-Student	-1.1013	-0.6528	0.2930
t-Student	Normal	0.0744	0.0833	0.1017
	t-Student	-0.7876	-0.2611	0.7218
Gumbel	Normal	0.0707	0.0783	0.0938
	t-Student	-1.4026	-0.9860	-0.0977
Clayton	Normal	0.0800	0.0895	0.1061
	t-Student	-0.8838	-0.3736	0.5509
Frank	Normal	0.0686	0.0751	0.0876
	t-Student	-1.5232	-1.1665	-0.4653

Table 18.10: TVaR of a portfolio composed by Bond A and Bond B.

		Tail VaR		
Copula	Marginal	99%	99.50%	99.90%
Gaussian	Normal	0.0926	0.1001	0.1166
	t-Student	-0.4732	-0.0525	0.8745
t-Student	Normal	0.0864	0.0943	0.1099
	t-Student	-0.0981	0.3525	1.2176
Gumbel	Normal	0.0810	0.0879	0.1015
	t-Student	-0.8366	-0.4607	0.2902
Clayton	Normal	0.0922	0.1003	0.1170
	t-Student	-0.2153	0.2315	1.1541
Frank	Normal	0.0773	0.0830	0.0943
	t-Student	-1.0429	-0.7274	-0.0961

Chapter 19

Credit Default Swap (CDS)

Credit derivatives are financial contracts that have been widely adopted by the credit market participants as a tool for exposure management or credit investments. Upon their introduction in the mid-1990s, the credit derivatives market expanded rapidly during the period of loose monetary policy and expanding credit from 2002 through 2007.

- The notional amount of credit derivative contracts outstanding at the end of 2003 stood at \$ 3.5 trillion from 2002, with an increase of 82%. At the end of 2007, outstanding contracts are estimated to be around \$ 42 trillion. However, it is still somewhat ten times less than the amount of the interest rate derivatives (those like IRSs), see Figure 19.1.

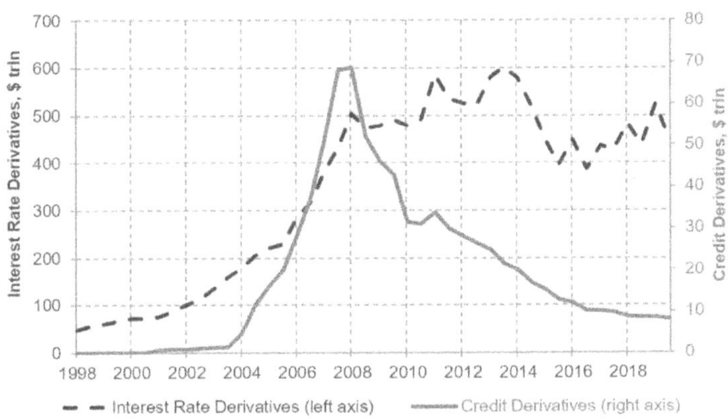

Fig. 19.1: Interest rate derivatives outperform the credit ones by ten times, though the credit derivatives sky-rocketed more on the event of the 2007-2009 financial crisis. *Sources: [BIS (2020)]*

- The growth in the credit derivatives market has been driven by the diversification of participants, the standardization of documentation, and the growth of product applications.

- Credit derivatives became mainstream and have been integrated with credit trading and risk management in many firms.

The growth of credit derivatives began slowly after the global credit crisis and during the Eurozone sovereign debt crisis in 2010 and 2011. In recent years, despite deliberate efforts by the *International Swaps and Derivatives Association (ISDA)* and by the market participants from the buyers and sellers side, the credit derivatives market contracted and shrunk substantially. However, they represent the third biggest over-the-counter (OTC) derivatives market in the world, with \$8 trillion notional value. Today, almost 60% of the total volume of credit derivatives consists of *Credit Default Swaps (CDSs)*, that are bilateral agreements between a protection buyer and a protection seller, in which the buyer agrees to make fixed periodic payments to the seller in exchange for protection against a credit event in front of an underlying asset or an assets portfolio. Because of the importance of the CDS market in the world financial system, our aim in this chapter is to describe the payoff structure for a CDS contract and the CDS pricing model. Concerning this last point, we will focus on the so-called *reduced-form* model.

19.1 CDS Terms and Definitions

A *Credit Default Swap (CDS)* is a financial instrument designed to offer protection against the default under the payment of a periodic premium.

Consider two parties A (the *protection buyer*) and B (the *protection seller*) that enter into a CDS deal with term $T - T_0$. The time window (T_0, T) is called the *protection time*, meaning that the protection will be negotiated for default happening between times T_0 and T. If a third part C (the *reference entity*) defaults at time $\tau \in (T_0, T)$, then A will be compensated by B at time τ or at T with a deterministic cash amount to cover the loss (LGD), so that the contract terminates. In exchange for this protection, A agrees to pay periodically a fixed amount, called *CDS spread*, to B. The CDS spread is fixed on the trade date and does not change over the life of the CDS contract. In a customized market, the CDS spread is the spread over such LIBOR that equates the discounted present value of coupon payments, following the occurrence of a credit event. These payments determine the premium leg of the CDS and they go to default at time τ if the latter occurs before T, or until T if no default occurs. When the protection seller agrees to pay the protection buyer not only in case of the default but to transfer all changes in the market value of the reference entity or asset, such a contract is another credit derivative. It is called *Total Return Swap (TRS)*.

The default, often called *credit event*, is usually defined by the two involved parties and it is one of the significant economic terms of a CDS. The most common credit events, as defined by the *International Swaps and Derivatives Association (ISDA)*, are:

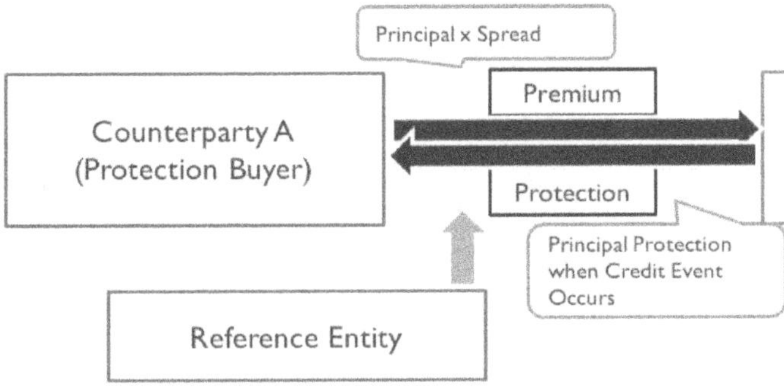

Fig. 19.2: Payoff structure of a CDS.

- *Bankruptcy*, that is the reference entity becomes insolvent or admitting in a regulatory, judicial, or administrative proceeding to its insolvency;
- *Failure to pay*, that is the reference entity fails to make a required payment when and where it is due on one or more of its obligations;
- *Debt restructuring*, that is a change in terms of the debt, which causes the debt to be less favorable to debt-holders. Common examples of debt restructuring include a decrease in the principal amount to be paid, a decline in the coupon rate, a postponement of payment obligations, a longer maturity time, or a change in the priority ranking of payment.

Other relevant covenants of a CDS are

i) Identity of the underlying reference entity;
ii) Contract's maturity and the time to maturity;
iii) Required payments (amounts and dates) by the protection buyer to the protection seller;
iv) Method of settlement for any obligation arising following the occurrence of a credit event. They are of three different kinds.

- *Physical Settlement*, in which the protection buyer must deliver any eligible deliverable obligation to the protection seller in return for a cash payment, equal to the notional amount of the swap;
- *Auction Settlement*, which converts physically settled CDSs into cash-settled CDSs, and defines the price at which cash settlement occurs through a rule-bound auction mechanism for the bonds underlying the defaulting reference entity;
- *Cash Settlement*, which involves a single payment by the protection seller to the protection buyer equivalent to the difference between the notional amount of the CDS and the expected recovery value.

For more details, a reader can refer to [Culp *et al.* (2016)].

Remark 19.1. Notice that the protection buyer and the protection seller take on *counterparty credit risk* when entering into a CDS, as described below:

- Protection buyer (A) takes the risk that the protection seller (B) may default. If B and the reference entity (C) default simultaneously, A loses the protection against default by C. If A defaults and C does not, B might need to replace the defaulted CDS at a higher cost;
- Protection seller (B) takes the risk that the protection buyer (A) may default. In that case, B might be deprived of the expected revenue stream.

However, in the future, this risk may be gone if regulatory reforms require that CDS be traded and settled via a clearing house, as it happens today also for other markets, such as commodities futures markets and stock exchanges.

Based on the given description, we want to determine the payoff of a CDS. For a related literature review, a reader can see, e.g. [Brigo *et al.* (2013)], [Jarrow and Turnbull (1995)], [O'Kane (2011)] and [Bielecki and Rutkowski (2013)].

19.2 CDS Payoff

Consider a CDS overtime interval $[0, T]$. The protection seller pays the protection buyer a cash flow amount if a default occurs till the maturity of the deal. In that case, for $t \in [0, T]$ its discounted payoff is equal to

$$Payoff_{\text{Protection Leg}}(t) = \begin{cases} N \cdot (1 - RR(t)) \cdot D(t, \tau) & t < \tau \\ N \cdot (1 - RR(t)) & t = \tau \\ 0 & \text{otherwise,} \end{cases}$$

where N denotes the notional of the deal, $RR(t)$ the recovery rate and $D(t, \tau)$ the value at time τ of rolled-up risk-free money-market account in which \$ 1 was deposited at time t. For details, if $B(t) = \exp\left(\int_0^t r(u)\,du\right)$ is the bank-account numeraire with continuously compounded risk-free short rate $r(t)$, then

$$D(t, \tau) = \frac{B(t)}{B(\tau)} = \exp\left(\int_t^\tau r(u)\,du\right).$$

We suppose that the recovery rate is constant during the time. The discounted payoff of the protection leg can be also written as

$$Payoff_{\text{Protection Leg}}(t) = N \cdot (1 - RR) \cdot D(t, \tau) \cdot \mathbb{1}_{\{t < \tau \le T\}}. \tag{19.1}$$

Since $\mathbb{1}_{\{t<\tau\le T\}} = \mathbb{1}_{\{\tau>t\}} \cdot \mathbb{1}_{\{\tau \le T\}}$, we can rewrite Eq. (19.1) as

$$Payoff_{\text{Protection Leg}}(t) = \mathbb{1}_{\{\tau>t\}} \cdot N \cdot (1 - RR) \cdot D(t, \tau) \cdot \mathbb{1}_{\{\tau \le T\}}. \tag{19.2}$$

The premium leg consists of coupon payments in case of no default and accrued premium, otherwise. Its discounted payoff is equal to

$$Payoff_{\text{Premium Leg}}(t) = Payoff_{\text{Premium Coupon}}(t) + Payoff_{\text{Premium Accrual}}(t), \quad (19.3)$$

where

$$Payoff_{\text{Premium Coupon}}(t) = -\mathbb{1}_{\{\tau>t\}} \cdot \sum_{i=1}^{n} Flow_i \cdot D(t,t_i) \cdot \mathbb{1}_{\{\tau>t_i\}},$$

$$Payoff_{\text{Premium Accrual}}(t) = -\mathbb{1}_{\{\tau>t\}} \cdot \sum_{i=1}^{n} \frac{\tau - t_{i-1}}{t_i - t_{i-1}} \cdot Flow_i \cdot D(t,\tau) \cdot \mathbb{1}_{\{t_{i-1}<\tau<t_i\}},$$

and we denote by

- t_{i-1} the start date of i-th cash flow $Flow_i$ for $i = 1, ..., n$;
- t_i the end date of i-th cash flow $Flow_i$ for $i = 1, ..., n$;
- $\alpha_i = t_i - t_{i-1}$ the day-count fraction of i-th cash flow $Flow_i$, for $i = 1, ..., n$ (it returns the calendar days between t_i and t_{i-1});
- R the credit default spread;
- $Flow_i = N \cdot \alpha_i \cdot R$ the i-th cash flow for $i = 1, ..., n$.

Formally, we may write the discounted payoff of a CDS at time t as:

$$\begin{aligned} Payoff_{CDS}(t) &= \mathbb{1}_{\{\tau>t\}} \cdot N \cdot (1 - RR) \cdot D(t,\tau) \cdot \mathbb{1}_{\{\tau\le T\}} \\ &\quad - \mathbb{1}_{\{\tau>t\}} \sum_{i=1}^{n} Flow_i \cdot D(t,t_i) \cdot \mathbb{1}_{\{\tau>t_i\}} \\ &\quad - \mathbb{1}_{\{\tau>t\}} \cdot \sum_{i=1}^{n} \frac{\tau - t_{i-1}}{t_i - t_{i-1}} \cdot Flow_i \cdot D(t,\tau) \cdot \mathbb{1}_{\{t_{i-1}<\tau<t_i\}}. \end{aligned} \quad (19.4)$$

Generally, we can compute the CDS price according to risk-neutral measure $\mathbb{Q}$ and the filtration $\mathcal{G}_t = \mathcal{F}_t \vee \mathcal{H}_t$, which represent the flow of information on whether the default occurred before time t and on the regular default-free market information up to t. For details, $\mathcal{F}_t = \sigma(\{\tau > u\}, u > t)$ is the filtration without default and represents the information flow of interest rates and other default-free market quantities, while $\mathcal{H}_t = \sigma(\{\tau < u\}, u \le t)$ is the filtration about default. If we denote $CDS(t)$ as the price at time t, we have

$$CDS(t) = \mathbb{E}[Payoff_{CDS}(t) \mid \mathcal{G}_t]. \quad (19.5)$$

The CDS price at time t is the sum of its conditional expectations. Thus, we have

$$\begin{aligned} CDS(t) = \mathbb{E}[Payoff_{\text{Protection Leg}}(t) \mid \mathcal{G}_t] &+ \mathbb{E}[Payoff_{\text{Premium Coupon}}(t) \mid \mathcal{G}_t] \\ &+ \mathbb{E}[Payoff_{\text{Premium Accrual}}(t) \mid \mathcal{G}_t]. \end{aligned} \quad (19.6)$$

For simplicity, we will use these notations in the rest of the discussion:

- $NPV_{\text{Protection Leg}}(t) = \mathbb{E}[Payoff_{\text{Protection Leg}}(t) \mid \mathcal{G}_t]$;
- $NPV_{\text{Premium Coupon}}(t) = \mathbb{E}[Payoff_{\text{Premium Coupon}}(t) \mid \mathcal{G}_t]$;
- $NPV_{\text{Premium Accrual}}(t) = \mathbb{E}[Payoff_{\text{Premium Accrual}}(t) \mid \mathcal{G}_t]$.

We observe that the information contained in $\mathcal{G}_t$ may not be available to a generic user who has only access to the smaller filtration $\mathcal{F}_t$. To solve this issue, we should change the filtration from $\mathcal{G}_t$ to $\mathcal{F}_t$. In this respect, the next lemma comes to be helpful.

Lemma 19.1. *For any $\mathcal{F}_T$-measurable function F, it holds*

$$\mathbb{1}_{\{\tau>t\}} \cdot \mathbb{E}[F \cdot \mathbb{1}_{\{\tau>T\}} \mid \mathcal{G}_t] = \frac{\mathbb{1}_{\{\tau>t\}}}{\mathbb{Q}(\tau > t \mid \mathcal{F}_t)} \cdot \mathbb{E}[F \cdot \mathbb{1}_{\{\tau>T\}} \mid \mathcal{F}_t]. \tag{19.7}$$

Thus, the price at time t of a CDS can be written as a conditional expectation upon the filtration on $\mathcal{F}_t$ as follows

$$CDS(t) = \frac{\mathbb{1}_{\{\tau>t\}}}{\mathbb{Q}(\tau > t \mid \mathcal{F}_t)} \cdot \mathbb{E}[CDS(t) \mid \mathcal{F}_t]. \tag{19.8}$$

In order to compute the conditional expectation of each component, we have to model the following two variables:

- Market rate $r(t)$;
- Default time τ.

We assume $r(t)$ satisfies $dr(t) = \mu(t,r)dt + \sigma(t,r)dW_t$, with W_t a Brownian motion under $\mathbb{Q}$. Moreover, there are two different approaches to model the default time:

- *Structural models*;
- *Reduced-form models.*

Both models are quantitative models of credit risk and their scope is to price and hedge financial contracts that are sensitive to credit risk, such as credit default swaps. In the structural approach, it is assumed that the default event is triggered by the market value of an obligor failing to meet its liabilities. In the reduced-form model, the default event is directly modeled by a stochastic arrival process. We will focus on the reduced-form method, also referred to as *intensity model*, because it is more flexible and tractable in the real market.

19.3 Reduced-Form Model

The model aims to describe the statistical properties of the default time as accurately as possible. Generally, the intensity models characterize the default as the first event (jump) of a Poisson counting process time with intensity $\lambda > 0$. If the intensity is assumed to be constant in time, the survival probability at time t is given by

$$\mathbb{P}(\tau > t) = e^{-\lambda t}.$$

However, the most popular form assumes the intensity to be time-varying, i.e. $\lambda = \lambda(t)$. In this case, the survival probability at time t is

$$\mathbb{P}(\tau > t) = \exp\left(- \int_0^t \lambda(u)\, du \right).$$

19.3.1 *Poisson Process for Modeling CDS*

We remind the reader that a Poisson process has been described in Chapter 2. In this section, we recall some useful properties and explain how defaults are modeled by the first jump of a Poisson process.

As mentioned, a Poisson process has the following properties

- *Superposition of independent Poisson processes*
- *Approximation of the Binomial distribution*
- *Likelihood equivalence, i.e.*

$$\mathcal{L} = \frac{(\lambda t)^x e^{-\lambda t}}{x!} \quad \propto \quad \lambda^x e^{-\lambda t}.$$

The latter property is particularly important when we deal with data that may be censored. Let us assume that there is no censoring and that assets until default are modeled as $Y_i \sim e^{\lambda}$. Then each element contributes by $\lambda e^{-y_i \lambda}$ to the likelihood

$$\prod_{i=1}^{n} \lambda e^{-y_i \lambda} = \lambda^n exp\left(-\lambda \sum_{i=1}^{n} y_i\right),$$

where n is the number of defaults and $\sum_{i=1}^{n} y_i$ is the number of assets. This likelihood stays the same when $n \sim Pois\,(-\lambda \sum_{i=1}^{n} y_i)$.

In case data is censored (e.g. in the dataset some assets will default at a later stage), the likelihood contribution for each event is $\lambda e^{-y_i \lambda}$ and the likelihood contribution for each censored observation is

$$\mathbb{P}(Y \geqslant y_i; \lambda) = \int_{y_i}^{+\infty} \lambda e^{-\lambda u} du = e^{-y_i \lambda}.$$

Combining censored and non-censored observations, we have that

$$\left(\prod_{non\text{-}censored\ i} \lambda e^{-y_i \lambda}\right)\left(\prod_{censored\ i} e^{-y_i \lambda}\right) = \lambda^x exp\left(-\lambda \sum_{i=1}^{n} y_i\right),$$

where x is the number of defaults, n-x is the number of censored observations and $\sum_{i=1}^{n} y_i$ is the total number of assets. This is exactly the same likelihood as modeling $X \sim Pois\,(\lambda \sum_{i=1}^{n} y_i)$.

We will use these results to compute the price of a CDS at time t.

19.3.2 *CDS Pricing*

In Section 19.2, we have seen that the price at time t of a CDS can be written as the following conditional expectation

$$CDS(t) = \frac{\mathbb{1}_{\{\tau>t\}}}{\mathbb{Q}(\tau > t \mid \mathcal{F}_t)} \cdot \mathbb{E}[CDS(t) \mid \mathcal{F}_t].$$

In order to compute the conditional expectation of each component, we have to define suitable models for the two variables, which are

- Market rate $r(t)$;
- Default time τ.

19.3.2.1 *Protection Leg Net Present Value*

Compute the *Net Present Value (NPV)* of the protection leg at time t, i.e.

$$\begin{aligned} NPV_{\text{Protection Leg}}(t) &= \frac{\mathbb{1}_{\{\tau>t\}}}{\mathbb{Q}(\tau > t \mid \mathcal{F}_t)} \cdot \mathbb{E}[N \cdot (1 - RR) \cdot D(t,\tau) \cdot \mathbb{1}_{\{t<\tau\leq T\}} | \mathcal{F}_t] \\ &= \frac{\mathbb{1}_{\{\tau>t\}}}{\mathbb{Q}(\tau > t \mid \mathcal{F}_t)} \cdot N \cdot (1 - RR) \cdot \mathbb{E}[D(t,\tau) \cdot \mathbb{1}_{\{t<\tau\leq T\}} | \mathcal{F}_t]. \end{aligned} \tag{19.9}$$

Given the interval $[t, T]$, we distribute the default as the sum of defaults in every disjoint subinterval $[s, s + ds)$ of $[t, T]$. Then,

$$[t, T] = \bigsqcup_{t\leq s<T} [s, s + ds).$$

If the default τ occurs in $[s, s + ds)$, the value of the protection leg cash flow is

$$\begin{aligned} NPV_{\text{Protection Leg}}(t) &= \frac{\mathbb{1}_{\{\tau>t\}}}{\mathbb{Q}(\tau > t \mid \mathcal{F}_t)} \cdot N \cdot (1 - RR) \cdot \mathbb{E}[D(t,s) \cdot \mathbb{1}_{\{s\leq\tau<s+ds\}} | \mathcal{F}_t] \\ &= \frac{\mathbb{1}_{\{\tau>t\}}}{\mathbb{Q}(\tau > t \mid \mathcal{F}_t)} \cdot N \cdot (1 - RR) \cdot \mathbb{E}[D(t,s) \cdot \mathbb{1}_{\{t<\tau\leq T\}} \cdot \mathbb{1}_{\{s\leq\tau<s+ds\}} | \mathcal{F}_t]. \end{aligned} \tag{19.10}$$

Thus, by summing all the protection leg cash flows for different instants, we may rewrite Eq. (19.9) as

$$NPV_{\text{Protection Leg}}(t) = \frac{\mathbb{1}_{\{\tau>t\}}}{\mathbb{Q}(\tau > t \mid \mathcal{F}_t)} \cdot N \cdot (1 - RR) \cdot \mathbb{E}\left[\int_t^T D(t,s) \cdot \mathbb{1}_{\{s \le \tau < s+ds\}} ds \,\middle|\, \mathcal{F}_t\right]. \tag{19.11}$$

Moreover, thanks to Fubini theorem we can switch the integral with the expectation, i.e.

$$\begin{aligned} NPV_{\text{Protection Leg}}(t) &= \frac{\mathbb{1}_{\{\tau>t\}}}{\mathbb{Q}(\tau > t \mid \mathcal{F}_t)} \cdot N \cdot (1 - RR) \cdot \mathbb{E}\left[\int_t^T D(t,s) \cdot \mathbb{1}_{\{s \le \tau < s+ds\}}\, ds \,\middle|\, \mathcal{F}_t\right] \\ &= \frac{\mathbb{1}_{\{\tau>t\}}}{\mathbb{Q}(\tau > t \mid \mathcal{F}_t)} \cdot N \cdot (1 - RR) \cdot \int_t^T \mathbb{E}\big[D(t,s) \cdot \mathbb{1}_{\{s \le \tau < s+ds\}} \mid \mathcal{F}_t\big]\, ds \\ &= \frac{\mathbb{1}_{\{\tau>t\}}}{\mathbb{Q}(\tau > t \mid \mathcal{F}_t)} \cdot N \cdot (1 - RR) \cdot \int_t^T \mathbb{E}\big[D(t,s) \mid \mathcal{F}_t\big] \cdot \mathbb{E}\big[\mathbb{1}_{\{s \le \tau < s+ds\}} \mid \mathcal{F}_t\big]\, ds \\ &= \frac{\mathbb{1}_{\{\tau>t\}}}{\mathbb{Q}(\tau > t \mid \mathcal{F}_t)} \cdot N \cdot (1 - RR) \cdot \int_t^T DF(t,s) \cdot \mathbb{Q}(\tau \in [s, s+ds) \mid \mathcal{F}_t)\, ds. \end{aligned} \tag{19.12}$$

We have used the independence between τ and interest rates, so that $DF(t,s) = \mathbb{E}\big[D(t,s) \mid \mathcal{F}_t\big]$ represents the discount factor between t and s. The integrand term $\mathbb{Q}(\tau \in [s, s+ds] \mid \mathcal{F}_t)$ can be rewritten as

$$\begin{aligned} \mathbb{Q}(\tau \in [s, s+ds) \mid \mathcal{F}_t) &= \mathbb{Q}(\{\tau < s+ds\} \cap \{\tau \ge s\} \mid \mathcal{F}_t) \\ &= \mathbb{Q}(\{\tau < s+ds\} \backslash \{\tau \le s\} \mid \mathcal{F}_t) \\ &= \mathbb{Q}(\tau < s+ds \mid \mathcal{F}_t) - \mathbb{Q}(\tau \le s \mid \mathcal{F}_t) \\ &= d\mathbb{Q}(\tau \le s \mid \mathcal{F}_t), \end{aligned} \tag{19.13}$$

thus, we get

$$NPV_{\text{Protection Leg}}(t) = \frac{\mathbb{1}_{\{\tau>t\}}}{\mathbb{Q}(\tau > t \mid \mathcal{F}_t)} \cdot N \cdot (1 - RR) \cdot \int_t^T DF(t,s) \cdot d\mathbb{Q}(\tau \le s \mid \mathcal{F}_t)\, ds. \tag{19.14}$$

In particular, the *Net Present Value* of the protection leg, at time $t = 0$, is equal to

$$\begin{aligned} NPV_{\text{Protection Leg}}(0) &= N \cdot (1 - RR) \cdot \int_0^T DF(0,s) \cdot d\mathbb{Q}(\tau \le s)\, ds \\ &= N \cdot (1 - RR) \cdot \int_0^T DF(0,s) \cdot d(1 - \mathbb{Q}(\tau > s))\, ds) \\ &= -N \cdot (1 - RR) \cdot \int_0^T DF(0,s) \cdot dNDP(s)\, ds. \end{aligned} \tag{19.15}$$

The differential of $NDP(t)$ is given by

$$dNDP(t) = \frac{d}{dt}e^{-\Gamma(t)} = -\frac{d}{dt}\Gamma(t)\cdot e^{-\Gamma(t)} = -\lambda(t)\cdot NDP(t).$$

By replacing the above relation into Eq. (19.15), we have

$$NPV_{\text{Protection Leg}}(0) = N\cdot(1-RR)\cdot\int_0^T DF(0,s)\cdot\lambda(s)\cdot NDP(s)\,ds. \quad (19.16)$$

Remark 19.2. Observe that the integral in Eq. (19.15) is a Stieltjes integral and it can be calculated through numerical approximations, such as the *trapezoid rule.* For $j = 0, ..., n$ and $0 = s_0 < s_1 ... < s_n = T$, with $s_j = \frac{j\cdot T}{n}$, it holds

$$NPV_{\text{Protection Leg}}(0) \approx -N\cdot(1-RR)\cdot\sum_{j=1}^{n}\frac{DF(0,s_{j-1})+DF(0,s_j)}{2}\cdot(NDP(s_{j-1})-NDP(s_j)). \quad (19.17)$$

19.3.2.2 *Premium Leg Net Present Value*

Similarly to Subsection 19.3.2.1, we compute the *Net Present Value (NPV)* of the premium accrual component at $t \geq 0$ by

$$\begin{aligned}
&NPV_{\text{Premium Accrual}}(t)\\
&= -\frac{\mathbb{1}_{\{\tau>t\}}}{\mathbb{Q}(\tau>t\mid\mathcal{F}_t)}\cdot\mathbb{E}\left[\sum_{i=1}^{n}\frac{\tau-s_{i-1}}{s_i-s_{i-1}}\cdot Flow_i\cdot D(t,\tau)\cdot\mathbb{1}_{\{s_{i-1}<\tau<s_i\}}\,\middle|\,\mathcal{F}_t\right]\\
&= -\frac{\mathbb{1}_{\{\tau>t\}}}{\mathbb{Q}(\tau>t\mid\mathcal{F}_t)}\cdot\sum_{i=1}^{n}Flow_i\cdot\mathbb{E}\left[\frac{\tau-s_{i-1}}{s_i-s_{i-1}}\cdot D(t,\tau)\cdot\mathbb{1}_{\{s_{i-1}<\tau<s_i\}}\,\middle|\,\mathcal{F}_t\right]\\
&= -\frac{\mathbb{1}_{\{\tau>t\}}}{\mathbb{Q}(\tau>t\mid\mathcal{F}_t)}\cdot\sum_{i=1}^{n}Flow_i\cdot\mathbb{E}\left[\int_{s_{i-1}}^{s_i}\frac{\tau-s_{i-1}}{s_i-s_{i-1}}\cdot D(t,s)\cdot\mathbb{1}_{\{s\leq\tau<s+ds\}}ds\,\middle|\,\mathcal{F}_t\right]\\
&= -\frac{\mathbb{1}_{\{\tau>t\}}}{\mathbb{Q}(\tau>t\mid\mathcal{F}_t)}\cdot\sum_{i=1}^{n}Flow_i\cdot\int_{s_{i-1}}^{s_i}\mathbb{E}\left[\frac{s-s_{i-1}}{s_i-s_{i-1}}\cdot D(t,s)\cdot\mathbb{1}_{\{s\leq\tau<s+ds\}}ds\,\middle|\,\mathcal{F}_t\right]ds\\
&= -\frac{\mathbb{1}_{\{\tau>t\}}}{\mathbb{Q}(\tau>t\mid\mathcal{F}_t)}\cdot\sum_{i=1}^{n}Flow_i\cdot\int_{s_{i-1}}^{s_i}\frac{s-s_{i-1}}{s_i-s_{i-1}}\mathbb{E}[D(t,s)\mid\mathcal{F}_t]\cdot\mathbb{E}[\mathbb{1}_{\{s\leq\tau<s+ds\}}\mid\mathcal{F}_t]\,ds\\
&= -\frac{\mathbb{1}_{\{\tau>t\}}}{\mathbb{Q}(\tau>t\mid\mathcal{F}_t)}\cdot\sum_{i=1}^{n}Flow_i\cdot\int_{s_{i-1}}^{s_i}\frac{s-s_{i-1}}{s_i-s_{i-1}}\cdot DF(t,s)\cdot\mathbb{Q}(\tau\in[s,s+ds]\mid\mathcal{F}_t)\,ds\\
&= -\frac{\mathbb{1}_{\{\tau>t\}}}{\mathbb{Q}(\tau>t\mid\mathcal{F}_t)}\cdot\sum_{i=1}^{n}Flow_i\cdot\int_{s_{i-1}}^{s_i}\frac{s-s_{i-1}}{s_i-s_{i-1}}\cdot DF(t,s)\cdot d\mathbb{Q}(\tau\leq s|\,\mathcal{F}_t)\,ds.
\end{aligned} \quad (19.18)$$

In the above steps we have used the Fubini theorem (to switch the integral with the expectation), and the independence between the interest rate and the default time τ. In particular,

$$\begin{aligned} NPV_{\text{Premium Accrual}}(0) &= -\sum_{i=1}^{n} Flow_i \cdot \int_{s_{i-1}}^{s_i} \frac{s - s_{i-1}}{s_i - s_{i-1}} \cdot DF(0,s) \cdot d\mathbb{Q}(\tau < s)\, ds \\ &= \sum_{i=1}^{n} Flow_i \cdot \int_{s_{i-1}}^{s_i} \frac{s - s_{i-1}}{s_i - s_{i-1}} \cdot DF(0,s) \cdot dNDP(s)\, ds \\ &= -\sum_{i=1}^{n} \int_{s_{i-1}}^{s_i} Flow_i \cdot \frac{s - s_{i-1}}{s_i - s_{i-1}} \cdot DF(0,s) \cdot NDP(s) \cdot \lambda(s)\, ds. \end{aligned} \tag{19.19}$$

Remark 19.3. Observe that $\int_{s_{i-1}}^{s_i} Flow_i \cdot \frac{s-s_{i-1}}{s_i-s_{i-1}} \cdot DF(0,s) \cdot dNDP(s)\, ds$ represents a Stieltjes integral, so we have

$$\int_{s_{i-1}}^{s_i} Flow_i \cdot \frac{s - s_{i-1}}{s_i - s_{i-1}} \cdot DF(0,s) \cdot dNDP(s)\, ds \approx \alpha_i \cdot \frac{DF(0,s_i)}{2} \cdot (NDP(s_{i-1}) - NDP(s_i)),$$

and consequently,

$$NPV_{\text{Premium Accrual}}(0) \approx N \cdot R \cdot \sum_{i=1}^{n} \alpha_i \cdot \frac{DF(0,s_i)}{2} \cdot (NDP(s_{i-1}) - NDP(s_i)). \tag{19.20}$$

Finally, compute the *Net Present Value* of the Premium Coupon component.

$$\begin{aligned} NPV_{\text{Premium Coupon}}(t) &= -\frac{\mathbb{1}_{\{\tau > t\}}}{\mathbb{Q}(\tau > t \mid \mathcal{F}_t)} \cdot \mathbb{E}\left[\sum_{i=1}^{n} Flow_i \cdot D(t,s_i) \cdot \mathbb{1}_{\{\tau > s_i\}} \middle| \mathcal{F}_t \right] \\ &= -\frac{\mathbb{1}_{\{\tau > t\}}}{\mathbb{Q}(\tau > t \mid \mathcal{F}_t)} \cdot \sum_{i=1}^{n} Flow_i \cdot \mathbb{E}[D(t,s_i) \cdot \mathbb{1}_{\{\tau > s_i\}} | \mathcal{F}_t] \\ &= -\frac{\mathbb{1}_{\{\tau > t\}}}{\mathbb{Q}(\tau > t \mid \mathcal{F}_t)} \cdot \sum_{i=1}^{n} Flow_i \cdot \mathbb{E}[D(t,s_i) | \mathcal{F}_t] \cdot \mathbb{E}[\mathbb{1}_{\{\tau > s_i\}} | \mathcal{F}_t] \\ &= -\frac{\mathbb{1}_{\{\tau > t\}}}{\mathbb{Q}(\tau > t \mid \mathcal{F}_t)} \cdot \sum_{i=1}^{n} Flow_i \cdot DF(t,s_i) \cdot \mathbb{Q}(\tau > s_i | \mathcal{F}_t). \end{aligned} \tag{19.21}$$

We have used the independence between interest rate and the default time τ, and the fact that the expected value of the indicator random variable for an event coincides with the probability of such an event. At time $t = 0$, we get

$$NPV_{\text{Premium Coupon}}(0) = -\sum_{i=1}^{n} Flow_i \cdot DF(0,s_i) \cdot NDP(s_i). \tag{19.22}$$

Hence, the Net Present Value of the premium leg at $t = 0$ can be approximated by

$$\begin{aligned} &NPV_{\text{Premium Leg}} \\ &\approx -N \cdot R \cdot \sum_{i=1}^{n} \alpha_i \cdot \left(DF(0, s_i) \cdot NDP(s_i) - \frac{DF(0, s_i)}{2} \cdot (NDP(s_{i-1}) - NDP(s_i)) \right) \\ &= -N \cdot R \cdot \sum_{i=1}^{n} \alpha_i \cdot DF(0, s_i) \cdot \frac{NDP(s_{i-1}) + NDP(s_i)}{2}. \end{aligned} \tag{19.23}$$

We would like to draw the reader's attention to the fact that we use the credit spread R whenever it is the *Premium leg* and the recovery rate RR whenever it is the *Protection leg*.

19.3.2.3 *CDS Net Present Value*

For any $t > 0$, the price of a CDS is given by

$$\begin{aligned} CDS(t) = \frac{\mathbb{1}_{\{\tau > t\}}}{\mathbb{Q}(\tau > t \mid \mathcal{F}_t)} \cdot \Bigg\{ & N \cdot (1 - RR) \cdot \int_t^T DF(t, s) \cdot d\mathbb{Q}(\tau \leq s \mid \mathcal{F}_t)\, ds \\ & - \sum_{i=1}^{n} Flow_i \cdot DF(t, s_i) \cdot \mathbb{Q}(\tau > s_i | \mathcal{F}_t) \\ & - \sum_{i=1}^{n} Flow_i \cdot \int_{s_{i-1}}^{s_i} \frac{s - s_{i-1}}{s_i - s_{i-1}} \cdot DF(t, s) \cdot d\mathbb{Q}(\tau \leq s | \, \mathcal{F}_t)\, ds \Bigg\}. \end{aligned} \tag{19.24}$$

If we set $D_2(t) = \int_t^T DF(t, s) \cdot d\mathbb{Q}(\tau \leq s \mid \mathcal{F}_t)\, ds$ and $D_3(t) = \int_{s_{i-1}}^{s_i} \frac{s - s_{i-1}}{s_i - s_{i-1}} \cdot DF(t, s) \cdot d\mathbb{Q}(\tau \leq s | \, \mathcal{F}_t)\, ds$, we can rewrite Eq. (19.24) as

$$\begin{aligned} CDS(t) = \frac{\mathbb{1}_{\{\tau > t\}}}{\mathbb{Q}(\tau > t \mid \mathcal{F}_t)} \cdot \Bigg\{ & N \cdot (1 - RR) \cdot D_2(t) - \sum_{i=1}^{n} Flow_i \cdot D_3(t) \\ & - \sum_{i=1}^{n} Flow_i \cdot DF(t, s_i) \cdot \mathbb{Q}(\tau > s_i | \mathcal{F}_t) \Bigg\}. \end{aligned} \tag{19.25}$$

A CDS agreed at time t has a fixed rate or credit spread R such that $CDS(t) = 0$. Solving Eq. (19.25) by R, under the assumption $Flow_i = N \cdot \alpha_i \cdot R(t)$, we find

$$R(t) = \frac{(1 - RR) \cdot D_2(t)}{\sum_{i=1}^{n} \alpha_i \cdot \left(D_3(t) + DF(t, s_i) \cdot \mathbb{Q}(\tau > s_i | \mathcal{F}_t) \right)}. \tag{19.26}$$

Since the integrals $D2$ and $D3$ cannot be solved explicitly, we have to use some approximation. More specifically, using Eqs. (19.17) and (19.23), we get

$$R(0) = \frac{(1 - RR) \cdot \sum_{j=1}^{n} (DF(0, s_{j-1}) + DF(0, s_j)) \cdot (NDP(s_{j-1}) - NDP(s_j))}{\sum_{i=1}^{n} \alpha_i \cdot DF(0, s_i) \cdot (NDP(s_{i-1}) + NDP(s_i))}. \tag{19.27}$$

In order to solve this equation, we need to know the zero coupon rate curve at time t, the recovery rate in case of default, and the survival probability at time t, representing the credit curve of the reference entity.

19.3.3 *Constant Hazard Rate Model*

In this subsection, we illustrate a simple formula to calibrate the (constant) intensity for a single CDS. Consider a CDS valid during the time horizon $[0, T]$. We assume the independence between the interest rates and the default time τ, and assume that the premium leg pays the credit spread R continuously until τ. This means that the premium leg pays $R\,dt$ in the interval $[t, t+dt]$. By discounting each premium flow by $D(0,t)$ and, by adding the premium flows at any $t \in [0,T]$, in which the default has not yet occurred ($\tau > t$), we obtain

$$\int_0^T D(0,s) \cdot \mathbb{1}_{\{\tau > s\}} \cdot R\,ds.$$

Thus, the Net Present Value of the premium leg is equal to

$$\begin{aligned} NPV_{\text{Premium Leg}}(0) &= \mathbb{E}\left[\int_0^T D(0,s) \cdot \mathbb{1}_{\{\tau > s\}} \cdot R\,ds\right] \\ &= R \cdot \int_0^T \mathbb{E}[D(0,s) \cdot \mathbb{1}_{\{\tau > s\}}]\,ds \\ &= R \cdot \int_0^T \mathbb{E}[D(0,s)] \cdot \mathbb{E}[\mathbb{1}_{\{\tau > s\}}]\,ds \\ &= R \cdot \int_0^T DF(0,s) \cdot \mathbb{Q}(\tau > s)\,ds. \end{aligned} \tag{19.28}$$

The Net Present Value of the protection leg is given by

$$\begin{aligned} NPV_{\text{Protection Leg}}(0) &= \mathbb{E}[(1-RR) \cdot D(0,\tau) \cdot \mathbb{1}_{\{\tau \le T\}}] \\ &= (1-RR) \cdot \mathbb{E}\left[\int_0^T D(0,s) \cdot \mathbb{1}_{\{s \le \tau < s+ds\}} ds\right] \\ &= (1-RR) \cdot \int_0^T \mathbb{E}[D(0,s) \cdot \mathbb{1}_{\{s \le \tau < s+ds\}}]\,ds \\ &= (1-RR) \cdot \int_0^T \mathbb{E}[D(0,s)] \cdot \mathbb{E}[\mathbb{1}_{\{s \le \tau < s+ds\}}]\,ds \\ &= (1-RR) \cdot \int_0^T DF(0,s) \cdot \mathbb{Q}(\tau \in [s, s+ds))\,ds \\ &= (1-RR) \cdot \int_0^T DF(0,s) \cdot d\mathbb{Q}(\tau \le s)\,ds \\ &= -(1-RR) \cdot \int_0^T DF(0,s) \cdot d\mathbb{Q}(\tau > s)\,ds. \end{aligned} \tag{19.29}$$

The constant intensity λ yields

$$\mathbb{Q}(\tau > s) = e^{-\lambda s},$$

and

$$d\mathbb{Q}(\tau > s)ds = -\lambda \cdot \mathbb{Q}(\tau > s)\, ds.$$

Hence, Eq. (19.29) becomes

$$NPV_{\text{Protection Leg}}(0) = \lambda \cdot (1 - RR) \cdot \int_0^T DF(0, s) \cdot \mathbb{Q}(\tau > s)\, ds.$$

Since the market quote R makes *fair* the CDS, we have

$$R \cdot \int_0^T DF(0, s) \cdot \mathbb{Q}(\tau > s)ds = \lambda \cdot (1 - RR) \cdot \int_0^T DF(0, s) \cdot \mathbb{Q}(\tau > s)\, ds. \quad (19.30)$$

Thus, we obtain

$$\lambda = \frac{R}{1 - RR}. \quad (19.31)$$

The above relationship is known as *credit triangle*. We deduce that the given constant hazard rate R can be interpreted as a credit spread, or a default probability PD. In particular, R is equal to the product between the loss given default and the probability of the instant default, i.e.

$$R = (1 - RR) \cdot \lambda.$$

Example 19.1. For a company with a spread curve at 200 bps, if we assume a recovery equal to 40%, then we get an implied hazard rate of 5% ($\lambda = \frac{0.02}{0.4}$). Consequently, the survival probability going out in 2 Y is equal to $NDP(2y) = \exp(-0.05 \cdot 2) = 0.9048$.

19.4 Credit Curve

In Subsection 19.3.3, we saw that a CDS can be priced once the survival curve (or credit curve), the zero-coupon rate curve and the recovery rate are known. The aim of this section is to show how to build a credit curve, that is able to replicate the structure of quoted CDS spreads using the bootstrap approach. The bootstrap is one of the most used approaches for constructing CDS survival curves. Generally, the bootstrap works starting from the shortest dated instrument and works out to the longest dated instrument. At each step, it uses the price of the next instrument to calibrate such parameter which determines how to extend the survival curve to the next maturity point. The result is a survival curve that can replicate exactly the market, and can be constructed very quickly.

However, bootstrapping cannot start from a single instrument to another one without having any information on what happens between their maturities. This is because a CDS contract, to calculate the time integral on the protection leg, requires the knowledge of the survival probabilities at any time between today and the CDS maturity.

Therefore, a bootstrap algorithm requires an interpolation scheme. We opt for linear interpolation. Recall that, for any function $f(t)$, given the points $(t_{i-1}, f(t_{i-1}))$ and $(t_i, f(t_i))$, the linear interpolation formula for $t^\star \in [t_{i-1}, t_i]$ is given by

$$f(t^\star) = f(t_{i-1}) + \frac{t^\star - t_{i-1}}{t_i - t_{i-1}} \cdot (f(t_i) - f(t_{i-1})). \tag{19.32}$$

19.4.1 *Linear Interpolation*

We set

$$f(t) = -\ln(NDP(t)). \tag{19.33}$$

The linear interpolation formula for $t^\star \in [t_{i-1}, t_i]$ becomes

$$\ln(NDP(t^\star)) = \ln(NDP(t_{i-1})) + \frac{t_{i-1} - t^\star}{t_i - t_{i-1}} \cdot (\ln(NDP(t_{i-1}) - \ln(NDP(t_i)).$$

Observe that $f(t) > 0$ since $0 < NDP(t) \leq 1$, thus, we can rewrite Eq. (19.33) as

$$f(t) = \int_0^t \lambda(u)\, du,$$

or, in a differential form,

$$\frac{df(t)}{dt} = \lambda(t).$$

Hence, we can write the interpolation scheme for $t^\star$, in terms of $f(t)$, by Eq. (19.32), i.e.

$$\lambda(t^\star) = \frac{f(t_i) - f(t_{i-1})}{t_i - t_{i-1}}. \tag{19.34}$$

Notice that $\lambda(t^\star)$ does not depend on $t^\star$, so $\lambda(t)$ is constant between the interpolation limits. As a consequence, we may write Eq. (19.34) as

$$\lambda(t^\star) = \lambda(t_{i-1}) = \frac{1}{t_i - t_{i-1}}(\ln NDP(t_{i-1}) - \ln NDP(t_i)) = \frac{1}{t_i - t_{i-1}} \ln\left(\frac{NDP(t_{i-1})}{NDP(t_i)}\right). \tag{19.35}$$

Thus, the survival probability at $t^\star$ is given by

$$\begin{aligned} NDP(t^\star) &= \exp\left(-\int_0^{t^\star} \lambda(u)\, du\right) \\ &= \exp\left(-\int_0^{t_{i-1}} \lambda(u) du - \int_{t_{i-1}}^{t^\star} \lambda(u)\, du\right) \\ &= NDP(t_{i-1}) \cdot \exp(-(t^\star - t_{i-1}) \cdot \lambda(t^\star)). \end{aligned} \tag{19.36}$$

We conclude that the linear interpolation of the logarithmic survival probability is equivalent to assume a piecewise constant intensity $\lambda(t)$.

However, we can also interpolate the survival probability; in this case, named $f(t) = NDP(t)$, the linear interpolation formula for $t^\star \in [t_{i-1}, t_i]$ becomes

$$NDP(t^\star) = NDP(t_{i-1}) + \frac{t_{i-1} - t^\star}{t_i - t_{i-1}} \cdot (NDP(t_{i-1}) - (NDP(t_i)).$$

Consequently, the intensity value at $t^\star$ is given by

$$\lambda(t^\star) = -\frac{\ln NDP(t^\star)}{t^\star}.$$

Based on these results, we will show how to build the survival curve using the bootstrap approach.

19.4.2 *Bootstrap Algorithm*

Let $R_1, R_2, ..., R_M$ be the CDS market quotes for contracts having maturities $T_1, T_2, ..., T_M$. Let RR be the recovery rate, which we assume to be the same for all contracts. Since we have to extrapolate the survival curve under the shortest CDS maturity and beyond the longest CDS maturity, we assume $\lambda(t)$ is flat between $t = T_0$ and $t = T_1$, and at its last interpolated value beyond the last time T_M. Below, we present the bootstrap algorithm.

i) Initialize the survival curve starting with $NDP(T_0) = 1$.
ii) Consider the contract with maturity T_1.
iii) Compute the value $NDP(T_1)$ that makes the CDS fair, at time T_0, with maturity T_1 and market quote R_1. This is done by solving

$$R_1 = \frac{(1 - RR) \cdot \sum_{i=1}^{n} (DF(0, t_{i-1}) + DF(0, t_i)) \cdot (NDP(t_{i-1}) - NDP(t_i))}{\sum_{i=1}^{n} \alpha_i \cdot DF(0, t_i) \cdot (NDP(t_{i-1}) + NDP(t_i))}, \tag{19.37}$$

where t_i $(i = 0, ..., n)$ denotes the premium payment dates, and $t_n = T_1$. The survival probabilities $NDP(t_i)$ can be interpolated between $(T_0, NDP(T_0))$ and $(T_1, NDP(T_1))$, as shown

$$\begin{aligned} NDP(t_i) &= NDP(T_0) + \frac{T_0 - t_i}{T_1 - T_0} \cdot (NDP(T_0) - NDP(T_1)) \\ &= 1 + \frac{T_0 - t_i}{T_1 - T_0} \cdot (1 - NDP(T_1)). \end{aligned} \tag{19.38}$$

Using Eq. (19.38), we have

$$\begin{aligned}NDP(t_{i-1}) - NDP(t_i) &= \frac{t_i - t_{i-1}}{T_1 - T_0} \cdot (NDP(T_0) - NDP(T_1))\\ &= \frac{t_i - t_{i-1}}{T_1 - T_0} \cdot (1 - NDP(T_1)),\\ NDP(t_{i-1}) + NDP(t_i) &= 2NDP(T_0) + \frac{2T_0 - t_i - t_{i-1}}{T_1 - T_0} \cdot (NDP(T_0) - NDP(T_1))\\ &= 2 + \frac{2T_0 - t_i - t_{i-1}}{T_1 - T_0} \cdot (1 - NDP(T_1)).\end{aligned}$$

Replacing these expressions in Eq. (19.37), we get

$$\begin{aligned}0 &= (1 - RR) \cdot \sum_{i=1}^{n} (DF(0, t_{i-1}) + DF(0, t_i)) \cdot (NDP(t_{i-1}) - NDP(t_i))\\ &\quad - R_1 \cdot \sum_{i=1}^{n} \alpha_i \cdot DF(0, t_i) \cdot (NDP(t_{i-1}) + NDP(t_i))\\ &= (1 - RR) \cdot \sum_{i=1}^{n} (DF(0, t_{i-1}) + DF(0, t_i)) \cdot \frac{t_i - t_{i-1}}{T_1 - T_0} \cdot (NDP(T_0) - NDP(T_1))\\ &\quad - R_1 \cdot \sum_{i=1}^{n} \alpha_i \cdot DF(0, t_i) \cdot (2NDP(T_0) + \frac{2T_0 - t_i - t_{i-1}}{T_1 - T_0} \cdot (NDP(T_0) - NDP(T_1)))\\ &= NDP(T_0) \cdot \left\{(1 - RR) \cdot \sum_{i=1}^{n} (DF(0, t_{i-1}) + DF(0, t_i)) \cdot \frac{t_i - t_{i-1}}{T_1 - T_0}\right.\\ &\quad \left. - 2R_1 \cdot \sum_{i=1}^{n} \alpha_i \cdot DF(0, t_i) - R_1 \cdot \sum_{i=1}^{n} \alpha_i \cdot DF(0, t_i) \cdot \frac{2T_0 - t_i - t_{i-1}}{T_1 - T_0}\right\}\\ &\quad - NDP(T_1)\left\{(1 - RR) \cdot \sum_{i=1}^{n} (DF(0, t_{i-1}) + DF(0, t_i)) \cdot \frac{t_i - t_{i-1}}{T_1 - T_0}\right.\\ &\quad \left. - R_1 \cdot \sum_{i=1}^{n} \alpha_i \cdot DF(0, t_i) \cdot \frac{2T_0 - t_i - t_{i-1}}{T_1 - T_0}\right\},\end{aligned} \tag{19.39}$$

that is equivalent to solve the following equation

$$\begin{aligned}NDP(T_0) \cdot &\left\{(1 - RR) \cdot \sum_{i=1}^{n} (DF(0, t_{i-1}) + DF(0, t_i)) \cdot \frac{t_i - t_{i-1}}{T_1 - T_0}\right.\\ &\quad \left. - 2R_1 \cdot \sum_{i=1}^{n} \alpha_i \cdot DF(0, t_i) - R_1 \cdot \sum_{i=1}^{n} \alpha_i \cdot DF(0, t_i) \cdot \frac{2T_0 - t_i - t_{i-1}}{T_1 - T_0}\right\}\\ &= \left\{(1 - RR) \cdot \sum_{i=1}^{n} (DF(0, t_{i-1}) + DF(0, t_i)) \cdot \frac{t_i - t_{i-1}}{T_1 - T_0}\right.\\ &\quad \left. - R_1 \cdot \sum_{i=1}^{n} \alpha_i \cdot DF(0, t_i) \cdot \frac{2T_0 - t_i - t_{i-1}}{T_1 - T_0}\right\} \cdot NDP(T_1).\end{aligned} \tag{19.40}$$

Given $NDP(T_1)$, by the relationship (19.35), we may evaluate $\lambda(T_0)$ by

$$\lambda(T_0) = \lambda(T_1) = -\frac{\ln NDP(T_1)}{T_1 - T_0}.$$

Then, we can compute the survival probabilities $NDP(t_0), NDP(t_1), ...,$ $NDP(t_{n-1})$ and the intensity values $\lambda(t_0), \lambda(t_1), ..., \lambda(t_{n-1})$ by the following credit triangle equation

$$\lambda(t_i) = -\frac{\ln NDP(t_i)}{t_i - T_0}.$$

iv) Once we have found the value $NDP(T_1)$, which reprices the CDS with maturity T_1, we add this time into our credit curve.

v) Consider the contract with maturity T_i for $i = 2, ...M - 1$.

vi) For $i = 2, ...M - 1$, in order to find the value of $NDP(T_i)$, we have to solve Eq. (19.37). More specifically, $NDP(T_i)$ can be computed by solving

$$\begin{aligned} &K + NDP(T_{i-1}) \cdot \Bigg\{(1 - RR) \cdot \sum_{T_{i-1} < t_j \leq T_i} (DF(0, t_{j-1}) + DF(0, j_i)) \cdot \frac{t_j - t_{j-1}}{T_i - T_{i-1}} \\ &- 2R_i \cdot \sum_{T_{i-1} < t_j \leq T_i} \alpha_j \cdot DF(0, t_j) - R_i \cdot \sum_{T_{i-1} < t_j \leq T_i} \alpha_j \cdot DF(0, t_j) \cdot \frac{2T_{i-1} - t_j - t_{j-1}}{T_i - T_{i-1}}\Bigg\} \\ &= \Bigg\{(1 - RR) \cdot \sum_{T_{i-1} < t_j \leq T_i} (DF(0, t_{j-1}) + DF(0, t_j)) \cdot \frac{t_j - t_{j-1}}{T_i - T_{i-1}} \\ &\quad - R_i \cdot \sum_{T_{i-1} < t_j \leq T_i} \alpha_j \cdot DF(0, t_j) \cdot \frac{2T_{i-1} - t_j - t_{j-1}}{T_i - T_{i-1}}\Bigg\} \cdot NDP(T_i), \end{aligned} \tag{19.41}$$

where K is a constant equal to the sum of premium and protection flows with payment date $t_j \leq T_{i-1}$, i.e.

$$\begin{aligned} K = (1 - RR) \cdot &\sum_{t_j \leq T_{i-1}} (DF(0, t_{j-1}) + DF(0, t_j)) \cdot (NDP(t_{j-1}) - NDP(j_i)) \\ &- R_i \cdot \sum_{t_j \leq T_{i-1}} \alpha_j \cdot DF(0, t_j) \cdot (NDP(t_{j-1}) + NDP(t_j)). \end{aligned} \tag{19.42}$$

Once $NDP(T_i)$ is known, we can find the intensity $\lambda(T_i)$ by

$$\lambda(T_i) = -\frac{\ln NDP(T_i)}{T_i - T_0}.$$

Thus, we can compute $NDP(t_j)$ and the intensities value $\lambda(t_j)$, for $T_{i-1} < t_j \leq T_i$, as shown before.

vii) For the contract with maturity T_M, we can repeat all the steps done for the contract with maturity T_1, due to the flat intensity.

viii) We end up with a survival curve consisting of $M + 1$ points with times $0, T_1, T_2, ..., T_M$ and values $NDP(0), NDP(T_1), NDP(T_2), ..., NDP(T_M)$.

19.4.3 *Example of Survival Curve Calibration*

Let us provide an example of a survival curve calibration based on the linear interpolation of $NDP(t)$.

Consider the market quotes *Allianz* issuer at 6M, 1Y, 2Y, 3Y, 4Y, 5Y, 7Y, 10Y, 15Y, with a 40% recovery rate. Hence, the loss given default (LGD) is 60%. Moreover, let us assume that each CDS contract defining the survival curve starts one business day (1 BD) after the trade date, i.e. *start Date* = *trade date* + *1 BD*; in this case, the trade date is 31/12/2020.

Start date	Issuer	Seniority	Rec. rate	Maturity date	Maturity	CDS spread
01/01/2021	ALLIANZ SE	Not Subordinated	40	20/06/2021	6m	0.000591550
01/01/2021	ALLIANZ SE	Not Subordinated	40	20/12/2021	1y	0.000719380
01/01/2021	ALLIANZ SE	Not Subordinated	40	20/12/2022	2y	0.001012720
01/01/2021	ALLIANZ SE	Not Subordinated	40	20/12/2023	3y	0.001396710
01/01/2021	ALLIANZ SE	Not Subordinated	40	20/12/2024	4y	0.001844100
01/01/2021	ALLIANZ SE	Not Subordinated	40	20/12/2025	5y	0.002292280
01/01/2021	ALLIANZ SE	Not Subordinated	40	20/12/2027	7y	0.003186100
01/01/2021	ALLIANZ SE	Not Subordinated	40	20/12/2030	10y	0.003992780
01/01/2021	ALLIANZ SE	Not Subordinated	40	20/12/2035	15y	0.004656210

Fig. 19.3: Structure of the survival curve.

Assume the accrual period always stretches between the coupon payment dates, except for the last accrual period, which uses the unadjusted maturity date (inclusive) for the end of the accrual. The day count convention is ACT/360. The *day count convention* expresses the number of days in the accrual period divided by the total number of days in the reference period. For details, ACT/360 convention counts the actual number of days within the accrual period and divides it by 360. The last two assumptions affect the computation of the day-count fraction α_i. In fact, given a trade with n coupons, α_i is computed as

$$\alpha_i = \begin{cases} \frac{T_i - T_{i-1}}{360} & i < n \\ \frac{T_n - T_{n-1} + 1}{360} & i = n, \end{cases}$$

where T_i for $i = 0, 1, ..., n$ is the payment date of the i-th coupon.

Example 19.2. Consider a CDS traded on 04/02/2021, maturing 05/02/2021, with the following coupons.

	Start Date	End Date
Flow 1	05/01/2021	05/02/2021
Flow 2	05/02/2021	05/03/2021

Fig. 19.4: CDS illustrative coupons.

Compute the day-count fraction of each coupon according to what we described before. We have

$$\alpha_1 = \frac{(05/02/2021 - 05/01/2021)}{360} = \frac{31}{360} = 0.086111$$

and

$$\alpha_2 = \frac{(05/03/2021 - 05/02/2021) + 1}{360} = \frac{29}{360} = 0.080556.$$

19.4.3.1 *MatLab*

In order to calibrate the curve in a simple way, we implemented a Matlab code that executes each step of the bootstrap algorithm described in Appendix B.5. The required inputs are:

- Pillars of survival curve;
- CDS spreads or the market quotes of survival curve;
- Coupons payment dates of premium leg;
- LIBOR discount factors at coupons payment dates;
- Loss given default.

The outputs are the survival probability and the value of λ, for each curve and each coupon payment date in Table 19.5 (all details about the code are available in Appendix B.5.1).

Start date	Issuer	Rec. rate	Maturity date	Maturity	NDP	lambda	CDS spread
01/01/2021	ALLIANZ SE	40	20/06/2021	6m	0.99952882	0.10059727	0.000591550
01/01/2021	ALLIANZ SE	40	20/12/2021	1y	0.99881847	0.12189669	0.000719380
01/01/2021	ALLIANZ SE	40	20/12/2022	2y	0.99663152	0.17128959	0.001012720
01/01/2021	ALLIANZ SE	40	20/12/2023	3y	0.99301471	0.23603103	0.001396710
01/01/2021	ALLIANZ SE	40	20/12/2024	4y	0.98769905	0.31156487	0.001844100
01/01/2021	ALLIANZ SE	40	20/12/2025	5y	0.98092047	0.38740066	0.002292280
01/01/2021	ALLIANZ SE	40	20/12/2027	7y	0.96308407	0.53946245	0.003186100
01/01/2021	ALLIANZ SE	40	20/12/2030	10y	0.93458241	0.67822703	0.003992780
01/01/2021	ALLIANZ SE	40	20/12/2035	15y	0.88781513	0.79443912	0.004656210

Fig. 19.5: Calibrated terms structure of survival probabilities, computed with Matlab.

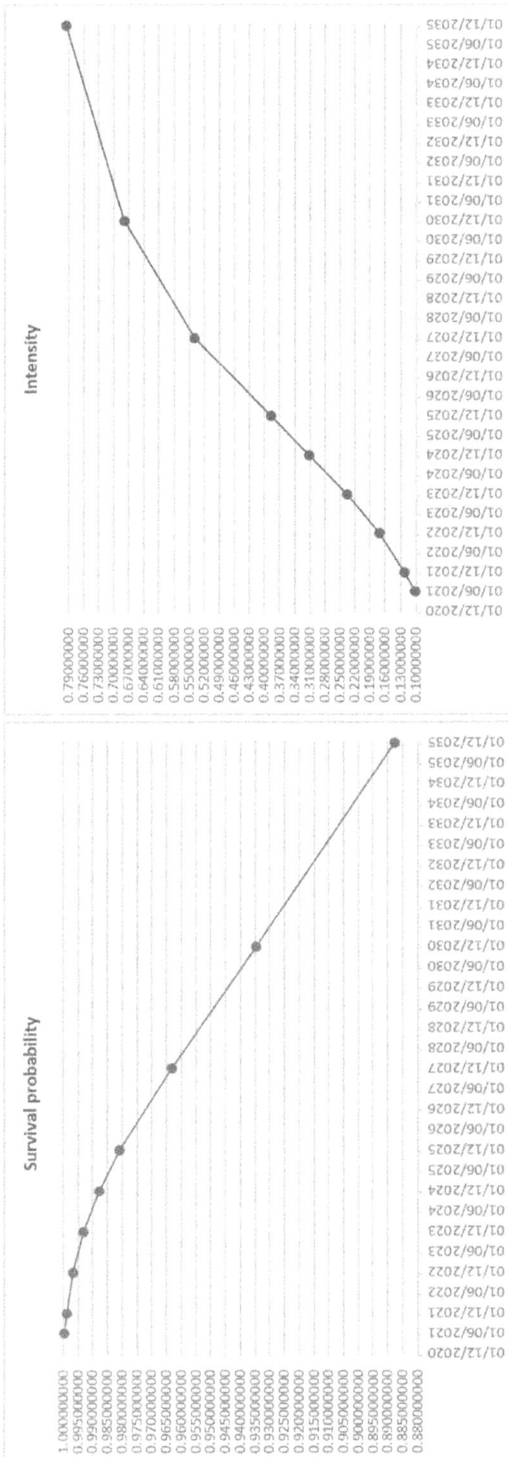

Fig. 19.6: Survival curve: No default probability is a decreasing function of the time, while the default intensity is an increasing function of the time.

19.4.3.2 *Murex*

Based on the same input data, we determine the calibrated terms structure of the survival curve by *Murex* in Table 19.7. Murex is a company that provides financial software for trading, treasury, risk, and post-trade operations for financial markets.

Start date	Issuer	Rec. rate	Maturity date	Maturity	NDP	lambda	CDS spread
01/01/2021	ALLIANZ SE	40	20/06/2021	6m	0.9995288	0.10059761	0.000591550
01/01/2021	ALLIANZ SE	40	20/12/2021	1y	0.9988185	0.12189482	0.000719380
01/01/2021	ALLIANZ SE	40	20/12/2022	2y	0.9966318	0.17127352	0.001012720
01/01/2021	ALLIANZ SE	40	20/12/2023	3y	0.9930152	0.23601391	0.001396710
01/01/2021	ALLIANZ SE	40	20/12/2024	4y	0.9876996	0.31155204	0.001844100
01/01/2021	ALLIANZ SE	40	20/12/2025	5y	0.9809207	0.38739544	0.002292280
01/01/2021	ALLIANZ SE	40	20/12/2027	7y	0.9630808	0.53951120	0.003186100
01/01/2021	ALLIANZ SE	40	20/12/2030	10y	0.9345651	0.67841280	0.003992780
01/01/2021	ALLIANZ SE	40	20/12/2035	15y	0.8877586	0.79486427	0.004656210

Fig. 19.7: Calibrated terms structure of survival probabilities, computed with Murex.

Comparing the results achieved in Table 19.8, we notice they are very similar. Indeed, regarding the Murex value as *theoretical* and the value returned by Matlab as estimated, the absolute and the relative errors for both NDP and λ are always less than 10^{-5} and 10^{-4}, respectively. This confirms the accuracy of our code.

	NDP				Lambda			
Maturity	Matlab Value (Estimated)	Murex Value	Absolute Error	Relative Error	Matlab Value (Estimated)	Murex Value (Theoretical)	Absolute Error	Relative Error
6m	0.999528820	0.999528818	1.60E-09	1.60E-09	0.100597270	0.100597612	3.42E-07	3.40E-06
1y	0.998818468	0.998818486	1.81E-08	1.81E-08	0.121896689	0.121894824	1.87E-06	1.53E-05
2y	0.996631516	0.996631831	3.15E-07	3.17E-07	0.171289592	0.171273525	1.61E-05	9.38E-05
3y	0.993014713	0.993015218	5.05E-07	5.08E-07	0.236031027	0.236013913	1.71E-05	7.25E-05
4y	0.987699048	0.987699552	5.03E-07	5.10E-07	0.311564870	0.311552043	1.28E-05	4.12E-05
5y	0.980920467	0.980920722	2.55E-07	2.60E-07	0.387400658	0.387395439	5.22E-06	1.35E-05
7y	0.963084068	0.963080794	3.27E-06	3.40E-06	0.539462448	0.539511196	4.87E-05	9.04E-05
10y	0.934582411	0.934565092	1.73E-05	1.85E-05	0.678227027	0.678412800	1.86E-04	2.74E-04
15y	0.887815130	0.887758596	5.65E-05	6.37E-05	0.794439123	0.794864274	4.25E-04	5.35E-04

Fig. 19.8: Comparison between the results obtained through Matlab and Murex.

Given the survival curve, we determine the spread value making fair a CDS traded with the following specifications:

- *Nominal*: €1.000.000,00;
- *Valuation date*: 31/12/2020;
- *Maturity date*: 15/05/2021;
- *Business day convention*: modified following

- *Rate convention*: linear with day count convention ACT/365
- *Payment schedule*: 3 M
- *Recovery rate*: 40%.

From the previous results, deduce that R must be equal to

$$R = \frac{(1-RR)\cdot\sum_{i=1}^{n}(DF(0,t_{i-1})+DF(0,t_i))\cdot(NDP(t_{i-1})-NDP(t_i))}{\sum_{i=1}^{n}\alpha_i\cdot DF(0,t_i)\cdot(NDP(t_{i-1})+NDP(t_i))}.$$

The discount factors and the survival probabilities at coupons payment dates (necessary to evaluate R) are shown in Table 19.9.

Schedule dates	Discount Factor	NDP
01/01/2021	1.0000130560	0.9999972446
15/03/2021	1.0008572431	0.9997960967
15/06/2021	1.0018690347	0.9995425954
15/09/2021	1.0027963194	0.9991911191
15/12/2021	1.0041848002	0.9988378937
15/03/2022	1.0055724902	0.9983092648
15/06/2022	1.0069661327	0.9977581081

Fig. 19.9: Survival probabilities and coupon payment dates.

Further, we find that the CDS spread value is 0.091169 bp and the (absolute) Net Present Value of each leg is €1348.5941. The respective Matlab code is available in Appendix B.5.2.

PART 6
Systemic Risk Implications

Chapter 20

Diversifying the Economy for Systemic Risk Reduction: The Case of the Kingdom of Saudi Arabia (KSA)

20.1 Introduction

This chapter,[1] through both a quantitative and quantitative analyses, investigates the resilience of the financial sector to the COVID-19 pandemic and the results of diversification efforts, particularly induced by the insurance sector. The analysis is carried out for the case of the Kingdom of Saudi Arabia (KSA) because its heavy dependence on oil and the relatively immature insurance sector that nevertheless played a positive role during the pandemic. The suggestion is that, during the crisis, systematic effects (i.e. members of the banking or insurance groups) prevail over idiosyncratic characteristics of each company. Furthermore, by identifying a key risk factor in oil volumes, exceptions are identified to the said rule for those instances in which idiosyncrasy still dominates group effects, which has policy implications. In particular, it is shown that the diversification induced by the insurance industry has benefited the economy during the COVID-19 pandemic, which could be used as an opportunity to consolidate players in the industry.

[Di Lorenzo and Sibillo (2020)] stressed the role of insurance companies in protecting against macroeconomic scenarios impacting families and firms. The COVID-19 pandemic could push towards "reward mechanisms for those companies that correctly implement strategies protecting the health and well-being of the community. Doing so would engender a virtuous cycle, able to stimulate the correct fulfilment of the rules imposed on companies for the protection of health. It would also contribute to verifying investments, especially when it comes to the funds that states allocate to economic recovery". Thus, "as has already been the case with Environmental, Social, and Governance (ESG) risks and consistent with an Enterprise Risk Management (ERM) approach, insurance companies will be able to expand the analysis of financial risks and returns in a Social Finance perspective, generating, that is, social impact with their products".

While the insurance industry has experienced financial difficulties and is affected by a number of issues, banking and financial supervision in the Kingdom

[1]This chapter has been partly published as [Orlando and Bace (2021)].

of Saudi Arabia (KSA), within its rather closed economy, it has demonstrated relative strength and stability over the past decades [Parkinson (2016)], [Ramsdale and Sakhri (2020)]. This period has also been relatively economically robust for the Kingdom [Dyck (2016)], [Diron and Perjessey (2019)]. This makes it worth studying the experience of the country and its financial system.

Severe challenges to the current stable and straightforward system have emerged, however, as the national economy slows, primarily due to depressed oil revenues [Friederich and Krustins (2020)]. This slowdown has been recently compounded by the COVID-19 pandemic. [Teresiene *et al.* (2021)] found that "the spread of the COVID-19 pandemic has a statistically significant negative effect on banking sector credit risk, financial distress, banking sector profitability, and solvency". In addition, "while the overall financial distress decreased and banking sector liquidity increased, the profitability and solvency decreased". The Saudi government is trying to take measures to diversify and open the economy, still so reliant on domestic hydrocarbon production and government spending, and to make it more efficient. This is needed to promote growth and reduce a growing budget deficit. While ambitious and long term with regard to expected results, some of these measures may prove counterproductive in the short term and are more likely to put pressure on the economy and the financial system [Friederich and Krustins (2020)]. There already have been signs of regulatory easing, including injection of liquidity and some loosening of lending criteria, which over time could threaten the stability of the system [Sharif (2016)], [Nereim and Al Othman (2020)]. This problem is exacerbated by economic weakness brought on by the COVID-19 pandemic, as many businesses shut down to comply with government restrictions. Borrowers affected most severely in the SME sector, will have difficulty servicing their loans, despite government measures to aid them (see [OECD (2020)], [Hussain *et al.* (2020)]). At the same time, the authorities are addressing thoroughly a poorly structured insurance industry, which still has too many players and less than adequate controls, resulting in financial problems for many of the insurance players [Fadaak and Alghamdi (2016)], [Toskas and Coutts (2020)]. Since key drivers of financial stability are the diversity, openness and efficiency of the economy, it is incumbent on the authorities to accelerate financial, economic and social reforms, and to open the economy faster and further, so that the Gulf region's largest economy has a chance of gaining competitiveness on regional and international scales [McKinsey (2015)]. Otherwise, the nation will be left further behind in the ever dynamic race for investment and progress, continuing to rely on a dwindling resource base and pilgrimage center, which ultimately could lead to serious financial and social disruption.

[Demirguc-Kunt *et al.* (2020)], by investigating a large dataset of more than 3000 financial companies, claim that a key risk factor is their exposure to oil prices. However, the statistical evidence is somehow weak. For this reason, in the panel data analysis presented here, this idea was retained but was declined differently.

20.2 Quantitative Analysis and the Exposure to Oil

In this section, a quantitative analysis is carried out of the performance of Saudi banks and insurers before and during the COVID-19 pandemic, and against the backdrop of oil prices.

20.2.1 *Data*

The database consists of stock price and trading volumes for 22 insurance and bank companies since March 2010 as retrieved from Bloomberg and Yahoo Finance. The company details (by number, name and ticker code) are available in Table 20.1. Notice that the insurance companies are numbered from 1 to 11 and banks are from 12 to 22. By including 22 names, we practically consider all financial institutions in the KSA because what we want to show is the difference between pre-COVID 19 and during COVID-19 for the whole economy. Notice that some factors (such as firm size) do not play a role in our analysis as they are invariant before and during the pandemic. In the remainder of this section, we will prove that the pandemic has caused a separation between banks and insurers or, in less technical words, that the pandemic has prompted a diversification in the economy.

In addition to the above mentioned data, for the same period we have retrieved the time series of the Saudi Stock Exchange Tadawul (coded as Tasi) and the Brent crude oil spot prices (BZ=F) traded at the New York Mercantile market.

20.2.2 *Cluster Analysis*

The database has been divided into two parts: from November 2014 to December 2018 and from the beginning of January 2019 to the end of January 2021. This is to analyse what happened during the COVID-19 pandemic.

(Z) returns the inconsistency coefficient for each link of the hierarchical cluster tree Z generated by the linkage function. The algorithm calculates the inconsistency coefficient for each link by comparing its height with the average height of other links at the same level of the hierarchy. The larger the coefficient, the greater the difference between the objects connected by the link. Notice that we use Ward linkage because it performs well in separating clusters when there is noise between clusters. The drawback of the Ward linkage is mainly related to its complexity of $O(N^3)$, making it not particularly scalable. However, that is not a problem in the context of this study because the dataset is composed only of 22 financial institutions.

Figure 20.1 displays the related dendrogram (i.e. a hierarchical cluster tree), and as shown there is no clear distinction between banks and insurance companies. As shown in Figure 20.2 the situation changed substantially during the COVID-19 pandemic as insurers and banks are rather distinguishable and the inconsistency coefficient is lower, [Jain and Ubes (1988)].

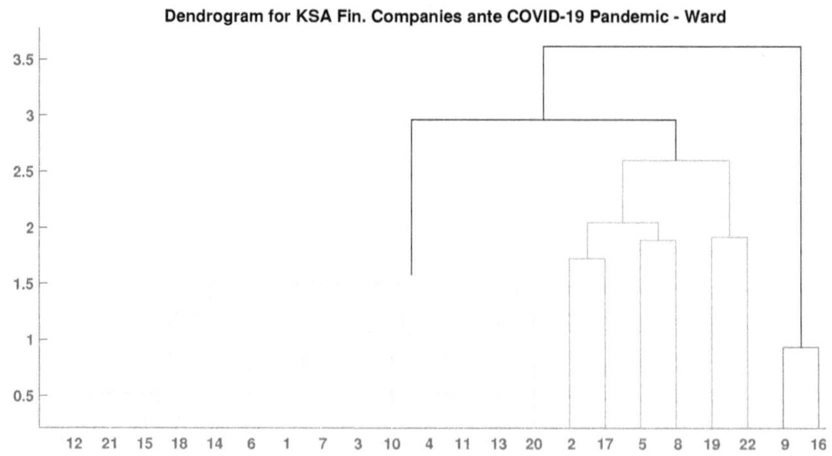

Fig. 20.1: Ex Ante COVID-19 pandemic hierarchical cluster tree on the performances of insurers (first 11 time series) and banks (from 11 to 22). Distance metric = euclidean, linkage = Ward. Mean of inconsistency coefficient (excluding zeros) = 0.8554. There is no clear distinction between banks and insurers.

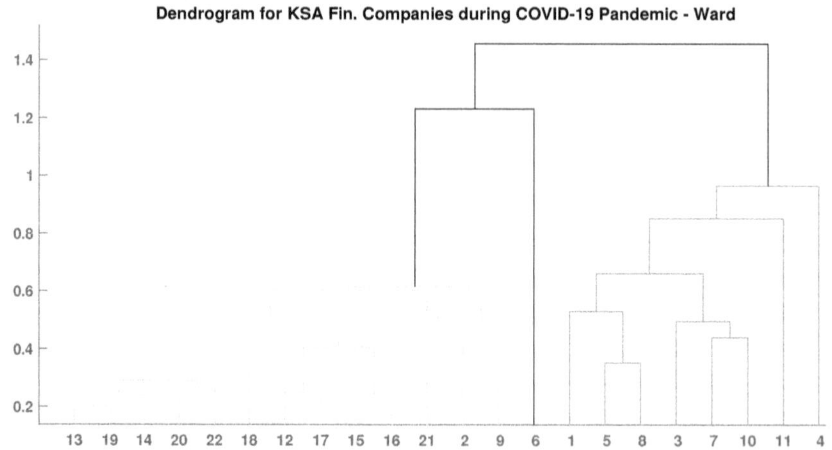

Fig. 20.2: COVID-19 pandemic hierarchical cluster tree on the performances of insurers (first 11 time series) and banks (from 11 to 22). Distance metric = euclidean, linkage = Ward. Mean of inconsistency coefficient (excluding zeros) = 0.8127. The pandemic has created a separation between banks and insurers.

So far hierarchical clustering has been applied to show how the same analysis produced different results before and during the pandemic. The result is that the pandemic produced a separation between banks and insurances. To measure the quality of clustering results, recurrence is made via the [Caliński and Harabasz

(1974)] index defined as

$$\textit{Calinski-Harabasz Index} = \frac{SS_B}{SS_W} \cdot \frac{N-k}{k-1}$$

where k is the number of clusters, N is the total number of observations, SS_W is the overall within-cluster variance and SS_B is the overall between-cluster variance. Figures 20.3 and 20.4 confirm that, while before the COVID-19 pandemic there was no clear-cut result on the number of clusters, the pandemic caused such a separation.

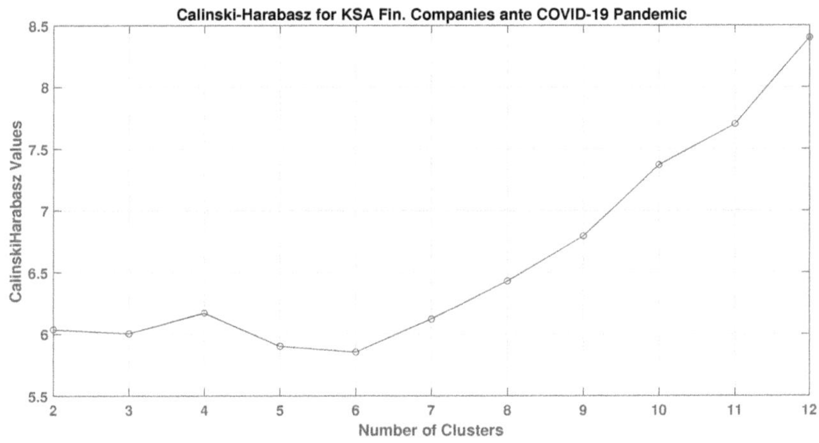

Fig. 20.3: Ex Ante COVID-19 pandemic. Calinski-Harabasz Index with Ward linkage. This figure shows no clear-cut on the number of clusters.

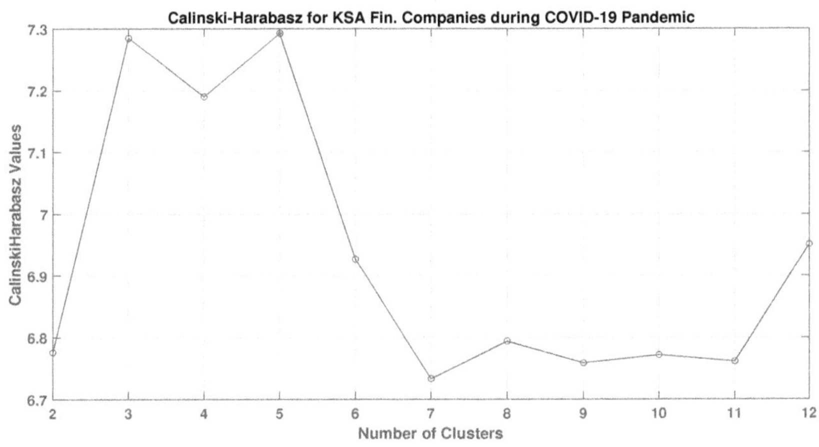

Fig. 20.4: During COVID-19 pandemic. This figure shows that the optimal number of clusters is either 3 or 5.

20.2.3 *Correlation*

While the economy of Saudi Arabia is clearly exposed to oil prices, the financial sector has its own rules. Figure 20.5 shows that, despite the recession caused by the pandemic, the performance of banks, insurers and the Tadawul stock market was positive.

Fig. 20.5: TASI vs. Insurance and Banking sectors since beginning 2019. In violet Tadawul index, in red the banking stock index, in blue the insurance stock index. Notice that banking (4.61%) underperformed the index (10.81%) while insurance strongly outperformed (40.71%). *Source:* [Argaam (2021)]

However, this varies considerably among periods and companies. For this reason a Kendall rank correlation was run to measure the ordinal association between the financial companies and both the Tadawul and the Brent price indices. Table 20.1 shows what really matters in terms of risk is the "oil exposure". In fact, while the correlation with the index is not a clear separator, the correlation with oil provides a clearer picture: only the two banks with a correlation lower than 0.5 significantly outperformed. On the other hand, insurers seem in general to be less correlated to both the stock market and oil.

Notice that Walaa Coop. Ins. before 2019 was the only insurer with a correlation above the threshold of 0.5. Arab National Bank, National Commercial Bank, Bank Albilad and Al Rajhi Bank were the only four banks below the threshold. Notwithstanding, while the first two increased the correlation (and underperformed) the other two did not (and had positive performances). This result is also explained by

Table 20.1: Kendall correlations for insurers and banks against the overall market and oil prices (from beginning of January 2019 to end of January 2021).

			Ante COVID-19		**With COVID-19**		
#	*Company*	*Code*	*Corr. with TASI*	*Corr. with Oil*	*Corr. with TASI*	*Corr. with Oil*	*Perf.*
1	Gulf Union Alahlia	8120	0.58	0.39	0.00	-0.19	41.65%
2	Bupa	8210	-0.07	-0.26	-0.18	-0.45	39.02%
3	Malath Coop. Ins.	8020	0.22	-0.06	0.17	-0.08	85.01%
4	Allianz Saudi Fransi	8040	0.16	-0.11	0.16	0.35	-19.09%
5	Arabian Shield	8070	0.37	0.34	0.28	0.10	48.89%
6	Salama	8050	0.51	0.36	-0.05	-0.19	56.68%
7	Walaa Coop. Ins.	8060	0.18	0.52	0.34	0.16	12.38%
8	Al-Etihad	8170	0.58	0.31	0.27	0.08	37.09%
9	Al Rajhi Ins.	8230	0.27	0.50	0.12	-0.07	23.21%
10	AXA Coop. Ins.	8250	0.57	0.48	-0.16	-0.43	68.71%
11	Wataniya Ins.	8300	0.27	-0.06	-0.00	-0.24	88.98%
12	Riyad Bank	1010	0.65	0.56	0.50	0.69	1.13%
13	Bank AlJazira	1020	0.70	0.57	0.35	0.54	-13.23%
14	Saudi Inv. Bank	1030	0.77	0.55	0.40	0.59	-22.05%
15	Banque Saudi Fransi	1050	0.65	0.53	0.50	0.65	-0.38%
16	Saudi British Bank	1060	0.65	0.52	0.38	0.78	-22.06%
17	Arab National Bank	1080	0.51	0.46	0.27	0.64	-11.32%
18	Samba Financial Group	1090	0.60	0.59	0.47	0.65	-8.09%
19	Al Rajhi Banking	1120	0.19	0.36	0.43	0.20	20.32%
20	Bank Albilad	1140	0.60	0.28	0.39	0.24	22.97%
21	Alinma Bank	1150	0.77	0.57	0.39	0.67	-30.13%
22	National Commercial Bank	1180	0.48	0.49	0.48	0.78	-6.52%

Highlighted in red the correlations higher than 0.5. In orange the companies with anomalous behaviour with respect to their industry.

the fact that Arab National Bank, National Commercial Bank and Bank Albilad were just below the threshold while Bank Albilad and Al Rajhi Bank were well below it.

20.2.4 *Econometric Analysis*

Let us define the extra-(log)return of the company i at the time t with respect to the market as

$$ExRet_{t,i} = Ret_{t,i} - \widehat{\alpha_i} - \widehat{\beta_i}\,MktRet_t \tag{20.1}$$

where $MktRet_t$ is the market return, $\widehat{\alpha_i}$ and $\widehat{\beta_i}$ are the intercept and slope coefficients, respectively, of the OLS regression carried out over our sample.

As mentioned, a key risk factor is exposure to oil of financial companies. [Demirguc-Kunt *et al.* (2020)] studied over 3,043 firms (896 commercial banks and 2,147 non-bank financials). The hypothesis is that volumes of both, stocks and oil contracts represent a proxy of liquidity, volatility and macroeconomic situations. For this reason, the econometric model intended to be tested is the linkage between extra-returns $ExRet_{t,i}$ and log-returns of trading volumes of each stock $TradVSt_{t,i}$, those of the Brent crude oil contracts $TradVBr_t$ and the interaction between trading volumes of each stock and trading volumes of oil (all in terms of log-returns).

That is

$$ExRet_{t,i} = \kappa_{1,i}\,TradVSt_{t,i} + \kappa_{2,i}\,TradVBr_t + \kappa_{3,i}\,TradVSt_{t,i}\,TradVBr_t + \varepsilon_{t,i} \tag{20.2}$$

where $\kappa_{j,i}$ for $j = 1,2,3$ are the variables' coefficients and $\varepsilon_{t,i}$ the error. The idea is that, in our case, individual effects are correlated with the explanatory variables (i.e. $COV(X_{t,i},\mu_i) \neq 0$), which motivates the use of the fixed-effects within estimation. In this way unobserved heterogeneity [Baltagi (2008)] can be captured.

Tables 20.2 and 20.3 show the statistics of the individual effects by company before and during the COVID-19 pandemic, respectively.

Table 20.2: Relationship between extra return, oil and trading volumes before the COVID-19 pandemic.

Panel: Individual Effects by Company				
ID	ieffect	Std. Error	t-stat	p-value
1010	-0.249415	0.02593	-9.6186	0***
1020	-0.016858	0.02593	-0.6501	0.516
1030	-0.073187	0.025947	-2.8206	0.005***
1050	-0.044353	0.025936	-1.7101	0.088*
1060	0.004819	0.025928	0.1859	0.853
1080	-0.02256	0.025929	-0.8701	0.384
1090	0.03074	0.025937	1.1852	0.236
1120	0.022084	0.02593	0.8517	0.395
1140	-0.027879	0.025972	-1.0734	0.283
1150	-0.125308	0.025941	-4.8305	0***
1180	0.005621	0.025941	0.2167	0.828
8020	-0.153727	0.02593	-5.9285	0***
8040	-0.087692	0.025931	-3.3818	0.001***
8050	0.014213	0.025929	0.5482	0.584
8060	-0.053373	0.025934	-2.058	0.04**
8070	-0.021558	0.025934	-0.8313	0.406
8120	-0.120458	0.025928	-4.6458	0***
8170	0.005591	0.025928	0.2156	0.829
8210	0.051687	0.025943	1.9923	0.047**
8230	0.013024	0.025955	0.5018	0.616
8250	-0.070516	0.025932	-2.7193	0.007***
8300	-0.177277	0.02593	-6.8367	0***
OVERALL	-0.049835	0.000261	-190.8164	0***

* $P \leq 0.05$, ** $P \leq 0.01$, *** $P \leq 0.001$.

Table 20.3: Relationship between extra return, oil and trading volumes during the COVID-19 pandemic.

Panel: Individual Effects by Company				
ID	ieffect	Std. Error	t-stat	p-value
1010	0.00244	0.022101	0.1104	0.912
1020	0.031266	0.022116	1.4137	0.158
1030	0.042878	0.022146	1.9362	0.053*
1050	0.068113	0.022088	3.0837	0.002***
1060	0.078135	0.02209	3.5372	0***
1080	0.092734	0.022132	4.19	0***
1090	0.068514	0.022098	3.1005	0.002***
1120	0.094865	0.022113	4.29	0***
1140	0.113965	0.022106	5.1554	0***
1150	-0.256709	0.022104	-11.6137	0***
1180	-0.081388	0.022108	-3.6813	0***
8020	-0.047632	0.022128	-2.1526	0.032**
8040	0.034045	0.022112	1.5397	0.124
8050	0.058896	0.022088	2.6665	0.008***
8060	0.019769	0.022142	0.8928	0.372
8070	0.05896	0.022111	2.6666	0.008***
8120	0.034966	0.02214	1.5793	0.115
8170	0.068463	0.022097	3.0983	0.002***
8210	0.292915	0.022133	13.2344	0***
8230	0.069564	0.022147	3.141	0.002***
8250	0.048067	0.022118	2.1732	0.03**
8300	0.019322	0.022221	0.8695	0.385
OVERALL	-0.049835	0.000261	-190.8164	0***

* $P \leq 0.05$, ** $P \leq 0.01$, *** $P \leq 0.001$.

20.2.5 *Panel Analysis*

As mentioned in [Demirguc-Kunt *et al.* (2020)], panel data analysis on banks tries to relate their extra-performance with bank's liquidity, capital, size, ownership and oil price. In that paper, Table 2 reports some results for the months of January, February, March and April. The highest (0.163) R-squared is in March and the lowest (0.027) is in April. In addition, while the estimated coefficients corresponding to oil and liquidity risks have very low *p*-value in March, in the other months, risk factors do not seem to be statistically significant. From those considerations, it seems that the model proposed in [Demirguc-Kunt *et al.* (2020)] can only capture the risk for a specific month.

Tables 20.4 and 20.5 report the analysis performed (with the toolbox by [Álvarez *et al.* (2017)]) on the model in Eq. (20.2). As shown, the regression is consistent across periods in terms of R-squared and p-values of the estimated coefficients. Individual effects are listed in Subsection 20.2.5. Notice that, in order to check whether multicollinearity was introduced (which implies that estimates are unstable and have high standard errors), the test is used as suggested by [Belsley *et al.* (2005)]. The so-called condition indices include the largest one which indicates weak dependencies when it is around 10, average when it is around 30 and high

Table 20.4: Relationship between extra return, oil and trading volumes before the COVID-19 pandemic.

Panel: Fixed effects (within) (FE)		
N = 1078	n = 22	T = 49 (Balanced panel)
R-squared = 0.095		
Wald F(3, 1053) = 36.755	p-value < 0.001	
RSS = 34.686	ESS = 12.274	TSS = 12.274

Stock Extra Perf.	Coefficient	Std. Error	t-stat	p-value
Stock Trad. Volumes	0.066	0.008	7.952	0.000 ***
Brent Trad. Volumes	-0.021	0.003	-6.699	0.000 ***
Interaction	-0.013	0.006	-2.345	0.019 **

* $P \leq 0.05$, ** $P \leq 0.01$, *** $P \leq 0.001$.
Cross-sectional regressions of monthly abnormal returns of banks and insurers in the KSA. Abnormal returns are the difference between realised returns and the expected returns implied by the market model (see Eq. (20.1)).
Belsley collinearity index = 1.133.

Table 20.5: Relationship between extra return, oil and trading volumes during the COVID-19 pandemic.

Panel: Fixed effects (within) (FE)		
N = 550	n = 22	T = 25 (Balanced panel)
R-squared = 0.088		
Wald F(3, 525) = 16.949	p-value = 0.000	
RSS = 6.402	ESS = 6.264	TSS = 6.264

Stock Extra Perf.	Coefficient	Std. Error	t-stat	p-value
Stock Trad. Volumes	0.010465	0.006042	1.7319	0.084 *
Brent Trad. Volumes	-0.01471	0.002449	-6.0084	0 ***
Interaction	-0.00558	0.002057	-2.711	0.007 ***

* $P \leq 0.05$, ** $P \leq 0.01$, *** $P \leq 0.001$.
Cross-sectional regressions of monthly abnormal returns of banks and insurances in the KSA. Abnormal returns are the difference between realised returns and the expected returns implied by the market model (see Eq. (20.1)).
Belsley collinearity index = 1.891.

when it is larger than 100. In our case, the Belsley collinearity diagnostics gives values between 1 and 2.

20.3 Discussion

The initial assumption of this work is that, while the financial system in the Kingdom of Saudi Arabia (KSA) has a history of relative soundness, the sector is facing challenges of a sluggish economy, need for reform and negative effects of the COVID-19 pandemic. The objective is to assess how well the government thus far has responded to the challenges in the financial sector. This entails an analysis of the performance of both banks and insurers. The working hypothesis is that the insurance industry has improved in efficiency and profitability and that its contribution has become evident during the pandemic.

The analyses in [Orlando and Bace (2021)] provide a comprehensive assessment of insurance and banking in the KSA. From that perspective, it is evident that especially insurers, have improved in all considered aspects (profitability, competition, capital, risk, etc.).

In addition to the above, quantitative analysis has expressively targeted the risk for the KSA financial system. For achieving this goal we performed cluster, correlation and panel data analysis. All of the above confirm the working hypothesis that the insurance industry has improved its position, resulting in higher efficiency and profitability and lower risk. Indeed, the obtained results evidence that progresses have been made in that industry in terms of helping to diversify the economy with the onset of the pandemic.

Cluster analysis confirms the induced diversification in the economy by insurers. This is because, while before COVID-19 pandemic there was no clear-cut result on the number of clusters, the pandemic caused such a separation. Such application to the financial industry in the KSA is new in literature.

To complement cluster analysis, we have added a correlation analysis to measure the risk that the economy of Saudi Arabia faces because of its exposure to oil. It is observed that insurers have contributed to the diversification of the economy as they appear much less correlated to oil than banks, thus reducing the risk of the whole KSA financial system, i.e. the systemic risk. Once again, such a result is new in literature. Still, in terms of exposure to oil of the KSA economy, an econometric analysis was carried out on panel data. In contrast to [Demirguc-Kunt *et al.* (2020)], it is shown that the risk factor for the financial sector in the KSA is the changes in oil volumes rather than the changes in oil prices.

In line with the KSA's economic transformation programme, reform and refinement of the financial system remain paramount. All financial sectors, including banking, insurance and asset management, need to adapt to the challenge of a more demanding economic and customer environment.

The quantitative analysis presented has shown how the diversification induced by the insurance industry has benefited the economy especially during the COVID-

19 pandemic where the separation between banks and insurers has become clearer. It is established that the COVID-19 pandemic presents an opportunity to consolidate players in the industry, with the result of contributing further to economic diversification. In this sense, the policy implications for the government, regulators and supervisors, are that the pandemic, having created a more competitive and "level" playing field, has highlighted those players who have demonstrated best performance and practice, in an idiosyncratic fashion, setting them apart from the systemic effects of the health crisis. From this, the authorities can extract elements of this best practice, in order to apply it in a more widespread manner across the industry.

Chapter 21

Systemic Risk Regulation

In the previous chapter, we considered an oil-exporting country where Islamic finance is prevailing. A reader may challenge us that our finding may have a limited scope for other countries with the western banking system. What about systemic risk and regulation in those counties? The current chapter[1] closes this gap.

21.1 Systemic Risk Concept

According to Figure 21.1, starting from 2020 there was a substantial increase in systemic risk, In fact, the systemic risk proxy equaled around USD 1.0 trln before the 2007-2009 crisis and it rose to USD 3.8 trln afterward. During the recent year of 2020, it was USD 5.6 trln at the highest point.

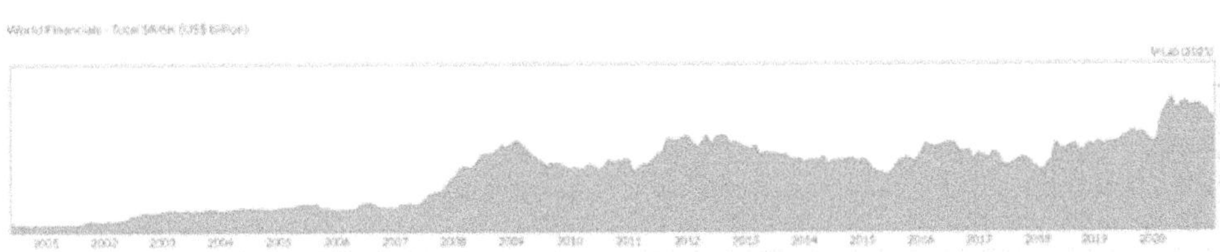

Fig. 21.1: Systemic risk increased worldwide during the pandemic times.
Source: [V-Lab of the New-York University Stern Business School (2021)]

The striking point here is that the post-2007-2009 banking regulation targeted reducing the systemic risk. We may read the following statements from the Basel III document (italics are added by us):

"...the Committee is introducing a number of macroprudential elements into the capital framework *to help contain systemic risks* arising from procyclicality and from the interconnectedness of financial institutions" [BCBS (2010a), p. 2, par. 7];

"...These reforms will raise the capital buffers backing these exposures, reduce procyclicality and provide additional incentives to move OTC derivative contracts to

[1]This chapter has been partly published as [Penikas (2021b)] where technical derivations on loan pricing are available.

central counterparties, thus *helping reduce systemic risk* across the financial system" [BCBS (2010a), p. 3, par. 13]);

Then comes a question. If the proxy for systemic risk continues to rise, is there something wrong with banking regulation of systemic risk? Is there something wrong with our measure of systemic risk? Or is there no problem at all?

For instance, we need to bear in mind that we do not know what the systemic risk was before systemic risk regulation was implemented. Perhaps, if we were able to observe it (and definitely if it was directly measurable), we could have seen a much larger increase in the absence of mitigating effects due to regulation. A simplistic "Before-After" analysis can be carried out by comparing the systemic risk proxy rise in 2009 and 2020. The former spike was $(3.8/1.0) - 1 = 280\%$, whereas the latter was only $(5.6/3.8) - 1 = 47\%$. Thus, we may wish to conclude that the systemic risk regulation might be efficient as the rise is smaller. Nevertheless, we should not forget that we are unable to control a comparable economic environment.

Thus the question is still there. What is the optimal banking regulation against systemic risk? To answer it, we wish to offer a stylized theory applicable to real life.

When studying systemic risk, we should depart from its concept. Then we wish to describe the current prudential approach to systemic risk treatment. We lay down the discussed alternative regulatory options. After that, we introduce the seemingly non-adjacent domains of the institutional analysis and development (IAD) and the natural monopoly regulation. This will help us to elaborate a stylized regulatory framework in Section 21.5.

The [Risk Hub (2021)] suggests that "[s]ystemic risk generally refers to the risk of a disruption to the flow of financial services that is (i) caused by an impairment of all or parts of the financial system and (ii) has the potential to have serious negative consequences on the real economy". [Tarullo (2011)] argues that it is the shadow banking that exacerbates the systemic risk implications.

It seems that the paper by [Penati and Protopapadakis (1988)] was the first to introduce the notion of systemic risk. After that, several authors tackled it. They include [Carey and Gordy (2004)], [Acharya (2009)], [Mayordomo *et al.* (2014)], [Li and Marin (2014)], [Acemoglu *et al.* (2015)], [Tente *et al.* (2019)], [Duprey and Ueberfeldt (2020)], [Meuleman and Vennet (2020)], [Fatica *et al.* (2020)]. Each of them justifies its quantitative measure of the systemic risk. In essence, they are similar in the sense that they measure the financial actors' interconnectedness. The employed tools include centrality measures, Shapley vector, etc. The key finding is that systemic risk cannot be directly observed so that one has to deal with its proxies.

21.2 Current Systemic Risk Regulation

The banking regulation with respect to the systemic risk departs from the theoretical findings on the interconnectedness and the "too big to fail" anti-concept. This means that conceptually the larger the financial institution is; the more transacts with other economic agents; the more jurisdictions are covered; the more systemic risk is borne; the more systemically important (SI) are the considerations. This is a concise idea of the assessment methodology adopted by the Basel Committee [BCBS (2014e)], recall its discussion in Subsection 7.3.4.

As already mentioned, one cannot evaluate whether the introduced systemic risk regulation was efficient in curbing systemic risk or not. This is because of the absence of the control observations for the same time and jurisdiction. Nevertheless, several authors claim that the regulation failed. For instance, [Moosa (2010)], [Dewatripont *et al.* (2010), p. 53, footnote 83], [Lall (2012)], [Cathcart *et al.* (2017)]. As a result, [Pettifor (2020)] proposed to once more tighten the banking regulation and create a supra-national regulator, though it remains unclear whether there should be a new body in addition, instead of or above the already existing Basel Committee. However, originally the [Pettifor (2020)] ideas were coined ten years in advance by [Dewatripont *et al.* (2010)] after the 2007-2009 crisis.

To counterbalance, once again, one can refer to Figure 21.1. There, the calculated systemic risk did not rise as much in 2020 in the presence of regulation, as it was in its absence in 2007-2009. Besides, one may hypothesize that the systemic risk could have been larger in 2020 in the absence of the discussed regulation. The key implication here is that it is not possible to evaluate the systemic risk regulation efficiency properly. Thus, one can neither agree, nor disagree with [Pettifor (2020)] when he claims that revision of the regulation is needed.

21.3 Systemic Risk Regulation Options

In the above, we have attempted to explain that we cannot observe the systemic risk directly and that we cannot robustly evaluate the efficiency of its regulation. Nevertheless, there are options discussed in the literature on how to alternatively regulate systemic risk. Those originate from the 2007-2009 crisis experience. There are two streams: legal and tax related ones. First, [Liikanen (2012)] suggested restoring the separation between commercial and investment banks. He argued that this should help in systemic risk reduction. Thus, he claimed for the revival of the Glass-Steagall Act. Interestingly, the US researchers indirectly support his proposal [Ludwig *et al.* (2020)]. Their rationale is that abolishing the Act in 1999 has led to a negative consequence for the economy as well as implied a significant increase in income inequality. Second, [ECB (2010)] proposed to tax banks according to the systemic risk they embed. The taxation rule is simple in concept. The larger the bank's contribution to the systemic risk, the larger the tax payment. [Poledna *et al.* (2017)] and [Ordonez (2018)] extend this idea. For instance, [Poledna *et al.* (2017)] argue that such a tax is more efficient than an increase in the capital ratio minimum requirement shown in Figure 7.4. [Ordonez (2018)] elaborates on the idea arguing that shadow banking (i.e. unregulated banking activities by intermediaries) "improves welfare because it provides a channel to escape excessive regulation that is asymmetrically more valuable for banks with access to efficient investment opportunities". Thus, by taxing "shadow activities, subsidizing regulated activities and allowing banks to self-select into being regulated or not" total welfare should increase. When thinking of these alternative regulatory options, we need to remember the following. To properly incentivize banks, it is needed to correctly evaluate the systemic risk and its contribution to it. However, we remember that we cannot observe the systemic risk by itself. That is why we switch to discussing the two domains that deal with the unobserved indicators. Such domains are the institutional analysis and development (IAD) and the natural monopoly regulation. Let us explain why these domains are important when dealing with systemic risk. This is the extension of some thoughts reported in [Selmier *et al.* (2016)] concerning the financial risk as a good.

21.4 Systemic Risk as a Public Bad

The foundation of the IAD is the goods taxonomy from Table 21.1. [Ostrom and Ostrom (1977)] first introduced it. The idea is to map all the goods (or bads) into a two-dimensional space. According to [Ostrom (2009)] examples of public goods might be peace, security, national defense, knowledge, etc. Regarding pure public goods, we observe that the notion of financial stability could be assimilated to the other general notions such as peace and security concepts. In fact, several authors defined the financial stability as a public good, see [Camdessus (1999)], [Shirakawa (2012)], [Demetriades (2012)], [Pettifor (2020)]. Systemic risk is then a public bad. There is a particular feature of the presented goods topology that is not explicitly discussed in [Ostrom (2009)]. The difference between the notion of financial stability and pure public goods is that the latter are intangible and immeasurable. Take peace as an example. However, we may use a proxy indicator for it. For instance, it could be the number of war conflicts in a particular geographic area. Alternatively, we may ask the expert panel to rank the regions by the degree of peace. However, all these approaches are mere peace proxies. The peace itself is felt but is not observed.

Now recall that the systemic risk is a public bad. The reader may easily trace how well it fits the above taxonomy. Primarily, this is due to the same discussed feature. As mentioned systemic risk by its nature is intangible, even though its realisations are quite tangible. Thus it is a stylized example of the public bad. To

Table 21.1: Original goods' topology accepted in IAD.

		Subtractability of Use	
Non-Excludability	High	Common-pool resource	[Pure] public good
	Low	[Pure] private good	Club good

Source: [Ostrom (2009), p. 413].

design the optimal regulatory framework for it, we need to review another domain that handles or regulates the public bad.

21.4.1 *Natural Monopoly Regulation*

The natural monopoly was the name originally given to a single entity in the economy that produces a natural resource. Subsequently, it was referred to as an industry in which high barriers of entry to the market give the largest supplier a decisive advantage over competitors.

Being a monopoly sets non-competitive price levels. Conventionally this implies the consumer welfare deterioration, also known as the deadweight loss (DWL). The governments wish to achieve competitive price levels and restore the welfare loss. However, the widespread anti-trust solutions are non-applicable because of the production process specifics. This means that the regulator cannot break down the company into smaller entities. A canonical reason might be the case that there is only a single oil well, for example. This implies the need for the government to coexist with the natural monopoly. Then the regulator decides to introduce restrictions to its activities. However, there is another challenge. On one hand, the regulator knows that the price equals marginal costs when there is perfect competition. On the other hand, in the presence of natural monopoly, the regulator does not know the true costs and cannot set competitive prices. The novelty of [Tirole (2014)] was the justification for the regulatory framework in such a case. He explained that when the costs are non-observable, the second-best solution is to request the natural monopoly to decrease its retail prices. From one side, when such a rule is a long-lasting one, the monopoly may adjust to its benefit, while also to the benefit of consumers. The natural monopoly may raise efficiency to earn profit even when the output tariffs gradually decrease. Nevertheless, there are opponents to the regulation of natural monopoly. For instance, [Posner (1999)] thinks that such regulation does not pay off and should be abolished. In contrast to him, [Avdasheva and Shastitko (2005), p. 32, par. 3] argue that no regulation is not a remedy. At worst, the regulation should be superseded by another one that distorts incentives to a lesser extent. The key implication here is the existence of a workable solution to handle the public bad negative consequences. The idea originates from the natural monopolies regulation. It suggests requesting steady end tariffs' decrease to de-stimulate high costs incurred by a natural monopoly.

21.4.2 *Conceptual Regulatory Framework*

According to the literature systemic risk exists as a concept and its realisation may bring devastating consequences. To prevent those, we have the existing regulation and the alternative proposals. However, all of them rely on the systemic risk proxy indicators. In the absence of the control observations, we fail to robustly evaluate the efficiency of the existing regulation. For sake of fairness, there are two types of evidence. The first type indicates that it may be efficient, the alternative ones show the opposite. At the same time, we learned that there is already experience in handling the negative consequences of the unobserved events. The natural monopoly regulation suggests demanding regular price decreases. Thus the entity is forced to work on cost optimization. Consequently, it may still earn a profit, whereas the end consumer benefits from the lower prices. To properly transplant the derivations from the natural monopoly regulation, we need to consider the following. We remind that the systemic risk is unobservable. However, we know that the more risks the bank takes on board, the more risks proliferate to the financial system. When every systemically important bank acts in this way, the risk augments economy-wise. The obstacle here is that we cannot properly measure it. There are only rare cases of its detrimental realisations at our disposal. Thus, the natural monopoly regulation experience suggests the following options — to regulate the risk-weights or the lending rates. If we wish for a systemically important bank to permanently decrease risk-weights, it will likely decrease indirectly the borrowers' default probability. However, the risk-weight has the same shortcoming as the systemic risk does. We do not observe it. We derive it analytically from a model, remember modeling approaches in Chapter 8. When we change a model, the risk-weight estimate may change as well.

Besides, we should recall the Volkswagen company scandal [Crete (2016)]. The company manipulated software estimates to get its cars sold to the US in larger quantities. This means when the regulation tackles the unobserved indicators, the indicator may be subject to manipulation. Of course, the observed indicators may be vulnerable to fraud actions too. We may recall the operational risk losses by the Barings Bank in 1994 or by the Societe Generale in 2007. Nevertheless, the observed indicator seems a preferred option. That is why one may suggest the regulator targeting lending rates by requiring banks to steadily curb them. For example, Figure 21.2 shows how a bank lowers the loan price from the time No. 9.

Then our research objective is to benchmark the suggested regulatory rule against the existing one. The suggested one prescribes to the regular cut of the lending rate. The existing one is the increase in the minimum capital ratio as in Figure 7.4. We would prefer the option that results in a lower probability of default for the approved bank borrowers.

21.5 Theoretical Model

The loan pricing rule of a typical bank is as follows:

$$r_A = r_D + (ROE - r_D) \cdot CAR \cdot RW, \tag{21.1}$$

where r_A is the interest rate offered on loans; r_D is the price paid for the deposits; ROE is the Return on Equity (ROE) targeted by the shareholders; RW is the portfolio average risk-weight.

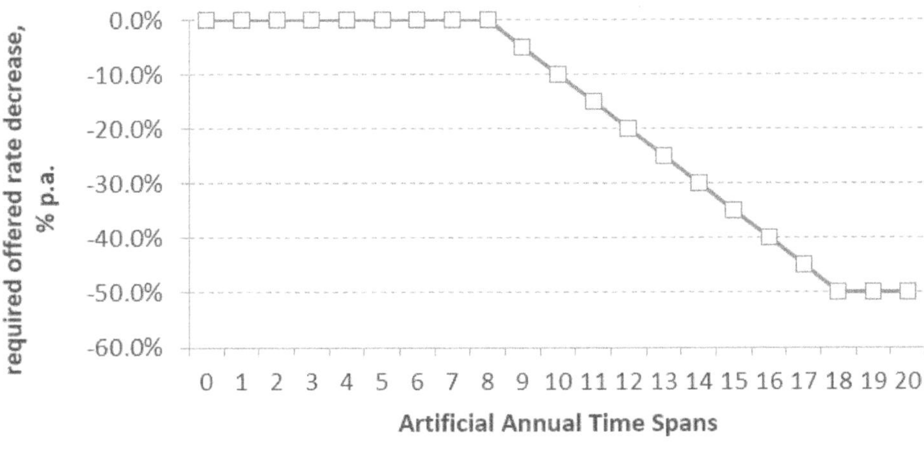

Fig. 21.2: The regulatory rule is to reduce the end rate by the predefined percentage as scheduled here.

From the above formula, we see that the larger the required capital ratio to minimum CAR is, the larger the lending rate r_A is. The larger the risk evaluation (the risk-weight, RW) is, the larger the end rate also is. This holds given the same deposit rate r_D and the profit target ROE. For calibration, we take two profit targets: 10% and 20% p.a. as a share of the invested capital. When thinking about the loan pricing and the lending market equilibrium properties, we should consider the two other facts. First, the larger the loan offered rate is, the less creditworthy borrowers come [Repullo (2013)]. That is why the bank stops granting loans when the rate is exorbitantly high. As a result, the loan supply curve is backward bending [Freixas and Rochet (2008), p. 174, fig. 5.2]. Second, the risk measure RW depends upon the borrower's creditworthiness degree. Namely, upon its probability of default (PD). We use the Basel Committee formula for the risk-weight from Eqs. (5.7) and (5.11). For simplicity, we assume that all loans have the same maturity of 2.5 years. The loss given default is 45% of the credit exposure amount. All loans are the standard corporate ones. The borrowers are the standard corporate firms, not SMEs. Third, for simplicity, we take the probability of default equal to the bank lending rate. The rationale is as follows. The higher the lending rate is, the riskier the borrower has to be. This means that the borrower has to earn more, as well as at the same time, he is more prone to default. Let us look at the two cases. Figure 21.3 shows the relationship between changes in the capital ratio and the default probability of the borrowers. Figure 21.4 mirrors the dependence by benchmarking the offered loan rate to the average borrower PD.

We may see that the implication of the existing regulatory rule is the permanent rise in the lending rates and consequently the borrower PD. Specifically, the larger the ROE target of a bank is, the larger the growth in PD is. For instance, the end

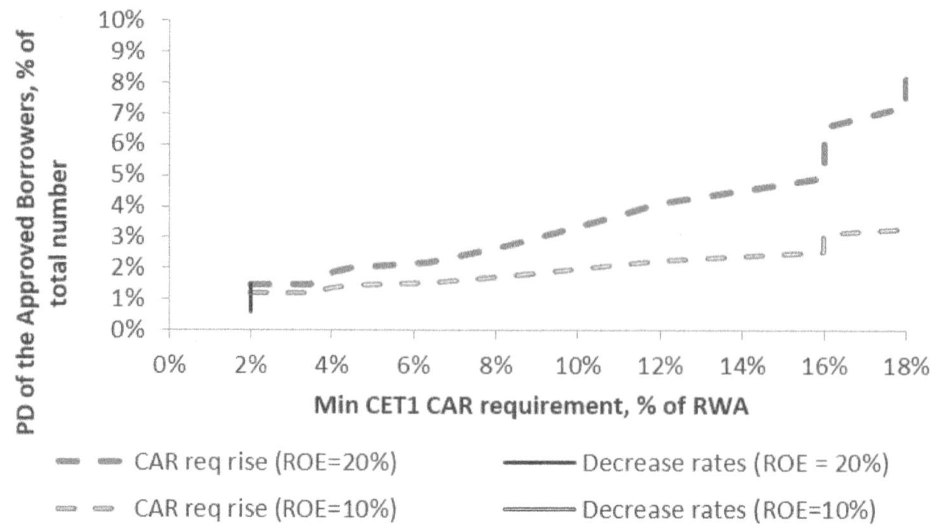

Fig. 21.3: The larger the capital ratio is, the higher the ultimate PD of the borrowers is.

minimum requirement of 18% of the risk amount results in PD equal to 3.6% for ROE of 10% and PD equal to 8.3% for ROE of 20%. The change in PD is non-linear in ROE. Of course, the bank shareholders may decide to downward adjust the profit targets. However, this may have a downward pressure on the bank valuations. The fall in the bank stock quotes may produce a cascade (contagion) effect. Then we will have another — earlier unforeseen — form of the systemic risk realisation, i.e. the fire sales.

The suggested regulatory rule has advantages over the existing one. When implementing it, we do not embed the schedule of the capital ratio increase. As we may see from Figure 21.3, banks experience a decrease in the borrowers' default probabilities with no decreases in capital ratio requirements. This is a mere reflection of the lending rate restriction, as may be seen from Figure 21.4. The difference in ROE targets implies different starting points. For instance, see point A for ROE equal to 10% and point B for ROE of 20% at Figure 21.4. The difference in ROE implies lending rate level variance, though it results in a comparable decrease of the end borrowers' default probabilities.

We have demonstrated that banking economics implies banks accumulate the total risks when the regulator asks to hold more and more capital as a proportion of risks taken. One of its reflections is the rise in the average borrowers' default probability. However, requesting an alternative, we end up with lower risks. When banks are forced to decrease their lending rates, all else being equal, they have to search for the more creditworthy borrowers to continue earning profits and not scoring losses. To generalize and implement the proposal in the real life, we should

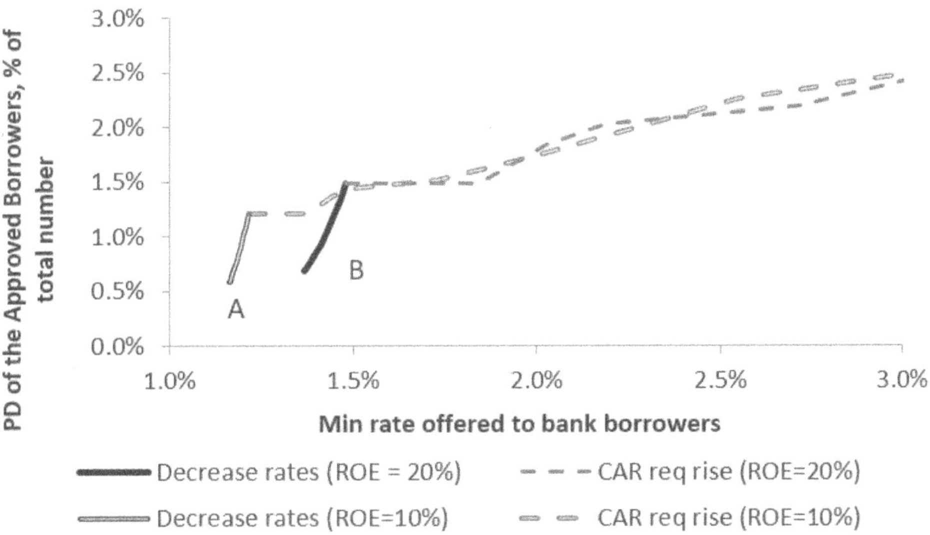

Fig. 21.4: Lower lending rates imply less borrowers with higher risk.

request the proportionate shrinkage in all the banking tariffs. This will assure us that the banks do not use cross-subsidies. This means that they do not reduce the tariffs for one product type while raising it for the other ones. For instance, to reduce the lending rates, do not also reduce the rates on deposits.

21.6 Discussion

The pandemic period is associated with the rise in the systemic risk proxy indicators. This is disregarding the presence of systemic risk regulation. We have no control data to evaluate the existing regulation efficiency. However, we may learn from the peer domains of institutional economics and the industrial organization how to reduce the unobserved systemic risk. To do so, we may request the banks to permanently decrease the cost of their services, e.g. to decrease the lending rates and increase those on deposits. In other words, make their tariffs lower and the products more affordable. We should apply these rules primarily to the systemically important banks. Our proposal could be applied not only to banks but to insurance companies as well.

21.6.1 *Internal Ratings-Based (IRB)*

We have demonstrated the benefits from the suggested regulatory framework over the existing approach using the assumption of the co-monotone dependence of the risk-weight and the default probability. This is definitely true for the IRB banks. When a bank uses the fixed risk-weights under the conventional standardized approach, such a rule may not yield the outcome as fast as expected. This is because the predefined risk-weights are less variable and there may be "cliff-effects", i.e. there may be discrete jumps between RW categories. Under the IRB those are smoother. That is why, we may suggest the following two-step solution. First, the systemically important banks all transit to IRB. Second, all of them are subject to regulation and regular price decreases' requirement.

21.6.2 *Globally Systemically Important Insurers (G-SIIs)*

In addition to G-SIBs, the international regulators delineated the globally systemically important financial institutions out of the insurance companies [FSB (2016)] by naming them Global Systemically Important Insurers (G-SIIs). A larger discussion on the identification can be found in [CIPR (2021)]. However, our principal findings hold for the insurance companies also. To reduce the systemic risks produced by them, the regulator has to request reducing the insurance tariffs. Similar to IRB, the Solvency II accord promotes the use of own data and models. Thus, all the systemically important insurance companies should run Solvency II and be subject to a requirement to regularly decrease their tariffs.

Concluding Remarks

The 2020-2021 pandemic has seriously impacted the economies worldwide. As for now, we do not see default proliferation, as mentioned in the Preface. In part, this is due to various stimulus measures undertaken by local governments. However, [Eckert *et al.* (2020)] reminded in mid-2020 that when the latter are lifted, the defaults might get noticeable. As a result, we already hear of the large car rental business of Hertz and the cosmetics l'Occitane having gone bust according to [Goldfine (2021)]. Typically, defaults start to mushroom one or two years after the financial crisis. On one hand, the representative of the Bank of International Settlements (BIS) [Borio (2020)] assured the global community that the international banks are solid as they have accumulated significant capital buffers. On the other hand, the Chairman of the Basel Committee [Hernandez de Cos (2021)] one year later warned that we should not relax that much. He explained that banks are not willing to utilize capital buffers. In fact, "only a few banks' capital ratios have fallen below their regulatory capital buffer level" and those banks which experienced downward pressures on their liquidity buffers "took management actions (such as borrowing from central banks) to preserve LCR levels well above the 100% minimum requirements". This prompted some "stakeholders, from both the industry and the regulatory community, to point out that buffers were not as usable as intended and thus to call for changes to the Basel III buffer framework". This is the so-called "taxi phenomenon" recognized, also, 40 years ago by another Basel Committee Chairman Peter Cooke according to [Goodhart (2011)]. That is why Pablo Hernández De Cos underlines that it is too early to call it a victory. The credit risks are still there and their level is unprecedentedly high.

To provide additional incentives for the economies, the global regulatory community might have decided to abandon the idea of up-lifting capital requirements in the final version of Basel III (see [Goel and Agarwal (2021)]). As [Penikas (2021a)] has shown, the credit money creation in the modern cashless economies is driven mostly by the capital ratio minimum requirements, and not by the mandatory reserve. That is why not lifting up the capital requirement may bring its benefits in the short-run, but could destabilize the economy in the long run as described by [Huerta de Soto (2006)]. That is why it is particularly important today — at the end of 2021 — that the banks worldwide can adequately model their credit risk.

In this book, we have offered various tools to capture the complexities in the credit risk dependence parameters. We explained the use of copulas for joint dependency modeling. When properly applied, copulas can improve credit risk modeling and henceforth its management for both balance sheet and off-balance sheet assets such as IRS, CDS, TRS. If copulas are wrongly applied, of course, there might be pioneers like [Salmon (2009)] and [MacKenzie and Spears (2012)] to blame the tool and not the risk analysts with poorly fitted models. Then there is also no wonder why the investors stay unable to cut through the unresolved complexity tree of [Haldane (2009)], even if risk managers did not do their best to develop proper models.

Last but not least, we strongly wish that our book helps regulators in driving financial stability and provides some guidance to banks running or planning to apply for the Internal Ratings-Based (IRB) approaches of Basel II and now of Basel III. Moreover, as Basel regulation has been taken as a benchmark for Solvency II, we believe that this book would be beneficial as well for the insurance industry and, thus, for the whole financial sector.

Giuseppe Orlando, Michele Bufalo, Henry Penikas, Concetta Zurlo
Bari, Rome, Milan (Italy),
Moscow (Russia)

October 11, 2021

Appendices

Appendix A

Financial Engineering: Coding in R

This appendix is meant to provide some examples and the related code in R to help the reader in learning the concepts exposed in the book.

A.1 R Code for Chapter 3

This code shows how to simulate copulas in R. The command "load()" loads in R, a previously installed package. In case the package has not been installed yet, execute the command "install.packages()" Note that most pseudo-random number generators (PRNGs) are build on algorithms based on recursive method starting from a base value that is determined by an input called the "seed". The default PRNG in many software (R, Python, Stata, Matlab, etc.) is the Mersenne Twister algorithm [Matsumoto and Nishimura (1998)]. For examples on how to code in R (including copulas) the reader may also refer to [r-bloggers (2020)].

A.1.1 *R Code 1*

```
# As an example we install a package before loading the corresponding library.
# From the next package onward we assume that libraries have been already installed.

#Install "scatterplot3d" which is a library that provides routines for producing 3D plots
install.packages("scatterplot3d")
# Once installed, load  "scatterplot3d"
library(scatterplot3d)
# Load "ggplot2" package useful to display plots next to each other
library(ggplot2)
# Load "grid" package useful to add a grid to a graph
library(grid)
# Set the seed number
set.seed(123)
# Load Copula package
library(copula)

# Build 3 copulas: Frank, Gumbel and Clayton
MyFrankC <- frankCopula(dim = 2, param = 6)
```

```
MyGumbelC <- gumbelCopula(dim = 3, param = 6)
MyClaytonC <- claytonCopula(dim = 4, param = 6)

# Generate random samples
MyFrankRnd <- rCopula(2000, MyFrankC)
MyGumbelRnd <- rCopula(2000, MyGumbelC)
MyClaytonRnd <- rCopula(2000, MyClaytonC)

# Plot the samples
Plot1 <- qplot(MyFrankRnd[,1], MyFrankRnd[,2], colour = MyFrankRnd[,1],
main="Frank copula random samples", xlab = "u", ylab = "v")
Plot2 <- qplot(MyGumbelRnd[,1], MyGumbelRnd[,2], colour = MyGumbelRnd[,1],
main="Gumbel copula random samples", xlab = "u", ylab = "v")
Plot3 <- qplot(MyClaytonRnd[,1], MyClaytonRnd[,2], colour = MyGumbelRnd[,1],
main="Clayton copula random samples", xlab = "u", ylab = "v")

# Define grid layout and print each graph
pushViewport(viewport(layout = grid.layout(1, 3)))
print(Plot1, vp = viewport(layout.pos.row = 1, layout.pos.col = 1))
print(Plot2, vp = viewport(layout.pos.row = 1, layout.pos.col = 2))
print(Plot3, vp = viewport(layout.pos.row = 1, layout.pos.col = 3))
```

Figure A.1 displays the graphs of the distributions obtained with Frank, Gumbel and Clayton copulas. Notice that, as the parameter θ is the same for all of them, the difference is only due to the type of copula.

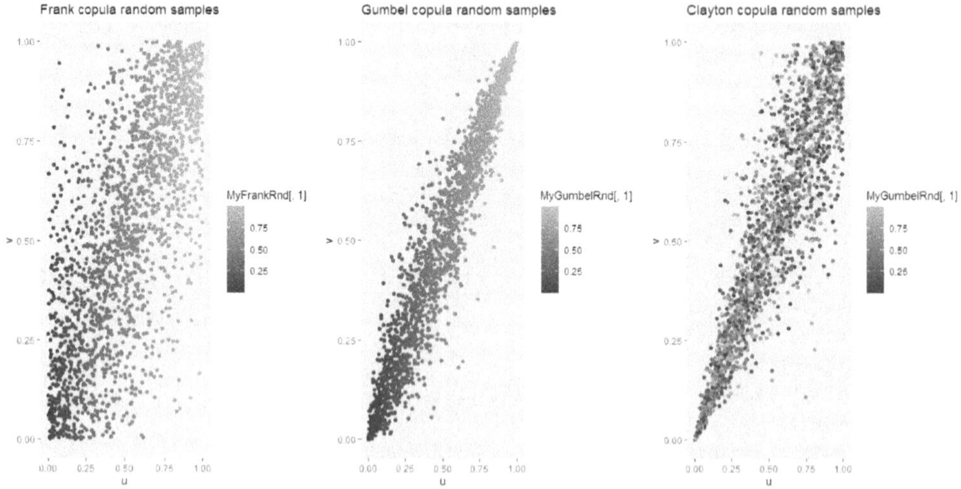

Fig. A.1: Frank, Gumbel and Clayton copulas, $\theta = 6$.

A.1.2 *R Code 2*

```
# Generate the Gaussian copula
MyGaussianCopula <- normalCopula(.7, dim = 2)
```

```
# Generate 2000 observations
MyGaussianCopulaRnd <- rCopula(2000, MyGaussianCopula)

# Compute the density
pdfMyGaussianCopula <- dCopula(MyGaussianCopulaRnd, MyGaussianCopula)

# Compute the CDF
cdfMyGaussianCopula <- pCopula(MyGaussianCopulaRnd, MyGaussianCopula)

# Divide the plot in 3 subplots
par(mfrow = c(1, 3))

# Gaussian copula: 3D plain scatterplot, plot of the CDF and contour plot
scatterplot3d(MyGaussianCopulaRnd[,1],MyGaussianCopulaRnd[,2], cdfMyGaussianCopula, color="red",
main="CDF", xlab = "u1", ylab="u2", zlab="Gaussian copula",pch=".")
persp(MyGaussianCopula, pCopula, main = "CDF")
contour(MyGaussianCopula, pCopula, xlim = c(0, 1), ylim=c(0, 1), main = "Contour plot")

par(mfrow = c(1, 3))
# Gaussian copula: 3D plain scatterplot, plot of the PDF and contour plot
scatterplot3d(MyGaussianCopulaRnd[,1], MyGaussianCopulaRnd[,2], pdfMyGaussianCopula, color="red",
main="Density", xlab ="u1", ylab="u2", zlab="Gaussian copula", pch=".")
persp(MyGaussianCopula, dCopula, main ="Density")
contour(MyGaussianCopula, dCopula, xlim = c(0, 1), ylim=c(0, 1), main = "Contour plot")
```

Figure A.2 displays the tridimensional scatter plot, the cumulative density and the contour plot of the Gaussian Copula obtained with the code above listed.

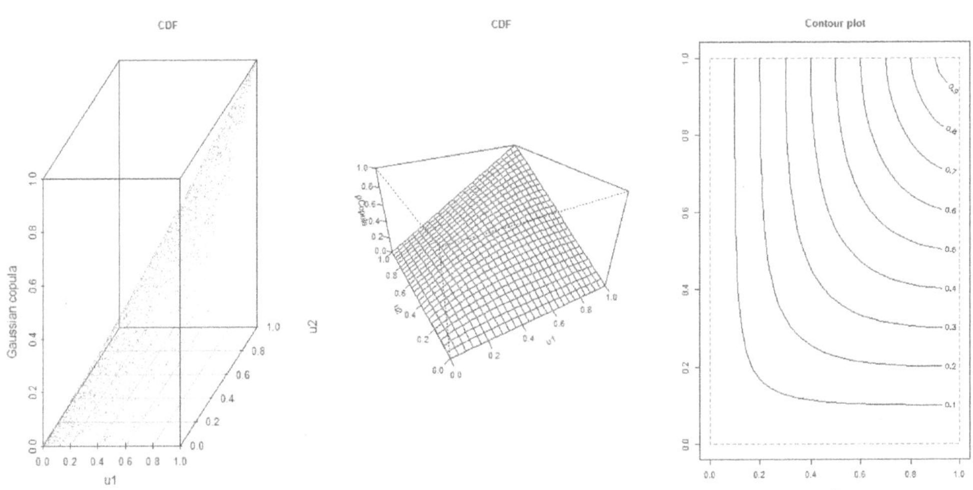

Fig. A.2: 3D scatter plot, plot of the CDF and contour plot.

Figure A.3 displays the tridimensional scatter plot, the probability density and the contour plot of the Gaussian Copula obtained with the code above listed.

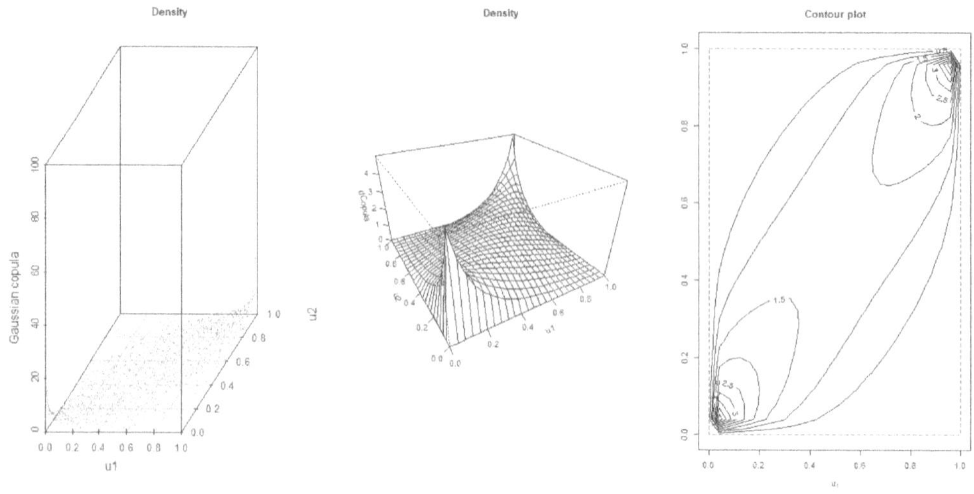

Fig. A.3: 3D scatter plot, plot of the PDF and contour plot.

A.1.3 *R Code 3*

```
# Generate a class of bivariate distribution with  marginals Gaussian and
# t-Student and the copula is normal
MultDist <- mvdc(copula = MyGaussianCopula,
                 margins = c("norm", "t"),
                 paramMargins = list(list(mean = 2),
                                     list(df = 2)))

# 3D PDF and CDF of the multivariate distribution
par(mfrow = c(1, 2))
scatterplot3d(MultDistRnd[,1],MultDistRnd[,2], pdfMultDist, color="red",
main="Density", xlab = "u1", ylab="u2", zlab="frequencies",pch=".")
scatterplot3d(MultDistRnd[,1],MultDistRnd[,2], cdfMultDist, color="red",
main="CDF", xlab = "u1", ylab="u2", zlab="frequencies",pch=".")
```

Figure A.4 displays the tridimensional plot of PDF and CDF of the multivariate distribution.

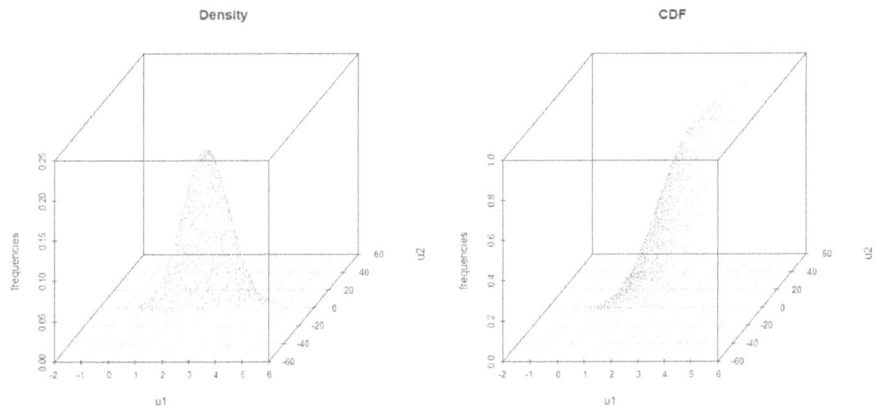

Fig. A.4: 3D PDF and CDF of the multivariate distribution.

A.1.4 *R Code 4*

```
# 3D prob. density and related contour of the multivariate distribution
persp(MultDist, dMvdc, xlim = c(-4, 4), ylim=c(0, 2), main = "Density")
contour(MultDist, dMvdc, xlim = c(-4, 4), ylim=c(0, 2), main = "Contour plot")
```

Figure A.5 displays the tridimensional plot of the probability density function and its contour of the multivariate distribution.

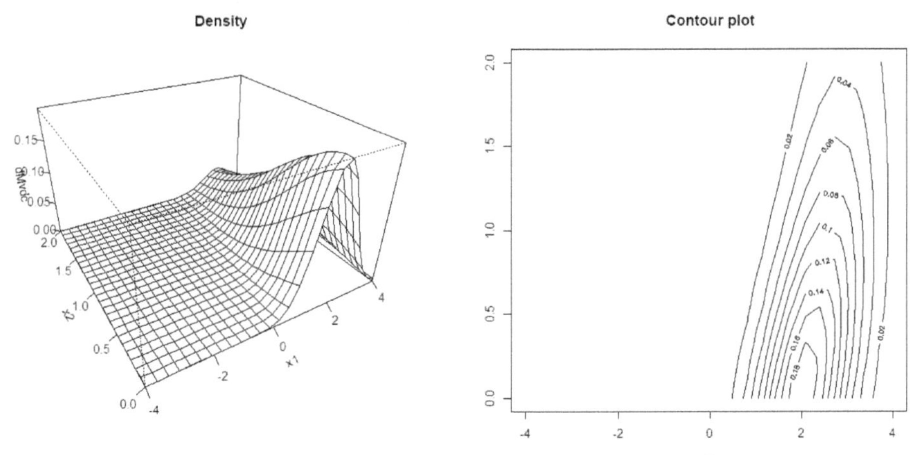

Fig. A.5: 3D probability density and contour of the multivariate distribution.

A.1.5 *R Code 5*

```
# 3D cum. density and related contour of the multivariate distribution
persp(MultDist, pMvdc, xlim = c(-4, 4), ylim=c(0, 2), main = "CDF")
contour(MultDist, pMvdc, xlim = c(-4, 4), ylim=c(0, 2), main = "Contour plot")
```

Figure A.6 displays the tridimensional plot of cumulative density function and its contour of the multivariate distribution.

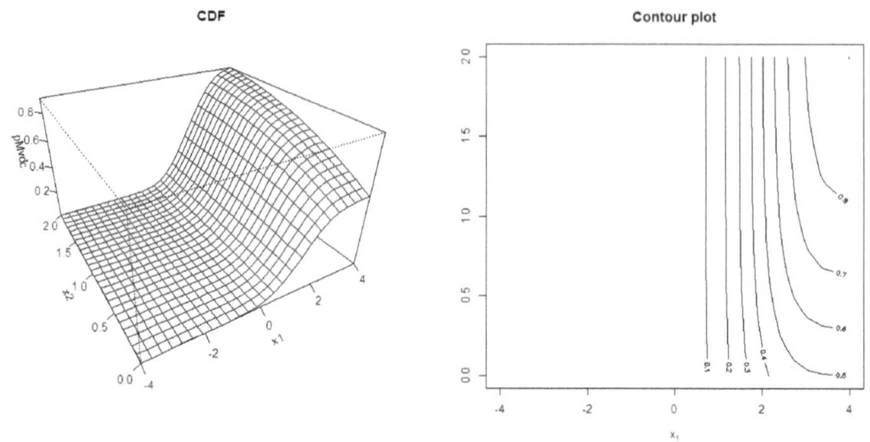

Fig. A.6: 3D cumulative and contour of the multivariate distribution.

A.1.6 *R Code 6*

```
# Build a Frank, a Gumbel and a Clayton copula
MyFrankC <- frankCopula(dim = 2, param = 3)
MyGumbelC <- gumbelCopula(dim = 2, param = 3)
MyClaytonC <- claytonCopula(dim = 2, param = 3)

# Density plot of the 3 copulas
par(mfrow = c(1, 3))
persp(MyFrankC, dCopula, main ="Frank copula density")
persp(MyGumbelC, dCopula, main ="Gumbel copula density")
persp(MyClaytonC, dCopula, main ="Clayton copula density")

# Contour plot of the densities of the 3 copulas
par(mfrow = c(1, 3))
contour(MyFrankC, dCopula, xlim = c(0, 1), ylim=c(0, 1), main = "Contour plot Frank")
contour(MyGumbelC, dCopula, xlim = c(0, 1), ylim=c(0, 1), main = "Contour plot Gumbel")
contour(MyClaytonC, dCopula, xlim = c(0, 1), ylim=c(0, 1), main = "Contour plot Clayton")
```

Figure A.7 displays the tridimensional plot of the density.

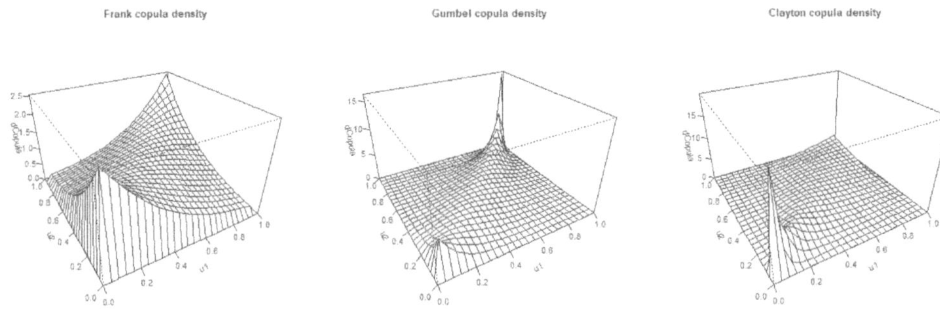

Fig. A.7: Density plot of the 3 copulas, $\theta = 3$.

Figure A.8 displays the contour for the Frank, Gumbel and Clayton copulas.

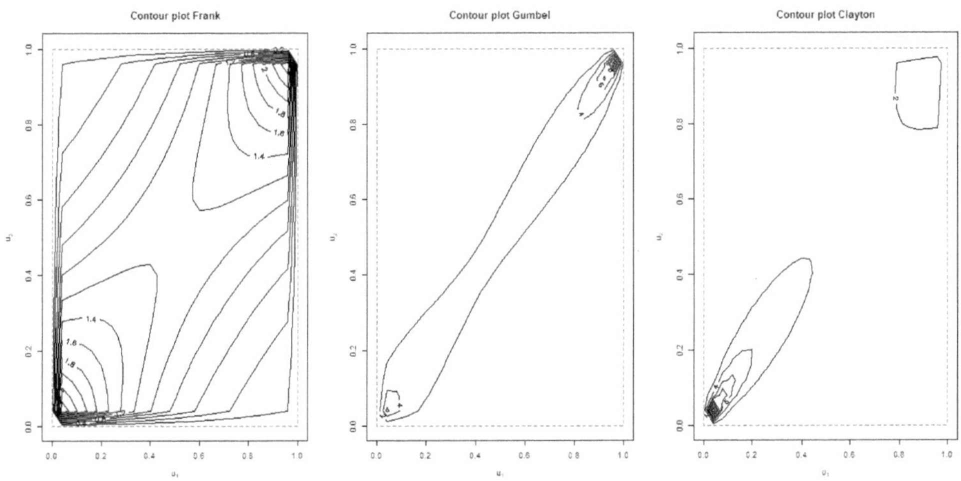

Fig. A.8: Contour plot of the 3 copulas, $\theta = 3$.

The package "mlCopulaSelection" provides useful tools to choose and fit a bivariate copula model (from a library of 40 models) to the data. The copula models in the library correspond to BB1, BB2,...,BB10 from [Joe (1997)] and their 90, 180 and 270 degree rotations. For example, the following code A.1.7 selects "CBB6" as the best model.

A.1.7 *R Code 7*

```
# Data: U and V uniform marginals
U <- c( 0.43, 0.1, 0.2, 0.33, 0.24, 0.29, 0.14, 0.4, 0.39, 0.8, 0.63, 0.16,
0.24, 0.14,0.71, 0.39, 0.48, 0.29, 0.38, 0.37)
V <- c(0.01, 0.26, 0.2, 0.36, 0.34, 0.43, 0.27, 0.61, 0.08, 0.25, 0.72, 0.15,
0.14, 0.12, 0.74, 0.18, 0.58, 0.15, 0.34, 0.13)
```

```
# Find the maximun likelihood estimates
res<-mlcbbsel(U,V)

# The best fitting copula model is:
res$copmax
[1] "CBB6"

# The parameters for the best fitting copula model are:
res$parmax
[1] 1.790219 1.824194

# Log-likelihood of the best fitting copula model with the above parameters
res$llmax
[1] 13.47008
```

A.2 R Code for Chapter 18

A.2.1 *R Code for Section 18.3.2*

This code has been developed for Subsection 18.3.2: risk evaluation of a fixed income portfolio.

This exercise considers a fixed income portfolio containing two secured bonds with ratings Aaa and Aa with a recovery rate equal to 60% and computes the VaR. Let us start by recalling the default transition probabilities matrix in Table A.1.

Table A.1: 1-year Rating transition matrix (cf. [Saldanha and Beers (2011), Table 1]).

	Aaa	Aa	A	Baa	Ba	B	Caa -C	NR
Aaa	94.2%	3.6%	0.0%	0.0%	0.0%	0.0%	0.0%	2.2%
Aa	1.7%	93.3%	2.1%	0.0%	0.0%	0.0%	0.0%	2.9%
A	0.0%	3.0%	91.7%	1.4%	0.0%	0.0%	0.0%	4.0%
Baa	0.0%	0.0%	3.8%	86.4%	3.2%	0.0%	0.0%	6.6%
Ba	0.0%	0.0%	0.0%	2.3%	88.9%	1.1%	1.5%	6.1%
B	0.0%	0.0%	0.0%	0.0%	12.8%	75.4%	3.8%	8.1%
Caa -C	0.0%	0.0%	0.0%	0.0%	0.0%	32.4%	62.1%	5.4%

A.2.1.1 *R Code 8*

```
# useful libraries
library(mlCopulaSelection)

# Define the marginals
BondRet <-read.table("MyBondData.csv", header=TRUE, sep=",")
```

```
r1 <- BondRet[,1]
r2 <- BondRet[,2]

# demonstrate scatterplot of joint returns (variables in levels)
plot(r1,r2, xlab = "Bond A return", ylab = "Bond B return")

# create an object of Spearman correlation
MyCorr <- c(cor(r1,r2, method = 'spearman'))

# demonstrate the Spearman correlation value
MyCorr #  +0.6449254

# obtain probability transformations
# extract empirical CDFs from observed return series
ecdf1 <- ecdf(r1)
p1    <- ecdf1(r1)

ecdf2 <- ecdf(r2)
p2    <- ecdf2(r2)

# demonstrate scatterplot of joint returns in probability transformation
plot(p1,p2, xlab = "Bond A return CDF", ylab = "Bond B return CDF")

#---------------------------------------------------------------------
# Find the copula model corresponding to the marginal with
# the function mlcbbsel in "mlCopulaSelection" package
res.12<-mlcbbsel(p1,p2)

# Display the best copula model and parameter corresponding to it
res.12$copmax
res.12$parmax

# introduce auxilliary variables depending on the fitted parameters
theta <- res.12$parmax[1]
delta <- res.12$parmax[2]

# demonstrate parameter values
theta # 3.16386
delta # 0.4517036
```

A.2.1.2 *R Code 10*

For any pair of parameters δ, θ compute the double integral of copula.

```
# useful libraries
library(pracma)

# compute Spearman correlation using copula
# for this purpose write the auxilliary function
```

```
Fn <- function(u,v)
{
u*v*dcbb9(theta,delta,u,v)
}

# use two-dimensional integration to arrive at Spearman correlation of interest
CorCop <- 12 * quad2d(Fn,0,1,0,1)-3
CorCop # +0.690851

# remind the value of the Spearman correlation calculated directly
MyCorr # +0.6449254

# uncomment to compare results for a zero copula-correlation situation
#CorCop <- -0.6
```

A.2.1.3 *R Code 11*

```
# useful libraries
library(CreditMetrics)

# Number of bonds in portfolio
N <- 2

# Number of simulations
n <- 100000

# Risk free
r <- 0.015

# Exposure at risk (equi-proportional portfolio, i.e., with equal weights)
EAD <- c(100,100)

# Rating category for transition matrix
RC  <- c("Aaa", "Aa", "A", "Baa", "Ba", "B", "Ca", "D")
RC_dim  <- 8

## Loss given default
LGD <- 0.4

# Rating of bonds in portfolio
Rating <- c("Aaa", "Aa")
BondNames <- c("Bond 1", "Bond 2")

# VaR confidence levels
alpha1 <- 0.95
alpha2 <- 0.99

## Transition matrix
TM <- matrix(
```

```
c(
94.2,3.6,0.0,0.0,0.0,0.0,0.0,2.2,
1.7,93.3,2.1,0.0,0.0,0.0,0.0,2.9,
0.0,3.0,91.7,1.3,0.0,0.0,0.0,4.0,
0.0,6.6,3.8,86.4,3.2,0.0,0.0,0.0,
0.0,0.0,0.1,2.3,88.9,1.1,1.5,6.1,
0.0,0.0,0.0,0.0,12.8,75.4,3.8,8.0,
0.0,0.0,0.0,0.0,0.1,32.4,62.1,5.4,
0.0,0.0,0.0,0.0,0.0,0.0,0.0,100.0
)/100, RC_dim, RC_dim, dimnames = list(RC, RC), byrow = TRUE)

#---------------------------------------------------------
# Use correlation from the above Part I
# Correlation matrix for the portfolio
rho <- matrix(c(1, CorCop, CorCop, 1),
N,N,dimnames = list(BondNames,BondNames), byrow = TRUE)

#----------------------------------------------------------
# VaR 95% confidence level
cm.CVaR(TM, LGD, EAD, N, n, r, rho, alpha1, Rating)

#       5%
# 0.4334493 # for +69% copula-correlation

# VaR 99% confidence level
cm.CVaR(TM, LGD, EAD, N, n, r, rho, alpha2, Rating)

#       1%
# 38.07774  # for +69% copula-correlation
#----------------------------------------------------------
```

A.2.1.4 *R Code 12*

Here we show how to model a portfolio of four bonds starting from Gaussian distributions, transitioning through the copulas to finally specifying four different marginals who, supposedly, best describe the risk profile of each bond. The end result is that the distributions of the four bonds, thanks to the copulas, are linked together according to the correlations originally specified.

```
# Load the library
library(MASS)
# Set the seed
set.seed(123)
m <- 4
n <- 2000

# Simulate 2000 observations for eac bond z <- mvrnorm(n,mu=rep(0, m),rho,empirical=T)
#z <- rmvt (n,delta=rep(0, m),sigma, df = 5)
```

```
# Load the library
library(psych)
# Compute the correlation of the Gaussian distributions and display them
cor(z,method='spearman')
pairs.panels(z)

# Given the correlation structure generate uniform distributions and display them
u <- pnorm(z)
pairs.panels(u)

# Show the distributions and compute the correlation
df <- cbind(Bond1,Bond2,Bond3,Bond4)
pairs.panels(df)
cor(df,meth='spearman')
```

Figures A.9, A.10 and A.11 show, respectively, four Gaussian, uniform and ad hoc distributions all keeping the assumed correlation.

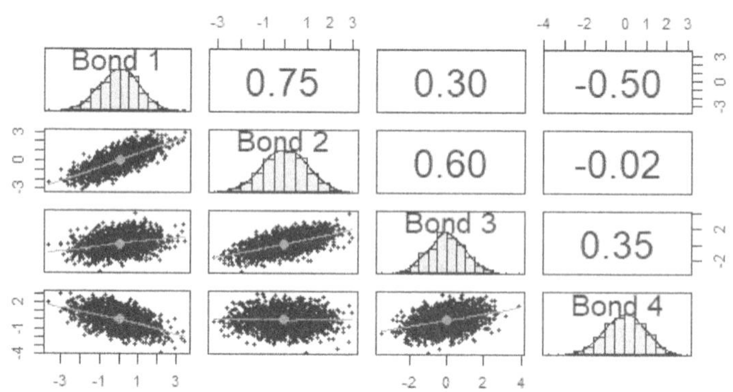

Fig. A.9: Randomly generated Gaussian distributions with a given correlation.

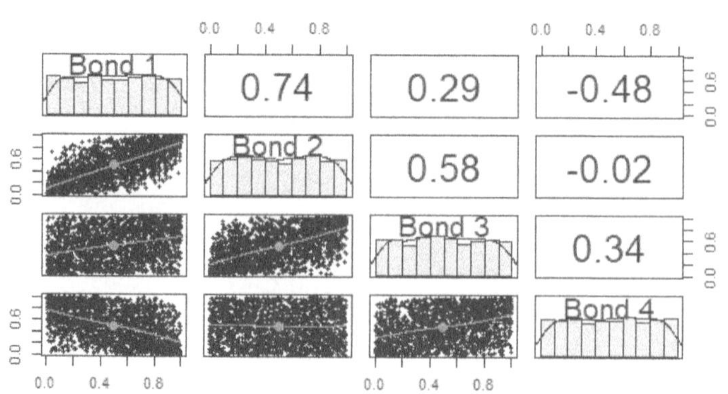

Fig. A.10: Randomly generated uniform distributions with the assumed correlation.

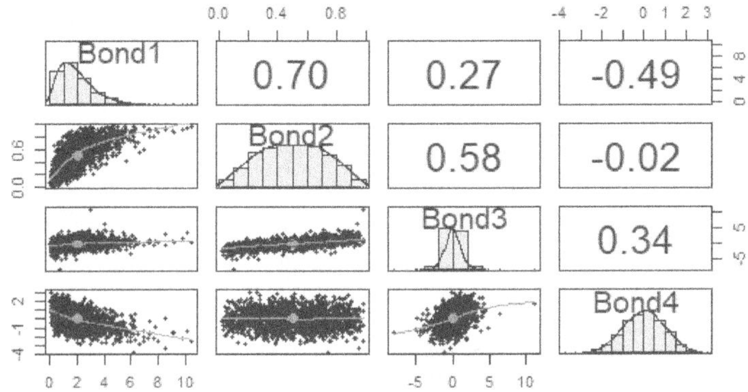

Fig. A.11: Four different types of distributions with the assumed correlation.

A.2.2 *R Code for Section 18.3.3*

This code has been developed for Subsection 18.3.3: portfolio risk evaluation on selecting the copulas.

Read data, and fit them to Gaussian, *t*-Student, Gumbel, Clayton and Frank for comparing which distribution suits best. Then build the marginals and compute the VaR (see [Bolancé Losilla *et al.* (2015)]).

A.2.2.1 *R Code 13*

Read data and look at their statistics.

```
# Load libraries
library(copula)
library(fCopulae)
library(QRM)
library(MASS)
library(VineCopula)
library(sn)
library(moments)
library(fitdistrplus)

# Read log-returns of BondA and BondB in a temporary variable
 TempBondRet <-read.table("MyBondData.csv", header=TRUE, sep=",")

# First column BondA, second BondB
 BondRet <- cbind(TempBondRet[1],TempBondRet[2])
 BondRet <- as.matrix(BondRet)
 n<-nrow(BondRet)

 head(BondRet) #Check the first columns
```

```
#             BondA        BondB
#[1,] -0.008456994 -0.002017764
#[2,] -0.000601343 -0.006685684
#[3,]  0.010204855  0.000952365
#[4,]  0.010105549  0.025253783
#[5,]  0.002320345  0.020562427
#[6,] -0.025831819 -0.008050608

summary(BondRet)

#     BondA                BondB
# Min.   :-0.137708   Min.   :-0.159453
# 1st Qu.:-0.006484   1st Qu.:-0.005565
# Median : 0.001140   Median : 0.001100
# Mean   : 0.001363   Mean   : 0.001312
# 3rd Qu.: 0.010273   3rd Qu.: 0.009699
# Max.   : 0.113157   Max.   : 0.132929

#Standard deviation

sd(BondRet[,1])
#[1] 0.01906022

sd(BondRet[,2])
#[1] 0.01719669

#Asymmetry
skewness(BondRet[,1])

#[1] -0.3402982

skewness(BondRet[,2])
#[1] -0.3480903

##Histograms
 par(mfrow=c(1,2))
 lo<-layout(matrix(c(1,1,2,2),byrow=T,ncol=2))
 hist(BondRet[,1],50, main="Histograms of log-returns")
 hist(BondRet[,2],50, main="")
 Udata <- pobs(BondRet)
 head(Udata) #Check the first columns

#           BondA     BondB
#[1,] 0.21065183 0.3624801
#[2,] 0.43561208 0.2233704
#[3,] 0.74642289 0.4888712
#[4,] 0.74324324 0.9531002
#[5,] 0.53577107 0.9197138
#[6,] 0.06041335 0.1995231
```

A.2.2.2 *R Code 14*

Compute the correlations and the parameters and fit the data to Gaussian, *t*-Student, Gumbel, Clayton and Frank copulas by using the adjusted distributions.

```
#Pearson correlation for Gaussian and t-Student copulas
 Rho<-cor(BondRet)
 Rho<-Rho[1,2]
 Rho
#[1] 0.7372308

#Kendall tau correlation for Gumbel and Clayton copulas

 RhoTau<-cor(BondRet, method = "kendall")
 RhoTau<-RhoTau[1,2]
 RhoTau
#[1] 0.4786596

 ParGum<-1/(1-RhoTau)
 ParGum
#[1] 1.918133

 ParClay<-(2*RhoTau)/(1-RhoTau)
 ParClay
#[1] 1.836265

############################
 # Gaussian copula
 NormCop <- normalCopula(Rho, dim = 2, dispstr = "un")
 NormCop # Info about Gaussian copula object

# Normal copula, dim. d = 2
# Dimension:  2
# Parameters:
#  rho.1   = 0.7372308

NormCopEst<-fitCopula(NormCop,Udata, method="mpl")
NormCopEst

#Call: fitCopula(copula, data = data, method = "mpl")
#Fit based on "maximum pseudo-likelihood" and 1257 2-dimensional observations.
#Copula: normalCopula
# rho.1
#0.6856
#The maximized loglikelihood is 395.1
#Optimization converged

# Set a temporary variable for the estimated rho
 Temp<-coef(NormCopEst)
 # Adjusted rho
```

```
 Adj.Rho<-Temp[[1]]
 Adj.Rho
#[1] 0.6856004
 logLik(NormCopEst) # value of the likelihood function
#'log Lik.' 395.1187 (df=1)

 AIC(NormCopEst) #AIC value
#[1] -788.2375
 BIC(NormCopEst) #BIC value
#[1] -783.101
 # Adjusted Gaussian copula
 NormCop <- normalCopula(Adj.Rho, dim = 2, dispstr = "un")
 NormCop
#Normal copula, dim. d = 2
#Dimension:  2
#Parameters:
#  rho.1   = 0.6856004

 # Shows that there is no dependency on the tails
 TailDep<-tailIndex(NormCop)
 TailDep

#Warning message:
#'tailIndex' is deprecated.
#Use 'lambda' instead.
#See help("Deprecated")

#lower upper
#    0     0

 ############################
 # t-Student copula
 tCop <- tCopula(Rho, dim = 2, dispstr="un", df.fixed=FALSE)
 tCop  # Info about t-Student copula object
#t-copula, dim. d = 2
#Dimension:  2
#Parameters:
#  rho.1   = 0.7372308
#  df      = 4.0000000

 tCopEst<-fitCopula(tCop, Udata, method="mpl", estimate.variance=TRUE)
#Warning message:
#In var.mpl(copula, u) :
#  the covariance matrix of the parameter estimates is computed \\
#  as if 'df.fixed = TRUE' with df = 2.62715767546228

 tCopEst
#Call: fitCopula(copula, data = data, method = "mpl", estimate.variance = TRUE)
#Fit based on "maximum pseudo-likelihood" and 1257 2-dimensional observations.
#Copula: tCopula
```

```
# rho.1     df
#0.6828 2.6272
#The maximized loglikelihood is 468.9
#Optimization converged

 # Set a temporary variable for the estimated rho
 Temp<-coef(tCopEst)

 # Adjusted rho
 Adj.tRho<-Temp[[1]]
 Adj.tRho
#[1] 0.6827558

 # Adjusted degree of freedom
 Adj.t.df<-Temp[[2]]
 Adj.t.df
#[1] 2.627158
 logLik(tCopEst) # value of the likelihood function
#'log Lik.' 468.8706 (df=2)

 AIC(tCopEst) #AIC value
#[1] -933.7413

 BIC(tCopEst) #BIC value
#[1] -923.4683

 # Adjusted t-Student copula
 tCop <- tCopula(Adj.tRho, dim = 2, dispstr="un", df=Adj.t.df)
 tCop
#t-copula, dim. d = 2
#Dimension:  2
#Parameters:
#  rho.1    = 0.6827558
#  df       = 2.6271577

 # Shows that the dependency on the tails is symmetric
 TailDep<-tailIndex(tCop)
 TailDep
#    lower     upper
#0.4591901 0.4591901

##########################
 # Gumbel copula
 GumbCop <- gumbelCopula(ParGum, dim =2)
 GumbCop
#Gumbel copula, dim. d = 2
#Dimension:  2
#Parameters:
#  alpha    = 1.918133
```

```
 GumbCopEst<-fitCopula(GumbCop,Udata, method="mpl")
 GumbCopEst
#Call: fitCopula(copula, data = data, method = "mpl")
#Fit based on "maximum pseudo-likelihood" and 1257 2-dimensional observations.
#Copula: gumbelCopula
#alpha
#1.893
#The maximized loglikelihood is 395
#Optimization converged

 # Set a temporary variable for the estimated alpha
 Temp<-coef(GumbCopEst)

 # Adjusted alpha
 Adj.G.alpha<-Temp[[1]]

 logLik(GumbCopEst) # value of the likelihood function
#'log Lik.' 395.0009 (df=1)

 AIC(GumbCopEst) #AIC value
#[1] -788.0018

 BIC(GumbCopEst) #BIC value
#[1] -782.8653

 # Adjusted Gumbel copula
 GumbCop <- gumbelCopula(Adj.G.alpha, dim =2)
 GumbCop
#Gumbel copula, dim. d = 2
#Dimension:  2
#Parameters:
#  alpha   = 1.893063

 # Shows dependency on the right tail
 TailDep<-tailIndex(GumbCop)
 TailDep
#    lower     upper
#0.0000000 0.5578268

############################
 # Clayton copula
 ClayCop<- claytonCopula(param =ParClay, dim = 2)
 ClayCop
#Clayton copula, dim. d = 2
#Dimension:  2
#Parameters:
#  alpha   = 1.836265

 ClayCopEst<-fitCopula(ClayCop,Udata, method="mpl")
 ClayCopEst
```

```
#Call: fitCopula(copula, data = data, method = "mpl")
#Fit based on "maximum pseudo-likelihood" and 1257 2-dimensional observations.
#Copula: claytonCopula
#alpha
#1.535
#The maximized loglikelihood is 393.4
#Optimization converged

 # Set a temporary variable for the estimated alpha
 Temp<-coef(ClayCopEst)
 # Adjusted alpha
 Adj.C.alpha<-Temp[[1]]
 logLik(ClayCopEst) # value of the likelihood function
#'log Lik.' 393.4172 (df=1)

 AIC(ClayCopEst) #AIC value
#[1] -784.8343

 BIC(ClayCopEst) #BIC value
#[1] -779.6978

 # Adjusted Clayton copula
 ClayCop<- claytonCopula(Adj.C.alpha, dim = 2)
 ClayCop
#Clayton copula, dim. d = 2
#Dimension:  2
#Parameters:
#  alpha   = 1.534542

 # Shows dependency on the left tail
 TailDep<-tailIndex(ClayCop)
 TailDep
#    lower     upper
#0.6365473 0.0000000

 ############################
 # Frank copula
 #We set rho = NA_real_  as we don't know it
 FrankCop<-frankCopula(param = NA_real_, dim = 2)
 FrankCop
#Frank copula, dim. d = 2
#Dimension:  2
#Parameters:
#  alpha   = NA

 FrankCopEst<-fitCopula(FrankCop,Udata,method="mpl")
 FrankCopEst
#Call: fitCopula(copula, data = data, method = "mpl")
#Fit based on "maximum pseudo-likelihood" and 1257 2-dimensional observations.
#Copula: frankCopula
```

```
#alpha
#5.471
#The maximized loglikelihood is 359.8
#Optimization converged

 # Set a temporary variable for the estimated alpha
 Temp<-coef(FrankCopEst)
 # Adjusted alpha
 Adj.F.alpha<-Temp[[1]]
 logLik(FrankCopEst) # value of the likelihood function
#'log Lik.' 359.7813 (df=1)

 AIC(FrankCopEst) #AIC value
#[1] -717.5627

 BIC(FrankCopEst) #BIC value
#[1] -712.4262

 # Adjusted Clayton copula
 FrankCop<-frankCopula(Adj.F.alpha, dim = 2)
 FrankCop
#Frank copula, dim. d = 2
#Dimension:  2
#Parameters:
#  alpha    = 5.470527

# Shows that there is no dependency on the tails
 TailDep<-tailIndex(FrankCop)
 TailDep
#lower upper
#    0     0
```

A.2.2.3 *R Code 15*

Compare between Gaussian, t-Student, Gumbel, Clayton and Frank for deciding which distribution suits best.

```
# (2) Comparison to check which model is the best
 AIC(NormCopEst)
#[1] -788.2375

 AIC(tCopEst)
#[1] -933.7413

 AIC(GumbCopEst)
#[1] -788.0018

AIC(ClayCopEst)
#[1] -784.8343
```

```
 AIC(FrankCopEst)
#[1] -717.5627

 BIC(NormCopEst)
#[1] -783.101

 BIC(tCopEst)
#[1] -923.4683

 BIC(GumbCopEst)
#[1] -782.8653

 BIC(ClayCopEst)
#[1] -779.6978

 BIC(FrankCopEst)
#[1] -712.4262
```

A.2.2.4 *R Code 16*

Estimate the Gaussian, *t*-Student, Gumbel, Clayton and Frank marginals.

```
 # Fit Gauss distribution for Bond A
 mod.GaussBondA <- fitdistr(BondRet[,1], "normal")
 mod.GaussBondA
#       mean             sd
#  0.0013633001   0.0190526395
# (0.0005373874) (0.0003799903)

 AIC(mod.GaussBondA) #AIC value for Bond A
#[1] -6385.61

 BIC(mod.GaussBondA) #BIC value for Bond A
#[1] -6375.337

 # Fit Gauss distribution for Bond B
 mod.GaussBondB <- fitdistr(BondRet[,2], "normal")
 mod.GaussBondB
#       mean             sd
#  0.0013122514   0.0171898455
# (0.0004848466) (0.0003428383)

 AIC(mod.GaussBondB) #AIC value for Bond B
#[1] -6644.268

 BIC(mod.GaussBondB) #BIC value for Bond B
#[1] -6633.995

# Fit t-Student distribution for Bond A
```

```
 mod.tBondA <- fitdistr(BondRet[,1], "t")
 mod.tBondA
#        m               s               df
#  0.0016503583   0.0113570954   2.7436875545
# (0.0003944037) (0.0004392449) (0.2558217321)

 # Bond A t-Student degree of freedom
 df.tBondA=d=mod.tBondA$estimate[[3:3]]
 AIC(mod.tBondA) #AIC value for Bond A
#[1] -6713.191

 BIC(mod.tBondA) #BIC value for Bond A
#[1] -6697.782

# Fit t-Student distribution for Bond B
mod.tBondB <- fitdistr(BondRet[,2], "t")
mod.tBondB

#        m               s               df
#  0.0015909254   0.0099198333   2.7084493917
# (0.0003462182) (0.0003729750) (0.2442727866)

# Bond B t-Student degree of freedom
 df.tBondB=d=mod.tBondB$estimate[[3:3]]
 AIC(mod.tBondB) #AIC value for Bond B
#[1] -7035.85

 BIC(mod.tBondB) #BIC value for Bond B
#[1] -7020.44
```

A.2.2.5 *R Code 17*

Risk estimation with Monte Carlo — Step 1: Set the seed, the number of simulations and generate them according to the chosen model.

```
 set.seed(123) # Set the seed
 N <-100000 # Number of simulated observations

 #############################
 # Gauss copula #
 # Model the class with previously calculated parameters
 GaussianClass <- normalCopula(param = Rho, dim = 2, dispstr = "un")
 # Monte Carlo simulations
 GaussianSims<-rCopula(N,GaussianClass)# Valores simulados

 #############################
 # t-Student copula #
 # Model the class with previously calculated parameters
 tStudentClass <- tCopula(Rho, dim = 2, dispstr = "un", df=Adj.t.df)
```

```
# Monte Carlo simulations
tStudentSims<-rCopula(N,tStudentClass)

##########################
# Gumbel copula  #
# Model the class with previously calculated parameters
GumbelClass<- gumbelCopula(dim =2,  param=Adj.G.alpha)
# Monte Carlo simulations
GumbelSims <- rCopula(N, GumbelClass)

##############################
# Clayton copula#
# Model the class with previously calculated parameters
ClayClass<- claytonCopula(param=Adj.G.alpha, dim = 2)
# Monte Carlo simulations
ClaySims<-rCopula(N,ClayClass)

############################
# Frank copula #
# Model the class with previously calculated parameters
FrankClass<- frankCopula(param = Adj.F.alpha, dim = 2)
# Monte Carlo simulations
FrankSims<-rCopula(N,FrankClass)
```

A.2.2.6 *R Code 18*

Risk estimation with Monte Carlo — Step 2: Define the confidence levels for the VaR.

```
#Set the confidence levels for the VaR
alfa <- c(0.99, 0.995,0.999)
w    <- cbind(1,1) #Risk weights
```

A.2.2.7 *R Code 19*

Risk estimation with Monte Carlo — Step 3: Compute Gaussian copula with Gaussian or t-Student marginals.

```
# GAUSSIAN COPULA with Gaussian or t-Student marginals #

 ### Gaussian marginals ###
 NCop.NMar.BondA <- qnorm(GaussianSims[,1],
mean=mod.GaussBondA$estimate[[1]], sd=mod.GaussBondA$estimate[[2]])
 NCop.NMar.BondB <- qnorm(GaussianSims[,2],
mean=mod.GaussBondB$estimate[[1]], sd=mod.GaussBondB$estimate[[2]])
 MC.data<-cbind(NCop.NMar.BondA, NCop.NMar.BondB)
 MC.Lsim <- (MC.data%*%t(w))
 #VaR
```

```
 quantile(MC.Lsim, alfa)
#       99%       99.5%       99.9%
#0.08150790 0.08944187 0.10594444

 #TVaR
 mean(MC.Lsim[MC.Lsim > quantile(MC.Lsim, alfa[1])])
#[1] 0.09260714

 mean(MC.Lsim[MC.Lsim > quantile(MC.Lsim, alfa[2])])
#[1] 0.1001398

 mean(MC.Lsim[MC.Lsim > quantile(MC.Lsim, alfa[3])])
#[1] 0.1166357

 cbind(mean(MC.Lsim[MC.Lsim > quantile(MC.Lsim, alfa[1])]),
mean(MC.Lsim[MC.Lsim > quantile(MC.Lsim, alfa[2])]),
mean(MC.Lsim[MC.Lsim > quantile(MC.Lsim, alfa[3])]))
#           [,1]      [,2]      [,3]
#[1,] 0.09260714 0.1001398 0.1166357

 ###  t-Student marginals ###
 NCop.tMar.BondA <- qst(GaussianSims[,1], mu=mod.tBondA$estimate[[1]],
sd=mod.tBondA$estimate[[2]],mod.tBondA$estimate[[3]])
 NCop.tMar.BondB <- qst(GaussianSims[,2], mu=mod.tBondB$estimate[[1]],
sd=mod.tBondB$estimate[[2]],mod.tBondB$estimate[[3]])
 MC.data<-cbind(NCop.tMar.BondA, NCop.tMar.BondB)
 MC.Lsim <- -(MC.data%*%t(w))
 #VaR
 quantile(MC.Lsim, alfa)
#       99%       99.5%       99.9%
#-1.1013261 -0.6527974  0.2929686

 #TVaR
 mean(MC.Lsim[MC.Lsim > quantile(MC.Lsim, alfa[1])])
#[1] -0.4731917

 mean(MC.Lsim[MC.Lsim > quantile(MC.Lsim, alfa[2])])
#[1] -0.05252179

 mean(MC.Lsim[MC.Lsim > quantile(MC.Lsim, alfa[3])])
#[1] 0.8745323

 cbind(mean(MC.Lsim[MC.Lsim > quantile(MC.Lsim, alfa[1])]),
mean(MC.Lsim[MC.Lsim > quantile(MC.Lsim, alfa[2])]),
mean(MC.Lsim[MC.Lsim > quantile(MC.Lsim, alfa[3])]))

#           [,1]        [,2]      [,3]
#[1,] -0.4731917 -0.05252179 0.8745323
```

A.2.2.8 *R Code 20*

Risk estimation with Monte Carlo — Step 4: Compute t-Student copula with Gaussian or t-Student marginals.

```
 # t-STUDENT COPULA with Gaussian or t-Student marginals#
 ### Gaussian marginals ###
 tCop.NMar.BondA <- qnorm(tStudentSims[,1],
mean=mod.GaussBondA$estimate[[1]],
sd=mod.GaussBondB$estimate[[2]])
 tCop.NMar.BondB <- qnorm(tStudentSims[,2],
mean=mod.GaussBondB$estimate[[1]],
sd=mod.GaussBondB$estimate[[2]])
 MC.data<-cbind(tCop.NMar.BondA, tCop.NMar.BondB)
 MC.Lsim <- -(MC.data%*%t(w))
 #VaR
 quantile(MC.Lsim, alfa)
#       99%      99.5%      99.9%
#0.0743550 0.0832773 0.1016548

 #TVaR
 mean(MC.Lsim[MC.Lsim > quantile(MC.Lsim, alfa[1])])
#[1] 0.0863761

 mean(MC.Lsim[MC.Lsim > quantile(MC.Lsim, alfa[2])])
#[1] 0.09432545

 mean(MC.Lsim[MC.Lsim > quantile(MC.Lsim, alfa[3])])
#[1] 0.1099356
 cbind(mean(MC.Lsim[MC.Lsim > quantile(MC.Lsim, alfa[1])]),
 mean(MC.Lsim[MC.Lsim > quantile(MC.Lsim, alfa[2])]),
 mean(MC.Lsim[MC.Lsim > quantile(MC.Lsim, alfa[3])]))

#          [,1]       [,2]      [,3]
#[1,] 0.0863761 0.09432545 0.1099356

 ### t-Student marginals  ###
 tCop.tMar.BondA <- qst(tStudentSims[,1],
mu=mod.tBondA$estimate[[1]],
sd=mod.tBondA$estimate[[2]],mod.tBondA$estimate[[3]])
 tCop.tMar.BondB <- qst(tStudentSims[,2],
mu=mod.tBondB$estimate[[1]],
sd=mod.tBondB$estimate[[2]],mod.tBondB$estimate[[3]])
 MC.data<-cbind(tCop.tMar.BondA, tCop.tMar.BondA)
 MC.Lsim <- -(MC.data%*%t(w))
 #VaR
 quantile(MC.Lsim, alfa)
#        99%        99.5%        99.9%
#-0.7875839 -0.2611348  0.7217623
```

```
#TVaR
 mean(MC.Lsim[MC.Lsim > quantile(MC.Lsim, alfa[1])])
#[1] -0.0980873

 mean(MC.Lsim[MC.Lsim > quantile(MC.Lsim, alfa[2])])
#[1] 0.3524529

 mean(MC.Lsim[MC.Lsim > quantile(MC.Lsim, alfa[3])])
#[1] 1.217587

 cbind(mean(MC.Lsim[MC.Lsim > quantile(MC.Lsim, alfa[1])]),
 mean(MC.Lsim[MC.Lsim > quantile(MC.Lsim, alfa[2])]),
 mean(MC.Lsim[MC.Lsim > quantile(MC.Lsim, alfa[3])]))

#           [,1]      [,2]     [,3]
#[1,] -0.0980873 0.3524529 1.217587
```

A.2.2.9 *R Code 21*

Risk estimation with Monte Carlo — Step 5: Compute Gumbel copula with Gaussian or *t*-Student marginals.

```
 # GUMBEL COPULA with Gaussian or t-Student marginals#
 ### Gaussian marginals ###
 GCop.NMar.BondA <- qnorm(GumbelSims[,1],
mean=mod.GaussBondA$estimate[[1]],
sd=mod.GaussBondA$estimate[[2]])
 GCop.NMar.BondB <- qnorm(GumbelSims[,2],
mean=mod.GaussBondB$estimate[[1]],
sd=mod.GaussBondB$estimate[[2]])
 MC.data<-cbind(GCop.NMar.BondA, GCop.NMar.BondB)
 MC.Lsim <- -(MC.data%*%t(w))
 #VaR
 quantile(MC.Lsim, alfa)
#        99%       99.5%      99.9%
#0.07071086 0.07826476 0.09375264

 #TVaR
 mean(MC.Lsim[MC.Lsim > quantile(MC.Lsim, alfa[1])])
#[1] 0.08104886

 mean(MC.Lsim[MC.Lsim > quantile(MC.Lsim, alfa[2])])
#[1] 0.08786275

 mean(MC.Lsim[MC.Lsim > quantile(MC.Lsim, alfa[3])])
#[1] 0.1015494

 cbind(mean(MC.Lsim[MC.Lsim > quantile(MC.Lsim, alfa[1])]),
mean(MC.Lsim[MC.Lsim > quantile(MC.Lsim, alfa[2])]),
```

```
mean(MC.Lsim[MC.Lsim > quantile(MC.Lsim, alfa[3])]))
#           [,1]       [,2]      [,3]
#[1,] 0.08104886 0.08786275 0.1015494

 ###  t-Student marginals ###
 GCop.tMar.BondA <- qst(GumbelSims[,1],
mu=mod.tBondA$estimate[[1]],
sd=mod.tBondA$estimate[[2]],mod.tBondA$estimate[[3]])
 GCop.tMar.BondB <- qst(GumbelSims[,2], mu=mod.tBondB$estimate[[1]],
sd=mod.tBondB$estimate[[2]],mod.tBondB$estimate[[3]])
 MC.data<-cbind(GCop.tMar.BondA, GCop.tMar.BondB)
 MC.Lsim <- -(MC.data%*%t(w))
 #VaR
 quantile(MC.Lsim, alfa)
#         99%        99.5%        99.9%
#-1.40261318 -0.98595282 -0.09772017
 #TVaR
 mean(MC.Lsim[MC.Lsim > quantile(MC.Lsim, alfa[1])])
#[1] -0.8365666
 mean(MC.Lsim[MC.Lsim > quantile(MC.Lsim, alfa[2])])
#[1] -0.4607118
 mean(MC.Lsim[MC.Lsim > quantile(MC.Lsim, alfa[3])])
#[1] 0.2901774
 cbind(mean(MC.Lsim[MC.Lsim > quantile(MC.Lsim, alfa[1])]),
mean(MC.Lsim[MC.Lsim > quantile(MC.Lsim, alfa[2])]),
mean(MC.Lsim[MC.Lsim > quantile(MC.Lsim, alfa[3])]))
#           [,1]       [,2]      [,3]
#[1,] -0.8365666 -0.4607118 0.2901774
```

A.2.2.10 *R Code 22*

Risk estimation with Monte Carlo — Step 6: Compute Clayton copula with Gaussian or t-Student marginals.

```
 # CLAYTON COPULA with Gaussian or t-Student marginals#
 ### Gaussian marginals ###
 CCop.NMar.BondA <- qnorm(ClaySims[,1],
mean=mod.GaussBondA$estimate[[1]],
sd=mod.GaussBondA$estimate[[2]])
 CCop.NMar.BondB <- qnorm(ClaySims[,2],
mean=mod.GaussBondB$estimate[[1]],
sd=mod.GaussBondB$estimate[[2]])
 MC.data<-cbind(CCop.NMar.BondA, CCop.NMar.BondB)
 MC.Lsim <- -(MC.data%*%t(w))
 #VaR
 quantile(MC.Lsim, alfa)
#       99%       99.5%       99.9%
#0.08002347 0.08945214 0.10609942
```

```
 #TVaR
 mean(MC.Lsim[MC.Lsim > quantile(MC.Lsim, alfa[1])])
#[1] 0.09221016
 mean(MC.Lsim[MC.Lsim > quantile(MC.Lsim, alfa[2])])
#[1] 0.1003122
 mean(MC.Lsim[MC.Lsim > quantile(MC.Lsim, alfa[3])])
#[1] 0.1170484
 cbind(mean(MC.Lsim[MC.Lsim > quantile(MC.Lsim, alfa[1])]),
mean(MC.Lsim[MC.Lsim > quantile(MC.Lsim, alfa[2])]),
mean(MC.Lsim[MC.Lsim > quantile(MC.Lsim, alfa[3])]))
#            [,1]      [,2]      [,3]
#[1,] 0.09221016 0.1003122 0.1170484

 ### t-Student  marginals ###
 CCop.tMar.BondA <- qst(ClaySims[,1],
mu=mod.tBondA$estimate[[1]],
sd=mod.tBondA$estimate[[2]],mod.tBondA$estimate[[3]])
 CCop.tMar.BondB <- qst(ClaySims[,2],
mu=mod.tBondB$estimate[[1]],
sd=mod.tBondB$estimate[[2]],mod.tBondB$estimate[[3]])
 MC.data<-cbind(CCop.tMar.BondA, CCop.tMar.BondB)
 MC.Lsim <- -(MC.data%*%t(w))
 #VaR
 quantile(MC.Lsim, alfa)
#       99%       99.5%       99.9%
#-0.8838350 -0.3735570  0.5508596

 #TVaR
 mean(MC.Lsim[MC.Lsim > quantile(MC.Lsim, alfa[1])])
#[1] -0.2153008
 mean(MC.Lsim[MC.Lsim > quantile(MC.Lsim, alfa[2])])
#[1] 0.2314888
 mean(MC.Lsim[MC.Lsim > quantile(MC.Lsim, alfa[3])])
#[1] 1.154052
 cbind(mean(MC.Lsim[MC.Lsim > quantile(MC.Lsim, alfa[1])]),
mean(MC.Lsim[MC.Lsim > quantile(MC.Lsim, alfa[2])]),
mean(MC.Lsim[MC.Lsim > quantile(MC.Lsim, alfa[3])]))
#            [,1]      [,2]      [,3]
#[1,] -0.2153008 0.2314888 1.154052
```

A.2.2.11 *R Code 23*

Risk estimation with Monte Carlo — Step 7: Compute Frank copula with Gaussian or t-Student marginals.

```
 # FRANK COPULA with Gaussian or t-Student marginals#
 ### Gaussian marginals ###
 FCop.NMar.BondA <- qnorm(FrankSims[,1],
mean=mod.GaussBondA$estimate[[1]],
```

```
sd=mod.GaussBondA$estimate[[2]])
 FCop.NMar.BondB <- qnorm(FrankSims[,2],
mean=mod.GaussBondB$estimate[[1]],
sd=mod.GaussBondB$estimate[[2]])
 MC.data<-cbind(FCop.NMar.BondA, FCop.NMar.BondB)
 MC.Lsim <- -(MC.data%*%t(w))
 #VaR
 quantile(MC.Lsim, alfa)
#       99%       99.5%      99.9%
#0.06863424 0.07508546 0.08763351

 #TVaR
 mean(MC.Lsim[MC.Lsim > quantile(MC.Lsim, alfa[1])])
#[1] 0.07728757
 mean(MC.Lsim[MC.Lsim > quantile(MC.Lsim, alfa[2])])
#[1] 0.08297538
 mean(MC.Lsim[MC.Lsim > quantile(MC.Lsim, alfa[3])])
#[1] 0.09425219
 cbind(mean(MC.Lsim[MC.Lsim > quantile(MC.Lsim,
alfa[1])]),mean(MC.Lsim[MC.Lsim > quantile(MC.Lsim,
alfa[2])]),mean(MC.Lsim[MC.Lsim > quantile(MC.Lsim,
alfa[3])]))
#            [,1]        [,2]        [,3]
#[1,] 0.07728757 0.08297538 0.09425219
 ### t-Student  marginals ###
 FCop.tMar.BondA <- qst(FrankSims[,1],
mu=mod.tBondA$estimate[[1]],
sd=mod.tBondA$estimate[[2]],mod.tBondA$estimate[[3]])
 FCop.tMar.BondB <- qst(FrankSims[,2],
mu=mod.tBondB$estimate[[1]],
sd=mod.tBondB$estimate[[2]],mod.tBondB$estimate[[3]])
 MC.data<-cbind(FCop.tMar.BondA, FCop.tMar.BondB)
 MC.Lsim <- -(MC.data%*%t(w))
 #VaR
 quantile(MC.Lsim, alfa)
#       99%       99.5%      99.9%
#-1.5232170 -1.1664677 -0.4653194

 #TVaR
 mean(MC.Lsim[MC.Lsim > quantile(MC.Lsim, alfa[1])])
#[1] -1.042933

 mean(MC.Lsim[MC.Lsim > quantile(MC.Lsim, alfa[2])])
#[1] -0.7273797

 mean(MC.Lsim[MC.Lsim > quantile(MC.Lsim, alfa[3])])
#[1] -0.09612818
```

```
 cbind(mean(MC.Lsim[MC.Lsim > quantile(MC.Lsim, alfa[1])]),
 mean(MC.Lsim[MC.Lsim > quantile(MC.Lsim, alfa[2])]),
mean(MC.Lsim[MC.Lsim > quantile(MC.Lsim, alfa[3])]))
#           [,1]       [,2]        [,3]
#[1,] -1.042933 -0.7273797 -0.09612818
```

Appendix B

Financial Engineering: Coding in Matlab

This appendix is meant to provide some examples and the related code in Matlab to help the reader in learning the concepts exposed in the book.

B.1 Asymptotic Single Risk Factor (ASRF) Model

Value-at-Risk (VaR) is widely used in finance to measure the worst loss given a confidence level within a time horizon. For example, in credit risk, the Asymptotic Single Risk Factor (ASRF) model by [Vasicek (1991)] is used to set the minimum bank regulatory capital standards and related to the credit VaR under the Basel II Internal Ratings-Based (IRB) approach. For more details, please, refer to Section 5.1.

B.1.1 *Matlab Code for the ASRF Model in Chapter 5*

Load the matrix of data in Table B.1.

Table B.1: Credit data.

EAD	PD	LGD	M
26.60	0.015	0.350	0.500
30.25	0.060	0.450	2.500
20.40	0.110	0.550	1.500
38.75	0.025	0.350	3.000
55.70	0.065	0.750	5.500

```
%Compute asset correlation

Rho = 0.12 * (1-exp(-50*PD)) / (1-exp(-50)) +...
    0.24 * (1 - (1-exp(-50*PD)) / (1-exp(-50)));

%Compute the asymptotic single risk factor capital.
```

```
Capital = asrf(PD,LGD,Rho,'EAD',EAD);

%Apply maturity and PD adjustment.
B = (0.11852 - 0.05478 * log(PD)).^2;

MatAdj = (1 + (M - 2.5) .* B) ./ (1 - 1.5 * B);

%Compute the adjusted capital for each asset.

AdjCapital = Capital .* MatAdj;

%Compute the sum of the adjusted capital at portfolio level.

PortfolioCapital = sum(AdjCapital)

%PortfolioCapital = 26.8781
```

B.2 Matlab Code for Chapter 15

The purpose of this code is to illustrate some applications of the CreditRisk + for portfolio with given exposures.

The dataset is available at `http://www.csfb.com`.

The first three examples are based upon a portfolio made up of 25 counterparties with different exposures, while the fourth example contemplates just two counterparties. More specifically, the four examples contain the following features:

- Each counterparty has the same (constant) default probability;
- All the counterparties belong to one of the two sectors. In this way, the sectors are the countries, i.e. *USA* and *Europe*. In other words, we are assuming each counterparty is subjected only to one systemic risk factor, which is responsible for the default probabilities variation;
- Counterparties are influenced by two sectors. In this way, the sectors are still the countries. We assume each counterparty *PD* is driven by more risk factors, which cause the default probabilities variation;
- Counterparties are classified according to both the rating and the country, which represent the sectors. In particular, we consider the ratings *AAA*, *BBB*, and the countries: *USA*, *Europe*. For convenience, we assume the first counterparty is focused on *AAA-USA*, while the second on

B.2.1 *Matlab Code 1*

```
% Consider a portfolio consisting of 25 counterparties
% with constant default probabilities.

clear
clc
```

```
% Input
E=xlsread('data.xlsx','A2:A26');
% Default probability of each counterparty
PD=xlsread('data.xlsx','B2:B26');
% Data initialization
l=length(E);
% Probability distribution of the default occurrences
n=PD'*ones(l,1);
k=0:l;% number of possible defaults, which belong to [0,g]
P=exp(-n)*n.^k./factorial(k);
figure(1)
bar(k,P)
title('Default probability distribution')
xlabel('Default occurrences (k)')
ylabel('Probability P(k)')

% Splitting the counterparties into exposure bands
% Choice of the unitary exposure
 L=1000000;
% Computation of the exposures nu(i)=E(i)/L
 nu=E/L;
% Exposures approximation

nu1=ceil(nu);
% Number of bands
 m=max(nu1);
% expected losses: eps(i)=E(i)*PD(i)/L
 eps=E.*PD/L;
% Computation of mu(i) by the amount of expected defaults in the i-th band
M=zeros(m,l);
for i=1:m
    for j=1:l
        if nu1(j)==i
            M(i,j)=1;
        end
    end
end
mu=M*PD;
% Computation of the expected losses for each band
% Eps(i)=mu(i)*nu1(i)
band=1:m;
Eps=mu'.*banda;
% PGF of the portfolio losses
syms z
a=mu'.*(z.^banda-1);
esp=a*ones(m,1);
GL=exp(esp); % Losses generating function

j=0:m;
% Factorials
```

```
fact=1./factorial(j);
% Derivatives of GL at point 0
A=sym(zeros(1,m+1));
C=sym(zeros(1,m+1));
A(1)=GL;
C(1)=subs(A(1),z,0); % GL evaluated at z=0

for i=2:m+1
     A(i)=diff(A(i-1),z,1);% first derivative of A(i-1)
     C(i)=subs(A(i),z,0);% A(i) evaluated at z=0
end
GLdiff0=eval(C); % Derivates array of GL evaluated at z=0
% Expected losses probability distribution
Ltilde=fact.*GLdiff0; % Loss probability
% for any k=0:l
figure(2)
bar(j*L,Ltilde)
title('Expected losses distribution')
xlabel('Losses ($)')
```

B.2.2 *Matlab Code 2*

```
% Consider a portfolio consisting of 25 counterparties
% which are focused into the same sector

% Input
% Exposures
E=xlsread('data.xlsx','A2:A26');
l=length(E);
% default probabilities
PD=xlsread('data.xlsx','B2:B26');
% Weights
w=xlsread('data.xlsx','D2:D26');
% Standard deviation of PD
S=PD/sum(PD);
sigma=S*std(PD);

% Specification of lambda_s and sigma_s
lambda_s=PD'*w;
sigma_s=sigma'*w;
% Specification of the Gamma distribution parameters alpha and beta
alpha=lambda_s^2/sigma_s^2;
beta=sigma_s^2/lambda_s;
% Let p=beta/1+beta
p_s=beta/(1+beta);

% Splitting the counterparties into exposure bands
% Choice of the unitary exposure
L=1000000;
```

```
% Computation of the exposures  nu(i)=E(i)/L
nu=E/L;
% Expected losses eps(i)=E(i)*PD(i)/L
eps=E.*PD/L;
% Exposures approximation nu(i)
% band size: 1
nu1=zeros(1,l);
for j=0:l
        for i=1:l
        if (j<nu(i)) && (nu(i)<= j+1)
            nu1(i)=j+1;
        end
        end
end
% Compute mu(i) by the sum of the PD's of the debtors staying in the i-th band
m=max(nu1);
M=zeros(m,l);
for i=1:m
    for j=1:l
        if nu1(j)==i
            M(i,j)=1;
        else
            M(i,j)=0;
        end
    end
end
mu=M*PD;
band=1:m;
% Computation of the expected losses for each band
Eps=mu'.*band;

% GMF of the portfolio losses
a=Eps./band;
syms z
b=a*(z.^band)';
GLtilde=((1-p_s)/(1-(p_s/lambda_s)*b))^alpha; % Generating function

% Probability distribution function of the portfolio losses
e=z.^(banda-1);
f=z.^banda;
% Polynomials setting
A=(p_s*alpha/lambda_s)*(e*Eps');
B=1-((p_s/lambda_s)*(f*mu));
c=coeffs(A,'All');
c=fliplr(c);   % Polynomial A - coefficients rearrangement
d=coeffs(B,'All');
d=fliplr(d);  % Polynomial B - coefficients rearrangement
z=1:length(c);
U=1./(z*d(1));
%
```

```
%
R=zeros(1,length(c));
R(1)=(1-p_s)^alpha;
S=zeros(1,length(c));
T=triu(toeplitz(R));
R(2)=U(1)*c*(T(:,1));
S(1)=R(2);
T=triu(toeplitz(R));
V=triu(toeplitz(S));
y=1:length(c);
Y=triu(toeplitz(y));
d(1)=[];
 for i=2:length(c)

     R(i+1)=U(i)*(c*T(:,i)-d*(V(:,i-1).*Y(:,i)));
     S(i)=R(i+1);
     T=triu(toeplitz(R));
     V=triu(toeplitz(S));
 end
 k=0:length(c);
 bar(k*L,R)
 title('Expected losses distribution')
 xlabel('Losses ($)')
```

B.3 Matlab Code for Chapter 16

B.3.1 *Matlab Code 3*

```
% Consider a portfolio consisting of 25 counterparties
% which are entirely focused in one of the two sectors
% The sectors are the countries USA and Europe
clear
clc
% Input
% Exposures
E=xlsread('dat.xlsx','A2:A26');
l=length(E); % Counterparties amount
% Counterparties default probabilities
PD1=xlsread('dat.xlsx','B2:B26');
PD2=xlsread('dat.xlsx','C2:C26');
PD=[PD1 PD2];
% Weights
w1=xlsread('dat.xlsx','G2:G26');
w2=xlsread('dat.xlsx','H2:H26');
w=[w1 w2];
% Standard deviations
s=size(PD,2);
S=sum(PD,1);
B=zeros(1,s);
```

```
sigma=zeros(1,s);
for j=1:s
    B(:,j)=PD(:,j)/S(j);
    sigma(:,j)=B(:,j)*std(PD(:,j));
end
% lambda_s and sigma_s
lambda_s=zeros(1,s);
sigma_s=zeros(1,s);

for j=1:s
    lambda_s(j)=PD(:,j)'*w(:,j);
    sigma_s(j)=sigma(:,j)'*w(:,j);
 end
% Parameters alpha_s and beta_s
alpha_s=lambda_s.^2./sigma_s.^2;
beta_s=sigma_s.^2./lambda_s;
p_s=beta_s./(1+beta_s);

% GMF of L
syms z
GL_s=((1-p_s)./(1-p_s*z)).^alpha_s;
GL=prod(GL_s); % Generating function of L
% Splitting into counterparty bands
% Choice of the unitary exposure
L=1000000;
% Exposures nu(i)=E(i)/L
nu=E/L;
% Exposures approximation
nu1=zeros(1,l);
for j=0:l
        for i=1:l
        if (j<nu(i)) && (nu(i)<= j+1)
            nu1(i)=j+1;
        end
        end
end

m=max(nu1);
M=zeros(m,l);
for i=1:m
    for j=1:l
        if nu1(j)==i
            M(i,j)=1;
        else
            M(i,j)=0;
        end
    end
end
% Expected losses
eps=zeros(1,s);
```

```
for j=1:s
eps(:,j)=E.*PD(:,j)/L;
end

% Probability distribution of portfolio losses
t_s=(p_s.*alpha_s)./lambda_s;
d_s=p_s./lambda_s;

band=1:m;
z1=z.^(band-1);
z2=z.^band;
AA=M*(w.*eps);
BB=M*(w.*PD);

for i=1:s
    A1(i)=z1*AA(:,i);
    B1(i)=z2*BB(:,i);

end

N=t_s.*A1;
D=1-d_s.*B1;

[NN,DD]=numden(sum(N./D));
c=fliplr(coeffs(NN,'All'));% Polynomial NN - sorted coefficients
d=fliplr(coeffs(DD,'All')); % Polynomial DD - sorted coefficients
z3=1:length(c);
U=1./(z3*d(1));

% Initialization
R=zeros(1,length(c));
R(1)=prod((1-p_s).^alpha_s);
S=zeros(1,length(c));
T=triu(toeplitz(R));
R(2)=U(1)*c*(T(:,1));
S(1)=R(2);
T=triu(toeplitz(R));
V=triu(toeplitz(S));
y=1:length(c);
Y=triu(toeplitz(y));
d(1)=[];
 for i=2:length(c)
     % Loss probability of amount (i+1)*L
     R(i+1)=U(i)*(c*T(:,i)-d*(V(:,i-1).*Y(:,i)));
     S(i)=R(i+1);
     T=triu(toeplitz(R));
     V=triu(toeplitz(S));
 end
% Plot of expected losses distribution
 k=0:length(c);
```

```
bar(k*L,R)
title('Expected losses distribution')
xlabel('Losses ($)')
```

B.3.2 *Matlab Code 4*

```
% Consider a portfolio consisting of 2 counterparties
% Assume each counterparty is classified according both to the rating and the country
% The ratings are AAA and BBB
% The countries are USA and Europe.

clear all
clc

% Input
% Exposures
E=[100,200]; % Total exposure=300;
% Matrix of counterparty weights for any sector
WS1=[1 0;0 0];
WS2=[0 1;0 0];
W=[WS1; WS2];
% Exposures weights
w=[1/3 2/3];
% Default probabilities
PD1=[0.2 0.4;0.3 0.6];
% Weighted default probabilities
PD=[w(1)*PD1; w(2)*PD1];
% Standard deviations
sgmaPD1=sqrt(PD1);
% Weighted standard deviations
sgmaPD=[w(1)*sgmaPD1; w(2)*sgmaPD1];

% Sector risks
lambda=sum(PD.*W,1);
sigma=sum(sgmaPD.*W,1);

% Parameters alpha and beta
alpha=lambda.^2./sigma.^2;
beta=sigma.^2./lambda;
p=beta./(1+beta);
% Choice the unitary exposure
L=100;
l=length(E);
% Splitting the counterparties into bands
nu=E./L;
nu1=zeros(1,l);
for j=0:l
        for i=1:l
        if (j<nu(i)) && (nu(i)<= j+1)
```

```
            nu1(i)=j+1;
        end
        end
end
m=max(nu1);
M=zeros(m,l);
for i=1:m
    for j=1:l
        if nu1(j)==i
            M(i,j)=1;
        else
            M(i,j)=0;
        end
    end
end
% Losses probability distribution
n=1-p;
u=p./lambda;
syms z
% for j=1:2
q=(PD.*W)*M;
band=1:m;
v=z.^band;
q1=size(q,1);
a=q1/m;
j=1:a:a*ceil(q1/a)+1;
i=length(j);
aa=[];
ab=[];
v=[];
b=sym(zeros(2,2));
for k=1:i-1
    ab=q(j(k):j(k+1)-1,:)*z^k;
    b(k,:)=sum(ab,1);
    v=['aa_', num2str(k)];
    vv = genvarname('v', who);
    eval([v '=ab']); % Generate a matrix series called aa_k, for any index k
end

b1=1-u.*sum(b,1);
GLi=(n./b1).^alpha;
GL=prod(GLi);  % PGF of losses
% losses distribution
GL1=diff(log(GL));
[A,B]=numden(GL1);
c=fliplr(coeffs(A,'All'));
d=fliplr(coeffs(B,'All'));
z1=1:length(c);
U=1./(z1*d(1));
```

```
R=zeros(1,length(c));
R(1)=prod((1-p).^alpha);
S=zeros(1,length(c));
T=triu(toeplitz(R));
R(2)=U(1)*c*(T(:,1));
S(1)=R(2);
T=triu(toeplitz(R));
V=triu(toeplitz(S));
y=1:length(c);
Y=triu(toeplitz(y));
d(1)=[];
for i=2:length(c)

     R(i+1)=U(i)*(c*T(:,i)-d*(V(:,i-1).*Y(:,i)));
     S(i)=R(i+1);
     T=triu(toeplitz(R));
     V=triu(toeplitz(S));
end
k=0:length(c);
bar(k*L,R)
title('Expexted losses distribution')
xlabel('Losses ($)')
```

B.4 Matlab Code for Chapter 18

B.4.1 *Code 5*

```
clear
clc
close all

% Default probabilities matrix
PD=[0.1 0.2;0.3 0.5; 0.6 0.8;0.7 0.9];
x=sort(PD); % Sorted PD
m=size(PD,2);
l=size(PD,1);
par=zeros(2,m);
y=zeros(1,m);
% Assume each PD follows a Gamma distribution and calibrate the parameters
for i=1:m
    par(:,i)=gamfit(PD(:,i)); % Estimated parameters marix
    % Theoretical CDF
    y(:,i)=cdf('gamma',x(:,i),par(1,i),par(2,i));
    % Empirical CDF versus theoretical CDF
    figure(1)
    subplot(2,1,i)
    % Plot empirical CDF
    cdfplot(x(:,i))
    title('Empirical CDF versus theoretical CDF, for the i-th sector')
```

```
    hold on
    plot(x(:,i),y(:,i)); % Plot theoretical CDF
    legend('Empirical','Theoretical','Location','NW');
end
% Theoretical approach
% Generate 1000 random numbers from a Gamma distribution with parameters
% set equal to the parameters estimated in the previous step
n=1000;
R=zeros(n,m);
for i=1:m
    R(:,i)=gamrnd(par(1,i),par(2,i),n,1); % Default events generated by
    % the above Gamma distribution
end
%
% Generate n=1000 random numbers from the Poisson distribution
% with parameters R(:,i), for any i in [1,m]
P=zeros(n,m);
for i=1:m
    P(:,i)=poissrnd(R(:,i));
    figure(2)
    subplot(2,1,i)
    plot(P(:,i))
    xlabel('Simulations number')
    ylabel('Default number')
end

% Theoretical copula
xx=P(:,1);
yy=P(:,2);
figure(5)
scatterhist(xx,yy,'Direction','out')
% Normalize the data by using the kerner estimator
u=ksdensity(xx,xx,'function','cdf');
v=ksdensity(yy,yy,'function','cdf');
figure(6)
scatterhist(u,v,'Direction','out')
xlabel('u')
ylabel('v')

% Estimate the Gaussian copula
rho=copulafit('Gaussian',[u v]); % Linear correlation matrix of
% gaussian distibution parameters
% Generate a random sample from the gaussian copula with correlation rho
r=copularnd('Gaussian',rho,1000);
u1=r(:,1);
v1=r(:,2);
figure(7)
scatterhist(u1,v1,'Direction','out')
xlabel('u')
ylabel('v')
```

```
set(get(gca,'children'),'marker','.')
% Bring back the data to their original range
xx1 = ksdensity(xx,u1,'function','icdf');
yy1 = ksdensity(yy,v1,'function','icdf');
figure(8)
scatterhist(xx1,yy1,'Direction','out')
set(get(gca,'children'),'marker','.')
% Computation of the Kendall rank correlation
tau_sample=corr([xx1,yy1],'type','kendall');
```

B.5 Matlab Code for Chapter 19

B.5.1 *Matlab Code 6*

```
function [NDP,lambda,ndp,Lambda] = CDS_Calibration(T,t,DF,LGD,R)
function [NDP,lambda,ndp,Lambda] = CDS_Calibration(T,t,DF,LGD,R)
% Calibration of a survival curve

% Input data
% T is the vector of survival curve tenors
% t is the vector of coupons payment dates
% DF is the vector of discount factors
% LGD is the loss given default
% R is the vector of CDS spreads

% Output
% NDP is the vector of survival probabilities
% lambda is the vector of intensities
% ndp is the vector of survival probabilities at coupons payment dates
% Lambda is the vector of intensities at coupons payment dates

% Computation of the day-count fraction
% (convention: LIN ACT/360, at the last payment date LIN (ACT+1)/360)

alpha=zeros(length(T)-1,length(t)-1);
for j=2:length(T)
    for i=2:length(t)
        if t(i)<T(j)
            alpha(j-1,i-1)=datenum((t(i)-t(i-1))/360);
        elseif t(i)==T(j)
            alpha(j-1,i-1)=datenum((t(i)-t(i-1)+1)/360);
        end
    end
end

% Discount factor matrix
A=zeros(length(T)-1,length(t));
for j=2:length(T)
    for i=1:length(t)
```

```
        if t(i)<=T(j)
            A(j-1,i)=DF(i);
        end
    end
end

% Matrix (DF_{i-1} + DF_{i})
B=zeros(length(T)-1,length(t)-1);
for j=2:length(T)
    for i=2:length(t)
        if t(i)<=T(j)
            B(j-1,i-1)=A(j-1,i-1)+A(j-1,i);
        end
    end
end

% Vector (T(i)-T(i-1))
TT=zeros(1,length(T)-1);
for j=1:length(T)-1
    TT(j)=datenum(T(j+1)-T(j));
end

% Matrices (t(i)-t(i-1)) and (2*T(i-1)-t(i)-t(i-1))
ZZ=zeros(length(T)-1,length(t)-1);
ZZ_sum=zeros(length(T)-1,length(t)-1);
for j=2:length(T)
    for i=2:length(t)
        if t(i)<=T(j)
            ZZ(j-1,i-1)=datenum(t(i)-t(i-1));
            ZZ_sum(j-1,i-1)=2*datenum(T(j-1)-T(1)) - datenum(t(i) -T(1))...
                - datenum(t(i-1)-T(1));
        end
    end
end

% Matrices (t(i)-t(i-1))/(T(i)-T(i-1)) and (2*T(i-1)-t(i)-t(i-1))/(T(i)-T(i-1))
CC=zeros(length(T)-1,length(t)-1);
CCC=zeros(length(T)-1,length(t)-1);
for j=1:length(T)-1
    for i=1:length(t)-1
        if T(j)<=t(i) && t(i)<= T(j+1)
            CC(j,i)=ZZ(j,i)/TT(j);
            CCC(j,i)=ZZ_sum(j,i)/TT(j);
        end
    end
end

% Matrix of the discount factor difference
AA=zeros(length(T)-1,length(t));
for j=2:length(T)
```

```
    for i=1:length(t)
        if T(j-1)<t(i) && t(i)<=T(j)
            AA(j-1,i)=DF(i);
        end
    end
end

% Vector of NDP
aaa=0;bbb=0;sum_a=0;sum_b=0;
NDP=zeros(1,length(T));
NDP(1)=1;
NDP(2)=(NDP(1)*(LGD*sum(B(1,:).*CC(1,:))-2*R(1)*sum(alpha(1,:).*A(1,2:61))...
    - R(1)*sum(alpha(1,:).*A(1,2:61).*CCC(1,:))))/(LGD*sum(B(1,:).*CC(1,:))...
    - R(1)*sum(alpha(1,:).*A(1,2:61).*CCC(1,:)));
for j=3:length(T)
    for i=3:length(t)+1
        if t(i-1)<=T(j-1)
            bbb(j-1,i-2)= R(j-1)*(NDP(j-2)*alpha(j-1,i-2)*AA(j-2,i-1)*...
                CCC(j-2,i-2)-NDP(j-1)*alpha(j-1,i-2)*AA(j-2,i-1)*...
                CCC(j-2,i-2) + 2*NDP(j-2)*alpha(j-1,i-2)*AA(j-2,i-1));
            aaa(j-1,i-2)=NDP(j-2)*LGD*B(j-1,i-2)*CC(j-2,i-2) - NDP(j-1)*...
                LGD*B(j-1,i-2)*CC(j-2,i-2);
            sum_a(j-1)=sum(aaa(j-1,:)) +sum_a(j-2);
            sum_b(j-1)=sum(bbb(j-1,:))+sum_b(j-2)*R(j-1)/R(j-2);
            elseif T(j-1)<t(i-1) && t(i-1)<=T(j)
            Num(j-2,i-2)= NDP(j-1)*(LGD*B(j-1,i-2)*CC(j-1,i-2)...
                -2*R(j-1)*alpha(j-1,i-2)*AA(j-1,i-1)...
                -R(j-1)*alpha(j-1,i-2)*AA(j-1,i-1)*CCC(j-1,i-2));
            Den(j-2,i-2)=LGD*B(j-1,i-2)*CC(j-1,i-2)....
                -R(j-1)*alpha(j-1,i-2)*AA(j-1,i-1)*CCC(j-1,i-2);
            sum_Num(j-2)=sum(Num(j-2,:))+sum_a(j-1) - sum_b(j-1);
            sum_Den(j-2)=sum(Den(j-2,:));
        end
    end
    NDP(j)=sum_Num(j-2)/sum_Den(j-2);
end

% Vector lambda
lambda=zeros(1,length(R));
for j=1:length(R)
    lambda(j)=-log(NDP(j+1))/datenum(T(j+1)-T(1))*365*100;
end
% Vector of NDP's at the coupons payment dates
ndp=zeros(1,length(t)+1);
ndp(1)=1;
for j=2:length(T)
    for i=1:length(t)
        if T(j-1)<=t(i) && t(i)<=T(j)
            ndp(i+1)=NDP(j-1)-datenum(t(i)...
                - T(j-1))/datenum(T(j)-T(j-1))*(NDP(j-1) - NDP(j));
```

```
        end
    end
end

% Vector of intensities at the coupons payment dates
Lambda=zeros(1,length(t));
for i=2:length(ndp)
    Lambda(i-1)=-log(ndp(i))/datenum(t(i-1)-T(1))*365*100;
end

end
```

```
% Example of survival curve calibration.
% Calibrate the survival curve using the developed Matlab function Calibration.m
% Firstly, define the input data: T,t,DF,LGD and R.
%
% Let LGD be the loss given default of the issuer
LGD=0.6;

% Let R be the vector of the survival curve market quotes
R=[0.00059155, 0.00071938, 0.00101272, 0.00139671, 0.0018441,....
   0.00229228, 0.0031861, 0.00399278, 0.00465621];

% Let T be the vector of the survival curve tenors
T=datetime({'2020-12-31','2021-06-20','2021-12-20','2022-12-20','2023-12-20', ...
            '2024-12-20','2025-12-20','2027-12-20','2030-12-20','2035-12-20'}, ...
             'InputFormat','yyyy-MM-dd');

% Let t be the vector of the payment dates of our CDS contracts, then define the survival curve
t=datetime({'2021-01-01','2021-03-22','2021-06-20','2021-09-20','2021-12-20',...
            '2022-03-21','2022-06-20','2022-09-20','2022-12-20','2023-03-20', ...
            '2023-06-20','2023-09-20','2023-12-20','2024-03-20','2024-06-20', ...
            '2024-09-20','2024-12-20','2025-03-20','2025-06-20','2025-09-22', ...
            '2025-12-20','2026-03-20','2026-06-22','2026-09-21','2026-12-21', ...
            '2027-03-22','2027-06-21','2027-09-20','2027-12-20','2028-03-20', ...
            '2028-06-20','2028-09-20','2028-12-20','2029-03-20','2029-06-20', ...
            '2029-09-20','2029-12-20','2030-03-20','2030-06-20','2030-09-20', ...
            '2030-12-20','2031-03-20','2031-06-20','2031-09-22','2031-12-22', ...
            '2032-03-22','2032-06-21','2032-09-20','2032-12-20','2033-03-21', ...
            '2033-06-20','2033-09-20','2033-12-20','2034-03-20','2034-06-20', ...
            '2034-09-20','2034-12-20','2035-03-20','2035-06-20','2035-09-20', ...
            '2035-12-20'},'InputFormat','yyyy-MM-dd');

% Let DF be the vector of the LIBOR discount factors at the payment date t(i)
DF=[1.00001305598169,1.00093966486187,1.00192884266539,1.00286745826889,...
    1.00425874133146,1.005661125367,1.0070412979052,1.00843614016285,...
    1.00979342436233,1.01111294812227,1.01228486593869,1.01343385545946,...
    1.01454962841278,1.01565215144742,1.01674861065046,1.0178252387039,...
```

```
    1.01887059110581,1.0198275595259,1.02076433403842,1.02169158606212,...
    1.02256038864315,1.02328825787068,1.02400935651754,1.0246680146275,...
    1.02528780903322,1.02580809467224,1.02627202456662,1.02669100806013,...
    1.02706498994146,1.02732737424853,1.02752724091645,1.02767524803175,...
    1.02777060729804,1.02776364280026,1.0276903125781,1.02756118244083,...
    1.02737858305629,1.02711429598524,1.02677950324768,1.02638698097381,...
    1.02594199849981,1.02547966573093,1.02495988670372,1.02437158677322,...
    1.0237470585272,1.02312655054315,1.02246541298068,1.0217534216207,...
    1.02099068331527,1.02025190178646,1.01948175333469,1.01865550745344,...
    1.01779124070569,1.01699089380832,1.01615200034201,1.01527021609931,...
    1.01435593310159,1.01354152748004,1.01270080522918,1.01182310305881,...
    1.0109186574044900];

% Calibrate the survival curve
[NDP,lambda,ndp,Lambda] = Calibration(T,t,DF,LGD,R)

% Plot of the survival probabilities and intensities
plot(T,NDP)
xlabel='Tenors'
ylabel='NDP'

% Plot of the intensities
plot(T(2:length(T)),lambda)
xlabel='Tenors'
ylabel='lambda'
```

B.5.2 *Matlab Code 7*

```
function [R] = Pricing_CDS(N,LGD,T,t,DF,NDP)
% This function returns the CDS spread value that makes fair a CDS contract
% with notional N, loss given default LGD (=1-RR) and premium payment dates
% at time t. To evaluate the contract consider a survival curve with
% tenors T, market quotes R and survival probabilities NDP

% Input data
% N is the notional of the trade
% LGD is the loss given default of the issuer
% T is the vector of survival curve tenors
% t is the vector of  payment dates for the premium flows
% NDP is the vector of the survival probabilities
% (output for the survival curve calibration)

% Output
% R is the CDS spread that makes fair the trade, that is given by
% R=[LGD*sum(DF(i-1)+DF(i))*(NDP(i-1)-NDP(i))]/[sum(alpha(i)*DF(i)*(NDP(i-1)+NDP(i))]

% Assume the day count convention actual/360
k=length(t);
```

```
% Compute the day-count fraction for each flow
alpha=zeros(1,k-1);
for i=2:k
    if t(i)<t(k)
        alpha(i-1)=datenum(t(i)-t(i-1))/360;
    elseif t(i)==t(k)
        alpha(i-1)=(datenum(t(i)-t(i-1))+1)/360;
    end
end

% Using the survival curve, compute the survival probabilities at time t(i)
% for each premium flow. Assume the survival probabilities are linearly interpolated
% i.e. NDP(t(i))=NDP(T(i-1))+(T(i-1)-t(i))/(T(i)-T(i-1))*(NDP(T(i-1))-NDP(T(i)))

ndp=zeros(1, k);
for j=2:length(T)
    for i=1:k
        if T(j-1)<t(i) && t(i)<=T(j)
            ndp(i)=NDP(j-1) + datenum(T(j-1)-t(i))/datenum(T(j) -...
                T(j-1))*(NDP(j-1) - NDP(j));
        end
    end
end

% Set LGD*(DF(i-1)+DF(i))*(NDP(i-1)-NDP(i)), that is the flow value
% of the protection leg, and alpha(i)*DF(i)*(NDP(i-1)+NDP(i), that is the
% flow value of the premium leg divided by the CDS spread R

Premium_flow=zeros(1,k-1);
Protection_flow=zeros(1,k-1);

for i=2:k
    Premium_flow(i-1)=N*LGD*(DF(i-1) + DF(i))/2*(ndp(i-1) - ndp(i));
    Protection_flow(i-1)=N*alpha(i-1)*DF(i)/2*(ndp(i-1)+ndp(i));
end
% Now, we can compute R
R=sum(Premium_flow)/sum(Protection_flow)

end


% CDS spread value computation for a CDS trade
% Application of the CDS_Pricing function
% First, define the input data:N,LGD,T,t,DF and NDP

% notional of the trade
N=10^6;

% Loss given default of the issue
LGD=0.6;
```

```
% Tenor of survival curve
T=datetime({'2020-12-31','2021-06-20','2021-12-20','2022-12-20','2023-12-20', ...
            '2024-12-20','2025-12-20','2027-12-20','2030-12-20','2035-12-20'}, ...
            'InputFormat','yyyy-MM-dd');

% No default probabilities of survival curve
NDP=[1,0.999528818117755,0.99881848572484,0.996631831229394,...
        0.993015217874217,0.987699551671771,0.980920721918289,...
        0.963080794066239,0.934565091989965,0.887758596039941];

% Payment dates of premium leg
t=datetime({'2021-01-01','2021-03-15','2021-06-15','2021-09-15', '2021-12-15', ...
            '2022-03-15','2022-06-15'},'InputFormat','yyy-MM-dd');

% Libor discount factors at payment dates t(i)
DF=[1.00001305598169,1.00085724308219,1.00186903467177,1.00279631942112,...
    1.00418480016563,1.00557249020212,1.00696613273659];

% Computation of CDS spread
R=CDS_Pricing(N,LGD,T,t,DF,NDP)
```

Appendix C

Dataset Used for Modeling Non-Performing Loans

Table C.1: Dataset for PD's estimate.

Firm	Net Debt to Equity Ratio	Y (dych.)	Current Ratio	ROI	Working Capital to Asset Ratio	Debt Ratio	Asset Turnover	ROA
Aeffe	0.16	0	1.454	0.130	0.293	0.881	1.503	0.073
Alkemy	0.30	0	1.372	0.106	0.275	1.049	1.456	0.069
Autogrill	0.91	1	0.696	0.106	−0.173	1.253	3.521	0.058
Basic Net	0.46	0	1.528	0.162	0.292	0.727	0.923	0.125
B&C Speakers	0.20	0	2.630	0.347	0.844	0.806	1.958	0.331
Bioera	3.37	1	0.721	−0.237	−0.397	1.954	2.994	−0.295
Brembo	0.11	0	1.138	0.241	0.102	0.935	1.920	0.173
Brunello Cucinello	0.05	0	1.853	0.230	0.462	0.683	1.818	0.167
Campari	0.39	0	2.352	0.127	0.296	0.804	0.569	0.098
Cairo Communication	0.26	0	0.791	0.137	−0.111	0.961	1.299	0.101
Centrale del Latte Italia	1.16	1	0.994	0.006	−0.003	1.022	1.279	0.003
Cellularline	0.13	0	3.031	0.086	0.403	0.539	0.592	0.077
Class Editori	2.51	1	0.587	−0.080	−0.632	1.650	0.676	−0.072
De Longhi	0.21	0	2.108	0.290	0.906	1.212	2.384	0.212
Elica	0.69	0	0.981	0.050	−0.014	1.168	2.627	0.013
Emak	0.57	0	1.936	0.105	0.487	0.921	1.380	0.077
Enervit	0.04	0	1.259	0.168	0.189	0.696	2.445	0.137
Fila	1.34	1	2.847	0.062	0.472	1.022	0.744	0.013
Geox	0.09	0	1.617	−0.025	0.654	1.083	2.510	−0.016
Giglio Group	2.28	1	0.758	−0.024	−0.385	1.357	1.239	0.020
Immsi	2.25	1	0.615	0.082	−0.337	1.357	1.239	0.020
I Grandi Viaggi	0.32	0	1.732	0.045	0.338	0.820	1.224	0.027
Ivs	0.90	0	0.951	0.076	−0.016	0.838	0.710	0.040
La Doria	0.47	0	1.690	0.098	0.495	1.107	1.952	0.076
Landi Renzo	0.89	0	1.162	0.100	0.118	1.214	1.661	0.040
Massimo Zanetti Beverage	0.55	0	1.347	0.074	0.189	0.977	1.788	0.040
Marr	0.48	0	1.654	0.206	0.623	2.098	3.408	0.140
Mondadori	0.89	0	1.162	0.175	0.152	1.227	2.504	−0.492
Monrif	1.27	1	0.561	0.029	−0.402	1.353	1.827	0.107
Netweek	1.09	1	0.802	−0.273	−0.323	2.319	2.361	−0.455
Newflat Food	0.22	0	1.128	0.214	0.290	2.844	5.019	0.098
Orsero	0.24	0	1.521	0.061	0.436	1.350	4.891	0.041
OVS	0.43	0	1.087	0.092	0.040	0.913	1.271	0.004
Piaggio	1.10	1	0.874	0.113	−0.091	1.384	1.743	0.042
Pininfarina	0.08	0	1.577	0.065	0.285	0.903	1.718	0.035
Piquadro	0.09	0	1.827	0.179	0.757	1.287	2.154	0.104
Pirelli	0.70	0	1.102	0.091	0.037	1.076	0.714	0.056
Poligrafici Editore	0.76	0	0.808	0.062	−0.173	1.384	1.988	−1.612
Ratti	0.04	0	2.260	0.265	0.912	1.371	1.986	0.187
Rcs	0.74	0	0.720	0.257	−0.222	1.310	2.077	0.178
Reno De' Medici	0.34	0	1.244	0.150	0.153	1.0052	2.080	0.092
Rosss	2.32	1	1.126	−0.015	0.275	2.844	3.912	−0.040
Salvatore Ferragamo	0.22	0	2.633	0.245	0.778	0.653	2.179	0.145
Sanlorenzo	0.21	0	1.280	0.178	0.440	2.071	2.872	0.096
Sogefi	1.24	1	0.852	0.141	−0.144	1.938	3.386	0.036
Technogym	0.17	0	1.185	0.437	0.215	1.600	2.556	0.378
Tod's	0.07	0	1.870	0.063	0.295	0.478	0.823	0.040
Triboo	0.17	0	0.849	0.076	−0.206	1.685	1.558	0.050
Unieuro	0.06	0	0.734	0.236	−1.692	7.683	2.026	0.118
Valsoia	0.32	0	3.006	0.182	0.738	0.565	1.822	0.219
Vianini	1.48	1	3.028	0.032	0.234	0.654	0.092	0.011

Table C.2: Dataset for LGD's estimate.

Loan ID	LGD	LGD*	Recov. Time	Collateral	Collateral*
101	0%	0	0.095	yes	1
102	0%	0	0.095	yes	1
103	89%	2	0.698	no	0
104	70%	2	0.593	yes	1
106	45%	1	0.753	no	0
107	85%	2	0.753	no	0
111	19%	0	0.095	no	0
112	86%	2	0.698	no	0
114	45%	1	0.632	yes	1
115	9%	0	0.181	yes	1
116	92%	2	0.632	no	0
119	80%	2	0.632	no	0
122	29%	0	0.451	yes	1
123	91%	2	0.503	no	0
124	71%	2	0.503	no	0
125	90%	2	0.503	no	0
127	64%	1	0.503	yes	1
128	16%	0	0.259	yes	1
130	63%	1	0.593	no	0
131	68%	1	0.593	no	0
133	87%	2	0.451	no	0
134	94%	2	0.451	no	0
135	90%	2	0.451	no	0
137	44%	1	0.593	yes	1
138	94%	2	0.817	yes	1
140	0%	0	0.593	yes	1
141	93%	2	0.503	no	0
142	40%	1	0.503	no	0
144	100%	2	0.503	yes	1
145	35%	1	0.451	yes	1
146	97%	2	0.451	no	0
148	61%	1	0.451	no	0
150	57%	1	0.503	no	0
151	60%	1	0.329	no	0
152	39%	1	0.329	yes	1
153	53%	1	0.329	no	0
155	94%	2	0.329	no	0
156	39%	1	0.329	no	0
158	46%	1	0.329	yes	1
159	57%	1	0.329	no	0
160	56%	1	0.329	no	0

* Variables expressed in categories for the purpose of the analysis

Table C.2: *Cont.*

Loan ID	LGD	LGD*	Recov. Time	Collateral	Collateral*
161	55%	1	0.259	no	0
162	56%	1	0.259	no	0
163	58%	1	0.259	no	0
164	97%	2	0.259	yes	1
165	92%	2	0.259	no	0
166	92%	2	0.259	no	0
167	55%	1	0.259	no	0
168	55%	1	0.259	no	0
169	55%	1	0.259	no	0
170	49%	1	0.181	no	0
171	51%	1	0.181	no	0
172	53%	1	0.181	no	0
173	54%	1	0.259	no	0
174	0%	0	0.095	yes	1

* Variables expressed in categories for the purpose of the analysis

Bibliography

Abedifar, P., Ebrahim, S. M., Molyneux, P., and Tarazi, A. (2015). Islamic Banking And Finance: Recent Empirical Literature and Directions for Future Research, *Journal of Economic Surveys* **29**, pp. 637–670.

Acemoglu, D., Ozdaglar, A., and Tahbaz-Salehi, A. (2015). Networks, shocks, and systemic risk. NBER Working Paper No. 20931, Retrieved from `https://www.nber.org/papers/w20931.pdf`.

Acharya, V. V. (2009). A theory of systemic risk and design of prudential bank, *Journal of Financial Stability* **5**, pp. 224–255.

Achleitner, A.-K., Braun, R., and Engel, N. (2011). Value creation and pricing in buyouts: Empirical evidence from europe and north america, *Review of Financial Economics* **20**, 4, pp. 146–161.

Altman, E. (2006). Default Recovery Rates and LGD in Credit Risk Modeling and Practice, `https://pages.stern.nyu.edu/~ealtman/UpdatedReviewofLiterature.pdf`.

Álvarez, I. C., Barbero, J., Zofío, J. L., *et al.* (2017). A panel data toolbox for Matlab, *Journal of Statistical Software* **76**, 6, pp. 1–27.

Aramonte, S. and Avalos, F. (2020). Corporate Credit Markets After the Initial Pandemic Shock, `https://www.bis.org/publ/bisbull26.htm`.

Argaam (2021). tradingview.com, `https://www.tradingview.com`.

Arnsdorf, M. (2011). Central Counterparty Risk, *Quantitative Research, J.P. Morgan.*

Artzner, P., Delbaen, F., Eber, J.-M., and Heath, D. (1999). Coherent Measures of Risk, *Mathematical Finance* **9**, pp. 203–228.

Avantage Reply Observatory on Banking System Solidity (2013). Capital Adequacy, Cost of Risk and Profitability: During a Crisis, A Real Puzzle for Banks, Retrieved on 17/9/2021 from `https://www.reply.com/Documents/AVANTAGE-REPLY-OBSERVATORY-ON-BANKING-SYSTEM-SOLIDITY_eng.pdf`.

Avdasheva, S. and Shastitko, A. (2005). *Developing competition in the industries with the natural monopoly component: foundations, options, limitations. TACIS project [in Russian]* (Moscow: Russian-European Centre for Economic Policy (RECEP)).

Baltagi, B. (2008). *Econometric analysis of panel data* (John Wiley & Sons).

Bank of England (2021). CP18/21 – Remuneration: Identification of material risk takers, Retrieved from `https://www.bankofengland.co.uk/prudential-regulation/publication/2021/september/remuneration-identification-material-risk-takers`.

Bank of Russia (2012). Draft Version for Public Consultation of the IRB Basel II Legislation No. 192-T [in Russian].

BCBS (1988). International Convergence of Capital Measurement and Capital Standards, http://www.bis.org/publ/bcbs04a.htm.

BCBS (1996). Amendment to the Capital Accord to incorporate market risks, http://www.bis.org/publ/bcbs24.htm.

BCBS (1999). Credit Risk Modelling: Current Practices And Applications, https://www.bis.org/publ/bcbs49.pdf.

BCBS (2000). Credit Ratings and Complementary Sources of Credit Quality Information. wp no. 3, https://www.bis.org/publ/bcbs_wp3.pdf.

BCBS (2001a). The internal ratings-based approach. consultative document. supporting document to the new basel capital accord, https://www.bis.org/publ/bcbsca05.pdf.

BCBS (2001b). Overview of The New Basel Capital Accord, https://www.bis.org/publ/bcbsca03.pdf.

BCBS (2003). Basel II: The New Basel Capital Accord – third consultative paper, http://www.bis.org/bcbs/bcbscp3.htm.

BCBS (2004). Basel II: International Convergence of Capital Measurement and Capital Standards: a Revised Framework, http://bis.org/publ/bcbs107.htm.

BCBS (2005a). An Explanatory Note on the Basel II IRB Risk Weight Functions, http://www.bis.org/bcbs/irbriskweight.htm.

BCBS (2005b). Basel II: International Convergence of Capital Measurement and Capital Standards: A Revised Framework, http://bis.org/publ/bcbs118.htm.

BCBS (2005c). Studies on the Validation on Internal Rating Systems, https://www.bis.org/publ/bcbs_wp14.htm.

BCBS (2006). Basel II: International Convergence of Capital Measurement and Capital Standards: A Revised Framework – Comprehensive Version, https://www.bis.org/publ/bcbs128.pdf.

BCBS (2008). Principles for Sound Liquidity Risk Management and Supervision, http://bis.org/publ/bcbs144.htm.

BCBS (2009). [Basel III Draft] Strengthening the Resilience of the Banking Sector – Consultative Document, http://bis.org/publ/bcbs164.htm.

BCBS (2010a). Basel III: A Global Regulatory Framework for More Resilient Banks and Banking Systems, http://bis.org/publ/bcbs189.pdf.

BCBS (2010b). Basel III: A Global Regulatory Framework for More Resilient Banks and Banking Systems (revised 2011), http://www.bis.org/publ/bcbs189_dec2010.htm.

BCBS (2010c). Developments in Modelling Risk Aggregation. Joint Forum, http://www.bis.org/publ/joint25.pdf.

BCBS (2011a). Capital Treatment for Bilateral Counterparty Credit Risk Finalised by the Basel Committee, http://www.bis.org/press/p110601.htm.

BCBS (2011b). Range of Methodologies for Risk and Performance Alignment of Remuneration, https://www.bis.org/publ/bcbs194.pdf.

BCBS (2012a). Basel III Regulatory Consistency Assessment (Level 2) – Japan, https://www.bis.org/bcbs/implementation/l2_jp.pdf.

BCBS (2012b). Capital Requirements for Bank Exposures to Central Counterparties, http://www.bis.org/publ/bcbs227.htm.

BCBS (2012c). Monitoring Indicators for Intraday Liquidity Management – consultative document, http://www.bis.org/publ/bcbs225.htm.

BCBS (2013a). Capital Requirements for Banks' Equity Investments in Funds – Final Standard, http://www.bis.org/publ/bcbs266.htm.

BCBS (2013b). Regulatory Consistency Assessment Programme (RCAP): Assessment of Basel III regulations – China, https://www.bis.org/bcbs/implementation/l2_cn.pdf.

BCBS (2014a). Basel III Leverage Ratio Framework and Disclosure Requirements, http://www.bis.org/publ/bcbs270.htm.

BCBS (2014b). Basel III: the Net Stable Funding Ratio, https://www.bis.org/publ/bcbs271.htm.

BCBS (2014c). Regulatory Consistency Assessment Programme (RCAP): Assessment of Basel III regulations – European Union, https://www.bis.org/bcbs/publ/d300.pdf.

BCBS (2014d). Regulatory Consistency Assessment Programme (RCAP): Assessment of Basel III regulations – United States of America, https://www.bis.org/bcbs/publ/d301.pdf.

BCBS (2014e). The G-SIB assessment methodology – score calculation, Retrieved from http://www.bis.org/bcbs/publ/d296.htm.

BCBS (2016a). Minimum Capital Requirements for Market Risk, https://www.bis.org/bcbs/publ/d352.pdf.

BCBS (2016b). TLAC Holdings. Standard. Amendments to the Basel III Standard on The Definition of Capital, http://www.bis.org/bcbs/publ/d387.pdf.

BCBS (2017). Finalising Basel III. In Brief, https://www.bis.org/bcbs/publ/d424_inbrief.pdf.

BCBS (2019). Basel Framework. BCP – Core Principles for Effective Banking Supervision. Principle 18, footnote 27, https://www.bis.org/basel_framework/chapter/BCP/01.htm?inforce=20191215&published=20191215#fn_BCP_01_33_27.

Bellotti, T. and Crook, J. (2012). Loss given default models incorporating macroeconomic variables for credit cards, *International Journal of Forecasting* **28**, 1, pp. 171–182.

Belsley, D. A., Kuh, E., and Welsch, R. E. (2005). *Regression diagnostics: Identifying influential data and sources of collinearity*, Vol. 571 (John Wiley & Sons).

Benzschawel, T., Lee, C.-Y., Hawker, B., and Craft, D. (2011). Market Default Probabilities and Credit Indexes, *Index Universe.*

Berman, S. e. a. (2012). Simpson's Paradox: A Cautionary Tale in Advanced Analytics, *Significance: Statistics Making Sense.*

Berskon, J. (1944). Application of the Logistic Function to Bio-Assay, *Journal of the American Statistical Association* **39**, 227, pp. 357–365, doi:10.1080/01621459.1944.10500699.

Bielecki, T. R. and Rutkowski, M. (2013). *Credit Risk: Modeling, Valuation and Hedging* (Springer Science & Business Media).

BIS (2009). Report on OTC Derivatives Data Reporting and Aggregation Requirements, https://www.bis.org/cpmi/publ/d100.pdf.

BIS (2013). Statistical Release: OTC Derivatives Statistics at end-December 2012, https://www.bis.org/publ/otc_hy1305.pdf.

BIS (2020). About Derivatives Statistics. OTC derivatives Notional Amount Outstanding by Risk Category, `https://www.bis.org/statistics/about_derivatives_stats.htm`.

Bliss, C. I. (1934). The Method of Probits, *Science* **79**, 2037, pp. 38–39, doi:10.1126/science.79.2037.38.

Blochwitz, S., Martin, M., and Wehn, C. (2006). Statistical Approaches to PD Validation, *B. Engelmann & R. Rauhmeier, eds. The Basel II Risk Parameters. Estimation, Validation, Stress-Testing — with Applications to Loan Risk Management*, pp. 289–306.

Bluhm, C., Overbeck, L., and Wagner, C. (2003). *An Introduction to Credit Risk Modeling* (Chapman & Hall).

Bolancé Losilla, C., Guillén, M., and Padilla Barreto, A. E. (2015). Estimación del riesgo mediante el ajuste de cópulas, *UB Riskcenter Working Paper Series, 2015/01.*

Borio, C. (2020). The Prudential Response to the Covid-19 Crisis. Retrieved from Speech on the Occasion of the Bank's Annual General Meeting, `https://www.bis.org/speeches/sp200630a.pdf`.

Borzykh, D. and Penikas, H. (2021). IRB PD Model Accuracy Validation in the Presence of Default Correlation: a Twin Confidence Interval Approach, *Risk Management* http://doi.org/10.1057/s41283-021-00079-2.

Breusch, T. and Pagan, A. (1979). A Simple Test for Heteroscedasticity and Random Coefficient Variation, *Econometrica.*

Brigo, D., Morini, M., and Pallavicini, A. (2013). *Counterparty Credit Risk, Collateral and Funding* (Wiley Finance).

Brown, L., Cai, T., and DasGupta, A. (2001). Interval Estimation for a Binomial Proportion, *Statistical Science* **16**, pp. 101–133.

Bruche, M. and González-Aguado, C. (2010). Recovery rates, default probabilities, and the credit cycle, *Journal of Banking & Finance* **34**, 4, pp. 754–764.

Caffo, B. (2007). Methods in Biostatistics. Lecture 27, `http://ocw.jhsph.edu/courses/methodsinbiostatisticsii/PDFs/lecture27.pdf`.

Caliński, T. and Harabasz, J. (1974). A dendrite method for cluster analysis, *Communications in Statistics-theory and Methods* **3**, 1, pp. 1–27.

Camdessus, M. (1999). International Financial and Monetary Stability: A Global Public Good?, Retrieved from IMF/Research Conference "Key Issues in Reform of the International Monetary and Financial System" `https://www.imf.org/en/News/Articles/2015/09/28/04/53/sp052899`.

Carey, M. and Gordy, M. (2004). Measuring Systematic Risk in Recoveries on Defaulted Debt I: Firm-Level Ultimate LGDs, Retrieved from `https://www.fdic.gov/analysis/cfr/2005/apr/mcarey-mgordy.pdf`.

Caruana, J. (2010). Strengthened Capital Framework: From Basel II to Basel III, `http://www.bis.org/speeches/sp100921a.pdf`.

Cathcart, L., El-jahel, L., and Jabbour, R. (2017). Basel II: An Engine without Brakes, *Journal of Banking Regulation* **18**, 4, pp. 359–74.

CBB (2015). Central Bank of Bahrain (CBB) Rulebook, `https://cbben.thomsonreuters.com/rulebook/ca-1117-4`.

Cherubini, U., Luciano, E., and Vecchiato, W. (2004). *Copula Methods in Finance* (John Wiley & Sons Ltd, New York).

CIPR (2021). Global Systemically Important Insurers (G-SIIs).

Cramer, J. S. (2003). *Logit models from economics and other fields* (Cambridge University Press).

Crete, R. (2016). The Volkswagen Scandal from the Viewpoint of Corporate Governance, *European Journal of Risk Regulation* **1**, pp. 25–31.

Crouhy, M., Galai, D., and Mark, R. (2000). A Comparative Analysis of Current Credit Risk Models, *Journal of Banking & Finance* **24**, 1, pp. 59–117.

Culp, C. L., Van der Merwe, A., and Staerkle, B. (2016). Single-name credit default swaps: a review of the empirical academic literature, *Johns Hopkins Institute for Applied Economics, AF/No* **11**.

Dahlin, F. and Storkitt, S. (2014). Estimation of loss given default for low default portfolios, Tech. rep., Royal Institute of Technology of Sweden, `https://www.math.kth.se/matstat/seminarier/reports/M-exjobb14/140512.pdf`.

Deblauwe, F. and Ha Le, T. (1997). Stability of Correlation between Credit and Market Risk over Different Holding Periods.

Demetriades, P. (2012). Financial stability in Europe: a European public good, Speech by Panicos Demetriades, Governor of the Central Bank of Cyprus, at the Fiduciary Future Cyprus 2012 Conference `https://www.centralbank.cy/en/the-governor/previous-governors/previous-governor-s-speeches/panicos-o.-demetriades/01112012`.

Demirguc-Kunt, A., Pedraza, A., and Ruiz-Ortega, C. (2020). Banking Sector Performance During the COVID-19 Crisis, *World Bank, Washington, DC.*

Demsetz, H. (1968). Why Regulate Utilities? *Journal of Law and Economics*, pp. 55–65.

Deutsche Bank (2015). Annual Report, `https://annualreport.deutsche-bank.com/2015/q2/management-report/risk-report/risk-profile.html`.

Dewatripont, M., Rochet, J.-C., and Tirole, J. (2010). *Balancing the Banks. Global Lessons from the Financial Crisis* (Princeton University Press).

Dewatripont, M. and Tirole, J. (1994). *The Prudential Regulation of Banks* (MIT Press).

Di Lorenzo, E. and Sibillo, M. (2020). Economic Paradigms and Corporate Culture after the Great COVID-19 Pandemic: Towards a New Role of Welfare Organisations and Insurers, *Sustainability* **12**, 19, p. 8163.

Diamond, D. and Dybvig, P. (1983). Bank Runs, Deposit Insurance, and Liquidity, *The Journal of Political Economy* **91**, pp. 401–419.

Diron, M. and Perjessey, A. (2019). Saudi Arabia's credit profile supported by very high fiscal and economic strength and external liquidity buffers, Moody's, `https://www.moodys.com/research/Moodys-Saudi-Arabias-credit-profile-supported-by-very-high-fiscal--PBC_1173724`.

Duprey, T. and Ueberfeldt, A. (2020). Managing GDP Tail Risk, Retrieved from Bank of Canada Staff Working Paper/Document de travail du personnel – 2020-03 `https://www.bankofcanada.ca/wp-content/uploads/2020/01/swp2020-3.pdf`.

Dyck, S. (2016). Saudi Arabia's fiscal position, Moody's, `https://www.moodys.com/research/moodys-PR_364481`.

EBA (2017). Draft Implementing Standards amending Implementing Regulation (EU) No 680/2014, `https://eba.europa.eu/regulation-and-policy/supervisory-reporting/implementing-technical-standard-on-supervisory-reporting`.

EBA (2019a). European Banking Authority (EBA) Report on MPLs. Progress Made and Challenges Ahead, Retrieved on 17/9/2021 from `https://www.eba.europa.eu/risk-analysis-and-data/npls`.

EBA (2019b). Instructions for Reporting the Validation Results of Internal Models. IRB Pillar I Models for Credit Risk, https://www.bankingsupervision.europa.eu/banking/tasks/internal_models/shared/pdf/instructions_validation_reporting_credit_risk.en.pdf.

ECB (2010). Financial Stability Review, Retrieved from https://www.ecb.europa.eu/press/pr/date/2010/html/pr100531.en.html.

Eckert, F., Mikosch, H., and Stotz, M. (2020). The Corona Crisis and Corporate Bankruptcies: Evidence from Switzerland, https://voxeu.org/print/66172.

Emery, K. and Ou, S. (2009). Corporate Default and Recovery Rates, 1920-2008, *Moody's Global Credit Policy*.

Engelmann, B., Hayden, E., and Tasche, D. (2003). Testing Rating Accuracy, *Risk*, pp. 82–86.

Ermolova, M. and Penikas, H. (2017). PD-LGD Correlation Study: Evidence from the Russian Corporate Bond Market, *Model Assisted Statistics and Applications* **12**, pp. 335–358.

Fadaak, T. and Alghamdi, S. (2016). Saudi insurance sector 2015, Albilad Capital.

FAO (2011). Recent Trends in World Food Commodity Prices: Costs and Benefits. Past and Future Trends in World Food Prices, http://www.fao.org/3/i2330e/i2330e03.pdf.

Fatica, S., Heynderickx, W., and Andrea, P. (2020). Banks, debt and risk: assessing the spillovers of corporate taxes, *Economic Inquiry* **58**, 2, pp. 1023–1044.

Ferrari, P. e. a. (2005). An Approach to Estimate Between- and Within-Group Correlation Coefficients in Multicenter Studies: Plasma Carotenoids as Biomarkers of Intake of Fruits and Vegetables, *American Journal of Epidemiology*.

Firth, D. (1993). Bias reduction of maximum likelihood estimates, *Biometrika*, pp. 27–38.

Fischer, W. and Meier-Hellstern, K. (1993). The Markov-Modulated Poisson Process (MMPP) Cookbook, *Performance Evaluation* **18**, pp. 149–171.

Fitch Ratings (2016). Recovery Ratings, https://www.fitchratings.com/site/definitions/recoveryratings.html, accessed: 2016-03-10.

FRB (2021). Charge-off and delinquency rates on loans and leases at commercial banks, https://www.federalreserve.gov/releases/chargeoff/delallsa.htm, accessed: 2021-06-10.

FRED (2012). S&P/Case-Shiller U.S. National Home Price Index (CSUSHPINSA), https://fred.stlouisfed.org/series/csushpinsa.

Freixas, X. and Rochet, J.-C. (2008). *Microeconomics of Banking*, 2nd edn. (Cambridge, Massachusetts: The MIT Press).

Friederich, J. and Krustins, K. (2020). Fitch rating of Saudi Arabia, Fitch Ratings, https://www.fitchratings.com/entity/saudi-arabia-81688867.

Frontczak, R., Jaeger, M., and Schumacher, B. (2017). From Power Curves to Discriminative Power: Measuring Model Performance of LGD Models, *Journal of Mathematical Finance*, pp. 657–670.

FSB (2016). 2016 List of Global Systemically Important Insurers (G-SIIs).

FSB (2019). 2019 List of Global Systemically Important Banks (G-SIBs), https://www.fsb.org/wp-content/uploads/P221119-1.pdf.

FSB (2020). 2020 List of Global Systemically Important Banks (G-SIBs), https://www.fsb.org/wp-content/uploads/P111120.pdf.

Fuster, A., Goldsmith-Pinkham, P., Ramadorai, T., and Walther, A. (2018). Predictably Unequal? The Effects of Machine Learning on Credit Markets, `https://ifin.usi.ch/assets/docs/seminars/a-fuster-338054.pdf`.

G20 State Leaders (2009). Leader's Statement, *Pittsburgh Summit of the G20 Leaders, 24-25 September 2009.*

Gim, T.-H. T. and Ko, J. (2017). Maximum likelihood and firth logistic regression of the pedestrian route choice, *International regional science review* **40**, 6, pp. 616–637.

Glößner, P., Steinbauer, A., and Ivanova, I. (2006). Internal LGD Estimation in Practice, *Wilmott Magazine.*

Goel, T. and Agarwal, I. (2021). Limits of Stress-test Based Bank Regulation. BIS Working Paper No. 953, `https://www.bis.org/publ/work953.htm`.

Goldfine, J. (2021). Here Are All the Companies That Went Bankrupt During the COVID Pandemic. More Than Ten Major Companies Have Already Declared Bankruptcy in 2021, `https://www.businessofbusiness.com/articles/companies-bankrupt-covid-pandemic-2021/`.

Goodhart, C. (2011). *The Basel Committee on Banking Supervision. A History of the Early Years 1974-1997* (Cambridge University Press).

Gordy, M. (2000). A Comparative Anatomy of Credit Risk Models, *Journal of Banking and Finance* **24**, pp. 119–149.

Gordy, M. B. and Howells, B. (2006). Procyclicality in Basel II: Can We Treat the Disease Without Killing the Patient? *Journal of Financial Intermediation* **15**, p. 395–417.

Haldane, A. (2009). Rethinking the Financial Network, `http://www.bis.org/review/r090505e.pdf`.

Han, C. and Jang, Y. (2013). Effects of debt collection practices on loss given default, *Journal of Banking & Finance* **37**, 1, pp. 21–31.

Hartmann-Wendels, T., Miller, P., and Töws, E. (2014). Loss given default for leasing: Parametric and nonparametric estimations, *Journal of Banking & Finance* **40**, pp. 364–375.

Heinze, G. and Schemper, M. (2002). A solution to the problem of separation in logistic regression, *Statistics in medicine* **21**, 16, pp. 2409–2419.

Hernandez de Cos, P. (2021). Evaluating the Effectiveness of Basel III During Covid-19 and Beyond, `https://www.bis.org/speeches/sp210420.pdf`.

Hernández de Cos, P. (2019). Post-Basel III: Time for Evaluation, `https://www.bis.org/speeches/sp191024.htm`.

Huerta de Soto, J. (2006). *Money, Bank Credit, and Economic Cycles* (MisesInstitute).

Hull, J. and White, A. (1998). Incorporating Volatility Updating Into the Historical Simulation Method for Value at Risk, *Journal of Risk.*

Hussain, M., Watson, J., and Dupont, E. (2020). Coronavirus rating impact: EMEA emerging market banks, Fitch Ratings, `https://www.fitchratings.com/research/banks/coronavirus-rating-impact-emea-emerging-market-banks-14-05-2020`.

IFSB (2013). Revised Capital Adequacy Standard for Institutions Offering Islamic Financial Services Excluding Islamic Insurance (Takāful) Institutions and Islamic Collective Investment Schemes (IFSB-15), `https://www.ifsb.org/download.php?id=4371&lang=English&pg=/published.php`.

IMF (2020). Law & Financial Stability, `https://www.elibrary.imf.org/doc/IMF071/23553-9781513523002/23553-9781513523002/Other_formats/Source_PDF/23553-9781513516813.pdf`.

Ingves, S. (2017). Remarks Given at IADI Conference on "Designing an Optimal Deposit Insurance System", https://www.bis.org/speeches/sp170602.htm.

Jain, D. D. and Ubes, D. (1988). *RC: Algorithms for Clustering Data* (Prentice-Hall Advanced Reference Series).

Jarrow, R. A. and Turnbull, S. M. (1995). Pricing Derivatives on Financial Securities Subject to Credit Risk, *The Journal of Finance* **50**, 1, pp. 53–85.

Joe, H. (1997). *Multivariate Models and Dependence Concepts, Monographs on Statistics and Applied Probability 73* (Chapman and Hall, London).

Jones, S. and Hensher, D. A. (2004). Predicting firm financial distress: A mixed logit model, *The Accounting Review* **79**, 4, pp. 1011–1038.

Jorion, P. (2007). *Value at Risk: The New Benchmark for Managing Financial Risk* (McGraw-Hill).

Kahf, M. (2005). Basel II: Implications for Islamic Banking. Paper Written for the 6th International Conference on Islamic Economics and Banking. Jakarta, Nov 22-24, 2005, http://monzer.kahf.com/papers/english/Basel_II_Implications_for_Islamic_Banking_FOR_6TH_CONFERENCE_IN_JAKARTA.pdf.

Kendall, M. G. (1948). *Rank correlation methods* (Griffin).

Kofman, J. (2011). Overcoming Challenges in PD/LGD Modelling in the Absence of High Quality and Rich Data, *Moody's Analytics Whitepaper.*

Koyluoglu, H. U. and Hickman, A. (1998). A Generalized Framework for Credit Risk Portfolio Models, http://www.bis.org/publ/bcbs225.htm.

Kuritzkes, A. and Schuermann, T. (2007). What We Know, Don't Know and Can't Know about Bank Risk: A View from the Trenches, *Princeton University Press.*

Lall, R. (2012). From failure to failure: The politics of international banking regulation, *Review of International Political Economy* **19**, 4, pp. 609–638.

Laviola, S. and Trapanese, M. (1997). Previsione delle insolvenze delle imprese e qualita del credito bancario: un'analisi statistica. Settembre 1997. Banca d'Italia Temi di Discussione No. 318 [in Italian], https://www.bancaditalia.it/pubblicazioni/temi-discussione/1997/1997-0318/tema_318.pdf.

le Roux, S. (2008). Measuring Counterparty Credit Risk: An Overview of the Theory and Practice, *Magister Scientia Dissertation.*

Leow, M., Mues, C., and Thomas, L. (2014). The economy and loss given default: evidence from two UK retail lending data sets, *Journal of the Operational Research Society* **65**, 3, pp. 363–375.

Li, D. (2000). On Default Correlation: A Copula Function Approach, *Journal of Fixed Income* **9**, pp. 43–54.

Li, S. and Marin, C. (2014). The use of financial derivatives and risks of U.S. bank holding companies, *International Review of Financial Analysis* **35**, pp. 46–71.

Liikanen, E. (2012). High level expert group on reforming the structure of the EU banking sector. Technical report, Retrieved from http://ec.europa.eu/internal_market/bank/docs/high-level_expert_group/report_en.pdf.

Longin, F. and Solnik, B. (2014). Extreme Correlation of International Equity Markets, *Journal of Finance* **LVI**, pp. 649–676.

Los Alamos Science (1987). Special Issue Dedicated to Stanislav Ulam, *Los Alamos Science. Special Issue* **15**, https://la-science.lanl.gov/lascience15.shtml.

Lozinskaia, A., Merikas, A., Merika, A., and Penikas, H. (2017). Determinants of the

Probability of Default: the Case of the Internationally Listed Shipping Corporations, *Maritime Policy & Management* **4**, pp. 837–858.

Ludwig, A., Monge-Naranjo, A., Slavik, C., and Sohail, F. (2020). Finance and Inequality: A Tale of Two Tails, Retrieved from `https://s3.amazonaws.com/real.stlouisfed.org/wp/2020/2020-044.pdf`.

Lütkebohmert, E. (2009). The asymptotic single risk factor model, *Concentration Risk in Credit Portfolios*, pp. 31–42.

Maarse, B. (2012). Backtesting Framework for PD, EAD and LGD, `https://essay.utwente.nl/61905/1/master_B._Maarse.pdf`.

MacKenzie, D. and Spears, T. (2012). 'The Formula That Killed Wall Street'? The Gaussian Copula and the Material Cultures of Modelling, `https://mathbabe.files.wordpress.com/2012/06/gaussian14.pdf`.

Marzban, C. e. a. (2013). Within-Group and Between-Group Correlation: Illustration on Noninvasive Estimation of Intracranial Pressure, *Preprint*.

Matsumoto, M. and Nishimura, T. (1998). Mersenne twister: a 623-dimensionally equidistributed uniform pseudo-random number generator, *ACM Transactions on Modeling and Computer Simulation (TOMACS)* **8**, 1, pp. 3–30.

Mayordomo, S., Rodriguez-Moreno, M., and Pena, J. (2014). Derivatives holdings and systemic risk in the U.S. banking sector, *Journal of Banking and Finance* **45**, pp. 84–104.

McKinsey (2015). Saudi Arabia beyond oil: the investment and productivity transformation, McKinsey Global Institute.

McNeil, A. J., Frey, R., and Tankov, P. (2005). *Quantitative Risk Management: Concepts, Techniques, and Tools* (Princeton Series in Finance).

Merika, A., Negkakis, I., and Penikas, H. (2021). Stress-Testing and Credit Risk Revisited: A Shipping Sector Application, *International Journal of Banking, Accounting and Finance* doi:10.1504/IJBAAF.2021.10040577.

Merton, R. (1973). Theory of Rational Option Pricing, *Bell Journal of Economics* **4**, 1, pp. 141–183, `https://econpapers.repec.org/article/rjebellje/v_3a4_3ay_3a1973_3ai_3aspring_3ap_3a141-183.htm`.

Merton, R. (1974). On the Pricing of Corporate Debt: The Risk Structure of Interest Rates, *The Journal of Finance* **29**, 2, pp. 449–470.

Metropolis, N. and Ulam, S. (1949). The Monte Carlo Method, *Journal of the American Statistical Association* **44**, 247, pp. 335–341.

Meuleman, E. and Vennet, R. V. (2020). Macroprudential policy and bank systemic risk, *Journal of Financial Stability* **47**.

Miron, P. and Swannel, P. (1991). *Pricing and Hedging Swaps* (Euromoney Books).

Mollenkamp, Carrick and Craig, Susanne and Ng, Serena and Lucchetti, Aaron (2001). Crisis on Wall Street as Lehman Totters, Merrill Is Sold, AIG Seeks to Raise Cash. Fed Will Expand Its Lending Arsenal in a Bid to Calm Markets; Moves Cap a Momentous Weekend for American Finance, *The Wall Street Journal* `https://www.wsj.com/articles/SB122139688846233147`.

Moosa, I. (2010). Basel II as a casualty of the global financial crisis, *Journal of Banking Regulation* **11**, 2, pp. 95–114.

Moscatelli, M., Parlapiano, F., Narizzano, S., and Viggiano, G. (2020). Corporate default forecasting with machine learning, *Expert Systems with Applications*, p. 113567.

Nawazish, M., Saeed, M. S., and Rizvi, K. A. (2013). The pricing of size, book to market and financial leverage in euro stocks, *Economic research-Ekonomska istraživanja* **26**, 2, pp. 177–190.

Nelsen, R. (2006). *An Introduction to Copulas*, 2nd edn. (Springer, New York).

Nereim, V. and Al Othman, R. (2020). Saudi Arabia less pessimistic than IMF as economy shrinks again, Bloomberg, `https://www.bloomberg.com/news/articles/2020-06-30/saudi-arabia-less-pessimistic-than-imf-as-economy-shrinks-again`.

Newman, R. (2015). We're Watching Trump's 7th Bankruptcy Unfold, `https://finance.yahoo.com/news/were-watching-trumps-7th-bankruptcy-unfold-171903858.html`.

OECD (2020). COVID-19 crisis response in MENA countries, OECD, `http://www.oecd.org/coronavirus/policy-responses/covid-19-crisis-response-in-mena-countries-4b366396/`.

O'Kane, D. (2011). *Modelling Single-name and Multi-name Credit Derivatives*, Vol. 573 (John Wiley & Sons).

Ong, M. K. (1999). *Internal Credit Risk Models: Capital Allocation and Performance Measurement* (Risk publications).

Ordonez, G. (2018). Sustainable Shadow Banking, *American Economic Journal: Macroeconomics* **10**, 1, pp. 33–56.

Orlando, G. and Bace, E. (2021). Challenging times for insurance, banking and financial supervision in Saudi Arabia (KSA), *Administrative Sciences* **11**, 3, p. 62.

Orlando, G. and Härtel, M. (2014). A Parametric Approach to Counterparty and Credit Risk, *Journal of Credit Risk* **10**, 4.

Orlando, G. and Pelosi, R. (2020). Non-Performing Loans for Italian Companies: When Time Matters. An Empirical Research on Estimating Probability to Default and Loss Given Default, *International Journal of Financial Studies* **8**, 4, p. 68.

Osadchiy, M. (2021). Vasicek Model Extension. Premature Default, `https://mpra.ub.uni-muenchen.de/108687/1/MPRA_paper_108687.pdf`.

Osadchiy, M. and Sidorov, A. (2020). From Default Distribution to Loss Distribution: Vasicek Mertonization, `https://mpra.ub.uni-muenchen.de/104138/1/MPRA_paper_104138.pdf`.

Ostrom, E. (2009). Prize Lecture, Retrieved in 2020 from Nobel Media AB: `https://www.nobelprize.org/prizes/economic-sciences/2009/ostrom/lecture/`.

Ostrom, V. and Ostrom, E. (1977). Public Goods and Public Choices, *E. Davas (Ed.), Alternatives for Delivering Public Services: Toward Improved Performance*, pp. 7–49.

Ou, S. (2011). Corporate Default and Recovery Rates, 1920-2010, *Moody's Global Credit Policy*.

Ozdemir, B. and Miu, P. (2009). *Basel II Implementation. A Guide to Developing and Validating a Compliant Internal Risk Rating System* (McGrawHill).

Parkinson, A. (2016). Saudi banks: peer review, Fitch Ratings, `https://www.fitchratings.com/site/re/889005`.

Penati, A. and Protopapadakis, A. (1988). The effect of implicit deposit insurance on banks' portfolio choices with an application to international 'overexposure', *Journal of Monetary Economics* **21**, pp. 107–126.

Penikas, H. (2014). Investment Portfolio Risk Modelling Based on Hierarchical Copulas [in Russian], *Applied Econometrics* **35**, pp. 18–38.

Penikas, H. (2015). History of Banking Regulation as Developed by the Basel Committee on Banking Supervision in 1974–2014 (Brief Overview), *Financial Stability Journal* **28**, pp. 9–47.

Penikas, H. (2020a). History of the Basel Internal-Ratings-Based (IRB) Credit Risk Regulation, *Model Assisted Statistics and Applications* **15**, pp. 81–98.

Penikas, H. (2020b). History of the World Largest Credit Risk Losses in 1972–2018, *HSE Economic Journal*, pp. 1–19.

Penikas, H. (2020c). Low Default Portfolios in Basel II and Basel III as a Special Case of Significantly Unbalanced Classes in Binary Choice Models, *Russian Journal of Money and Finance* **79**, pp. 101–128, doi:10.31477/rjmf.202002.101.

Penikas, H. (2020d). The Review of the Open Challenges in the IRB Loan Portfolio Credit Risk Modeling, *Model Assisted Statistics and Applications* **15**, pp. 371–388.

Penikas, H. (2021a). Money Multiplier Under Basel Capital Ratio Regulation: Implications for Counter-COVID-19 Stimulus, *Journal of Sustainable Finance & Investment*.

Penikas, H. (2021b). Natural Monopoly Regulation Principles' Application to Reduce Systemic Risk in Bankin, *Finance and Business* **17**, 3.

Penikas, H. and Simakova, V. (2014). Interest Rate Risk Management Based on Copula-GARCH Models [in Russian], *Applied Econometrics* **13**, pp. 3–36.

Penikas, H., Skarednova, A., and Surkov, M. (2021). How Do Investors Prefer Banks to Transit to Basel Internal Models: Mandatorily or Voluntarily? `http://cbr.ru/StaticHtml/File/124474/wp-74_e.pdf`.

Penman, S. H., Richardson, S. A., and Tuna, I. (2007). The book-to-price effect in stock returns: accounting for leverage, *Journal of accounting research* **45**, 2, pp. 427–467.

Pettifor, A. (2020). Rebuild the ramshackle global financial system. Economic researchers neglect the role of financialization in global, *Nature* **582**, p. 461.

Phongmekin, A. and Jarumaneeroj, P. (2018). Classification models for stock's performance prediction: A case study of finance sector in the stock exchange of thailand, in *2018 International Conference on Engineering, Applied Sciences, and Technology (ICEAST)* (IEEE), pp. 1–4.

Poledna, S., Bochmann, O., and Thurner, S. (2017). Basel III capital surcharges for G-SIBs are far less effective in managing systemic risk in comparison to network-based, systemic risk-dependent financial transaction taxes, *Journal of Economic Dynamics and Control* **77**, pp. 230–246.

Polizatto, V. P. (1989). A Generalized Framework for Credit Risk Portfolio Models. Background Paper for the 1989 World Development Report WPS 340, `http://documents1.worldbank.org/curated/en/389501468764981235/pdf/multi-page.pdf`.

Porto, R. F. (2011). A brief note on implied historical loss given default, *Journal of Credit Risk* **7**, 2, pp. 73–81.

Posner, R. A. (1999). *Natural Monopoly and Its Regulation* (Cato Institute).

Preisser, J. S. and Qaqish, B. F. (2014). A Comparison of Methods for Simulating Correlated Binary Variables with Specified Marginal Means and Correlations, *Journal of Statistical Computation and Simulation* **84**, pp. 2441–2452.

Pykhtin, M. (2004). Portfolio Credit Risk Multi-Factor Adjustment, *Risk* **17**, pp. 85–90.

Pykhtin, M. and Zhu, S. (2007). A Guide to Modelling Counterparty Credit Risk, *Global Association of Risk Professionals.*

r-bloggers (2020). R code, https://www.r-bloggers.com/, accessed: 2020-03-10.

Radkov, P. and Minkova, L. (2011). Assessing bank's default probability using the ASRF model, *International Journal of Technology Modeling and Management* **2**, 1, pp. 29–34.

Ramsdale, R. and Sakhri, A. (2020). Saudi banks: 2019 results dashboard, Fitch Ratings, https://www.fitchratings.com/research/banks/saudi-banks-2019-results-dashboard-20-05-2020.

Repullo, R. (2013). Banking Theory and Regulation. CEMFI Lecture Course, https://www.cemfi.es/studies/css/course.asp?cu=20.

Risk Hub, S. (2021). Retrieved on 9/2/2021 from http://www.systemic-risk-hub.org/.

Ross, S. M. (2014). *Introduction to Probability Models*, 11th edn. (Academic Press).

Ryden, T. (1996). An EM Algorithm for Estimation in Markov-Modulated Poisson Processes, *Computational Statistics & Data Analysis* **21**, pp. 431–447.

Saldanha, L. and Beers, D. (2011). Default, Transition, and Recovery: International Local and Regional Governments Default and Transition Study, *Standard & Poor's.*

Salmon, F. (2009). Recipe for Disaster. The Formula That Killed Wall-Street, https://www.wired.com/2009/02/wp-quant/.

Schroeck, G. (2002). *Risk Management and Value Creation in Financial Institutions* (Wiley Finance).

Segoviano, M. A. and Singh, M. (2008). Counterparty Risk, Impact on Collateral Flows, and Role for Central Counterparties, *International Monetary Fund, IMF Working Paper.*

Seidler, J. and Jakubik, P. (2009). Implied Market Loss Given Default in the Czech Republic. Structural-Model Approach, *Czech Journal of Economics and Finance* **59**, 1, pp. 20–40.

Selmier, W. T., Penikas, H. I., and Vasilyeva, K. (2016). Financial Risk as a Good, *Procedia Computer Science* **31**, pp. 115–123.

Sharif, A. (2016). Reality check for Saudi banks, Bloomberg, https://bloomberg.com/news/articles/2016-05-09/.

Shemyakin, A. and Kniazev, A. (2017). *Introduction to Bayesian Estimation and Copula Models of Dependence*, 1st edn. (John Wiley & Sons).

Shirakawa, M. (2012). International financial stability as a public good, Retrieved from high-level seminar, co-hosted by the Bank of Japan and the International Monetary Fund https://www.bis.org/review/r121015c.pdf.

Shleifer, A. (2012). *The Failure of Judges and the Rise of Regulators* (MIT Press).

Siarka, P. (2011). The Issue of PD Estimation–a Practical Approach, *Mathematical economics* **7**, 14, pp. 199–212.

Singh, M. (1999). Collateral, Netting and Systemic Risk in the OTC Derivatives Market, *International Monetary Fund, IMF Working Paper.*

Singh, M. and Aitken, J. (2009). Counterparty Risk, Impact on Collateral Flows, and Role for Central Counterparties, *International Monetary Fund, IMF Working Paper.*

Sironi, A. and Resti, A. (2007). *Risk Management and Shareholders' Value in Banking: from Risk Measurement Models to Capital Allocation Policies*, Vol. 417 (John Wiley & Sons).

S&P Dow Jones Indices (2012). The S&P CoreLogic Case-Shiller Home Price Indices, https://www.spglobal.com/spdji/en/index-family/indicators/sp-corelogic-case-shiller/sp-corelogic-case-shiller-composite/#overview.

SRB (2021). Minimum Requirement For Own Funds and Eligible L (MREL). Single Resolution Board (SRB) under the Banking Package, https://www.srb.europa.eu/en/system/files?file=media/document/mrel_policy_may_2021_final_web.pdf.

Szepannek, G. and Luebke, K. (2021). Facing the Challenges of Developing Fair Risk Scoring Models, *Frontiers in Artificial Intelligence* doi:10.3389/frai.2021.681915.

Tarashev, N. A. and Zhu, H. (2007). Modeling and calibration errors in measures of portfolio credit risk, *BIS Working Papers*.

Tarullo, D. K. (2011). Regulating Systemic Risk, Retrieved from https://www.bis.org/review/r110401b.pdf?frames=0.

Tente, N., von Westernhagen, N., and Slopek, U. (2019). M-PRESS-CreditRisk: Microprudential and Macroprudential Capital Requirements for Credit Risk under Systemic Stress, *Journal of Money, Credit and Banking* **51**, 7, pp. 1923–1961.

Teresiene, D., Keliuotyte-Staniuleniene, G., and Kanapickiene, R. (2021). Sustainable Economic Growth Support through Credit Transmission Channel and Financial Stability: In the Context of the COVID-19 Pandemic, *Sustainability* **13**, 5, p. 2692.

Tetereva, A. (2012). Distance-to-Default (According to KMV model), http://home.lu.lv/~valeinis/lv/seminars/Tetereva_05042012.pdf.

Tian, S. and Yu, Y. (2017). Financial ratios and bankruptcy predictions: An international evidence, *International Review of Economics & Finance* **51**, pp. 510–526.

Tirole, J. (2014). Prize Lecture, Retrieved from Nobel Media AB https://www.nobelprize.org/uploads/2018/06/tirole-lecture.pdf.

Toskas, P. and Coutts, G. (2020). Industry profile and operating environment: Saudi Arabian insurance, Fitch Ratings, https://www.fitchratings.com/research/insurance/industry-profile-operating-environment-saudi-arabian-insurance-18-06-2020.

Tsai, B.-H. (2013). An early warning system of financial distress using multinomial logit models and a bootstrapping approach, *Emerging Markets Finance and Trade* **49**, sup2, pp. 43–69.

Upadhyay, R. (2014). Information Value (IV) and Weight of Evidence (WOE) – A Case Study from Banking (Part 4), http://ucanalytics.com/blogs/information-value-and-weight-of-evidencebanking-case/.

V-Lab of the New-York University Stern Business School (2021). Retrieved on 9/2/2021 from https://vlab.stern.nyu.edu/welcome/srisk.

Vasicek, O. (1987). Probability of Loss on Loan Portfolio, https://www.moodysanalytics.com/-/media/whitepaper/before-2011/02-12-87-probability-of-loss-on-loan-portfolio.pdf.

Vasicek, O. (1991). Limiting loan loss probability distribution, Tech. rep., KMV working paper.

Vasicek, O. (2002). The Distribution of Loan Portfolio Value, https://www.bankofgreece.gr/MediaAttachments/Vasicek.pdf.

Vasicek, O. (2012). Structural Models in Credit Valuation: The KMV Experience, https://w4.stern.nyu.edu/finance/docs/pdfs/Seminars/123w-vasicek.pdf.

Wagner, C. (1982). Simpson's Paradox in Real Life, *The American Statistician* **36**, pp. 46–48.

Wang, X. (2014). Firth logistic regression for rare variant association tests, *Frontiers in Genetics* **5**, p. 187.

White, H. (1980). A Heteroscedasticity-Consistent Covariance Matrix Estimator and a Direct Test for Heteroscedasticity, *Econometrica* **48**, pp. 817–838.

Witt, G. (2014). A Simple Distribution for the Sum of Correlated, Exchangeable Binary Data, *Communications in Statistics – Theory and Methods*, pp. 4265–4280.

Yao, X., Crook, J., and Andreeva, G. (2014). Modeling Loss Given Default in SAS/STAT, `http://support.sas.com/resources/papers/proceedings14/1593-2014.pdf`.

Yashkir, O. and Yashkir, Y. (2013). Loss given default modelling: comparative analysis, *The Journal of Risk Model Validation* **7**, 1, pp. 25–59.

Ye, H. and Bellotti, A. (2019). Modelling recovery rates for non-performing loans, *Risks* **7**, 1, p. 19.

Zhong, R. (2013). Andrew Haldane: The Banker Who Cried 'Simplicity', *The Wall Street Journal* `https://www.wsj.com/articles/SB10001424052702304858104579263190940438738`.

Index

About the Authors

Giuseppe Orlando, PhD, currently works at the Department of Economics and Finance (DEF) and at the Department of Mathematics (DM) of the University of Bari (Italy). He does research in Economics, Finance, Actuarial Science and Econometrics in which he obtained the "Bruno De Finetti" Award in Mathematics Applied to Economics. His current projects are on Nonlinear Dynamics in Economics, Natural Catastrophes (NatCat) Modeling and Interest Rates Forecasting. He was also Senior Risk Manager, Risk Consultant, Chief Risk Officer and Head of Risk and Quantitative Research for financial institutions such as Allianz, ING, HSBC, State Street, etc.

Michele Bufalo is from the University of Rome "La Sapienza" where he obtained his PhD in Economics and Finance under the supervision of Rosa Maria Mininni and Giuseppe Orlando. He is fellow at Department of Economics and Finance (DEF) of the University of Bari, where he has been appointed professor of Stochastic Processes. His research interests include option pricing, interest rates forecasting, derivatives, incomplete markets, and numerical algorithms in which he has published numerous articles.

Henry Penikas, PhD, is a project leader within the Bank of Russia (BoR) Research and Forecasting Department. Before he worked for the BoR Banking Regulation Department, he also worked for the risk management divisions of the Russia's largest banks (Alfa-Bank and Sberbank). He participated in the working groups of the Financial Stability Board and the Basel Committee on Banking Supervision. Henry also carries out research at the National Research University of Higher School of Economics (HSE) and the P.N. Lebedev Physics Institute of the Russian Academy of Sciences (LPI). He taught at the University of Pavia (Italy).

Concetta Zurlo received a Master's degree in Mathematics at the University of Bari where she studied credit and counterparty risk with Rosa Maria Mininni and Giuseppe Orlando. Concetta works in Accenture (ICEG division) as Murex analyst in the Financial Services Industry for one of most leading European banking groups since she graduated. She currently acts as a Team Leader on the *"Benchmark Reform"* project that involves the introduction of new alternative reference rates to replace existing benchmark rates to become compliant with the EU Benchmarks Regulation. Concetta has experience as the Front Office Functional Consultant in Commodities, Interest Rate and Credit Derivatives. Thanks to her job, she has accumulated knowledge on evaluation methods of OTC Derivatives in terms of pricing and sensitivities analysis.

Note: *Opinions expressed in the book are solely those of the authors and may not reflect the official positions of the affiliated institutions.*

CPSIA information can be obtained
at www.ICGtesting.com
Printed in the USA
BVHW062225030222
627290BV00005B/11

9 789811 252358